D1602892

THE ROMANCE
LANGUAGES

Other published works in the series:

The Celtic Languages
The Slavonic Languages
The Germanic Languages
The Semitic Languages

Forthcoming:

The Indo-European Languages
The Dravidian Languages
The Uralic Languages
The Turkic Languages

440
R758l

28 3.50

THE ROMANCE LANGUAGES

EDITED BY

MARTIN HARRIS
AND
NIGEL VINCENT

San Diego Christian College
2100 Greenfield Drive
El Cajon, CA 92019

London and New York

First published 1988
by Routledge

Reprinted 1997, 2000
by Routledge
2 Park Square, Milton Park, Abingdon, Oxon, OX14 4RN
270 Madison Ave, New York NY 10016

Transferred to Digital Printing 2006

© 1988 Selection and editorial matter Martin Harris and Nigel Vincent

Routledge is an imprint of the Taylor & Francis Group

Typeset in Times by Leaper and Gard Ltd, Bristol

All rights reserved. No part of this book may be reprinted or
reproduced or utilized in any form or by any electronic,
mechanical, or other means, now known or hereafter
invented, including photocopying and recording, or in any
information storage or retrieval system, without permission in
writing from the publishers.

British Library Cataloguing in Publication Data
A catalogue record for this book is available from the British Library

Library of Congress Cataloguing in Publication Data
A catalogue record for this book is available from
the Library of Congress

ISBN 0–415–16417–6

Publisher's Note
The publisher has gone to great lengths to ensure the quality of this reprint
but points out that some imperfections in the original may be apparent

Contents

Abbreviations

abl.	ablative	ELeng.	East Lengadocian
acc.	accusative	Eng.	English
adj.	adjective	EP	European
Am.	American		Portuguese
Ann.	Annobonese (fa	f.	feminine
	d'ambó)	fam.	familiar
AR	Arumanian	Fr.	French
art.	article	fut.	future
attr.	attributive	Gasc.	Gascon
aug.	augment	GBi.	Guinea-Bissau
Auv.	Auvernhat		Crioulo
BP	Brazilian	gen.	genitive
	Portuguese	ger.	gerund
Byz.	Byzantine	Gk.	Greek
Cab.	Caboverdiano	GR	Gallo-Romance
Cal.	Calabrese	Gua.	Guadeloupéen
Camp.	Campidanese	Guy.	Guyanais
Cat.	Catalan	Hai.	Haitian
Cha.	Chabacano	imp.	imperative
CLat.	Classical Latin	imperf.	imperfect
compl.	complement	impers.	impersonal
cond.	conditional	ind.	indicative
conj.	conjugation	indef.	indefinite
dat.	dative	indir.	indirect
decl.	declension	inf.	infinitive
def.	definite	IR	Istro-Rumanian
dem.	demonstrative	It.	Italian
det.	determiner	Lat.	Latin
dir.	direct	Lem.	Lemosin
disj.	disjunctive	Leng.	Lengadocian
Dom.	Dominican	Log.	Logudorese
DR	Daco-Rumanian	Lou.	Louisianan

Luc.	Lucano	pres.	present
m.	masculine	pret.	preterit
Mar.	Martiniquais	Pri.	Principense
Mau.	Mauritian	pron.	pronoun
Mil.	Milanese	pros.	prospective
Mod.	Modern	Prov.	Provençal
n.	neuter	PWR	Proto-Western-
Nap.	Naples		Romance
neg.	negative	refl.	reflexive
nom.	nominative	Réu.	Réunionnais
Nuor.	Nuorese	R-R	Rhaeto-Romance
obj.	object	Rum.	Rumanian
Occ.	Occitan	Sard.	Sardinian
OLat. etc.	Old Latin etc.	Sey.	Seychellois
Osc.	Oscan	sg.	singular
p.	person	Sic.	Sicilian
pal.	palatal	SIt. etc.	Southern Italian etc.
Pal.	Palenquero	Sl.	Slavic
Pap.	Papiamentu	SLu.	Saint Lucian
part.	participle	Sp.	Spanish
perf.	perfect(ive)	STo.	São Tomense
pers.	personal	su.	subject
Pied.	Piedmontese	subj.	subjunctive
p.-in-p.	prospective-in-past	suff.	suffix
pl.	plural	Sur.	Surselvan
pluperf.	pluperfect	SVO etc.	subject–verb–
pol.	polite		object etc.
Port.	Portuguese	Tusc.	Tuscan
pos.	position	VC	verb–complement
pp.	past participle	Vegl.	Vegliote
pred.	predicative	Ven.	Venetian
prep.	preposition		

Preface

It may not come amiss, in a book where matters diachronic and synchronic are inextricably intertwined, to begin by saying a few words about its genesis before considering its structure. The immediate origin of the volume may be traced to the fact that a number of the contributors had previously been invited to write chapters for Bernard Comrie's encyclopaedic compilation *The World's Major Languages* (Croom Helm, 1987). This invitation had the effect of forcing each of us to think hard about which aspects of the structure, history and sociology of our chosen languages should, and/or could, be included within the inevitable length restrictions. At the same time, it was clear that the format of Comrie's volume, while perfectly understandable and justifiable in its own terms, was likely to misrepresent the Romance language family as a whole for two distinct reasons. In the first place, the individual chapters were not always long enough to allow a full treatment of certain key aspects. Second, a number of languages were excluded which, albeit minor on politico-demographic grounds, were nonetheless of major significance in providing the evidence necessary to a successful reconstruction of the historical evolution of the family and to a proper appreciation of its current typological diversity. We therefore decided to go ahead with a project which took as its goal the characterisation of one particular language family, where the material for inclusion was determined principally on linguistic and historical grounds internal to the family itself, and for the most part independent of external political considerations. To this end, the chapter lengths in the present volume are roughly twice those to be found in Comrie's and the number of Romance languages has been expanded from the original five — French, Spanish, Portuguese, Italian and Rumanian — to encompass Catalan, Occitan, Sardinian and Rhaeto-Romance. Of course, there are still exclusions. Some might argue for a separate chapter on Galician or Istro-Romance, or for more detailed coverage of 'dialects' such as Andalusian or Sicilian or Brazilian Portuguese. With even more space, it might have been possible to give way to these, and other conceivable and similar, demands, but one must always stop somewhere on the continuum from idiolect to language family. As things stand, we believe that the present volume achieves a reasonable coverage of the linguistic diversity of both ancient and modern Romania.

Since in other respects the model of the chapters prepared for *The World's Major Languages*, with their mixture of the synchronic and diachronic, their relative theoretical neutrality and their adherence to a discursive style of narrative, appeared satisfactory, there was every incentive to keep the same nucleus of authors, who have in several cases incorporated some of the material from their earlier pieces. Naturally, however, new recruits had to be found for the new chapters. In addition, we decided to prepare a new chapter on Latin, where the emphasis was on looking forward to the ways in which that language has changed in the course of its development and fragmentation into the Romance languages. At the same time, it also seemed a good idea to gather into one introductory chapter facts of distribution and numbers of speakers, thus leaving each single chapter to be organised according to mainly structural linguistic criteria. Finally, in view of the recent rapid expansion of interest in the topic of pidgin and creole languages, we felt it would be useful, and indeed genuinely innovatory in a work of this kind, to add a chapter surveying and synthesising current research into Romance-based pidgins and creoles.

One respect in which we have departed from the model of Comrie's volume is in our attempt to impose a degree of uniformity of coverage on the central descriptive chapters. Not only do they fall into the same major sections, namely phonology, morphology, syntax and lexis, but within each section we have tried to ensure that a similar range of core topics has been covered. Thus, anyone wishing to look up say the sequential constraints on clitic pronouns or the historical evolution of tonic vowels in all the languages represented should not be disappointed. We have, however, deliberately refrained from going further in this direction. Thus, the reader will find that the individual chapters differ in the selection of non-core topics dealt with, in the mix of diachrony and synchrony, in the relative balance between the sections and in the types of theoretical approach adopted. While some may lament such heterogeneity, our own feeling is that it enhances the value of the work by demonstrating how differences of perspective may lead to varying assessments of significance with respect to broadly similar bodies of data.

How, then, might this book be used? A number of possibilities spring to mind. On the one hand it might serve as a work of reference for points of information ranging from the very particular — e.g. how many phonemically distinct laterals are there in Catalan? — to the more general — e.g. what are the main sources of loan vocabulary in Spanish? — and so on. Another reader might wish for a general overview of the history and structure of a particular language, either for linguistic purposes such as typological investigation or as background to a study of the history, literature or whatever of the region concerned. Yet again a third type of reader might wish to check out a given phenomenon such as basic word order in all the members of the family.

As regards intended level of readership, we have tried to ensure that the book is both sufficiently clear and expository for it to be used for general reference or as a textbook on undergraduate or graduate courses in Romance linguistics. Yet we also cherish the hope that it will offer information and occasional insights of value to scholars in linguistics and allied disciplines. To aid the reader, we have included both an analytical index and a system of cross-reference within the main body of the text. Each chapter concludes with a select list of essential reference works and further reading.

At this point, it is perhaps worth adding a word of advice aimed particularly at readers of the whole book or at those who use the index and the cross-references to follow up a given theme or area of data across a number of chapters. The multiple authorship, which distinguishes this work from the usual run of Romance linguistic manuals, brings with it obvious advantages in terms of breadth and depth of coverage, but also some attendant complications which derive from the contributors' differing perspectives and ranges of interest. The latter are easier to cope with than the former. It is clear, for example, that the more developed treatment of lexis in the Spanish chapter is not due so much to any intrinsic features of the history and structure of that language's vocabulary as to John Green's authorial decision to give special prominence to this topic in his chapter. Interested readers may then use the model of extended coverage Green provides and the data from the corresponding sections of other chapters to construct for themselves more detailed accounts of, say, loanwords in French or word-formation in Rumanian. Similarly, one author may have used a technique which could have potentially interesting results when applied to data from another language. Thus, Wheeler offers on page 206 a brief description of a method for compiling an inventory of typically Catalan core vocabulary. It would be intriguing to see this applied more generally. In the field of syntax, Haiman's detailed analysis of word-order in Rhaeto-Romance has obvious and as yet inadequately explored implications for the analysis of northern Italian dialects and their relation to the standard language. These are questions which are only briefly hinted at in the Italian chapter, though there is some interesting related discussion *vis-à-vis* Sardinian (pp. 338ff). More generally, all the relevant sections in the different chapters could be read consecutively, and the patterns of recurrence and diversity assembled into a single account of word order in Latin and Romance. All these, and — we hope — many more, represent ways in which the contents of the present volume will serve not just to document the results of current and previous work but also to stimulate new research into the extraordinarily rich data, both synchronic and diachronic, which the Romance languages offer.

Elsewhere, the differences between chapters lie not in emphasis but in the contrasting ways contributors have chosen to solve a problem of presentation. For example, in languages like Occitan or Sardinian, where for social and historical reasons there is no recognised standard or norm, how is one to state the facts? For Occitan phonology Wheeler opts for 'a basically diasystemic and somewhat abstract approach' (p. 246–7). Jones prefers to supplement his general overview of Sardinian phonology with a detailed treatment of the dialect of one village. Or compare with both of these the problem in the case of Rhaeto-Romance where there is a complex pattern of standardisation based on the recognition of different dialects at different periods in different places. This has necessitated a presentation in parallel of a number of systems in Haiman's chapter.

Despite the foregoing, the enterprising reader may still be puzzled, if not by differences of emphasis and presentation then by apparent contradictions between chapters. Yet it is in the nature of linguistic inquiry that analysts will at times disagree about how to interpret a given example or construction. In the case of a closely related group like the Romance languages, there is the additional complication that linguist A might propose a particular analysis of a phenomenon in language x, while linguist B might offer a different account of an apparently identical phenomenon in language y. Thus, to take a case in point, Vincent in his chapter on Italian (pp. 306ff) gives a semantically based treatment of the distribution of the various complement types in that language. Green, by contrast, suggests that complement selection in Spanish (pp. 117–18) is for the most part lexically arbitrary. Do such instances represent structural differences between the languages or theoretical differences between the linguists? The question matters both synchronically and diachronically. Vincent (pp. 65ff) also gives a semantic account of complementation in Latin, suggesting therefore that the change between Latin and Italian involves the development of a new pattern of semantic motivation which goes hand-in-hand with the emergence of a new set of formal exponents. On Green's view, either the lexical arbitrariness has to be projected back to the Latin stage, or else the history of Spanish — and indeed of Italian, if Green's analysis can be successfully generalised — is one of successive loss of semantic motivation. As it happens, in this instance the complete resolution of these differences is not possible, since much of the necessary detailed linguistic analysis has not yet been carried out. Once again, our hope is that allowing the different perspectives to stand side by side will serve to highlight areas for potential future research.

While we obviously cannot claim that everyone who consults this volume will find their queries answered, we believe that it will take its place on the shelves of both libraries and individuals as a reliable and up-to-date guide to the history and structure of the Romance languages and to the way they are currently being investigated.

In conclusion, we would like to acknowledge the cooperation of the individual contributors not only in preparing the versions of their own chapters on time, but for putting up with queries and requests for changes, and for cross-reading other chapters and providing often invaluable comments and corrections. Thanks too to numerous friends and colleagues who read drafts and offered advice, and to an anonymous referee for a number of helpful observations. We are particularly grateful to Christy MacHale for drafting the maps, to Jenny Potts for her skilful and informed copy-editing, to Mark Barragry on the production side and last, but certainly not least, to our editor, Jonathan Price.

Martin Harris   Nigel Vincent
University of Essex   *University of Manchester*

1 The Romance Languages

Martin Harris

The Romance languages, whose history, structure and present-day distribution are the subject of the chapters which follow, share a common source: their development in each case may be traced back to Latin. Latin for its part developed from a form of Italic spoken originally in a number of small communities in Latium (Lazio) in central Italy, probably settled by Proto-Latin speakers around 1000 BC. The Italic branch of Indo-European appears to have been brought to the peninsula towards the end of the second millennium BC, and included Oscan (spoken over much of southern Italy at least until the time of the Pompeii disaster, as graffiti clearly testify), Umbrian (spoken in the north Tiber valley) and a number of other more or less well known varieties in addition to the Latin group of dialects. The label 'Latin' may be said to refer initially to this group of related dialects (including, for instance, Faliscan, spoken around what is now Civitá Castellana, some fifty miles from Rome on the north bank of the Tiber), but it soon came firstly to designate the speech of Rome — attested since the sixth century BC — and then to be used as an increasingly broad cover term for a range of related varieties differing along temporal, geographical and social dimensions (see below). Latin was, as we have seen, bordered to the south and east by cognate tongues, while to the north its principal neighbour was the non-Indo-European Etruscan. Farther north still, by the fourth century BC — the time at which Rome was establishing her dominance in central Italy — the Po plain had been settled by speakers of varieties of Celtic (p. 3), a separate Indo-European family, but one which bears a number of striking structural parallels to Italic. In the extreme south, on the other hand, Greek was a recurrent source of external but still Indo-European influence.

As Roman military, political and economic influence spread during the period of expansion of the Roman Empire, firstly within Italy and then beyond, the Latin language also flourished, coming to be spoken in much of western and central Europe, and western north Africa, only Greek (spoken in the eastern Mediterranean and the Middle East) being a serious linguistic rival within the imperial boundaries. In particular, in addition to

1

those areas of Europe which are currently Romance-speaking, much of southern Britain, the rest of what is now Belgium, Holland, much of Germany, Austria, Yugoslavia and Albania, and a fairly narrow coastal strip in what is today Morocco, Algeria, Tunisia and Libya were also Latin-speaking to a greater or lesser extent. The subsequent retreat of Romance from part of the territory it once occupied — which has of course in recent centuries been vastly more than offset by its expansion overseas — came about mainly in the period after the end of the Empire in the west during the fifth century AD (earlier north of the Danube; cf. p. 23), largely to the profit at that time of Germanic and Slavic languages within Europe and, from the later seventh century onwards, of Arabic in north Africa.

Despite the military and political collapse of the Western Empire and the subsequent loss of territory by Romance, Germanic and Slavic actually made less headway within Europe than might have been expected. In Iberia, for instance, the incoming Visigoths were already Latin-speaking before they arrived, and retained many aspects of the civilisation they found there, with themselves now in a dominant role; the continued use of Romance is therefore hardly surprising. In northern Gaul, to take a second example, a Catholic Frankish kingdom under Clovis emerged by the end of the fifth century, in which Latin was established from the outset as the language of both religion and administration and where a Romance vernacular — with a significant Frankish overlay — rapidly began to develop. The persistence — or reintroduction — of Romance in the area of present-day Rumania, on the other hand, is more difficult to account for, and is discussed in some detail below (pp. 2–3). The survival or otherwise of Romance when political mastery passed into other hands can be ascribed partly to the extent and profundity of earlier Latinisation and partly to the density and pattern of settlement of the newcomers; the use by the Christian church as its 'official' language of Latin/Romance (what some scholars call 'Late Latin' is the same as what others call 'Early Romance') is certainly also a relevant factor. It is with the subsequent fate of Romance in those areas where it did persist that this chapter is primarily concerned.

Of course, as was indicated earlier, even when Roman power was at its height there was not one single homogeneous form of Latin used by all speakers throughout the Empire: social and regional variation, particularly in the spoken language, would have been apparent at all times. There would, for example, have been considerable differences between the speech of Cicero and that of his slaves, or between the Latin spoken by a Roman provincial governor and that of his subjects, and the question of how such varieties should be distinguished and denominated is discussed below (pp. 26–7). During the period between the collapse of the Empire in the west and the emergence of the first Romance vernacular texts in various parts of Europe, one must envisage a situation in which this ever-present variation within Latin was accentuated as the language developed in ever more divergent ways in different localities. There are three main reasons for this. The first is simply the general tendency towards linguistic fragmentation inherent in the language acquisition process, counter-balanced at all times by the need to communicate with others within a shared speech community. Given the loss of a single uniform education system, and given the increasing separation of various groups of Romance speakers from one another, particularly after the rise of the Moslems in the eighth century shook the cohesiveness of the Western Romance world, this shared speech community must have grown progressively smaller for most speakers; thus the pressures offsetting fragmentation weakened and dia-lectalisation proceeded apace.

Secondly, there were already during the Empire incipient divergences between the Latin of various provinces, partly at least because of the dif-ferent language or languages which were spoken (and often continued to be spoken for centuries) in various regions before Latin became the pre-dominant language. Thus there are, for example, considerably more words of Celtic origin in contemporary French and north Italian dialects than in Spanish, standard Italian or (even more so) Rumanian, reflecting the Celts' domination before Rome's expansion both of Italy north of the river Po (*Gallia Cisalpina*: 'Gaul this side of the Alps') and of most of present-day France (*Gallia Transalpina*: 'Gaul beyond the Alps'). One representative example may be found in derivatives of a Latinised Celtic word RUSCA 'bark' (cf. Welsh *rhysg* 'rind'), surviving with various meanings ranging from 'peel' and 'skin' through 'bark' to 'cork' and '(cork) bee-hive' in Gallo-Italian dialects, throughout Gaul, and in Catalan. Within Iberia there seem to have been several languages spoken in various parts before the arrival of the Romans, including (in addition to Celtic) both Basque, a non-Indo-European language still spoken in the western Pyrenees on either side of the Spanish–French frontier, and also another language or language family, Iberian, of unknown provenance and genetic relationship. Very often, the precise source of a word peculiar to all or part of Iberia is unclear; for this reason, those lexical items found in Ibero-Romance that are clearly of long standing and which are apparently neither of Latin nor Celtic origin — such as Sp. and Port. *cama* 'bed' (cf. pp. 118, 165) — seem best labelled simply 'pre-Romance'. In much of central and southern Italy, most of the 'substrate' languages were themselves, as we have seen, of the Indo-European Italic group closely related to Latin itself, although there are limited traces of the influence of Etruscan. From the eighth century BC, there was significant settlement by speakers of Greek in southern Italy and Sicily, with some borrowing of lexical items into early Latin (p. 75), but while one or two Greek-speaking communities survive to this day (p. 19), the effects of this on local Romance dialects appear to have been minimal. As for possible pre-Roman influences on Rumanian, these are lost in the mists of time, partly because the present-day location of Rumanian is very probably not identical with that where Latin was first learnt (p. 23) and partly because we know virtually nothing of any pre-Roman languages in this entire area (cf. pp. 412–13).

The third reason for the increased linguistic divergence following the break-up of the Empire lies in the languages of the conquerors, whether immediate or subsequent. Thus one expects, for instance, to find most words of Germanic origin in French, particularly in those dialects — such as Walloon — nearest to the eventual Romance–Germanic frontier, with fewer in those other Romance-speaking areas where Germanic settlement was less dense. In Spanish (and to a lesser extent Catalan and Portuguese), one finds a substantial Arabic element (p. 119), reflecting the occupation of significant parts of the peninsula by Arabic speakers for nearly eight centuries, while in the case of Rumanian the constant contacts with Slavic and other non-Romance languages have led to a substantial non-Romance lexical element in the language even in everyday vocabulary (pp. 413–14).

The previous paragraphs have discussed the problem of linguistic divergence as though it were exclusively a lexical phenomenon: this is of course far from the case. Much has been written about the extent to which phonological, morphological and syntactic differences can be attributed to substrate or to adstrate factors, but in very few, if any, cases is general agreement reached. The pronominal use of *on* 'one' (< HOMO 'man') in French (p. 221) is a structure once regarded as certainly of Frankish origin; but while the parallel with modern German *man* 'one' (cf. *Mann* 'man') is indisputable, the direction of any influence between Germanic and Romance — and indeed whether such influence need be postulated at all — remains a contentious issue. Very often too, one finds that exactly the change or pattern under discussion is to be found also in some other Romance variety, or indeed in a totally different language family, in a situation in which the postulated external influence is wholly lacking. Such an instance is the passage of prevocalic initial [f] in Castilian (and Gascon) via [φ] and [h] to ∅ ('the loss of initial [f]'), a development once confidently attributed to the influence of Basque or a Basque-related substrate, but parallelled in part at least in a number of southern Italian dialects, where a comparable cause cannot of course be adduced. In short, most non-lexical divergences, in Romance and elsewhere, seem best attributed to internal linguistic evolution, though of course the 'selection' of one change rather than another may be unconsciously favoured by structures found in other languages still actually in use in a multilingual community.

All of these reasons, then, led to the emergence of a number of linguistically distinct areas within the Romance-speaking world. The process of fragmentation, however, went much further. As we have seen, a language as it evolves is subjected always to two conflicting pressures simultaneously: the pressure towards convergence or homogeneity, which facilitates communication within a perceived speech community, and the pressure towards divergence or heterogeneity (p. 3), caused by the very nature of the language acquisition process, which ensures that no one generation or individual learns their native language in exactly the form in which it has been internalised by their elders. Enhanced social mobility, a high level of education and greater frequency and range of travel and communication strongly favour the former pressure, as the recent retreat of many non-standard dialects clearly indicates; social and geographical immobility on the other hand, with very limited possibilities for education and travel, favour dialectalisation, with each community developing a form of language peculiar to itself, as part of a strong local identity. This process of course never goes so far as to prevent communication with those in the near vicinity; local dialects range along a spectrum, even in districts perceived as being on either side of a major dialect division. (Consider, for instance, the gradation from French to Tuscan via a whole set of French, Franco-Provençal and Gallo-Italian dialects spoken in adjacent parts of France, Switzerland and Italy.) Nevertheless the particular social context of the period between the end of the Roman Empire and the beginning of the Middle Ages did bring about marked linguistic divergence, the dialectal consequences of which remain, albeit now often rather marginally, in all of the present-day Romance-speaking areas within Europe.

From the early part of the Middle Ages, however, at least in the western part of the Romance-speaking world, the first signs of a new phase of linguistic evolution could be discerned, namely the gradual emergence in a particular area of one dialect more favoured for various reasons than any other; from these favoured varieties, at different speeds in different territories, a series of national languages has developed. The precise timing and result of this development, which affected written forms of the language markedly sooner than the everyday spoken idiom, depended on a whole variety of historical factors, in particular the establishment or otherwise of a nation-state in a given region and the policy, explicit or otherwise, of the linguistically dominant group towards those whose native form of speech was other than theirs; these factors are considered in detail below. At this stage we will simply contrast by way of example the fates of Portuguese and Occitan, the former now a major world language and the latter having little official status even in those areas of rural southern France where it is still in use. Portuguese, originating from the Galician dialect spoken in the north-west of the Iberian peninsula, came to be the language of an area which since the mid-twelfth century has been — apart from a brief period from 1580 to 1640 — politically independent of Spain, and has flourished accordingly, whereas Occitan, despite the high standing of medieval 'Provençal' (p. 16) as the literary language of the troubadours and the fact that Occitan dialects were once spoken over more than a third of France, could not compete with the strong desire which developed in the highly centralist post-revolutionary France for there to be a single national language. We return to this theme at several points in what follows.

We shall now look in turn at each of the branches of the Romance family of languages.

The Romance of Iberia

Within the Iberian peninsula, the major early division, apparent (with the usual caveat about dialect gradation) as early as the ninth century, was between Catalan on the one hand — which had and has close affinities with Occitan north of the Pyrenees (p. 16) and whose speakers were within the Frankish domains for several centuries — and the other dialects of Spain and Portugal, collectively referred to as Hispano-Romance. This latter group includes both the dialects of the Christian north (limited in the tenth century roughly to the northwestern third of the peninsula) and those of the Arab-dominated south, collectively known as Mozarabic. In linguistic terms we may observe that the eight centuries from the first Arab invasion in 711 near Gibraltar (< Arabic *gebel al-Tariq* 'mount of Tariq') to their final expulsion from Granada in 1492 can be characterised as a period involving firstly the gradual divergence of the dialects of the Arabised south from those of the north and then, slowly at first but later with greater speed, the recapture of Mozarabic- or Arabic-speaking territory by speakers of 'Christian' northern dialects. Simultaneously with these developments, we find at first the familiar process of linguistic fragmentation between the Christian kingdoms and then the gradual emergence of two of the resultant dialects, Castilian and Portuguese, to become in due course the national languages of Spain and Portugal.

More specifically, we may observe that as the Reconquest got underway, there was a range of Hispano-Romance dialects, traditionally grouped, largely because of the political divisions of the time, into four, these being, from west to east, Galician, Leonese, Castilian, and (Navarro-)Aragonese, with Catalan still further to the east. Speakers of each of these dialects gradually reoccupied territory to the south, but the central Castilian-dominated swathe gradually grew broader, to the point of cutting off the southward expansion of Catalan, Aragonese and Leonese at points close to Alicante in the east and Badajoz in the west, with a substantial strip further west christianised by speakers of Galician-Portuguese, who reached and recaptured the Algarve by the mid-thirteenth century, at which point modern Portugal may be said to have taken shape. At first, it was largely Mozarabic that these incoming dialects replaced (albeit possibly with some residual influence from Mozarabic on the dialects of Andalusia), but in much of the southern third of the country, from the latter part of the twelfth century onwards, it was often non-Romance languages, in particular Arabic and Berber, which gave way to Castilian, coming in from the north and now very much in a dominant position. Furthermore, along those eastern and western flanks of Spanish territory initially reconquered by speakers of Aragonese and Leonese respectively, Castilian gained ground fairly rapidly, a process helped no doubt by the fact that the differences between the dialects at that time were significantly less than those found now between standard (Castilian) Spanish and those forms of Aragonese and Leonese which continue to be spoken today.

There are three questions arising from this greatly truncated account which need a brief response. Firstly, why did the Christian dialects of the north have such an easy task in defeating both the Mozarabic forms of Spanish spoken in the reconquered areas and also the non-Romance languages of the occupiers? Secondly, why, within the central group of dialects, did Castilian fairly early emerge as dominant? And thirdly, why and to what extent have Galician and Catalan escaped Castilian hegemony?

The first of these questions is relatively easily answered: Mozarabic could not compete in prestige with the speech of the newcomers, and given the 'religious crusade' nature of the Reconquest, this was clearly even more true of Arabic or Berber. Further, in Arab Iberia, Mozarabic had the status of a spoken patois, the languages of culture and administration having been Arabic and, to a significant extent, Hebrew. All in all, the victory of the northern forms can readily be explained, and the principal long-term effect of Mozarabic on Spanish and Portuguese was as a medium whereby a considerable number of lexical items of ultimately Arabic origin passed in due course into the two national languages of the peninsula.

The second question reflects simply the central role played by Castilian in the Reconquest within what is now Spain. After the recapture of Toledo in 1085, and in particular after the reunion of León with Castile in 1230, this pre-eminence increased, to the point where, when Mozarabic was abandoned, as we have already seen, in favour of the language of the incomers, it was in fact, except of course where the new ruling elite spoke Portuguese or Catalan, Castilian which was inevitably adopted. As elsewhere, the social prestige associated with the court, particularly during the reign of Alfonso X el Sabio (1252–84), reinforced the position established by military success.

The third question is more complex. We have already observed that the southern extension of the most northwesterly Hispanic dialect, Galician, developed into Portuguese, and we shall discuss the present fortunes of that language shortly. Perhaps as a consequence of the success of its offspring, perhaps because of its geographical remoteness, perhaps because of its own distinctiveness and the strong literary and cultural tradition dating back to the flourishing lyrical poetry of the Middle Ages (often written by non-Galicians, as for example Alfonso X), Galician has arguably survived more strongly than either Leonese or Aragonese, the other major medieval dialects, although a variant of the former, spoken in Asturias around Oviedo and known as Bable, has recently enjoyed something of a resurgence. The fact remains, however, that from the sixteenth to the nineteenth century, Galician was frequently represented as a mere rural patois, and indeed one particularly low in social standing. It needed a literary revival in the nineteenth century and a linguistic revival in the twentieth to restore Galician's fortunes to some extent, although the long-term position is far from clear. Alongside this, one notes the current resilience of Catalan, the only language in Western Europe not the official language of a modern nation-state which can truthfully be said to be secure and whose present position is more fully discussed below.

Spanish (Castilian)

Spanish is not only the official language of Spain (including the Canary Islands and the north African enclaves of Ceuta and Melilla) but is spoken also in 19 republics in Central and South America and the Caribbean (Argentina, Belize — where English is also found — Bolivia, Chile, Colombia, Costa Rica, Cuba, Dominican Republic, Ecuador, El Salvador, Guatemala, Honduras, Mexico, Nicaragua, Panama, Paraguay, Peru, Uruguay and Venezuela) as a result of the colonisation of that region — and indeed significant parts of what is now the USA — by Spanish speakers from the sixteenth century onwards, with constant reinforcement by incoming Hispanophones since that date. In addition, Spanish is spoken in the US-associated Caribbean territory of Puerto Rico and residually in the Philippines. Not to be overlooked either is the very substantial number of Spanish speakers within the USA itself, a number maintained and augmented primarily from Mexico, from Puerto Rico and from Cuba; officially estimated at some 14 million people, the real figure seems likely to be very significantly higher, perhaps approaching 20 million. Finally, one should note groups of Spanish speakers in Morocco and Western Sahara, and also in Equatorial Guinea, where Spanish is the official language. It is estimated that in all some 280 million people have Spanish as their native tongue or (in parts of both Spain and Latin America) as a second language alongside Catalan or an Amerindian language; it is worth noting that by far the largest number of Hispanophones — well in excess of 70 million — are to be found in Mexico, almost twice the total to be found in Spain. Recent figures suggest that some 12 million people, widely scattered but with a particular concentration in the central Andean region, speak a South American Indian language (of which over 1,500 have been listed), although many of these speakers also have at least some knowledge of Spanish (or, in the case of Brazil, Portuguese). Particularly resilient are Quechua, an official language of Peru alongside Spanish, spread far beyond its original homeland by the Incas in pre-Spanish times, and Guaraní, which shares official status with Spanish in Paraguay, partly at least as a result of its widespread use by the early Jesuit missionaries; there are, however, also significant Amerindian-speaking communities from Chile northwards to Mexico.

In linguistic terms, the Spanish of Latin America shares a number of features, especially at the phonological level, with the southern variant of peninsular Castilian, Andalusian, which, given the provenance of most of the early settlers, is hardly surprising. There has been much controversy about the influence of substrate languages on aspects of the Spanish of Latin America other than the obvious lexical input, but almost all the phonological and morphosyntactic characteristics examined have counterparts in areas where the proposed source language was not spoken. That is not to say, of course, that there is not mutual influence, especially in bilingual areas — but taken as a whole the linguistic developments of Spanish in America seem best attributed to the normal processes of change, with only marginal effects from the Amerindian substrate.

In comparison with French and Portuguese, Spanish forms the base of relatively few creoles. The most significant group is to be found in the Philippines, known collectively as Chabacano, and deriving to a significant extent at least from Ternateño, a creole which developed in Ternate in the Moluccas from interaction between Spanish and an already existing Portuguese-Malay creole, and which was taken to the Philippines in the middle of the sixteenth century. This seems to have been the principal source of four major Spanish creole dialects in the Philippines, none of which, however, are prospering in the face of constant pressure from English. There are small numbers of speakers of Spanish-based creoles in various parts of the north-west of South America, the best known of these being perhaps Palenquero, showing features derived also from Portuguese and spoken by some 2,000–3,000 people in northern Colombia; for Papiamentu see p. 12. One should also note briefly the existence of an Italianised form of Spanish used by Italian immigrants in the Buenos Aires area (Cocoliche) and a range of Spanish–English hybrids spoken in the American south-west; none of these, however, are sufficiently developed to qualify as true creoles, and appear to have a limited future.

Finally, one should briefly note Judeo-Spanish, the language of the Sephardic Jewish communities who fled from or were expelled from Spain during the fifteenth century. Judeo-Spanish, the collective name for a range of mutually comprehensible variants, shows both conservative and innovatory features, the former above all at the level of phonology and the latter particularly in the lexicon, as would be expected. The best known Judeo-Spanish communities, in the Balkans, suffered greatly during the Second World War, but significant numbers are to be found in Morocco (where the influence of contemporary Spanish is strong), in the United States, particularly New York City (where the pressure to linguistic conformity is also strong), and in Israel, where the Spanish-speaking community is large enough to support radio broadcasts and a journal *Aki Yerushalayim.* Recent estimates suggest a total of some 200,000 speakers in all.

Portuguese

Portuguese, as we have already seen, developed as a concomitant of the southward movement of speakers of Galician, with which as a result it still has the closest of affinities. The inhabitants of Portugal currently number some 10.5 million, and metropolitan Portuguese is generally said to have two principal dialect groups, northern and southern (broadly reflecting the different times at which Moslem occupation ended), with transitional varieties spoken in the provinces of Beira Alta and Beira Baixa. From Portugal, the language was taken to Brazil, the effective colonisation of which got under way from the middle of the sixteenth century, and has gradually become the native language of almost the whole of the population, currently estimated to be in excess of 150 million. As elsewhere in Latin America, there was in Brazil a prolonged period of interaction between speakers of Portuguese and speakers of indigenous languages, the most important of the latter being Tupi, one dialect of which, like Quechua and Guaraní noted earlier, came to be used for missionary and other purposes well outside its own original territory. This *lingua geral*, however, has not persisted, and was already losing ground to Portuguese by the end of the seventeenth century. Portuguese in Brazil, influenced by the diverse origins of both the immigrants and the administrators sent from Lisbon, rapidly developed norms of its own, particularly in the more popular registers. The overall position is that while the official and literary standards on both sides of the Atlantic do vary, not least because of the changes which took place in metropolitan but not Brazilian Portuguese from the seventeenth century onwards, apparently as part of a process of fairly conscious linguistic distancing from Castilian, ease of communication ensures that this variation is kept within limits; no such constraints affect common speech, however, in which divergences at all linguistic levels can readily be perceived. Again as elsewhere, there have been attempts to demonstrate that the divergences between Brazilian Portuguese and that of Portugal are due to the influence either of Tupi and/or of the Portuguese-based creole (see below) which developed subsequent to the importation of black slaves; but whereas as usual no influences other than on the lexicon have been established to general satisfaction in respect of the standard language, the widespread simplification of suffixed morphology in particular in spoken Brazilian Portuguese is strongly reminiscent of a typical result of the process of creolisation.

Brazilian Portuguese is, for the reasons we have indicated, relatively homogeneous, although there are differences between a northern and a southern group of dialects. This division apparently goes back to the pattern of early settlement and to subsequent patterns of economic and cultural evolution.

After Brazil, the biggest concentration of speakers of varieties of Portuguese and of Portuguese-derived creoles outside Portugal is in Africa. We should, however, note first the two Atlantic archipelagoes of Madeira and the Azores, both colonised in the first half of the fifteenth century, with populations of some 300,000 and 350,000 respectively: their speech is generally grouped together as 'Insular Portuguese', and is fairly close to the European standard. The Portuguese of Madeira has a number of marked phonological characteristics and a clearly recognisable local intonation, while the Azores embrace a number of varieties of Portuguese, that of São Miguel being the most distinctive.

Within Africa itself, one thinks first of the former Portuguese colonies of Angola and Mozambique, with populations of some eight million and 12 million respectively. Recent estimates suggest that somewhere between a quarter and a half of these populations, particularly those in the major urban areas, speak at least some Portuguese, the norms of the more educated being essentially those of European Portuguese but with an admixture of features more reminiscent of the Portuguese of Brazil, whether through common divergence from the metropolitan norm or from the effects of (partial) creolisation or both. Creoles today appear to be of limited incidence, but one does find references, particularly in respect of Angola, to the existence, above all around the towns and cities, of varieties often known collectively as *pequeno português*, parallel to the *petit-nègre* or *petit français* of Francophone Africa mentioned below (p. 16).

One group of Portuguese-based creoles is to be found in the Cape Verde islands and on the nearby mainland, in Guiné-Bissau. The islands were colonised in the fifteenth century, and served as the centre where slaves were collected, auctioned and despatched; hence they necessarily played an important role in the formation and diffusion of Portuguese-derived creoles, particularly to Brazil. Among the present population of some 250,000 one finds a linguistic spectrum ranging from near-standard Portuguese to a fully fledged creole (though decreolisation is apparently well advanced). Of the two principal varieties of creole, one, Sotavento, is very similar to that of Guiné-Bissau, with over half a million inhabitants, most of whom use this *crioulo* as their language of everyday communication, as do some 60,000 persons in neighbouring Senegal. Further south in the Gulf of Guinea are the islands of São Tomé and Príncipe, with some 70,000 inhabitants, whose creole is described as 'increasingly lusitanised' by one observer, and Pagula (formerly Annobon), whose creole shows clear signs of Spanish influence.

Looking further east, there were significant Portuguese settlements in India and Ceylon. Leaving aside such former colonies as Goa, with some half a million inhabitants, where the local Portuguese is, or was, fairly close to the European standard, one finds remnants, or historical records, of Portuguese-derived creoles along much of the Indian coastline, and again much further east, in Timor and Java (and indeed many other islands in this region), in Malaysia, where there are still in Malacca some 3,000 speakers of a creole known as Malaqueiro (or similar names) and a community of speakers of a related variety in Singapore, and in Macao, where standard Portuguese appears largely to have ousted Macaísta, although this survives as a popular medium of communication among some 2,000 descendants of creole speakers who moved from Macao to Hong Kong.

The 'oriental' Portuguese-based creoles, formerly very much more widely diffused than at present, display a sufficient number of points of similarity with those of Cape Verde and Guiné-Bissau, noted above, for many to argue that they share a common 'pidgin' or 'proto-creole' ancestor, which has undergone relexification to a greater or lesser extent in different actual contact situations, to yield the varieties at present in existence. (A similar argument, the monogenesis theory, has been advanced more generally, cf. p. 425.) It can certainly be demonstrated that there were significant trading and other links between the Portuguese-creole-speaking areas, and while the observed similarities may with some plausibility be attributed to the directly comparable historical and socio-linguistic circumstances in which pidgins arise and are then creolised, there was certainly a Portuguese-based *lingua franca* in common use throughout the relevant period.

One should note also two other Portuguese-based creoles found in the Americas: one, Papiamentu, spoken by upwards of 200,000 speakers on Curaçao and another, Saramacano, spoken on the nearby mainland in upper Surinam. These creoles are both in some ways atypical, the former because of complex influences on its lexicon (above all from Spanish, but also from Dutch and to a lesser extent English) and the latter because it manifests an unusually high proportion of words of African origin. In addition, there have been reports of Portuguese-derived creoles in Brazil itself among rural speakers of African origin, for instance Fronteiriço spoken on the Brazil–Uruguay border, though these are apparently on the point of extinction if not already totally lost. Finally, one should note the existence of small Portuguese-speaking settlements in both the USA and in Canada, in all of which language-shift is apparently well advanced.

Catalan

Catalan, with some six million speakers, has not experienced the great overseas expansion of its two sister languages within the peninsula. We have already noted that Catalan, from its homeland in the medieval Counties, including almost all the present-day French department of *Pyrénées Orientales*, was carried as far south as Alicante during the Reconquest (albeit with little headway on its western flanks, despite a lengthy period of political union with Aragon from 1137), and that the inhabitants of the Balearics (conquered between 1229 and 1235) and a declining number of older inhabitants in the Sardinian town of Alghero (occupied in 1355) are Catalan-speaking to this day. It has to be said, however, that Castilian has made substantial headway in the *País Valencià*, particularly in Alicante and the other southern coastal resort towns. Recent surveys suggest a figure of some 40 per cent of Catalan speakers in the *País Valencià*, and 50 per cent in Catalonia proper, where there has been very high immigration of Castilian speakers from the south of Spain into industrial towns around Barcelona over the last thirty years or so. In the province of Tarragona, south of Barcelona, on the other hand, some 70 per cent are speakers of Catalan, while to the north the number is as high as 80 per cent.

The language is fairly homogeneous, although two principal dialect groups are generally distinguished, western (which includes Valencian and the eastern fringe of Aragon) and eastern, which includes the Catalan of Roussillon, the Balearics and Alghero but also, much more significantly, that of the great city of Barcelona. It is not exaggerating to say that it is above all the fidelity of the majority of the inhabitants of this city, of all social groups, to their native tongue which has ensured that its fate has been so unlike that of Occitan across the border in France; and indeed it is difficult to point to any language in Europe which has not become the official language of a nation-state which is as strongly placed as Catalan today.

The Romance of Gaul

As will be apparent from what has already been said, a major division developed within Transalpine Gaul between the French dialects of the north and centre (and part of modern Belgium), known collectively in medieval times as the *langue d'oïl*, and the Occitan dialects of the south, the *langue d'oc* (*oïl* (> *oui*) and *oc* being the markers of affirmation in their respective areas). The fate of Occitan is discussed below (pp. 16–17), as is that of Franco-Provençal (p. 17), the collective name for the dialects of a smaller intermediate area in the south centre of eastern France together with the varieties originally spoken in parts of Switzerland and the Val d'Aosta in Italy. The northern group of dialects is one of the most innovative branches of Romance, partly because of the intensity of the Germanic superstrate influence referred to earlier and partly because of radical changes within French itself in the post-medieval period.

French

Within the three major areas just noted, linguistic fragmentation continued, and a wide variety of dialects emerged, the principal ones being shown in Map V. One northern dialect was Norman, which has had such a profound influence on the development of English, and from this source developed those varieties of French spoken in Jersey, Guernsey and Sark, estimated to have 15–20,000 speakers between them in the early nineteen-eighties; few if any of these, however, are under 40 years of age, and the loss of these forms of French spoken within the British Isles seems certain in due course. Another French dialect to emerge was Francien, the dialect of the Ile de France, and it is from this dialect that, once circumstances arose which favoured the growth of a national language, modern standard French has developed. The establishment of a fixed royal court in Paris, the development of an educational and of a legal system centred on that same city, and the fact that the abbey at Saint-Denis, close by, was in effect the spiritual centre of the kingdom were all factors which tended to favour the dialect of Paris and the surrounding area for the status of national language. Since the twelfth and thirteenth centuries, when Francien (a modern name) gradually came to be accepted as a norm to aim towards, at least in writing and in cultivated speech in northern and central France, its advance has been slow but steady, although, as we shall observe later, it was not until the nineteenth and twentieth centuries, particularly in the south, that French came to be so wholly dominant within the boundaries of France, at first among the bourgeoisie and in the cities, and later also in the remoter rural areas. Indeed, French's long period of predominance as the major international language of culture and diplomacy long antedates its general use as a spoken language within France: by the end of the seventeenth century, French had in effect replaced Latin in the former role, to the point that the Berlin Academy was able to ask, as a matter of fact, in 1782, at a time when Francien was the native tongue of perhaps a quarter of the population of France, 'Qu'est-ce qui a rendu la langue françoise universelle?' ('What has made the French language universal?'). This enhanced role for French persisted until the First World War and even beyond.

Within Europe, French is now spoken by some 51 million people within France (and Monaco), and by some four million Walloons in Belgium, principally in the four francophone districts of the south, Hainaut, Namur, Liège and Luxembourg, and in the bilingual district of Brussels the capital. Somewhat less than half a million people live in the Grand-Duchy of Luxembourg, where the native language of most speakers is a Germanic dialect but where French is the language of education and administration, whereas in Switzerland the most recent figures suggest that some 18 per cent of a total population of some 6.4 million, mostly living in the Suisse romande, are French speakers. In northern Italy, the Val d'Aosta has a population of around 100,000, some two-thirds of whom use French and/ or a local variety of Franco-Provençal according to the register.

Outside Europe, indigenous French speakers are to be found in almost every continent. In Canada, there are some six million Francophone descendants of the original colonists, three-quarters of these living in the province of Quebec, where they form some 80 per cent of the total population. Strenuous efforts are made to preserve and strengthen French, particularly in Quebec, within what has been since 1867 officially a bilingual country. Descendants of another group of French colonists in Acadia (the easternmost provinces of Canada), driven out in the mid-eighteenth century, carried their language southwards down the eastern seaboard of the United States, a few travelling as far as Louisiana, which had earlier been claimed for France by explorers coming southwards down the Mississippi. As a result, although there are relatively few French speakers in Acadia today except in New Brunswick (some 200,000), there are significant numbers — approaching one million — in New England, where there is a major admixture also directly from Quebec. Further, in Louisiana, a French possession until 1803, where as we have seen the immigrants were primarily from Acadia, and are indeed called 'Cajuns' (< *(a)cadien*), *français acadien* is in regular use by perhaps a further one million people, together with both a small elite speaking more or less standard French and also a French-based creole, sometimes known as Gombo, spoken by a declining number of people in eastern Louisiana and a small part of eastern Texas and earlier also in a few communities in Mississippi.

Elsewhere, French is generally in competition not with another European language but with indigenous non-European languages and/or with French-based creoles in former French (or Belgian) colonies. In the West Indies, French is found for instance in Haiti, where it is the official language of approaching five million people but where the great majority actually speak creole, and in various islands such as Martinique and Guadeloupe, where also French-based creoles have been documented and described; similarly, in Guyane, there are upwards of 50,000 creole speakers. Important also are the countries of the Maghreb (Algeria, Morocco and Tunisia), where French appears to be holding its own since independence: in Algeria, for example, it is estimated that some 20 per cent of the population can read and write French as a first or second language, with a much higher proportion able to speak it, above all in the cities. In black Africa, there are sixteen independent Francophone states comprising a great swathe across the west and the centre of the continent from Senegal to Zaire, together with the Malagasy Republic. There is a further group of French and French-creole-speaking islands in the Indian Ocean, for example Mauritius (approaching one million speakers), Seychelles (c. 40,000 speakers) and Reunion (450,000 speakers). In most of these countries, the future of French as a second language, used for a variety of official, technical or international purposes in place of one or more indigenous languages, seems secure. In Syria and Lebanon, however, the use of French as a second language has declined greatly, while in Vietnam, Laos and Cambodia, French and French-derived creoles appear to have been almost entirely lost.

Like all languages with any significant degree of diffusion, French is not a single homogeneous entity. Just as in France itself there is within most regions a spectrum of variation from 'pure' patois (the original local dialect, now often moribund) through *français régional* (largely the standard grammar, with a more or less regionally marked phonology and a greater or lesser number of non-standard lexical items) to the standard language (which itself has a wide range of styles and registers), so too one finds a similar spectrum in most if not all of the areas discussed above, often with the added dimension of a French-based creole. In Quebec, for example, one finds 'educated Quebec French' shading imperceptibly through to the fully popular variant known as *joual* (from the local pronunciation of *cheval* 'horse') associated primarily with Montreal. French-based creoles are spoken not only in Louisiana (alongside Cajun, discussed earlier), Haiti and various islands mentioned earlier, but arguably also in parts of black Africa, in the form of such variants as *petit-nègre* or *petit français*, though there the precise boundary between a pidgin and a creole is not always clear in practice. As in the case of *français régional*, there is very frequently a standard–creole continuum, with more educated speakers tending perhaps increasingly towards the metropolitan norms.

Occitan

The other major branch of Romance found within present-day France is Occitan, the generic name for all those varieties other than Franco-Provençal and Catalan spoken south of the major east–west line in Maps V and VI, forming a great swathe from Provençal through Lengadocian, Auvernhat and Lemosin to the very distinctive Gascon south of the Garonne. (This group of dialects is still at times referred to by English speakers as Provençal, this being a widely used name in the medieval period for the *koine* which was at that time a major literary language, with significant output, particularly in the twelfth and thirteenth centuries, of lyric poetry, narrative verse and prose: today, however, Provençal refers properly only to the local dialect of Provence.) While Old Occitan and Old French were certainly more similar than their modern descendants, not least because many of the radical changes which characterise French post-date the medieval period, there are in fact far closer parallels, both synchronic and diachronic, between Occitan and Catalan than between Occitan and French; as one observer put it, whereas a 'Proto-Occitan-Catalan' is a quite plausible concept, a 'Proto-Occitan-French' (excluding Catalan) certainly is not.

Forms of Occitan remained in general use in the southern part of the country until the end of the fifteenth century and beyond; indeed, only the edict of Villers-Cotterets in 1539 really ousted it (and indeed Latin) as an official written language, though by this time French was widely seen as having greater prestige, with all the consequences which follow from such an attitude. Occitan remained however as virtually the sole everyday spoken language in its home territory until the new social and political climate which followed the Revolution, after which French made rapid headway, above all in the cities and among the upwardly socially mobile. Various attempts have been made to re-establish some form of Occitan as a literary language, most notably by the ninteenth-century Felibrige movement associated with Mistral, a movement hindered, however, by the essentially conservative and folklorist attitudes of its adherents. Attempts to form a standard written Occitan are also fraught with difficulty, given the diversity of the varieties of Occitan in use today. More recently, effort has been directed rather towards the restoration of local pride in spoken variants of Occitan, both in their own right and as vehicles for the maintenance and transmission of local culture, perhaps the one strategy with any hope of success. The fact remains, however, that there are today probably only some two to three million people still happy to converse in their own form of Occitan, none of these being monolingual. Various relaxations in the absolute hegemony of French within France have been tolerated since the last war, above all by virtue of the Loi Deixonne (1951) with subsequent amendments which permitted the teaching of local forms of language at all educational levels, as a result of which some 14,000 secondary school children were following courses in Occitan during the school year 1983–4. However, given that it is now common for parents to speak to their children in French rather than Occitan, there are very few true native speakers below the age of 40, a fact which must call into question the long-term future of all varieties of Occitan.

Franco-Provençal

Franco-Provençal is the name given to the group of dialects spoken in south-east central France, roughly in a triangle bounded by Grenoble, Geneva and Lyon, in Suisse romande and in the Val d'Aosta in Italy, thence shading fairly sharply into the Gallo-Italian dialects of the far north of that country. Sharing certain features of French, Occitan and indeed of Italo-Romance, these dialects, having lost their hold on the cities mentioned earlier, are now reduced to the status of patois, the formerly relatively unified language based on the usage of Lyon having fragmented. It is worth noting that the separate treatment accorded to Franco-Provençal is due at least as much to its geographical diffusion over three countries and its characterisation as a zone of linguistic transition as to its linguistic distinctiveness; Gascon, for instance, is notably more different from the other forms of Occitan, of which it is nevertheless traditionally treated simply as one variety.

Italian, Sardinian, Rhaeto-Romance

Crossing Italy to the north of Florence, one finds a major phonetic isogloss relating to the voicing or otherwise of Latin intervocalic voiceless plosives. Forms of Romance found north and west of this line, traditionally referred to as the La Spezia–Rimini line, generally show voicing in this environment while those to the south and east do not. (Consider for example the derivatives of Lat. SALUTARE 'to greet', which gives Fr. *saluer* (with the consonant lost entirely), Sp., Cat., Occ. *saludar* (with [ð] in the first two and variably [d] or [ð] in Occitan) but It. *salutare* and Rum. *a săruta* (the modern meaning in the latter case being 'to kiss').) Within Italy, one finds to the north of this line the Gallo-Italian dialects (Piedmontese, Ligurian, Lombard and Emilian), which have already been mentioned as shading into Franco-Provençal and thence into the dialects of present-day France, and also Venetian, which is linguistically, although not geographically, transitional between the Gallo-Italian dialects and Tuscan. To the south of the line, where voicing does not typically occur, one must distinguish on the one hand Tuscan and on the other hand a range of central and southern dialects from Umbria through the Abruzzi to Campania, Calabria and Sicily, with Sardinian so distinct as to warrant the separate treatment accorded to it in this volume (Chapter 9). Apart from the La Spezia–Rimini line itself, there are no abrupt divisions between these dialects, but rather a spectrum the ends of which are markedly distinct from one another. Partly within Italian territory and partly in Switzerland, one finds those forms of Romance traditionally labelled Rhaeto-Romance, similar in many ways to the dialects of northern Italy but sufficiently distinct from them to deserve description in their own right (Chapter 10).

Italian

The position of the dialects in Italy today is much more solid than elsewhere in Romance-speaking Europe. While one can truthfully say that from the time of Dante, Petrarch and Boccaccio — that is, from the early part of the fourteenth century — Tuscan, and in particular the Tuscan of Florence, came to be firmly established as the literary language of Italy, this had little or no effect on the speech even of educated people elsewhere in the peninsula, except in the capital city, where the usage of the Papal court appears to have influenced the local educated norm as early as the fifteenth century.

With this one major exception, there was no historical process comparable to the Reconquest in Spain and Portugal and no socially cohesive pressure such as that experienced in post-Revolutionary France to lead to the diffusion of Tuscan outside its home territory other than as the literary language of a very small minority. While the *questione della lingua* — the debate about the form of Italian most appropriate for literary usage — continued for centuries, it was not until after the political unification of Italy in

1861 that the question of a national language for educational and administrative purposes was seriously tackled. Despite the controversial recommendation of a commission headed by Alessandro Manzoni that the basis of this new truly national language should be contemporary Florentine, it was in fact, perhaps inevitably, literary Tuscan which was disseminated through the school system, a tendency reinforced by a strong prescriptivist tradition which has only begun to recede within the last couple of decades. It should at all times be borne in mind that in Italy, more perhaps than anywhere else in Europe today, there is a gradation from the indigenous dialects of isolated rural communities through regional dialects to regional standard Italian, with the national standard language superimposed and with the vast majority of native speakers able to practise code-switching over at least part of this range. Certainly, a number of regional standards are still in everyday use by even the most educated of speakers, reflecting the deep regional loyalties and long-standing cultural traditions of the different parts of what is now Italy. (The survival of Catalan, it will be recalled, has been attributed to similar factors.) As against this, however, the normal pressures exerted by a national education system, by military service — a great linguistic leveller — and by increased geographical and social mobility together, in the twentieth century, with the all-pervasive influence of radio and television, have contributed to the fact that standard Italian is now understood virtually everywhere in a country where it is only very recently that, for the first time, more than half the population claim 'Italian' rather than a regional variety as their native language.

It has recently been suggested that Roman may be tending to supplant Florentine as the basis of the standard language. Such a view, however, would be rather too dramatic. We noted above that educated Roman speech was to a very considerable extent Tuscanised well before the process was felt elsewhere in the country, the indigenous centre-south dialect, *romanesco*, being downgraded socially and increasingly limited to rural areas surrounding the city. When one talks, therefore, of 'Roman' in this context, one is speaking in effect of a form of speech not so different from the standard, but with certain originally local features of phonology and lexis, which is certainly now widely diffused over the national radio and TV networks.

Italian today, in the very broad sense outlined here, that is, including all the dialects, is spoken by some 60 million Italians within Italy and San Marino, only some three-quarters of a million now having some other language as their mother tongue (see p. 14 for French, p. 21 for Ladin and Friulan, p. 13 for Catalan). Non-Romance languages spoken within Italy include German in the Alto Adige (South Tyrol), Greek in Puglia and Calabria, Albanian, Slovenian and Serbo-Croat (see Map VII). Italian is spoken also by some 10 per cent of the population of Switzerland, including around 250,000 people in one Italophone canton, Ticino, by a number of people in Corsica (see next section) — where, however, the official language has been French since 1769 — and in not insignificant Italian-speaking communities of Venetian origin in Istria and Dalmatia, now within the borders of Yugoslavia. In Malta, the popular spoken language has always been a local form of Arabic, but Italian was an official language until 1934, although it had long been losing ground to English, a process accelerated by the Second World War. In recent years, the availability of Italian television in the island has tended to restore at least a passive knowledge of the language to many Maltese. Elsewhere there is a large Italian-speaking minority of some four million in the USA, second only to the even larger group of Hispanophones noted earlier, and sharing with them a renewed interest in their linguistic and cultural heritage. Italian is spoken also by a declining linguistic minority in Eritrea, where it also forms the basis of probably the only surviving Italian-based creole. We have already mentioned the Italianised Spanish of Buenos Aires, Cocoliche, and there is apparently a rudimentary Italian-based creole known as Fazendeiro which is, or was, spoken in São Paulo in Brazil. These are both reflexes of significant Italian immigration into various South American countries, where recent figures suggest one and a half million italophones in Argentina and half a million in Brazil; there are also at least half a million Italian speakers in each of Canada and Australia. Italian does not, however, have anything like the same degree of diffusion across the world as Spanish, Portuguese or French.

Sardinian

Sardinian, the most conservative of all the Romance languages in a number of respects, is spoken by some one million people, all (apart from emigrants) within the island of Sardinia. The inhabitants of this island were largely divorced from the historical and cultural development of the former Roman Empire from the end of the fifth century, and the language which developed locally was used for almost all purposes until the end of the fourteenth century. Since that time it has been rivalled by various forms of Italian, by Catalan, by Spanish and latterly by standard Italian for all purposes other than everyday speech and here too, except perhaps in the remotest rural areas, it is now losing ground, especially among younger speakers. The net result has been on the one hand the implantation of non-Sardinian forms of Romance in certain areas and on the other hand the failure of any one dialect to emerge as standard Sardinian.

The first of these factors accounts for the small Catalan-speaking settlement at Alghero mentioned earlier, for two Genoese-speaking settlements, Carloforte and Calasetta, on islands off the southwestern corner of Sardinia, and for the fact that the two most northerly dialects, those of Gallura and Sassari, are so heavily influenced by Tuscan as to be best regarded as variants of Italian rather than Sardinian (p. 314). (The same applies to an even greater extent to the Italian of Corsica, formerly very similar to Sardinian.) The second factor is responsible for the existence in the remainder of the island of three principal dialects, Campidanese (spoken over most of the south), Nuorese (centre and east) and Logudorese (north-west), none of which can really claim to be predominant (see Map IX). In recent years, in Sardinia as elsewhere, there has been a revival of interest in local languages and cultures; nevertheless, the long-term future of Sardinian as such looks far from secure (p. 349).

Rhaeto-Romance
The name Rhaeto-Romance is that conventionally given to a number of Romance speech forms found in the eastern part of Switzerland and northeastern Italy, characterised more by their differences from the major Romance language groups than by a set of shared features common only to themselves (p. 35). Indeed, it is certain that the areas in which these tongues are spoken have never formed a single administrative unit, and virtually certain that they have never been a homogeneous linguistic or cultural entity either. Equally, it is not possible to point to a common substrate or a common superstrate which would justify the tradition of treating these dialects together. It is perhaps simplest to think merely in terms of a set of dialects most closely related to those of the north of Italy, with each one showing a particular subset of a group of both conservative and innovative features said to characterise Rhaeto-Romance. Chapter 10 opens with an attempt to indicate these characteristics, but proceeds to talk on almost every page of the divergences between one form of Rhaeto-Romance and another.

There are three principal subtypes of Rhaeto-Romance (p. 351). Firstly, in the Swiss canton of the Grisons, one finds some 40,000 speakers of what is usually known as Romantsch, a number of related dialects of which the best known is probably Surselvan. Romantsch has been a 'national' (though not an 'official') language of Switzerland since 1938, and considerable work has been done on codifying the dialects and providing them with a standardised orthography; they are also taught in both primary and secondary schools. The fact remains, however, that the pressure of German, both standard and regional, is strong and incessant.

Secondly, there are, around Ampezzo and Bolzano in a number of valleys in the Dolomites and the Alto Adige in the eastern part of central northern Italy, something in excess of 10,000 speakers of Ladin. Much more significant, however, are some half a million speakers of Friulan, spoken in the region of Friuli-Venezia Giulia, around the cities of Udine and Gorizia. Neither of the forms of Rhaeto-Romance spoken within Italy enjoy the status or protection of Romantsch, and the influence of standard Italian and, in the case of Friulan, of Venetian also, is ever-present, and growing.

All in all, then, there are somewhat less than 600,000 speakers of

Rhaeto-Romance in a limited and non-contiguous geographical area, of whom probably none are now monolingual. The pressures of two high-status languages — German and Italian — on varieties which are essentially isolated from each other, coupled with the lack of any official support for what is numerically by far the most important variant probably bode ill for the long-term future of any member of this group of Romance languages, although some or all of them may well survive for a considerable time in informal spoken usage.

Balkan Romance

Dalmatian

Before passing on to look at the last major branch of the Romance family of languages, we should glance briefly at a group of dialects which has fared notably less well than Rhaeto-Romance, to the point of being totally lost at the end of the nineteenth century. On the coastal areas of what is now Yugoslavia and on the offshore islands, there existed a form of Romance generally known as Dalmatian, which was in a number of ways structurally intermediate between Italo- and Daco-Romance. This form of Romance, which should be confused neither with (Venetian) Italian introduced into Istria and Dalmatia from the Middle Ages onwards as a result of trade and settlement (see p. 20) nor with the tiny output of Istro-Rumanian found not far from Rijeka (see below), is best represented in records from Dubrovnik and the surrounding areas. Even the earliest records, however, show Venetian influence, and the indigenous Romance speech of that area is no longer attested after the end of the fifteenth century, ousted by the combined pressure of Venetian on the coast and Serbo-Croat inland. The last place where this form of Romance survived was apparently the island of Krk (Veglia), and the standard description of the local Dalmatian dialect, Vegliote, published in 1906, is based on personal interrogation of its last-known speaker — or rather of a son who claimed to remember it well!

Rumanian

The history of the easternmost branch of the Romance family of languages is rather more complex than that of the varieties we have discussed hitherto. Deriving from the Latin spoken in the Roman province of Dacia — and hence often known as Daco-Rumanian — the antecedent of modern Rumanian, although mentioned as early as the thirteenth century, is attested in texts only from the sixteenth century, with consequential uncertainty as to its precise history during the preceding thirteen centuries or so. In essence, there are two views about the persistence of a Romance tongue in what is today Rumania: one is that Latin was preserved without a break north of the Danube, although this province was abandoned by Rome as early as AD 271; the other is that Latin was lost in this region but later reintroduced by Romance speakers from south of the Danube (an area much longer in Roman hands), as these migrated northwards under pressure from incoming speakers of Slavic languages. The second view is broadly speaking more plausible, given both the fact that the northern province was one of the last to be occupied and one of the first to be abandoned and also the dispersal of pockets of Romance speakers, as we shall see, well outside the boundaries of present-day Rumania, a distribution consistent with northward migration. This does not, of course, in any way rule out the possible persistence of a form of Romance north of the Danube, which would have reinforced, or been reinforced by, an influx of Latin speakers from the south.

Balkan Romance is generally divided into four principal types, of which one, Daco-Rumanian, is, as we have seen, the antecedent of modern Rumanian (see Map XI). The three other principal sub-Danubian variants are Istro-Rumanian, spoken by fewer than two thousand speakers around Ucka Gora in the eastern part of the Istrian peninsula not far from Rijeka, Megleno-Rumanian, also spoken by a few thousand speakers north-west of Salonika in Greece, and Arumanian (Macedo-Rumanian), spoken by far more — some 350,000 — in northern Greece, parts of Albania and southwestern Yugoslavia. This group is not helped by the fact that it is spread over three countries, one of these being virtually cut off from the other two for political reasons, and that it has no single focus or national base, or official support in any of the countries in which it is spoken.

The northern branch of Balkan Romance has prospered considerably, Rumanian today having some 21 million speakers. There are two principal dialects: Moldavian, spoken in the northern part of the country and indeed right up to the Dniester river within the two Soviet republics of Moldavia and Ukraine, and Muntenian (Wallachian), spoken in the south of the country and underlying the literary language developed during the latter part of the eighteenth and the first part of the nineteenth century and based on the language of Bucharest. There are those who argue also for a third dialect, spoken in Transylvania, but most analysts prefer to see this rather as a transitional area between the two principal dialects.

Standard Rumanian shows no readily identifiable substrate influences but does of course bear very considerable marks of its long period of interaction with Slavic. (For lexical borrowings from other sources, see pp. 414–16). Rumanian also has more than one morphosyntactic feature characteristic of the Balkan *Sprachbund.* During the nineteenth century, serious attempts were made as a result of a (relatively brief) period of 'Romance nationalism' to reduce the Slavic element in the lexicon, but changes were largely limited to specialist registers, with little effect on everyday vocabulary; one countervailing pressure favouring Slavic has always been that of religious language, Old Church Slavonic being the liturgical language of the orthodox church in the Balkans. One lasting effect of the pro-Romance movement, however, was the change within Rumania from the Cyrillic to the Latin alphabet, begun early in the nineteenth century and completed by the time of the union of the principalities of Moldavia and Walachia in the early 1860s.

Rumanian, then, is spoken by some 21 million people, in Rumania (18 million), in adjacent parts of the USSR (where it is often claimed to be a separate language and the Cyrillic alphabet is used) and of Yugoslavia (the Banat), and in a number of villages just across the borders of Bulgaria and Hungary. In addition, there are substantial communities of Rumanian speakers abroad, in particular in Australia and the USA, but Rumanian was not involved in the great period of colonial expansion, so there are no areas speaking Rumanian or Rumanian-derived creoles in the New World.

Conclusion

We have briefly surveyed in this chapter some of the historical, social and cultural factors underlying both the present patterning and the current distribution of the Romance languages as we see this today. Some branches of Romance — for instance in Britain or north Africa — died out before the attested emergence of any local vernacular; one other, Dalmatian, has died out almost within living memory, and the long-term future for several others must be at best doubtful. On the other hand, while none of the Romance languages can rival the claims of English to be the international language of the second part of the twentieth century, it should not be forgotten that among the dozen or so languages in the world with the greatest number of speakers, one finds no fewer than three Romance languages, with a continuum of variants from the metropolitan norm through regional standards to more or less creolised local forms. What the Roman Empire did for Latin, colonial expansion and contemporary ease of travel and communication have done for Romance. It is a more detailed examination of these languages severally to which we shall now turn.

Bibliography

Agard, F.B. (1984) *A Course in Romance Linguistics* 2 vols. Georgetown University Press, Washington DC.
Anderson, J.M. and J.A. Creore (eds.) (1972) *Readings in Romance Linguistics.* Mouton, The Hague.
Bal, W. and J. Germain (1982) *Guide bibliographique de linguistique romane.* Cabay, Louvain.
Bourciez, E. (1967) *Eléments de linguistique romane* 5th edn. Klincksieck, Paris.
Dittmar, N. and B. Schlieben-Lange (eds.) (1982) *Die Soziolinguistik in romanischsprachigen Ländern.* Narr, Tübingen.

Elcock, W.D. (1975) *The Romance Languages.* Faber and Faber, London.
Hall, R.A. Jr (1974) *External History of the Romance Languages.* Elsevier, New York.
Hope, T.E. (1971) *Lexical Borrowing in the Romance Languages* 2 vols. Blackwell, Oxford.
Iordan, I., J. Orr, and R. Posner (1970) *An Introduction to Romance Linguistics.* Blackwell, Oxford.
Kontzi, R. (ed.) (1982) *Substrate und Superstrate in den romanischen Sprachen.* Wissenschaftliche Buchgesellschaft, Darmstadt.
Lüdtke, H. (1956) *Die strukturelle Entwicklung des romanischen Vokalismus.* Romanisches Seminar an der Universität Bonn, Bonn.
Malkiel, Y. (1978) 'The Classification of Romance Languages'. *Romance Philology* 31: 467–500.
—— (1978) 'Factors in the Unity of Romania', *Romance Notes* 18: 263–71.
Manoliu-Manea, M. (1985) *Tipología e historia: elementos de sintaxis comparada románica.* Gredos, Madrid.
Posner, R. and J.N. Green (eds.) (1980–2) *Trends in Romance Linguistics and Philology* 4 vols. Mouton, The Hague.
Rohlfs, G. (1971) *Romanische Sprachgeographie.* Beck, Munich.
Sampson, R. (1980) *Early Romance Texts: An Anthology.* Cambridge University Press, Cambridge.
Tagliavini, C. (1972) *Le origini delle lingue romanze* 6th edn. Patron, Bologna.
Vincent, N. and M. Harris (eds.) (1982) *Studies in the Romance Verb.* Croom Helm, London.
Weinrich, H. (1958) *Phonologische Studien zur romanischen Sprachgeschichte.* Aschendorffsche Verlag, Münster.

2 Latin

Nigel Vincent

1 Introduction

Latin differs most obviously from the other languages that are dealt with in this volume in that it is a dead language, for which direct recourse to the phonetic output and intuitive judgements of native speakers is by definition not available. Nor, of course, is it possible to conduct surveys into the correlation of linguistic and social variables, language attitudes and the like. Rather, our knowledge of Latin grammar, lexis and phonology has to come from the evidence of surviving texts, admittedly available in generous quantity and over a long period, supplemented by the occasional explicit comments of native grammarians and authors. To this may be added the data retrievable by the backward projection, through the techniques of reconstruction, of the evidence of the daughter languages, these in turn offering us a combination of living data and a variably rich textual tradition. The integration of the two sorts of evidence, attested and reconstructed, takes place in the further context of those general principles and constraints that have emerged, and are still emerging, from the various subdisciplines of general linguistics. For our understanding of the social, cultural and ethnic factors governing the use of Latin, we must turn to the evidence of history, where once again the surviving records have to be matched against the current state of affairs and interpreted in the light of our general knowledge of social, political and economic processes.

A further caveat is necessitated by the fact that the term Latin is often employed as a convenient designation for a broad range of related but distinct varieties. Thus, in origin, Latin refers to the speech of the city-state of Rome as it emerged towards the middle of the first millennium BC (p. 1); yet it may still be appropriately used a thousand years later as the name of the dominant administrative language of the Roman Empire at the time of its collapse, conventionally taken to date from the deposition of Romulus Augustulus by the Huns in AD 476. Add to this the social and geographical variation also discussed earlier (pp. 2–5), and it will be clear that the potential for terminological confusion is considerable. The traditional means of resolving the ambiguities of the term Latin has been to use the expression Classical Latin to refer to the language of the educated classes of Rome in the period of Cicero and Caesar (first century BC) and a variety of other labels — Late, Popular, African, etc. — to distinguish different eras, regions and social levels as necessary. Of these alternative epithets, the most abused by far has been 'Vulgar', which, although it might seem on etymological grounds to delimit a social variety, has come to be used by scholars in such a wide range of senses as to be virtually useless. In this book, therefore, we shall follow both the more ancient and the more modern practice and employ the undifferentiated term Latin. Only in cases where ambiguity or confusion seems likely to arise will more precise (and transparent!) designations be adopted.

Our aim, then, in the present chapter is to narrate the structural transformations that Latin underwent in the course of the passage towards the modern Romance languages. Unfortunately, this task is not made any easier by the fact that the chronology of the texts, from which a large part of our evidence is of course drawn, does not necessarily reflect what must be presumed, on internal criteria, to be the natural sequence of linguistic developments. Thus, the evidence of an early but innovative writer like Plautus (254–184 BC) will often tell us more about the sorts of direction linguistic evolution must have taken by the fifth century AD than we could learn from a contemporary but conservative writer such as Boethius (AD 480–524). It will be important to remember, therefore, in what follows that there are two distinct stages involved in describing the linguistic history of Latin. First, the evidence, culled from such sources as are available, has to be integrated into a linguistically plausible diachronic sequence; only at a second stage can that sequence be projected back onto a sociolinguistic model of Rome and the Empire at the various stages of its history. Of course, much of this latter task remains to be done, and it should be clear that the present chapter is concerned primarily with the former exercise.

As an example of the separability of internal and external factors, consider the development of the tonic vowel system. Structurally, we must explain as far as possible how a system based on a phonemic opposition of vowel quantity with predictable assignment of word stress came to be replaced by a number of systems where the crucial factors were vowel quality and free, or partially free, stress. Such an account can, in part at least, stand or fall independently of our ability to date precisely the changes involved, or to say when and where there was a historical overlap of systems, or to be able to identify sociolinguistic parameters of stratification, even though these are all important questions, to which answers must ultimately be sought. Similarly, in the realm of grammar, a strictly linguistic history needs to explicate and, if possible, explain how the classical 'accusative and infinitive' with verbs of saying and thinking (p. 67) came to be replaced by the emergent pattern of finite complementation with QUID/QUOD + embedded sentence. An increased use of the former over the latter in the prose of a Boethius or a Claudian will simply be taken as an index of their conservative usage, not as indicating the need to revise our relative chronology of the two constructions.

Two dangers, apart from that of incompleteness, threaten too strict a separation of internal and external history. The first is that we might take as a starting point or intermediate stage of a diachronic linguistic trajectory a usage which never existed outside the confines of the written page or the rhetorician's manual. Consider, for example, the freedom of adjective position, and in particular the distance between noun and associated adjective, as derivable from an analysis of classical poetry. On the one hand, it might be argued that this is no more than a literary artifice; certainly, the position of the adjective seems to be a good deal less free in prose. On the other hand, the position of the adjective is considerably more constrained in all of the modern Romance languages than in even the most colloquial of prose. It must also be said, moreover, that a number of the world's languages seem to exhibit positively Virgilian degrees of freedom even in the absence of a written tradition, so we must be on our guard against ruling out all poetic usage simply on the grounds that it is poetic usage.

The second danger alluded to above is that in some circumstances a structural argument will require the contemporaneity of two or more linguistic patterns. There is a grave risk of circularity if the only evidence for such contemporaneity is the necessity of completing the argument, and in such cases — say as regards the relative order of the pairs auxiliary + verb and verb + object — specific attention will have to be paid to establishing as accurately as possible the absolute as well as the relative chronology.

With these considerations and caveats in mind, we turn now to a treatment of individual aspects of Latin phonology, morphology, syntax and lexis. The general format of each section will be a synchronic description of the relevant Latin structures, followed by a diachronic account of how those structures were transformed into the patterns, call them Late Latin or Early Romance, which underlie the development of the modern Romance vernaculars, whose individual properties will form the contents of the succeeding chapters.

2 Phonology

The phoneme inventory of Latin is set out in Table 2.1. Latin orthography provides a one-to-one representation for the phonemes of the language, except for its failure to indicate the systematically contrastive length of vowels. It has also, of course, provided the basis for most West European orthographies and thence for the International Phonetic Alphabet (IPA), so that given the sound–letter equivalences c = /k/ and x = /ks/ and making due allowance for the special cases to be discussed below, it is a

Table 2.1: The Phoneme Inventory of Latin

Consonants

p	b	t	d	k	g	kʷ	gʷ		
f		s						h	
m		n							
		l							
		r							

Vowels						Diphthongs	
ī	ĭ			ŭ	ū	ai	(written *ae*)
	ē̆	ĕ		ŏ	ō	au	
		ā	ă			oi	(written *oe*)

straightforward matter to read off the phonemic structure from the spelling. Among the special cases, note first that we have listed /kʷ, gʷ/ (orthographically *qu, gu*) as separate phonemes rather than as clusters of /k g/ plus /w/. This decision is based partly on morphophonemic evidence (/kʷ/ alternates with /k/ as in RELĪNQUO 'I leave' vs RELĬCTUS 'left', and /gʷ/ alternates with /k/ and /w/ as in NĪNGUIT 'it snows' vs NĬX 'snow (nom. sg.)' and NĬVEM 'snow (acc. sg.)' and partly on phonotactic evidence (initial clusters of the form /Cw/ are otherwise absent in the language apart from a handful of words in /sw/ such as SUĀDEO 'I urge', and SUĀVIS 'sweet'). Next, there is the problem of the status, phonemic or otherwise, of [ŋ], generally agreed to be the phonetic value of the *g* in the orthographic sequence *gn* in DĬGNUS 'worthy', RĒGNUM 'kingdom', etc. (and perhaps also in *gm*, as in TĔGMEN 'cover', etc.). Minimal pairs such as AGNUS 'lamb' [aŋnus] vs ĂNNUS 'year' [annus] on the one hand and AGGERE 'earthwork (abl.)' ['aggere] vs ANGERE 'to choke' ['aŋgere] on the other are sometimes adduced to show that [ŋ] cannot be an allophone of either /n/ or /g/ and must therefore be accorded phonemic status in its own right. It seems preferable, however, to follow the lead of the orthography and say that we have here a case of partial overlapping with [ŋ] as the allophone of /n/ before velars and of /g/ before nasals. The orthography also seems to be right in treating as variants of /i u/ the values [j w] which must be attributed to *i* and *u* (the systematic use of a separate lower case *v* is a Renaissance innovation) in words like IAM 'now', IŎCOR 'I jest', VŎLO 'I wish', VĀDO 'I go', etc. The conditioning factor here is the syllable structure: [i u] when the item is in nuclear position and [j w] in onset or (more rarely) coda position.

In the absence of any orthographic marking of vowel length, we have assembled some minimal contrasts in the chart of vowel length contrasts.

Vowel Length Contrast

(a) Lexical

mălum	'evil'	mālum	'apple (acc. sg.)'
lătus	'side'	lātus	'broad'
ĕsse	'to be'	ēsse	'to eat'
lĕgo	'I read'	lēgo	'I send as ambassador'
pŏpulus	'people'	pōpulus	'poplar'
ŏs	'bone'	ōs	'mouth'

(b) Morphological

rosă   'rose (nom. sg.)'   rosā   'rose (abl. sg.)'
    (and similarly for all 1st decl. nouns)
lĕgit   'he reads'   lēgit   'he read'
    (and similarly for a number of verbs)
gradŭs   'step (nom. sg.)'   gradūs   'step (gen. sg.)'
    (and similarly for all 4th decl. m./f. nouns)

(c) Lachmann's Law

dŭctus	'past part. of *duco*'	lūctus	'past part. of *lugeo*'
frĭctus	'past part. of *frico*'	frīctus	'past part. of *frigo*'
lĕctus	'past part. of *-licio*'	lēctus	'past part. of *lego*'
făctus	'past part. of *facio*'	āctus	'past part. of *ago*'

The examples given here show that length oppositions were functional both in maintaining lexical contrasts and in the working out of nominal and verbal morphology. Of particular interest are the length alternations introduced by so-called Lachmann's Law, according to which the stem vowel of the past participle is long if the root ends in a voiced consonant and short otherwise, even though the consonant voicing opposition is subsequently neutralised before the past participle suffix -TUS. Note, too, that vowel length in closed syllables, as in the examples of Lachmann's Law and elsewhere (cf. *nōsco* 'I discover' vs *pŏsco* 'I demand'), can only be discovered through the testimony of grammarians and through subsequent historical development, since both orthographically and metrically such quantities are 'hidden'.

Latin also had the three diphthongs of Table 2.1., which always counted as equivalent to long vowels. Of these, /oi/ was already recessive in the classical language, most instances having shifted to /ū/ (e.g. OLat. OINOS > ŪNUS), just as the Old Latin diphthong /ei/ had given /ī/ (OLat. DEICO > DĪCO). The cases of /oi/ that did survive, e.g. POENA 'punishment' (cf. PŪNIO 'I punish'), later shift to /ē/ and are thenceforth indistinguishable from primary /ē/ — thus Fr. *peine* 'suffering' (< POENA) beside *veine* 'vein' (< VĒNA). On the later fate of /ai, au/ see below.

Of crucial importance in integrating the consonant and vowel phonology of Latin were two suprasegmental factors: stress and syllable structure. The position of stress in Latin was predictable in terms of the segmental composition of the word. If we allow that a short vowel contributes one unit of phonological 'weight', a post-vocalic tautosyllabic consonant likewise one unit, and a long vowel two units, and if we agree that a syllable with two or more units of 'weight' is heavy and a syllable with one unit is light, then we can easily see the logic behind the traditional rule that stress falls on the penultimate syllable if that is heavy, and otherwise on the antepenultimate syllable. Note, however, that such a formulation is not inconsistent with the existence of stressed light syllables — e.g. ÁNĬMA — since the antepenultimate must be stressed regardless, as must the penultimate of disyllables, e.g. CĂNIS 'dog', FĬDES 'faith', nor with the existence of so-called hypercharacterised syllables, having a long vowel plus a post-vocalic consonant (three units of weight), e.g. SCRĪPSI 'I wrote', MĪLLE 'thousand'. Nonetheless, there is evidence within the development of Latin of a tendency to eliminate such situations, either by shortening the vowel, e.g. ĀMĀNTEM > ĂMĀNTEM, or by reducing a geminate consonant, e.g. CAUSSA > CAUSA (a diphthong in Latin is always counted as two units and therefore long), CĂSSUS > CĀSUS, *DĪVĬDTOS > DĪVĪSSUS > DĪVĪSUS. Similarly, the process of iambic shortening, whereby a sequence ᴜ – becomes ᴜ ᴜ is well attested, e.g. BĔNĒ > BĔNĔ, ĔGŌ > ĔGŎ, DŬŌ > DŬŎ, and serves to eliminate the anomaly of a long vowel after a stressed light syllable. Such tendencies eventually dictate a new norm in spoken Latin, according to which stressed syllables are never more nor less than two units in weight. The consequences are twofold: stressed short vowels in open syllables lengthen, e.g. CĂNEM > /ka:ne(m)/, and long vowels in closed syllables shorten, e.g. ĀCTUM > /aktu(m)/. We have deliberately cited words with [a] in this connection, since with this vowel no difference in phonetic quality accompanies a difference in quantity. This is easily seen in the fact that, for example, in Italian the pairs *cane* 'dog' and *pane* 'bread', *fatto* 'fact' and *atto* 'act' rhyme even though their Latin etyma differ in vowel length (CĂNEM/PĀNEM; FĂCTUM/ĀCTUM). In the case of the mid and high vowels, however, differences in length were accompanied by differences in quality, according to the general phonetic principle that short vowels tend to be laxer (more open) than their long congeners. Thus, the phonetics of the Latin vowel system is best represented as in Figure 2.1.

Figure 2.1: Phonetic Values of Latin Vowels

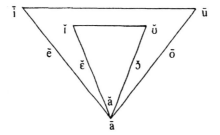

Each pair of non-low vowels is doubly distinguished — by quality and by quantity. Suppose now that, as a result of the changes described above, the differences of quantity become tied to the structure of the syllable. Two possibilities ensue. The first is that the loss of the quantity opposition entails the loss of the quality opposition since the two are linked. If that happens, the two triangles in Figure 2.1 will, as it were, be superposed, and where previously there were ten distinctive vowels, there will now only be five. Exactly this situation obtains in the Sardinian vowel system, also attested in a small area of Calabria (see below). Hence:

The Sardinian Vowel System

(For examples, see p. 317.)

The second alternative is that the quality contrasts will outlive the loss of the length distinction (except of course for the low pair /ă ā/), and we will get a nine-vowel system thus:

'Transitional' Late Latin Vowel System

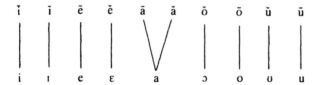

Although this system does not survive as such, it is a necessary transitional stage in the development of the other Romance vowel systems. Evidence for early variation between the two possibilities can be found in examples such as CAUDAM > It. c[o]da, (contrast AURUM > It. [ɔ]ro); LŪRĬDUM > LŪRDU(M) > It. l[o]rdo, Fr. lourd (contrast NŪLLUM > It. nullo, Fr. nul); FRĪGĬDUM > FRĪGDU(M) > It. fr[e]ddo, Fr. froid (contrast MĪLLE > It. mille, Fr. mille). These developments suggest that after a change /au/ > [ɔ], the subsequent change may go with quantity, viz. [ɔ] > [o], or with quality, viz. [ɔ] > [ɔ]. Similarly, the long high vowels /u i/ may shorten (but not centralise) to give [ŭ ĭ] (not [ʊ ɪ]), which subsequently develop to either [u i] or [ʊ ɪ], as the examples above testify.

The possibility of variation is eliminated, however, once the inter-predictability of length and quality is disrupted by the merger of /ĭ/ and /ē/, attested in early inscriptions at Pompeii and elsewhere in the southern half of Italy, and plausibly attributable to Osco-Umbrian substrate influence. The effect is that the reflexes of Latin pairs such as PĬRA/VĒRA rhyme in all the Romance languages:

Rum.	pere	vere
It.	pera	vera
Fr.	poire	voire
Sp.	pera	vera
Port.	pera	vera

The exception of course is Sardinian (see the diagram above), where we find *pira* but *bera*. A parallel merger in the back series of /ŭ/ and /ō/ is later and does not affect the Latin/Romance of the Balkans (pp. 391ff) and of a small area of Lucania. Thus, whereas the reflexes of Latin NŬCEM/VŌCEM rhyme in Fr. *noix/voix*, It. *noce/voce* and Port. *noz/voz*, they remain distinct both in Sardinian, *nuge/boge*, and in Rumanian, *nucă/voce*. The effects of these various mergers are set out in Table 2.2, where the Rumanian (or Balkan) system can be clearly seen to parallel the Sardinian system in the back series and what we will henceforth call the Proto-Western-Romance (PWR) system in the front series. The Sardinian

Table 2.2: Romance Vowel Systems

Latin	ĭ	ī	ē	ĕ	ā̆	ŏ	ō	ŭ	ū
Sardinian	i		e		a		o		u
Balkan	i		e	ɛ	a		o		u
PWR	i		e	ɛ	a	ɔ		o	u

system therefore represents the 'default' development of the classical vowel system consequent upon the loss of distinctive quantity, but this is interrupted by two waves of merger spreading outwards from Rome and/or Campania at different times. That all three systems were copresent in the Italian peninsula is strongly suggested by the survival of the 'Balkan' and 'Sardinian' systems in residual dialect areas of Southern Italy, as Map VIII indicates. In dealing with Romance vowel systems, manuals traditionally cite a fourth, so-called 'Sicilian' system, where Lat. /ī ĭ ē/ all merge to /i/ and in parallel fashion /ū ŭ ō/ yield /u/, Thus, we find Sicilian rhyming triplets such as:

vinu	'wine'	(< Lat. VĪNUM)	luci	'light'	(< Lat. LŪCEM)
sinu	'breast'	(< Lat. SĬNUM)	nuci	'nut'	(< Lat. NŬCEM)
kinu	'full'	(< Lat. PLĒNUM)	vuci	'voice'	(< Lat. VŌCEM)

This pattern, however, is probably best viewed not as an independent system evolving directly from Latin but as a subsequent development in Sicily (and parts of Calabria) of Proto-Western-Romance, involving the merger of the Proto-Western-Romance oppositions /i e/ and /u o/. Its explanation is plausibly to be sought in the strong substrate/adstrate effects in this area of the pentavocalic Greek pattern.

Within this pattern of tonic vowel developments the two Latin diphthongs /ai/ and /au/ had rather different roles. The former for the most part monophthongised to /ɛ/, and in so doing must have helped to blur the correlation between vowel quality and quantity, since /ɛ/ was normally the reflex of Latin /ĕ/, whereas any vowel deriving from /ai/ (or /au/ for that matter) would retain the diphthong's inherent length. Indeed some scholars have gone so far as to argue that it is the monophthongisation of /ai/ which finally brings about the collapse of the Classical Latin quantity-based system. Unfortunately, the inscriptional evidence militates against this view, which in any case imposes a rather heavy burden on a minor sound change affecting a small number of items, and which even then is not without exceptions. Thus, It. *seta*, Sp. *seda*, Fr. *soie*, etc. 'silk' presuppose /e/ not /ɛ/ from Lat. SAETA, and note It. *preda* 'booty' with /ɛ/ from PRAEDA, where the French cognate *proie* requires an earlier /e/.

The diphthong /au/ by contrast resisted monophthongisation in a large part of Romania, including Rumanian, southern Italian dialects, most varieties of Rhaeto-Romance, Occitan and Portuguese (where it has subsequently become /ou/). Elsewhere, by a development parallel to that of /ai/, /au/ yields a long open vowel, /ɔ̄/. The exception is Sardinian, where we find /a/. Thus, Lat. TAURUM 'bull' > Rum. *taur*, Cal. *tauru*, Occ. *taur*, Port. *touro* vs Sp. and It. *toro* and Sard. *trau*, this last by metathesis from **taru* (cf. Sard. *laru* < LAURUM 'laurel'). In a few cases, however, even /au/ monophthongised early. Hence Lat. FAUCES 'jaws' > It. *foci*, Sard. *foge*, Occ. *fotz*, Sp. *hoz*, Port. *foz*, which presuppose Lat. /o/ and not /ɔ/, as do forms like It. *c[o]da*, Fr. *queue*, etc. from Lat. CAUDAM.

A much debated issue in Romance historical phonology has concerned the nature and unity of Romance diphthongisation. The facts are relatively straightforward, even if their interpretation is not, and may be encapsulated in the following two generalisations:

(a) a number of languages and dialects, including French, Rhaeto-Romance and northern Italian, have developed so-called 'falling diphthongs' (i.e. having a vowel nucleus as the first element followed by an offglide) from Latin stressed monophthongs, principally /ē/ and /ō/: e.g.

Lat. PĬLUM 'hair' > Fr. *poil* (subsequently [pwal] (cf. p. 211)), R-R *peil*, Vegl. *pail*; Lat. TĒLAM > Fr. *toile*, R-R *teila*; Lat. GŬLAM 'throat' > Fr. *gueule*, R-R *gula* (both with subsequent remonophthongisation); Lat. -ŌSUM 'adj. suff.' > Fr. *-eux*, R-R *-us* (again with remonophthongisation). Vegl. *-aus.*

(b) Many languages and dialects have undergone a process of metaphony, whereby the stressed vowel, usually, but not necessarily, /ĕ/ and /ŏ/, has diphthongised (often with subsequent raising and remonophthongisation) before unstressed, usually final, /i/ and/or /u/, the end product being a rising diphthong (i.e. an on-glide preceding a stressed nucleus): e.g. VĔNTUM 'wind' > SIt. *vientu*, *DĔNTI 'teeth' > *dienti* vs DĔNTEM 'tooth' > *dente*, or PŎRCUM (m.) 'pig' > Port. *porco* vs PŎRCAM (f.) > *p[ɔ]rca*.

This second type of diphthong is more widespread in Romance, and is generally thought to be older, in all probability attributable to a period before the break-up of Latin into the individual vernaculars. It also seems clear that the two phenomena must have different explanations, since metaphony is essentially a harmonising or assimilatory effect between a stressed and an unstressed vowel, and therefore occurs regardless of syllable structure, while falling diphthongs are best seen as due to phonetic lengthening, a conclusion endorsed by the fact that they are limited to open syllables. To see the historical problem, consider now the patterns of standard Italian and of Spanish:

Latin	Italian	Spanish	
BŎNUM	buono	bueno	'good (m. sg.)'
BŎNAM	buona	buena	'good (f. sg.)'
MŎRT(U)UM	morto	muerto	'dead (m. sg.)'
MŎRT(U)AM	morta	muerta	'dead (f. sg.)'
CAECUM	cieco	ciego	'blind (m. sg.)'
CAECAM	cieca	ciega	'blind (f. sg.)'
DEFĔNDIT	difende	defiende	'defends (ind.)'
DEFĔNDAT	difenda	defienda	'defends (subj.)'

Both languages have the rising (putatively metaphonic) diphthong, but Italian has it only in open syllables, the classic falling (non-metaphonic) diphthong environment. Spanish, by contrast, has the metaphonic type of diphthong in open and closed syllables, but regardless of the final vowel. The Spanish pattern can be explained fairly straightforwardly as being due to the analogical extension of the originally metaphonic pattern to all stressed syllables. The Italian, more strictly Tuscan, pattern is more puzzling. It can be quite neatly explained, however, according to Schürr, if one sees the diphthongs as borrowings from surrounding metaphonic dialects, specifically those to the north-west, with the borrowing being mediated by native phonotactics that forbid long vowels (to which diph-thongs are equivalent) in closed syllables. Once borrowed the diphthongs would then generalise by analogy to the non-metaphonic environments. Alternatively, one might see metaphony as original in Tuscan, but with the effects having been obscured by the local developments in syllable structure which filtered out those diphthongs which did not conform phonotactically. Either way it seems clear, as most scholars would agree, that we should seek a unified solution for rising diphthongs in Romance, though whether or not in terms of the operation of metaphony is more controversial, while treating the development of falling diphthongs under a separate heading.

Whereas the tonic vowels, despite the kinds of shift discussed in the pre-ceding sections, tend to preserve their segmental identity as the nucleus of the stressed syllable in a word, the vowels in the unstressed or secondarily stressed syllables tend to be subject to a wide range of elisions, assimi-lations, reductions, and so forth, which it would be impossible conveniently to summarise in a short chapter such as the present one. We will content ourselves, therefore, with an indication of the main types of process involved. Two in particular were important:

(a) *Syncope*: the loss of the immediately pre- or post-tonic vowel, as in ŎC(Ŭ)LUM 'eye' > Fr. *oeil*, It. *occhio*, Sp. *ojo*, Rum. *ochi*; BŎN(Ĭ)TĀTEM > Fr. *bonté*, Cat. *bontat*, R-R *bundet*. The evidence for this is already to be found in documents such as the third-century *Appendix Probi*. The pattern is attested in all the Romance languages but is less widespread in the east than the west — cf. for example, in comparison to the foregoing, Rum. *bunătate*, Sard. *bonidade*, or It. *dodici* beside Fr. *douze*, Port. *doze* < DŬŎDĔCĬM 'twelve'.

(b) *Glide formation*: this occurred when a Latin unstressed /i/, /e/, or /u/ was in hiatus with another vowel: e.g. FĪLĬUM 'son', CĀSĔUM 'cheese', BĂTTUO 'I beat'.

These changes are less important in themselves than because they trigger many other changes such as palatalisation, gemination and cluster reduction due to the new sequences that are thereby created. Other changes are significant because of the way they interact with marking of morphological categories, as in the general late Latin loss of the opposition between /u/ and /o/ in final syllables or the differential loss of final vowels in French (all except /a/), Spanish (all except /o/ and /a/ and some /e/), or the frequent tendency in southern Italy to reduce the final syllable inventory to /i u a/ (and even to just [ə]).

It is a commonplace of historical phonology that sounds change in dif-ferent ways in different environments. We have seen that the principal determining environments in the case of vowels are the location of stress and the nature of the syllable structure. Occasionally, too, the vocalic context may be relevant, as in the case of metaphony. Less commonly, vowels may also change under the influence of adjacent consonants. Thus, rounding due to the following or preceding labial consonant has occasioned the changes in the development of It. *dovere* < DĒBĒRE, *nuvolo* < NŪBĬLUM, *-evole* < -ĒBĬLEM, etc. Even here, mention must be made of stress, since only atonic vowels are affected — contrast *deve* < DĒBET. When we come to consonant changes, we find three principal types of influence: position in the word, position in the syllable, and the nature of the adjacent segment (vocalic or consonantal). To these we may add two further, minor and usually sporadic, effects: metathesis (It. *formaggio* vs Fr. *fromage* < FŌRMĀTĬCUM) and dissimilation (IR *irimă* < ĂNĬMAM, Sp. *cárcel* < CARCĔREM).

The influence of position in the word is perhaps most dramatically obvious in the almost total loss of word-final consonants. Already in Latin the inventory of consonants in this position was severely reduced from that set out in Table 2.1. No words end in /p g kʷ gʷ f h/. We can easily add /b/ to this list since the only possible instances would be ĂB, SUB and OB, which could only occur proclitically. Likewise /d/ is final in the prepositions ĂPŬD, ĂD and the conjunction SĒD, to which the same reasoning applies, and in a few pronominal forms (ĬLLŬD, QUĬD, etc.), all of which are neuter and thus destined to disappear anyway. Note too that inflectional -D in the Old Latin ablative (-ĀD, -ŌD, etc.) had already been lost. Final /k/ has a slightly wider range of occurrence, being found in the demonstrative HĪC (whose neuter HŌC gives *oc* as in *langue d'oc* (p. 13)) and in adverbial forms such as ĬLLĪNC, ĬSTŬC, etc. (in all these instances the final consonant is the residue of an Old Latin deictic particle -CE) and in a few imperative forms of verbs (FĂC, DĪC, etc.) and in the exceptional noun LĂC 'milk'. We have the explicit testimony of contemporary grammarians that /m/ in final position was at most realised as nasality on the preceding vowel and often completely absent, so that it is really only the dental series /t s n l r/ that show up regularly at the end of words. Of these /t/ is lost everywhere except in Sardinian (p. 326), although the final consonant, now protected by a paragogic vowel, in forms such as Cal. *vividi* < BĬBIT may be a relic and not a secondary development. The resonants /n l r/ likewise lose their word-final position by virtue of a paragogic /-e/: hence, CŎR > *CŎRE > It. *cuore*, etc.; MĔL > *MĔLE > It. *miele*, etc. with the classic diphthongal outcome in an open syllable. Compare the French reflexes of these etyma, *coeur*, *miel*, whose vocalism indicates a formerly open syllable, even though, in line with normal French developments, the paragogic vowel has now been lost, and the syllable thereby closed again (p. 213). This leaves only /-s/, whose survival marks one of the classic diagnostics for the division of the Romance languages, not simply on phonological grounds but because of the morphological consequences (cf. pp. 59, 63). Thus, to take by way of example two representative languages, compare the following forms of the verb 'to sing':

	Spanish	Italian
2 p. sg. pres. ind.	cantas	canti
1 p. pl. pres. ind.	cantamos	cantiamo
2 p. pl. pres. ind.	cantáis	cantate
2 p. sg. past subj.	cantases	cantassi

Contrast, too, the pattern of plural formation in the two languages:

	Sg.	Pl.		Sg.	Pl.	
Spanish	casa	casas	Italian	casa	case	'house'
	libro	libros		libro	libri	'book'
	monte	montes		monte	monti	'mountain'

The survival of /-s/, again in paragogic contexts, in those same southern Italian dialects that are claimed to preserve /-t/ is probably an independent phenomenon: e.g. Luc. *kàntasi* < CANTAS, Cal. *yèrasi* < ERAS.

There are also a few word-final clusters in Latin, namely /-ns, -rs, -ks, -ps/ (the last two may be preceded by a sonorant). There are also /-nk/ only in adverbs, /-nt/ only as a verbal inflection, and /-ls, -ms, -rt, -st/ attested in scarcely more than one word each. None of these survives in Romance.

Word-final is generally taken as a weak position in the structure of a word, and one where changes may be expected in any language. It is, of course, equivalent to final position in the last syllable of the word, and it is perhaps no surprise, therefore, to find another series of changes taking place in the final position of internal syllables. We may distinguish three types of pattern:

(a) assimilation to following dentals, characteristic of central and southern Italy and Sardinia: e.g. It. *otto* 'eight' < ŎCTŌ, Sard. *mannu* 'big' < MĂGNUM;

(b) palatalisation of velars, typical of Western Romance in the case of syllable-final stops as witness the reflexes of ŎCTŌ like Fr. *huit*, Sp. *ocho* 'eight', etc., but also of Italian in the case of nasals, e.g. *le[ɲɲ]o* 'wood' < LĬGNUM;

(c) labialisation of velars before dentals found in southern Italian dialects and normal in Balkan Romance, whence Rum. *opt* 'eight', *lemn* 'wood' (cf. p. 397).

The series of consonant changes traditionally known as lenition relate to the segmental rather than the syllabic environment. They occur when original stops are in intervocalic position, or followed by a liquid (CĂPRA >

Sp. *cabra*, Fr. *chèvre*), and involve a set of shifts generally characterisable as:

	Voiceless stop		Voiced stop		Voiced fricative		zero
	p t k	>	b d g	>	β ð γ	>	∅
VĪTA 'life'	It. *vita*		Mil. *vida*		Sp. *vi*[ð]*a*		Fr. *vie*

As can be seen from the above example, the Romance languages can be set out according to the extent to which they undergo the change. Generally speaking Italian and Rumanian do not exhibit the change at all (although see p. 287 for a qualification on this point), while the Western Romance languages, including northern Italian dialects, all do so, but to differing degrees. The extent of the change also differs according to the place of articulation of the consonant, with labials being the most resistant to total loss and the velars least so: SĂPĔRE 'to know' > It. *sapere.*, Sp.,Port.,Cat. *saber*, Fr. *savoir*, ĂMĪCAM 'friend' > It. *amica*, Sp., Port., Cat. *amiga*, Fr. *amie*. Note that voiced stops usually follow the same paths as their voiceless congeners, so that, say, Sp. [ð] from /-t-/ and from /-d-/ are not synchronically distinguishable, and Fr. *devoir* < DĒBĒRE 'to owe' shares the same final syllable as *savoir* < SĂPĔRE. Note, too, that those languages which exhibit lenition also show reduction of geminates to single consonants: CŬPPAM > Fr. *coupe*, Sp. *copa* but It. *coppa*; CATTUM > Fr. *chat*, Sp. *gato*, It. *gatto*; SĬCCUM > Fr. *sec*, Sp. *seco*, It. *secco*. This strongly suggests a chain-shift effect connecting the two developments.

The above changes serve in part to alter the distributional possibilities of existing phonemes and allophones and in part to introduce new elements — e.g. voiced fricatives — into the inventory of Romance sound types. However, by far the most radical effects on segmental inventories are those wrought by palatalisation. The segments affected, the environments and the eventual outcomes are subject to considerable regional variation (for details, see the individual chapters), but the pan-Romance nature of the phenomenon indicates that its beginnings must be sought in the pronunciation of Latin, and specifically in the tendency of certain sound types to change their place and manner of articulation when adjacent to front vowels and glides. Table 2.3 seeks to summarise the relevant parameters. Some comments on and clarifications of this schematic representation are necessary. First, we must specify the geographical bounds of the double reflexes of /ki ke/, namely /ts s/ in Portuguese, Spanish, Catalan, Occitan French and some northern Italian dialects versus /tʃ ʃ/ in Rhaeto-Romance and contiguous Italian dialects, standard Italian and Rumanian. The fricatives /s ʃ/, and also their voiced congeners /z ʒ/, simply represent a further stage of weakening, or more precisely de-affrication, of /ts tʃ dz dʒ/, and are not strictly part of the palatalisation process itself. In the voiced series, the distribution of /dz z/ is much more limited than /ts s/, being

Table 2.3: Romance Palatalisation

Palatalising segment	Potentially affected segments	Areas affected	Outcome
j	all	all	various
i	k g	all but Sardinian	ts/s; ʧ/ʃ;dz/z; ʤ/ʒ
e	k g	all but Sard./Vegl.	ts/s; ʧ/ʃ; dz/z; ʤ/ʒ
a	k g	Gallo- and Rhaeto-Romance	ʧ/ʃ; ʤ/ʒ

restricted to Istrian and northeastern Italian dialects. Whereas the differences in outcome — palato-alveolar as opposed to dental affricates/fricatives — are not easy to rank on phonetic grounds, the triggering environments form a neat hierarchy with the highest element, the palatal glide /j/, having the most widespread effect, and the lowest element /a/ showing the most limited geographical range (cf. p. 212). Furthermore, there is a genuine implicational relation in that no dialect or language shows palatalisation induced by a given segment and not by all higher segments. Note, however, that /a/ induces as reflexes palato-alveolars and not dentals, thus Fr. *cent* < CĔNTUM 'hundred' beside *chant* < CĂNTUM 'song'.

As noted, the palatalising effects induced by /j/ are the most far-reaching of all. Among the stops, /t d k g/ are affected everywhere, and in French and in many Italian dialects (but not the standard language) /p b/ are likewise involved (cf. Sp. *rabia*, It. *rabbia* beside Fr. *rage* < RĂBĬAM 'anger', or It. *sappia* but Fr. *sache*, Sic. *saccia* < SĂPĬAT 'he knows (subj.)'). Nasals behave similarly, with /nʤ/ or /ɲ/ being the regular reflex of /nj/: Fr. *vigne*, Sp. *vina*, It. *vigna* but Camp. *bingia* < VĪNĔAM. Occasionally, the sequence with a labial, viz /mj/, is affected too: Fr. *vendange*, Cal. *vinnigna* < VĪNDĒMIA 'wine harvest'. /sj/ does not regularly palatalise in French, Occitan, Catalan and Spanish: BĂSIUM > Occ. *bais*, Cat. *bes*, Sp. *beso* vs. It. *bacio*, Sard. *bazu*, Port. *beijo*. /lj/ usually yields /ʎ/: Port. *filha*, It. *figlia* < FĪLĬAM 'daughter', though often the laterality is subsequently lost altogether, e.g. Sp. *hija* [ixa] and Fr. *fille* [fij] (cf. p. 212). Finally, the palatal element in the sequence /rj/ either raises the preceding vowel, or displaces the rhotic or disappears without trace, or metathesises as in the following forms of the suffix -ĀRĬUM: Sp. *-ero*, It. *-aio* or *-aro*, Fr. *-aire*, Port. *-eiro*.

3 Morphology

Latin still retained to a large degree the type of inflectional morphology to be found in the older stages of all the Indo-European languages. Such a pattern of inflection includes: (a) a nominal subsystem, comprising the traditional classes of nouns, adjectives, the lower numerals, and various kinds of pronouns and pronominal adjectives, all marked for case, gender and number; (b) a verbal subsystem marked for tense, aspect, mood and voice; and (c) a range of indeclinable words or particles, including prepositions, conjunctions and underived adverbs.

Nominal Morphology

It is traditional to divide Latin nouns into five declensions as set out in the chart of noun morphology. Useful as a tabular presentation like this is, however, it fails to bring out a number of important generalisations. In particular, it should be noted that several morphological formations are common to all declensions (e.g. for all neuter nouns there is syncretism of the nominative and the accusative; all masculine and feminine accusative singular forms end in -*m* and accusative plural in -*s*; neuter nominative/accusative plural is always in -*a*; no noun is distinct in dative and ablative plural, etc.). Moreover, there is a natural division between declensions I and II with a nominative plural in /-i/ (recall that the spelling -*ae* in the first declension represents /-ai/) and declensions III, IV and V with a nominative plural in -*s*. There is also a split between declensions I and II (and V — later to be absorbed into I anyway) with genitive singular -*i* and genitive plural in -*rum* as opposed to III and IV with genitive singular in -*is* and genitive plural without -*r*-. Add to this the fact that IV and V are vanishingly small closed classes and that I (predominantly feminine) and II (predominantly masculine and neuter) are complementary in gender, while

Latin Noun Morphology

	I (a-*stems*)	II (o-*stems*)	IIIa (C-*stems*)	IIIb (i-*stems*)	IV (u-*stems*)	V (e-*stems*)
Singular						
Nom.	stell-a 'star'	lup-us 'wolf'	urb-s 'city'	av-is 'bird'	man-us 'hand'	sp-es 'hope'
Voc.	-a	-e	-s	-is	-u	-es
Acc.	-am	-um	-em	-em	-um	-em
Gen.	-ae	-ī	-is	-is	-us	-eī
Dat.	-ae	-ō	-ī	-ī	-ui	-eī
Abl.	-ā	-ō	-e	-ī	-u	-ē
Plural						
Nom.⎫ Voc.⎭	-ae	-i	-ēs	-ēs	-ūs	-ēs
Acc.	-ās	-ōs	-ēs	-ēs	-ūs	-ēs
Gen.	-ārum	-ōrum	-um	-ium	-uum	-ērum
Dat.⎫ Abl.⎭	-īs	-īs	-ibus	-ibus	-ibus	-ēbus

III contains nouns of all genders, and it becomes clear that the core of Latin declensional structure can be represented thus:

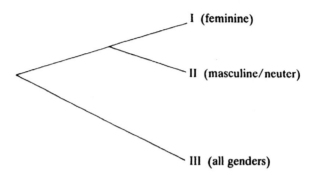

I (feminine)

II (masculine/neuter)

III (all genders)

Such a view is reinforced by the morphology of Latin adjectives, which fall into two groups: those with a single set of forms for all genders (so called third declension adjectives, e.g. *facilis* 'easy', *vetus* 'old' and the present participle in -*ans/-(i)ens*) and those which combine the inflections of I for feminines and II for masculines and neuters (e.g. *bonus* 'good', *miser* 'wretched', and the past participle in -*tus/a/um*). Pronouns, although they have some special inflectional quirks of their own such as masculine singular in -*e* (due to reinterpretation of an encliticised particle) and genitive singular in -*ius*, nevertheless essentially follow the I/II pattern:

Inflection of Some Latin Pronouns

Personal pronouns

	1st p. sg.	2nd p. sg.	1st p. pl.	2nd p. pl.	3rd p. refl. sg./pl.
Nom./voc.	ego	tū	nōs	vōs	—
Acc.	mē	tē	nōs	vōs	sē
Gen.	meī	tuī	nostrī	vestrī	suī
			nostrum	vestrum	
Dat.	mihi	tibi	nōbīs	vōbīs	sibi
Abl.	mē	tē	nōbīs	vōbīs	sē

[Note: non-reflexive third person pronouns were frequently left unexpressed both as subject and object. When necessary, forms of the anaphoric/demonstrative *is, ea, id* were used in the classical language, later replaced by *ille, illa* (see p. 53).]

Demonstrative pronouns

	proximal Singular			distal (2nd p.)			distal (3rd p.)		
	m.	f.	n.	m.	f.	n.	m.	f.	n.
Nom./Voc.	hic	haec	hoc	iste	ista	istud	ille	illa	illud
Acc.	hunc	hanc	hoc	istum	istam	istud	illum	illam	illud
Gen.		huius			istīus			illīus	
Dat.		huic			istī			illī	
Abl.	hōc	hāc	hōc	istō	istā	istō	illō	illā	illō

	Plural								
Nom./Voc.	hī	hac	haec	istī	istae	ista	illī	illae	illa
Acc.	hōs	hās	haec	istōs	istās	ista	illōs	illās	illa
Gen.	hōrum	hārum	hōrum	istōrum	-ārum	-ōrum	illōrum	-ārum	-ōrum
Dat.	hīs				istīs		illīs		
Abl.	hīs				istīs		illīs		

Other pronouns

	Anaphoric			Identitive			Emphatic			Relative		
Singular												
	m.	f.	n.	m.	f.	n.	m.	f.	n.	m.	f.	n.
Nom.	is	ea	id	īdem	eadem	idem	ipse	ipsa	ipsum	quī	quae	quod
Acc.	eum	eam	id	eundem	eandem	idem	ipsum	-am	ipsum	quem	quam	quod
Gen.		eius			eiusdem			ipsīus			cuius	
Dat.		cī			cīdem			ipsī			cui	
Abl.	eō	eā	eō	eōdem	eādem	eōdem ipsō	ipsā	ipsō		quō	quā	quō

Plural												
Nom.	iī	eae	ea	īdem	eaedem	eadem ipsī	-ae	ipsa	quī	quae	quae	
Acc.	eōs	eās	ea	eōsdem	eāsdem	eadem ipsōs	-ās	ipsa	quōs	quās	quae	
Gen	eorum (m., n.) eārum (f.)			eōrundem (m., n.) eārundem (f.)			ipsōrum (m., n.) ipsārum (f.)			quōrum (m., n.) quārum (f.)		
Dat.	eīs/iīs			eīsdem/iīsdem			ipsīs			quibus		
Abl.	eīs/iīs			eīsdem/iīsdem			ipsīs			quibus		

[Note: the forms *huius, huic,* etc. for the genitive and dative singular and *hīs,* etc. for the dative/ablative plural are the same for all genders.]

The model of Latin declensional structure outlined above is also supported by subsequent diachronic developments in Romance. Already in classical times a number of fifth declension nouns had parallel first declension forms — e.g. *materies/materia* 'matter', *mollities/mollitia* 'softness' — and some members of IV — e.g. *domus* 'house', *colus* 'distaff' — had variant second declension forms. It was but a short step for nouns in these two classes to be absorbed into the larger, productive declensions or to be replaced by new formations — e.g. *spes* 'hope', but It. *speranza,* Sp. *esperanza,* Rum. (via It.) *speranṭa* (< SPERANTIA); Fr. *espoir,* Cat. *espera* (backformed from the verb). The modern Romance languages likewise bear witness to a number of gender shifts which serve to increase the correlation between form and gender. Several tree names ended in *-us* but were feminine: *fagus* 'beech', *morus* 'mulberry bush', *pirus* 'pear tree' (contrast forms in *-a* for fruit: *mora, pira*). The form has either been retained with a gender shift, e.g. It. *pero* (m.), or again new formations have been found, e.g. Sp. *peral,* Fr. *poirier.* An interesting minimal contrast is Sp. *haya* and It. *faggio* 'beech' which derive from *fageam* and *fageum,* feminine and masculine forms respectively of the adjective from *fagus.* Likewise, a number of Greek borrowings in Latin were feminine but in *-us,* e.g. *atomus, dialectus, methodus, periodus,* whereas their Romance counterparts are usually masculine (but cf. Fr. *méthode* (f.)). A curious exception is *manus* 'hand', which has remained feminine everywhere, even when, as in Sp. and It. *mano,* it is clearly masculine in form.

Readjustments were also provoked by the loss, as yet not satisfactorily explained, of the neuter gender. In the case of the third, mixed gender, declension, the status of masculine as the unmarked gender meant that it absorbed most of the neuters. Apart from the gender of the modern words, such shifts are evidenced in forms like Fr. *lait*, Sp. *leche*, Port. *leite*, It. *latte*, Rum. *lapte*, 'milk', all of which presuppose an etymon *LACTEM, a well formed accusative only on the assumption that the classical neuter stem LAC had been treated as masculine (or feminine − cf. Sp. *la leche*). In other instances, the modern forms derive from the Latin neuter nominative/accusative form and not from a putative analogical accusative: for example, It. *cuore*, Fr. *coeur*, Cat. *cor*, etc. 'heart' must come from Lat. COR and not *CORDE(M); It. *nome*, Rum. *nume*, Fr. *nom*, etc. 'name' presuppose NOME(N) and not *NOMINE(M). In some circumstances, there is a declensional shift linked to a formal overlap. Thus, Latin third declension nouns in -*us* were neuter. The surviving forms like It. *corpo*, Fr. *corps*, Sp. *cuerpo* 'body' (< CORPUS), It. *tempo*, Fr. *temps*, Sp. *tiempo* 'time' (< TEMPUS) and occasional late Latin forms like a genitive singular *corpi* (instead of expected *corporis*) reveal a change of both gender and declension, and reinforce the view of an overall diachronic pressure to make the two categories overlap. Interesting confirmation also comes in the analogical reinterpretation of neuter plurals in -*a* as a feminine singular: FOLIA 'leaves' > Fr. *feuille*, It. *foglia*, Sp. *hoja*; GAUDIA 'pleasures' > Fr. *joie*, It. *gioia*. In Italian and Rhaeto-Romance the situation is a little more complex in that many neuter plurals in -*a* have become feminine but remained plural, thereby creating a class of mixed nouns with masculine singulars and feminine plurals: e.g. R-R *il vierv* (m. sg.) 'the word', *la viarva* (f. pl.) 'the words'; the neuter plural is used collectively, while a new masculine plural *ils viervs* has sprung up for use in counting. This is the only sense in which it can be said that Romance exhibits a change in the Latin system of number, since such nouns permit a three-way distinction singular/plural/collective. That this was once fully productive is witnessed by the fact that even originally masculine nouns like DIGITUS 'finger', RAMUS 'branch' have entered into the pattern. Note, too, the large class of nouns in Rumanian, including those deriving from Latin neuters, e.g. *timp*, pl. *timpuri*, which are masculine in the singular and feminine in the plural (cf. p. 401).

While changes in declension and gender affect principally the morphological and lexical levels of the language, changes in the case system are intimately bound up with other syntactic developments and will be treated together with those in section 4 below.

Verbal Morphology
Latin verbs are marked for tense (past, present, future), aspect (perfective, imperfective), mood (indicative, subjunctive), voice (active, passive), person (first, second, third), and number (singular, plural). In addition, every

verb has a number of non-finite forms, including two imperatives (singular, plural), two infinitives (present, perfect), three participles (past, present, future), and a gerund and gerundive. On the basis principally of differences in the characteristic thematic vowel but also of some differences in inflectional endings, the verbs are traditionally divided into five classes or conjugations. The present indicative active and principal parts of specimen verbs are set out in the chart of verb morphology. Once the principal parts of any verb are known it is possible, except in cases of extreme irregularity (see below), to construct all other forms. Thus the imperfect is formed for all verbs by addition of the suffix -b- followed by the endings -am, -as, -at, -amus, -atis, -ant; the future by the addition of the same -b- suffix plus the endings -o, -is, -it, -imus, -itis, -unt for verbs of the first two conjugations and by the direct addition, without an intervening suffix, of the endings -am, -es, -et, -emus, -etis, -ent for the third and fourth conjugations. There

Latin Verb Morphology

	I (a-*stems*)	II (e-*stems*)	IIIa (*C-stems*)	IIIb (i-*stems*)	IV (i-*stems*)
Inf.	rogāre 'to ask'	habēre 'to have'	legere 'to read'	facere 'to do'	audīre 'to hear'
Present					
1 sg.	-ō	-eō	-ō	-iō	-iō
2 sg.	-ās	-ēs	-is	-is	-īs
3 sg.	-at	-et	-it	-it	-it
1 pl.	-āmus	-ēmus	-imus	-imus	-īmus
2 pl.	-ātis	-ētis	-itis	-itis	-ītis
3 pl.	-ant	-ent	-unt	-iunt	-iunt
Perf.	rogāvī	habuī	lēgī	fēcī	audīvī
Pp.	rogātum	habitum	lēctum	factum	audītum

are, moreover, certain overlaps, such as the syncretism of all forms except the first person singular of the future perfect indicative and the present perfect subjunctive, and of the second person and imperative forms in the passive. Furthermore, the combination of properties 'future + subjunctive' is unrealised, at least within the core verbal system, and certain other formations — notably the perfect passives and the future infinitives — are expressed periphrastically. Hence the total number of inflectionally distinct forms for any (non-defective) verb is 85, to which may be added nine non-finite formations (or 14 if the rare future imperatives are added). Note too that, since the participles and gerund(ive)s are really verbal adjectives or nouns, they in turn are further susceptible to all the inflectional modifications that befit those classes. A complete list of all the parts of a typical a-stem verb is given in the paradigm of *rogare* 'to ask'.

Full Conjugation of Specimen Verb — *rogare* 'to ask'

		Active Indicative	Subjunctive	Passive Indicative	Subjunctive
Pres.	1 sg.	rogo	rogem	rogor	roger
	2 sg.	rogas	roges	rogaris	rogeris
	3 sg.	rogat	roget	rogatur	rogetur
	1 pl.	rogamus	rogemus	rogamur	rogemur
	2 pl.	rogatis	rogetis	rogamini	rogemini
	3 pl.	rogant	rogent	rogantur	rogentur
Imperf.	1 sg.	rogabam	rogarem	rogabar	rogarer
	2 sg.	rogabas	rogares	rogabaris	rogareris
	3 sg.	rogabat	rogaret	rogabatur	rogaretur
	1 pl.	rogabamus	rogaremus	rogabamur	rogaremur
	2 pl.	rogabatis	rogaretis	rogabamini	rogaremini
	3 pl.	rogabant	rogarent	rogabantur	rogarentur
Fut.	1 sg.	rogabo	—	rogabor	—
	2 sg.	rogabis		rogaberis	
	3 sg.	rogabit		rogabitur	
	1 pl.	rogabimus		rogabimur	
	2 pl.	rogabitis		rogabimini	
	3 pl.	rogabunt		rogabuntur	
Pres. perf.	1 sg.	rogavi	rogaverim	rogatus sum	rogatus sim
	2 sg.	rogavisti	rogaveris	es	sis
	3 sg.	rogavit	rogaverit	est	sit
	1 pl.	rogavimus	rogaverimus	sumus	simus
	2 pl.	rogavistis	rogaveritis	estis	sitis
	3 pl.	rogaverunt	rogaverint	sunt	sint
Past perf.	1 sg.	rogaveram	rogavissem	eram	essem
	2 sg.	rogaveras	rogavisses	eras	esses
	3 sg.	rogaverat	rogavisset	erat	esset
	1 pl.	rogaveramus	rogavissemus	eramus	essemus
	2 pl.	rogaveratis	rogavissetis	eratis	essetis
	3 pl.	rogaverant	rogavissent	erant	essent
Fut. perf.	1 sg.	rogavero	—	ero	—
	2 sg.	rogaveris		eris	
	3 sg.	rogaverit		erit	
	1 pl.	rogaverimus		erimus	
	2 pl.	rogaveritis		eritis	
	3 pl.	rogaverint		erunt	

| Imperative | sg. | roga | | rogare | |
| | pl. | rogate | | rogamini | |

Inf.	pres.	rogare		rogari	
	perf.	rogavisse		rogatus esse	
	fut.	rogaturus esse		rogatum iri	

Part.	pres.	rogans, -tis
	perf.	rogatus, -a, -um
	fut.	rogaturus, -a, -um
Gerund		rogandum
Gerundive		rogandus, -a, -um

Comparing the formal resources of Latin with those of the modern Romance languages in the area of verb morphology, four different circumstances may be identified:

(a) the Latin forms — with due allowances being made for the effects of sound change — may survive in more or less their original function. For example, the Romance present tenses are for the most part direct reflexes of the Latin present, though with a fair sprinkling of analogical formations — e.g. Mod. Fr. *trouve/trouvons* vs OFr. *truef/trouvons* (contrast Mod. Fr. *meurs/mourons* and cf. p. 224) — and neutralisations — e.g. It. first person plural *-iamo* (<Lat. II/III conjugation subjunctive *-e/iamus*) for the indicative and subjunctive of all conjugations. Similarly, the imperfect as a category remains, but with more or less differentiation amongst the persons. After the loss of final consonants had eliminated the distinction between Latin *amabam* and *amabat*, Spanish (*amaba*) and Old Italian (*amava*) were left with a single form. Italian, but not Spanish, has restored the distinction by importing the first person ending of the present to create a new form *amavo*.

(b) Some Latin forms may survive but with a change of function. For instance, the characteristic -ss- marker of Romance past subjunctives (Fr. *aimasse*, It. *amassi*, Sp. *amase*, Port, *amasse*, etc.) betrays its origin in the Latin suffixes *-issem*, etc. of the pluperfect subjunctive. The reason here seems to lie in the fact that on the one hand the pluperfect subjunctive had a phonologically very distinctive ending, which was nevertheless made redundant by the new analytic perfect forms (see below p. 56), while, on the other hand, sound changes had threatened the phonetic identity of the original imperfect subjunctive *amarem*, etc. The morphological shift then exploited the first situation to resolve the second. We may also cite as an example in this connection the alternative Spanish past subjunctive forms *amara*, etc. (p. 99), which are reflexes of the Latin pluperfect indicative. Note, finally, how the French participle suffix *-ant* represents a conflation of two Latin forms, the gerund *-andum* and the participle *-antem* (thus Fr. *aimant*, but It. *amando* and *amante*).

(c) Some Latin forms disappear altogether, such as the already mentioned imperfect subjective, which only survives in Sardinian (p. 332) and in the Portuguese personal infinitive (p. 154). The Latin pluperfect indicative has similarly few Romance reflexes. However, the biggest casualties under this heading must without doubt be the inflected passive and future (OFr. *ier*, OProv. *er* are two relic forms from the irregular Latin future ERO series of the verb 'to be'). Homonymic clashes induced by sound changes — *amavi/amavit/amabit* all become *amavi* — and the inconsistent nature of the inflectional pattern across the conjugations — *amabo* but *regam* — are the deciding factors here. Amongst the non-finite forms, the future participle is a clear casualty, surviving only in adjectival usages such as It. *venturo* 'next, coming' and of course in the term 'future' (< FUTURUM) itself! Lost too are the perfect and passive infinitives.

(d) Many Romance verb forms are not the direct reflexes of Latin verb forms but result from the grammaticalisation, and in some cases eventual fusion, of the elements of a periphrastic construction. We may identify three subtypes here:

(i) The new form more or less corresponds in function to an old one. This seems to be the case for the periphrasis infinitive + HABET, which comes to take over the role of the Latin synthetic future, and whose constituent parts eventually fuse into the inflected futures of most but not all modern Romance (Fr. *aimera*, Port. *amará*, etc.).

(ii) The new forms partially replace old ones but at the same time there is a reorganisation of the system of morphosyntactic oppositions. Thus, the periphrasis HABET + past participle in part replaces the Latin inflected perfect, and in part coexists with it to create a new grammatical contrast. Similarly, the Latin inflected passive gives way to the periphrasis EST + past participle, but new patterns are created in so far as the same periphrasis is used for the perfect of some intransitive verbs while passive meanings are also signalled by an extended use of the reflexive.

(iii) A genuinely new constellation of form and meaning is created. The obvious example here is the conditional, a Romance formation which has no single correspondent in the Latin system.

(For further discussion of the particular factors at work in each of these examples, see Section 4.)

In summary, then, the person/number categories remain essentially unchanged in Romance, while the categories of tense, mood and aspect undergo considerable reorganisation both in terms of the grammatical oppositions and of their formal expression. The conjugational structure remains but in a slimmed down form. Thus, most verbs in *-io* with an infinitive in *-ĕre* realign with either *-ire* or *-ēre* verbs: e.g. Lat. *fugere* but Sp. *huir*, Rum. *a fugi*, etc.; Lat. *rapere* but It. *rapire*, Fr. *ravir*; Lat. *mori* (not **moriri*) but Sp. *morir*, Fr. *mourir*, etc. on the one hand, and Lat. *sapere* but Sp. *saber*, It. *sapere*, etc., on the other. There are also occasional shifts from *-ĕre* to *-ēre* (e.g. Lat. *cadĕre* but It. *cadére*, Sp. *caer*, etc.) and vice versa (e.g. Lat. *ridēre* but It. *rídere*, Fr. *rire*, etc.). What these kinds of development suggest is an emergent tripartite pattern of -*are*, -*ere*, -*ire* verbs, with the middle class showing lexically arbitrary division into stem-stressed and ending-stressed subclasses. Indeed, we may go further and suggest a binary split between -*are* verbs and all other verbs, whether -*ere* or -*ire* (cf. the treatment of Italian conjugational structure, pp. 294–5).

Before concluding, some mention must be made of irregularity in the verbal paradigm. Latin, like any other language, had its share of irregular verbs, and the present tenses of some of the most common ones are listed in the chart given here. Some have survived with their irregularity intact, most notably perhaps *esse* 'to be', though even here there has been suppletive interaction with forms of Lat. STARE and SEDERE (see the chart for 'be' in Latin and Romance). Others — e.g. *malle* 'to prefer', *nolle* 'to be unwilling', *ferre* 'to bear' — have simply disappeared. More complex is the circumstance where some of a verb's forms survive while others do not. Consider Latin *ire* 'to go', and the Romance verbs with the same meaning set out in the chart of paradigms. This, of course, is a classic instance of suppletion with *vadere* 'to go' and a verb of disputed etymology, perhaps *ambulare*, providing most of the forms that do not derive from *ire*. Note too in the case of Spanish and Portuguese the penetration of part of the 'be' paradigm (cf. the English usage *have you been to France?*).

Present Tenses of Some Latin Irregular Verbs

	posse 'be able'	ēsse 'eat'	velle 'wish'	malle 'prefer'	ire 'go'	fieri 'become'	ferre 'bear'
1	possum	edo	volo	malo	eo	fio	fero
2	potes	ēs	vis	mavis	is	fis	fers
3	potest	ēst	vult	mavult	it	fit	fert
4	possumus	edimus	volumus	malumus	imus	(fimus)	ferimus
5	potestis	ēstis	vultis	mavultis	itis	(fitis)	fertis
6	possunt	edunt	volunt	malunt	eunt	fiunt	ferunt

The Verb 'be' in Latin and Romance

	Lat.	Sp.	Port.	Cat.	Fr.	Occ.	It.	Sard.	R-R (Sur.)	Rum.
Inf.	esse	ser	ser	ésser	être	èsser	essere	essere	èsser	a fi
Present										
1 sg.	sum	soy	sou	só(c)	suis	soi	sono	sòe	sun	sînt
2 sg.	es	eres	és	ets	es	ès	sei	ses	cis	eşti
3 sg.	est	es	é	és	est	es	è	est	ci	e(ste)
1 pl.	sumus	somos	somos	som	sommes	sèm	siamo	semus	essan	sîntem
2 pl.	estis	sois	sois	sou	êtes	sètz	siete	sedzis	essas	sînteţi
3 pl.	sunt	son	são	són	sont	son	sono	sun	cin	sînt

Romance Paradigms of Verbs Meaning 'to go'

	Spanish	Portuguese	Catalan	French	Occitan	Italian	Sardinian	Rhaeto-Romance (Surselvan)
Present								
1	voy	vou	vaig	vais	vau	vado	ando	mondel
2	vas	vais	vas	vas	vas	vai	andas	vas
3	va	vai	va	va	va	va	andat	va
4	vamos	vamos	anem	allons	anam	andiamo	andamus	mein
5	vais	ides	aneu	allez	anatz	andate	andaes	meis
6	van	vão	van	vont	van	vanno	andan	van
Imp.	ve/id	vai/ide	ves/aneu	vas/allez	vas/anatz	va/andate	vae/vadzi	va/mei
Imperf.	iba	ia	anava	allais	anavi	andavo	andabo	mavel
Pret.	fui	fui	aní	allai	aneri	andai	–	–
Subj.	vaya	vá	vagi	aille	ane	vada	ande	mondi
Fut.	iré	irei	(an)iré	irai	anarai/irai	andrò	–	–
Inf.	ir	ir	anar	aller	anar	andare	andare	i
Pp.	ido	ido	anat	allé	anat	andato	andau	ius
Ger.	yendo	indo	anant	allant	anant	andando	andande	–

Note: forms of VADERE, IRE and AMBULARE do not survive in Rumanian, where the normal verb for 'to go' is *a merge*, a regular verb derived from Lat. MERGERE 'to sink'.

Many verbs, on the other hand, are not irregular in Latin but become so in Romance because of the disruptive effects of sound change. Lat. *habere* is an inconspicuous member of the second conjugation, but its descendants in Romance show manifold irregularities; likewise: *debere* 'to have to', *venire* 'to come', *tenere* 'to hold', etc. An interesting case involves *velle* 'to wish', one of the most irregular of Latin verbs in its present tense, as the leftmost column below shows. Yet the Italian forms in the rightmost column require us to reconstruct an intermediate Late Latin stage as in the middle column: In other words, the verb has been regularised by the force of analogy, and then disrupted anew by the effects of sound change.

Classical Latin	Late Latin	Italian
volo	*voleo	voglio
vis	*voles	vuoi
vult	*volet	vuole
volumus	*volemus	volemo (OIt.)
vultis	*voletis	volete
volunt	*voleunt	vogliono

The above examples all concern the present tense, where most Latin irregularities, apart from those discussed, were eliminated and where the irregularities in Romance have largely arisen in the course of the development of the separate languages. The situation with regard to the past tense and the past participle is rather more complex. In Latin there were four principal ways of forming the perfect stem:

(a) by reduplication — e.g. *cecini* 'I sang', *momordi* 'I bit', etc.;

(b) by the suffixation of -*u*-, of which there were two allomorphs, namely /-w-/ post-vocalically — e.g. *amavi, delevi, audivi* — and /-u-/ post-consonantally — e.g. *monui, volui*;

(c) by the suffixation of -*s*- (the so-called sigmatic perfect) — e.g. *dixi* 'I said', *scripsi* 'I wrote', *clausi* 'I shut';

(d) by the direct addition of the perfect inflections to the stem (with or without concomitant lengthening of the stem vowel) — e.g. *movi* 'I moved', *vidi* 'I saw', *bibi* 'I drank', *volvi* 'I rolled'.

Of these, the first was a minor formation in Latin, although it had been widespread in Indo-European, and has left virtually no trace in Romance (one example is It. *diedi* < DEDI). The last also disappeared for the most part (but cf. Port. *fiz* < FECI, Cat. *viu* < VIDI), presumably because of existing homonymies and of the even greater number that were to come with the loss of distinctive vowel length. The sigmatic and -*u*- patterns accordingly both expanded considerably the latter particularly in Italian and Rumanian (p. 296), and account for the vast majority of so-called irregular past tenses and past participles in the modern languages.

Particles

Under this heading we have grouped an assortment of minor classes, whose chief unifying properties are first that they are indeclinable and second that they straddle the boundary between grammar and lexis. This latter point is illustrated by the role of these items within the grammar of Latin: e.g. the use of *ab* to mark the agent in a passive construction, or the overlaps between the vestigial locative case, *humi* 'on the ground', and a prepositional construction such as *in humo*. It can be seen again in the way a number of semantically independent items in Latin — e.g. *de* 'about', *quod* 'because' — develop into grammatical functions in Romance — e.g. Fr., Sp., It. etc. *de/di* as a marker of dependent nouns and infinitives (cf. pp. 68–9); Fr., Sp., It. etc. *que/che* as a marker of dependent clauses of various kinds, or, in more recent terminology, a complementiser.

Traditionally, this class includes adverbs such as *iam* 'already', *saepe* 'often', *hic* 'here', *ibi* 'there', *paene* 'almost', etc.; discourse particles such as *etiam* 'even', *enim* 'for', *modo* 'only', etc.; interrogative words such as *ubi* 'where', *quo* 'whither', *unde* 'whence', *quando* 'when', *cur* 'why', etc.; prepositions such as *in* 'in, on', *per* 'through', *trans* 'across', *cum* 'with', *post* 'after', etc.; conjunctions such as *cum* 'when', *si* 'if', *dum* 'while', *quamquam* 'although', etc. Relatively few of these items survive directly into Romance with unchanged meaning or function. Commonly, there is either a semantico-syntactic shift — e.g. Lat. TRANS 'across' > Fr. *très* 'very', Lat. PER 'through' > It. *per* 'for', Fr. *par* 'by (marker of the agent in passives)' — or the original Latin form is taken up as part of a new compound item. Thus, Latin *cras* 'tomorrow' survives in Sardinian and, as *crai*, in a number of southern Italian dialects, but in general the concept comes to be expressed by compounds containing the element *mane* 'in the morning': Fr. *demain*, It. *domani*, Sp. *mañana*, Port. *amanhã*, Rum. *mîine*, etc.

For more details of the role of prepositions in relation to the breakdown of the case system, see below p. 217, and for the changing patterns of complementation and subordination, see pp. 65ff.

4 Syntax

Nominal Group

In dealing with the changes in nominal syntax from Latin to Romance it will be convenient to distinguish between 'external' syntax, that is to say the way the noun and its modifiers fit into the general patterns of sentence structure, and 'internal' syntax, the patterns of relationship between the noun and its modifiers. We shall deal with the former topic under sentence structure (see p. 59).

In regard to internal syntax, perhaps the most salient difference between Latin and Romance is the absence in Latin of articles, both definite and indefinite. This has the twofold effect first that certain semantic categories had to be signalled in a different way or not at all and second that there is no obvious evidence for a Latin NP with internal constituent structure based on the obligatory ordering relations between determiners, adjectives and nouns such as it is normal to set up for any of the Romance languages. We therefore have two types of change: reorganisation in the system of grammatical categories and the emergence of fixed constituent structure.

If Latin did not have articles, it is natural to ask what were the etymological sources of this category in Romance. The indefinite article derives from the numeral 'one', with the result that decontextualised phrases such as Fr. *un chien*, Sp. *un perro*, etc. can mean either 'a dog' or 'one dog'. Indeed it is only infrequently that we find a formal differentiation of the article and numeral as, for instance, in Cal. *nu cani* 'a dog' vs *unu cani* 'one dog'. The situation of the definite articles is different in that the use of descendants of ILLE, and more rarely IPSE, has led to the replacement of those items in their original senses, a question we discuss further below. IPSE in fact survives as an article only in Sardinian *su, sa*, Balearic Catalan *es, sa*, and in a few southern Italian dialects, which remains an unexplained puzzle in view of the fact that IPSE predominates over ILLE in the Late Latin texts. ILLE emerges as the definite article via the semantic attrition of the remote deictic pronoun/adjective, a type of change well documented from many other language families. At the same time there is a parallel development of ILLE as a third person pronoun.

The development of ILLE as an article impeded its continued use as a demonstrative. At the same time, another pronoun/adjective in that series, HIC, was under threat by virtue of the effects of the sound changes which delete both initial /h/ and many final consonants. As a result the Latin system of demonstratives which had separate exponents for the deictic categories corresponding to the three personal pronouns (HIC 'near the speaker', ISTE 'near the addressee', ILLE 'near neither speaker nor addressee') underwent a reorganisation. The outcome was the grammaticalisation of a reinforced form of ECCU/E+ILLE, literally 'behold that', ancestor of the remote demonstrative in all the daughter languages (cf. p. 221 for subsequent transformations in French). Meanwhile ISTE, similarly reinforced by ECCU/E, expanded its semantic range to become a general proximal ('near the speaker and the addressee') marker. Such a two-term demonstrative system survives in Gallo-Romance, Rhaeto-Romance and Balkan Romance. Elsewhere, however, reinforced ECCU+IPSE provided a third term (see for instance Catalan, p. 178), so that the structure of the Latin system remains unchanged even though the exponents are new. An interesting hybrid is Tuscan, which retains a three-term system but with a special (now moribund) second person form *codesto* (< *ECCU+TIBI+ISTE). Structurally, the demonstrative series fills the same syntagmatic slot as the articles — hence no Romance language permits *il

questo cavallo 'the this horse' or the like (though cf. Catalan, p. 192) —
and provides more evidence for a prenominal determiner position, and
thus for the emergence of NP-like constituency.

A third category of determiner in a number of languages is the
possessive, hence the absence of, say, Fr. **le mon cheval* 'the my horse'.
The Romance languages are not, however, united in this respect. The
equivalent It. *il mio cavallo*, Port. *o meu cavalo*, OProv. *lo mieus cavals*,
Cat. *el meu cavall* are impeccable, as are forms such as It. *questo mio
cavallo*, literally 'this my horse', *un mio cavallo* 'one of my horses'. For
these languages, then, the possessive must be treated as either a straightforward adjective or as occupying a separate syntactic position between
articles and adjectives. Possessives also differ from articles and demonstratives in that their more usual position in Latin was post-nominal, a state
of affairs reflected in emphatic uses such as Sp. *en presencia tuya* 'in your
(not someone else's) presence', in the normal unstressed Rum. *calul meu*
'my horse' (note that *-ul* is the postposed clitic article — cf . p. 400), and
southern Italian dialect uses like *figliomo* 'my son'. The attraction of the
possessive to the determiner position in languages like French therefore
represents a significant change of order, which once more reflects emergent
NP structure.

Next in regard to the NP, mention must be made of the position of the
adjective. Latin was particularly flexible on this score, permitting not just
pre- and post-nominal uses, but also complete separation of noun and
adjective: *magno cum periculo* 'with great danger', *non satis credidi, tuam,
hominis prudentis, tam valde esse mutatam voluntatem* 'I could not believe
that you, as a prudent man, had so radically changed your intention', literally 'that your (f. sg. acc.) ... had changed intention (f. sg. acc.)'. These
latter possibilities were greatly exploited in poetry where metrical considerations were paramount, but they are found in sufficient numbers in more
mundane prose (the second example above is from Cicero's letters) to
suggest that they were not unrepresentative of ordinary usage. In Romance,
by contrast, we find that adjectives occupy only the positions immediately
adjacent to the noun. The extent to which both positions are exploited
varies from language to language, and depends on the semantics of the
adjectives in question (for some particular discussion in relation to Italian,
see p. 299). However, certain points recur in all or most languages,
including the fact that common adjectives of size, worth and age precede;
that there are cases of adjectives with two different meanings dependent
on position — It. *vecchio*, *vario*, *certo*, Fr. *propre*, *même*, etc.; that
adjectives being used evaluatively and metaphorically precede, while in a
more literal and distinguishing sense they follow (cf., for example, p. 105
or pp. 191–2).

Thus, a typical Romance NP structure is: (Det) (Adj) N (Adj). To this
may be added dependent PPs, which follow the second adjective slot.

These include genitives which are now expressed phrasally via the grammaticalisation of Latin DE 'about' to mark nominal dependence. Relatives followed the noun in Latin and continue to do so throughout Romance. Indeed, in some respects the syntax of relatives has changed comparatively little since Latin. Thus, all the Romance languages have a system of relative pronouns which continues the Latin QUI series, and the standard languages at least continue the strategy of not marking the position of the relativised item by a resumptive pronoun. Nonetheless, certain points are worthy of mention. Whereas in Latin all the grammatical properties of the relativised noun — case, gender and number — could be recovered from the form of the relative pronoun, in Romance the possibilities are considerably more limited. Among the pronouns that descend from Latin QUI, case (or more accurately grammatical function) is to some extent retrievable, but the patterns differ from language to language. Thus, French has *qui* after prepositions only for animates but *qui* for subjects and *que* for objects regardless of animacy; Italian has *che* for subjects and objects and *cui* after prepositions, similarly without regard to animacy; Portuguese has *que* for subjects, objects and after prepositions if the head-noun is inanimate, and *quem* after prepositions if the noun is animate (*quem* also has a number of other uses); and so on. In fact, to the extent that words like French, Portuguese, Spanish *que*, Italian *che* have the same form as the items which introduce sentential complements, comparatives and other kinds of adverbial clauses, it may even be argued that they are no longer true relative pronouns but simply complementisers whose function is to signal the beginning of a subordinate clause. Such a view is especially well supported in those dialects and spoken registers which adopt an alternative strategy for identifying grammatical function according to which clitic pronouns serve to identify the grammatical function of the deleted noun leaving the relative marker simply to indicate the beginning of the clause: e.g. Mil. *quell fioeu che te gh'hee faa el regall,* literally 'that son that you to-him have given the present'. Such a pattern has become standard in Rumanian (p. 409). Note that in the above Milanese example gender and number are still not recoverable since *ghe* is a generalised indirect object clitic for all third person nouns, singular or plural, animate or inanimate, masculine or feminine. These properties can, on the other hand, be retrieved if the alternative strategy of using the definite article plus the reflex of Latin QUALIS 'what' is adopted. Compare, for example, the situation in Catalan discussed on pp. 199–201, but similar patterns are found in most of the individual languages, and clearly reflect a late Latin innovation concomitant with the emergence of the definite article.

Typologically, the organisation of the NP in the Romance languages, with the exception of the use of prenominal adjectives (more or less extensive according to the language) and the occurrence of post-nominal articles in Rumanian, conforms very well to what has come to be seen by many scholars as characteristic of SVO languages. These patterns may be set beside the more flexible ordering properties of Classical Latin and the marked tendency in early Latin for certain modifiers, in particular adjectives and dependent genitives, to precede rather than follow the noun.

Verbal Group

The system of temporal and aspectual oppositions in Latin is given in the following chart, where the third person singular indicative active forms of CANTĀRE 'to sing' are conventional labels for the complete classes of forms obtainable by varying person, number, mood and voice as appropriate. We return to these last two categories in particular below. Such a chart brings out clearly the existence of two series of forms, one built on the imperfective stem CANTA- and the other built on the perfective stem

Tense and Aspect in the Latin Verb

	Past	Present	Future
Imperfective	CANTABAT	CANTAT	CANTABIT
Perfective	CANTAVERAT	CANTAVIT	CANTAVERIT

signalled by the suffix -V-. As we have indicated (p. 51), the perfective stem could be formed in a variety of ways, some of them quite irregular, but only a handful of defective verbs lacked the inflectional resources necessary to support a system of this kind. In one respect, however, the chart is misleading, namely in that it does not bring out the dual function of the form CANTAVIT, which could serve both as a present perfective ('he has sung') and as a past simple ('he sang'). While the latter meaning survived in the Romance reflexes of this form variously called preterits or past historics (Fr. *chanta*, It. *cantò*, etc.), the present perfective came increasingly to be expressed through the grammaticalisation of the periphrasis HABET CANTATUM (> Fr. *a chanté*, It. *ha cantato*, etc.). In such a construction, the expression of perfectivity is contained in the participle, while person, number, tense and mood can be realised on the auxiliary, so that an entire series of forms HABEBAT CANTATUM, HABEAT CANTATUM, etc. becomes available and supplant the original CANTAVERAT (past perf. indic.), CANTAVERIT (pres. perf. subj.), etc.

From the foregoing it should be clear that this wholesale transfer of functions to the new series of forms cannot take place if those forms are not available, something which might happen for either a morphological reason — the verb in question simply did not have a past participle — or a semantic one — the verb's meaning was not compatible with the original meaning of the grammaticalised periphrasis. The former was not uncommon in Latin, and was rectified by the creation of new analogical participles. Thus, for the classical BIBERE 'to drink' with no past participle, the evidence of Romance attests two competing forms: BIBITUM, whence Sp./Port. *bebido*, and BIBUTUM, whence Cat. *begut*, Fr. *bu*, etc. Less easily remedied was the circumstance in which the necessary periphrasis could not arise for semantic reasons. This was inevitable with any intransitive verb whose subject expressed the role of patient, such as verbs expressing motion, location, change of state, etc. (cf. the discussion of such verbs in Italian (p. 301). Whereas it is easy to see how the meaning 'I have written the letter' can emerge from 'I have the letter written' (cf. pp. 101–2), there is no corresponding way to produce 'I have gone' from *'it has me gone' or the like. These verbs therefore developed periphrases based on an auxiliary which itself took a patient subject, namely *essere* 'be'. This complementary distribution of auxiliaries remains almost intact in Italian (p. 301), but has been gradually eroded elsewhere so that for example *haber* has generalised to all verbs, even *ir*, in Spanish, though this last stage of the change is only about five hundred years old. A relic of this development which has not yet disappeared even in Spanish is the tendency with verbs of this class to place the subject post-verbally, the inherited position for patients (cf. p. 115).

For rather different reasons, the Latin future inflections were also threatened (cf. p. 48). The remedies adopted vary from none at all in Sicilian and southern Italian dialects, where futurity is generally expressed by the present tense plus appropriate time adverbs, to the development of a number of periphrases constructed from an auxiliary (e.g. VELLE 'to want' in Rumanian, DEBERE 'to have to' in Sardinian) plus the infinitive. By far the most successful of these involved HABERE. Thus, CANTARE + HABET yields Fr. *chantera*, Sp. *cantará*, It. *canterà*, etc. Again the mechanism engenders a whole series of forms. Thus, if CANTABIT gives way to CANTARE HABET, then HABEBIT will yield to HABERE HABET, in which case a putative future perfect such as *HABEBIT CANTATUM (replacing an earlier CANTAVERIT) will in turn become *HABERE HABET CANTATUM, the ancestor of modern Fr. *aura chanté*, etc. One particular form which is produced in this way, and which on one view may even have been the trigger of the whole process, is CANTARE HABEBAT, clearly identifiable as the past of CANTARE HABET and used precisely to indicate the 'future-in-the-past' of reported speech. This, then, is the origin of the so-called conditional, which rapidly developed a range of modal values initially in the apodoses of conditional sentences (p. 72) and then in main clauses. Indeed, the interaction of the conditional form and the subjunctive mood forms a recurrent theme in the following chapters (see, for instance, p. 231). Before finishing this section, we should note that not all forms supplanted by these periphrastic formations disappeared entirely. We have already alluded to the survival of the past perfective subjunctive in -ISSET (p. 47), and we should note too the continuance of the past perfective indicative as one

form of the imperfect subjunctive in Spanish (p. 99) and the future perfective as the probable source of the Portuguese future subjunctive (p.
155).

The final periphrasis that we will consider in this section is that of the
passive. Recall that in Latin the passive was principally an inflectional category; it is only in the perfective that the periphrasis CANTATUM EST 'it has
been sung' makes an appearance. Yet the preponderance of the evidence
of the Romance languages tells a different story, one in which the passive is
formed with the appropriate tense of the verb ESSERE followed by the past
participle. The motivation for this change is not hard to find in the inroads
made on the inflectional system by sound change, but important too —
perhaps more so — is the increasing role of the perfect periphrasis, and this
for two reasons. First, by providing a model in which the auxiliary verb
gives expression to the appropriate categories of tense, mood, etc., it
ensures that CANTATUM EST should be interpreted as a present imperfective, not perfective. (It can also plausibly be seen as causing the change
of word order underlying Fr. *est chanté*, etc.) But if EST CANTATUM is the
present imperfective, then the corresponding perfective must be *EST
STATUM CANTATUM (recall that in origin ESSERE takes ESSERE as its
auxiliary), the future is *ESSERE HABET CANTATUM and so forth. Second,
the emergent use of ESSERE with patient subject verbs matches well with
ESSERE as the general auxiliary of the passive, the archetypical construction
in which the patient becomes the subject. For reasons that are not entirely
clear, the periphrasis with ESSERE + past participle does not survive in
Balkan Romance (the modern Rumanian construction is due to a
nineteenth-century literary imitation of French), with the double consequence that we find there no evidence for two perfect auxiliaries and no
periphrastic passive. Instead, we find the other main passivising construction attributable to Late Latin: the use of the reflexive pronoun *se*,
particularly flourishing in Italian and Spanish, somewhat less so in French.
The Rumanian evidence thus confirms what is also clear from the surviving
texts, namely that from a very early stage *se* had extended from its purely
reflexive use to include a number of uses in which the agent remains
unexpressed: *Myrina quae Sebastopolim se vocat* 'Myrna, which is called
(literally 'calls itself') Sebastopol'; *mala rotunda toto anno servare se
possunt* 'round apples can be kept (literally 'keep themselves') all year
round'. That the usage could even extend to inherently intransitive verbs
can be seen in the following example from the fifth-century *Peregrinatio*:
recipit se episcopus et vadent se unus quisque 'the bishop withdrew and
everyone went away' (compare here the Fr. *s'en aller*, It. *andarsene*, Sp. *irse*
Port. *ir-se*, etc.). The subsequent developments in the individual languages
are discussed at various points in the chapters which follow.

Sentence Structure

A simple sentence may be regarded as consisting in the first place of a nucleus made up of the verb plus its dependents, where the form and number of the latter is determined by the verb's semantico-syntactic class, and in some cases by arbitrary lexical properties. When the dependents of the verb are single nominal groups, one of these is always in the nominative case. However, this nominative noun or pronoun may, in some circumstances, be omitted, its reference being determined by context and its grammatical properties of person and number being deducible from the inflection of the verb. The second nominal dependent is in the accusative case unless a different case is determined by lexical properties of the verb, and other arguments are either expressed by a particular case or by a prepositional phrase. Thus: *surrupuistin uxori tuae pallam istanc?* 'did you not steal this cloak (acc.) from your wife (dat.)?'; *miles gladio usus est* 'the soldier (nom.) used a sword (abl.)'; *Caesar Aeduos frumentum flagitabat* 'Caesar (nom.) kept demanding the corn (acc.) of the Aedui (acc.)'; *praedam militibus donat* 'he presents the booty (acc.) to the soldiers (dat.)'; *civem de vi accusavit* 'he accused the citizen (acc.) of violence'. As with the first dependent of the verb, so the second, if recoverable from context, can be freely omitted, although it is worth noting that in this instance there is no way in which the missing element's grammatical features can be marked on the verb: *Pompeius interfecit* 'Pompey killed him', *nego* ' I deny it'. As this last example shows, a single Latin verb form can thus constitute a complete sentence (even when the verb in question is transitive), with the inflection marking the subject and the object omitted. Several Romance languages, including Spanish, Italian and Portuguese, retain the ability to omit subjects — the so-called pro-drop phenomenon (p. 334) — but a similar omission of the object pronoun is only possible in Portuguese (cf. p. 158), where the pattern is clearly an innovation and not a retention from Latin. It is worth noting, however, that apparently empty arguments are to be found in examples such as It. *tutto induce a pensare che ...* 'everything leads (one) to think that ...' (contrast the need for 'one' or 'people' to make a grammatical translation into English). Analogous examples are to be found in a wide range of Romance languages, and suggest that the problem of object deletion in Latin and Romance needs to receive some of the considerable scholarly attention that has traditionally been accorded to the issue of subject deletion (see pp. 231–2). This last point has always been seen in connection with two other notable Romance developments, namely the emergence of a fixed word order and the change from synthesis to analysis, two issues to which we now turn.

Word Order

The order of words and/or constituents which make up a sentence is one of the more obvious respects in which the grammar of Latin differs from that of its descendants. These differences may in turn be divided into those that reflect a more fixed order of elements in Romance than in Latin, and those which betoken a genuine change of order. For example, the Romance articles — with the exception of Rumanian (p. 400) — occur in a fixed prenominal position. They derive, as we have seen (p. 53), from the Latin adjectives ILLE (generally) and IPSE (occasionally), which already in the classical language tend to occur before rather than after the noun they accompany. Thus, the Romance pattern may be seen as a 'freezing' of a preferred Latin pattern, while Rumanian has undergone an exceptional change attributable to areal influence. On the other hand, modal verbs such as *debere* 'to have to' and *posse* 'to be able' more commonly followed rather than preceded their dependent infinitive — e.g. *satis intellegere non possum* 'I cannot sufficiently understand', whereas the modern languages are all agreed in requiring the order modal + infinitive: *je ne peux pas comprendre, non deve venire, no podia confirmar nada*, etc. Of course, the two situations cannot be completely separated. If the overall change is from a language such as Latin with fairly flexible word order to languages with more fixed orders, then any fixed order is bound to represent a change with respect to one or more of the earlier possibilities. Thus, in Latin *non possum satis intellegere* was also possible (cf. *si nollem aut non possem tueri* 'if I would not or could not defend it') as was *homo ille*, while in French *comprendre je ne peux pas* and *homme le* are not. Indeed, our distinction breaks down completely if one regards word order in Latin as entirely conditioned by pragmatic and discourse factors, since in such a circumstance there would be no 'neutral' or 'unmarked' word order to take as a reference point for evaluating subsequent developments, which would all therefore involve fixing rather than changing of order. On this view, which is not without its advocates, Latin is a genuine 'free' word order language, structurally akin in this respect to a number of Australian and other 'exotic' languages described in the general linguistic literature. The following description is based on the assumption that such a view is not tenable, flying as it does in the face of all the evidence derived from both philological and statistical study of the texts, and therefore imposing too great a strain on the discrepancy between spoken and written Latin (see section 1). This is not to say, of course, that pragmatic and discourse factors are not relevant — they clearly are — but that they are not of themselves decisive in determining word order in Latin.

The key issue, in fact, concerns the place of the verb. If, as the traditional account would have it, the natural place for the Latin verb is sentence-final, then there is a genuine word order change to be explained, since the one place one does not expect to find the verb in modern Romance is in final position (though it is sometimes claimed that patterns such as Sicilian *cunzumati siti* 'you are lost' and Sardinian *mandikatu asa* 'you have eaten' (p. 338) are relics of Latin final position). Alternatively, it has been argued that the heavy statistical predominance of verb-final patterns in writers such as Caesar and his contemporaries is simply the consequence of strict prescriptive control over the written language, and that the genuine spoken pattern is more closely attested in such writers as Plautus or Petronius. On this account, the puristic insistence on verb-final structures represents an overgeneralisation of archaic religious and legal texts. Such a view, however, only pushes the same change back to an earlier stage. Unless the archaic texts are genuinely discrepant, and represent a pattern that was never normal — a possibility that, quite rightly, no-one seems prepared to envisage — we are still faced with the need to explain first a change from an early, predominantly verb-final, stage to Plautine Latin with its greater freedom in the positioning of the verb, and second a further change to the more rigid verbal syntax of modern Romance.

Let us therefore try the alternative tack of projecting backwards from the Romance languages to see precisely what patterns are in need of explanation. We find:

(a) Uniformly in all the Romance languages, the verb precedes the object in a transitive sentence.

(b) With equal regularity, the unmarked position for the subject of a semantically unified class of intransitive verbs expressing motion, location and change of state is after rather than before the verb (for examples and further discussion concerning the individual languages, see the following chapters). An apparent exception here is French, where *arrive Pierre and kindred patterns are not found, but this is the result of later developments in the language (pp. 235–6): OFr. vendrat li jurz 'the day will come' is entirely normal. Note further that this same class of verbs has — or has had — ESSERE as a perfect auxiliary (p. 57). What unites the verbs in questions is that the subject fulfils the role of patient, in other words that the subject has the same role as the object of a transitive verb.

Seen from this perspective, the first change appears to have been a semantically driven one, whereby the verb comes to be followed by the NP which fills the role of patient. In other words, we have a pattern which, in the way it unites the objects of transitives and the subjects of certain intransitives, is reminiscent of ergative languages, and correlates with other ergative traits which have been pointed out in Latin, such as the occasional formal identity of nominatives and genitives (cf. the chart of Latin noun morphology above), the difficulty in deciding the relative markedness of accusative and nominative (and note that it is the accusative which by and large survives in Romance), and the existence of so-called intransitive passives such as curritur 'people run' (literally 'it is run'). Meanwhile, initial position remains the locus of the topical element in the clause, whether this is an NP, an adverbial expression or even the verb itself. Of course, not all sentences will have specific topics and in that case the unassigned noun of an agent- or experiencer-taking verb will fill the first position, which will, however, remain empty in the case of patient-taking intransitives. The resultant word order pattern, for which there is considerable evidence already in the Latin of Plautus and which may be taken as the departure point for subsequent Romance developments, can be schematised thus: (Topic)–Verb–Patient.

Thereafter we can point to three main changes:

(a) The formation of a VP constituent, consisting of the verb and its patient, plus any auxiliaries and adverbial elements. One piece of evidence of the emergence of such a constituent, in addition to the increasing fixedness of order between auxiliaries, verbs and pronouns, consists in the relative rarity of VSO patterns either in the modern Romance languages or in Old French (the VSO structures of modern spoken French are a later and different development — see p. 236) compared to the possibility of VOS. The latter results from movement of the subject to a position following the new VP, whereas the former would require interruption of the VP, something which can still only happen in Spanish and Italian in the most marked circumstances (cf. p. 115 and p. 305). The agglomeration of elements around the verb to form a VP is exactly parallel to the emergence of internal NP constituency described above.

(b) The gradual grammaticalisation of the topic position to produce a sentence-initial subject position, something which happened in French, but is arguably not yet complete in any of the other Romance languages. Once this change has taken place, then even the patient arguments of verbs like *venir, mourir*, etc. will be attracted to first position, and all trace of the ergatively motivated word order will have been lost.

(c) A third development is the emergence of a verb-second (V2) constraint, characteristic of French (p. 235) and Rhaeto-Romance (pp. 369ff), and not implausibly attributed to Germanic influence.

One characteristic of the V2 pattern is that where there is no other element to occupy the initial slot the unstressed subject clitic takes on that role. Clitic pronouns also permit other NPs and PPs to be moved to pre-subject position (so-called left dislocation) or to absolute final position (so-called right dislocation), while track can still be kept of their grammatical roles in the sentence. These possibilities are increasingly exploited in the Romance languages, particularly in French (p. 236), as the discussions in the individual chapters will show.

Before moving on, mention should briefly be made of the contribution from typological studies to the question of Romance word order change. We have already noted (p. 55) how the elements within the nominal group tend both in Latin and in Romance to fall into the order head–modifier. An equivalent ordering principle elsewhere in the sentence would require nominals to follow their governing prepositions, objects to follow verbs, adverbs to follow verbs and auxiliaries to precede verbs, all properties which hold of the vast majoriy of constructions in the vast majority of the Romance languages. It has therefore been suggested that there is a single motivating principle behind all the changes of order between Latin and Romance, namely the move towards a consistent manifestation of the order head–modifier (sometimes referred to by the German term *Postdeterminierung*). The account given here is rather more cautious, preferring to recognise separate and logically independent developments in nominal and verbal/sentential syntax, subject only to the proviso that perhaps the most noticeable feature in both sets of circumstances is not so much change in word order as the increasing rigidification of linear patterning that comes with the growth of constituent structure. In current grammatical parlance, the Romance languages have all become clearly configurational in contrast to the predominant non-configurationality of Latin syntax.

The fixing of word order is often treated in traditional accounts as part of the general tendency in Romance to replace synthetic patterns with analytic ones, that is to say the tendency to use syntactic means (fixed sentence position) for the expression of morphosyntactic categories in place of morphological ones (nominal case inflection). The survival of case in Romance is interestingly various. The conventional view, for which there is very strong support, is that for the most part Latin nouns persist into Romance in their accusative form, hence the practice in this volume (and elsewhere) of citing Latin etyma in the accusative case. This is perhaps most obvious in the singular in the forms of those third declension nouns which differ between nominal and oblique stems: e.g. none of the forms Fr. *nuit*, Sp. *noche*, It. *notte*, Rum. *noapte*, could be derived from Lat. NOX 'night'. If necessary, the Italian and Rumanian forms could be derived from the genitive, since final -s does not survive in the east (cf. pp. 398–9), but the Spanish and French forms require either NOCTE (abl.) or NOCTEM (acc.) as their source. General linguistic considerations of morphological markedness would argue in favour of the reconstruction of the accusative in this situation, as would the errors which predominate in inscriptions. If the singular is from the accusative, it makes sense to assume the plural is too, and this is corroborated by the fact that the plural in the western part of Romania is signalled by -s, marker of accusative plural in all declensions. Nonetheless, there are clear indications that in the east the plurals derive from nominatives (e.g. It. *-e* < -AE (f. pl.), *-i* < -I (m. pl.)), presumably since, with the loss of -s in that area the accusative singular in -AM, -EM, etc. would have been non-distinct from the accusative plural in -AS, -ES, etc. Be that as it may, the implication is that case markings were ceasing to serve their previous role and so could be subverted to mark number. If this is true, one may presume it was either because the word order was already tolerably well fixed or because of an emergent ergative system (see p. 61), where the classical system of distinguishing nominative and accusative would be less functional. Note, however, that it makes more sense to assume some other grammatical change prior to loss of case marking, or else we are forced into the dubious position of accepting an intervening period when neither is functional. (For more on the role of case in Old French, see pp. 216–17, and for Rumanian p. 400).

Other commonly cited examples of the synthesis to analysis pattern of development include the periphrastic passive, perfective and future discussed above (pp. 56–8) and such phenomena as:

(a) the adverbs in -*ment/mente/menti* etc. found throughout the Romance area, though only marginally in Rumanian, which derive from a Latin syntagm adjective + MENTE 'mind', and which replace the inherited suffixal patterns: e.g. MISER 'wretched', MISERE 'wretchedly'; FORTIS 'brave', FORTITER 'bravely'; etc.

(b) Comparatives, which in Latin are usually suffixal — ALTUS 'high', ALTIOR 'higher'; FACILIS 'easy', FACILIOR 'easier'; FACILE or FACILITER 'easily', FACILIUS 'more easily' — but which are marked in Romance by reflexes of the particles PLUS or MAGIS 'more': Fr. *plus*, It. *più*, Sp. *más*, Rum. *mai*, etc. Similarly, the standard of comparison in Latin was indicated either by the ablative case: *nihil est virtute* (abl.) *amabilius* 'nothing is more lovable than virtue', or by the use of *quam* + noun: *utilior quam scientia* 'more useful than knowledge', while in Romance only the latter survives in the guise of the general complementiser *que/che*, etc.

(c) a number of prepositional uses, including not only reflexes of DE 'about' for the expression of possession and other kinds of grammatical dependence previously marked by the genitive, and reflexes of AD 'to' for abstract goals in addition to literal locative ones, but also a whole range of other prepositions in the individual languages to express agents, instruments, etc.

Similar to the above sorts of situation and often discussed together with them is the emergence of articles and clitic pronouns. The difference is that these latter categories did not exist as such in Latin, and their development, by very similar processes of grammaticalisation, serves therefore to refute the naive view that analytic constructions simply replace the corresponding synthetic ones. Nor is it easy to maintain the equally traditional view that analysis vs synthesis is a sort of equipollent opposition, and that languages oscillate between the two at different periods in their histories. Rather, it should be clear that if a language is of a broadly synthetic type, and thus has a relatively high proportion of bound morphology, there are only two things that can happen (apart from stasis). The first is reanalysis of the suffixal structure, as, for example, when the Latin past perfective subjunctive comes to be a simple past subjunctive or the inchoative marker -ESC- becomes part of the inflection of -IRE- verbs (p. 101). The second and more common possibility is the loss of the inflections themselves, something which may come about as a result of sound change, especially since inflections are rarely under the main stress of the word, or as a consequence of other syntactic changes. Conversely, any periphrastic structure is likely to be susceptible to fusion and consequent phonological adjustment as the elements of the periphrasis come to be treated as a single unit. Given these universal tendencies, and given the fact that whatever state it is in, a language will tend to change, it follows automatically that a predominantly 'synthetic' language like Latin can only stay as it is or engender 'analytic' structures. These in turn can either persist as separable periphrastic formations or 'resynthesise', and if the latter, they may do so at different rates. The Romance languages, as we have seen, show, in differing degrees, developments of all the kinds adumbrated above, but there is no macroshift of 'synthetic' to 'analytic' or vice versa which is in need of a single, unified, explanation.

Limitations of space prevent us going further into the structure of the Latin simple sentence. We note only that to the nucleus consisting of the verb plus its lexically determined dependents may be added a number of adverbials expressing time, place, manner, etc. These will consist of specific adverbs (*hodie* 'today', *illic* 'there'), special case forms (e.g. *illa nocte* 'on that night (abl.)') or prepositional phrases (e.g. *in insula Samo* 'on the island of Samos'). Complex sentences arise when a verb in a non-finite form (infinitive, gerund(ive) or participle) or a full sentence expresses an argument of the verb (complementation) or an adverbial (subordination), and it is to these that we now turn our attention.

Complementation

Just as verbs can be classified by virtue of the number and forms of the nouns with which they may be constructed, so they may also be grouped according to whether they may take, in addition to or instead of a nominal, a sentential or infinitival complement. Thus, in *deterrere ne scribat parat*, literally 'to frighten (him) lest he write he prepares', i.e. 'he is preparing to frighten him from writing', the selection of the clause consisting of the negative complementiser *ne* 'lest' plus the subjunctive verb *scribat* is dictated by the governing verb *deterrere*, here occurring in its infinitive form as in turn required by the main verb *parat*. There are, therefore, two questions which need to be addressed: what different forms could complement structures take in Latin? and what, if any, were the principles which dictated which forms went with which verbs? The proviso 'if any' is necessary since it is possible that the choice may be a matter of more or less arbitrary lexical selection, as appears to be the case for *iubere* 'to order' which takes the infinitive, while *imperare* 'to command' more usually takes *ut* + subjunctive (compare English *to forbid someone to do something* but *to prevent someone from doing something*). Correspondingly, there may be two types of change, namely in the forms of complementation and in the principles that determine their assignment.

We begin then with a survey of Latin complement patterns:

(a) *Ut/ne* + subjunctive: this construction may be freely used to express purpose (a so-called final clause) after any type of verb: *oportet esse ut vivas, non vivere ut edas* 'you must eat in order to live, not live in order to eat'; *gallinae pennis fovent pullos, ne frigore laedantur* 'hens keep their chickens warm with their wings so that they are not hurt by the cold'. However, the same construction is used with many verbs where the sense is not as much one of purpose but simply one of futurity, in that the action/state identified in the *ut/ne* clause follows that expressed in the governing verb. Thus, *Ubii Caesarem orant ut sibi parcat* 'the Ubii beg Caesar to spare them', *sententiam ne diceret recusavit* 'he refused to give an opinion'. This is one of the most widespread of Latin complement types, and is found regularly after verbs of ordering (*imperare, praedicere*), desiring (*optare, studere,* and sometimes even *velle,* though this more normally takes an infinitive), warning (*monere*), requesting (*rogare, petere*), urging (*persuadere*), fearing (*timere, vereri*) and so on. With verbs of hindering (*impedire, prohibere*) another conjunction, *quin* (< QUI-NE) is often found, but the construction is essentially the same. The generalisation which seems to hold here is that all these verbs express an attitude towards, or an attempt to bring about/forestall, an event which is yet to come. Accordingly, we will call them 'future-oriented'. This orientation towards the future, with its implied uncertainty or unreality, helps also to explain the fact that these clauses contain the conjunctive (see below p. 70). Note finally that many verbs in this class would take a following, so-called pro-lative, infinitive (see below) if the subjects of both actions were the same: *vereor laudare praesentem* 'I am afraid to praise someone who is present', *precor recipi* 'I beg to be received'.

(b) (Prolative) infinitive: in origin the Latin infinitive is a verbal noun able to fill the role of subject or object of another verb. The subject function is seen in an example like *legere difficile est* 'to read is difficult', and in the use of the infinitive with many impersonal verbs *libet scribere* 'it is pleasing to write'. When used as an object, the infinitive soon came to be reanalysed as a dependent verbal form with an implied subject coreferential with that of its governing verb. Thus, *volo vincere* was originally to be understood as 'I want victory' but later as 'I want (I) win'. Other verbs which would permit such a construction are: *malle* 'to prefer', *audere* 'to dare', *conari* 'to try', *incipere* 'to begin', *scire* 'to know how to', *posse* 'to be able to'. Beside these are a smaller group where the infinitive may serve as a second accusative, e.g. *tondere filias suas docuit* 'he taught his daughters to shave (him)', literally 'he taught them shaving'.

(c) Accusative + infinitive: the use of an infinitive and an accusative as the codependents of a single verb exemplified in the last example, must be sharply distinguished from an instance such as *dicit te errare* 'he says that you are going wrong'. Here the accusative *te* is semantically subject of *errare*, and bears no direct relation to *dicit*. Compare the acceptability of *filias suas docuit* 'he taught his daughters' versus **dicit te*. A simple test that reveals this difference is the fact that a coreferential subject is not omitted in examples of the latter type: *te abisse hodie hinc negas?* 'do you deny that you left here today?' would be ungrammatical with *te* omitted whereas it is the presence of *te* which rules out ** vis te abire*. The so-called 'accusative and infinitive' construction is normal with verbs whose complement is logically a proposition, i.e. verbs of saying, thinking, hoping, perceiving, etc.: *audire* 'to hear', *videre* 'to see', *intellegere* 'to understand', *nuntiare* 'to announce', *simulare* 'to pretend', *promittere* 'to promise' and many more. Note too that if a verb has different senses it may take different constructions. Thus, *scire* in the sense of 'to know how to' takes a simple infinitive, but when it means 'to know that', it is followed by the accusative and infinitive. A variant of the accusative + infinitive is the nominative + infinitive, which is derived by passivisation, as in *traditur Homerus caecus fuisse* 'Homer is said to have been blind'.

(d) *Quod* + indicative: just as *ut* is in origin a marker of purpose, but comes to be used in complement clauses in an attenuated sense, so *quod* 'because' introduces the complement of a class of so-called verbs of emotion where in a loose sense the complement can be said to express the cause or origin of the emotion: *dolet mihi quod tu nunc stomacharis* 'it pains me that (i.e. because) you are angry now', *iuvat me quod vigent studia* 'I am pleased that studies are flourishing'. The dividing line between this class and that of the accusative and infinitive is an uncertain one, and it is not surprising to find the same verb taking both, with no discernible difference of meaning: *gaudet miles quod vicerit hostem* 'the soldier rejoices. that he has conquered the enemy' and *salvom te advenisse gaudeo* 'I rejoice that you have come home safe'.

(e) Indirect questions: for any verb with the appropriate meaning — e.g. *mirari* 'to wonder', *quaerere* 'to inquire', *nescire* 'not to know' — the complement may be an indirect question introduced by an interrogative word, (e.g. *num* 'whether') and with the verb in the subjunctive.

What we have described in the preceding paragraphs is a range of possible complement structures, with the choice of which one goes with which verb being dictated largely by semantic considerations. When we come to look at the situation in the Romance languages we find the following changes have taken place:

(a) *ut/ne/quin* + subjunctive have been lost altogether;

(b) *quod* as the introducer of a finite clause has greatly increased its range and is followed freely by either indicative or subjunctive;

(c) the indirect question structure continues but with loss of the mandatory subjunctive;

(d) the accusative and infinitive is limited to perception verbs;

(e) a causative construction with *facere* + infinitive has emerged;

(f) the prepositions *ad* and *de* have developed specialised uses as introducers of dependent infinitives;

(g) the infinitive, unsupported by an introductory particle, survives but with a greatly reduced number of verbs.

The combined effect of these changes is to give rise to a system of complementation which is constructed according to entirely different principles from those which obtained in Latin, and thus makes it difficult to narrate the changes as a series of continuous evolutions. Rather, we will try to group the phenomena listed above under a number of headings to show how they provide evidence for the restructuring that has taken place.

In the first place it is important to underscore the severely reduced role of the 'bare' infinitive, which occurs with fewer verbs in all Romance languages than in Latin. Comparing the individual languages with each other, and excluding some southern Italian dialects and Rumanian, where the infinitive does not survive for independent reasons (see p. 411), we find some interesting differences (e.g. It. *andare a fare* vs Fr. *aller faire*; Sp. *rehusar trabajar* vs. Fr. *refuser de travailler*, etc.), which it is not possible to examine here in full detail.

With regard to AD and DE, it is clear that the motivations behind the two particles are rather diverse. AD occurs most frequently with those verbs that we earlier characterised as 'future-oriented' — Fr. *inviter, hésiter, obliger*; It. *convincere, preparare, cominciare*; Sp. *enseñar, persuadir, arrancar* — and for this reason may be seen as inheriting the role of the *ut* clause in Latin. Such a development is also in line with the semantics of AD as the preposition of goal or motion towards, and indeed we may note the possible analogical influence of an alternative Latin expression of purpose — AD + gerund(ive), particularly favoured with verbs of motion: *legatos mittit ad pacem petendam* 'he sends ambassadors to sue for peace'. For a typological comparison we may adduce the fact that in English also *to* is the marker both of purpose and of direction, and thence becomes a general infinitive particle.

If the role of AD with infinitives is to be explained, in origin at least, on semantic grounds, the role of DE seems to be more structural, and must be linked to the emergence of QUOD/QUID as a finite complementiser. The alternation between the two items can be seen in cases such as Fr. *avante de*,

Sp. *antes de*, It. *prima di* + infinitive versus *avant que, antes que, prima che* + clause, and in the Italian contrast between *più ricco di me* 'richer than me' and *più ricco che non si pensi* 'richer than one thinks'. In the area of complementation, the French structures *il a décidé de nous accompagner* 'he decided to accompany us' vs *il a décidé que son fils nous accompagnera* 'he has decided that his son will accompany us' are typical and could be replicated from any other Romance language except, as we have said, for Rumanian. The general principle which emerges is that as the role of the Latin complement pattern with QUOD + clause generalised, largely at the expense of the accusative and infinitive, so a parallel pattern with DE + infinitive emerged beside it and in complementary distribution to it. This linked role of QUOD and DE is at the heart of the new Romance system of complementation.

Where the bare infinitive did remain, it tended to form a closer nexus with its controlling verb than had previously been the case. In the most extreme instance the two fuse, as happened with the development of the future periphrasis (see p. 57). More usually, however, they remain formally separate, but their connection can be seen in the fact that clitic pronouns logically dependent on the infinitive may be placed before or attached to the controlling verb. Modern French is an apparent exception in this regard, since it is normal to say *je peux le voir* 'I can see it' and not **je le peux voir* (contrast It. *lo posso vedere*). However, the modern French usage arose with the normative reforms of the seventeenth century, and Old French usage paralleled that of the other languages. A further index of this close connection is the fact that in Italian the compound tenses of modals may be formed using the auxiliary appropriate to the syntactico-semantic class of the following infinitive (see p. 301).

One characteristic construction that has emerged through an increasingly close connection of verb and infinitive is the causative. This is found in all the languages, and is unique in that although an infinitive is involved, there is no missing argument. Contrast, therefore, *Paul veut venir* 'Paul wants to come', where *Paul* is subject of both verbs, and *Paul fera venir son frère* 'Paul will make his brother come', where the erstwhile subject of the infinitive, *son frère*, becomes the object of the causative complex *fera venir*. If the infinitive already has an object, the underlying subject is further displaced into a prepositional phrase: *Paul fera nettoyer la chambre à son frère* 'Paul will make his brother clean the room'. If the nouns here are replaced by clitics, they must attach to *faire* — thus *Paul la lui fera nettoyer* (cf. p. 234), again exactly as if we were dealing with a single verb (compare *Paul la lui donnera* 'Paul will give it to him'). Moreover in Italian, though not in French or Spanish, the compound causative verb can be passivised: *Giorgio fu fatto entrare* 'George was made (to) enter'. Historically, the interest of this construction lies in the fact that causatives in Latin were expressed by one of *facere, efficere, curare*, followed by *ut* + subjunctive.

The Romance development therefore represents the emergence of a pattern closely akin to the otherwise moribund accusative + infinitive, even where an explicit clausal structure might seem to be called for in view of the fact that there are no missing arguments. All of which suggests, contrary to a view sometimes expressed, that there was no internal inadequacy in the accusative and infinitive which led to its demise, and that its replacement by the QUOD structures we have described is simply a consequence of a major reorganisation in the patterns of Romance complementation.

We should note, moreover, that a further result of the emergence of the new complement structures is to free the subjunctive from its obligatory dependence on the conjunction (*ut/ne/quin*) or the interrogative word in indirect questions, and to establish a pattern whereby the subjunctive and the indicative alternate according to the semantic circumstances here as in main clauses. Thus, subjunctives are normal with governing verbs of fearing, doubting, believing, and of emotional attitude (wonder, surprise, sorrow, etc.), and when the controlling predicate is interrogative or negative, but indicatives are required after verbs of saying and in more generally affirmative contexts. It is only at a later stage that in some languages the subjunctive may come to be regarded as a formal rather than a semantic category, as the discussion of that mood in the following chapters demonstrates.

Finally, the interaction of word order and complementation is of some interest. When the complement is an infinitive it normally precedes its governing verb, e.g. *emori cupio* 'I want to die', whereas finite complements with *ut* or *quod* and indirect questions tend to follow. Perhaps not surprisingly, the accusative and infinitive, which is formally non-finite but nevertheless has an explicit subject, is ambivalent. Compare two Plautine examples: *te abisse hodie hinc negas?* 'do you deny that you left here today?' and *audivistin tu me narrare haec hodie?* 'did you hear me say these things today?'. With the loss of the accusative and infinitive the rightward concatenation of complement structures becomes the norm and is well illustrated in the following example: *faxo ut scias quid pericli sit dotatae uxori vitium dicere* 'I'll make sure you know what danger there is in speaking ill of so well endowed a wife'. Such patterns must clearly have reinforced the tendency for objects to follow the verb which was described above.

Subordination

As noted earlier, complementation may be considered as involving subordinate clauses which fulfil a role as one of the verb's nuclear dependents. In other circumstances, subordinate clauses may have an essentially adverbial function, and it is the latter which will be the topic of the present section. Attention will be focused particularly on those clauses which are of interest either in Latin itself or because of changes which occur between Latin and Romance.

Mention has already been made (p. 66) of *ut* in its function as the introducer of adverbial clauses of purpose. We argued there that in this use the following subjunctive was semantically justified in that the expression of purpose is inevitably tinged with a degree of epistemic uncertainty, something which it is precisely the role of the subjunctive to signify. Note too, however, that result clauses are expressed in the same way: *ita pulchra est ut omnes deam putent* 'she is so beautiful that everyone thinks she is a goddess'. Here the content of the *ut*-clause is factual and might be thought, therefore, to require an indicative. The generalisation seems to be that *ut* takes a subjunctive whenever it introduces a clause expressing an event determined by or consequential upon another (cf. our treatment of complementiser *ut* above, p. 66). Interestingly, the modal opposition has been widely restored in Romance: cf., for instance, the discussion of French *de sorte que* 'so that' (p. 231).

In fact, *ut* only occurs with the indicative in Latin on the relatively rare occasions that its function is purely temporal, e.g. *Pompeius, ut equitatem suum pulsum vidit, acie excessit* 'Pompey, when he saw his cavalry beaten, left the line of battle'. In this case the verb *vidit* is a perfect indicative, the normal mood with almost all the frequent temporal conjunctions indicating that the event in the matrix clause occurred at the same time or after that in the embedded clause: cf., for example, *postquam* 'after', *cum* in its purely temporal senses, *ubi* 'when' (or 'where' — note the same polyvalency in uses of its direct descendant Fr. *où* like *le jour où ...* 'the day when ...'). When it is the subordinate clause which expresses the prior event, as with *antequam* or *priusquam* 'before', the indicative is in principle required, but already in classical authors the subjunctive is frequently used especially when the event concerned is to be seen as generic ('whenever'): thus, *antequam ludi fierent* (subj.), *servus per circum ductus est* 'before the games began, a slave was led through the streets'. The subjunctive has tended to gain ground in such cases in Romance, being normal with, for instance, Fr. *avant que*, It. *prima che*, Port. *antes (de) que*, etc. The subjunctive as marking prior circumstance may also help to explain its use in conditionals (see below) and with *cum* in examples like *cum Caesar Anconam occupavisset, urbem reliquimus* 'when Caesar had occupied Ancona, we left the city'. The conjunction *cum*, however, disappears throughout Romance, generally being replaced by reflexes of *quando*, originally used only in interrogatives, which is normally followed by the indicative (though note cases such as It. *quando piova* (subj.) 'when (and if) it rains').

Concessive clauses in Latin are marked by three principal conjunctions: *quamquam, quamvis* (literally 'as you wish'), and later *licet* (literally 'let it be conceded that'). The first of these was regularly used with the indicative, although its nearest equivalent (but not direct descendant), Fr. *quoique* (p.

240), is used with the subjunctive, at least according to the rules of pre-scriptive grammarians. The other two, reflecting their volitive origin, are regularly followed by the subjunctive, as are typical Romance creations such as Fr., Sp. *bien que,* It. *benché,* etc. The history of modal usage in clauses of this type provides a particularly clear illustration of how the choice of mood in an adverbial clause is subject to the conflicting pressures of semantic motivation (what exactly the clause in question means), syn-tactic consistency (all clauses within a given category should share the same mood), and, as here, the precise etymology of the individual conjunction concerned. As the following chapters show, these conflicts are only rarely resolved in a consistent fashion in any of the Romance languages.

We conclude this section by examining the development of conditional sentences. These differ from other matrix clause/adverbial clause sequences in that the two constituents, the protasis and the apodosis, com-bine more or less equally to produce a single logical proposition: 'if *x*, then *y*'. There is thus a potential conflict between a tendency for the protasis to behave as a subordinate clause, and to take where necessary a different mood/tense from the main clause, and a countervailing tendency for both clauses to be in the same mood/tense, thereby giving formal recognition to their equal status in the semantics of the whole complex sentence. If the first possibility prevails, we get patterns such as Lat. *flectere si nequeo* (pres. ind.) *superos, Acheronta movebo* (fut.) 'if I can't sway the gods above, I'll rouse all hell below' and *si valeant* (pres. subj.) *homines, ars tua, Phoebe, iacet* (pres. ind.) 'if men stay well, your art, Phoebus, is helpless'. The independent choice of tense, and to a lesser extent mood, is especially common in so-called 'real' conditionals, where it is likely, or at least not unlikely, that the necessary conditions will be fulfilled. The alternative possibility of two matching forms is particularly favoured in Latin for unreal or hypothetical conditionals such as *si ibi te esse scissem, ad te ipse venissem* 'if I had known you were there, I would have come to you myself', *sapientia non expeteretur, si nihil efficeretur* 'wisdom would not be sought after if it did no practical good'. Uses such as these are perhaps the commonest circumstance in which Latin exhibits the subjunctive in a main clause, and the pattern survives essentially unchanged in Sicilian, Sardinian and some southern Italian dialects (see p. 304). Elsewhere, however, the subjunctive has retreated from apodoses in favour of the conditional or conditional perfect, a development which certainly goes back as far as Late Latin, where it accounts for one of the earliest uses of the CANTARE HABEBAT syntagm (p. 57). In French alone of the standard languages, the subjunctive has also been definitively ousted from unreal protases (p. 240), although similar developments can be observed in the popular registers of the other languages. In colloquial usage and despite vigorous purist objections, it is increasingly common to find conditionals or conditional perfects in both clauses (cf. p. 240), an interesting restoration of the pattern of temporal/modal parallelism in the two halves of the conditional sentence, but now via the extension of an originally main clause form into the protasis rather than vice versa.

5 Lexis

Latin, as we have said, is an Indo-European language, and it will therefore come as no surprise to see many of the common Indo-European roots represented in its core of inherited vocabulary. Table 2.4 sets out some examples with cognates from other members of the family. Equally there are words in Latin which have cognates in the other Italic languages, but which are not attested in the broader Indo-European family, such as UTI 'to use' (cf. Osc. *uittiuf* 'use (nom. sg.)'), or are not found with this particular meaning, such as DICERE and Osc. *deikum* 'to say' beside the older meaning 'to point, show' which survives in INDICARE. Internal loans from other Italic languages include: BOS 'ox', RUFUS 'red' (cf. the directly inherited RUBER in Table 2.4), POPINA 'cook-shop' (beside inherited COQUINA, whence Romance *cuisine, cucina*, etc. 'kitchen'). There are words too, though fewer than one might expect, from the powerful early neighbours, the Etruscans: SATELLES 'bodyguard', PERSONA 'mask', SPURIUS 'son of an unknown father', TABERNA 'shop'.

Table 2.4: Latin and Indo-European: Some Cognates

Latin	Greek	Sanskrit	Germanic
tres	treîs	trayas	three
septem	hepta	sapta	seven
centum	(he)katon	satam	hundred
genus	genos	janas	kin
ager	agros	ajras	acre
ruber	eruthros	rudhiras	red
video	eidon	veda	wit
facio	tithemi	dadhami	do
est	esti	asti	is

Yet in the context of the present volume perhaps greater interest attaches to the patterns of survival and replacement which have affected the vocabulary of Latin on its way into the Romance languages. Let us begin by noting that many common Latin words did not in fact survive. Thus, Latin for 'fire' is IGNIS, but the evidence of Romance is that the word was replaced, presumably at a fairly early date, by FOCUS (whence *feu, fuego, foc*, etc.) which originally meant 'hearth'. In turn, forms such as It. *camino* 'fireplace', Fr. *cheminée* 'chimney' go back to CAMINUS 'oven, forge', itself originally a Greek borrowing. Likewise, the classical word for 'beautiful', PULCHER, is nowhere inherited directly, although, of course, it may well survive as a later learned borrowing from Latin (compare in this regard an 'English' word such as *pulchritude*). Instead, we find an interesting pattern whereby the central Romance languages have forms deriving from BELLUS (< *BONELLUS): thus Fr. *beau*, It. *bello*, Cat. *bell*, R-R *bal*, whereas the languages on the western or eastern edge of the imperial territory show reflexes of FORMO(N)SUS (< *forma* 'shape' — cf. Eng. *shapely* for a similar semantic development): Sp. *hermoso*, Port. *formoso*, Rum. *frumos*. Such geographical patterning of the lexis is often taken to betoken a situation in which lexical innovations spread out from the centre of the Empire so that a relic form may well persist at either extreme. Other common items of Latin vocabulary which have not continued into Romance include PUER 'boy', PUELLA 'girl', VIR 'man', CRUS 'leg', HIEMS 'winter', INGENS 'huge', TUTUS 'safe', DIVES 'rich', VEHERE 'to carry', LUDERE 'play', LINQUERE 'to leave', as well as innumerable particles and 'small' adverbs.

It will often not be possible to put a sure finger on the motive behind particular losses, but one can note with more certainty the mechanisms of replacement. A common one is for the root itself to continue, but in a different derivational form. Thus, although direct reflexes of HIEMS 'winter' are not attested, the derived adjective HIBERNUS yields Fr. *hiver*, Sp. *invierno*, etc. Similarly, Fr. *jour*, It. *giorno* 'day' are from DIURNUS 'daily'. though this time beside Occ., Cat., Sp. and Port. *dia* from DIES 'day'. The verbs SPUERE 'to spit' and CANERE 'to sing' have disappeared leaving behind Romance formations based on their participles SPUTUM, CANTUM: OFr. *espuer*, R-R *spüder*, It. *sputare*, Cat., Sp., Port. *cantar*, Rum. *cînta*. An especially common type of replacement involves the use of a diminutive: thus to the Latin AURIS 'ear', AVIS 'bird', VETUS 'old' correspond the derivatives AURICULA, AVICELLUS, VETULUS, from which in turn descend forms such as Sp. *oreja*, Fr. *oreille*; It. *uccello*, Cat. *ocell*; Rum. *vechi*, Occ. *vielh*, etc.

In other instances the replacing form results from an internal semantic shift of the kind we noted above for FOCUS. Such a mechanism may, of course, be triggered if the original Latin word itself shifts in meaning without being lost. Thus, everywhere except Sardinia the word DOMUS has disappeared in its original sense of 'house'. The motivation seems fairly clear: DOMUS, which in any case had always meant a rather grand private residence, was increasingly used in the technical religious sense 'house of god', hence It. *duomo* 'cathedral'. The first replacement was probably *casa*, originally 'hut' or 'hovel', which is still present in Spanish, Italian, Rumanian and Portuguese. French attests *casa* but only in the semantically shifted preposition *chez* 'at the house of, in' while that language's normal word for a domestic residence, *maison*, reveals a concrete use for what is in origin a verbal abstract, MANSIO from MANERE 'to remain' (cf. Eng. *dwelling* for a parallel development). Meanwhile, in French the word *dôme* has become specialised to a part of the building (cf. Eng. *dome*), and has been replaced by *cathédrale*, a derivative of CATHEDRA '(the bishop's) chair', in turn a borrowing from Greek.

More than once in discussing the patterns and processes by which semantic and lexical changes took place we have had cause to cite cases of borrowing, a common means of lexical replacement and enrichment particularly in the language of a centre so cosmopolitan as Rome and of a territory so geographically extensive and culturally diverse as the Empire. Some borrowings seem to relate to everyday items and concepts, and presumably reflect a regional usage: e.g. It. *scaffale* 'shelf' and *spaccare* 'to split' of Langobardic origin, or the Spanish items of unknown provenance, *cama* 'bed' and *perro* 'dog'. In other cases, borrowings from a given source cluster in certain semantic fields and hint at a specific type of cultural contact. Thus, there is a considerable body of Romance lexis which derives from the Greek of the early Christians. Some such items reflect the technicalities of Christian practice and belief: e.g. ANGELUS 'angel', EPISCOPUS 'bishop', BAPTIZARE 'to baptise', ECCLESIA 'church', and have remained as such. Others have since had their religious association overlaid by further semantic change as Fr. *parler*, It. *parlare* 'to talk' < PARABOLARE 'to tell parables'. (We may contrast here the converse effect of semantic specialisation due to religious association already noted with DOMUS or to be seen in the case of PEREGRINUS now 'pilgrim' but once simply 'stranger'.) Of course, Greek loans are not limited to those connected with Christianity, since there had been long-term cultural contact with Greece virtually ever since the beginnings of the Roman state. Some examples are: PETRA 'stone' which virtually displaces Latin LAPIS (Fr. *pierre*, Rum. *piatră*, etc.); COLAPHUS 'blow' (It. *colpo*, Sp. *golpe*); PLATEA 'square' (Fr. *place*, Occ. *plasa*, etc.) and CAMERA 'room' (Cat. *cambra*, It. *camera*, etc.).

Celtic was also a prolific source of loan vocabulary, again reflecting inevitable cultural contacts over a period of nearly a millennium. Thus, the word for the typically Celtic garment, CAMISIA 'shirt', remains in Fr. *chemise*, Occ., Cat., Sp., Port. *camisa*, It. *camicia*, Rum. *cămaşă*, and the name of a Celtic weapon, LANCEA 'throwing spear' has given rise not just to Fr. *lance*, It. *lancia*, Sp. *lanza*, etc. 'spear', but also to one of the common words for 'to throw', Fr. *lancer*, It. *lanciare*, Sp. *lanzar*, etc. Other Celticisms include: CARRUS 'cart', CAMMINUS 'road', CAMBIARE 'to change', ALAUDA 'lark', BECCUS 'beak'. What is less certain is whether a number of older items which are attested only in Italic and Celtic — e.g. CANO 'I sing' beside Irish *canim*, LOQUOR 'I speak' and Irish -*tluchur* — are due to a period of common inheritance (the so-called Italo-Celtic hypothesis), as used to be thought, or to early cultural diffusion, the currently more favoured view. Other examples of this close equivalence between Italic and Celtic are: CULUS 'arse' and Irish *cul*, TERRA 'land' and Irish *tir*,

METERE 'to reap' and Welsh *medi* (this root is attested elsewhere but not in this meaning), SAECULUM 'century' and Welsh *hoedl*, etc.

Finally, mention must be made of the considerable number of words in Latin of Germanic origin. In fact, the label 'Germanic' is too vague, since it refers to a large family of related languages spoken in different areas and therefore impinging differently on the various parts of the Empire. Thus, loans from Scandinavian are more common in northern French than in those languages spoken along the Mediterranean shore (though, of course, many of these loans were later transmitted to the Mediterranean via the Norman presence in Sicily and southern Italy in the eleventh and twelfth centuries). Loans from Frankish are also frequent in French, from Langobardic in Italian, from Visigothic in Spanish and so on (see the relevant chapters for further details and examples). We will concentrate instead on those items which, by their presence in a number of different Romance languages, must be treated as loans into the general Latin of the Empire. Thus, consider, for example, a group of colour terms of Germanic origin: *BLANK- 'white' mostly replaces Lat. ALBUS, whence Fr., Occ., Cat. *blanc*, Port. *branco*, Sp. *blanco*, though note Rum. *alb*, R-R *alf*; *BRUN- 'brown' gives Fr., Occ. *brun*, Sp., Port., It. *bruno*; *GRIS- 'grey' is seen in Fr., Occ., Cat. *gris*; FALWA 'tawny' in Fr. *fauve*, Occ. *falb*; *BLUND- 'blonde' in Fr. *blond*, It. *biondo*. Semantically more heterogeneous are a group of words which betray their Germanic origin in the initial cluster /gw-/, a nativisation of original /w-/ (recall that Latin /w/ had developed to /v/). Thus, WARDON 'to observe' > Fr. *garder*, Occ. *gardar*, Cat./Sp. *guardar*, It. *guardare*; WARNJAN 'to provide' > Fr. *garnir*, Sp./Port. *guarnir*, It. *guarnire*; WARJAN 'to defend oneself' > Fr. *guérir*, Cat./Port. *guarir*, It. *guarire*; WAIDANJAN 'work, earn' > Fr. *gagner*, Cat. *guanyar*, R-R *guadagner*, Port. *ganhar*; WISA 'manner' > Fr. *guise*, Sp./Cat./Port./It. *guisa*. The list of Germanisms is long and cannot be done proper justice in a paragraph or two. What is clear, however, is that the penetration of vocabulary from this source is considerable and is not limited to a few special semantic areas, suggesting that at the level of everyday usage spoken Latin readily accommodated foreign vocabulary, which then went on to become the basis of some of the most everyday items in the Romance languages.

Items from other sources than those discussed in this section are usually typical of one area rather than another (e.g. Arabisms in Spain and southern Italy, Slavic loans in Rumanian) and will be dealt with in the appropriate chapters. The reader is also referred to the discussion of general principles of borrowing and vocabulary formation in Chapter 3 (pp. 188ff).

6 Conclusion

It is important to emphasise in concluding that in some respects what has been described in this chapter is not a uniform language, but rather a series of diachronic trajectories that point forward to the developments in the individual Romance languages that are documented in the succeeding chapters. For instance, we can be sure, both on the basis of the textual material and of the comparative evidence of cognate languages, that an inflectional verb system of the kind described in sections 3 and 4 gradually evolved into the type of Romance system where a large part of the grammatical work is done by periphrastic means. It is much harder, and in many cases, impossible to know the relative, let alone the absolute, chronology of the changes: did the rise of the periphrastic passive antedate or postdate the rise of the periphrastic perfect? What is the chronological relation of either to the loss of the neuter gender? Did the expansion of QUOD + indicative as a pattern of complementation come before or after the emergence of clitic pronouns? Some of these and other questions may acquire answers as our grammatical understanding becomes more sophisticated or as our reading of the philological data becomes more subtle (the two are naturally not unconnected); in the meantime the approach adopted here seems the most suited to our goal of charting the first stages in the transformation of Latin into Romance. The subsequent chapters will take up the remainder of the story.

Bibliography

Latin
Allen, W.S. (1970) *Vox latina*. Cambridge University Press, Cambridge.
Ernout, A. (1927) *Morphologie historique du latin*. Klincksieck, Paris.
—— and F. Thomas (1951) *Syntaxe latine*. Klincksieck, Paris.
Gildersleeve, B.L. and G. Lodge (1895) *Latin Grammar*. Macmillan, London.
Glare, P.G.W. (ed.) (1968–82) *Oxford Latin Dictionary*. Clarendon Press, Oxford.
Leumann, M., J. Hoffman, and A. Szantyr (1972–7) *Lateinische Grammatik* 2 vols. Beck, Munich.
Löfstedt, E. (1959) *Late Latin*. Aschehoug, Oslo.
Marouzeau, J. (1922–49) *L'ordre des mots dans la phrase latine* 3 vols. Champion, Paris.
Mihaescu, M. (1978) *La langue latine dans le sud-est de l'Europe*. Les Belles Lettres, Paris.
Palmer, L.R. (1954) *The Latin Language*. Faber and Faber, London.
Scherer, A. (1975) *Handbuch der lateinischen Syntax*. Carl Winter, Heidelberg.
Väänänen, V. (1981) *Introduction au latin vulgaire* 3rd edn. Klincksieck, Paris.
Woodcock, E.C. (1959) *A New Latin Syntax*. Bristol, Bristol Classical Press.

Romance
Elcock, W.D. (1975) *The Romance Languages* 2nd edn. Faber and Faber, London.
Lausberg, H. (1969) *Romanische Sprachwissenschaft* 3 vols. De Gruyter, Berlin. (Italian trans. revised and expanded by author, *Linguistica romanza*, Feltrinelli, Milan, 1971.)

Meyer-Lübke, W. (1890–1902) *Grammatik der romanischen Sprachen* 4 vols. Reisland, Leipzig.
—— (1935) *Romanisches etymologisches Wörterbuch* 3rd edn. Carl Winter, Heidelberg.
Posner, R. and J. Green (eds.) (1980–2) *Trends in Romance Linguistics and Philology* 4 vols. De Gruyter, Berlin.
Wright, R. (1982) *Late Latin and Early Romance in Spain and Carolingian France.* Francis Cairns, Liverpool.

3 Spanish

John N. Green

1 Introduction

Spanish is by far the most widely spoken of the modern Romance languages, and as an international vehicle for commerce and diplomacy is fast encroaching on the preeminent position long enjoyed by French. (Details of its geographical distribution together with speaker statistics will be found in Chapter 1. See also Map I.) In most Spanish-speaking regions the terms *español* and *castellano* are used interchangeably, but a useful distinction can be drawn between 'Spanish' as a diasystem and 'Castilian' as its prestige form in Europe, the basis of the standard language and still, for many speakers, the model for pronunciation.

In common with all spatially diffused languages, Spanish is subject to regional and sociolinguistic variation and also — in its international role — to conflicting normative pressures, but despite some well-publicised divergences of pronunciation and vocabulary (discussed in sections 2 and 5 below), the range of variation is not very great and only rarely disrupts mutual comprehensibility. In Spain, the 'purest' form of Castilian is traditionally identified with Burgos, but in practice the norm has long been the educated usage of Madrid, which has consistently been more open to outside influences. In Latin America, the prestige formerly attaching to Colombian Spanish (perhaps because Colombia was the first ex-colony to establish its own language Academy in 1873) has now unquestionably moved northwards to Mexico City, by far the most populous Spanish-speaking conurbation in the world.

The modern focus of the two 'norms' does not, however, mean that their geographical boundary can be neatly located between Europe and the New World, since Andalusian in southern Spain and the dialects of the Canary Islands share many of the distinguishing features of Latin American. Despite the vast discrepancy in populations, the Castilian norm continues to be highly valued — though not necessarily imitated — in most of Latin America. An ironical recent development in Spain, however, has been the spread, among younger speakers, of modes of pronunciation whose origin is unmistakably Andalusian.

2   Phonology

In this sketch of Spanish phonology we shall concentrate on the Castilian norm, making reference as appropriate to variant articulations and socio-linguistic status. An arrangement of material adopted in the interests of economy should not, however, be taken to imply that other varieties of Spanish are deviations from, nor yet dialects of, Castilian.

Auditory Impression

Before considering the segmental units, we should say a little about pro-sodic characteristics and general auditory impression. Spanish has often been quoted as a textbook example of a syllable-timed language, with a delivery sometimes likened to a recalcitrant machine gun. A newer pro-posal suggests Spanish would be more accurately described as 'segment timed' since the delivery, though perceptually regular, does not always produce isochronous syllabification or isochronous stress intervals. The rhythmic pattern, naturally, has implications for intonation, which tends to avoid abrupt changes and readily accommodates melodic units of ten to fifteen syllables. Castilian, whose everyday register is confined to little more than an octave, has a basic rise–fall for simple declaratives, a sustained rise for most yes-no questions, and the characteristic Western Romance level or rising tone to mark enumerations and sentence-medial clause boundaries. A prominent feature of Castilian is its 'dynamic' or intensity accent, which is noticeably free from tonal modulation. Most writers also comment on the resonant quality that Castilians and northern dialect speakers impart to their everyday speech. This has been variously ascribed to an unusual articulatory setting, to the rhythmic structure, to the predominance of low, open vowels, and to the stability of vowel sounds in both stressed and unstressed positions. Though all these factors may be contributory, the principal cause must be articulatory setting, since many other regional varieties of Spanish are produced with a less marked resonant quality despite sharing the other structural features of Castilian.

Consonants

The segmental consonant system of Castilian, given in Table 3.1, can be presented as neatly symmetrical, with four articulatory positions and five degrees of aperture, but this disguises some interesting irregularities in distribution. While, for instance, the absence of any point-of-articulation opposition between oral stops and affricates argues for a merger of the categories, they differ in that /dʒ/ is by no means securely established in the system, and neither palatal enters into syllable-initial clusters, which the stops do freely. The reintroduction of [dʒ], which was present in Old Spanish probably as an allophone of /ʒ/, is comparatively recent and its phonemic status remains doubtful. Since, as we shall see (p. 84), it occurs as the exponent of two distinct phonemes, its incorporation would neces-

Table 3.1: The Castilian Consonant System

	Bilabial		Dento-alveolar	Palatal	Velar	
Oral stops						
[−voice]	p		t		k	
[+voice]		b	d			g
Affricates						
[−voice]				ʧ		
[+voice]				(ʤ)		
Fricatives						
[−voice]		f	θ s		x	
Nasal stops	m		n	ɲ		
Laterals			l	ʎ		
Vibrants						
[+tense]			r			
[−tense]			ɾ			

sarily provoke a realignment of the system.

The Castilian voiceless stops are unaspirated plosives. The voiced series is in complementary distribution with a corresponding set of voiced spirants, the plosives occurring word-initially and medially after nasals, and the spirants elsewhere: *boca* 'mouth' ['boka] but *cabo* 'end' ['kaβo], *donde* 'where' ['dɔnde] but *nudo* 'knot' ['nuðo], *grande* 'big' ['grande] but *magro* 'lean' ['mayɾo]. A word-initial plosive, however, is also liable to replacement by the corresponding spirant when intervocalic within a breathgroup: *la boca* [la'βoka]. Moreover, in indigenous words neither /b/ nor /g/ occurs word-finally, and orthographic -*d* is weakened to [ð̞] or lost completely. It has traditionally been assumed that the spirants are the subordinate members of these pairs, since the weakening of plosives to fricatives in comparable environments is well attested as a historical process in Romance. But the distinction is equally amenable to analysis as a strengthening of spirants in group-initial or post-nasal position, and recent research on language acquisition among Mexican children seems to show that the spirants are acquired first and remain dominant.

The future of the medial spirants is, however, less secure than their present frequency implies. The Latin intervocalic voiceless plosives from which many of them derive have in French often undergone a third stage of lenition resulting in their complete loss and a consequent syllabic merger (see p. 39), compare VĪTAM 'life' > Sp. ['biða], Fr. [vi]; MĪCAM 'crumb' > Sp. ['miya], Fr. [mi]. There are a number of pointers to a similar outcome in Spanish. One is the very lax articulation often given to intervocalic /-g-/ especially when followed by the labio-velar glide /w/; in a word like *agua* 'water' the *g* is rarely more than a frictionless velar approximant and is sometimes lost altogether. Another sign is the disappearance of /-d-/ from past participles in -ado/-ido. This change, which is now virtually complete among younger speakers, has been the subject of intense normative disapproval, giving rise in turn to amusing hypercorrections like [baka'laðo] for bacalao 'cod'. Curiously, the same change has gone unnoticed in the reflexive imperative, where the coalescence of levantad + os as ¡levantaos! 'stand up' (familiar plural) is even accepted by the standard orthography. The loss of /-d-/ in these contexts is still clearly dependent on morphological factors (in the past participle, it affects the feminine form -ada less frequently than the corresponding masculine -ado), but it may signal the first stage of a more general phonological process.

The three Castilian sibilants are the remainder of what was in Old Spanish a much larger set, including a voiced phonemic series whose demise is still not wholly explained. The absence of phonemic voiced sibilants now sets Spanish apart from most other Romance varieties, though [ʒ] is used by some speakers as an alternative realisation of /ʎ/ (see below), and [z] occurs infrequently as an allophone of /s/ before voiced obstruents, but not intervocalically, thus desde 'from/since' ['dɛzðe] but esposa 'wife' [ɛs'posa] — compare Port. ['ʃpozɐ], It. ['spɔːza] and Fr. [e'puz]. In many non-Castilian varieties, the inventory of sibilants, or their frequency, is further reduced, for example, by the aspiration and sometimes complete loss of syllable-final /-s/ (see p. 85). Moreover, American Spanish and most varieties of Andalusian lack the distinctive Castilian opposition between /θ/ and /s/, as in cima 'summit' /θima/ : sima 'abyss' /sima/, caza 'hunt' /kaθa/ : casa 'house' /kasa/, haz 'bundle' /aθ/ : as 'ace' /as/. Throughout South America and in most of Andalusia, only [s] is found — a feature popularly called seseo. The converse, using only [θ] and duly known as ceceo, is confined to scattered locations in Andalusia.

The assumption has been quite widely made that the majority seseante territories lost an earlier opposition between /θ/ and /s/ and therefore represent innovatory tendencies in relation to the conservatism of Castilian. (It has indeed been suggested that American Spanish still maintains an opposition at underlying level which is always neutralised in phonetic representation — an idea further discussed on p. 101 below.) The truth is certainly more complex. From the available documentary evidence it cannot be conclusively established whether or not a phonological opposition between two front sibilants was present in the Spanish of the first colonists, but it is now almost certain that the interdental fricative articulation [θ] was a Castilian innovation which significantly post-dated the early phase of settlement. Seseante regions may, therefore, have eliminated something since the sixteenth century, but not specifically the [θ] sound. How then did it arise in Castilian? The most plausible explanation is: as a way of increasing the auditory distinctiveness of an opposition which was in danger of coalescing. The loss of distinctive voicing had reduced the six medieval sibilants to three by the fifteenth century; let us call them S_1, S_2 and S_3. Suppose now that S_1 had been simplified from a medieval affricate /ts/ to a dorso-alveolar or laminal /s/; that S_2 represented a less common apico-alveolar /s/; and that S_3 was a palatal /ʃ/. The distance — both articulatory and auditory — between the three sounds would have been very small. In the circumstances a natural development would be the 'splaying out' of tongue positions into: front apical [θ], mid apical [s] and back dorsal [x]. These values are very similar to the ones now found in modern Castilian, except that the /x/ phoneme is often realised even further back as a uvular [χ], probably to maximise the difference between /x/ and /s/, whose unusual apico-alveolar articulation gives a slight auditory impression of palatality. By contrast, Mexican Spanish has a noticeably forward articulation of velar /x/, which is in no danger of coalescing with the only other sibilant, a forward laminal /s/ whose distribution echoes that of the former S_1 and S_2.

If the reconstruction we have just outlined is correct, we shall have to say that *seseante* dialects are innovatory in relation to late medieval Spanish (having eventually reduced six sibilants to two), whereas Castilian is conservative in its phonology (having maintained a three-way opposition) but still innovatory in its phonetics! The merger of S_1 and S_2 in *seseante* varieties, whatever its exact date, naturally created homophones, some of which have persisted. But in other cases it seems to have led to lexical substitutions in order to avoid ambiguity: the Castilian minimal pair *coser* 'to sew' /koseɾ/ : *cocer* 'to cook' /koθeɾ/ poses no problem in America, where *coser* is maintained, but *cocinar* /kosinaɾ/ is the verb 'to cook'.

Let us now turn to the Castilian sonorants. The three nasals contrast intervocalically, where there are numerous permutations of minimal pairs and a few triads: *lama* 'slime' /lama/ : *lana* 'wool' /lana/ : *laña* 'clamp' /laɲa/. Elsewhere, the opposition is incomplete. Word-initially, /ɲ-/ is very rare, confined to a few affective terms and borrowings from Amerindian languages; among Latinate items, only /m-/ and /n-/ are possible. Nasals combine freely with obstruents to form heterosyllabic clusters, in which seven or more phonetic variants can be detected, always homorganic with the following consonant and therefore neutralising the opposition — *infeliz* 'unhappy' [iɱfeˈliθ], *incierto* 'uncertain' [iɲ̟θjɛɾto], *incapaz* 'unable' [iŋkaˈpaθ], and so on. The opposition is also neutralised in word-final position, where only /-n/ occurs. A variant pronunciation, previously common in Andalusia and parts of Latin America, is now spreading rapidly in Spain, though it remains sociolinguistically marked: word-final and sometimes syllable-final /-n/ is realised as velar [-ŋ], with appreciable nasalisation of the preceding vowel. (For similar developments in Italian, see p. 282.) It has been argued that the weak articulation of final

[-ŋ] may be the prelude to phonemic nasalisation of the vowel, a development Spanish has so far resisted.

Table 3.1 shows an opposition between two lateral phonemes, a dento-alveolar /l/ and a palatal /ʎ/. Though it does not carry a high functional load, the opposition is regularly maintained in such pairs as *loro* 'parrot' : *lloro* 'I weep'. The phonetic realisation of /ʎ/, however, is subject to wide variation, and for many speakers the pronunciation [ʎ] is now characteristic only of very formal or careful delivery. The delateralisation of /ʎ/ to [j] as in French (p. 212), long familiar in Latin America under the name *yeísmo*, and now spreading rapidly in Spain, has created an allophonic overlap with the glide /j/, and consequently a new set of homophones — like ['pojo] for both *pollo* 'chicken' and *poyo* 'bench' — affording rich possibilities for confusion and hypercorrection. A secondary development of *yeísmo* strengthens the [j] derived from /ʎ/ to [ʒ] or even [dʒ], but in Spain these further stages remain sociolinguistically marked: whereas in Madrid the pronunciation of words like *calle* 'street' as ['kaje] is now virtually standard, the fricative variant ['kaʒe] is often regarded as uneducated and the affricate realisation ['kadʒe] is usually stigmatised as vulgar. Less stigma, however, seems to attach to an earlier, and apparently independent, strengthening of certain initial [j] sounds to [dʒ], a prominent example being the pronunciation of the personal pronoun *yo* 'I' as [dʒo] rather than [jo]. The long-term effects of this series of changes are by no means clear. The generalisation we can properly draw in the interim, is that only syllable-initial [j], whatever its source, is a possible input to strengthening. For as long as this holds good, there will not be a complete coalescence of /j/ and /ʎ/.

The vibrants /ɾ/ and /r/ are the only sonorants to contrast at the same point of articulation, but the opposition is only intervocalic — *caro* 'expensive' /kaɾo/ : *carro* 'cart' /karo/; elsewhere the two sounds are in complementary distribution. In standard Castilian the difference seems to be one of tenseness rather than length: /-ɾ-/ is usually a flap and /-r-/ a full-bodied aveolar trill. The /ɾːr/ opposition is maintained in all dialects, but with a very wide range of phonetic exponents. Particular mention should be made of the fricativisation of /r/ to velar [x] or uvular [ʁ] in Puerto Rico and Colombian coast Spanish, together with its realisation in some other American varieties as a weak trill with palatal friction [ɾ]. This latter development (also observed in Brazilian Portuguese, p. 138) suggests an intriguing historical parallel with the palatals /ɲ/ and /ʎ/, since all three derive principally from Latin intervocalic geminates and appear to have evolved via a stage of tenseness. A second parallel could be drawn between /ʎ/ and /r/ in that their most recent (and still sociolinguistically marked) evolution seems likely to remove them from the class of sonorants.

Vowels

As is apparent from Table 3.2, the five simple vowels of modern Spanish form a classic symmetrical triangle. Their frequency of occurrence in running prose also follows a regular pattern: low vowels are more frequent than high, front more so than back (hence in ascending order /u, i, o, e, a/). All five occur as independent words, with /e/ and /a/ both representing homophones. All occur both stressed and unstressed, in open and closed syllables, though /i/ and /u/ are rare in word-final position. As we noted above, there is little tendency to weakening or centralisation in unstressed syllables, a feature which sets Spanish clearly apart from its peninsular neighbours Portuguese and Catalan. Regardless of the presence or absence of stress, however, all vowels are represented by laxer variants in closed syllables; the high and mid series are lowered slightly and /a/, which in citation has a central low articulation, may be displaced forward or backward depending on the adjacent consonant: *presté* 'I lent' /pres'te/ [prɛs'te], *cortó* 'it cut' /kor'to/ [kɔr'to], *jaulas* 'cages' /'xawlas/ ['χɑwlæs].

Table 3.2: Vowels and Semi-vocalic Glides

	Vowels		Glides	
High	i	u	j	w
Mid	e	o		
Low		a		

This unexceptional laxing has paved the way for a change in Andalusian and some Latin American varieties which may have far-reaching consequences for the vowel system and for plural marking. The great majority of Spanish nouns in the singular end in open /-a/, /-o/ or /-e/, but the addition of the plural marker /-s/ closes the syllable and produces the regular allophonic variation in the vowel:

hermano(s) 'brother(s)' /er'mano/ [ɛr'mano] + /s/ = [ɛr'manɔs]
hermana(s) 'sister(s)' /er'mana/ [ɛr'mana] + /s/ = [ɛr'manæs]
madre(s) 'mother(s)' /madre/ ['maðre] + /s/ = ['maðrɛs]

In Andalusian, syllable-final /-s/ often weakens to an aspirate [-h], so *los hermanos* becomes [lɔʰ ɛr'manɔʰ] and so on. This substitution, though phonetically salient, does not affect the phonemic status of the vowels. In a more 'advanced' variety of Andalusian, however, the aspiration is lost altogether and with it the conditioning factor for the vowel alternation. Now [la 'maðre] contrasts functionally with [læ 'maðrɛ] in a new system of plural marking not too far removed from the vocalic alternations of Italian (see p. 289). The implications for the phonological inventory are disputed: on the one hand the new functional contrasts argue for the recognition of three new vowel phonemes, but this has been countered by the claim that Andalusian plurals are now marked by a prosody of laxing which affects all vowels in the word, not merely the one in contact with historical /-s/.

Table 3.2 above shows no diphthongs or triphthongs. On the phonetic level, combinations of vowels and vowel-like elements are common, but their phonemic status has always been among the most controversial areas of Spanish linguistics. Eighteen monosyllabic combinations can be distinguished, eight with a glide onset /ja, je, jo, ju, wa, we, wi, wo/, six with an off-glide /aj, aw, ej, ew, oj, ow/, and a further four with both on- and off-glides /waj, wej, jaw, waw/ of which the last two are very rare. The analyst's task is complicated by the existence of numerous other combinations, both within and across word boundaries, of vowels 'in hiatus' — pronounced as two syllables in careful speech, but readily coalescing into monosyllables in rapid or informal delivery. To explain the controversy, we must make a brief foray into stress assignment.

Stress Assignment

Stress in Latin was non-phonemic and predictable from syllable structure (see p. 31). Throughout the history of Spanish, stress has remained extraordinarily faithful to its etymological syllable, though as a result of phonetic evolution that syllable may no longer bear the same relation to the whole word as it did in Latin. A good example is provided by Latin words regularly stressed on the antepenultimate syllable, almost all of which have lost their intertonic vowel and now conform to the majority pattern of penultimate stress: SALĬCEM /'sa-li-ke/'willow' > *sauce* /'sawθe/. Like Latin, modern Spanish does not use stress to differentiate lexical items, but the cumulative effect of phonetic change has been to remove some of the previous conditioning environments, so that stress placement is no longer wholly predictable from surface phonetic structure. The simplest phonological treatment thus entails marking stress as an inherent property of lexical items. Most linguists nevertheless feel this root-and-branch approach denies significant generalisations.

In this belief they are supported by the standard orthography, which uses a written accent only when stress deviates from the expected position, defined as follows: words ending in a consonant other than -*s* or -*n* are stressed on the final syllable, others (the great majority) on the penultimate. The exemption of -*s* and -*n*, which serve as plural markers for nouns and third person verbs respectively, is designed to accommodate the fact that plurals almost invariably maintain the stress pattern of their corresponding vocalic singulars: *la(s) chica(s) corre(n)* 'the girl(s) run(s)' /la(s) 'tʃika(s) 'kore(n)/. The orthographic rules automatically define as an exception any form stressed earlier than the penultimate syllable, including the not insignificant number of proparoxytones (known in Spanish metrics as *esdrújulas*) reintroduced into the language by lexical borrowing. In practice, the orthographic conventions work reasonably well, but they do leave a residue of quite common nouns and adjectives which appear to be stressed in the 'wrong' place: *árbol* 'tree', *cárcel* 'prison', *césped* 'turf', *lápiz* 'pencil', *mártir* 'martyr', *útil* 'useful', all have penultimate stress where final might be expected, and the converse applies in: *holgazán* 'lazy', *país* 'country', *preguntón* 'inquisitive', and so on.

Some allegedly phonological analyses clearly derive from these orthographic conventions. The properly phonological generalisations thus captured are: that the preferred stress position in Spanish is penultimate; that stress can move further back than the antepenultimate syllable only if the word is clearly composite, like *entregándomelo* 'handing it to me' or *fácilmente* 'easily' (though such adverbs have a secondary stress in the expected position); that plurals maintain the pattern of singulars even when this entails creating proparoxytones like *jóvenes* 'youths'; and that otherwise antepenultimate stress is not phonologically predictable (the open penultimate syllable common to all such forms being a necessary, but not sufficient, condition). Even so, it should be clear from the examples already quoted that the seemingly capricious stress-assigning properties of -*n*, -*r* and -*s*, in fact depend on whether these segments form part of the lexical stem, or represent suffixal morphemes. Whatever interpretation is placed on this correlation, the fairly straightforward account of stress we have so far envisaged will necessarily be complicated when we turn to verbal inflection. Here, stress operates functionally to differentiate otherwise identical forms of the same lexeme — *hablo* 'I speak' : *habló* '(s)he spoke', *¡cante!* 'sing!' : *canté* 'I sang', *tomara* '(s)he would take' : *tomará* '(s)he will take'. It follows that an analysis wishing to view stress as generally predictable must make reference to morphological information. Some theories, of course, rule this out by axiom.

Semi-vocalic Glides
The status of the semi-vocalic glides is problematic because, although [j, w] appear to be in complementary distribution with the vowels /i, u/ respectively, this economical analysis requires prior knowledge of stress position: /i/ is realised as [j] (or becomes [-syllabic]) if and only if it is unstressed and adjacent to some other vowel. The neatest analysis of all would thus need to show that glide formation and stress assignment are both predictable. Can it be done? Consider these examples:

amplio ['am-pljo] : amplío [am-'pli-o] : amplió [am-'pljo]
'ample'   'I broaden'   '(s)he broadened'
continuo [kɔn-'ti-nwo] : continúo [kɔn-ti-'nu-o] : continuó [kɔn-ti-'nwo]
'continuous'   'I continue'   '(s)he continued'

Here, the occurrence of the full vowel or glide is predictable, once stress is known. But the converse is not true: stress cannot be predicted using only the phonological information given here. Nor can it be made predictable by including general morphological conditions, since other verbs behave differently in the middle form of the series: *cambiar* 'to change' and *menguar* 'to lessen' conjugate respectively as ['kam-bjo] and ['mɛŋ-gwo] not *[kam-'bi-o] or *[mɛŋ-'gu-o]. For reductionists, the consequences are uncomfortable: neither glide formation nor stress assignment can be predicted on phonological criteria alone.

Systematic Alternations

An allied debate has raged around the predictability or otherwise of the verb stem alternations traditionally called 'radical changes'. The two most frequent ones involve glides and stress assignment. The verb *poder* 'to be able' has two stems: /pod-/ when the following vowel is stressed and /pwed-/ when the stem itself is stressed. This results in a heterogeneous paradigm, very striking in the present indicative, with 1 sg. *puedo* alongside 1 pl. *podemos*. Similarly, *helar* 'to freeze', has the stressed stem *hielo* /jelo/ alongside *helamos* /elamos/. Some 400 verbs follow these two patterns, far more than one would normally wish to describe as 'irregular'. In any event, the observable changes are perfectly regular once the stress assignment is known. But the interesting question is whether membership of the radical changing pattern is itself predictable. It used to be. The seven-term vowel system inherited by most West Romance dialects (p. 33) maintained a phonemic contrast between the pairs of mid vowels /e : ɛ/ and /o : ɔ/. In northern Spain, /ɛ/ and /ɔ/ diphthongised when stressed. This was a regular phonological change, affecting all word classes equally and all types of syllable (in northern French, the same vowels diphthongised only in open syllables; see p. 211). So, Spanish verbs with /ɛ/ or /ɔ/ as their stem vowel were regularly subject to diphthongisation under stress, that stress in turn being positioned according to the number of syllables in the inflection.

What has changed between early and modern Spanish is the loss of the phonemic opposition between the mid vowels in favour of an allophonic variation predictable from syllable structure. It is no longer possible to tell, from an infinitive, whether a verb will be radical changing or not: the stem vowel of *podar* 'to prune' is identical to that of *poder* but does not diphthongise; neither does the *e* of *pelar* 'to peel', although it is phonetically indistinguishable from that of *helar*. These facts are susceptible of various competing analyses.

Some linguists, arguing that so common an alternation must result from a regular productive rule, have postulated underlying vowels /ɛ, ɔ/ for radical changing verbs and thus claim the synchronic process is identical to the historical change. The theoretical elegance of this treatment is not in doubt, but it is by no means clear that Spanish language learners could reconstruct from imperfect synchronic alternations an underlying opposition which is always neutralised in phonetic representation. Their task, indeed, would be even harder: the opposition they need to reconstruct — and later neutralise — is apparently present at the phonetic level as a result of the laxing process routinely affecting closed syllables (see p. 85). The phonetic input is thus most confusing. Not only do learners have to postulate underlying /ɔ/ in *poder* but not *podar* when both are actually pronounced with [o]; they also need to distinguish between *torcer* 'to twist', which diphthongises, and *cortar* 'to cut', which does not, even though both have phonetic [ɔ] in the infinitive!

Other linguists, opposed in principle to such abstract analyses, have argued that the alternation is real, but works synchronically in the opposite direction. If forms such as *hiela* or *puede* are taken to be basic, rather than the traditional infinitive, then the diphthong can be made to 'revert' automatically to a simple vowel whenever stress is displaced to another syllable. For the data so far adduced, this proposal works well, though there would be a handful of exceptions: *juega* '(s)he plays' alternates with *jugar* not *jogar, and a verb like *licuece* 'it liquifies', whose diphthong derives from a different historical source, does not revert to *licocer. The proposal fails, however, to accommodate a less common radical change in which unstressed /e/ alternates with stressed /i/, as in *pedir* 'to request' : *pide*, *medir* 'to measure' : *mide*. If the /i/ alternants here are taken as basic, it becomes impossible to explain why *vive* '(s)he lives' has its infinitive in *vivir* rather than *vevir. Even if these difficulties could be overcome, the proposal would — like the abstract analysis it aims to supersede — still require access to morphological information. This is because the alternation is much less regular outside the verb system than within it. The adjective *bueno* 'good' has an associated noun *bondad* in which the final syllable is stressed and the diphthong duly replaced, but its superlative may be either *bonísimo* or *buenísimo*. Other derivational processes are undermining the earlier phonological regularity of diphthongisation: *deshuesar* 'to remove bones/pits' is a verb coined from the noun *hueso*, but the diphthong which regularly occurs under stress in the noun is irregular in the infinitive, where it is unstressed. Parallel examples are *ahuecar* 'to hollow out' from *hueco*, or *amueblado* 'furnished' from *mueble*.

Not surprisingly, a third body of opinion believes that Spanish speakers cannot predict these alternations at all, and must learn them as inherent features of the individual word. This view is supported by the observation that speakers of some varieties stigmatised as substandard, notably Chicano, regularly keep the diphthongised stem throughout a paradigm regardless of stress placement, saying *despiertamos* for standard *despertamos* 'we wake up' and *recuerdamos* for standard *recordamos* 'we remember'. A recent experiment with speakers of standard American Spanish has provided further corroboration. Informants were given a set of connected sentences containing nonce verb forms and asked to complete other sentences which required different grammatical forms of the made-up verbs. The informants proved most reluctant to 'create' diphthongs or other irregularities even in the nonce verbs very reminiscent of frequent 'real' verbs; but more surprisingly, many also resisted replacing a given diphthong by its corresponding simple vowel in unstressed positions.

All told, it looks as though a process which at first was phonologically regular has passed through a stage of morphological conditioning and is now giving way to lexical marking on individual words. As often happens in linguistic change, this will preserve analogical relationships at the expense of phonological regularity.

Orthography

Spanish orthography, though popularly reputed to be 'phonetic' (by which is meant 'phonemic') is in fact quite highly conventionalised. The correspondence of letters to sounds is skewed by the preservation, and occasionally restoration, of etymological spellings. Once the conventions have been mastered, it is relatively easy to read aloud the written language; but transcribing from speech is altogether trickier, as attested by the difficulty Spanish schoolchildren experience with dictation exercises. Standard orthography is also biased towards the Castilian norm, making its acquisition more difficult for the great majority of speakers who have no phonological opposition between /s/ and /θ/ (see p. 82).

As can be seen from Figure 3.1, which assumes a conservative articulation, only six letter–sound correspondences can be considered strictly biunique. Obvious difficulties for transcription are: the invariably mute *h*, the velar consonants, the alternation of *c* : *z* and *g* : *j*, and the distribution of *b* : *v*. Since *b* and *v* correspond to only one phoneme and are not in the same distribution as its two allophones — *beber* 'to drink' = /beber/ [be'βɛɾ], *vivir* 'to lie' = /bibir/ [bi'βiɾ] — it is hardly surprising that words containing these letters are often misspelled, even on public notices; two recently observed in Segovia province read *Se prohive aparcar* [= *prohibe*] 'no parking' and *Coto pribado de caza* [= *privado*] 'private hunting'.

Among the velars, the orthographic contexts for the two values of *c* and *g* recapitulate the phonetic environment for early Romance palatalisation, but preserving this relationship in the modern language results in asymmetries. For instance, the reluctance to employ *k* in native words requires the use of the digraph *qu* to represent /k/ before front vowels. This produces a somewhat spurious parallel in verbs which, though morphologically regular, require a modification in spelling when the vowel of the ending changes, hence: *indicar* 'to indicate' becomes *indique* in the subjunctive and *otorgar* 'to grant' becomes *otorgue*. But *qu*, which occurs only before *i*, *e*, is a genuine digraph, while *gu* is bivalent: in *gui*, *gue* /gi, ge/ it acts as a digraph, but before non-front vowels it represents the sequence /gw/,

Figure 3.1: The Principal Letter-Sound Correspondences of Castilian

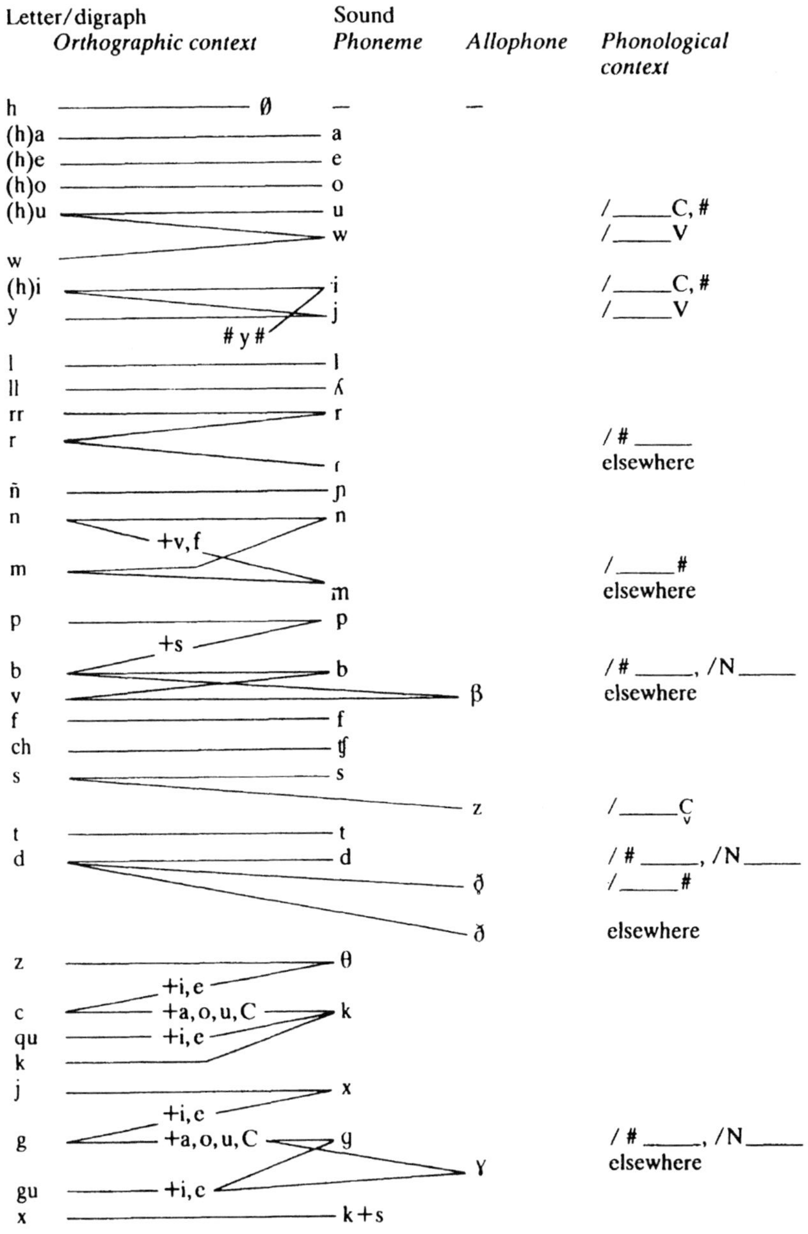

Letter/digraph Orthographic context	Sound Phoneme	Allophone	Phonological context
h	Ø —	—	—
(h)a	a		
(h)e	e		
(h)o	o		
(h)u	u		/ ____C, #
	w		/ ____V
w			
(h)i	i		/ ____C, #
y	j		/ ____V
	# y #		
l	l		
ll	ʎ		
rr	r		
r			/ # ____
	ɾ		elsewhere
ñ	ɲ		
n	n		
	+v,f		/ ____#
m			elsewhere
	m		
p	p		
	+s		/ # ____ , /N ____
b	b		elsewhere
v		β	
f	f		
ch	ʧ		
s	s		
		z	/ ____Ç
t	t		
d	d		/ # ____ , /N ____
		ð̞	/ ____#
		ð	elsewhere
z	θ		
c	+i,e		
	+a,o,u,C k		
qu	+i,e		
k			
j	x		
	+i,e		
g	+a,o,u,C g		/ # ____ , /N ____
		γ	elsewhere
gu	+i,e		
x	k+s		

Key: / = in the environment; , = or; # = word boundary; + = followed by; V = any vowel; C = any consonant; Ç̬ = any voiced consonant; N = any nasal consonant.

which in turn requires the sequences /gwi, gwe/ to be spelled with a diaeresis as *güi, güe*. A further asymmetry arises in the verb system as a result of the preference for representing /θ/ as *c* before front vowels, in which environment *z* is restricted to a few foreign words such as *zinc* and *zebra*. Hence, verbs like *alzar* 'to raise' are spelled with *c* in the subjunctive (*alce*), perhaps to counterbalance verbs like *esparcir* 'to scatter' which in the corresponding forms have no alternative to using *z* (*esparza*). But the parallel does not hold good for *g* and *j* as representations of /x/: while *acoger* 'to welcome' must use *j* in the subjunctive (*acoja*), *dejar* 'to leave' retains its *j* (*deje*), spurning the available alternative of **dege*.

These and other anomalies are the indirect consequences of the wish to maintain an etymological relationship elsewhere in the system. Sometimes, more than one etymological 'layer' is preserved: *h*, for instance, represents Latin *h* in *hombre* 'man' < HOMINE (variously spelled *omne/ omre/ ombre* in Old Spanish), Latin *f* in *hablar* 'to speak' < FABULARE (see p. 121), Arabic /ħ/ in *alheña* 'henna' < /al+ħinnaa?/, and Arabic /f/ in *alhóndiga* 'granary' < /al+funduq/. Whether current Spanish orthography is the most efficient representation of the spoken language remains a matter of debate, since the answers vary according to desiderata. If the prime aim is to preserve the world-wide visual uniformity of Spanish, some departure from phonemic principles is unavoidable. One should not underestimate the impact of a spelling reform, particularly one not shared by all Spanish-speaking countries: at first sight *Djudeo-espanyol*, in its near-phonemic Israeli orthography, is a different language. We should also note that if etymological relics were eliminated from all Romance languages, their visual relatedness would disappear overnight.

3   Morphology

It is difficult in many languages to draw a principled distinction between morphology and syntax, and in Spanish the difficulty is exacerbated by historical shifts between inflection and parataxis, not all of which have been unidirectional (see below). In this section we shall concentrate on the inflectional morphology of modern Spanish, including periphrastic tenses and forms of address (in the interests of a unified presentation of verb morphology), but postponing the main discussion of clitics and derivational processes to sections 4 and 5 respectively.

Analytic Tendencies

Because Spanish has shared the general Romance drift away from synthesis towards more analytical forms of expression, and has accordingly swept away whole areas of Latin inflection (notably the entire morphological passive and most of the substantival declension system), the impression is sometimes given that it is a morphologically simple language. This is misleading. Derivation has always been a favoured and vigorous method of enriching the lexicon, with the effect of creating numerous forms whose overall morphological structure, while reasonably transparent, can hardly be described as simple. An abstract nominal like *desaprovechamiento* 'negligence' probably consists of six synchronic morphemes, *des-a-provech-a-mient-o*, with a further historical division *-pro(-vech)-* fossilised in the root. Most substantives also continue to be inflected for number and gender, and the verb system remains highly inflected in its most frequent paradigms, the trend towards analysis having affected the periphery much more than the core. Numerous complete utterances can be made using a single verb form: *llueve* 'it is raining', *¿saldrás?* 'will you go out?', *sonreíamos* 'we were smiling'. Quite complex ideas can be expressed using only a verb and clitic: *se escribían* 'they used to write to one another'. This concision is largely owed to inflection. Even in the periphrastic forms, where tense, aspect and voice can be 'unpacked' into as many words, the auxiliary remains highly inflected.

In the modern language, only interjections and functors (conjunctions, prepositions and a subset of adverbs) are immune to both inflection and derivation. Spanish, consequently, is far from being an isolating language: very few words consist of only one morph. True, in comparison with the formal registers of Latin, the inventory of inflected paradigms is appreciably smaller, but the frequency of the surviving inflections in continuous text has been maintained or even increased. The development of definite and indefinite articles, for instance, means that most Spanish noun phrases have one number and one gender marker more than their Latin counterparts. The 'synthesis index' of Spanish (calculated by dividing the number of morphemes in running text by the number of words) now falls between 1.9 and 2.2 depending on the complexity of the register.

Gender and Number in Substantives
The canonical structure of Spanish substantives is: (derivational prefix(es)) + lexical root + (theme vowel) + (derivational suffix(es)) + (gender marker) + (number marker). Theme vowels only occur in substantives derived from verbs. Gender is overtly marked on a large proportion of nouns, and number on almost all. Only a tiny handful of nouns like *crisis* 'crisis' consist of a single, unanalysable morph and remain uninflected for plurality; those which do are borrowings.

Gender in modern Spanish is a two-term grammatical category with important syntactic functions. It does not correspond to natural gender and must be regarded as inherent and semantically unmotivated for inanimate nouns. (There would, indeed, be a good case for replacing the traditional terms 'masculine', 'feminine' and 'gender' by something less specific, like 'noun classes 1 and 2'.) The sex of animate beings is normally respected — *tio : tia* 'uncle : aunt', *zorro : zorra* 'fox : vixen' — but *victima* 'victim' is feminine regardless of the sex of the referent, and the names of less common birds, animals and insects are often invariable, so that to refer to a 'male eagle' or 'female beetle' one must say respectively *águila macho* and *escarabajo hembra*, not *águilo or *escarabaja. A small number of nouns are bivalent, like *el/la cliente* 'customer', but none are neuter. The combination of the so-called 'neuter' article *lo* with an adjective — as in *lo alto* 'the highest point', *lo peor* 'the worst of the matter', *lo triste* 'the sad part' — is best regarded as a kind of syntactic nominalisation in which *lo* functions as a [-count] marker. Historically, it represents a Spanish innovation, not a continuation of the Latin neuter gender, which was eliminated before the Old Spanish period from substantives, usually in favour of masculine, though faint traces of it persist in the pronoun system (see p. 95).

The mismatch between natural and grammatical gender is compounded in Spanish by a mismatch between grammatical gender and morphological marking. The markers *-o* and *-a* show a high degree of correlation with masculine and feminine respectively. Only one native noun in *-o* is feminine: *la mano* 'hand', which remains faithful to its etymological gender. (Modern clipped forms like *la foto* 'photograph', *la moto* 'motorcycle' and *la radio* 'radio' are now rallying to its support.) The reliability of *-a* as a feminine marker is almost as good; *el dia* 'day' is a latinate exception, but nearly all others are borrowings, such as *el guía* 'guide' from Germanic, *el sofá* 'sofa' from Arabic probably via French, and *el poeta* 'poet' and several others from Greek. A recent source of exceptions, however, has been the popularity of the agentive suffix *-ista*: nouns like *ciclista* 'cyclist' and *paracaidista* 'parachutist', which are obviously bivalent, can be used in Spanish with either *el* or *la*, but retain their *-a* ending when referring to men. The predictability of gender from most other endings is much lower, though it can be greatly improved by reference to etymological and derivational information. For example, of the 200-odd words ending in *-ez*, over 80 per cent are feminine; but *-ez* is 100 per cent feminine if it signals an abstract noun derived from an adjective — *la delgadez* 'slimness', *la palidez* 'pallor', *la sensatez* 'common sense', and 100 per cent masculine in borrowings from Arabic — *el ajedrez* 'chess', *el ajimez* 'window arch', *el alférez* 'sub-lieutenant', *el jaez* '(ornate) harness'. Whether such information is systematically available to language learners, however, must be doubted.

The categories of gender and number are for the most part overtly marked on determiners, demonstratives, pronouns and adjectives of all kinds, as well as nouns. In Castilian, all plural substantives and determiners end in /-s/, though the derivation of plurals from singulars is not quite so straightforward as this implies, since a sizable minority adds the full syllable /-es/ and a few already ending in /-s/ remain unchanged. (The /-e-/ of the syllabic plurals is now generally considered to be epenthetic, an analysis sometimes — though less consensually — applied to /-e/ as a singular ending.) We have already seen the drastic effect on plural marking in those dialects which have lost final /-s/ (see p. 85 above). It should be noted, however, that this development does not affect the inflectional character of plural marking: it merely replaces an additive mechanism by an alternation.

Determiners

Most nouns in connected discourse are preceded by a determiner inflected for number and gender, of which the most common are the articles:

	Definite		Indefinite	
	m.	*f.*	*m.*	*f.*
Singular:	el	la	un	una
Plural:	los	las	unos	unas

As in most western varieties of Romance (p. 53), the definite articles are semantically attenuated reflexes of the demonstrative ILLE and the indefinites derive from the numerical UNU 'one' (the Spanish masculine is truncated before substantives but appears as *uno* when used pronominally). Since determiners automatically acquire number and gender from their head noun and usually have unambiguous exponents for these categories, it could be argued that their presence renders the morphological marking of the noun redundant. But there is a minor complicating factor in the apparent mismatch of article and noun which occurs when a feminine singular noun begins with stressed /a-/ (sometimes spelled *ha-*); thus, *el agua* 'the water' not ** la agua*, *un águila* 'an eagle' not ** una águila*, *el hacha* 'the axe' not ** la hacha*, and so forth. Historically, these determiners seem to have developed regularly from ILLA and UNA in this specific phonetic environment, and are therefore accidental homonyms of the masculine forms. Whether Spanish speakers now perceive this pattern underlying the surface syncretism, seems very doubtful. If not, perhaps the correct synchronic analysis is to treat *la/una* as marked feminine singulars, contrasting with *el/un*, both unmarked for gender.

The Spanish demonstratives form a three-term system which correlates with grammatical person: *este* 'this (of mine)' : *ese* 'that (of yours)' : *aquel* 'yonder (of his/hers/theirs)'. One set of forms doubles up for adjectives and pronouns (the latter take an orthographic accent in the masculine and feminine) and the system is essentially identical to its Latin forerunner (p. 53), though with different exponents. As pronouns, the demonstratives each have a further form, *esto* : *eso* : *aquello*, deriving from the Latin neuter. These are used as anaphors for complete sentences or propositions; they can therefore be considered neutral in gender, but no longer specifically 'neuter' since they have no adnominal functions.

Subject Pronouns and Forms of Address

In addition to the grammatical categories of number and gender found in the substantives and determiners, the pronoun system encodes person and arguably case (though not as a continuation of Latin case functions). There is, however, both syncretism and asymmetry, as can be seen from the subject pronouns presented in Figure 3.2. Here, gender is neutralised in the first and second persons singular. In the plural, the /-as/ forms are used to refer to exclusively female sets, and those in /-os/ are therefore better described as 'gender-neutral' than 'masculine' (in much the same way that 'masculine' is better described as the unmarked gender for substantives).

Figure 3.2: The Castilian Subject Pronoun System

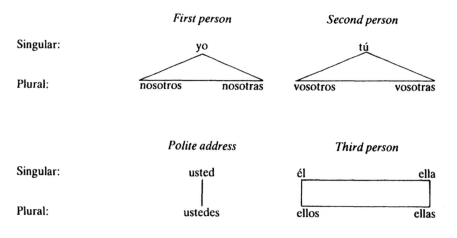

The first and third person subject pronouns are common to all varieties of Spanish, but Castilian is sharply distinguished from most others in its treatment of the semantic category of addressee. In the late medieval period, the physical distance encoded in the person category (and in demonstratives) came to be exploited metaphorically as a marker of social distance, the 'polite' address forms *usted/ustedes* (see p. 119) colligating with third person verb inflections in order to emphasise the differential status accorded by the speaker to the addressee. Quite subtle shades of social relationship can be conveyed by this system. Symmetrical usage by speaker and addressee connotes social equality, plus familiarity if *tú* is chosen, or respectful formality if *usted* is preferred. Asymmetrical usage by consent encodes a relationship of social inequality, even dominance/subservience. Unnegotiated asymmetrical usage can therefore be employed as an instantly recognisable signal of contempt or aggression. The system remained stable in most of Spain for at least two centuries, but has recently been undergoing significant change. The morphological aspects are not affected, but whereas *usted* was previously the unmarked form, employed in all contexts not specifically judged to be familiar or intimate, it has now become positively marked for deference. Unless there are gross discrepancies of age and status, a stranger will now be addressed in Spain as *tú*.

This recent development has the effect of widening the earlier discrepancy in usage between Castilian and other varieties. In grammatical terms, the Castilian system rests on a clash between second person semantics and third person morphology. This clash is resolved in west Andalusian and Canary Island dialects by colligating *ustedes* with second person morphology, as in *ustedes sois* 'you are'. In Latin America, the position is more complicated. Almost all regions lack the European 'familiar' plural *vosotros* (whether they have eliminated the form, or never had it, is disputed). Instead, *ustedes* is used, with third person inflections, as a generalised plural. In the singular, there is more diversity. Standard Mexican Spanish uses *tú* opposing *tú hablas* 'you speak' in the singular to *ustedes hablan* in the plural. Standard Argentinian uses as its generalised singular *vos* (which in medieval Spain had been used as a polite singular, just as modern French *vous*), colligated with inflections which derive from the second person plural but are no longer identical to their European counterparts, hence *vos ponés* 'you put', *vos andás* 'you walk'. Between Mexican and Argentinian, a wide array of permutations is possible, colligating pronouns with inflections which are historically both singular and plural, sometimes even blends. The stable *voseo* of Argentina is not a recent phenomenon; its roots must be sought in the colonial period, and archival research has revealed that it was well established in educated Buenos Aires usage by the beginning of the nineteenth century. This suggests that *voseo*, which is found in Uruguay, Paraguay and most of Central America as well as Argentina, and preserves the essentials of fifteenth-century peninsular usage, may originally have been the principal, if not uniform, model throughout Latin America. The pattern now found in Mexico and most of the Caribbean probably represents the historical overlay of later Castilian changes, diffused through better contacts with the Viceroyalty, and meeting more or less resistance as they filtered southwards.

Verbal Inflection
We turn now to a discussion of the simple tense-forms of the verb. In the standard language verbs are traditionally said to belong to one of three conjugations, with infinitives in *-ar*, *-er* and *-ir*. The *-ar* group, deriving from the Latin first conjugation in -ARE, is by far the largest and the one which accommodates almost all new coinings (compare *alunizar* 'to land on the moon' with French *alunir*, p. 223). The distinction between the *-er*

and -ir patterns is more apparent than real: aside from the future and conditional paradigms (which necessarily diverge since they take the infinitive as their stem) their endings are identical in all but four instances. We shall therefore distinguish only two basic conjugations for regular verbs, as set out in the chart of simple tense-forms.

In Castilian, as in Latin, each paradigm consists of six forms representing three grammatical persons in both singular and plural (most American varieties, as we have seen, have only five forms). In general, all

The Simple Tense-forms of Regular Verbs, Showing the Stress and a Possible Morphological Analysis

Conjugation I: tomar 'to take'   Conjugation II: comer 'to eat'

(a) Present

Indicative	Subjunctive	Indicative	Subjunctive
tóm-Ø-o	tóm-e-Ø	cóm-Ø-o	cóm-a-Ø
tóm-a-s	tóm-e-s	cóm-e-s	cóm-a-s
tóm-a-Ø	tóm-e-Ø	cóm-e-Ø	cóm-a-Ø
tom-á-mos	tom-é-mos	com-é-mos	com-á-mos
tom-á-is	tom-é-is	com-é-is	com-á-is
tóm-a-n	tóm-e-n	cóm-e-n	cóm-a-n

(b) Imperfect

Indicative	Subjunctive (1)	or (2)	Indicative	Subjunctive (1)	or (2)
tom-á-ba-Ø	-á-se-Ø	-á-ra-Ø	com-í-a-Ø	-ié-se-Ø	-ié-ra-Ø
tom-á-ba-s	-á-se-s	-á-ra-s	com-í-a-s	-ié-se-s	-ié-ra-s
tom-á-ba-Ø	-á-se-Ø	-á-ra-Ø	com-í-a-Ø	-ié-se-Ø	-ié-ra-Ø
tom-á-ba-mos	-á-se-mos	-á-ra-mos	com-í-a-mos	-ié-se-mos	-ié-ra-mos
tom-á-ba-is	-á-se-is	-á-ra-is	com-í-a-is	-ié-se-is	-ié-ra-is
tom-á-ba-n	-á-se-n	-á-ra-n	com-í-a-n	-ié-se-n	-ié-ra-n

(c) Preterit or simple past (indicative only)

tom-Ø-é	(?é = á+i)	com-Ø-í	(?í = í+i)
tom-á-ste		com-í-ste
tom-Ø-ó	(?ó = á+u)	com-i-ó
tom-á-mos		com-í-mos
tom-á-ste-is		com-í-ste-is
tom-á-ro-n		com-ié-ro-n

(d) Future indicative (all verbs)   Conditional (all verbs)

tom-a-r-é	com-e-r-ía
tom-a-r-ás	com-e-r-ías
tom-a-r-á	com-e-r-ía
tom-a-r-émos	com-e-r-íamos
tom-a-r-éis	com-e-r-íais
tom-a-r-án	com-e-r-ían

six forms are distinct, though there is some syncretism in first and third persons singular, and more in dialects which have lost final /-s/. As already noted (see p. 87), stress operates functionally to differentiate otherwise identical forms. The unmarked paradigm is the present indicative and the unmarked person the third singular, which is the morphological shape assumed by the handful of verbs that do not accept animate subjects (*nieva* 'it is snowing', *acontecio* 'it happened'). It is useful to distinguish a 'theme vowel' after the lexical stem, /-a-/ for the first conjugation and for the second /-e-/ or /-i-/, in a rather complicated phonological distribution. It can then be seen that the distinction between the present indicative and subjunctive rests on a reversal of the theme vowel.

The order of morphemes is fixed: (derivational prefix(es)) + lexical stem + theme vowel + tense marker (sometimes including an empty morph) + person marker. Some forms, however, have fused in the course of history and a neat segmentation is not always possible. The preterit is the most difficult paradigm to analyse, since the theme vowel is sometimes indistinguishable, and segmenting the second and third person plural markers in the regular way, /-is, -n/, leaves an awkward residue which occurs nowhere else in the system. The future and conditional pose a rather different problem: both have evolved during the history of Spanish (see below) from combinations of the infinitive with either the present or imperfect of the auxiliary *haber* 'to have', and despite considerable phonetic reduction the 'endings' still contain traces of this verb's lexical stem. This secondary derivation explains the identity of the conditional endings with those of the second conjugation imperfect.

Spanish is in the unusual position of having alternative forms for the past subjunctive, neither of which is a reflex of the original paradigm. The *-se* series derives from the Latin pluperfect subjunctive, and the *-ra* from the pluperfect indicative (see p. 46). In northwestern dialects and parts of Latin America, *-ra* is still occasionally found as a pluperfect. In standard Spanish, the two forms are not quite interchangeable: in the 'attenuating' sense *quisiera* 'I should like' and *debiera* 'I really ought' cannot be replaced by the *-se* counterparts, and elsewhere their distribution may be determined by considerations of symmetry or by sociolinguistic factors.

Limits of Regularity
By the strictest criteria, almost 900 Spanish verbs are irregular in one or more of the simple tense-forms (excluding those which undergo merely orthographic alternations, discussed on p. 90). This disconcerting figure includes a very few with anomalies in their endings, for instance the empty morph *-y* which appears in *doy* 'I give' and only three other verbs (see the chart of irregular verbs). All the others are subject to stem alternations, with varying degrees of predictability. Over half the total are 'radical

Five Irregular Verbs Used as Auxiliaries Reproduced in Standard Orthography

ser 'to be'   estar 'to be'   haber 'to have' tener 'to have' ir 'to go'

(a) Present indicative

soy	estoy	he	tengo	voy
eres	estás	has	tienes	vas
es	está	ha	tiene	va
somos	estamos	hemos	tenemos	vamos
sois	estáis	habéis	tenéis	vais
son	están	han	tienen	van

(b) Present subjunctive (endings regular, same stem throughout)

sea	esté	haya	tenga	vaya
seas	estés	hayas	tengas	vayas
sea	esté	haya	tenga	vaya
seamos	estemos	hayamos	tengamos	vayamos
seáis	estéis	hayáis	tengáis	vayáis
sean	estén	hayan	tengan	vayan

(c) Imperfect indicative (endings regular, same stem throughout)

era	estaba	había	tenía	iba
eras	estabas	habías	tenías	ibas
era	estaba	había	tenía	iba
éramos	estábamos	habíamos	teníamos	íbamos
erais	estabais	habíais	teníais	ibais
eran	estaban	habían	tenían	iban

(d) Future indicative (endings regular, infinitival stem throughout)

seré	estaré	habré	tendré	iré

(e) Conditional (endings regular, infinitival stem throughout)

sería	estaría	habría	tendría	iría

(f) Preterit indicative (endings slightly irregular, preterit stem throughout)

fui	estuve	hube	tuve	fui
fuiste	estuviste	hubiste	tuviste	fuiste
fue	estuvo	hubo	tuvo	fue
fuimos	estuvimos	hubimos	tuvimos	fuimos
fuisteis	estuvisteis	hubisteis	tuvisteis	fuisteis
fueron	estuvieron	hubieron	tuvieron	fueron

(g) Imperfect subjunctive (endings regular, preterit stem throughout)

(1) fuese	estuviese	hubiese	tuviese	fuese
(2) fuera	estuviera	hubiera	tuviera	fuera

changing', of the three types discussed earlier (p. 88); some others, like *huir* 'to flee', insert a glide under predictable conditions. A significant minority retain a Latin stem alternation which is no longer predictable or productive, contrasting the preterit and the non-present subjunctive paradigms with all others; these verbs, as can be seen from the chart, have slightly different endings in the preterit, with an alternating stress pattern. A number of verbs, some of which are otherwise regular, preserve a Latin anomaly in the past participle — *abrir* 'to open' : *abierto* < APERTUM, *romper* 'to break' : *roto* < RUPTUM; while the common irregular participles like *hecho* 'done' < FACTUM show no sign of change, others seem likely candidates for analogical replacement, as has happened with *torcer* 'to twist', now conjugated with *torcido* though its old participle *tuerto* survives as an adjective meaning 'one-eyed/squint-eyed'. Some twenty verbs of conjugation II modify the infinitival stem used as the basis of the future and conditional, mostly as a regular phonological adjustment following the loss of the theme vowel before a stressed inflection, as in *saldré* < *salir* + *é* 'I shall go out', *valdría* < *valer* + *ía* 'it would be worth'. Finally, a handful of very frequent verbs are totally eccentric and even undergo stem suppletion.

One class, amounting to some 200 including compounds, deserves special mention. Polysyllabic verbs which end in *-cer* or *-cir* preceded by a vowel, like *conocer* 'to know' or *relucir* 'to flaunt', have an extra velar consonant before non-front vowels, *conozco* being pronounced [ko-'noθ-ko] in Castilian and [ko-'nos-ko] in *seseante* districts of Andalusia and throughout Latin America. The intriguing question is: where does the velar come from? Is it part of the underlying stem but lost before front vowels? Or is it epenthetic, and if so under what conditions? The first answer is historically correct: all these verbs contain an originally inchoative infix -SC- (for French, see p. 223), whose velar regularly palatalised before a front vowel and assimilated to the preceding sibilant. But it seems unlikely that contemporary speakers recapitulate this process to produce the less frequent of the two alternants. If the velar is regarded as epenthetic (though phonetically unmotivated), it remains predictable in Castilian but only by reference to the phoneme /θ/. In *seseante* dialects, which lack the /θ : s/ opposition, the alternation is unpredictable: speakers cannot know from the phonological structure that *reconocer* 'to recognise' [re-ko-no-'seɾ] requires [-k-] while *recoser* 'to sew up' [re-ko-'seɾ] does not. They must, in other words, learn the alternation as an inherent lexical feature of the verb.

Periphrastic Forms and Auxiliaries
In addition to its simple paradigms, Spanish is particularly well endowed with periphrastic forms, more so than any other standard Romance language. Usually, these consist of an inflected auxiliary followed by a nonfinite form of the lexical verb (an infinitive or participle), but more complex combinations are also possible. Virtually all are Romance creations, though some embryonic models are attested in Latin (pp. 56–8). The most far-reaching innovation was the compounding of HABERE, originally meaning 'to possess', with a past participle. HABEO CENAM PARATAM first meant 'I have the supper here, already prepared', but with increased use and a

change of word order, it soon came to mean simply 'I've prepared the supper'. The new construction provided a powerful model: in principle, any paradigm of HABERE could be combined with the past participle to make a new tense-form. This remains true in modern Spanish: all eight simple paradigms of *haber*, including the almost extinct future subjunctive, can be used as auxiliaries. Although the periphrases with *haber* were flourishing in Old Spanish, they could only be used with transitive verbs, a direct consequence of their etymology; intransitives were conjugated with *ser* (see p. 57). It was only at the end of the fifteenth century that *haber* ousted *ser* for all verbs, and the past participle became invariable. Alongside the now fully grammaticalised periphrases with *haber*, however, Spanish has had since its earliest texts an alternative construction making use of *tener* < TENERE 'to hold' closely reminiscent of the prototype: *tengo preparada la cena*, with agreement, means the same as the Latin expression from which we set out. (For the use of cognate *ter* in Portuguese, see p. 150.)

The chart of irregular verbs, detailing the most common auxiliaries, shows not only two verbs 'to have' but also two verbs 'to be', a notorious difficulty for foreign learners of Spanish. At some risk of oversimplification we shall say that *ser* is the normal copula, denoting inherent qualities, while *estar* focuses on resultant states; compare *la pimienta es picante* 'pepper is hot' (inherently) with *la sopa está fría* 'the soup's cold' (because it's cooled down). Both verbs can be used as auxiliaries, in conjunction with a past participle, to make analytic passives. This results in a plethora of forms, since any paradigm of *ser* or *estar* can be used, including those which are already composite. Nor are the two passives synonymous: *ser* denotes the action or process, as in *el dinero ha sido robado (por un atracador)* 'the money has been stolen (by a gangster)', whereas *estar* denotes the subsequent state, as in *la tienda estaba abierta* 'the shop was open' (because it had been opened). *Estar* also combines with a present participle to create a range of progressive forms. In turn, these may combine with other periphrases, without grammatical restriction, but nevertheless with increasing markedness, so that three-term verbs like *había estado andando* 'I'd been walking' are not frequent, and monsters like *ha estado siendo construido* 'it's been being built' are usually avoided in compassion for the listener.

Evolutionary Trends

To conclude this section on morphology, we should pose the twin questions: how secure is inflection? and could the elaborate verb inflection system be reduced or eliminated? So drastic a change is inconceivable in the near future, and it would be wrong to assume that Spanish is necessarily evolving along the same pathways as other Romance varieties, notably French, where inflection has been reduced. Indeed, in the course of its history, Spanish has created new morphology. One example is the adverbial ending *-mente*, deriving from the ablative of the feminine noun

MENS 'mind/manner' used with a feminine adjective, thus STRICTA MENTE > *estrechamente* 'narrowly'. In modern Spanish *-mente* is no longer perceived as a noun (its congener *miente* 'mind' is now confined to a few idiomatic expressions), but it can still be detached from its host adjective in order to avoid awkward repetition: *lenta(*mente) y cuidadosamente* 'slowly and carefully'. Even clearer examples are the future and conditional paradigms, both general Romance innovations (see p. 57), which in Old Spanish were still separable into their component parts — witness *conbidar le ien de grado* 'they would willingly invite him', *Mio Cid* 21 — and in Portuguese have still not fully coalesced (see p. 150). Although the new future paradigm is, in its turn, tending to be replaced in colloquial Spanish by a periphrasis (*voy a ver* 'I'm going to see/ I'll see') which better accords with general analytic tendencies in the language, the conditional paradigm is under no threat of substitution — on the contrary, it appears to be extending its range of functions.

Against this, we must set a theoretical prediction and a tentative observation. In typological theory, VO syntax and suffixal inflection may be viewed as cross-category disharmonies. On a syntactic level, there is no doubt that Spanish has been moving towards VO structure and has attained a reasonable consistency (see section 4); its verbal inflections constitute a prominent exception. Their demise, if it did come about, would have to be the consequence of a major syntactic reorganisation. Such a reorganisation occurred in the sparsely documented period between Latin and Old Spanish, when the development of determiners and the increased use of prepositions made most of the case system redundant. Something similar happened in Middle French (p. 231), when the use of subject pronouns became obligatory and the verb endings, now redundant, began to coalesce and disappear. Spanish, as we have seen, shows little syncretism in its inflections and, unlike French, rarely needs subject pronouns to avoid syntactic ambiguity, though they are regularly used for emphasis and contrast. But any move to increase the use of subject pronouns — and there is some evidence that this is happening in colloquial registers — would undermine the need to preserve number and person inflections in the verb, and could thereby threaten the entire inflectional edifice.

4 Syntax

Typological Consistency

On most of the criteria favoured by typological theory, modern Spanish is a consistent VO language. Briefly: in simplex sentences objects or complements follow the main verb; noun phrase relationships are expressed exclusively by prepositions; genitive constructions take the form of prepositional phrases and always follow their head noun; the standard follows the comparative; most adjectives, and all attributive phrases and relative clauses, follow their head noun; most adverbs follow the verb they modify; auxiliaries are frequent and always precede the lexical stem even when they are themselves composite; quantifiers and negatives precede the item they qualify and have only forward scope; interrogative words are always phrase-initial. Needless to add, there are some complications. We have already noted one major discrepancy with VO typology: the vigour of suffixal inflection in the verb system, a vigour which has been fed rather than starved by the evolution of auxiliaries. We shall examine below some apparent inconsistencies both in the effects of adverbial scope and in the operator : operand relations of derived lexical forms and compounds. Despite these reservations, there can be no doubt that, during the period of its documented history, Spanish has evolved in ways which increase, rather than disturb, its typological consistency.

While the chief distributional facts of Spanish syntax are relatively uncontentious (when due allowance is made for some regional variation), it is nevertheless difficult to present a theoretically neutral description of some core features which are susceptible of competing analyses. The key difficulties are: word order, constituency and concord. We shall assume a model which, like typological theory, recognises syntactic relations as primes. It is clear, for instance, that grammatical mobility is an attribute of subjects in Spanish, not a general property of noun phrases. As we shall see, subject and object phrases are formally differentiated in ways which obviously relate to their sentential functions.

The Nominal Group

Subjects
The minimal overt structure of a subject noun phrase in Spanish is a proper noun or single personal pronoun (see Figure 3.2 above). For subject NPs with common nouns as their heads, the structure is: determiner + (numeral) + (adjective or conjoined adjectives) + noun + (adjectival modifier(s)). In Spanish, the determiners — articles, demonstratives and (unlike Italian, pp. 54, 298) possessives — form a mutually exclusive set, only one being possible in prenominal position. Articles always precede the noun and have done so quite consistently since the earliest documented stages of the language. Demonstratives and possessives may, however, be used as postposed adjectives, in which case the preposed article is retained, so *ese libro* 'that book (of yours/near you)' alternates with *el libro ese* which is more colloquial and sometimes pejorative. Most of the possessives have several alternants, with a short form, inflected only for number and restricted to prenominal position, opposed to a longer form, inflected for both number and gender, and used as a postnominal adjective. Hence: *mi hermano* 'my brother', *mi hermana* 'my sister', *mis parientes* 'my relatives',

un libro mio 'a book of mine/one of my books', *unas sobrinas tuyas* 'some of your nieces'. When used pronominally, the demonstratives stand alone (embellished by an orthographic accent) — *éste* 'this man', *aquélla* 'that woman'; but the possessives must be combined with an article — *el mio* 'mine (of masculine singular possessions)', *las nuestras* 'ours (of feminine plural possessions)'.

Quantifiers and negatives form a special class sharing some characteristics with adjectives and others with determiners, and therefore cut across the schema given above. Both precede the noun they modify (a possible exception is discussed below), but a negative is not compatible with a determiner — *ningunos libros* 'no books' (**los/*unos ningunos libros*), whereas a quantifier can cooccur with a definite determiner — *(tus) muchos amigos*, '(your) many friends', *(los) pocos árboles* 'the (few) trees'. Combinations of quantifiers and indefinite articles are not usually permissible — **unos muchos* '*some many', **un cada* '*an each'; but *unos pocos* 'some/a few' is not only perfectly grammatical but also very frequent. Faced with this apparent exception, some linguists have reanalysed *unos/unas* as a special kind of quantifier, rather than as the plural of the indefinite article *un/una*.

Adjectival Modifiers and Relatives

In Spanish, adjectives but not adjectival phrases or relative clauses may precede the head noun. The handful of quantifiers and negatives already mentioned are the only adjectives to be invariably fixed in prenominal position. Some common adjectives have clearly differentiated meanings depending on position: *un buen hombre* 'a good chap' contrasts with *un hombre bueno* 'a morally upright man', as does *un viejo amigo* 'a long-time friend' with *un amigo viejo* 'an elderly friend'. The semantic and pragmatic conditions for adjective placement have long been a matter of debate in Spanish linguistics and a limited consensus has emerged that prenominal adjectives indicate known, expected or figurative qualities whereas those following the noun convey new, unexpected or distinguishing information; compare *las verdes hojas* 'the green leaves' with *las hojas azules* 'the blue leaves'. But semantic generalisations about the content of individual adjectives are quite often falsified by usage in extended contexts. A recent proposal based on discourse analysis claims that the relative order of adjective and noun is itself meaningful: postnominal order denotes contrast, the establishment of a difference, whereas prenominal order merely provides a characterisation without implying any contrast. It should be noted that this analysis works well not only for conventional adjectives, but also for any pairs of substantives, like *obra maestra* 'masterpiece', in which the first slot is reserved for the element being characterised and the second for the characteriser.

Relative clauses in Spanish must follow their head noun or dummy head and be introduced by an overt relativiser. *Que*, the unmarked complementiser, is also the particle most often used to introduce relatives. During the documented history of Spanish, *que* has been increasing its domain at the expense of *quien(es)* 'who', and the supposed prehistorical opposition of inanimate *que* to animate *quien* has now been so far undermined that combinations like *el hombre quien* ... 'the man who ...' sound over-formal and stilted in many contexts. For many Spanish speakers, however, it remains ungrammatical to use *que* in oblique relatives with human antecedents; hence *el chico a quien* ... (*a que ...) 'the boy to whom ...', *el abogado con quien* ... (*con que ...) 'the lawyer with whom ...'. To indicate a possessive relative, *de quien* 'of whom' may be used, but much more common is *cuyo* which derives from the invariable Latin genitive pronoun CUIUS, but has been reanalysed as an adjective and now agrees with the item possessed, hence *el chico cuyas hermanas* ... 'the boy whose sisters ...'. This historical reanalysis allows modern Spanish to 'access' prepositional objects of possessives for relativisation much more easily than can be achieved in some other Romance languages: *el chico con cuya hermana hablabas* 'the boy whose sister you were talking to'.

Objects

Many of the characteristics of subject noun phrases, including the behaviour of their adjectival modifiers, carry over to object or complement phrases, but there are some important exceptions. In particular, for nonsubject NPs, determiners are distributed according to semantic criteria: there are few purely syntactic constraints on their presence. For mass nouns no determiner is used: *compré vino/arroz* 'I bought (some) wine/rice'; there is no equivalent of the 'partitive' article obligatory in French in comparable environments (see p. 227). Singular count nouns do require a determiner — *compré un libro/el libro que querías* 'I bought a book/the book you wanted'; but in the plural it may be omitted, producing a slight semantic difference between *compré libros* (= some, an indetermiate number) and *compré unos libros* (= a few, a small number of specific books). In the case of possessive pronouns, the article is obligatory for direct objects — *¡dale el tuyo!* 'give him yours', but is usually omitted in complements — *este lápiz es mío* 'this pencil is mine' — resulting in a neutralisation of the potential distinction between adjectival and pronominal complements.

A further peculiarity of Spanish object NPs is illustrated by *vi a Carmen* 'I saw Carmen' and *vi a tu primo* 'I saw your cousin', as opposed to *vi la calle* 'I saw the street' or *vi (unas) montañas* 'I saw (some) mountains'. When the object refers to a particular human being, it is obligatorily introduced by the preposition *a*, popularly known as 'personal a'. This construction is by no means confined to humans; it is common when the referent is an animal, a place name or country, or even an inanimate object if there is any possibility of confusion with the grammatical subject, hence:

reconocía a Roma 'she could recognise Rome', *la rata cazó al gato* 'the rat hunted the cat', *la bicicleta dobló al camión* 'the bicycle overtook the lorry'. This usage has been increasing during the documented history of Castilian, where *a* now seems to function as a generalised object marker, with the important proviso that the object so marked must be particularised or referential. Preserving the distinctiveness of subjects and objects is an evident desideratum in Spanish syntax (and, as we shall see, one of the main guarantors of relatively free word order), but its maintenance is not achieved without wider repercussions. In particular, the 'personal *a*' construction has the effect of converting many object NPs into prepositional phrases and, since *a* is also the preposition used to introduce datives, of removing any overt distinction between direct and indirect objects for the great majority of animate NPs; witness *vi a Juana* 'I saw Jane' and *di a Juana el recado* 'I gave Jane the message'.

Object Pronouns and Clitics
The grammar of object pronouns in Spanish is notoriously complex and also liable to considerable regional variation; we shall be able to present only a schematic outline here. The pronouns themselves are of two morphological types: disjunctive free forms and clitic particles bound to the verb (though the clitics also derive historically from free pronouns). Object pronominalisation in Spanish never consists merely of substituting a free pronoun for a full NP in the identical syntactic frame. In many sentences two coreferential pronouns occur, one disjunctive and the other clitic; of these, it is the clitic which is obligatory. The inclusion of the matching disjunctive pronoun signals emphasis, contrast or diasmbiguation. So, the neutral pronominal equivalent of *vi a Juana* 'I saw Jane', is *la vi* 'I saw her', with an emphatic or contrastive variant in *la vi a ella* 'I saw HER'; but *vi a ella* is ungrammatical, unlike the equivalent structure in Italian (p. 290).

So-called 'clitic doubling' is widespread in Spanish and is not confined to examples of the above type. Full NPs with human referents also commonly occur with a clitic: *la vi a Juana* 'I saw Jane', *le dije a Miguel que ...* 'I said to Michael that ...'. This results in a skewed manifestation of 'doubling'. When the direct or indirect object is a proper noun or definite phrase with a human referent (and sometimes, by extension, any animate referent), doubling consists of inserting a clitic 'copy' of the object, a process which is optional but often preferred. But when the object is human and pronominal, the clitic is obligatory, so that doubling consists of optionally including the disjunctive pronoun. Doubling, in both contexts, is clearly gaining ground, and for a few verbs has become almost mandatory: for many speakers, *gustar* 'to please', now requires a clitic even when its indirect object is a human proper noun — *le gustan a María las cerezas* (*gustan ...*) 'Mary likes cherries' (literally 'to-her are-pleasing to Mary the cherries'). On the other hand, doubling is not permissible when the object NP is inanimate. The third person deictic clitics *lo, la, los, las* cannot cooccur within a simplex sentence with the full NP, hence *compró el libro* 'she bought the book', *lo compró* 'she bought it', but not **lo compró el libro*. (In this respect, Spanish is rather unlike French; see p. 236.)

We noted above that the use of 'personal *a*' precludes an overt distinction between direct and indirect objects with animate referents. What is true of full NPs is also true of disjunctive pronouns and furthermore of most clitics: compare *me vio a mí* 'she saw ME' with *a mí me dijo que ...* 'she said to ME that ...'. Only in the third person clitics is an overt distinction made between direct and indirect objects (or 'accusatives' and 'datives' in different terminology): *la vi (a ella)* 'I saw her' versus *le dije (a ella) que ...* 'I said to her that ...'. This distinction, though potentially useful, is unique within the pronoun system and is now being subjected to analogical levelling. Since, however, there are competing targets for the process, levelling may well result in regionally differentiated patterns. The reason is that the third person system inherited from Latin distinguishes direct from indirect, but not always animate from inanimate — a dichotomy which is very important in other parts of the grammar. *La vi*, without further context, is ambiguous between 'I saw her' and 'I saw it' (any feminine-gender inanimate object).

The changes in progress are schematised in Figure 3.3. A Castilian innovation using *le* < dative ILLI as the animate masculine direct object clitic, has spread rapidly and in Spain is now virtually standard. This usage, called *leísmo*, has not penetrated to some remoter parts of Spain or to most of Latin America, which remains faithful to the etymological model, called appropriately *loísmo*. In Castilian, the logical extension of *lo* > *le* is for plural *les* to oust *los* as the animate masculine direct object; this too is happening, though a little more slowly. A further development, called *laísmo*, now clearly established in parts of Old Castile but still stigmatised elsewhere, uses *la* and *las* to mark animate feminine indirect objects as well as direct, hence *la di el libro* 'I gave her the book'. If both *leísmo* and *laísmo* eventually become standard in the prestige dialect, the effect will be to eliminate all overt trace of the Latin accusative : dative opposition. Clear differentiation of gender will have been a target attained at the expense of case. But the resulting system will still not be symmetrical, since the animate : inanimate distinction will be overtly marked for masculines, but not for feminines. Therein may lie the seeds of a further readjustment in the future.

Cliticisation of pronouns to the verb is by no means a recent process in Spanish; it appears well established at the time of the earliest texts. What has changed is the position of clitics with respect to the verb. Enclisis was frequent in older stages of the language, and even in the late nineteenth century it was regarded as elegant (albeit slightly precious) in novelistic style to preserve enclitic reflexives especially in the preterit; so, for

Figure 3.3: Variation in the Third Person Clitic System

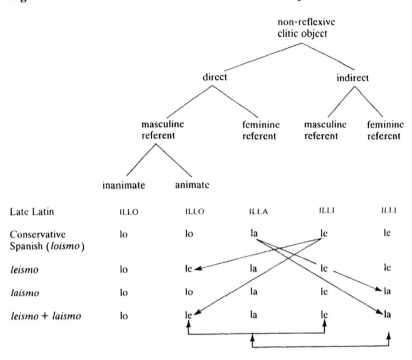

Note: An overt distinction between animate and inanimate operates only where shown. For plural forms, add /-s/ throughout. All the above items are mutually exclusive; no two *l*-forms may co-occur in any variety of Spanish (see p. 110).

instance, Galdós frequently writes, in sentence-initial position, *sentóse* 'he sat down' instead of the more prosaic *se sentó*, and *levantóse* 'he stood up' instead of *se levantó*. Reference grammars of contemporary Spanish customarily list three conditions under which enclitic position is maintained: in the positive imperatives — *¡dámelo!* 'give it to me', and after infinitives and present participles — *voy a verlo* 'I'm going to see it', *sigue cantándolo* 'he goes on singing it'. In fact, in colloquial Spanish, the last two examples would be *lo voy a ver* and *lo sigue cantando* respectively. Increasingly too, clitics 'climb' from a lower clause to the front of the main verb, sometimes hopping over an intermediate element; compare formal *quiero hacerlo* 'I want to do it' and *tiene que traérmelo* 'he must bring it for me' with colloquial *lo quiero hacer* and *me lo tiene que traer*. Despite the frequency of such examples, there are a number of contexts in which climbing is not possible, some apparently determined by lexical properties of the individual verb, others relatable to more general features like the presence of an intervening preposition. For instance, *creer* 'to believe' and *sentir* 'to regret' do not normally accept climbing from a lower clause: *creo haberlo dicho/*lo creo haber dicho* 'I believe I said it', *siento haberlo hecho/*lo siento haber hecho* 'I'm sorry I did it'; while the linking prepositions *en* and *con* seem regularly to block climbing: *insisto en hacerlo/*lo insisto en hacer* 'I insist on doing it', *sueño con verlo/*lo sueño con ver* 'I dream of seeing it'. While the overall frequency of clitic climbing seems to be increasing in Spanish, there is some tentative evidence that the number of individual sites permitting the movement has declined since the medieval period, as has certainly been true of French; again, there seem to have been competing targets for analogical levelling.

Curiously, voice is the verbal category with which pronominals have been most closely linked during the history of Spanish. The connection is essentially due to the cliticisation of the reflexive pronouns, a development which seems likely to result in the emergence of a new set of medio-passive paradigms. In modern Spanish reflexivity can be marked unambiguously on disjunctive pronouns by the addition of *mismo* 'self, same', as in *(a) ti mismo* 'yourself'; but most of the clitics, which cannot co-occur alone with *mismo*, are ambiguous in this respect (as also between direct and indirect interpretation). Reflexivity is distinguished, if at all, only in the third person *se*, which contrasts with the non-reflexive deictics in *l-* (see Figure 3.3), but itself neutralises the direct : indirect opposition, and also number and gender.

Recently, *se* and its congeners in other Romance languages have been the focus of intense linguistic debate. The problem is whether *se* should be treated as one single morpheme or a set of homophonous forms. Traditional accounts distinguish four or more functions of *se* which can be traced, more or less directly, to Latin SE, SIBI, or a fusion of the two: a true reflexive pronoun — *se lavó* 'he washed himself'; a reciprocal marker — *solían escribirse* 'they used to write to one another'; a passive marker — *el congreso se inauguró* 'the congress was opened'; and an impersonal marker — *se habla inglés* 'English spoken'. In addition, Spanish uses a *se*, known to have a different historical origin, as a means of circumventing the prohibition, dating from the earliest texts, on the cooccurrence of any two *l*-clitics; hence *se lo dio* 'she gave it to him', not **le lo dio*. (This strategy for avoidance is peculiar to Spanish, though the prohibition itself is not.) The difficulty for synchronic analysis is that several of the above functions appear to be semantically compatible, but Spanish never in practice permits more than one *se* per verb. The combination, for example, of an 'impersonal' *se* with a 'lexically reflexive' verb is ungrammatical — **se se esfuerza por ...* 'one struggles to ... ', as are many other apparently reasonable pairs. If *se* were only one morpheme, the problem would not arise; but can such disparate meanings be reconciled? Two accounts are now available which solve most of the problems. In one, *se* is viewed as a pronoun with very little inherent meaning ('third person, low deixis'), which acquires significance from contextual inferences. In the other, *se* is seen as part of a new medio-passive paradigm, its third person impersonal use paralleling that of Latin: VIVITUR = *se vive* = 'one lives'. In neither treatment is *se* a reflexive pronoun!

The Verb

Tense and Aspect

Spanish verbs, as we pointed out above (p. 93), are highly inflected and can often stand alone to form a complete utterance. As such, they are necessarily the principal carriers of tense, aspect and modality, though this information can be devolved upon an auxiliary and supplemented from various adverbial structures. If the 'core' system of Latin is viewed as the interaction of three time values (past, present, future) with two aspects (imperfective, perfective; see p. 56), then a substantial continuity of functions is discernible in modern Spanish, despite some notable modifications in morphology. The morphological changes have, however, imposed considerable strain on the semantic relations simply by making available more candidates for core membership than can be accommodated within the Latin six-cell matrix. Especially problematic in this respect are the past and conditional paradigms.

The emergence of HABERE as an auxiliary not only provided a neat morphological marking of perfective aspect, which in Latin had been dependent on a stem alternation, but also resolved the bivalency of the Latin 'perfect' as between present perfective and simple past (aorist) functions (see pp. 56 and 228). Thus VIVI in the sense of 'I have seen' was replaced by HABEO *VISTU > *he visto*, leaving *vi* to denote unambiguously 'I saw/I caught sight of'. It would be difficult, in modern Spanish, to argue for the exclusion of either of these forms from the core system, though the inclusion of both requires the recognition of a third aspect (punctual) which is nevertheless only opposed to the other two on the past time axis. (The so-called 'past anterior tense', as in *hube visto* < HABUI *VISTU, which is restricted to a subset of temporal adverbial clauses in the literary language, cannot be considered a member of the core system; nor does it systematically mark punctuality.) The resulting asymmetry has led some commentators to suppose that Spanish might follow French (p. 228) or northern Italian (p. 300) in extending the domain of the periphrastic paradigm to the point where it ousts the simple past from everyday speech and recreates the bivalency of Latin; but the Spanish evidence is difficult to interpret. The essential denotation of forms like *he visto* is 'completion of an action or process which remains relevant at the moment of speaking', but there are well known regional differences in usage according to the time lapse between completion and moment of speaking. In Castilian and central peninsular dialects the tolerated time lapse is longer, so that *he visto* is semantically compatible with time adverbials like *esta mañana* 'this morning' and, for some speakers, even with *ayer* 'yesterday'. In other peninsular dialects such collocations are not found, and in many Latin American varieties, notably Mexican, the periphrastic forms are reserved for immediate past time, so that *ayer he visto* . . . would simply be ungrammatical. The obvious conclusion that Castilian is the innovating variety is, however, checked by very recent observation of the educated norm, in which the preterit *vi* is increasingly being used to refer to the immediate past. It is too early to tell whether this represents a temporary aberration, or a genuine trend imitated from a newly prestigious conservative cognate.

Another source of tension in the core system has been the ambiguous status of the conditional. A plausible pathway for its incorporation is sketched below in relation to French (p. 229). If the absolute time values 'past : present : future' are reconceptualised as relative values 'anteriority : simultaneity : posteriority', this opens the way for a reanalysis of aspect in terms of 'now : then' axes. The new framework allows the conditional *vería* 'I should see' to be incorporated as the signal of 'posteriority' on the 'then' axis, in the same way that the future *veré* 'I shall see' represents 'posteriority' on the 'now' axis. This accurately reflects the distributional match of the two forms in indirect and direct speech respectively. If we take the argument one stage further and recognise a dimension of 'anticipated anteriority', we can also accommodate *habría visto* 'I should have seen' on the 'then' axis, to match *habré visto* 'I shall have seen' on the 'now'. Again, the distribution of the two forms in indirect and direct speech runs parallel.

The difficulty with this neat analysis is that conditionals carry not only temporal–aspectual meaning, but also modality (as, to a lesser extent, do futures; see below). One of their major functions is to evoke a hypothetical or unreal state of affairs. This usage appears to be a more recent historical development of the 'basic' temporal–aspectual meaning, and is probably due to a general tendency for markers of 'posteriority' to acquire modal connotations simply because the state to which they refer is unverifiable at the moment of speaking. In this function, Spanish conditionals are progressively encroaching on the domain of the subjunctive and have therefore a claim to be considered as an independent mood, but one which in relation to the indicative has a very restricted range of tense-forms.

Some developments in the 'peripheral' system are also noteworthy. In the core paradigms, imperfective aspect neutralises the potential distinction between habitual and durative meaning, so that *hacía* can mean either 'I was doing' or 'I used to do', depending on general context or the presence of a disambiguating adverbial like *en aquel momento* 'at that moment' or *todos los días* 'every day'. So much was true of Latin, but Spanish has now evolved symmetrical periphrases to differentiate the meanings, respectively: *estaba haciendo* and *solía hacer* (literally 'I was accustomed to do'). The composite forms are not only more specific in aspectual meaning than their simple counterparts; they are also more clearly differentiated in time reference, so that, for example, the present durative cannot combine with a future adverbial to refer to immediate futurity — *mañana voy a Londres* 'I'm going to London tomorrow', but not **mañana estoy yendo.*

In connection with the development of passives, we alluded earlier (p. 102) to the slow emergence of a stative aspect using *estar* which now seems to have attained a stable distinctiveness in relation both to the *ser*-passive and to the reflexive medio-passive. These latter are now principally differentiated by register: *ser*-passives, though common in journalistic and technical writing, have been virtually ousted from speech to the advantage of the clitic forms. Nevertheless, there is a syntactic difference in that, for most speakers, only the *ser*-passive can cooccur with an explicit agentive phrase; and also a semantic difference in that the deontic modality of the Latin passive now attaches only to the reflexive forms: *eso no se hace* 'that isn't done'. There may be a connection between the two distributions, deontic modality being inferred from the absence of agency: 'that isn't done (by anyone)' implying 'that mustn't be done'.

Modality and Mood

As we have seen, modality in Spanish is conveyed by various mechanisms, but the language is not usually considered to possess a discrete set of modal verbs. The chief exponents of possibility and volition are respectively *poder* 'to be able' and *querer* 'to want', which have only minor morphological irregularities and share syntactic properties with many other verbs. Moral obligation is expressed by *deber* 'ought', and external obligation, weakly by *haber de,* and more strongly by *tener que,* both translatable as 'to have to'. *Deber,* which seems to have had a continuous history as a deontic modal, has also developed an epistemic sense which, at least in the simple paradigms, is formally marked: *debe matricularse* 'he must register (= is obliged to)', *debe de matricularse* '(I infer that) he must be registering'. An interesting parallel can be found in the Romance replacement futures (see p. 57), which began as periphrases marking weak deontic modality and have now generally developed an epistemic sense: *estará en el despacho* 'she must be in the office'.

All varieties of Spanish preserve a vigorous subjunctive mood (see the charts of regular and irregular verbs for the morphology). Opinion is divided, however, on whether the subjunctive should be viewed as an independently meaningful category or as a 'mere' marker of subordination. Its use in many contexts is undoubtedly determined by grammatical factors; for example, a clause dependent on *querer* or any other expression of volition invariably requires a subjunctive — *quiero que lo hagas/*haces* 'I want you to do it'. In others, the conditioning is more subtle: indicative *sale* 'she goes out' certainly means something different from subjunctive *¡salga!* 'get out!', but it has been argued that the imperative sense derives from an underlying volitive, '(I want you to) get out', in which the presence of the subjunctive is more readily explicable. Something similar happens in a subset of restrictive relatives, where subjunctive *busco un hombre que hable árabe* 'I'm looking for a man who speaks Arabic' (= any Arabic speaker) contrasts with indicative *busco a un hombre que habla árabe* 'I'm looking for a (particular) man who (I know) speaks Arabic'. Here it could again be argued that the alternation of indicative and subjunctive correlates with the presence or absence of 'personal *a*', which establishes the referentiality of the antecedent noun. There are, however, a few instances where a genuine alternation is possible: *¿crees que vendrá?* and *¿crees que venga?* can both be translated as 'do you think he'll come?', but the first is neutral in implicature while the second conveys the speaker's belief that he won't. If such examples are taken as criterial, the 'grammatical marker' hypothesis cannot be sustained. Nevertheless, it remains very difficult to find a single, uniform meaning for the subjunctive, the traditional labels of 'doubt' and 'uncertainty' matching some, but by no means all, of its functions.

Word Order and Cohesion

Let us now turn to the combinatorial possibilities of the nominal and verbal groups we have examined separately. The minimal complete utterance, as we have seen, consists of a single verb, but a verb inflected for person and number. Most analysts assume this marking is not autonomous, but 'copied' from an underlying subject by virtue of the complex system of concord inherited from Latin. Although some exponents of concord, notably nominal case, have been eliminated during the history of Spanish, the system still marks number and gender on all modifiers within the noun phrase, and number and person (and in analytic passives gender too) between subject and verb. Concord thus guarantees the cohesion of sentential constituents and in most cases unambiguously assigns a subject to a verb. Subjects and objects that are morphologically identical can almost always be differentiated by the presence or absence of determiners and 'personal *a*', or by their position relative to the verb.

In Spanish simplex sentences, nominal objects and complements always follow their verb: *Elena compró un coche* 'Helen bought a car', *el libro parecía interesante* 'the book seemed interesting'. In everyday language, the VO/VC order is fixed; objects cannot precede their verbs, **Elena un coche compró*. It is certainly possible to topicalise an object consisting of a definite noun phrase or a proper noun by moving it to the front of the sentence, but when this happens there is an intonation break after the topic, and an object clitic is obligatorily inserted before the verb: *el coche, lo compró Elena* '(as for) the car, Helen bought it'. The result is no longer a simple sentence; *lo compró Elena* is a complete structure in its own right.

In the light of these observations and the typological statements at the head of this section (pp. 103–4), it is puzzling that Spanish has acquired a reputation for free, or comparatively free, word order. If VO order is obligatory, and the internal structure of noun phrases largely invariable, where lies the freedom? It is due to one salient characteristic which differentiates Spanish sharply from French but is common to most of the southern Romance group, namely that subject NPs are not fixed by grammatical requirements at a particular point in the sentence. SVO, VSO and VOS orders are all found, their syntactic transparency being guaranteed in almost all cases by the operation of concord, itself corroborated by unambiguous suffixal inflections. Of course, the position of subject NPs is not random: it is heavily influenced by pragmatic and sometimes stylistic considerations. As a general rule, topics precede comments, and new information is located towards the end of the sentence. Because of the marked tendency in speech for the topic to coincide with the grammatical subject, SV order is probably the most frequent, especially if the subject consists of a single proper noun or a very short phrase. So ?*compró Elena el coche* would sound very odd in speech, and *compró el coche Elena* would tend to be reserved for contradiction or contrast: 'It was Helen (not Jane) who bought the car'. Nevertheless, VSO and VOS orders are common in more formal registers, and in all registers VS is obligatory in existential statements: *viven gitanos en las cuevas* 'there are gypsies living in the caves'. There is also a strong tendency for unusually long or 'heavy' subject phrases to appear on the right of the verb, *han llegado (en Madrid) todos los transeuntes de la Compañia X* 'all passengers travelling with Company X have now arrived (in Madrid)' and VS order is the norm in many types of subordinate clause even when the subject consists of a single word: *no vi lo que leia Juana* 'I didn't see what Jane was reading'.

The mobility of subjects is not, in itself, a serious difficulty for a typological description and does not affect most of the features implied by VO structure, but it does cause problems in assigning a 'basic' word order to Spanish: SVO, VSO and VOS are all possible candidates. For generative linguists, the mobility of the first NP has proved more problematic, since both leftward and rightward movement rules are in this case difficult to constrain, and a rightward rule would often break up the presumed inviolability of the VP constituent. We have so far avoided the term 'verb phrase', precisely because the existence in Spanish of such a sentential constituent remains undemonstrated and possibly undemonstrable.

Aside from subject NPs and adjectives, the elements enjoying most syntactic freedom are adverbial clauses and phrases, and the quantifier *todo* 'all' which may 'float' from a subject NP to postverbal position. In conditionals, for instance, the protasis normally precedes the apodosis, but either order is acceptable. Likewise, temporal adverbial clauses tend to precede the main clause as an iconic reflection of chronology, but *sali luego que hubo terminado la cena* 'I went out as soon as he'd finished eating supper' is perfectly grammatical in Spanish, as in English. Simple adverbs, on the other hand, tend to be functionally located and any movement, when possible, may affect their scope relations. Thus, an adverb acting as a sentence modifier is usually placed in initial position — *Desgraciadamente ...* 'Unfortunately ...' — and its scope extends rightwards throughout the sentence; an adverb modifying an adjective similarly precedes and has rightward scope — *muy perezoso/*perezoso muy* 'very lazy'; but an adverb qualifying a verb normally follows and therefore has leftward scope — *corre rápidamente/?rápidamente corre* 'runs fast'.

Negatives and Interrogatives

Negatives and interrogatives have virtually no freedom of word order. Spanish is a '*wh*-fronting' language which obligatorily 'piedpipes' any accompanying preposition to initial position: *¿con quién salieron?* 'who did they go out with?/with whom ...?'. *¿salieron con quién?* is permissible only as an incredulous echo question and *¿quién salieron con?* is ungrammatical. Yes-no questions in speech often rely entirely on intonation to differentiate between interrogatives and statements. Both VS and SV orders are found, but VS cannot be assumed to be the result of syntactic inversion, since VS order is usually acceptable in the corresponding statement. VS order is normal in questions beginning with an interrogative word: *¿qué quieren ustedes?* 'what would you (pl.) like?', but some Caribbean varieties regularly show an SV order, *¿qué ustedes quieren?*, that would be rejected by the metropolitan standard.

Sentential negation in Spanish is expressed by inserting *no* immediately before the verbal group (including clitics). Anything to the right of *no* may fall within its scope. If the intention is to negate the verb contrastively, a break in intonation or a syntactic permutation like topicalisation may be used to exempt items normally to the right of the verb from the unwanted negation. Phrasal negation is likewise achieved by a preposed *no* and demarcative intonation. (Occasionally *no* is found after quantifiers and in sentence-final position, apparently with leftward scope, as in *los otros merendaron pero yo no* 'the others had tea, but I didn't'; but such examples are best treated as ellipses.) Multiple negation is quite acceptable in Spanish: *no dice nunca nada a nadie* 'he never says anything to anyone' (literally 'he doesn't never say nothing to nobody'). For negative pronouns and adverbs, there is a choice of construction: 'nobody came' can be rendered either as *no vino nadie* or *nadie vino*, but some form of preverbal negation is obligatory — *vino nadie* is ungrammatical. Since multiple negation is the norm rather than the exception, extra negatives cannot be added in order to intensify the effect. The curious alternative is to combine a preconstituent negator with a following positive modifier: *sin duda alguna* 'without any doubt/without the slightest doubt'.

Complementation
Several aspects of complex sentence structure have by now been mentioned under different headings, notably relativisation in connection with noun phrase organisation and modality (pp. 106 and 114) and adverbial clauses in connection with word order constraints (p. 115). In some others, particularly coordination, Spanish does not differ significantly from Latin or from its Romance neighbours. In the structure of complementation, however, there have been some notable changes. The principal classical Latin patterns of accusative + infinitive, or finite subjunctive clauses in continuous indirect speech, have given way progressively to analytic constructions on the model of QUOD > que + indicative, or to infinitival complements (see pp. 65ff). In modern Spanish, verbs of saying, thinking and believing take the que complementiser followed by a finite indicative while those suggesting a stronger emotional state, such as volition, exhortation, demand or fear, require que plus a finite subjunctive. In both cases there are 'sequence of tense' constraints which limit the range of tense-forms in the subordinate clause by reference to the main verb. In both cases also, the finite clause may be substituted by an infinitive when the subjects of both clauses are coreferential. Yet this strategy is used much more frequently to avoid a subjunctive clause than an indicative. *Quiero que (yo) lo haga* 'I want that I should do it', though grammatical, is clumsy and improbable; *quiero hacerlo* 'I want to do it' is far more natural. On the other hand, to replace *creo que me he equivocado* 'I think I've made a mistake' by *creo haberme equivocado* signals much greater formality of register. So too does the last remnant of the Latin accusative + infinitive in: *la creo inteligente* 'I believe her (to be) intelligent', as opposed to *creo que es inteligente* 'I think she's intelligent'.

Despite this minor anomaly, infinitival complementation with coreferential subjects has made great strides in Spanish, to the point where the infinitive has become one of the most frequent forms of the verb. Complementation of this kind often requires a 'linking' preposition. Sometimes, the presence or absence of a linkage appears to correlate with some other grammatical property: for instance, all lexically reflexive verbs require a preposition, perhaps as a signal that the infinitive does not represent the direct object. Occasionally, the preposition itself continues an earlier metaphor which has now become opaque, as in *abstenerse de hacer* 'to abstain from doing' (= 'to hold oneself away from'). Sometimes, too, the preposition echoes the derivational structure of the verb, as in *insistir en* 'to insist on'. But more usually the linkage seems quite arbitrary and must be learned as an idiosyncratic feature of the verb. There seems to be no semantic reason for *decidir* 'to decide', *intentar* 'to try' and *pensar* with the meaning 'to intend', all to take a bare infinitive, when *decidirse* and *resolverse* 'to decide/resolve' both require *a*, *optar* 'to opt' requires *por*, *tratar* 'to try' requires *de*, and *pensar* with the meaning 'to think about' requires *en*, even though 'to dream about' is *soñar con*. It is not unusual for languages to be left with arbitrary anomalies of this kind as a result of divergent historical processes, but it is very puzzling to find a language creating irregularity on this scale. So far, no satisfactory explanation has been proposed.

5   Lexis

Spanish, like other world languages, preserves in its lexicon a multi-layered record of historical contacts, both direct and indirect. For ease of exposition we shall divide Spanish vocabulary into three categories: inherited, borrowed and created items. It must, however, be borne in mind that these diachronic categories are by no means always delimitable by criteria of synchronic analysis, nor recognisable to untrained native speakers.

Inherited Items

By 'inherited' vocabulary is meant: the stock of Latin words introduced during the main phase of colonisation and continuously in use from that date to the present, plus the few items surviving from the pre-Roman substratum. Since little is known of the indigenous Iberian languages, attribution of a term to this source is often rather tentative, when other origins have been investigated and eliminated. Such etymological puzzles include: *barro* 'mud', *cama* 'bed', the adjective *gordo* 'fat', *manteca* 'lard', *páramo* 'moor', *pizarra* 'slate' and *vega* 'river plain'. *Izquierdo* 'left' has congeners throughout the peninsula and in south-west France, and is cognate with Basque *ezker*, but may be a borrowing there too. No satisfactory etymology has been found for *perro* 'dog', which until the sixteenth century seems to have been a popular alternative to Latin *can*, now restricted to a few rural and astronomical contexts. A number of common words derive from Celtic, including: *cambiar* 'to change', *camino* 'road', *camisa* 'shirt', *cerveza* 'beer', and *carro* — 'cart' in Spain, though in much of Latin America it has come to mean 'car', by contamination from English (see p. 241). These and similar words, however, are widely distributed in Romance and may therefore be borrowings into Latin from Gaulish. Direct survivals from the Celtic spoken in north and central Iberia probably include: Sp., Port. *álamo* 'poplar', Sp., Port. *gancho* 'hook', Sp. *engorar*, Port. *gorar* 'to addle', Sp. *serna*, Port. *seára* 'sown field', with *berro* 'watercress' and *légamo* 'slime' apparently exclusive to Spanish.

Borrowings

A significant number of Germanic words remain in regular use, nearly all of them widespread in Western Romance; they were probably diffused via Latin before the main period of invasions, as a result of Roman contact with 'confederate' Germanic peoples. They include military terminology — *guerra* 'war', *guardia* 'guard', *tregua* 'truce', *espuela* 'spur', *estribo* 'stirrup', *yelmo* 'helmet' — but also some everyday words, like *ropa* 'clothing', *falda* 'skirt', *jabón* 'soap', *ganso* 'goose', *ganar* 'to win', together with a set of common adjectives, *fresco* 'fresh/cool', *rico* 'rich', *blanco* 'white', and *gris* 'grey'. Some other words of ultimately Germanic origin were borrowed much later from French, Occitan and Catalan, including: *orgullo* 'pride', *galardón* 'reward' and *guante* 'glove'.

Direct contact between Germanic and Hispano-Romance speakers seems not to have been extensive. The early waves of invaders left few permanent settlements and the later Visigoths, who ruled substantial areas of Hispania for over two centuries, had long been in contact with Romans first as confederates then as founders of the kingdom of Toulouse, and were almost certainly bilingual, if not monolingual, Romance speakers at the time of their arrival in the peninsula (see p. 2). It is in place and personal names that Germanic elements have most vividly survived. *Andalucía* owes its name (after a little Arabic readjustment) to the Vandals who briefly settled there; numerous villages are called *Suevos* (after Swabians) and *Godos* (after Goths) or some still-recognisable variant like *Villagodos.* Common personal names include: *Alfonso, Alonso, Álvaro, Elvira, Fernando, Gonzalo, Ramón* and *Rodrigo.* It is likely that the Visigoths were responsible for the increase in use of the patronymic suffix *-ez* (probably calqued from the Latin genitive -ICI) in, for instance: *Fernández, Gómez, González, Hernández, López, Martínez,* and so on.

Approaching four thousand words can be traced to Arabic, almost all of them nouns and a high proportion beginning with *a-* or *al-,* representing the agglutination of the Arabic definite article. An important group relates to horticulture and water management: *acequia* 'irrigation channel', *noria* 'water wheel', *aljibe* 'cistern', *aceite* 'olive oil', *alcachofa* 'artichoke', *algodón* 'cotton', *arroz* 'rice', *azafrán* 'saffron', *azúcar* 'sugar', *berenjena* 'aubergine', *naranja* 'orange', *zanahoria* 'carrot'. Others concern civil administration: *aduana* 'customs', *alcaide* 'governor/gaoler', *alcalde* 'mayor', *alguacil* 'constable'; and still others have been assimilated, via Spanish, into international scientific vocabulary: *alcohol, algebra, cifra* 'figure/cipher', *cénit* 'zenith', *nadir,* and so on. In southern Spain, where the period of contact was longest and most intense (see pp. 6–7), some of the features most often cited as 'typical' are designated by Arabic words: *azahar* 'orange blossom', *azotea* 'flat roof', *azucena* 'lily', and *azulejo* 'ceramic tile' (so called because the basic colour was a deep blue — *azul*). In categories other than nouns, Arabic has given the adjectives *baldío* 'fallow' and *mezquino* 'mean', the verbs *achacar* 'to accuse' and *halagar* 'to flatter' (all of them well adapted to Romance grammatical patterns), the preposition *hasta* 'up to', and the exclamative *ojalá* 'would that ...' (literally: 'may Allah grant ...'). An interesting disputed case is that of *usted(es),* the polite form of address (see pp. 96–7), often explained as a contraction of *vuestra merced* (= approximately 'Your Grace'; compare Port.

você, Cat. *vostè*), but now thought to have been blended with Arabic /ustaď/ 'lord, master'.

During the colonial era, from the sixteenth to mid-nineteenth centuries, words were assimilated from Amerindian languages, those denoting new concepts often going on to become internationalisms: *cacao, chicle, chocolate, coyote, tomate,* from Nahuatl; *maíz, patata, tobaco,* from Arawak; *alpaca, cóndor, llama,* from Quechua; *ananá(s)* 'pineapple', *petunia, tapioca, tucán,* from Guaraní. In general, Castilian has retained Amerindian terms only for new concepts; a rare exception is Nahuatl *tiza* 'chalk' (as a writing material) which has restricted Romance *greda* < CRETAM to the rock itself. As is to be expected, Latin American varieties have borrowed more extensively from the indigenous languages with which they continue to be in contact. In much of Mexico, for instance, Nahuatl *tianguis* is the ordinary word for 'market', and *zacate* and *zopilote* may be preferred to designate 'grass' and 'vulture' respectively. Likewise in common usage in Peru are some Quechuan words (*charaque* 'cured meat', *chuño* 'potato flour', *poroto* 'bean', *soroche* 'mountain sickness') and in Paraguay others from Guaraní (*cobaya* 'guinea pig', *tapera* 'ruins, debris', *yacaré/yaguaré* 'alligator').

Since the Renaissance, Spanish has enriched its lexicon, mainly in the formal and technical registers, by extensive borrowing from Latin and other Romance languages; and to the present day, Latin and Greek continue to be favoured sources for the creation of new terminology. (We shall examine below some linguistic consequences of widespread borrowing from cognate languages.) Borrowing from English, relatively minor before the nineteenth century, has accelerated rapidly in the twentieth and affects all varieties, most particularly those in the Caribbean and Central America in regular contact with the USA. Although the recent influx of words (and cultural artifacts) from this source has been considerable, the proportion of non-specialist words permanently incorporated into Spanish is likely to be much lower than purists fear.

Degrees of Assimilation
The degree to which borrowings are intuitively recognised as intrusive depends on such factors as their adjustment to native phonological and orthographic patterns, their date of acquisition, and the level of education of the person making the judgement. Spanish school children are sometimes taught to think of *j* and *z* as 'the Arabic consonants' especially when both occur in the same word; while there is some truth in the generalisation, it also makes false predictions — so *ajimez* 'window arch' and *ajedrez* 'chess' are correctly identified as Arabic but *juez* 'judge', from IUDICEM, is wholly Romance. One possible measure of assimilation is participation in regular morphological processes. Notice that the vast majority of borrowings are nouns and as such require relatively little morphological

adjustment; most participate readily in plural inflection, but a recent acquisition like *jersey* can pluralise either regularly as *jerseyes* or as *jerseys*, presumably in imitation of English. Derivation is a particularly effective means of integration: the Germanic borrowings quoted above, *guerra* and *orgullo* regularly form adjectives *guerrero* and *orgulloso*; the Arabic *halagar* forms *halagüeño*; and in much of Central America a 'peasant farmer' is called *milpero*, an agentive derivation from the indigenous word *milpa* 'maize field'.

The gradual blurring of distinctions between inherited and borrowed categories, often abetted by lexical creativity, confronts descriptive linguists with an intriguing problem in the specific case of late borrowings from Latin, many of which are related to words that have had a continuous history in the language. This relationship, however, is no longer immediately apparent because the inherited items have generally undergone more extensive phonological modification than the late-comers, which have tended to be admitted in a hispanised pronunciation of the original spelling. Some idea of the scale of borrowing of 'learned' vocabulary from Latin can be gained from the list given here, which shows only a subset of the common verbs and nouns that underwent the phonological change f- $>$ h- $>$ zero, a change completely bypassed by their associated high register adjectives. The question is therefore whether the relationship is psycholinguistically real and, if so, whether it should be recreated by productive rules in synchronic morphophonemics. While attempts to relate 'doublets' of this kind are particularly associated with the abstract phase of generative phonology and are nowadays less often attempted or even deemed desirable, we should note that any across-the-board phonological solution, whether concrete or abstract, is liable to run foul of mixed derivational sets: *humo* 'smoke' has as its regular derivatives *humoso* 'smoky' and *ahumar* 'to preserve food by smoking', but it is also manifestly related to *fumar* 'to smoke' (of fires or of people).

Popular and Learned Word Pairs

hierro 'iron'	: férrico	heder 'to stink'	: fétido
hijo 'son'	: filial	hembra 'female'	: femenino
hado 'fate'	: fatal	hongo 'mushroom'	: fungoso
hambre 'hunger'	: famélico	hormiga 'ant'	: fórmico
harina 'flour'	: farináceo	huir 'to flee'	: fugaz
hastío 'distaste'	: fastidioso	hurto 'theft'	: furtivo

A further example of overlapping categories and progressive reanalysis is provided by Spanish negatives (see p. 116 for syntactic aspects of negation). Most derive ultimately, but not directly, from Latin NE, once the universal negator, but by the classical period more familiar as a prefix creating a whole family of compound negatives, including NON < NE + OINOM 'not one, not a single'. This resulted in a series of synchronic alternations, all of which have been disrupted by subsequent lexical replacements. So, USQUAM 'anywhere'/NUSQUAM 'nowhere' were eliminated before the earliest Spanish texts in favour of periphrases meaning 'in any place/in no place'; UMQUAM 'ever' was likewise rejected in favour of a periphrasis meaning 'at no time', despite the continuing vigour of NUMQUAM 'never' as *nunca*; and ULLUM 'any' gave way to ALICUNUM > *alguno*, despite the survival into Old Spanish of NULLUM 'no, not any' as *nul* (modern *nulo/ nulidad* are much later high-register borrowings). One might thus expect the derivational transparency of Latin negatives to have been edited out of Spanish; but this is not entirely the case.

In Old Spanish, the basic negators *non* and *ni* 'neither, nor' < NEC (< NE + QUE), together with *nunca* and *nul*, seem to have been perceived as a synchronic set. One indication is that *non*, whose final -*n* persisted until the early fifteenth century, apparently exerted an analogical pull on *ni*, which is frequently written *nin* during the same period. Likewise *neguno* < NEC + UNUM, the Romance rival to *nul*, is attested from the earliest texts with the alternative spellings *niguno* and *ninguno*. Also Romance creations were the pronouns *nada* 'nothing' and *nadi* 'nobody', both variants of the past participle *nado* of the verb *nacer* 'to be born', used colloquially as an intensifier ('not a born man would do it', 'we saw not a born thing') but having no etymological connection with negation. The success of *nada* and *nadi* is due to a combination of factors: their reinterpretation as negatives was provoked by frequent collocation, later colligation, with the true negator *no*, a development paralleled in French (see p. 237) but boosted in Spanish by the quite fortuitous initial /n-/. Their consolidation was assured when *nado* was displaced as the past participle of *nacer* by the analogical creation of a regular form *nacido*, which effectively severed the lexical and metaphorical links between the verb and the new negative pronouns.

The modern Spanish negatives are thus the result of inheritance, analogy and sheer accident. Even so, *no, ni, nada, nunca, ninguno* and *ninguna parte* 'nowhere' (the analytic replacement for NUSQUAM) give an appearance of systemic cohesion. The pattern in turn has been bolstered by lexical survivals, borrowings and derivations. *Negar* 'to deny' < NEGARE is attested in Old Spanish, with derivatives *negativo* and *negación* following in the fifteenth century, and *negable* much more recently. *Neutro* 'neuter' < NEUTRUM (literally 'neither one nor the other') is not attested before the fifteenth century, but has now acquired: *neutral, neutralidad, neutral- izar*, and *neutrón*. Alongside the obviously learned borrowings *nefando/ nefasto* 'nefarious' (literally 'not to be spoken of'), *nihilismo* and *nimio* 'excessive', we find the more popular coinings *nonada/ nadería* 'trifle, mere nothing'. The consequence is that words of very different dates and pro- venance now conspire to associate initial /n-/ with an obvious semantic component of negativity, to the point where it is most unlikely that native speakers would fail intuitively to recognise the coincidence. Whether /n-/ can be considered to be a synchronic morpheme is more doubtful, since it is no longer productive (unlike, for instance, the negative prefixes *in-* and *des-*) and its segmentation would create a large number of unanalysable roots with unique or near-unique distributions. It seems best, therefore, to treat /n-/ as a submorphemic marker of negation.

Creativity and Rates of Replacement
The proportions of inherited, borrowed and created words within the total word stock differ appreciably from their relative frequencies in continuous discourse. In the total stock, for instance, the words directly inherited from Latin constitute a small, if important, minority; they are proportionately much more frequent in discourse. This is especially true for functors (grammatical items such as determiners, pronouns, prepositions and conjunctions), which represent a tiny proportion of the total, but can nevertheless account for over two thirds of the words in running text. A recent study of the 5,000 most frequent words found that they were composed of some 24 per cent inherited items, 35 per cent created and 41 per cent borrowed (with both the latter categories in turn heavily reliant on Romance roots), but that the 24 per cent of inherited words accounted for 81 per cent of all occurrences. Functors make a major contribution to this high total, all but one — the Arabic preposition *hasta* 'until' — being derived from Latin roots.

Figure 3.4: Lexical Relationships

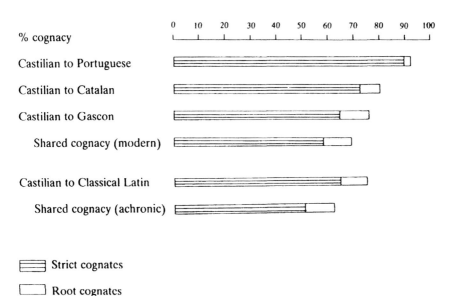

Strict cognates

Root cognates

This impression of relative conservatism in the lexicon (or, alternatively, of a low replacement rate), is corroborated by the standard lexicostatistical test of 100 'core' concepts, which in turn provides a yardstick for comparing Spanish with neighbouring varieties of Romance. Figure 3.4 shows the relative cognacy rates as established by this method. The percentage of shared items for each pair of languages varies depending on the inclusion or otherwise of root cognates. For example, Port. *frio*, Sp. *frio*, Cat. *fred*, Gasc. *hred*, Fr. *froid*, It. *freddo*, Rum. *frig* 'cold' are all fully cognate with Latin FRIGIDUM; whereas Port. *cabeça*, Sp. *cabeza* 'head' are fully cognate with each other, but only root cognates of Cat., Gasc. *cap*, and CLat. CAPUT. By the looser criterion, modern Spanish still shares 75 per cent of its core vocabulary with Classical Latin, a figure which falls only to 64 per cent if the stricter criterion is adopted.

This already high retention rate could, however, be increased if instead of comparing Spanish with Classical Latin, we compared it with the presumed lexicon of Proto-Romance. In Figure 3.4, the discrepancy of eight items between the synchronic and achronic cognacy rates, is almost certainly due to shared innovations of early Romance rather than to subsequent borrowing. Five of the eight result from semantic shifts or lexical replacements using Latin roots, for example FOCUM, originally 'hearth', displaces classical IGNEM 'fire' to give Port. *fogo*, Sp. *fuego*, Cat. *foc*, Gasc. *huec*; and BUCCAM, originally 'cheek', displaces OREM 'mouth' to give Port., Sp., Cat., Gasc. *boca*. Two involve derivation without lexical change: Port. *orelha*, Sp. *oreja*, Cat. *orella*, Gasc. *aurelha* 'ear', all derive from AURICULAM rather than classical AUREM. Only one is an external borrowing: the Germanic word BLANK 'white' gives Port. *branco*, Sp. *blanco*, Cat./Gasc. *blanc*, though reflexes of classical ALBUM survive in literary registers (Sp. *alba* 'dawn') and in numerous derivatives, both popular and technical (Sp. *albero* 'tea/dish towel', *albuminoide* 'albuminoid').

In terms of synchronic relationship, the lexical overlap of Spanish and Portuguese is very striking, at 89 per cent strict cognacy and 92 per cent root cognacy. Spanish is progressively less well related to Catalan (72 per cent strict cognacy), Gascon (64 per cent) and standard French (61 per cent), along a scale which obviously correlates with geographical distance. In the few items of core vocabulary where Spanish and Portuguese differ, Spanish is usually the innovating member of the pair, though not always in a way that matches its easterly neighbours. So, Sp. *perro* 'dog' (origin uncertain; see above) contrasts with Port. *cão* and Gasc. *can* < CANEM, but also with Cat. *gos*; while Port. *joelho*, Cat. *genoll*, Gasc. *jolh* < GENUCULUM 'knee' all contrast with Sp. *rodilla*, originally a metaphor 'little wheel, pivot' (compare Fr. *rotule* 'kneecap') which took over when OSp. *hinojo* became homophonous with *hinojo* < FENUCULUM 'fennel'. A more frequent pattern, however, finds both Spanish and Portuguese behaving with the conservatism typical of peripheral areas, in face of central innovations which peter out in Gallo-Romance or Catalan. Examples are: Port. *pássaro*, Sp. *pájaro* < PASSAREM 'bird' versus Cat. *ocell*, Gasc. *ausèth* < AVICELLUM; Port., Sp. *comer* < COM+EDERE 'to eat' versus Cat. *menjar*, Gasc. *minjar* < MANDUCARE; Port. *areia*, Sp. *arena* < ARENAM 'sand' versus Cat. *sorra*, Gasc. *sable*; Port. *pequeno*, Sp. *pequeño* 'small' verus Cat., Gasc. *petit* (classical PARVUM does not survive); Port., Sp. *rabo* < RAPUM 'tail' verus Cat. *cua*, Gasc. *coda* < CAUDAM; and Port. *mulher*, Sp. *mujer* < MULIEREM 'woman' versus Cat. *dona*, Gasc. *hemna*. In rarer instances, Portuguese and Spanish have innovated eccentrically: Port., Sp. *garra* 'claw', probably an Arabic–Romance blend, contrasts with Cat., Gasc. *urpa*; and Port. *amarelo*, Sp. *amarillo* 'yellow', derivatives of AMARUM 'bitter', contrast both with Cat. *groc* < CROCEUM 'saffron coloured' and with Gasc., Fr. *jaune* < GALBINUM 'yellowish green'.

Creative Mechanisms
In previous stages of the language, the gender markers -*o*/ -*a* (see pp. 93–4) have been highly productive. In the kinship system, for example, mechanisms as diverse as ellipsis, analogy, back formation and borrowing have reduced the irregularities and suppletions of Latin, to the benefit of the -*o*/ -*a* alternation. Adjectival ellipsis is responsible for Sp. *hermano/hermana* < (FRATREM) GERMANUM/(SOROREM) GERMANAM 'real, full (brother/ sister)' (i.e. siblings with both parents in common); for *cuñado/cuñada* 'brother/sister-in-law' < (FRATREM) COGNATUM/(SOROREM) COGNATAM (originally 'half-brother/sister'); and for *primo/prima* 'cousin' < PRIMUM (SOBRINUM))/PRIMAM (SOBRINAM) (literally 'first (cousin)'). These ellipses in turn eliminated the FRATER : SOROR suppletion (though the roots survive in religious contexts as *fraile* 'monk' and *Sor Merced* 'Sister Mercy'); freed *sobrino/sobrina* to take over the meanings 'nephew/niece'; but required the use of a derivative PRIMARIUM > *primero* 'first' to form an ordinal distinct from the new kinship term. Analogy is responsible for *suegra* 'mother-in-law' < SOCRAM, reformed from the apparently irregular fourth declension SOCRUM to match *suegro* 'father-in-law' < SOCERUM. *Nieto* 'grandson' appears to be a back formation from *nieta* 'granddaughter' < NEPTAM, itself an analogical readjustment of classical NEPTEM. *Tio/tia* 'uncle/aunt' are borrowings from Greek.

Against this generalisation of the -*o*/ -*a* pattern, we should note the persistence of suppletion in the most common kinship pair: *padre* 'father' < PATREM : *madre* 'mother' < MATREM. Among animal names, suppletion has likewise persisted in *toro* 'bull' < TAURUM: *vaca* 'cow' < VACCAM; and one has been introduced by the adoption of *caballo* 'horse' < CABALLUM (originally 'nag') to replace classical EQUUM, even though EQUAM 'mare' survives as *yegua*. An aspect of the -*o*/ -*a* alternation that has proved highly contentious is the treatment of a small number of masculine/feminine pairs like *barco/barca* 'ship' and *cesto/cesta* 'basket'. In these, the feminine is usually the older form, and the denotational differences relate to size, shape and function; but the correlation of these features with gender is, at best, tentative. Overall, the *-o/-a* alternation, though extremely frequent in Spanish, has long passed its peak as a creative mechanism and seems now to be on the verge of non-productivity. Many recent neologisms are neutral in gender — like *astronauta* 'astronaut', *izquierdista*, 'leftist', *racista* 'racist' — and rely on the determiner to mark the sex of the referent, if need be. Since all neologisms of this kind take plural marking, the trend does not seem to signal a more general move towards morphological invariability.

Created Items: Derivation and Composition
Throughout the history of Spanish, derivational processes have played a major role in extending the lexicon and increasing the range of 'motivated' vocabulary. (Conversely, the widespread borrowing of partial synonyms of higher register that we examined above, may well have increased lexical opacity.) Prefixation, very common in Latin, has left numerous traces in inherited vocabulary, though it is not always clear that segmentation is synchronically valid: *concebir* 'to conceive', *percibir* 'to perceive' and *recibir* 'to receive' embody prefixes which are still productive (very much so in the case of *re-*), but which, if segmented here, neither have their modern meanings nor leave a coherent semantic value for the root. Recently, prefixation has regained considerable momentum. *Super-/hiper-* can now be prefixed to almost anything as superlatives (*supermercado* 'supermarket', *hiperraquítico* 'extremely thin/weak'); smallness is indicated by *mini-* (*minibus, minitrén* 'minitrain, shuttle'); forward position by *ante-* (*anteojos* 'goggles') or *pre-* (*preescolar* 'pre-school'); opposition or protection by *anti-* (*antinuclear, antirresbaladizo* 'antiskid', *faro antiniebla* 'fog lamp'); and reflexivity by *auto-* (*autoservicio* 'self-service', *autodestrucción* 'self-destruction', *autocargante* 'self-charging'). Infixation is a rarer process, and one open to competing interpretations, as is so-called 'parasynthesis'. Both are illustrated by *enfurecerse* 'to get angry', transparently derived from *furia*, but variously argued to result from the conscious use of an infix (-SC-; see p. 101) or of a reanalysed inchoative suffix (*-ecer*), coupled simultaneously or later with a prefix and reflexivisation. A similar difficulty is posed by verbs like *lloriquear* 'to whimper', which may appear to have a pejorative infix when compared with a base form like *llorar* 'to weep', but are probably better analysed as having one of a range of affective suffixes which behave in morphologically similar, but not identical ways. So, *traquetear* 'to rattle' along with its noun *traqueteo* is related to the onomatopoeic *trac* 'clang', but has no base verb on which infixation could operate. Similarly, *llovizznar* 'to drizzle' is clearly related to the basic *llover* 'to rain', but the change in conjugation membership implies the use of a

ready-made suffix, rather than a two-stage process of infixation.

Suffixation has always been particularly vigorous in Spanish, as a method of both changing morphological class and adding expressive nuances. Among function changers we should note: adjectivals -ero, -oso, -able/-ible (inoxidable 'stainless', but also presidenciable 'suitable to be president'); the abstract nominals -ancia/-encia, -ación/-ición, -ez, -miento and -aje (borrowed from French and cognate with the rather rare negative -azgo; compare andamiaje 'scaffolding' with noviazgo 'courtship'); the vogue nominal -ota (pasota 'drop-out', drogota 'junkie'); and the agentive -dor, which in the feminine and after the ellipsis of máquina 'machine' has coined labels for a whole gamut of labour-saving devices (afeitadora 'shaver', embotelladora 'bottling machine', licuadora 'liquidiser', secadora 'spin dryer', among many others). Spanish also possesses a bewildering array of so-called 'diminutives' and 'augmentatives', but these seem always to have carried affective connotations rather than strict denotation of size. Still highly productive are the diminutives -ito, -ino (usually implying affection) and -illo (often, though not always, pejorative). The augmentatives -ón and -azo generally indicate some kind of excess rather than mere size: hombrón 'hulk of a man', solterona 'old maid'; but the excess can also connote approval, as in colloquial molón 'great, fantastic', from molar 'to go well, really swing'. Some idea of the mixed flavours of these suffixes can be gauged from the series: casa 'house', casita 'cottage', caseta 'weekend cottage', casilla 'hut', casuca 'shack' (both affectionate and pejorative depending on context), casucha 'hovel', casón 'rambling country house', caserón 'dilapidated old pile'. Nor are such suffixes confined to nominal stems; adjectives and adverbs are quite frequent hosts — gordo 'fat' : gordito 'chubby', ahora 'now' : ahorita mismo 'this very second', despacio 'slowly' : ¡despacito! 'gently does it!'.

By comparison with the exuberance of derivational mechanisms in Spanish, compounding is often unjustly represented as a minor process. In fact, compounding has been used as a source of neologisms at all stages of the language, and recently there has been a notable upsurge in the process. Long-established two-term patterns are illustrated in: agridulce 'bittersweet', bienvenida 'welcome', caradura 'cheek, insolence' (literally 'hard face'), dondequiera 'wherever', madreselva 'honeysuckle' and mediodía 'midday'. Phrasal compounds include: correveidile 'gossip' (literally 'run-go-and-tell-him/her'), hazmerreir 'jester, laughing stock' (literally 'make-me-laugh') and sabelotodo 'know-all'. One very productive pattern creates a compound adjective from a part of the body plus its attribute: pelilargo 'long-haired', cejijunto 'beetle-browed', labihendido 'hare-lipped', barbirrojo 'red-bearded', piernicorto 'short-legged'. But by far the most common mechanism for recent neologism is the compounding of verb + object, where the object is often plural, of either gender, but the resulting noun is masculine singular. Well entrenched examples are: abrelatas 'tin-opener', cascanueces 'nut-cracker', engañabobos 'booby-trap', espantapájaros 'scarecrow', sacacorchos 'cork-screw'; together with humorous pejoratives like sacamuelas 'dentist, tooth-puller'.

We end this section on a note of optimism. Although purist hackles have been raised by the recent influx of anglicisms (as in France, see p. 243), the productive patterns of the language remain resolutely Romance. The best evidence is that new concepts and artifacts which might easily have attracted a foreign label are so often named from indigenous roots, whether by derivation or compounding. Urbanización 'housing development', currently to be seen on builders' placards all over Spain, is made up of impeccably classical roots. Calientaplatos 'plate-warmer', lavaplatos 'dishwasher', limpiaparabrisas 'windscreen-wiper', and even, alas, cartabomba 'letter-bomb' use only indigenous material. Through developments of this kind, Spanish is becoming more, not less, Romance in its structure.

6 Conclusion

Comparing the two principal norms of Spanish, we have noted a number of differences in phonology, morphosyntax and lexis, but have nevertheless argued that the mainstream varieties can be grouped together as a diasystem, a shared underlying structure with relatively minor surface divergences. How has this come about? And where should the diasystemic limits be set?

If membership of hispanidad is determined by mutual intelligibility, we are obliged to exclude the creoles of Colombia and the Far East which, though often loosely described as 'Spanish creoles', appear on closer scrutiny to have autonomous grammatical systems (for further discussion see Chapters 1 and 12). More problematic are the 'Hispanic' varieties of the United States which range on a continuum between lightly dialectal puertorriqueño and the basilectal form of chicano, which has undergone some of the morphological modification usually associated with creolisation and has assimilated numerous calques of American English lexical and idiomatic structures. These internal characteristics, together with the frequent code-switching between Spanish and English common to all Hispanic variants in the USA, can render chicano totally impenetrable to monolingual Spanish speakers. On the other hand, there is usually mutual comprehensibility between standard and Judeo-Spanish speakers, perhaps with some difficulty and depending — because of the large numbers of lexical borrowings from adstrate languages — on the topic of discourse. But djudeo-espanyol in present-day Israel is a cover term for a continuum of variants ranging from the standard seseante Spanish (see p. 82) delivered with a slight regional accent which is used in broadcasts by Boz de Israel radio, to the unmistakably different version chosen for the associated quarterly magazine Aki Yerushalayim which has its own morphosyntax, vocabulary and highly distinctive orthography (see p. 92). Mutual comprehensibility here is less a matter of intralinguistic features than of cultural choice.

The maintenance of a shared orthography and written standard (for which normative organisations such as the *Real Academia de la Lengua* and its corresponding Academies in Latin America must be given some credit) has probably been the crucial factor in the survival of *hispanidad* and in preventing a repetition of the linguistic fragmentation that followed the dissolution of the Roman Empire (see pp. 2–5). In the colonial era, the political, religious and administrative bonds linking Spain to its Latin American territories were not designed (any more than their Roman predecessors had been) to keep the colonies in close contact with one another, and there is evidence of quite rapid divergence as vocabulary, grammatical calques and phonetic traits were assimilated from Amerindian languages. Fragmentation could easily have gone hand in hand with nineteenth-century independence movements. But cultural and linguistic links with Spain survived political independence, and those same factors which in Europe caused the decline of rural dialects — improved communications and the spread of literacy — not only maintained the essential unity of the written language, but actually brought about convergence in formal and technical registers. Today, an Argentinian novelist can unambiguously evoke an Argentinian setting through dialogue and to a lesser extent narrative; but it is often impossible to tell, on linguistic grounds alone, whether a newspaper leader, legislative text or set of instructions for some domestic appliance, originated in Spain or in any of the nineteen Latin American countries where Spanish is the national language.

Spanish is now firmly enshrined in the Constitutions of Spain and most countries of Latin America, and is viewed by the respective governments as a symbol of national unity. It is also, with Portuguese, one of only two Romance languages to be increasing rapidly its numbers of speakers; on those grounds alone its future seems assured. But in the process of expansion from minor dialect to major world language, Spanish has become a little more like some of the varieties it once rivalled.

Bibliography

Amastae, J., and L. Elías-Olivares (eds.) (1982) *Spanish in the United States.* Cambridge University Press, Cambridge.

Canfield, D.L. (1981) *Spanish Pronunciation in the Americas* 2nd edn. Chicago University Press, Chicago.

Cano Aguilar, R. (1981) *Estructuras sintácticas transitivas en el español actual.* Gredos, Madrid.

Contreras, H. (1976) *A Theory of Word Order with Special Reference to Spanish.* North-Holland, Amsterdam.

Corominas, J. and J.A. Pascual (1980–6) *Diccionario crítico etimológico castellano e hispánico* 6 vols. Gredos, Madrid.

Cressey, W.W. (1978) *Spanish Phonology and Morphology: A Generative View.* Georgetown University Press, Washington DC.

Fant, L. (1984) *Estructura informativa en español. Estudio sintáctico y entonativo.* Uppsala University Press, Uppsala.

Fontanella de Weinberg, M.B. (1976) *La lengua española fuera de España. América, Canarias, Filipinas, Judeo-español.* Paidós, Buenos Aires.

Galmes de Fuentes, A. (1983) *Dialectología mozárabe.* Gredos, Madrid.

García, E.C. (1975) *The Role of Theory in Linguistic Analysis. The Spanish Pronoun System.* North-Holland, Amsterdam.

Harris, J.W. (1983) *Syllable Structure and Stress in Spanish.* MIT Press, Cambridge, Mass.

Haverkate, H. (1979) *Impositive Sentences in Spanish.* North-Holland, Amsterdam.

Lapesa, R. (1980) *Historia de la lengua española* 8th edn. Gredos, Madrid.

Lloyd, P.M. (1968) *Verb–Complement Compounds in Spanish.* Niemeyer, Tübingen.

Lorenzo, E. (1971) *El español de hoy, lengua en ebullición* 2nd edn. Gredos, Madrid.

Luján, M. (1980) *Sintaxis y semántica del adjetivo.* Ediciones Cátedra, Madrid.

Macpherson, I.R. (1975) *Spanish Phonology: Descriptive and Historical.* Manchester University Press, Manchester.

Malkiel, Y. (1970) *Patterns of Derivational Affixation in the Cabraniego Dialect of East-Central Asturian.* University of California Press, Berkeley.

—— (1972) *Linguistics and Philology in Spanish America.* Mouton, The Hague.

Martín Zorraquino, M.A. (1979) *Las construcciones pronominales en español.* Gredos, Madrid.

Menéndez Pidal, R. (1972) *Orígenes del español* 7th edn. Espasa-Calpe, Madrid.

Moliner, M. (1982) *Diccionario de uso del español* 2 vols. Gredos, Madrid.

de los Mozos, S. (1984) *La norma castellana del español.* Ámbito Ediciones, Valladolid.

Patterson, W.T. (1982) *The Genealogical Structure of Spanish: A Correlation of Basic Word Properties.* Georgetown University Press, Washington DC.

Quilis, A. (1981) *Fonética acústica de la lengua española.* Gredos, Madrid.

Real Academia Española (1973) *Esbozo de una nueva gramática de la lengua española.* Espasa-Calpe, Madrid.

Resnick, M.C. (1975) *Phonological Variants and Dialect Identification in Latin American Spanish.* Mouton, The Hague.

Rivero, M.-L. (1977) *Estudios de gramática generativa del español.* Ediciones Cátedra, Madrid

Sala, M. (1976) *Le Judéo-espagnol.* Mouton, The Hague.

—— (1982) *El español de América: 1 Léxico.* Instituto Caro y Cuervo, Bogotá.

Seco, M. (1982) *Diccionario de dudas de la lengua española* 8th edn. Aguilar, Madrid.

Suñer, M. (1982) *Syntax and Semantics of Spanish Presentational Sentence-Types.* Georgetown University Press, Washington DC.

Wright, R. (1982) *Late Latin and Early Romance in Spain and Carolingian France.* Francis Cairns, Liverpool.

Zamora Vicente, A. (1967) *Dialectología española* 2nd edn. Gredos, Madrid.

4 Portuguese

Stephen Parkinson

1 Introduction

Portuguese, like English, has spread too far and wide to be described solely in terms of its European forms. The polarisation of European Portuguese varieties (abbreviated EP) and Brazilian Portuguese varieties (BP), and the relative decline in the cultural and economic position of Portugal are such that the Brazilian standard must be given equal status with the European. Accordingly, divergences between Brazilian and European Portuguese are noted wherever relevant. In general, European Portuguese forms are used for exemplification and phonetic transcriptions reflect Lisbon Portuguese, which is the *de facto* European standard, though the traditional definition of standard EP as 'the educated speech of Lisbon and Coimbra' still has many adherents. The twin standards of Rio de Janeiro (Carioca) and São Paulo (Paulista), followed by the north and south of the country respectively, dominate Brazilian Portuguese usage. No attempt will be made to distinguish them on a systematic basis. The main dialect areas of Portugal and Brazil are shown in Maps II and III.

Galician, from which Portuguese ultimately derives (pp. 6ff), is not given a systematic treatment here: standardisation has been long in coming, and the emerging standard emphasises the divergence between Galician and Portuguese. The term Galician-Portuguese is used as a convenient way of referring to common features of the two languages, during the period 1200–1350, when there was considerable cultural and linguistic unity between Portugal and Galicia. The most significant divergences of the two languages took place in the period 1350–1500, a time of radical change in Portuguese, indubitably linked with the political upheaval resulting from the emergence of the new royal house of Avis, in 1383, and the population movements resulting from the establishment of Lisbon as capital, and (according to a recent theory) the aftermath of the Plague of 1348.

2 Phonetics and Phonology

Portuguese is characterised by a complex vowel system incorporating a large number of units (oral and nasal, monophthongal and diphthongal) and a range of vowel alternations conditioned by stress and morphology.

Vowels

The vowel phonemes of Portuguese are represented in Tables 4.1 and 4.2. Not all the vowel contrasts implied by this system are of equal weight. The phoneme /ɐ/ is only found in the European Portuguese system, and there in a marginal role. Both European and Brazilian Portuguese have two non-high central vowels in their phonetic inventories, a low [a] and a higher vowel usually transcribed [ɐ], traditionally labelled 'open a' and 'closed a' respectively, and distinguished orthographically by the acute and circumflex accents (p. 143). In Brazilian Portuguese, [ɐ] is an allophone of /a/, in atonic final position and in nasal contexts; in European Portuguese, [ɐ] is likewise tied to atonic and nasal contexts, but the exclusion of [a] from the same contexts is not absolute, leading to occasional contrasts not found in Brazilian Portuguese, e.g. *nação* [nɐ'sɐ̃ũ] 'nation' — *acção* [a'sɐ̃ũ] 'action'; *a* [ɐ] 'to' and feminine singular definite article vs *à* [a] (contracted form of *a + a*; see the chart of contractions, p. 149) 'to the (f. sg.)'; *-amos* ['ɐmuʃ] 1 pl. pres. ind. first conjugation vs *-ámos* ['amuʃ] ibid., pret.; *cadeira* [kɐ'dɐirɐ] 'chair' vs *caveira* [ka'vɐirɐ] 'skull'. In European Portuguese the contraction of atonic /ɐ+ɐ/ can also produce an atonic /a/ which contrasts with a single atonic /ɐ/: *casa suja* ['kazɐ'suʒɐ] 'dirty house' – *casa azul* ['kaza'zul] 'blue house'. In Lisbon EP [ɐ] is found preceding the palatal consonants /ʃ ʒ ʎ ɲ/, where other accents have [e], and the diphthongs /ɐi/ and /ɐ̃ĩ/ correspond to /ei/ and /ẽĩ/ in other accents.

Table 4.1: Portuguese Vowels

Monophthongs

High	i	ĩ			ə*		u	ũ
High-mid	e	ẽ					o	õ
Low-mid	ɛ			ɐ*	ɐ̃		ɔ	
Low					a			

Diphthongs

iu						ui	ũĩ	
eu	ei	**ẽĩ		**ou	oi	õĩ		
ɛu	ɛi				ɔi			
	ai	ɐ̃ĩ	au	ɐ̃ũ				

Note: *distinct phoneme in European Portuguese only; **distinct phoneme in some accents only.

Table 4.2: Atonic Vowel Systems

	EP			BP		
Final	ə	u		i		u
(including clitics)		ɐ		a = [ɐ]		
Non-final	i	ə	u	i		u
		(o)		e		o
	(ɛ)	ɐ	(ɔ)			
		(a)			a	

The contrasts between high-mid and low-mid vowels (/e/-/ɛ/; /o/-/ɔ/) are very frequently neutralised. Low-mid vowels rarely occur under nasality and in final syllables closed by /r/; high-mid vowels are excluded from syllables closed by /l/ (with very few lexical exceptions). Mid-vowel contrasts are virtually absent from atonic systems, and are widely neutralised by morphophonemic rules in nominal and verbal paradigms (see section 3).

In atonic syllables (Table 4.2) there is large-scale neutralisation of vowel quality contrasts in the front and back vowel series. In addition, atonic vowels are reduced by centralisation and raising. This is most noticeable in the case of /a/ (reduced to [ɐ]) and in the European Portuguese neutralisation vowel /ə/ (morphophonemic /e/), where its effects are phonemic; reduction nevertheless affects the phonetic realisation of all atonic vowels. In final syllables each series is represented by a single vowel: the front vowels by EP /ə/, BP /i/, the back vowels by /u/. (In European Portuguese atonic final /i/ is very rare, and can usually be replaced by /ə/, e.g. *táxi* 'taxi' ['taksi], ['taks(ə)].)

In European Portuguese (and to a lesser extent in Brazilian Portuguese) the rules relating tonic and atonic systems are the source of widespread allomorphic variation in inflectional and derivational morphology:

casa	['kazɐ]	'house'	casinha	[kɐ'ziɲɐ]	'little house'
mora	['mɔrɐ]	'(s)he lives'	morara	[mu'rarɐ]	'(s)he had lived'
				(BP [mo'rarɐ])	
bate	['batə]	'(s)he hits'	bater	[bɐ'ter]	'to hit'
peso	['pezu]	'weight'	pesar	[pə'zar]	'to weigh'
				(BP [pe'zaχ])	

In atonic diphthongs there is no contrast of high-mid and low-mid vowels, but no reduction (raising and centralisation) of /e a/; a similar situation obtains with nasal vowels and diphthongs, and in syllables closed by /l/, except that the neutralisation of mid-vowel contrasts is the result of a general rule applying in tonic syllables as well. In some variants of Brazilian Portuguese pretonic /e o/ are raised to /i u/ in a wide and variable range of contexts, particularly when a high vowel (usually /i/)

follows, e.g. *dormir* [duχˈmiχ] 'to sleep'; *medida* [miˈdidɐ] 'measurement'. In European Portuguese there are many 'irregular' forms in which pretonic /ɛ ɔ o a/ appear (hence the brackets enclosing them in Table 4.2). Most are explicable as originating in vowel sequences or diphthongs, e.g. *pregar* 'to preach' [prɛˈgaɾ] < *preegar* < PRAEDĬCARE; *corado* 'red, blushing' [kɔˈɾadu] < *coorado* < CŌLŌRĀTUM; *roubar* 'to steal' [ʀoˈbaɾ] (EP), [χoˈbaχ] (BP) < OPort. *roubar*. Other cases of pretonic /ɛ ɔ a/ occur in syllables closed by plosives e.g. *secção* [sɛkˈsɐ̃ũ], *optar* [ɔpˈtaɾ] 'to choose' where Brazilian Portuguese has open syllables and atonic /e o a/. Atonic vowels are also involved in a major feature of European Portuguese phrasal phonetics, the contraction of vowels across word-boundaries. This most typically takes the form of the fusion of word-final atonic vowels or clitic articles with word-initial vowels or clitics, and results in a wide range of diphthongs and monophthongs: *o uso* 'the custom' /u uzu/, [uːzu]; *uma amiga* 'a friend' /umɐ ɐˈmigɐ/, [umaˈmigɐ]; *é o Pedro* 'it's Pedro' /ɛ u ˈpedru/, [ɛuˈpedɾu].

Portuguese shares with French (p. 211) the feature of an extensive series of vowels with distinctive nasality. The nasal vowels /ĩ ẽ õ ũ ɐ̃/ contrast phonemically with the corresponding oral vowels: e.g. *mudo* [ˈmudu] 'dumb' – *mundo* [ˈmũdu] 'world'; *ri* [ʀi] 'laugh' – *rim* [ʀĩ] 'kidney'. There is no contrast between nasal vowels and homosyllabic vowel + nasal consonant sequences, nasal vowels being very frequently followed by a more or less consonantal nasal off-glide, e.g. *mundo* /ˈmũdu/ = [ˈmũⁿdu], so that it is frequently argued that nasal vowels can be analysed phonologically or morphophonologically as VN sequences. The open vowels /a ɛ ɔ/ are not found in the nasal series, and are generally excluded when a nasal consonant follows. This restriction is absolute in Brazilian Portuguese, while in European Portuguese it is overridden by morphophonemic processes leading to open vowels (notably verb stem alternations (p. 152)) and in neologisms with antepenultimate stress. Thus a verb such as *comer* 'to eat' shows alternations in European but not in Brazilian Portuguese, and BP *tônico* [ˈtoniku] 'tonic' corresponds to EP *tónico* [ˈtɔniku]. There is a general phonetic tendency for nasal consonants to cause nasalisation of preceding and following vowels; in Brazilian Portuguese the resulting nasality can be as strong as phonemic nasality.

Portuguese has a larger inventory of falling diphthongs than other Romance languages, in addition to a host of rising diphthongs which are no more than phonetic variants of vowel sequences. /ẽĩ/ (Lisbon /ɐ̃ĩ/) is a word-final variant of /ẽ/, as can be seen from the doublet *cento* 'hundred' [ˈsẽtu], *cem* 'hundred' [sẽĩ], and also occurs preceding inflectional -*s*: *nuvem* 'cloud' [ˈnuvẽĩ], plural *nuvens* [ˈnuvẽĩʃ]. (The orthographic change of *m* to *n* is without phonetic significance.) In most dialects there is a distinction between /ẽĩ/ and the relatively uncommon /ɐ̃ĩ/: *quem* 'who' /kẽĩ/ vs *cães* 'dogs' /kɐ̃ĩʃ/: in Lisbon the centralisation of /ẽ/ eliminates this distinction by realising all cases of /ẽĩ/ as /ɐ̃ĩ/. Some dialects (notably northern European Portuguese) retain the diphthong /ou/ distinct from /o/; others (southern European Portuguese, some Brazilian Portuguese) monophthongise /ei/ to /e/. In Brazilian Portuguese the vocalisation of post-vocalic /l/ creates a new series of falling diphthongs, e.g. *sol* 'sun' [sɔu] (BP), [sɔl] (EP).

Most diphthongs have a limited distribution. /ũĩ/ is found only in *muito* 'much, many' (and is often realised as [wĩ]); /iu/ is only found in preterit forms of third conjugation verbs; /ɛu/, /ɛi/, /ẽĩ/, /ẽũ/, /õĩ/, /ui/, /õĩ/ and /ɔi/ are found almost exclusively in stem-final position, and are closely associated with inflectional patterns.

At first glance the Portuguese vowel system might seem to have undergone little historical change. Portuguese preserves the seven tonic vowels of PWR (cf. p. 33), with no diphthongisation of mid vowels:

mudo	/mudu/	< MŪTUM	vida	/vida/	< VĪTAM
todo	/todu/	< TŌTUM	cabelo	/kabelu/	< CAPĬLLUM
porta	/pɔrta/	< PŎRTAM	cego	/segu/	< CAECUM
(cf. Sp. *puerta*)			(cf. Sp. *ciego*)		
		gato	/gatu/	< CATTUM	

The correspondence between Portuguese and PWR vowels is not as simple as this schema would lead one to believe. A large number of processes, notably metaphonic changes of mid vowels, have affected vowel quality.

Mid vowels were raised by a variety of metaphonic processes. A yod in the following syllable raised low-mid /ɛ ɔ/ to high-mid /e o/, *cereja* 'cherry' [sɐ'reʒɐ] < CERĔSIAM; *soberba* 'pride' [su'berbɐ] < SUPĔRBIAM; *hoje* 'today' ['oʒə] < HŎDIE; *força* 'strength' ['forsɐ] < FŎRTIAM and sporadically raised /e o/ to /i u/, *vindima* 'grape harvest' [vĩdimɐ] < VINDĒMIAM; *siba* 'cuttlefish' < SĒPIAM; *cunho* ['kuɲu] 'stamp' < CŬNEUM, though some putative cases of the raising of Latin /ĭ ŭ/ might be the semi-learned derivation of /i u/ from /ĭ ŭ/, e.g. *cruz* 'cross' < CRŬCEM. A high /i/ in a following syllable similarly raised /e o/ to /i u/ (with the same caveat): *vinte* 'twenty' [vĩtə] < viĭti < VĪGINTI; *fiz* 'I did' [fiʃ] < *fizi* < FĒCI; *pus* 'I put (pret.)' [puʃ] < *pusi* < *posit* < PŎSUIT; OPort. *u* 'where' < ŬBI. A third process raised low-mid /ɛ ɔ/ to /e o/ when the following syllable contained a reflex of Lat. /ŭ/: *medo* 'fear' < MĚTUM; *ovo* 'egg' ['ovu] < ŎVUM (vs *ovos* 'eggs' ['ɔvuʃ] < ŎVOS). This process, for which the label *metafonia* is usually reserved in Portuguese linguistics, is problematic because it implies a preservation of the distinction between Latin /ŭ/ and /ō/ in atonic final syllables, for which there is no other evidence in Portuguese. (If Portuguese metaphony is seen as a special case of Romance diphthongisation (cf. p. 35), the problem is less acute, as the origins of the process will be that much earlier in time.) Metaphony has also been very widely morphologised, with the resulting alternations spread by analogy to forms with etymological /o/. Similar patterns have developed in verbal and deverbal morphology, further confusing the historical development.

The extensive range of nasal vowels in Portuguese arose from the nasalisation of vowels followed by tautosyllabic /n m/ or by heterosyllabic /n/, with concomitant effacement of the nasal consonant: SŬM > OPort. *som* [sõ] 'I am'; PANEM > **pan* > OPort. *pã* 'bread'; MANUM > *mão* 'hand'. Progressive nasalisation accounts for the nasal vowels of *mãe* 'mother' < MATREM, *muito* 'very, much' < MŬLTUM, *mim* 1 sg. obj. pron. < MIHI, *nem* 'nor' < NĔC, and for the palatal nasals of *ninho* 'nest' ['niɲu] < *nĩo* < **nio* < NĪDUM and *nenhum* 'no, not any' < *nẽ ũu* < NĔC ŪNUM. One of the most noteworthy developments of the fourteenth and fifteenth centuries was a series of changes resulting in the merger of the word-final nasal vowels -[ã], -[õ], with -[ãũ] (> [ɐ̃ũ]), e.g. *cão* (sg.) 'dog' (< *cã* < CANEM; *falam* ['falɐ̃ũ] 'they talk' (< FABŬLANT); *razão* (sg.) 'reason' (< *razõ* < RATIŌNEM). This phonological change, whose morphological effects are described in section 3, was effectively morphologised when it was obscured by the subsequent reintroduction of final /õ/ and /ã/ resulting from the contraction of -/õo/ and -/ãa/ (e.g. *bom* < *bõo*, *irmã* < *irmãa*) in the fifteenth century.

Most Portuguese diphthongs are relatively late creations, resulting from the reduction of vocalic hiatuses, in which Galician-Portuguese was very rich, a factor which contributed greatly to its predominance as a vehicle for lyric poetry (p. 7). These hiatuses resulted mainly from the effacement of intervocalic consonants, e.g. BŎNUM > OPort. *bõo*, 'good', MALUM > OPort. *mao* 'bad', MŎLĪNUM > OPort. *moĩo* 'mill', PĔDEM > OPort. *pee* 'foot'. Many of these hiatuses were resolved as falling diphthongs or (following assimilation) as monophthongs: *mao* > *mau*; *pee* > *pé*; *bõo* > *bõ*; SŌLA > OPort. *soa* > *soo* > *so* [sɔ] 'alone'; SAGĬTTAM > OPort. *saeta* > *seeta* > *seta* [sɛta] 'arrow'. Hiatuses not reduced in this way were frequently broken by glide epenthesis, e.g. CRĒDO > *creo* > *creio* 'I believe'; LAUDARE > **lo(u)ar* > *louvar* 'to praise'. Nasal vowels in unresolved hiatuses were denasalised (BONA > OPort. *bõa* > *boa* 'good' (f.); **PANATARIUM* > *pãadeiro* > *paadeiro* > *padeiro* 'baker') except for the sequences [ĩo], [ĩa] where the hiatus was broken by a palatal nasal glide [j̃] which subsequently developed into the nasal [ɲ], e.g. *moinho* 'mill' [mu'iɲu] < OPort. *moĩo*.

A conservative feature of Portuguese is its preservation of Lat. /au/ as a diphthong /ou/. (In standard European Portuguese this has monophthongised to /o/ in tonic syllables, but betrays its diphthongal origin by being exempt, like the diphthongs, from reduction in atonic syllables.) Other diphthongs resulted from fusions between vowels and semi-vowels, principally late Lat. /j/, e.g. *ribeira* 'river bank' < RIPARIAM. The vocal-

isation of syllable-final /k/ yielded both /w/ and /j/, e.g. ACTUM > *auto*,
aito 'deed, act'; NŌCTEM > *noute, noite* 'night', which resulted in free
variation between the diphthongs /oi/ and /o(u)/, producing the now
standard forms *toiro* 'bull', *coisa* 'thing', *dois* 'two', *doido* 'foolish, crazy'
beside *touro* < TAURUM, *cousa* < CAUSAM, *dous* < DŪOS, *doudo*
(possibly originating in English *dolt*, certainly borrowed back as the name
of the ill-fated dodo).

The effacement of atonic vowels, which is a notable feature of modern
European Portuguese, is not widely found in the history of Portuguese.
Post-tonic penults which had not fallen in late Latin are often retained
in Old Portuguese (compare *velho* 'old' < VĚT(Ŭ)LUM with *povo* 'people'
< *poboo* < PŎPŬLUM). Final atonic /e/ was only lost by apocope when
it followed single /r l n z/:

Apocope	*No apocope*
amor < AMŌREM	torre < TŬRREM
casal < CASÁLEM	verdade < VĒRĪTATEM
paz < PACEM	urze < ŬRTĬCEM
OPort. pã < PANEM	carne < CARNEM

The chronology of the raising and reduction of atonic vowels is one of
the most intractable problems of Portuguese phonology. In Old Portuguese
pretonic /e o/ were frequently raised to /i u/ by a process of vowel harmony similar to that found in some accents of modern Brazilian Portuguese, but there is no firm evidence to permit an earlier dating of the raising of final /e o/, which probably took place independently in Portugal
and Brazil after the sixteenth century. The general raising of pretonic
/e o/, and the emergence of atonic /ə/ were even later developments of
European Portuguese.

Consonants
The consonant phonemes of Portuguese are displayed in Table 4.3. Further
discussion is needed to do justice to the semi-vowels, vibrants and sibilants.

The semi-vowels /j w/ are marginal phonemes. In most cases /j w/
result from the semi-vocalisation of atonic /i u/ in hiatus: *diário* ['djarju]
(=[di'ariu]) 'daily', *suar* 'to sweat' [swar] (=[su'ar]), except for a few
borrowings, especially Brazilian Portuguese forenames (e.g. *iate* 'yacht'
['jatə], *Ueber* BP ['webeχ]). /kw gw/ (in *quando* 'when' ['kwẽdu], *guarda*
'policeman' ['gwardɐ]) are perhaps better analysed as labialised velars
/kʷ gʷ/.

In European Portuguese there are two contrasting vibrant phonemes, a
weak tap /ɾ/ and a strong uvular trill /ʀ/. The uvular articulation of the
strong vibrant (perhaps the latest manifestation of the retraction of *r*-

Table 4.3: Consonants

	Bilabial/ labiodental	Dental/ alveolar	Palatal	Velar	Uvular
Plosives: voiceless	p	t		k	
voiced	b	d		g	
Fricatives: voiceless	f	s	ʃ		χ*
voiced	v	z	ʒ		
Nasals	m	n	ɲ		
Laterals		l	ʎ		
Vibrants		ɾ			ʀ*
Semi-vowels	(w)		(j)		

Note: * these sounds are mutually exclusive variants.

sounds that earlier affected French and German) is a recent innovation of Lisbon European Portuguese, where it was a stigmatised variant
until the end of the nineteenth century. Many dialects retain the older post-
alveolar trill [r]. The corresponding contrast in Brazilian Portuguese is
between the tap and a fricative /χ/, whose range of phonetic variants
includes [χ ʁˈ ʀ ɣ x h]. As in Spanish, the contrast between the two
phonemes is realised only in intervocalic position, e.g. *caro* 'dear' [ˈkaɾu]
vs *carro* 'car' EP [ˈkaʀu], BP [ˈkaχu]. Elsewhere the contrast is always
neutralised. /ʀ/ (/χ/) is always found in syllable-initial position; in
European Portuguese syllable-final positions are invariably filled by /ɾ/,
while in Brazilian Portuguese (especially Rio) /χ/ is preferred. (This is
consistent with a general tendency to use the weaker member of the pair
(/ɾ/ in EP, /χ/ in BP) in weak syllable positions.) In both languages
syllable-final *r* is subject to further weakening; EP /ɾ/ may be an approximant [ɹ], while BP /χ/ is frequently effaced.

The sibilants /s z ʃ ʒ/ contrast only intervocalically (inside the word)
and word-initially; elsewhere they are subject to complex distributional (or
morphophonemic) rules, in which European Portuguese (and following
European Portuguese, Rio de Janeiro Brazilian Portuguese) differ radically
from Brazilian Portuguese (São Paulo). Before a voiceless consonant, only
/ʃ/ (EP) or /s/ (BP) is found; before a voiced consonant only /ʒ/ (EP) or
/z/ (BP); before a word-initial vowel only /z/ (EP and BP). *Voz* 'voice'
thus takes the following forms:

Citation form	Plural	Preconsonantal	Prevocalic
voz	*vozes*	*voz baixa*	*voz alta*
		'low voice'	'loud voice'
EP [vɔʃ]	[ˈvɔzəʃ]	[vɔʒˈbaiʃɐ]	[vɔˈzaltɐ]
BP [vɔs]	[ˈvɔzis]	[vɔzˈbaiʃɐ]	[vɔˈzaltɐ]

The main historical factors in the development of Portuguese consonants are the processes of lenition and palatalisation (cf. p. 38ff).

Portuguese continued the development of intervocalic consonants initiated in late Latin, with the effacement of /d/, the vocalisation of palatalised /g/, the weakening of /b/ to /v/ (merging it with /v/ < CLat. [w]), the voicing of voiceless single obstruents and the simplification of geminates. In addition, intervocalic /l/ and /n/ were effaced, and geminate /ll nn/ reduced to single /l n/. This development can be seen as an extension of lenition, if lenition is characterised as progressive vocalisation of consonants. The weakened laterals and nasals were not simply lost but fused with the preceding vowels (much as syllable-final /l/ in Brazilian Portuguese appears as /u/), the lateral losing all its distinguishing features, while the nasal transmitted its nasality to the vowel. A preceding diphthong or following yod generally blocked lenition, although some instances of [-kj-] and [-tj-] underwent voicing (see the chart of palatalisations).

b > v	FABAM	fava		bb > b	ABBĀTEM	abade
d > ∅	SĒDEM	see > sé		dd > d	ADDŪCO	adugo
g > ∅	SĬGĬLLUM	seelo > selo				
g > j	RĒGEM	rei				
p > b	LŪPUM	lobo		pp > p	CAPPAM	capa
t > d	RŎTAM	roda		tt > t	MĬTTĔRE	meter
k > g	LACUM	lago		kk > k	SACCUM	saco
f > v	AURIFĬCEM	ourives				
s > z	CASAM	casa		ss > s	ŌSSUM	osso
l > ∅	MALUM	mao > mau		ll > l	GĂLLUM	galo
n >˜	MANUM	mão		nn > n	PANNUM	pano

The effacement of intervocalic /l n/ has been morphologised, in the inflection of nouns and adjectives with root-final /l/, e.g. azul 'blue', plural azuis, and in derivational morphology, partly as the result of the introduction of unevolved forms: céu 'heaven, sky' (< CAELUM) corresponds to celeste 'heavenly'; fim [fĩ] 'end' (< FĪNEM) to final 'final'; beside irmão 'brother' there is a familiar form mano (borrowed from Castilian hermano).

Latter-day manifestations of lenition can be found in the effacement of intervocalic /d/ in second person plural verb forms (a fifteenth-century development, see p. 156) and the weakening of intervocalic /b d g/ (a relatively modern phenomenon, little found in Brazilian Portuguese).

A wide range of palatal and dental consonants resulted from the palatalising influence of front vowels and yod, as shown in Table 4.4. The development of an affricate /ʧ/ from obstruent + lateral clusters is an innovation peculiar to Galician-Portuguese and Leonese, and stands in strange contrast to the absence of delateralisation in /ʎ/ < /lj/ (compare Port. chave (OPort. [ʧave]), filho and Sp. llave, hijo (p. 84)). The affricate /ʧ/ later merged with the fricative /ʃ/ in southern dialects (as in French, cf. p. 212). Palatalisation reappears in Brazilian Portuguese, where in many varieties the dental plosives /t d/ are realised as palato-alveolar affricates [ʧ dʒ] when followed by /i/: *o meu tio vende um lote* 'my uncle sells a piece of land' [u meu ʧiu vẽdʒi ũ lɔʧi].

Palatalisations

ʎ	< -lj-		filho	< FĪLIUM	'son'
	-Cl-		velho	< VĚT(Ŭ)LUM	'old'
			olho	< ŎC(Ŭ)LUM	'eye'
ɲ	< -nj-		vinha	< VĪNEAM	'vine'
	-jn- < -gn-		lenha	< LIGNAM	'wood'
	epenthetic j		vinho < vĩo	< VĪNUM	'wine'
s < ts	< kj		braço	< BRACHIUM	'arm'
	tj		paço < paaço	< PALATIUM	'palace'
			-ção	< -TIŌNEM	
	kke		aceitar	< ACCĔPTĀRE	'to accept'
	Cdj-	OPort.	vergonça	< VĔRĒCŪNDIAM	'shame'
z < dz	< Vke		fazer	< FACĔRE	'to do'
	-kj-		juizo	< JŪDĬCIUM	'judgement'
	-tj-	OPort.	vezo	< VĬTIUM	'vice'
			razão	< RATIŌNEM	'reason'
ʃ < ʧ	< Cl	OPort.	chantar	< PLANTĀRE	'to plant'
			chave	< CLAVEM	'key'
			chuva < chuiva	< PLŪVIAM	'rain'
ʃ	< js < ps,ks		caixa	< CAPSA	'box'
			seixo	< SAXUM	'stone'
	jss < ssj		baixar	< *BASSIARE	'to lower'
	js < sk		peixe	< PĬSCEM	'fish'
			faixa	< FASCIAM	'band'
ʒ	< -sj-		queijo	< CASĔUM	'cheese'
	VdjV		hoje	< HŎDIE	'today'
			vejo	< VĬDEO	'I see'
	ge		gente	< GĔNTEM	'people'
	-gj-		fujo	< FŪGIO	'I flee'
	-dj-		esponja	< SPŎNDEAM	'sponge'
	-j-		cujo	< CŪIUM	'whose'

In the sibilant system, the result of the Romance palatalisations was similar to the situation in Old Spanish, with a contrast of (lamino-)dental, (apico-)alveolar and palato-alveolar fricatives. Only northern European Portuguese dialects have retained this contrast: southern dialects merged the alveolars with the dentals, in the Portuguese equivalent of Spanish *seseo* (p. 82) (unremarked because standard); in central dialects the dentals were eliminated in favour of the apico-alveolars, which are traditionally known as *s beirão* by their association with the speech of the Beira Alta and Beira Baixa.

Stress and Syllable Structure

At the phonological level there are severe restrictions on consonant clusters. Syllable onsets can consist of a single consonant or a cluster of obstruent (/p t k b d ɡ f/) and liquid (/r l/); releases can consist of a single liquid or sibilant if the nucleus is an oral monophthong, or only of a sibilant if the nucleus is nasal or diphthongal. (Diphthongs and nasal nuclei function in the same way, as complex nuclei rather than closed syllables, in their resistance to resyllabification and atonic vowel reduction.)

In a large number of neologisms, many of common currency, the release consists of an obstruent, e.g. *absurdo, advogado.* European Portuguese allows more syllable-final consonants than Brazilian Portuguese (compare EP *facto* 'fact' ['faktu], BP *fato* ['fatu]; EP *secção* [sɛk'sẽũ], BP *seção* [se'sẽũ]) and freely uses them in acronyms (e.g. *CUF* [kuf] *Companhia União Fabril* compared to BP *PUC* ['puki] *Pontifícia Universidade Católica*); in Brazilian Portuguese preconsonantal /k/ is rarely found, and other such clusters of obstruents are resyllabified following epenthesis (*abstrato* [abi'stratu]; *advogado* [adʒivo'gadu]), which gives Brazilian Portuguese a much stronger tendency towards a simple CV syllable structure.

Sibilants in medial clusters (*estar, estrela*) are traditionally shown as syllable-final, but are really ambisyllabic, especially in compounds where the sibilant is root-initial (*abstrato, inscrever*). In European Portuguese the effacement of initial atonic /i/ leaves /ʃ/ in initial position: *estar* ['ʃtar], *estrela* ['ʃtrelɐ].

Portuguese is nominally a free-stress language, with stress being nonetheless predictable in the majority of words by a complex of grammatical and morphophonological factors. Stress generally falls on the penultimate syllable. If the final syllable is closed by any consonant except inflectional -*s* (/z/) or contains as its nucleus a diphthong or nasal vowel, final stress is the rule. The chart given here exemplifies regular and irregular stress patterns. In most nouns and adjectives, where the vowel of the final syllable is a gender marker, the stressed syllable corresponds to the final syllable of the root. In simple verb forms stress generally falls on the thematic vowel (see section 4). If the thematic vowel is word-final, or followed only by one of the person–number suffixes -*s* (/z/) and -*m* (morphophonemic /N/, realised as nasalisation of the vowel), or if there is no thematic vowel, the general rule of penultimate stress applies. These rules do not correspond to the orthographic conventions for stress-marking, because the orthography incorporates some covert stress-marking devices: -*z*, -*ão*, -*i*, -*u* in final syllables indicate oxytonic stress, while the otherwise equivalent graphs -*s*, -*am*, -*e*, -*o* in final syllables indicate penultimate stress. Final -*em* is interpreted as atonic (like -*am*); the absence of a separate graph for stressed /ẽi/ forces the orthography to mark it as irregular.

Phonetically, European Portuguese is a clear case of a stress-timed

Stress

Noun and Adjective Stress

Regular penultimate stress	Regular final stress	Marked stress
banana(s)	ananás	câmara, Canadá
posta(s)	postal	apóstol
maço(s)	maçã(s)	órfã(s)
malha	calhau	peru (/pcˈru/)
avaro	alvor	árvore

Verb Stress
Theme Vowel Stress

Penultimate	Final	Antepenultimate	Penultimate Stress
falamos (pres. ind.)	falar (inf.)	falávamos (imperf.)	falo (pres. ind.)
falavas (imperf.)	falou (pret.)	falássemos (imperf. subj.)	falas (pres. ind.)
falaram (pret.)	falei (pret.)	faláramos (pluperf.)	falam (pres. ind.)

Orthographic Stress Conventions

Penultimate		Final		Antepenultimate
Unmarked	Marked	Unmarked	Marked	Marked
carros	ténis	arroz	cirós	cântaros
falamos				falávamos
juro		peru	paletó	pálido
bate	júri	bati		
	líder	bater		
nuvem		catalães	vintém	
falaram		falarão		
	órfã	irmã		
	hóquei	saquei		
amores			jacarés	árvores

language, in that its rhythmic pattern is based on the occurrence of stressed syllables at regular intervals. This entails that atonic syllables are considerably shorter than tonic ones. In addition, atonic vowels are centralised and raised, and [ə] and [u] are frequently effaced or reduced to secondary articulation of preceding consonants, resulting in frequent consonant clusters and syllabic consonants at the phonetic level, e.g. *restaurantes* /ʀəʃtauɾãtəʃ/, [ʀʃtaurẽtʃ], *perfeito* /pərfɐitu/, [pɾfɐit]. Brazilian Portuguese is mainly syllable-timed, with atonic syllables more equal in length to tonic syllables, little vowel reduction, few syllable-final consonants, weakening of syllable-final /l r/, and breaking of medial clusters by vowel epenthesis. The rhythm of European Portuguese is the result of relatively recent developments: Portuguese verse metre reflects the older state of affairs, and is based on syllable-counting.

Orthography

Modern Portuguese orthography (summarised in Table 4.4) is phonological rather than narrowly phonemic or phonetic, assuming knowledge of the main phonological and morphophonemic processes of the language.

Table 4.4: Portuguese Orthography

	EP	BP		EP	BP
a	/a ɐ/	/a/	-m	nasality	
á		/a/	m-	/m/	
ã		/ẽ/	-n	nasality	
â	/ɐ/	/a/ = [ɐ]	n-	/n/	
ãe		/ẽĩ/	nh	/ɲ/	
ão		/ẽũ/	o	/o ɔ u/	
b		/b/	ó	/ɔ/	
c ᵃ		/k/	ô	/o/	
c '		/s/	ou	/o/	
ç		/s/	õe	/õĩ/	
ch		/ʃ/	p	/p/	
d		/d/	qu ᵃ	/kw/	
e	/e ɛ ɐ i ə/	/e ɛ i/	qu '	/k/	
é		/ɛ/ ,	-rr-	/ʀ/	/χ/
ê		/e/	r-	/ʀ/	/χ/
f		/f/	r	/ɾ/	/ɾ χ/
g ᵃ		/ɡ/	-s	/ʃ z ʒ/	/s z/
g '		/ʒ/	-s-	/z/	
gu ᵃ		/ɡw/	s-	/s/	
gu '		/ɡ/	t	/t/	
h	silent (but see ch, lh, nh)		u	/u w/	
i		/i j/	v	/v/	
j		/ʒ/	x	/ʃ/ (/s z ks ɡz/)	
l		/l/	-z	/ʃ z ʒ/	/s z/
lh		/ʎ/	z-	/z/	

The written accents are used to indicate irregular stress patterns, including all cases of antepenultimate stress. These accents also indicate vowel quality (often redundantly). The circumflex accent ˆ indicates closed vowels [ɐ e o], while the acute accent ´ indicates open vowel qualities [a ɛ ɔ] and is also used to mark stress on *i*, *u*, which are deemed to have no 'closed' phonetic values. In a few cases these two accents are still used to indicate vowel quality in regularly stressed words (e.g. *três* 'three', *pôde* '(s)he could', vs *pode* '(s)he can', *pó* 'dust') and to distinguish stressed monosyllables from clitics, e.g. *dê* [de] 3 sg. present subjunctive of *dar* 'give' – *de* [də] 'of'. The grave accent, formerly used to indicate unreduced atonic vowels, now has very limited use to indicate morphologised vowel contractions (see the chart of contractions, p. 149) most notably *à* (preposition *a* + article *a*).

The *til* is used as a marker of nasality from the earliest documents, while still retaining its earlier function as an abbreviation for nasal consonants: in many cases (e.g. *tã* = *ta(n)*?) its interpretation is a matter of dispute between linguists and paleographers. The graphs *nh* and *lh* were introduced on the Provençal model in the second half of the thirteenth century, to deal with the problem of palatal liquids, Galician retaining the Castilian graphs *ll, nn* (*ñ*). Etymological and pseudo-etymological spellings were rife in the nineteenth century, until some degree of order was restored by twentieth-century spelling reforms. Brazilian and Portuguese orthographies have been progressively harmonised by agreements between the respective governments and Academies, beginning with the *Acordo Ortográfico Luso-Brasileiro* of 1945, which failed to gain ratification from the Brazilian Government, and latterly with 1971 decrees in both countries, in which the distinctively Brazilian convention of marking unpredictable closed mid vowels with the circumflex was abandoned, as part of a rationalisation of the use of accents. The orthographic differences that remain reflect phonological differences between European and Brazilian Portuguese.

3 Morphology

Nouns and Adjectives

The basic grammatical categories of Portuguese nominal inflection are gender and number.

Grammatical gender is in Portuguese a two-term noun classification system whose categories, traditionally labelled 'masculine' and 'feminine', correlate to some extent with the semantic feature of (natural) gender, in animate nouns. The principal exceptions are of nouns with semantic common gender but a single grammatical gender (e.g. *tigre* (m.) 'tiger', *criança* (f.) 'child', *cônjuge* (m.) 'spouse') distinct from the class of common nouns where masculine and feminine forms are identical (e.g. *parente* (m. and f.) 'relative'), and from morphological anomalies such as *guarda* (m.) 'policeman' where the usual correspondence of gender and stem-ending do not obtain.

Stem-final -*o* (/u/), usually corresponds to masculine gender, stem-final -*a* to feminine. Noun endings other than these can correspond to either gender, e.g. *amor* (m.) 'love', *cor* (f.) 'colour', *rapaz* (m.) 'lad', *paz* (f.) 'peace', *estudante* (m. and f.) 'student'; the corresponding adjectives are similarly invariable, e.g. *contente* 'happy', *doce* < DULCEM 'sweet', *final* 'final', *simples* 'simple, plain', or follow the pattern of animate nouns in which masculine is marked by final -*e* or the absence of a gender marker, and feminine is marked by -*a*: *inglês* – *inglesa* 'English', *cru* – *crua* 'raw', *professor* – *professora* 'teacher'.

Portuguese follows the Western Romance pattern of unmarked singular number contrasting with plural number marked by -*s* (morphophonemic /z/ realised as [s z ∫ ʒ] according to the sibilant system p. 138). A few nouns and adjectives are invariable for number, e.g. *arrais* 'bo'sun', *simples*. All such forms end in -*ais* or -*es*, the absence of a plural marker being explained by haplology, *simples-es → *simples*.

The simplification of Portuguese noun morphology has been so great that it is hardly surprising that few vestiges remain of the Latin declensional system. As elsewhere in Hispano-Romance, the Latin case system was not preserved, except in personal pronouns, and neuter gender has only survived, in a much modified form, in demonstrative pronouns. Nouns and adjectives are uniformly derived from the accusative singular, except for sporadic cases of derivation from the nominative singular, e.g. *Deus* < DEUS 'God', *Carlos* < CAROLUS. A few non-nominal forms preserve relics of other cases e.g. *agora* 'now' < HAC HORA 'at this time' (ablative). The predominant masculine *-o* and feminine *-a* endings derive from the Latin second and first declensions respectively, with few changes of declension (e.g. *contente* <. CONTENTUM). Other endings have had a more chequered history. Adjectives ending in *-ês* were invariable for gender in Old Portuguese, feminines in *-esa* being generalised only in the fifteenth century. Similarly feminines in *-e* have been replaced by forms in *-a*, e.g. *infanta*, *estudanta* (popular), *equipa* (alternative form of *equipe* < Fr. *équipe*) 'team'. Adjectives in *-um* were analogically remodelled in the opposite direction, OPort. *comũu – comua* < COMUNEM 'common' becoming invariable *comum* (m./f.).

Apocope and its interactions with other historical processes (see section 2) have given rise to a host of stem alternations associated with number inflection. The apocope of /e/ in singular forms established *-es* (EP /ɔz/, BP /iz/) as a surface allomorph of the plural, e.g. *flor – flores* 'flower(s)'; *raiz – raizes* 'root(s)'. In combination with nasalisation it gave alternations such as OPort. *pã – pães* < PANE(S) 'bread, loaf', *naçõ – nações* < NATIONE(S) 'nation(s)'. The subsequent merger of final nasals (p. 136) and fusion of vowels in hiatus turned these and other alternations into opaque correspondences between nasal diphthongs *pão – pães*, *nação – nações* (compare *irmão – irmãos* < GERMANO(S) 'brother(s)', *rã – rãs* < RANA(S) 'frog(s)'). Of these, the alternation between *-ão* (sg.) and *-ões* (pl.) is dominant, due to the high frequency of the suffixes *-ção* < -TIONEM and *-ão* < -ONEM, and has been extended analogically, e.g. *verão*, pl. *verões* < VERANUM 'summer'. In stems with final -/le/, apocope blocked *l*-deletion in the singular, while the plural underwent *l*-deletion and fusion of the resulting vowel sequence, giving a series of alternations between vowel + *l* and diphthongs: *sol – sóis* < SOLE(S) 'sun(s)'; *casal – casais* (OPort. *casaes*) < CASALE(S) 'married couple'; *paul – pauis* < PADULE(S) 'marsh'.

On a more limited scale, stem alternations have become associated with gender marking. Denasalisation at the end of the Old Portuguese period differentiated masculine and feminine forms: *bom – boa* (OPort. *bõa*) < BONUM 'good'; *leão – leoa* (OPort. *leõ – leõa*) < LEONEM 'lion'. Metaphonic alternations also act as a subsidiary marker of gender and number, as illustrated in the chart of noun metaphony. The alternation between /o/

and /ɔ/ differentiates between masculine and singular forms on the one hand and feminine and/or plural forms on the other, in both nouns and adjectives. The corresponding alternation between /e/ and /ɛ/ complements masculine -o and feminine -a in nouns only.

Noun Metaphony

		o-*stems*		e-*stems*	
Nouns		porco < PORCUM 'pig'		capelo < CAPELLUM 'hood, cowl'	
		porca < PORCAM 'sow'		capela < CAPELLAM 'chapel, garland'	
		m.	*f.*	*m.*	*f.*
	sg.	porco	porca	capelo	capela
		[o]	[ɔ]	[e]	[ɛ]
	pl.	porcos	porcas	capelos	capelas
		[ɔ]	[ɔ]	[e]	[ɛ]
Adjectives		novo < NOVUM 'new'		No alternating forms	
	sg.	novo	nova		
		[o]	[ɔ]		
	pl.	novos	novas		
		[ɔ]	[ɔ]		

Determiners

The class of determiners comprises articles, demonstratives and possessives, as indicated in the chart opposite. In modern Portuguese, all forms in this class are used pronominally as well as prenominally, without formal differentiation. The Old Portuguese possessive forms *ma, ta, sa* were weak forms found in prenominal position. The demonstratives show regular gender endings, supplemented by metaphonic alternations. In addition, in their pronominal function they contrast a neuter (more precisely indefinite inanimate) gender ending -*o* with masculine -*e* and feminine -*a*, this also supplemented in modern Portuguese by a metaphonic alternation which is restricted to this grammatical category. The values and occurrence of second and third person possessives are determined by the address system, described below.

The definite article and demonstratives are the result of a reorganisation of the Latin deictic system (p. 53). The Latin demonstrative ILLE gave not only the Portuguese definite article but also the homophonous weak object pronouns, as well as providing the base for the third person demonstratives. The second person demonstratives originated in Lat. IPSE, whose identity function was taken over by derivatives of the expanded form *METIPSIMUM, *mesmo* < OPort. *meesmo* (cf. Fr. *même*), or *METIPSE (OPort. *medês*). HOC survives only in adverbs: HOC ANNO > Oport. *ogano* 'this year', HAC HORA > *agora* 'now', PER HOC > *pero* 'but'

Articles, Demonstratives and Possessives

Articles

Definite	ILLUM, ILLAM etc.	o, a	
Indefinite	UNUM, UNAM	um, uma (hũu, hũa)	

Demonstratives

		Determiner/pronoun	*Indefinite pronoun*
'1st person'	ISTE etc.	este, esta	isto (esto)
	*ACCU ISTE etc.	(aqueste, aquesta)	(aquesto)
'2nd person'	IPSE etc.	esse, essa	isso (esso)
	*ACCU IPSE etc.	(aquesse, aquessa)	(aquesso)
'3rd person'	*ACCU ILLE etc.	aquele, aquela	aquilo (aquelo)

Possessives

1 sg.	MEUM	meu, minha (mia, mha, ma)
2 sg.	TUUM	teu (tou), tua (ta)
3 sg./pl.	SUUM	seu (sou), sua (sa)
1 pl.	*NOSSUM	nosso, nossa
2 pl.	*VOSSUM	vosso, vossa

Note: Old Portuguese forms are enclosed in parentheses.

(showing, like its Spanish counterpart, an interesting shift from causal to concessive).

The system of place adverbs consisted originally of only two terms, *aqui* (first person) and *ali* (third person), but developed a third term, second person *ai*, to match the three-term demonstrative system: *aqui* (=*este*) – *ai* (=*esse*) – *ali*(=*aquele*).

Both the articles show abnormal phonetic developments. In the indefinite article, derived from the numeral UNUM, the feminine forms would ordinarily have been denasalised, as *[ua], *[uas], but retain their nasality, by analogy with the masculine. The modern feminine forms developed in the seventeenth century, through glide epenthesis ũa > uw̃a > *uma* possibly influenced by the orthographic form of the masculine, (*h*)*um*. (In Galician, with a different orthographic tradition, the feminine is either *unha* [uŋa], or *umha* [uma], beside masculine *un* [ũ], [uŋ].)

The exceptional deletion of intervocalic /ll/ in derivatives of ILLE (cf. also *eis* (dialectal OPort.) < *eles*) may be put down to the acceleration of phonetic changes in high-frequency grammatical morphs, especially clitics. The original lateral remains in the sandhi forms *lo, la*. In modern Portuguese these allomorphs are only found in contracted forms of the atonic object pronouns (see the chart of personal pronouns). The possessives *teu* and *seu* were analogically formed on the basis of the first person singular form, from inherited *tou* < TUUM, *sou* < SUUM; the feminines *mia* < MEAM, *tua*, *sua* < TUAM, SUAM show the regular raising of mid vowels in hiatus.

Pronouns

Portuguese has three series of pronouns: subject pronouns derived from

Latin nominatives, prepositional objects derived from Latin datives in the three instances where these are distinct from the subject forms, and verbal objects derived from Latin accusatives. The first two series are strong or tonic forms, the third are weak and enclitic, and subject to vowel reduction. The distinction between dative and accusative pronouns is retained only in the third person series, where *lhe* < ILLI contrasts with *o, a.* Modern Galician preserves *che* as a second person non-reflexive dative distinct from accusative and reflexive *te.* *Che* was a common Galician-Portuguese variant of *te*; the contraction of *ti* (*te*) and *se* with the direct object pronouns *o* and *a* led to palatalised contractions, *ti-o* > *tjo* > [tʃo] *cho, se-o* > *sjo* > [ʃo] *xo*, from which Galician-Portuguese *che* and the now obsolete *xe* were backformed.

Personal Pronouns

	Strong Pronouns		Weak Pronouns		
	Subject	*Object*	*Dir. Obj.*	*Ind. Obj.*	*Reflexive*
1 sg.	eu	mim	me	me	me
2 sg.	tu	ti	te	te	te
3 sg.	ele (m.), ela (f.)	ele, ela	o (m.), a (f.)	lhe	se
	você	você, si (EP)	lhe (BP)		
	o senhor (EP)	o senhor (EP)			
1 pl.	nós	nós	nos	nos	nos
2 pl.	vós	vós	vos	vos	vos
3 pl.	eles, elas	eles, elas	os, as	lhes	se
	vocês	vocês, si (EP)	lhes (BP)		
	os senhores (EP)	os senhores (EP)			

In addition to its already extensive range of values, the enigmatic monosyllable *o* combines with the universal complementiser *que* to give the interrogative relative *o que*, e.g. *o que deseja?* 'what do you wish?'. The same form appears in headless relative clauses, *esqueci o que me disse* 'I forgot what he said', though in other contexts *o que* functions alongside *os que, a que* and *as que* as a regular combination of demonstrative pronoun and relative pronoun, e.g. *não vi a que procuras* 'I haven't seen the woman you are looking for'.

Clitic pronouns and articles developed a wide range of sandhi forms, including contraction, when proclitic, as displayed in the chart of personal pronouns. The processes concerned were productive in Galician-Portuguese over a wide range of forms, e.g. *todolos* (= *todos* 'all' + *os*), and are still productive in Galician.

The pronoun and possessive system has been radically affected by the development of the address system. Second person plural forms are no longer used except in a religious or highly formal ceremonial context; second person singular forms are used for familiar address in European Portuguese (and conservative Brazilian Portuguese dialects): otherwise

Contractions

		Masculine	Feminine	Indefinite
Preposition +	a + def. art.	ao	à (OPort. aa)	
determiner/pronoun	a + demonstrative	àquele	àquela	àquilo
	de + def. art.	do	da	
	de + indef. art.	dum	duma	
	de + demonstrative	deste	desta	daquilo
		desse	dessa	disso
		daquele	daquela	daquilo
	de + personal pronoun	dele	dela	
	em + def. art.	no	na	
		(OPort. eno	ena)	
	em + indef. art.	num	numa	
	em + demonstrative	neste	nesta	nisto
		nesse	nessa	nisso
		naquele	naquela	naquilo
	em + personal pronoun	nele	nela	
	por + def. art.	pelo	pela	
		(OPort. polo	pola)	
	para + def. art.	prò	prà	
	(colloquial)			
Verb + 3rd person	infinitive + o, a	metê-lo	metê-la	
clitic	final -s + o, a	mete-lo	mete-la	
	final nasal + o, a	metem-no	metem-na	
Clitic + clitic	me + o, a	mo	ma	
	te + o, a	to	ta	
	lhe(s) + o, a	lho	lha	
	nos + o, a	no-lo	no-la	
	vos + o, a	vo-lo	vo-la	

third person verb forms, with the pronoun *você(s)* (< *vossa mercê* 'your grace', cf. dialectal *vossemecê*) or (in European Portuguese) the partly pronominal *o senhor* (m.), *a senhora* (f.), are used for all formal (and plural) address in European and all address in Brazilian Portuguese. In addition, a wide range of titles can be used as address forms with third person verbs, with the result that third person object pronouns *o(s)*, *a(s)*, have also acquired second person reference, as has *si* < SIBI, now used as the formal second person prepositional object in European Portuguese (*é para si* 'it's for you'), as well as retaining its original third person reflexive value in *si mesmo* 'himself, itself etc.'. Brazilian Portuguese has been more resistant to this last development: there is a tendency for *lhe*, exclusively used as an indirect object in European Portuguese, to be used for second person functions. Alternatively, the second person object pronoun *te* is used even where the corresponding subject pronoun and verb forms are missing, or else weak forms are avoided altogether: *eu vi ele* 'I saw him', *eu vi você* 'I saw you'. Ambiguities in the reference of the possessive *seu* are resolved by the use of *dele, dela, de você* etc., instead of or as well as the possessive, especially in Brazilian Portuguese.

Verbs

Most Portuguese verb forms are synthetic (morphologically simple), with the structure: stem + tense/aspect/mood + person/number. The stem is usually composed of the root and a conjugation-class marker known as the theme (or, in recognition of the fact that all themes are single vowels, thematic vowel).

As in Spanish, the Latin quadripartite conjugational system reduces to three paradigms, with the merger of the Latin second and third conjugations, a fusion that leaves no traces except in irregular verbs. Portuguese verbs fall into three conjugational classes, identified by the thematic vowels /a/ (first conjugation) /e/ (second) and /i/ (third), most prominently in the infinitive forms, where the thematic vowel is stressed. The second and third conjugations are closely linked, in opposition to the first, by being non-productive and metaphonic, as well as by the frequent neutralisation of the contrast between their thematic vowels, for instance in the past participle in -*ido* (inherited in the third conjugation, replacing older -*udo* in many second conjugation verbs) and in the imperfect indicative and present subjunctive forms. A number of verbs have indeed changed from the second to the third conjugation, e.g. *cair* < *caer* (< CADERE) 'to fall'. Irregular verbs have idiosyncratic stems, with no thematic vowel and with consonantal alternations. The infinitive, composed of stem + *r*, can be considered a special type of stem in so far as it is *r* the base of the future and conditional paradigms, where clitic pronouns (see p. 148) are mesoclitic (affixed between stem and ending) rather than enclitic, e.g. *amar-me-á* '(s)he will love me'. This feature is not found in Brazilian Portuguese, where either the pronoun is proclitic to the whole verb form or evasive action is taken, as in European Portuguese, by the use of an alternative verb form (the present or a periphrasis, see p. 160): in Brazilian Portuguese the infinitive ending /r/ can be analysed as a mood marker, beside independent markers for the future and conditional forms.

Alongside the synthetic past tenses (imperfect, preterit, pluperfect), there exists a series of analytic forms, made up of the auxiliary *ter* (< TENERE) and the past participle: perfect, pluperfect and future perfect tenses (indicative and subjunctive) are formed using the present, imperfect and future tense forms of *ter*. This development follows the general Hispano-Romance pattern, though Portuguese has been more loath to abandon older synthetic forms and uses a different past tense auxiliary. In both Portuguese and Galician, *ter* has replaced *haver* (< HABERE, p. 57) not only as the verb of possession but also, except in literary styles, as auxiliary. In some forms of Brazilian Portuguese even the existential *há* 'there is' has been taken over by *tem*. The synthetic and analytic forms of the pluperfect are grammatically equivalent but the synthetic form is effectively limited to written forms of European Portuguese.

For all person/number categories except first person plural there are two sets of person markers, one set peculiar to the preterit (and sometimes the only marker of preterit forms) and the other found in the remainder (or majority) of verbal forms, as shown in the chart given here.

The first person singular is unmarked in present subjunctive forms, where the final morph is the reversed thematic vowel /e/ or /a/.

Person/Number

		Affix	Regular verbs 1st conj.	Regular verbs 2nd/3rd conj.	Irregular verbs 1st conj.	Irregular verbs 2nd/3rd conj.
1 sg.	General (imperf. subj.)	Ø	falasse /falase-Ø/	metesse /metese-Ø/	estivesse /stivese-Ø/	dissesse /disese-Ø/
	Present	-o	falo /fal(a)-o/	meto /met(e)-o/		digo /dig-o/
	Irregular present	-u			estou /sta-u/	
	Preterit	-i, Ø	falei /fala-i/	meti /mete-i/	estive /stive-Ø/	disse /dise-Ø/
2 sg.	General	-s	falas /fala-z/	metes /mete-z/	estas /sta-z/	dizes /dize-z/
	Preterit	-ste	falaste /fala-ste/	meteste /mete-ste/	estiveste /stive-ste/	disseste /dise-ste/
3 sg.	General	Ø	fala /fala-Ø/	mete /mete-Ø/	esta /sta-Ø/	diz(e) /dize-Ø/
	Preterit	-u	falou /fala-u/	meteu /mete-u/		
	Irregular preterit	root change			esteve /steve-Ø/	disse /dise-Ø/
1 pl.		-mos	falamos /fala-muz/	metemos /mete-muz/	estamos /sta-muz/	dizemos /dize-muz/
2 pl.	General	-is	falais /fala-iz/	meteis /mete-iz/	estais /sta-iz/	dizeis /dize-iz/
	Personal infinitive	-des	falardes /falar-dez/	meterdes /meter-dez/	estiverdes /stiver-dez/	disserdes /diser-dez/
	Preterit	-ste	falaste /fala-ste/	meteste /mete-ste/	estiveste /stive-ste/	disseste /dise-ste/
3 pl.	General	-m = /˜/	falam /fala-˜/	metem /mete-˜/	estão /sta-˜/	dizem /dize-˜/
	Preterit	-ram /rã/ = [rṽũ]	falaram /fala-rã/	meteram /mete-rã/	estiveram /stive-rã/	disseram /dise-rã/

Note: all verb forms are present indicative unless otherwise stated.

The development of the address system (pp. 148–50) has effectively removed all morphological second person forms from Brazilian Portuguese, and made second person plural forms practically obsolete in European Portuguese. The second person plural preterit ending -*stes* is commonly used as a second person singular form in European Portuguese, by analogy with the -*s* ending of other second person plural forms. Many Brazilian dialects nevertheless retain second person imperative forms, e.g. *canta!* 'sing!', as emphatic imperatives, beside the normal third person *cante!*; the corresponding emphatic negative, *não canta!* 'do not sing!' (also found in colloquial European Portuguese) stands beside the neutral (normatively preferred) *não cantes!*

Person marking is supplemented by metaphonic alternations in the second and third conjugations, as illustrated in the chart of verb metaphony. The general effect of metaphony is that the distinction between low-mid and high-mid root vowels is eliminated. The only exceptions to the alternations are verbs where the root vowel quality is invariable or where mid-vowel distinctions are neutralised by a basic phonological rule. In abstract morphophonemics it is possible to account for these alternations by metaphonic rules assimilating the first person singular root vowels to the thematic vowel, thus giving high vowels when the theme is /i/, high-mid when it is /e/, and low when it is /a/.

Verb Metaphony

	2nd conjugation		3rd conjugation		
	meter	*correr*	*servir*	*dormir*	*fugir*
Present indicative					
1 sg.	meto	corro	sirvo	durmo	fujo
	[e]	[o]	[i]	[u]	[u]
2 sg.	metes	corres	serves	dormes	foges
	[ɛ]	[ɔ]	[ɛ]	[ɔ]	[ɔ]
3 sg.	mete	corre	serve	dorme	foge
	[ɛ]	[ɔ]	[ɛ]	[ɔ]	[ɔ]
1 pl.	metemos	corremos	servimos	dormimos	fugimos
	[ə]EP	[u]EP	[ə]EP	[u]EP	[u]EP
	[e]BP	[o]BP	[e]BP	[o]BP	[u]BP
3 pl.	metem	correm	servem	dormem	fogem
	[ɛ]	[ɔ]	[ɛ]	[ɔ]	[ɔ]
Present subjunctive					
1 sg.	meta	corra	sirva	durma	fuja
	[e]	[o]	[i]	[u]	[u]
1 pl.	metamos	corramos	sirvamos	durmamos	fujamos
	[ə]EP	[u]EP	[i]EP	[u]EP	[u]EP
	[e]BP	[o]BP	[i]BP	[u]BP	[u]BP

Tense, aspect and mood are always represented in a single portmanteau morph, in synthetic forms. The range of tense/aspect/mood markers is displayed in the chart given here. The preterit is unique in having no overt marker. It is indicated in regular verbs by its idiosyncratic person/number morphs, and in irregular verbs by the selection of the distinctive stem form, which is also used for the pluperfect, past subjunctive and future subjunctive forms.

Tense/Aspect/Mood

Tense	Stem	Affix	1st conj.	2nd/3rd conj.	Irregular
Present indicative	Present	Ø	fala /fala-Ø/	mete /mete-Ø/	diz(e) /dize-Ø/
	Present (1 sg.)	Ø			digo /dig-Ø-o/
Present subjunctive	Present (1 sg.)	e,a	fale /fala-e/	meta /mete-a/	diga /dig-a/
Imperfect	Present	va,a	falava /fala-va/	metia /mete-a/	dizia /dize-a/
Preterit (examples 1 pl.)	Present	Ø	falamos /fala-Ø-muz/	metemos /mete-Ø-muz/	
	Preterit	Ø			dissemos /dise-Ø-muz/
Pluperfect	Present	ra	falara /fala-ra/	metera /mete-ra/	
	Preterit	ra			dissera /dise-ra/
Past subjunctive	Present	sse	falasse /fala-se/	metesse /mete-se/	
	Preterit	sse			dissesse /dise-se/
Future subjunctive	Present	r	falar /fala-r/	meter /mete-r/	
	Preterit	r			disser /dise-r/
Future indicative	Infinitive	a	falará /falar-a/	meterá /meter-a/	
	Irregular	a			dirá /dir-a/
Conditional	Infinitive	ia	falaria /falar-ia/	meteria /meter-ia/	
	Irregular	ia			diria /dir-ia/

Note: all examples are third person singular unless otherwise stated.

The morphological symmetry of the tense and aspect system conceals great semantic complexity. Events and processes in the present are usually expressed by the present continuous, the simple present representing timeless states, as well as indicating the immediate future in colloquial registers: *a reunião começa agora* 'the meeting is just about to begin' vs *a reunião está começando* 'the meeting is just beginning (has just begun)'. The synthetic preterit (much more frequently used than its Romance counterparts) is essentially perfective rather than past. On the one hand, it represents a non-durative past tense, in opposition to the durative imperfect; on the other, it is a present perfect, e.g. *morreu o meu pai* 'my father has died', in contrast to the little used analytic perfect which represents only continued or repeated action in the near past (*tenho tomado banho todos os dias* 'I've been bathing every day'). The remaining analytic past tenses have only perfect (or relative past) reference: the perfect subjunctive for instance, is a genuine present perfect (*não é possível que ele tenha feito isso* 'he cannot have done that' (literally, 'it is not possible that he has done that').

Portuguese is virtually unique in the Romance family in having an infinitive with person/number endings, the 'personal' or 'inflected' infinitive (*infinitivo pessoal, infinitivo flexionado*), as well as a plain (impersonal) form. (A similar form is found in Sardinian, p. 332.) The forms of the personal infinitive derive from the Latin imperfect subjunctive (p. 47), *falarem* < FAB(U)LARENT, *dizerem* < DICERENT; being identical with the infinitive in its first and third person singular forms, (e.g. *falar* < FAB(U)LARE (infinitive), FAB(U)LAREM (1 sg. imperf. subj.), FAB(U)LARET (3 sg. imperf. subj.), it was soon reanalysed as an infinitive, with the extension of its functions discussed in section 3.

The present subjunctive is marked by a reversed thematic vowel (the first conjugation theme /a/ for the second and third conjugations, the second conjugation theme /e/ for the first conjugation). The reversed theme is usually said to replace theme and tense/aspect/mood marker, but if we accept the analysis of first person singular present indicative forms, where the thematic vowel is assumed to be deleted by morphophonemic rule when followed by a vocalic suffix, the present subjunctive morph will follow the thematic vowel and trigger its deletion by the same rule in all forms. This is supported by the fact that present subjunctive forms almost invariably have the same stem form as first person singular present indicatives, even when that form has no thematic vowel (the exceptions, *seja* (*ser*), *esteja* (*estar*), *dê* (*dar*) being odd in that they are verbs of no fixed conjugation, whose first person singular present forms have been analogically remodelled); the subjunctive marker also resists fusion with the root, while the thematic vowel does not (compare *rói* /ʀo+e+Ø/ (3 sg. pres. ind., *roer* 'to gnaw'), [ʀɔi] and *voe* /vo+(a)+e/ (3 sg. pres. subj., *voar* 'to fly'), ['voə]).

The future subjunctive is morphologically anomalous in that it patterns with past tense verb forms (DIXERINT > *disserem* cf. pret. *disse*). Its 'future' label reflects the fact that it generally cooccurs with explicit indications of future time, without itself expressing futurity. The problems of the meaning of the subjunctive mood in general, and particularly of the future subjunctive, are essentially syntactic and are discussed in the next section.

A considerable number of verbs have one or more of a limited set of irregularities which are consistent enough to constitute minor paradigms (and as such have exerted analogical influence). These features are tabulated in the chart of verb irregularities, with a sample of irregular verbs analysed for irregular components. There is a nucleus of irregular verbs resisting easy incorporation in any conjugation; *ser* 'to be' *ir* 'to go', which incorporate forms from more than one Vulgar Latin verb, and *ter* 'to have', *vir* 'to come', *pôr* 'to put' (OPort. *tēer* < TENERE; *viir* < VENIRE; *pōer*, *poer* < PONERE), which incorporate nasal root vowels with a variety of realisations. These verbs, together with *dar* and *estar*, the only first conjugation irregular verbs, also form a cohesive group with many analogical links, e.g. the first person singular present indicative forms *sou, dou, estou* formed on the model of *vou* < VADO. A larger number of verbs have an idiosyncratic stem form in the first person singular present indicative (which as we have seen also acts as the base for the present subjunctive) and/or the preterit and related tenses (pluperfect, past subjunctive, future subjunctive).

Verb Irregularities

	estar	ter	por	saber	poder	fazer	dizer	querer
Present tense								
1 sg. ind. stem	+	+	+	+	+	+	+	+
subjunctive stem	+			+				+
1 sg. ind.	estou	tenho	ponho	sei	posso [ɔ]	faço	digo	quero [ɛ]
3 sg. ind.	está	tem	pôe	sabe	pode	faz(e)	diz(e)	quer
1 sg. subj.	esteja	tenha	ponha	saiba	possa	faça	diga	queira
Preterit								
1 sg.	estive	tive	pus	soube	pude	fiz	disse	quis
1 sg. fut. subj.	estiver	tiver	puser	souber	puder	fizer	disser	quiser
3 sg. pret.	esteve	teve	pôs		pôde	fez		
Past participle			posto			feito	dito	(quisto) OPort.
Short future			(porrei) OPort.			farei	direi	(querrei) OPort.

Many of the complexities of Portuguese verbal inflection can be traced to the major phonological developments described in section 2. In regular preterits the person–number affix fused with the thematic vowel (*-ei* < *ai*, *-i* < *ei*, *ii*) as was the case with the third person singular ending (*-ou* < *au*, *-eu*, *-iu*). In irregular preterits final *-i* was often lost by apocope (*fiz* < **fizi* < FECI) after causing metaphonic raising of the root vowel. The second person plural was *-des* until the fifteenth century, when the plosive was effaced in intervocalic position *falades* > *falais*; *partides* > *partiis* > *partis*; *batedes* > *batees* > *bateis* (dialectal *batês*). It remains only where the consonant was protected by a preceding consonant (personal infinitive *falardes*) or nasality (*vindes*) and in a few verbs with monosyllabic roots, e.g. *ide* (imperative *ir*), *credes* (*crer*), *sede* (imperative *ser*).

Vowel alternations in the verbal system, while clearly originating in metaphony (see section 2) show less clear phonological conditioning, so that the precise interplay of sound change and analogy that caused them must remain conjectural. In third conjugation verbs the effect of yod in first person singular present indicative forms was to raise low-mid vowels to mid, SERVIO > *s[e]rvo* vs *s[ɛ]rve* < SERVIT, DORMIO > OPort. *d[o]rmo* vs *d[ɔ]rme* < DORMIT, and high-mid /o/ to /u/, SUBIO > *subo* vs OPort. *s[o]be* < SUBIT. These two patterns seem to have merged to give a single alternation between high and low-mid vowels, *sirvo*, *durmo* vs *s[ɛ]rve*, *d[ɔ]rme*, which was analogically extended to verbs with root vowels /i u/, e.g. *destruir* (*destruo*, *destrói*). The resulting general rule that all second and third person singular, and third person plural forms have low vowels was extended to the second conjugation, whose few cases of the survival of -EO and -IO endings in the first person singular resulted only in palatalisation of root consonants (*ponho* < PONEO, cf. 3rd conj. *minto*, *menço* < MENTIO); from there the alternation of high-mid and low-mid root vowels spread to verbs with low-mid root vowels, and the whole of the first conjugation.

Metaphony is also responsible for the alternation in root vowels which distinguishes first and third person singular forms in irregular preterits: *fiz* (1 sg. *fazer*) < FECI vs *fez* < FECIT. The high vowel of the first person singular form was analogically extended to the whole preterit stem paradigm: *fizemos* (OPort. *fezemos*), *fizera* (pluperfect, OPort. *fezera*), obliterating its metaphonic origin.

4 Syntax

Word Order

The basic word order of Portuguese simplex sentences is subject–verb–object (SVO): *o gato comeu a galinha* 'the cat ate the hen'. This pattern represents the unmarked order rather than the norm: divergences from it are nearly always grammatically or stylistically marked.

Like Spanish, Portuguese displays many of the features which characterise VO languages: objects, complements and adverbs almost always
follow the verb; relative clauses, genitives, attributive phrases and (with
more exceptions) adjectives follow their head noun; auxiliaries precede the
lexical stem; and quantifiers and negatives precede the element they
qualify.

The order of subject and verb is mainly determined by functional considerations. The theme (or topic) of the sentence, usually 'old' or given
information, is placed before the rheme (or comment). This accounts not
only for the predominance of SV orders (themes being usually grammatical
subjects) but also for many of the cases where VS is the unmarked order.
These include intransitive verbs, especially those of temporal or locative
content, e.g. *chegou o domingo* 'Sunday came', *apareceu um homem no
jardim* 'a man appeared in the garden'; reflexives, *libertaram-se os escravos*
'the slaves freed themselves' (or 'the slaves were freed'); and sentences with
heavy subject phrases, *entraram dois homens gordos e um rapaz loiro*, 'two
fat men and a fair-haired boy came in'. It also explains the obligatory post-
position of the noun phrase in sentences with the existential *haver* (*há um
senhor aqui* 'there is a gentleman here', *houve uma reunião* 'a meeting took
place') where it could be said that there is no theme as such. (It is in any
event questionable whether the single nominal argument of *haver* is its subject. The existential does not agree in number with the noun; the pronominal counterpart of the noun is an object pronoun, e.g. *há caracóis? —
não os há* 'are there any snails? — there aren't any'.)

Noun phrases may be dislocated for thematic prominence, though
objects cannot usually be preposed without a pronoun copy and intonation
break, as illustrated by the possible modifications of our initial SVO
sentence: *comeu a galinha, o gato* (VOS), 'THE CAT ate the hen', *a galinha,
o gato comeu-a* (OSVpron.), *a galinha, comeu-a o gato* (OVpron.S), 'the
hen, the cat ate'. In informal speech there are numerous ways of giving an
NP prominence without disturbing SVO order. These involve periphrases
incorporating *é que*, cleft and pseudocleft constructions: *o gato é que
comeu a galinha, foi o gato que comeu a galinha, o que comeu a galinha foi
o gato* all give prominence to the subject *o gato*; *foi a galinha que o gato
comeu*; *o que o gato comeu foi a galinha* and the elliptical pseudocleft *o
gato comeu foi a galinha* give prominence to the object *a galinha*.

No doubt as a result of the functional value of VS orders, interrogation
does not rely heavily on word order. Subject–verb inversion was apparently
the main marker of polar interrogatives in Old Portuguese (e.g. *queredes
vos seer cavaleiro?* 'do you wish to be a knight?') but modern European
and Brazilian Portuguese, like French (p. 237), prefer constructions which
retain SV(O) order. In speech polar questions can be identified entirely by
rising intonation (*o seu pai está aqui?*); or more explicitly by tag question

(*o seu pai está aqui, não é?* 'your father is here, isn't he?'); or by means of *é que*: *é que o seu pai está aqui?* (cf. French *est-ce-que*). In non-polar questions inversion is the rule in European Portuguese after non-pronominal interrogatives: *quando morreu o seu pai?* literally 'when died your father'; *onde mora você?* 'where live you?', where Brazilian Portuguese has *quando seu pai morreu?*, *onde você mora?*. SVO order can be preserved in European Portuguese by use of the *é que* periphrasis: *quando é que o seu pai morreu?*. As the interrogative pronouns *quem* 'who(m)', *o que* 'what' have no case marking, inversion is avoided and the *é que* form used in object interrogation, again as with Fr. *est-ce que*: *o que* (*é que*) *matou a galinha?* 'what killed the hen?'; *o que é que o gato matou?* 'what did the cat kill?'. Replies to yes-no questions take the form of an echo of the main verb: (*você*) *tem lume?* — *tenho* (*sim*)/*não tenho*, 'do you have a light' — '(yes) I have'/'no I have not' (the appropriate response to an *é que* question being *é* or *não é*).

The principal means of negation is the negative particle *não* < *nõ* < NON, inserted before the auxiliary or verb, although spoken Brazilian Portuguese often postposes *não*, instead of or in addition to preposed *não*. Multiple negation occurs with additional negative elements following the verb: *não veio ninguém* 'nobody came'; *não fiz nada* 'I did nothing'. Where a negative pronoun precedes the verb, as subject or preposed object, no further negative particle is needed; *ninguém veio, nada fiz*. The indefinite *algum* 'some' may be used as an emphatic negative, *não vi homem algum*, 'I didn't see any man whatsoever', compared with *não vi nenhum homem* 'I didn't see any man'. The pronoun *nada* (< (REM) NATAM literally 'a born thing') is following the same course as French *pas*: having become a negative by association with *não*, it is now losing its pronominal status: *não gostei nada da comida* 'I didn't like the food at all'.

Weak object pronouns are usually enclitic to the verb in European Portuguese and proclitic in Brazilian Portuguese: *o pai deu-me um bolo* (EP), *o pai me deu um bolo* (BP) 'father gave me a cake'. In written Brazilian Portuguese, as in European Portuguese, sentence-initial clitics are excluded, but this does not hold for spoken Brazilian Portuguese. In both varieties the clitic will invariably precede the verb if any item except a lexical subject NP precedes; negatives, subordinating conjunctions (notably *que*), relative pronouns, interrogative pronouns and (in literary language) preposed adverbs, all require clitics to precede the verb, e.g. *não me deu o bolo* (*não deu-me o bolo*) 'he did not give me the cake', *se me der o bolo* 'if he gives (fut. subj.) me the cake', *quero que me dê o bolo* 'I want him to give me the cake', *quando lhe deram o bolo?* 'when did they give him the cake?', *sempre o amava bem* '(s)he always loved him dearly'. Interestingly, in contexts where the object is linguistically or pragmatically recoverable, Portuguese, especially Brazilian, tolerates, as did Latin, the total omission of direct object pronouns, e.g. *me dá* (EP *dá-mo*) 'give it to me', *eu vi ontem na*

TV 'I saw (it/them) on TV yesterday', *é preciso levar gasolina — eu levo* 'someone has to get petrol — I'll get it', a characteristic shared by no other contemporary Romance language (cf. p. 59). Clitic-climbing from embedded sentences is optional: in Brazilian Portuguese the pronoun is proclitic either to the infinitive, *o médico quer me examinar* or, in more literary style, to the matrix verb, *o médico me quer examinar*, 'the doctor wants to examine me'; in European Portuguese it is enclitic, *o médico quer-me examinar, o médico quer examinar-me.*

The Nominal Group
Determiners (articles and demonstratives), possessives and quantifiers typically precede the noun, while postnominal position is the norm for adjectives, *todos estes livros novos* 'all these new books'. Prenominal possessives combine with definite determiners, e.g. *o meu carro* 'my car', *estes nossos livros* 'these books of ours', and, at least in spoken Brazilian Portuguese, with the indefinite article *?um meu livro.* The possessive may occur without the definite article when denoting family relationships, *meu filho* 'my son', especially as forms of address; in Brazilian Portuguese omission of the article is more general. As in Spanish and Italian, prenominal adjectives are semantically distinct from their apparent postnominal counterparts, and in some cases should be considered distinct lexical items, e.g. *uma simples bebida* 'just a drink' vs *uma bebida simples* 'a single (vs double) drink'; *o maior escritor* 'the greatest writer' vs *o irmão maior* 'elder brother'; *um grande livro* 'a great book' vs *um livro grande* 'a big book'. Even where there is no lexical difference, preposed adjectives have a much reduced qualifying function, notably in literary epithets, *a branca neve* 'the white snow', *a fiel Penelope* 'faithful Penelope'; conversely, postposed possessives, *um livro meu* 'a book of mine' (in many varieties the only permissible combination of possessive and indefinite article), *notícias tuas* 'news of you' give prominence to the relation of possession or origin, with concomitant reduction of their deictic value. A different construction preposes adjectives for thematic purposes, *o coitado do rapaz* 'the poor boy' (cf. French, pp. 227–8).

The basic distinction between definite and indefinite articles is, as in English, a question of definiteness of reference. In European Portuguese the zero article occurs only in plural object and postposed subject NPs, as an indefinite: *vi homens na praia* 'I saw men on the beach', *alugam-se quartos* 'rooms to let', or a generic *gosto de mulheres brasileiras* 'I like Brazilian women'. In Brazilian Portuguese, especially in informal styles, the zero article can indicate generic reference in other types of NP (singular objects, singular and plural subjects): *gosto de mulher brasileira* 'I like Brazilian women', *mulher brasileira canta bem, mulheres brasileiras cantam bem* 'Brazilian women sing well', in contrast with European Portuguese usage which requires the definite article *as mulheres brasileiras cantam bem, a mulher brasileira canta bem.* The plural indefinite article has connotations of paucal number, especially when it contrasts with the zero article: *foi brincar com (uns) amigos* 'he went to play with (a few) friends'. This is distinct from its deictic (usually pronominal) use: *uns (gatos) comiam, outros dormiam* 'some (cats) ate, others slept'.

Number and gender are marked concordially on all NP constituents, except in basilectal and colloquial Brazilian Portuguese, where number marking can be restricted to the initial prenominal constituent *muitas garota bonita* 'many pretty girls', *os meu velho amigo* 'my old friends', and absent altogether in predicative adjectives, *os engenheiro são alemão* (vs standard Brazilian Portuguese *os engenheiros são alemães*) 'the engineers are German' (cf. French, p. 226).

The infinitive (personal and impersonal) functions as verbal noun in nominalisations, often marked with the definite article: *lamentou terem os amigos saido* 'he regretted that the friends had gone out', *lamentou o eles terem saido* 'he regretted their having gone out'. As in Spanish, the so-called gerund (*saindo, tendo saido*) has no nominal functions, but is used as an active participle, *sairam rindo* 'they went out laughing', or as a non-finite verb form in elliptical adverbial phrases *saindo, encontraram uns amigos* 'as they were leaving they met some friends', as well as forming part of numerous verbal periphrases (p. 162).

Verbal Syntax

Subject pronouns are duplicated by verb inflection (except in basilectal Brazilian Portuguese where there is a tendency for third person singular forms to be used for all persons) and are frequently omitted, especially in the unambiguous first and second person forms. Third person forms are more ambiguous. The use of third person grammatical forms as the main form of address restricts the omission of pronouns to clear cases of anaphora or address. Otherwise, subjectless third person verbs are interpreted as having indefinite subjects: *é horrivel* 'it is terrible', *dizem que é proibido* 'they (people) say that it is forbidden'.

The extensive set of verb forms outlined in section 3 is rarely utilised in spoken forms of Portuguese, with the morphologically anomalous future and conditional forms (p. 150) the main casualties. The present indicative has a wide range of uses: it is very frequently used in place of the future, e.g. *se tiver* (fut. subj.) *tempo, falo* (pres. ind.) *com você* 'if I have time I will talk with you', as well as being used as a narrative tense, e.g. *(ele) entra, fecha a porta e dispara,* 'he comes in, closes the door and fires'. By contrast, present tense reference is made explicit by the use of the present continuous forms, especially in Brazilian Portuguese. The imperfect indicative is frequently used in place of the conditional in temporal and modal functions: *eu disse que vinha* (imperf.) vs *eu disse que viria* (conditional) 'I said I would come', *eu queria* (imperf.)/*querria* (cond.) *pedir um favor* 'I would like to ask a favour'. The most common explicit future form is the periphrasis using *ir*, e.g. *vou continuar* 'I will (literally, am going to) continue' which provides an analytic future-in-the-past for the temporal functions of the conditional: *eu disse que ia vir* 'I said I would (literally, was going to) come'.

Reflexive pronouns have a wide range of functions. As well as indicating identity of subject and object (reflexivity *sensu stricto*) and reciprocity of subject and object relations, they occur in three other contexts. A large number of verbs are lexically specified as reflexives without any necessary semantic connotations (e.g. *arrepentir-se*, *ir-se*) traditionally labelled intrinsic reflexives. Reflexive verb forms are widely used with passive force, leading to considerable indeterminacy between reflexive and reflexive passive interpretations. When the subject is inanimate (*abriram-se as portas* 'the doors were opened'), a passive reading is the only possible one; when it is animate, a reflexive/reciprocal reading is preferred except when this would be semantically anomalous (compare *mataram-se os candidatos* 'the candidates killed themselves/each other', *fuzilaram-se os prisioneiros* 'the prisoners were shot by firing-squad'). An additional function of third person singular reflexives (traditionally referred to as 'indeterminate *se*') is to indicate indeterminate animate subjects (cf. *se* in Spanish and Italian, *on* in French). Indeterminate *se* is formally distinct from the reflexives in that it only occurs with singular verbs, regardless of the number of the noun, and occurs in intransitive and passive constructions where reflexives are impossible: *aluga-se quartos* 'rooms to let' (i.e. there is someone (here) who lets rooms), *é-se tentado pelo diabo* 'one is tempted by the devil', *gosta-se da praia* 'one likes the beach', *se se estava sorteado, servia-se* 'if you were called up (to the army), you served', *dá-se livros a si mesmo* 'one gives books to oneself'. Many varieties of Brazilian Portuguese systematically avoid reflexives, with the result that the set of verbs taking intrinsic *se* is drastically reduced, and subjectless third person singular verbs are interpreted as indefinites, in the same way as subjectless third person plural forms, e.g. *aqui (se) come bem = aqui comem bem* 'you (people) eat well here'.

Portuguese, like Spanish, boasts two verbs with copular functions, *ser* derived from a blend of SEDERE (OPort. *seer*) and ESSERE, and *estar* (< STARE, cf. p. 102). (Both verbs also function as auxiliaries, as described below.) The distinction between them is primarily one of aspect. *Ser* is used in non-progressive expressions and *estar* in progressive expressions (consistent with its use as an auxiliary). The traditional characterisation of *ser* as denoting inherent or permanent qualities, and *estar* as denoting non-inherent qualities follows from this. In the majority of cases the choice of verb is conditioned rather than contrastive: *o João é bombeiro* 'João is (ser) a fireman', *o Pedro está zangado* 'Pedro is (estar) angry'; *o João é um desempregado habitual* 'João is permanently unemployed', *o Pedro está* *desempregado* 'Pedro is unemployed'; *o João é esquisito* 'João is an awkward person', *o Pedro está (sendo) esquisito (hoje)* 'Pedro is (being) awkward (today)'. The aspectually neutral verb *ficar* 'to be, become' is often used in locative expressions (where Portuguese otherwise tends to prefer *ser* to *estar*, e.g. *Lisboa é/fica/?está em Portugal* 'Lisbon is in Portugal') and with adjectives otherwise requiring *estar*: *fiquei doido* 'I was crazy'. In this last use it retains some of its original permansive and resultative connotations, which are preserved in its use as a full intransitive verb, e.g. *eu vou ficar em casa* 'I will stay at home'. *Ficar* derives ultimately from *FIGICARE 'to fix', the original transitive meaning being preserved by *fincar* (cf. Sp. *hincar*).

Analytic past tenses are formed with the auxiliaries *ter* and *haver* (OPort. *aver*), the latter being now only used in literary forms of the language. In Old Portuguese both verbs were used with adjectival past participles which agreed with the noun object: *eles tiinham as azes paradas* 'they had their battle-lines made ready', *huũs arcos que eles aviam derrubados* 'some arches which they had knocked down'. The two verbs were differentiated to some extent semantically (*ter* 'to possess', *aver* 'to acquire'), but were often in free variation. The clear emergence of these verbs as auxiliaries dates from the fifteenth century, when they began to be used intransitively and with non-agreeing past participles. *Ser* was used in Old Portuguese to form analytic past tenses with a small number of intransitive verbs (*chegar* 'to arrive', *partir* 'to depart') but this construction was lost earlier and more completely than in the rest of Western Romance. As in Spanish, there is a large number of 'semi-auxiliary' verbs which pattern syntactically like auxiliaries, while retaining some of their own semantic features in verbal periphrases expressing temporal, modal and aspectual values. Progressive aspect is represented by *estar* (and the verbs of motion — *andar* literally 'to walk', *ir* 'to go', *vir* 'to come') combined with the present participle (BP) or *a* + infinitive (EP), *estou trabalhando* (BP), *estou a esperar* (EP) 'I am working'; the future tense by *ir* + infinitive; predictive and obligative mood by *haver de* + infinitive, *eu hei de matá-lo* 'I will surely kill him', and *ter que* + infinitive, *tenho que matá-lo* 'I must kill him'.

Ser functions as the main auxiliary for the passive construction, *a casa foi construída por J. Pimenta,* 'the house was built by J. Pimenta'. As in Spanish, *estar* and a range of semi-auxiliaries including *ficar, ir, vir*, can be used in 'stative' passive constructions with past participle and agent clause: *a casa esteve cercada ontem pelos soldados* 'yesterday the house was surrounded by the soldiers', refers to a past state, compared with *a casa foi cercada ontem pelos soldados* 'the house was surrounded by the soldiers yesterday', referring to a past event, and possibly to the present state. Where verbs have two forms of the past participle, e.g. *prendido, preso* from the verb *prender* 'to arrest', there is a tendency (by no means absolute) for the strong form to be used in passive constructions while the weak form is used in analytic past tenses, e.g. *o Pedro foi preso ontem* 'Pedro was arrested yesterday', *tinham prendido o Pedro na véspera* 'they had arrested Pedro the day before'.

The only modal contrast not expressed by auxiliaries is the distinction between indicative and subjunctive. The problem of the 'meaning' of the subjunctive is the familiar one of interpreting a formal category whose use is nearly always determined by context. There is rarely any direct contrast between subjunctive and indicative forms. In main clauses, subjunctives are only in direct contrast with indicatives when they represent the imperative: *venha cedo* 'come soon' (the normal imperative for Brazilian Portuguese dialects lacking morphological second person forms), *(que) o ceu te proteja* (pres. subj.) 'may Heaven protect you', otherwise the modality is marked adverbially: *oxalá venha* (pres. subj.) *cedo* 'may he come soon', *talvez venha amanhã* 'perhaps he will come tomorrow'. In these cases the verbal mood is clearly subordinate to the adverb: when *talvez* follows the main verb, the subjunctive is not used: *virá* (fut. ind.) *talvez amanhã*.

The subjunctive is, however, primarily a form associated with subordinate clauses. It is required in all subordinate clauses which refer to states or events so as to deny, or at least not to affirm, their existence. These include expressions of volition, *quero que venha* 'I want him to come', *mando que venha* 'I order him to come'; probability and necessity, *é provável que venha* 'it is probable that he (will) come', *é preciso que venha* 'it is necessary for him to come'; potential and counterfactual conditional sentences, *se vier* (fut. subj.) *não nos encontrará* 'if he comes he will not find us', *se viesse* (imperf. subj.) *não nos encontraria* (cond.) 'if he came he would not find us'; and adverbial clauses of future or non-temporal reference, *quando vier, não nos encontrará* 'when he comes, he will not find us', *vamos embora, para que não nos encontrem/antes que nos encontrem* 'let's go so that they do not find us/before they find us'. The subjunctive is used even when the truth of the proposition is presupposed rather than asserted, e.g. *lamento que sejam incomodados,* 'I am sorry that you are (should be) inconvenienced', *não me aflige que os meus filhos bebam vodka* 'I am not upset that my children drink (should drink) vodka'; or when it is asserted elsewhere in the sentence, *eu sei que os meus filhos bebem vodka, mas não me aflige que o façam* 'I know that my children drink vodka, but it doesn't upset me (that they do)'.

The subjunctive and indicative only contrast when the context is indeterminate or ambiguous as regards assertion or non-assertion, and it is left to the verb modality to express doubt or certainty. Typical examples are found with ambiguous main verbs such as *dizer* interpreted as 'to say' with the indicative, *diz que eu trabalho bem* 'he says that I work well' and as a verb of command when followed by the subjunctive, *diz que eu trabalhe bem* 'he tells me to work well'; the conjunction *quando* with habitual reference, *quando o vejo, fujo* 'whenever I see him, I run', or future reference *quando o vier* (fut. subj.), *fujo* 'when I see him I will run'; and when the main clause directly questions the proposition, and the modality of the verb expresses the questioner's expectations, e.g. *você crê que virá?* (future), *você crê que venha?* (pres. subj.) 'do you believe he will come?'. A more complex contrast is found in relative clauses with a definite but unspecified antecedent. All the following sentences can be translated as 'I am looking for a woman who has money': the use of the future subjunctive, *procuro a mulher que tiver dinheiro*, implies that the woman sought exists but has not been identified, as opposed to the indicative, *procuro a mulher que tem dinheiro*, which indicates that she is identified, and the combination of indefinite article and present subjunctive, *procuro uma mulher que tenha dinheiro*, which does not assert her existence.

In practice, Portuguese makes extensive use of non-finite verb forms in such contexts, using the infinitive, and especially the personal infinitive, to circumvent problems of tense/mood selection. Many of the earlier examples of subjunctives in subordinate clauses can be recast using the personal infinitive: *não me aflige os meninos beberem vodka*; *vamos embora, antes de nos encontrarem*; *lamento serem incomodados*. Where the infinitive has an overt subject, both personal and impersonal infinitives are found, e.g. *vi os rapazes fazer* (inf.)/*fazerem* (pers. inf.) *comida*, 'I saw the boys prepare food', except when the subject is a raised clitic *ela nos mandou calar* (inf.) 'she told us to be quiet'. Use of the personal infinitive characterises high-prestige varieties, at least in Brazilian Portuguese, so that hypercorrect forms often appear as a marker of linguistic insecurity: ?*ela nos mandou calarmos* (pers. inf.).

Portuguese retains the future subjunctive form which Spanish has all but discarded. It is used in temporal or conditional clauses when the main verb has future reference (not necessarily expressed by the future tense): *quando vier o pai, teremos comida* (future)/*avisa-me* (imperative)/*vou-me embora* (present) 'when Father comes we will have some food/tell me/I'll go away'. It has no intrinsic temporal value (futurity always being expressed in the main verb) and is rarely in contrast with the present subjunctive: the difference between them, as illustrated above, is that the future subjunctive refers to predicted but unrealised events or states, while the present subjunctive implies greater uncertainty. Unlike the formally identical personal infinitive, the future subjunctive is consistently used in all registers, and in some is used to the exclusion of the present indicative as the only non-past verb form following *se* and *quando*.

5 Lexis

The bulk of the Portuguese lexicon is predictably of Latin origin, either directly transmitted through Hispanic Latin or borrowed from ecclesiastical or literary Latin at a later date. Of the 2,217 entries in the European Portuguese *Português Fundamental*, over 90 per cent are of Latin origin. (Terms found in the *Português Fundamental* are identified by + in this section.) Pre-Romance and Germanic vocabulary generally entered through Latin, as in the case of +*camisa* (< CAMISIA, probably of Celtic origin) 'shirt', found also in French and Italian. Not surprisingly, most such terms are common to Portuguese and at least Castilian: *barro* 'mud', +*cama* 'bed', +*manteiga* 'butter' are Pre-Romance terms shared with Castilian; +*guerra* 'war', +*guardar* 'guard', +*roubar* 'steal', +*branco* 'white' are common Germanic items. Portuguese has its share, perhaps smaller than Castilian, of the Arabic vocabulary left by the Arabic domination of the Iberian Peninsula (p. 6). French and Provençal terms were borrowed into Old Portuguese in the wake of cultural contacts with French monasticism (encouraged by the Burgundians of the first royal dynasty) and Provençal literature. Castilian borrowings were prevalent at times of political *rapprochement*, notably in the thirteenth century and during the Spanish hegemony of 1580–1640. The voyages of discovery of the fifteenth and sixteenth centuries led to intense contacts with African, Asian and Oriental cultures and languages, though many terms borrowed in this way remain exoticisms. Even in Brazilian, which is commonly believed to have a strong African element in its vocabulary, African terms are usually linked to Afro-Brazilian culture, and constitute a separate register rather than supplanting European terms. In modern times French and English (especially American English, for Brazilian) have been the dominant lexical influences.

The Latin element in Portuguese is largely common to the group of Hispanic Romance languages. This includes examples of lexical conservatism such as +*falar* < FABULARE; +*queijo* < CASEUM; +*querer* < QUAERERE; +*medo* < METUM; +*verão* < VERANUM (common to other conservative forms of Romance) and +*coração* < CORATIONEM; +*almoço* < *ADMORDIUM is peculiar to Ibero-Romance. The smaller body of words peculiar to Galician-Portuguese includes *adro* < ATRIUM 'square', *abegão* < ABIGONEM 'herdsman'.

Borrowings from ecclesiastical Latin are present from the earliest records, and account for the many 'semi-learned' forms which are unaffected, or only partly affected, by early sound changes, such as *cruz*, +*bispo*, *virgen*, +*missa* (characterised by the retention of /i u/ for CLat. /ī ū/) + *igreja* < ECCLESIAM (with no palatalisation of /kl/), and + *escola* < SCOLAM (with retention of intervocalic /l/). The names of the days of the week preserve the old Judeo-Christian framework, Portuguese being the only Romance language to reward the early church's efforts to oust pagan day-names: after +*domingo* 'Sunday', first day of the week, come the weekdays numbered two to six: +*segunda-feira* (< FERIAM SECUNDAM) 'Monday', +*terça-feira* 'Tuesday', +*quarta-feira* 'Wednesday', +*quinta-feira* 'Thursday', +*sexta-feira* 'Friday' until +*sábado* 'Saturday' ushers in the weekend. (The weekdays are often reduced to their number, *chegará na quinta* 'he will arrive on Thursday'.)

More conscious latinising by the learned prose-writers of the fifteenth and sixteenth centuries brought a spate of neologisms (often characterised by antepenultimate stress and obstruent clusters), which often supplanted popular terms, e.g. *martírio* for *marteiro*; *obter* for *gaançar*. In derivational morphology, Portuguese has many learned derived forms related to popular simple roots: +*mão* – *manual*; +*céu* – *celeste*; +*cor* – +*colorido*; +*ouro* – *áureo*. The same Latin etymon can thus surface in several different phonetic and semantic guises; ARTICULUM was the source for *artelho* (OPort.) 'ankle', +*artigo* (< *artigoo*) 'article' and *articulo* 'joint'; the agentive suffix -ARIUM appears as popular -*eiro*, semi-learned -*airo* and learned -*ário*.

The number of Arabic terms in Portuguese is estimated as somewhat over 1,000. Arabic borrowings are concentrated in areas such as agriculture (+*alface* 'lettuce', +*arroz* 'rice', +*laranja* 'orange'), administration (+*bairro* 'quarter', +*aldeia* 'village') and commerce (+*armazém* 'warehouse, store', +*loja* 'shop' +*alfândega* 'customs'). Many terms of medieval science and warfare were of Arabic origin.

The African element is strong in Brazilian Portuguese in those areas of popular culture and belief with strong African roots: *macumba* 'voodoo ritual', the musical terms *samba, marimba, batuque* 'rhythmic dance (literally, hammering)', and *moleque* 'lad' are common Brazilian Portuguese terms, and *cachimbo* 'pipe' has passed into common European Portuguese usage.

Tupi contributes a large vocabulary of Brazilian Portuguese flora and fauna: *acajú* 'mahogany', *maracujá* 'passion-fruit', *piranha* 'piranha fish'.

Contacts with the Far East contributed +*chá* 'tea' (borrowed from Mandarin: English *tea* is the Fujiang form); *mandarim* 'Mandarin' from Malay *mantri* contaminated by Port. *mandar* 'to order'.

Early Provençal borrowings include *afan* 'desire' (one of the few words to escape the change of final -*ã* to -*ão*); *segre* 'world' (supplanted by the fifteenth-century coining +*século* 'century'); *monge* 'monk' (replacing OPort. *mogo* (*moogo, meogo*) < MONACHUM); *freire* 'friar'; +*chapéu* (< *chapel*) 'hat'. Modern gallicisms are often distinguished by irregular stress or lack of regular gender marking: +*bidé* 'bidet', +*guiché* 'ticket window', +*duche* 'shower', +*greve* 'strike', +*cabine* '(telephone) booth', +*equipe* 'team', (the latter words having gender-transparent alternative forms +*cabina*, +*equipa*). Italian contributed literary and musical terms *soneto, arpejo*, and some navigational vocabulary, e.g. *bússola* 'compass'. English and American terms show the same lack of assimilation as their French counterparts. Many sporting terms are borrowed, e.g. +*futebol* 'football', +*golo* 'goal', +*ráguebi* 'rugby', +*ténis* (BP *tênis*) 'tennis', with other cultural imports: +*bife* 'steak (any meat)', +*sandes* 'sandwich', occasionally +*sanduiche,* +*lanche* 'snack'; +*pulôver,* +*filme* replacing earlier *fita* 'film' literally, 'ribbon'.

Modern Portuguese makes extensive use of derivational suffixes for lexical expansion. As well as the common stock of noun- and verb-forming suffixes derived and borrowed from Latin (e.g. -*izar* (verb-forming), -*eiro,* (-*airo,* -*ário*), -*ano,* -*ão* (< -ANUM and < -ANEM), -*ismo,* -*ista* (noun-forming), -*ção* (-TIONEM) (nominalising)), there is a large stock of pro-ductive and semi-productive suffixes with semantic (rather than grammatical) content, frequently involving emotive as well as referential meaning. Prominent among these are diminutive and augmentative suf-fixes. The most productive diminutives are -(*z*)*inho* (feminine -(*z*)*inha*) and -(*z*)*ito* (-(*z*)*ita*): *pedra* 'stone', *pedrinha* 'pebble', *pedrazinha* 'small stone'; *casa* 'house', *casita* 'little house'. These diminutives have con-notations of endearment or disparagement (according to situational con-text) which become prominent when they are applied to humans: *mulher* 'woman', *mulherinha* 'scheming woman'; *avó* 'grandmother', *avózinha* '(dear old) granny'; and especially when used to modify adverbs or inter-jections: *adeus* 'goodbye', *adeusinho* 'bye-bye' (familiar); *devagar* 'slowly', *devagarinho* 'little by little'. Augmentative suffixes have strong pejorative overtones: *mulher* 'woman', *mulherona* 'stout woman'.

A further set of suffixes has a very wide range of meanings (including augmentatives, collectives and instrumentals), such that the suffix can only be taken as signalling the morphological link between the derived form and the base, while the precise meaning of the word is an independent lexical unit: the suffix -*ada* is identifiable in *palmada* 'slap' (*palma* 'palm of hand'); *colherada* 'spoonful' (*colher* 'spoon'); *rapaziada* '(gang of) kids' (*rapaz* 'boy'); *marmelada* 'quince conserve'(source of English *marmelade*) from *marmelo* 'quince'; *noitada* 'night out' (*noite* 'night').

In those suffixes with alternative forms incorporating the augment -*z*- (e.g. -(*z*)*inho*), the unaugmented variant functions as an internal suffix, forming a complex stem which is stressed like simple forms, while the aug-mented suffix functions as an external suffix, forming compounds in which the base and the suffix both have gender and number markers (the latter being overt only when plural number is realised by stem mutations as well as suffixes, e.g. *pãozinho* 'roll', plural *pãezinhos*) and are both stressed. A similar structure is found in the adverbs formed with -*mente*, e.g. *novamente* [nɔvɐ'mẽtə] 'recently, newly', where the suffix is affixed to the feminine form of the adjective *novo* 'new' and the base vowel quality is preserved. The augmented suffixes thus give a morphological transparency, which is matched by a semantic transparency: forms incorporating internal suffixes are more likely to have unpredictably restricted meanings, e.g. *folha* 'leaf, sheet of paper', *folhazinha* 'small leaf', *folhinha* 'calendar'.

6 Conclusion

The processes of convergence and divergence inside the Portuguese-speaking world are still working themselves out. While European and Brazilian varieties are drawing closer together, partly through the realisation that Brazilian norms need not be opposed to Portuguese ones, partly through the influence of Brazilian television on Portugal, the former Portuguese colonies in Africa are looking for linguistic independence in the recognition of local standards. Portuguese can nevertheless claim 'unity in diversity' (*unidade na diversidade*) and as such can only increase in prominence as a major world language.

Bibliography

Azevedo, M.M. (1981) *Passive Sentences in English and Portuguese*. Georgetown University Press, Washington DC.

Barbosa, J. Morais (1983) *Études de phonologie portugaise* 2nd edn. University of Évora, Évora.

Bortoni-Ricardo, S. (1985) *The Urbanization of Rural Dialect Speakers. A Sociolinguistic Study in Brazil*. Cambridge University Press, Cambridge.

Câmara, J. Mattoso (1972) *The Portuguese Language*, translated A.J. Naro. University of Chicago Press, Chicago.

Carvalho, J.G. Herculano de (1964–84) *Estudos linguísticos*. Vol. 1, Verbo, Lisbon, 1964; vol. 2, Almedina, Coimbra, 1969; vol. 3, Coimbra Editora, Coimbra, 1984.

Casteleiro, J.M. (1981) *Sintaxe transformacional do adjectivo*. Instituto Nacional de Investigação Científica, Lisbon.

—— et al. (1984) *Português Fundamental. Vocabulário e Gramática*, vol. 1, *Vocabulário*. Instituto Nacional de Investigação Científica, Lisbon.

Cintra, L.F.L. (1972) *Sobre formas de tratamento na língua portuguesa*. Horizonte, Lisbon.

—— (1983) *Estudos de dialectologia portuguesa*. Sá da Costa, Lisbon.

Congresso sobre a situação actual da língua portuguesa no mundo, Actas, vol. 1. Instituto de Língua e Cultura Portuguesas, Lisbon, 1985.

Cunha, C. (1968) *Língua portuguesa e realidade brasileira*. Tempo Brasileiro, Rio de Janeiro.

—— and L.F.L. Cintra (1984) *Nova gramática do português contemporâneo*. João Sá da Costa, Lisbon.

Instituto da Lingua Galega e Real Academia Galega (1982) *Normas ortográficas e morfolóxicas do idioma galego*. Instituto da Lingua Galega, Vigo.

Kremer, D. and R. Lorenzo (1982) *Tradición, actualidade e futuro de galego. Actas do Colóquio de Tréveris*. Xunta de Galicia, Santiago de Compostella.

Lemle, M. (1984) *Análise sintática*. Ática, Rio de Janeiro.

Lopes, O. (1972) *Gramática simbólica do português*. Gulbenkian Foundation, Lisbon.

Machado, J.P. (1967) *Dicionário etimológico da língua portuguesa* 2nd edn. Confluência, Lisbon.

Mateus, M.H.M. (1982) *Aspectos da fonologia portuguesa* 2nd edn. Instituto Nacional de Investigação Científica, Lisbon.

—— et al. (1983) *Gramática da língua portuguesa*. Almedina, Coimbra.

Maurer, T. (1951) *Dois problemas da lingua portuguesa: o infinito pessoal e o pronome se.* University of São Paulo, São Paulo.
Perini, M. (1977) *Gramática do infinitivo português.* Vozes, Petrópolis.
Quicoli, A.C. (1980) *The Structure of Complementation.* Story-Scientia, Ghent.
Schmidt-Radefeld, J. (1976) *Readings in Portuguese Linguistics.* North-Holland, Amsterdam.
Silva Neto, S. (1970) *História da lingua portuguesa* 2nd edn. Livros de Portugal, Rio de Janeiro.
Teyssier, P. (1982) *História da língua portuguesa.* Sá da Costa, Lisbon.
—— (1984) *Manuel de langue portugaise (Portugal-Brésil)* 2nd edn. Klincksieck, Paris.
Thomas, E.W. (1969) *The Syntax of Spoken Brazilian Portuguese.* Vanderbilt University Press, Nashville.
Vázquez Cuesta, P. and M. Luz (1971) *Gramática portuguesa* 3rd edn. Gredos, Madrid. Portuguese translation, *Gramática da lingua portuguesa*, Edições 70, Lisbon, 1980.
Viana, A.R. Gonçalves (1973) *Estudos de fonética portuguesa.* Imprensa Nacional, Lisbon.
Williams, E.B. (1962) *From Latin to Portuguese* 2nd edn. University of Pennsylvania Press. Philadelphia.

5 Catalan

Max W. Wheeler

1 Introduction

Catalan dialects fall into two groups (pp. 12–13): Western Catalan, which consists of the dialects of western Catalonia and of Valencia, and Eastern Catalan, which includes North Catalan (spoken in France), the dialects of eastern Catalonia, Balearic and *alguerès*. The boundary between the two groups runs a little west of due south from Andorra (see Map IV). The standard language is based on the dialects of eastern Catalonia, though regional standards in Valencia and the Balearics admit alternative forms, mostly traditional ones, which are not current in eastern Catalonia. Examples given are standard Catalan (educated Barcelona pronunciation) unless otherwise specified.

2 Phonology

The phonemic system of Catalan is shown in Table 5.1, which presents a slightly abstract diasystem. The labio-velar plosives are phonetically [kw] and [gw] and have traditionally been regarded as diphonemic. The arguments for their monophonemic status are essentially distributional. The phonemic status of the prepalatal affricates is rather dubious. They generally correspond to diphonemic /tʃ/ and /dʒ/, and there is no contrast between affricate and fricative in word-initial, or in post-consonantal position. In Valencian there is no contrast at all between [ʒ] and [dʒ] (generally [dʒ]) but [ʃ] and [tʃ] show a marginal contrast word-initially (which is not reflected in standard orthography), which would support contrasted /ʃ/ and monophonemic /tʃ/ for that dialect; e.g. *Xàtiva* (place-name), *xarop* 'syrup' with /ʃ/, *Xelva* (place-name), *xiular* 'to whistle' with /tʃ/. Labio-dental /v/ is now absent from mainland dialects from Tarragona northwards, and from central Valencian. It has merged with /b/ (though underlying /v/ is still subject to different rules, see below). In central Valencian (*apitxat*) the voiced sibilants have merged with their voiceless counterparts (probably under Spanish influence). The voiced plosives have fricative or approximant allophones in many environments, and /r/ has

170

Table 5.1: Catalan Phonemes

Consonants	Labial	Dental/ alveolar	Prepalatal	Palatal	Velar	Labio-velar
Stop						
[−voice]	p	t	(tʃ)		k	(kʷ)
[+voice]	b	d	(dʒ)		g	(gʷ)
Fricative						
[−voice)	f	s	ʃ			
[+voice]	v	z	ʒ			
Nasal	m	n		ɲ		
Trill		r				
Lateral		l		ʎ		
Glide				j		w

Vowels

i		u
e	ə	o
ε	a	ɔ

both trill [r] and tap [ɾ] allophones (details below). The alveolar lateral /l/ is inclined to be velarised. Favouring environments for this are syllable codas, back vowels and preceding low vowels. The lexical incidence of /ʎ/ and /j/ differs dialectally; /ʎ/ from one source, namely Latin /l-/, /-ll-/, is realised as a lateral everywhere, but /ʎ/ from other origins has merged with /j/ in Balearic and in the central part of eastern Catalonia, though this merger is recessive in the latter region. Only Balearic has the full eight-vowel system. Items with Balearic /ə/ (< PWR /e/) in stressed syllables have /ε/ in eastern Catalonia and /e/ in Western Catalan and *alguerès*.

The maximal permitted syllable is CCVCCC (e.g. *glaucs* 'greenish grey (m. pl.)'), where C includes semi-vowels. Any single consonant can begin a syllable (though no word begins with /w/) and any single consonant can end a syllable or a word, underlyingly, at least (see below). Other onsets consist of a plosive or /f/ + an alveolar liquid, but not *tl- or *dl-, Internal codas consist of a consonant or a consonant + s: (C(s)). Final codas may add an additional consonant to this: (C(s)(C)), or may consist of two consonants + s, where the /s/ is often the plural morpheme: ((C(C(s))). Apart from /s/, which evidently plays a special role in codas, and from /tʃ/ and /dʒ/, which are realised as phonetic affricates, consonant sequences in codas are restricted to those permitted by the following sonority hierarchy, in which an interior consonant must be more sonorant: liquid – semi-vowel – nasal – fricative – plosive. There are also many limitations on consonant sequences, whether of coda + onset or within codas. For example, palatal consonants are excluded from most sequences except when /ʃ/ or /ʒ/ is preceded by a [+coronal] consonant. The only geminates found lexically are [+consonantal] sonorants, i.e. /rr/, /ll/, /ʎʎ/, /mm/, /nn/ (but not */ɲɲ/), for example, *corre* 'runs', *til.la* 'linden tea', *espatlla* 'shoulder', *setmana* 'week', *tarannà* 'character'. The medial sequences /bl/ and /gl/ seem to have two possible syllable divisions, lexically distinguished. Commonly we find /b.l/ [bbl] and /g.l/ [ggl], e.g. *poble* 'people, town', *regla* 'rule'; but there are also examples of /.bl/ [βl] and /.gl/ [ɣl], e.g. *biblia* 'bible', *ègloga* 'eclogue'. Some major phonological rules depend on syllable structure. There are two which do so exclusively. A rule turns /v/ into /w/ in syllable codas, e.g. *bevem* 'we drink' ~ *beure* 'to drink'. Another neutralises voicing in coda obstruents, e.g. *llarga* (f. sg.) ~ *llargs* [ʎarks] (m. pl.) 'long', *anglesa* [əŋglɛzə] (f.) ~ *anglès* [əŋglɛs] (m.) 'English', *trobada* (f.) ~ *trobat* (m.) 'found'. The realisation of voice in coda obstruents is determined by the phonetic context (see below, p. 175).

Historical Phonology
Catalan participates in many of the sound changes common to Western Romance, with occasional differences of detail, for example, the development of a seven vowel tonic system, syncope, lenition, and palatalisation (of velars before front vowels and of non-labials before /j/). Among the consonant changes typical of Catalan can be mentioned: /l-/ > /ʎ/, e.g. LŪPUM > *llop* 'wolf', LĒGĔRE > *llegir* 'to read'. Initial /l-/ is here treated like geminate /-ll-/; note the parallelism with the obstruent stops and /r/. The change of /-mb-/ > /-m-/, e.g. *CAMBAM > *cama* 'leg', is shared with Spanish and Gascon, while that of /-nd-/ > /-n-/, e.g. MANDĀRE > *manar* 'to order', is shared with Gascon. A set of typical changes which involve neutralisation in syllable codas is displayed in the chart given here. Also typical of Catalan is the loss of /-n/ in post-vocalic, absolute word-final position, e.g. TĒNET > *té* 'has', MŎLĪNUM > *molí* 'mill' (but pl. *molins*), IŬVĔNEM > *jove* 'young'.

There are some distinctive vowel changes showing the raising effect of a following /j/ from various sources: /ɛ/ regularly becomes /i/, for example, FĒRĬAM > *fira* 'fair', LĔCTUM > *llit* 'bed', ĔXIT > *ix* 'goes out'. Similarly, /ɔ/ becomes /u/ in this environment, e.g. FŎLĬAM > *fulla* 'leaf', CŎLLĬGIT > *cull* 'picks', ŎCŬLUM > *ull* 'eye'. Diphthongisation, as in Occitan (pp. 247–8), is a likely intermediate stage in these changes. Apparently similar is /a/ > /e/ before /j/, e.g. ĀRĔAM > *era* 'threshing floor', AXEM > *eix* 'axle', but numerous exceptions here, such as PĂLĔAM > *palla* 'straw', show that the details are much more complicated. Several changes affecting mid front vowels have profoundly upset the pattern of lexical incidence of /e/ and /ɛ/ inherited from Latin. The changes can be

Some Typical Catalan Consonant Changes

Lat. cons.	Internal onset /V_V	Coda /V_C, /V_#	
v	v	w	e.g. NǑVAM > nova, NǑVUM > nou 'new'
g	g	w	e.g. LĪGAT > lliga 'ties', IŪGUM > jou 'yoke'
d	∅	w	e.g. PĒDŬCŬLUM > poll 'louse', PĒDEM > peu 'foot'
tj	∅	w	e.g. RĂTĬŌNEM > raó 'reason', PŪTĔUM > pou 'well'
c	∅	w	e.g. RĔCĬPĔRE > rebre 'to receive', DĪCIT > diu 'says'

([c] = Lat. /k/ before i, e)

summarised as follows: (1) /ɛ/ > /e/ except before Proto-Catalan /ð/ in codas; (2) /e/ > /ɛ/ before /l/, before /r/ followed by a coronal consonant, or before /n'r/; (3) /e/ > /ə/ except as in (2); (4) /ə/ > /ɛ/. Of these changes, (1) and (2) are pan-Catalan and in themselves would almost have resulted in phonemic merger, but for a few cases such as DĔCEM > */dɛð/ > deu 'ten' vs DĔUM > déu 'god'. Eastern Catalan as a whole is characterised by having undergone (3), which has diverted many cases of potential merger of /e/ and /ɛ/; (4), which affects the output of (3), is characteristic of North Catalan and eastern Catalonia, and recently some of Balearic. Many neologisms have increased the incidence of /ɛ/, which was rare in Western Catalan as a result of the previous changes. Examples of (1): TĔMPUS > temps /tems/ 'time', HĔRBAM > herba /ɛrba/ 'grass', but PRĔTĬUM > */prɛð/ > preu 'price'. Examples of (2): VĒLAM > vela /vɛla/ 'sail', VĬRĬDEM > verd /vɛrd/ 'green', CĬNĔREM > cendra /sɛndra/ 'ash'. Examples of (3) without (4), in Balearic: CATĒNAM > [kəðənə] 'chain', STRĬCTUM > [əstrət] 'narrow', giving, with (4) on the eastern mainland, [kəðɛnə], [əstrɛt]. In its atonic vocalism Catalan shares with Gallo-Romanic the loss of Lat. post-tonic /e/ and /o/ (examples passim), but is distinctive in its change of post-tonic /a/ to /e/ before a consonant, e.g. CĀSAS > cases 'houses', PAUSAS > poses 'you put', LĪGANT > lliguen 'they tie', *PŎRTÁBAMUS > portàvem 'we brought', ŎRPHĂNAM > òrfena 'orphan (f.)'.

Stress

Stress in Catalan is fairly conservative. It falls on one of the last three syllables of a word. Oxytone stress is unmarked for consonant-final words, paroxytone stress for vowel-final words. No verb stem has marked stress, which means that verb stems are never stressed further back than the final syllable. Clitics do not affect the stress position of words they are attached to — queda-te-me-la 'keep it for me' retains initial stress — but in North Catalan and Balearic the final post-verbal clitic receives stress on a second cycle (after vowel reduction), e.g. porta(-me)-la ['pɔrtə(mə)'lə] 'bring (me) it (f.)'. There are some unstressed words: the VP clitics themselves, definite determiners, *que* relative pronoun and complementiser, atonic prepositions, obsolescent possessives *mon, ton, son*, etc., and a few verb forms, namely, the perfect auxiliary *has, ha, han*, and *ets* 'are (2 sg.)', *és* 'is' in certain contexts. There are also quite a few stressed non-words, or combinable stems, for the most part either Latinate prepositional prefixes (e.g. *ex-, extra-, sobre-* 'over', *sub-, supra-*) or Greek stems (e.g. *arxi-, astro-, hètero-*). Such elements are not always treated consistently, and sometimes occur unstressed with reduced vowels.

Phonological Rules
Vowel reduction is the phenomenon in which vowel contrasts are reduced in unstressed syllables. A pan-Catalan (and arguably Proto-Romance) vowel reduction rule neutralises the contrast between half-open and half-close vowels in unstressed syllables, where only the latter are found. Eastern Catalan is affected by a more radical vowel reduction rule merging /e/, /ɛ/, /a/, (also Balearic /ə/) as [ə] in unstressed syllables (see the chart of Eastern Catalan vowel reduction). Continental Eastern Catalan likewise merges unstressed /ɔ/, /o/, and /u/ as [u]. Within Catalonia vowel reduction as in the chart is prestigious and is spreading to western Catalonia.

Eastern Catalan Vowel Reduction

té [te]	tenim [tənim] 'hold (3 sg.), (1 pl.)'
creu [krɛw]	creiem [krəjɛm] 'believe (3 sg.), (1 pl.)'
mana [manə]	manem [mənɛm] 'order (3 sg.), (1 pl.)'
posa [pɔzə]	posem [puzɛm] 'put (3 sg.), (1 pl.)'
dóna [donə]	donem [dunɛm] 'give (3 sg.), (1 pl.)'
juga [ʒuɣə]	juguem [ʒuɣɛm] 'play (3 sg.), (1 pl.)'

The phoneme /r/ is a trill in word-initial position and syllable-initially after a consonant (i.e. in strong positions), and also generally in a coda. Elsewhere a tap [ɾ] is found. Intervocalic geminate /rr/ is pronounced [r], as the preceding principles plus the rule of geminate contraction (see below) would lead one to expect. The so-called voiced plosives are in fact realised as fricatives [β], [ð], [ɣ], or approximants, in syllable onsets when preceded by a [+continuant] sound, or, in the case of [β] or [ɣ], by /l/ too, e.g. *a donar-me'l* 'to give me it', *és breu* 'is short', *cada* 'each', *el gos* 'the dog'. They are plosives elsewhere, e.g. *dóna-me'l* 'give me it', *tan breu* 'so short', *calda* 'heat', *un gos* 'a dog'.

Sandhi Phenomena
An unstressed vowel in word-initial or word-final position which is adjacent to another vowel is liable to elision or, if high, to glide formation. As within words, however, a glide does not occur between a consonant and a

vowel. For example, *sortie ₫ venure* 'to go to see', *aquest₫ illa* 'this island', *venure-hi clar* [-əj-] ~ [-i-] 'to see clearly', *ella ho sap* [-əw-] ~ [-u-] 'she knows it', *hi havia* [jə-] ~ [i-] 'there was', *ho anava a fer* [wə-] ~ [u-] 'was going to do it', *no hi va ser* [-oj-] 'wasn't there', *va ofendre* [-aw-] 'offended', *no hi era* [-oje-] 'wasn't there'. Word-final obstruents are neutralised with respect to voice contrasts. When a consonant begins a following word, the final obstruent takes on its voicing specification, as expected. When a vowel begins the next word, final plosives are voiceless, but final fricatives (and affricates) are voiced. (It is odd that plosives in this environment appear to be stronger than word-internally, while fricatives are weaker. Occitan and Portuguese seem to share this phenomenon, and French has vestiges of it, p. 213.) In utterance-final position all obstruents are voiceless. Long (geminate) stops, whether sonorants or obstruents, can arise in sandhi, but continuant consonants (fricatives and /r/) are not pronounced long in this environment. A characteristic feature of Balearic, however, is affrication of fricative sequences in these cases. Only dental/alveolar stops (including nasals) regularly assimilate to the place or manner of following consonants. The following examples illustrate assimilations typical of normal style: *aquest periode* [-pp-] 'this period', *al costat meu* [-mm-] 'at my side', *tan poc* [-mp-] 'so little', *tan clar* [-ŋk-] 'so clear', *s'ha fet gran* [-gg-] 'has grown big', *tan fresc* [-ɱf-] 'so fresh', *dit llarg* [-ʎʎ-] 'long finger', *del tot legal* [-ll-] 'quite legal', *hem fet cami* [-kk-] 'we've made headway'. Balearic, however, goes much further, assimilating labial and velar stops as well: *sac buit* [-bb-] 'empty sack', *som grans* [-ŋg-] 'we are big', *cap jove* [-dʤ-] 'no young person'.

Morphophonemic Rules
Underlying stem-final /ʒ/ never appears in a syllable coda or in any word-final position, being replaced by /dʒ/; that is, the contrast between /ʒ/ and /dʒ/ is neutralised. The phenomenon is somewhat opaque, since phonetic [ʒ] can appear word-finally, as the realisation of underlying /ʃ/ in a voicing environment (e.g. *el mateix home* [əl mateʒ ɔmə] 'the same man'). The affrication of /ʒ/ is isolated and inexplicable synchronically. It reflects the outcome of a sound change, /dʒ/ > [ʒ] between vowels, which got interrupted in its lexical spread, making /ʒ/ and /dʒ/ contrastive in that position (see the chart on p. 176). Sequences of sonorant + homorganic plosive (also /-st/) are liable to elision of the final consonant in certain circumstances, which vary somewhat according to the particular consonants involved. In all dialects the sequence sonorant + plosive + consonant is phonotactically ill-formed. The plosive is deleted, both before plural /+s/ and before a consonant-initial following word, for example, in *llamps* 'flashes of lightning', *molts* 'many', *verd fosc* 'dark green', *sang freda* 'cold blood'. In Catalonia this process has been generalised to word-final prevocalic and to utterance-final environments. Deletion is obligatory when the sonorant is an

Phonemic Contrast of /ʤ/ and /ʒ/

/ʤ/	/ʒ/
lletja 'ugly (f.)'	boja 'mad (f.)'
lleig 'ugly (m.)'	boig 'mad (m.)'
desitjar 'to desire'	assajar 'to rehearse'
desig 'desire'	assaig 'rehearsal'

anterior nasal, e.g. *llamp* 'lightning', *profund* 'deep', *és un sant* 'he's a saint'. There are a few lexically governed exceptions in closely collocated phrases, such as *amb això* [əmb əʃɔ] 'with that', *quant és?* 'how much is it?', *Sant Andreu* 'St Andrew'. When the sonorant is a velar nasal, deletion of the following velar stop is optional in utterance-final position, e.g. *cinc* [siŋ(k)] 'five', and does not occur prevocalically: *cinc homes* [siŋk ɔməs] 'five men'. When the sonorant is an alveolar lateral, deletion seems to be lexically governed, occurring in a few common words such as *alt* 'high', *molt* 'much', *malalt* 'ill', but not in e.g. *tumult* 'tumult' *indult* 'reprieve'. After alveolar continuants, deletion is socially and stylistically governed; non-deletion is more prestigious and formal.

In many words underlying /r/ is deleted before inflectional /+s/ or a word boundary, for example, *darret*, *darrets*, *darrera* 'last (m. sg.), (m. pl.), (f. sg.)', cf. *endarrerir* 'get behind'; *clat* 'clear', *flots* 'flowers', *agrait* 'thank', cf. *agrair-li* 'thank her'. The phenomenon is commoner in poly-syllables than in monosyllables, and is subject to regional variation. But in many equally common words /r/ remains: *sospir* 'sigh', *amor* 'love', *car* 'dear'. Valencian dialects do not generally show r-deletion. On the other hand, it is lexically more extensive in Balearic, which has *car* [ka], *amor* [ɔmo]. Medieval textual evidence suggests that r-deletion began in the environment before /+s/, i.e. as an assimilation rule.

3   Morphology

Nominal Categories

Gender

The category of gender, with a binary masculine : feminine distinction, is generally relevant to all nominal parts of speech, in that it determines agreement phenomena, though it may not be overtly marked on all items in each class. There are two groups of exceptions: the so-called indefinite pro-nouns (see p. 192) which are always unmarked for gender, and the neuter deictics and clitic *ho*. Where gender contrast is formally marked, the feminine inflection is /+a/ in the singular, /+e/ (a regularly conditioned allomorph of the former) in the plural, while the masculine inflection is most commonly zero, but not infrequently /+e/ or /+o/.

Gender and Number Marking

f. sg.	m. sg.	f. pl.	m. pl.	
gossa	gos	gosses	gossos	'dog'
còmoda	còmode	còmodes	còmodes	'comfortable'
flonja	flonjo	flonges	flonjos	'flabby'

Masculine gender is, as usual, semantically and grammatically unmarked and hence appears in plural forms referring to sets containing members of both genders, for example, *els rossos* 'fair-haired men, fair-haired people', *els reis* 'the kings, the king and queen'. A very few words (all adjectival) are overtly marked for gender in the plural but not in the singular, e.g. *feroç* sg., *feroces* f. pl., *feroços* m. pl. 'fierce'; *cent, -cents, -centes* 'hundred'. Masculine forms also appear in nominals of neuter or unspecified gender. There is a truly neuter third person clitic pronoun *ho*, which contrasts with both masculine and feminine clitics. It is anaphoric (a) to the deictic pronouns *açò* 'this', *això* 'this/that', *allò* 'that'; (b) to whole propositions, including *wh*-questions; (c) to nominal predicate phrases, e.g. *són metges? — si que ho són* 'are they doctors? — yes, they are'.

Number
Plural is generally marked overtly in all the nominal parts of speech, the exceptions being, not surprisingly, the indefinite pronouns and the neuter deictics again, together with certain quantifiers, and the numeral adjective *mil* 'thousand'. The plural inflection is word-final /+s/ (or possibly /+z/ since voice is neutralised in word-final position). Oxytone words of masculine gender ending in /s/, /z/, or /ʃ/ show the masculine gender allomorph /+o/ before the plural /+s/, thereby preventing the regular phonological absorption of /s/ by a preceding sibilant, for example, *capaç, capaços* 'capable'; *pis, pisos* 'apartment'; *peix, peixos* 'fish'. This is widely applied in the spoken language in the case of masculine stems in final /dʒ/ also, though the standard language accepts forms without /+o/: *desig, desitjos ~ desigs* 'desire'. Many varieties also incorporate /+o/ in the plural of masculine words ending in /-sk/ or /-st/, e.g. *disc, discos ~ discs* 'record'; *text, textos ~ texts* 'texts'. Feminine words and non-oxytone words ending in sibilants, and compound words whose second element is itself plural, are uninflected for plural (though an orthographic *-s* is added if the word doesn't already end in one): *falç* f. sg., *falçs* [fals] f. pl. 'scythe'; *cactus* m. sg./pl. 'cactus'; *índex* m. sg., *índexs* m. pl. 'index'; *llevataps* m. sg./pl. [*lleva* + *taps*] 'corkscrew'. A few other words (lexical exceptions) which end in *-s* are invariable in the plural, such as *dilluns* m. sg./pl. 'Monday(s)', *temps* m. sg./pl. 'time(s)'.

Deixis
Classical and modern normative Catalan have a standard three-term

system of deictics. The system is effectively current, however, only in Valencia (where the preferred forms for the first and second person adjectives are *este, -a* and *eixe, -a*). Other varieties have merged the first and second person categories, preferring *això* as the pronoun, *aquí* as the adverb, and either *aquest* or *aqueix* as the adjective, depending on region. Usage is fairly strictly person-based, so, in correspondence and on the telephone, *aquí* refers ambiguously either to where the addressor is or to where the addressee is.

	Adjective	Neuter pronoun	Locative adverb
1st person	aquest, -a	açò	ací
2nd person	aqueix, -a	això	aquí
3rd person	aquell, -a	allò	allí ~ allà

Person and Case

Catalan has three pronouns of singular address (semantic second person): *tu, vós* and *vostè*, and two pronouns of plural address *vosaltres* and *vostès*. Grammatically, *tu* is second person singular, *vós* and *vosaltres* are second person plural, and *vostè* and *vostès* are third person singular and plural respectively. *Vosaltres* is the plural corresponding to both *tu* and *vós*. In those varieties in which all three pronouns of singular address are used *vós* is used reciprocally and connotes equal status without solidarity. *Vós* is also used as the general pronoun of address in formal letters and in public notices. As in much of the rest of Europe, status-dominated pronoun usage (non-reciprocal *tu/vostè*), which was customary even between parents and children until recently, is fast being replaced by usage in which solidarity dominates, that is, displaying solidary reciprocal *tu*, and non-solidary reciprocal *vostè*, or even, among younger people in non-status-marked settings, by universal *tu*.

Each personal pronoun has a distinct, stressed, subject form, an unstressed, clitic, non-subject form, and a possessive adjective/pronominal. There are also distinct indirect object forms for the third person non-reflexive clitics, and distinct prepositional object forms for first person singular and for third person reflexive/reciprocal; use of the latter form is optional. Catalan is a 'pro-drop' language (cf. p. 334), in which subject pronouns are used only contrastively. Certain locative adverb/prepositions (e.g. *davant* 'in front of', *darrere* 'behind', *dins* 'inside', *vora* 'beside', *prop* 'near'), which are optionally followed by a PP with *de*, must, when governing a personal pronoun, be followed by either the possessive form of it, or by *de* + prepositional object form, as follows: *davant del bisbe ~ davant el bisbe* 'before the bishop', *davant seu* 'before him/her(self)', *davant d'ell* 'before him(self)', *davant de si* 'before him/her(self)', **davant ell, *davant si*. The origin of the *davant seu* construction seems to be in a cross between the expected *davant d'ell* and the still current *al davant seu* 'at his

Personal Pronouns and Case Forms

	Subject	Prep. object	Non-subject clitic		Ind. obj. clitic	Possessive
1 sg.	jo	mi		-me		meu
2 sg. (fam.)	tu			-te		teu
3 pl. refl.	—	si		-se		
3 sg. m.	ell		-lo			
2 sg. (pol.)	vostè		-lo/-la		-li	seu
3 sg. f.	ella		-la			
3 sg. n.	això		-ho		-hi	
1 pl.	nosaltres			-nos		nostre
2 pl.	vosaltres			-vos		vostre
2 sg.	vós					
3 pl. m.	ells		-los			
2 pl.	vostès		-los/-les		-los	seu ~ llur
3 pl. f.	elles		-les			

Contextual Variants of Clitic Pronouns

	1 Proclitic or enclitic /V_{‖, C}	2 Proclitic or enclitic /_[vV,ho,hi	3 Proclitic or enclitic /{‖, C}_	4 Reinforced proclitic/ enclitic on form 3
1 sg.	'm	m'	me	em
2 sg.	't	t'	te	et
3 reflexive	's	s'	se	es
3 sg. dir. obj. m.	'l	l'	lo	el
3 sg. dir. obj. f.	la	l'		
3 sg. ind. obj.	li			
1 pl.	'ns		nos	ens
2 pl.	-us [ws]		vos	us ~ [əws]
3 pl. dir. obj. m.	'ls		los	els
3 pl. dir. obj. f.	les			
Partitive/ablative	'n	n'	en ~ ne	en
3 dir. obj. n.	-ho [w]	ho	ho ~ [əw]	
Locative/prep.	-hi [j]	hi	hi ~ [əj]	

(Column 4 rows 1 sg.–3 sg. dir. obj. m. grouped: em, et, es, el } /_[vC)

front', though it is unclear why *davant ell should have become ungrammatical. Colloquial Catalan extends the preposition + possessive case construction to certain other prepositions, so that we find, for example, *contra meu* 'against me', *sobre seu* 'on him/her'. The forms of the clitics given in the chart of personal pronouns and case forms are the post-consonantal enclitic variants. Their conditional allomorphs are given in the chart of contextual variants of clitic pronouns and discussed below. Possessives are inflected for number and, with the exception of *llur*, for gender of the thing possessed. The forms *meu, teu, seu* have, in the standard language as used in Catalonia, corre-

sponding feminines *meva, teva, seva. Llur* (cf. French *leur*) is now purely
literary; *seu* etc. is normally used for both singular and plural possessors, as
with Spanish *su* etc. There are obsolescent atonic possessive adjectives
mon/ma/mos/mes 'my', *ton/ta/tos/tes* 'your (2 sg.)', *son/sa/sos/ses* 'his/
her/its/your (pol.)/their', which are restricted in current use almost
entirely to close family terms, e.g. *mon pare* 'my father', *sa germana* 'her
(etc.) sister'.

Clitics

The standard system of Catalan clitics is, with respect both to conditioned
variation of forms and to breadth of usage, a rather conservative one in the
Romance context. The original formal variation corresponded not so much
to whether the elements were proclitic or enclitic to the verb as to whether
they were preceded or followed by consonants or vowels. This traditional
system, the product of regular sound change, which is set out in columns 1–
3 in the chart of contextual variants of clitic pronouns, is still to a large extent that of conservative dialects. The conditions of columns 1–3 in the
chart are to be applied in order, disjunctively. Column 1 provides the
default case. The environments include those provided by other clitics in a
sequence. In standard Catalan the 'reinforced' forms (4) (derived abduct-
ively from those of column 1) are used in proclitic position in the context
indicated. In colloquial varieties the reinforced forms are now found in
post-consonantal enclitic environments as well, instead of type 3, e.g.
promet-em 'promise me', *cull-el* 'pick it', *venent-els* 'selling them'. In
dialects, too, invariant 1 pl. *mos* and 3 pl. indirect object *lis* are found. The
order of pronouns in a sequence is nowadays basically this: third person
reflexive, second person, first person, third person indirect object, third
person direct object, *ne, ho, hi*. Examples are: *se te'ls menja* 'she eats yours
up', *us l'hi envien* 'they send it to you there', *quedeu-vos-ens-la* 'keep it
(for us)', *dóna-me'n* 'give me some'. In the medieval language, and still in
Balearic varieties, the third person direct object precedes other clitics. In
spoken varieties except Valencian, the expected sequences of *li* (3 sg. ind.
obj.) plus a following clitic *x* are replaced by *x* + /i/, with *x* → /l/ if it contains no other consonant, as follows: *li'l* → [li] (*l'hi*), *li la* → [li] (*la hi*), *li'ls*
→ [əlzi] (*els hi*), *li les* → [ləzi] (*les hi*), *li'n* → [ni], *li ho* → [li] (*l'hi*), *li hi* →
[li]. Only the outputs in parentheses above are standard. Note that four of
the output combinations are homophonous with each other and with the
clitic *li* itself. In most spoken varieties outside Valencia this model has been
extended to *els* (3 pl. ind. obj.) and combinations of *els* plus a following
clitic, all of which are realised [əlzi], except *els* + *en* [əlzəni], i.e. *els, els el,
els la, els els, els les, els ho, els hi*, all → [əlzi]. A new analysis is well on the
way to crystallising, in which /+l/ corresponds to 'third person non-
reflexive', /+z/ to 'plural' and /+i/ to 'indirect object or locative', with
each of these concepts being marked only once in a clitic sequence, and

gender being expressed only inconsistently (cf. the Spanish developments discussed on p. 108).

Determiners

The expected forms of the definite determiners deriving from Latin ILLUM etc. would be *lo, los, la, les*, with the first two being reduced to *l, ls*, respectively, in enclitic position, and with *lo* and *la* being reduced to *l* in prevocalic position. This state of affairs is largely retained in the dialects of western Catalonia (*lo pare, los pares, del pare, dels pares* etc.). Elsewhere, *lo, los*, have been replaced by 'reinforced' forms *el, els*, abducted from the enclitic variants. Parallel forms deriving from Latin IPSUM etc. (p. 53) are current in the Balearics and a few places on the Costa Brava. They are *s'* sg. prevocalic, *es* m. sg., *es* m. pl. before a consonant, *ets* m. pl. before a vowel, *sa* f. sg., *ses* f. pl.; m. *so, sos*, are retained after the preposition *amb* 'with'. In fact, both /l/ and /s/ sets of determiners are current in the Balearics. The differences in their use are (a) stylistic and (b) semantic/pragmatic. Only /l/ determiners are appropriate in formal styles. In Majorcan literature it is common for /s/ forms (*parlar salat*) to be restricted to the dialogue of the Majorcan characters, /l/ articles being used elsewhere. Even within *parlar salat*, /l/ determiners are often used when the definiteness comes from uniqueness of reference, e.g. *el cel* 'the sky', *el bisbe* 'the bishop (sc. of Majorca)'. A distinction is possible, for example, between *la Mort* 'Death' and *sa mort* 'the death (which we were talking about)'. A third set of singular definite determiners, derived from Latin DOMINUM etc. 'master', namely *en, na* (both *n'* before vowels), is used generally in the Balearics, and in official styles elsewhere, before proper names of persons (either Christian names, e.g. *Na Joana*, or surnames, e.g. *En Fuster*). In Catalonia, the form *en* is widely used, but *n'* and *na* have been replaced by *l', la*. *En* may, non-standardly, be replaced by *el* likewise.

Adjectives

Except as specified below (p. 192), all adjectives are inflected for number. The majority are inflected for gender too. Those that are not are almost exclusively derived from Latin adjectives which were also unmarked for gender, e.g. *atroç* 'atrocious', *semblant* 'similar', *jove* 'young', *celta* 'Celtic'. Adjectives can appear in headless (elliptical) NPs. If the NP reference is not contextually determined, humans are assumed. Thus: *els alts* 'the tall ones/tall people/tall men', *aptes i inútils havien de lluitar* 'fit and unfit had to fight'. Comparison of adjectives (and adverbs) is expressed by means of the degree adverb *més* 'more'. A few adjectives/adverbs have synthetic comparatives, e.g. *millor* 'better', *pitjor* 'worse', *major* 'greater', *menor* 'smaller', *menys* 'less'; their use is optional, though common. There is no grammatical category of superlative distinct from comparative.

Prepositions

Phonological and morphological criteria allow us to divide prepositions into three classes: tonic prepositions such as *sobre* 'over', *fins* 'up to', compound tonic prepositions such as *des de* 'since', *cap a* 'towards', and atonic prepositions. The atonic prepositions are: *a* 'to, at', *amb* 'with', *en* 'in', *de* 'of, from', *per* 'by' and the compound atonic *per a* 'for'. It is the phonology and syntax of this group which give rise to most of the PP problems. Many spoken varieties confuse some of these atonic prepositions. Valencian has replaced *amb* with *en*. Eastern Catalan generally has merged *per a* with *per*, and confusion reigns between *a*, *en*, and *amb*, particularly before vowels. The problem with *a* in Eastern Catalan is that, being unstressed, it is subject to vowel reduction, and to elision when adjacent to a vowel on either side, for example, *escriu a en Pere* [əskɾiw əmpeɾə] 'is writing to Pere'. (Valencian has a prevocalic variant *ad* which avoids some of these difficulties.) Already in Old Catalan there had become established the current use of *en* 'to (locative)' preceding *aquest/aqueix/aquell*, *un*, and *algun*, e.g. *anirem en algun indret desconegut* 'we'll go to some unknown spot'. Colloquial speech extends this use, which has sometimes been written *an* or *a n'*, both to replace non-locative *a*, and before other vowel-initial words than the ones mentioned above: *escriu an en Pere* (non-standard) 'is writing to Pere'. This use of *en* has extended from a position before the masculine definite determiner to the parallel position before the feminine determiner, such as *digues-ho a(na) les companyes* 'tell it to your mates (f.)', where simple *a* was not phonologically endangered, creating a bisyllabic [ənə]. An alternative strategy to avoid disappearing *a* is to substitute it with *amb* (especially, though not exclusively, in indirect object function), for example, *li va dir amb ella* 'he told her'. The Eastern merger of *per* and *per a* is perhaps due in part to the distinction, a relatively late one in Romance terms, never having become firmly established. But phonological facts evidently have some part to play, in particular, the regular elision of prevocalic [ə], together with the general tendency to reduce [əɾəC] to [ərC].

Verbal Categories

In the chart are shown the paradigms of *perdre* 'to lose', a regular verb of conjugation class II. Each of the subparadigms is identified by a label corresponding to its major tense, aspect, or mood use. To be considered first are various morphological and morphophonemic aspects which have no syntactic or semantic significance. Verbs are traditionally divided into three conjugation classes on the basis of which thematic vowels are maximally distinguished. Class I has thematic vowel /a/ (e.g. *comprares, comprant, comprar* 'buy') and derives from Latin first conjugation verbs. Class II has thematic vowel /e/ (*perderes, perdent*), and derives from Latin second and third conjugation verbs. Class III has thematic vowel /i/

Paradigms of a Regular Verb

Present indicative
   perdo, perds, perd, perdem, perdeu, perden
Non-past subjunctive
   perdi, perdis, perdi, perdem, perdeu, perdin
Future
   perdré, perdràs, perdrà, perdrem, perdreu, perdran
Prospective-in-past/conditional
   perdria, perdries, perdria, perdríem, perdríeu, perdrien
Past imperfective indicative
   perdia, perdies, perdia, perdíem, perdíeu, perdien
Past perfective indicative (synthetic)
   perdí, perderes, perdé, perdérem, perdéreu, perderen
Past perfective indicative (periphrastic)
   vaig ..., vas ..., va ..., vam ..., va ..., van perdre
Past subjunctive
   perdés, perdessis, perdés, perdéssim, perdéssiu, perdessin
Past perfective subjunctive
   vagi ..., vagis ..., vagi ..., vàgim ..., vàgiu ..., vagin perdre
Positive imperative
   perd, perdi, perdem, perdeu, perdin
Present perfect/anterior relative tenses:
   Finite paradigms of haver *'have'* + perdut
Non-finite forms:
   Infinitive: perdre
   Gerund: perdent
   Participle: perdut [±f., ±pl.]

(*dormires, dormint, dormir* 'sleep') and derives from Latin fourth conjugation verbs. There are a few athematic verbs, best seen as a subgroup of class II. Class III has two major subclasses. The majority group (IIIb) is of verbs which exhibit a post-root affix -*eix*- /ɛʃ/ (cf. French, Occitan, Italian) in those present forms which would otherwise be rhizotonic (e.g. *ofereix* 'offers' but *oferim* 'we offer'). The minority group (IIIa) consists of some 24 verbs which lack this -*eix*- affix. Class II has, for the most part, inflections which are identical either to those of class I or to those of class IIIa. Where classes I and II go together, against III, they share a theme vowel /ɛ/ (I *comprem* 'we buy', II *temem* 'we fear') or /e/ (e.g. in the past subjunctive: *comprés, temés*). Historically what has happened here is the extension of theme vowels from II to I, with a contribution from the original class I non-past subjunctive morph. Where II and III (especially IIIa) go together, against class I, it is in having ∅ theme vowel in, for example, present indicative 2 sg. II *tems* 'fear', IIIa *dorms* 'sleep' — the convergence is due to regular sound change — and in having the theme vowel /i/ in the past imperfective: 1 sg. II *temia*, III *dormia*. The latter reflects a widespread Romance morphological change. The unique forms of class II, in addition to those mentioned above which show thematic /e/, are the infinitive, in -re or -er (perdre 'lose', témer 'fear'), and its weak participles in -ut (perdut 'lost', temut 'feared'). Class II can also be divided into two subgroups. Class IIa consists of those which take a post-root /g/ affix (variant /k/) (cf. Spanish, p. 101) in the non-past subjunctive stem or the 'preterit stem' — generally both. Class IIb lacks this affix (perdre, whose paradigms are given in the chart, is a IIb verb). Class IIa contains a few verbs (IIa1) with /ɛ/ in the infinitive and gerund (all that remains distinct of the Latin second conjugation), viz haver 'have', poder 'can', saber 'know', soler 'be accustomed to', valer 'be worth', and voler 'want'. Class IIa2 is the remainder. Many class II verbs have athematic ('strong') participles, e.g. atès from atènyer 'reach', cuit from coure 'cook'. There are about 80 class II verbs in common use, not counting prefixal derivatives. The conjugation classes are not distinguished in the third person plural present indicative (compren, temen, dormen) or in the first person singular past perfective indicative (synthetic): comprí, temí, dormí; or, in most dialects, in the rhizotonic forms of the non-past subjunctive, e.g. 1 sg. comprí, temi, dormi.

Most verbs, including all of class I (except anar 'go') and all of class IIb, have no stem variation at all other than that resulting from entirely regular phonological processes like vowel reduction and final obstruent devoicing. (The so-called 'future stem' is not treated here as an aspect of stem variation.) Verbs of class IIa (which contains all class II verbs in root-final /n/, /l/, /j/, /w/ or /v/, plus a few others) together with estar 'be' (II athematic) and eixir 'go out' (IIIa) use a 'preterit stem' in the past perfective indicative (synthetic), the past subjunctive, and class II weak participle; e.g. from deure 'owe', 3 sg. past perfective degué, past subjunctive degués, participle degut. In nearly all cases the preterit stem displays the addition of /g/ to the present stem (= root). (Other preterit stems are, for instance, /kresk/, /merɛsk/, /nask/, /vɛj/ ~ /vɛʒ/, /fo/, /isk/, corresponding to créixer 'grow', merèixer 'deserve', néixer 'be born', veure 'see', ser 'be', and eixir 'go out' respectively.) And in nearly all cases this stem form with /g/ is the one also found in the first person singular present indicative and throughout the non-past subjunctive; e.g. from deure, 1 sg. pres. ind. dec, non-past subj. degui. The origin of the /g/ in the preterit stem and in forms of the present stem is different. It has developed from the Latin perfect /-u-/ morph in the first case (POTUIT > OCat. pog), and has been extended from Latin stem-final /k/ or /g/ in the latter (DICO > dic, PERTANGO > OCat. pertanc), but the two elements have been identified so that their distribution is assimilated to the same verbs. In non-standard varieties also the present /g/ stem spreads to the infinitive and gerund of IIa2 verbs: voler ~ volguer 'want', valent ~ valguent 'be worth', and indeed to others: dient ~ diguent 'say'. Before the /g/ stem-extension, stem-final /n/ and /l/, together with /j/ after /a/, are retained, but other consonants are dropped. This gives rise, among other things, to indicative – subjunctive stem contrasts such as the following: *movem – moguem* 'we move', *plou – plogui* 'rains', *podem – puguem* 'we can', *coneixem – coneguem* 'we know'. Present stem alternations in class III verbs are associated with stress patterns. In addition to the *-eix-* stem extension mentioned above, whose function in class IIIb appears to be to avoid root stress, vowel alternations appear in some verbs of class IIIa. In these, unstressed /e/, /o/, correspond to stressed /i/, /u/, respectively: e.g. 1 pl. pres. ind. *eixim*, 1 sg. *ixo* 'go out', 1 pl. *cosim*, 3 sg. ind. *cus*, subj. *cusi* 'sew'. The raised vowels /i/, /u/, were originally appropriate where stressed /ɛ/, /ɔ/, were followed by Lat. [j] in the next syllable onset, but this etymological distribution has been obliterated. Valencian, which conjugates more verbs according to pattern IIIa than other dialects, has quite a few verbs of this type: *afegir* 'add', *llegir* 'read', *teixir* 'weave', *vestir* 'dress' make their third person singular present indicatives *afig, llig, tix, vist*, respectively. This pattern of present stem alternation based on stress (viz one stem in first to third person singular and third plural, another stem in first and second person plural), is also found in several irregular class II verbs where stress is not directly implicated, e.g. *estar* 'be': *estàs, està, estan*, but *estem, esteu*; and has been profoundly influential in conditioning the distribution of innovative forms of the present subjunctive (pp. 190–1).

Other stem-final consonant alternations in Class IIa verbs are, firstly, /v/ ~ /w/, e.g. *bevem ~ beu* 'drink'. This reflects the regular phonological process whereby /v/ → /w/ in syllable rimes (see above, p. 172). A second alternation, /j/ ~ /w/, e.g. *caiem ~ cau* 'fall', seems to show underlying stem-final /j/ becoming /w/ in the same environment, though this is not a regular phonological alternation. Thirdly there is Ø ~ /w/, e.g. *plaem ~ plau* 'please', also an irregular alternation, which, by elimination, seems to reflect underlying /w/ → Ø in syllable onsets. The distinction between the latter two alternation types is, in fact, a relatively recent one, and has different lexical distribution (if it is found at all) in different dialects. Both alternations go back to Proto-Catalan [ð] ~ [w] alternation, in which both phones are reflexes of Latin intervocalic /-tj-/, /-d-/, /-c-/. Class II /-j-/-stem verbs have developed a curious past imperfective where stress is shifted on to the root, and in which non-rounded vowels are replaced by /ɛ/. Hence we find (1 pl.) *quèiem* 'fell', *crèiem* 'believed', *dèiem* 'said', *dúiem* 'brought', *fèiem* 'made', *jèiem* 'lay', *rèiem* 'laughed', *sèiem* 'sat', *vèiem* 'saw'. And in the Balearic dialect, verbs of this group have rhizotonic forms of the first and second person plural present indicative also, with a special second plural person/number inflection, e.g. *creim, creis* 'believe', *feim, feis* 'do'.

Person/Number Inflections

The person/number inflectional suffixes are: 1 pl. /-m/, 2 pl. /-w/, 3 pl. /-n/, 2 sg. /-s/ (except in the positive imperative where it is Ø), 3 sg. Ø. The first person singular is expressed by (a) distinct variants of tense and aspect markers, e.g. future *perdré* 'I will lose', past perfective (synthetic) *perdí* 'I lost'; (b) in the present indicative either by stem variants (= non-past subjunctive stem), e.g. *prenc* 'I take', *vaig* 'I go', or by /+o/: standard *tallo* 'I cut' (Valencian /+e/: *talle*; North Catalan /+i/: *talli*). Otherwise the first singular person/number inflection is Ø. Hence in the past imperfective, prospective-in-past/conditional, and both subjunctives, the first singular is identical to third person singular. The same is true in Balearic and Valencian in the case of the present indicative of verbs of classes IIb and IIIa, where there is no suffix at all.

Auxiliary Verbs

Catalan has no well defined class of auxiliary verbs or modals. There is only one unquestionable auxiliary: the *va-* formative which participates in the past perfective (periphrastic). It has only two paradigms: an indicative and a subjunctive. The periphrastic past perfective indicative is cognitively synonymous with the synthetic form. The commonest indicative inflections of *va-* (*vaig, vas, va, vam, vau, van*) most closely resemble those of an athematic class II present, except that even the first and second person plural forms have no theme vowel, while the first and second person plural subjunctives *vàgim, vàgiu*, have a suffix vowel typical of the past subjunctive and a stress pattern typical of past tense paradigms in general. Alternative forms of the indicative (*vares, vàrem, vàreu, varen*) resemble synthetic past perfectives. Though historically derived from the present of *anar* 'go', only the singular and third person plural forms of the indicative (of the first set above) and of the subjunctive are now shared with that verb. *Va-* has no other 'tenses' or non-finite forms. The perfect/anterior set (*haver* + participle) is somewhat less grammaticalised. In this construction *haver* has virtually the full paradigm set of a regular verb, and its forms are largely identical with those of the verb used in the *haver de* 'have to' construction, though both of these paradigms now diverge somewhat from those of the transitive main verb *haver* ~ *heure* 'get'. Like the *va-* auxiliary, however, *haver* has unusual forms of the non-past subjunctive: 1-2pl. *hàgim, hàgiu*, whose pattern these two share with no other verb. Its second and third person singular and third person plural present indicative, in perfect aspect use, are atonic, and consequently subject to vowel reduction and liable to sandhi elision in Eastern Catalan: *has* [əs], *ha* [ə], *han* [ən]. *Haver* + participle differs from other verb + participle constructions in that it is active; the others are stative/passive and occur only with transitive verbs (see below, pp. 194ff). The perfect/anterior *haver* + participle construction is well integrated into the tense/aspect system and shares with inflectional affixes the expression of relative tense. The balance seems on the whole on the side of *haver*'s being an auxiliary verb, and it will be treated as such below among the tense and aspect verb categories.

Non-finite Forms

The infinitive consists of: the verb root + thematic vowel in class I (/a/), III (/i/), and IIa2 (/ɛ/), + /r/. In classes IIa1 and IIb the contiguity of root-final consonants with the + /r/ inflection gives rise to certain phonological processes largely concerned with syllabification; /-Cr/ is not a well formed syllable rime. The sequences of /n+r/, /l+r/, provoke epenthesis of /d/ before the /r/. This is not entirely a phonotactic process, since outside verbs these sequences are acceptable, although uncommon. If, given this epenthesis, the /C+r/ is an acceptable internal sequence — it is when the consonant is a plosive or a semi-vowel — syllabification is achieved by a final unmarked vowel: /bat+r/ *batre* 'strike', /kɔw+r/ *coure* 'cook', /rɛb+r/ *rebre* 'receive'. If the resulting /C+r/ is not phonotactically acceptable, an unmarked vowel is inserted between them: /tem+r/ *témer* 'fear', /kreʃ+r/ *créixer* 'grow', /vɛns+r/ *vèncer* 'defeat'.

The gerund consists of the verb root + theme vowel (I /a/, IIa1–IIb /e/, IIa2 /ɛ/, III /i/) + /nt/.

The participle consists of the preterit stem + theme vowel (I /a/, II /u/, III /i/) + /d/. Athematic (strong) participles, all of which are in verbs of classes II and III, consist of present stem (often with deletion of the final consonant) + /t/ or /z/ (rarely /st/).

Tense

Intersections of tense with aspect and mood categories will be discussed with the latter.

The present tense paradigm is morphologically the least marked. Only the affix *-eix-* in class IIIb verbs can be said to be an exponent of the present tense exclusively. The first person singular suffix *-o* and the stem variants found in the first person singular present indicative together with the non-past subjunctive are also associated with present tense in a non-exclusive way. Otherwise present indicative consists of the verb root + theme vowel (/a/ in class I rhizotonic forms; /ɛ/ in class I and II first and second person plural; /i/ in class III first and second person plural) + person/number endings (/C+n/ → /Cen/). The inherited stress pattern, consisting of rhizotonic forms in the singular and third person plural and suffix stress in the first and second person plural, is characteristic of the present system as a whole (indicative, subjunctive, and imperative). Present is unmarked relative to future, and appears in contexts of neutralisation, for instance in the protasis of conditionals (*si vens* 'if you are coming/come (present habitual)/come (future)').

The future paradigm still clearly reveals its origin in infinitive of main verb + present indicative of *haver*. The only differences are that class IIa1 verbs with thematic /ɛ/ in the infinitive lack it in the future stem, and that *tenir* 'have', *venir* 'come' with class III infinitives have class II future stems: *tindr-*, *vindr-*. In addition the 'infinitive' part of the future is unstressed.

The future paradigm is distinctive in having oxytone stress throughout. In contrast to many European languages (including most Romance ones), the future in Catalan (and similarly the prospective, or relative future, tenses) is not normally used for inferential senses ('that'll be the postman'/'that must be the postman'). This meaning is expressed by the quasi-modal *deure* 'must', e.g. *això deu ser el carter* 'that must be the postman' (present inference); *això deurà ser el carter* 'that must be the postman' (future inference).

Restricting the terms 'past' and 'future' to times relative to the speaker's present, we may distinguish, in the relative tense categories, anterior, referring to time previous to some other reference point, and prospective, referring to time subsequent to some other reference point. In Catalan, as widely in Romance, anterior is expressed by means of the auxiliary *haver* + participle, and prospective by means of the /+r/ future/prospective inflectional morpheme (see the chart of relative tense). The paradigm used in (1) in the chart is conventionally called 'conditional', and indeed one of its main uses is in the apodosis of conditional sentences. But it is plausible to argue that prospective-in-past is its 'basic meaning' (cf. the presentation for French, p. 240), which is also reflected in its structure and etymology, i.e. future/prospective stem (containing /+r/ morph) + past imperfective suffix of class II–III verbs. In this, the latter part is a reduced form of the past imperfective of *haver*. Two verbs, *ser* 'be' and *haver* 'have', have in current use (I suspect more as conditionals than as prospective-in-past) alternative forms, derived from the Latin pluperfect indicative: *fóra, fores, fóra, fórem, fóreu, foren*; *haguera, hagueres, haguera, haguérem, haguéreu, hagueren*.

Relative Tense

(1)   Prospective-in-past   'Conditional'
va dir que em sustituiria 'she said she would take my place'
(2)   Anterior-in-future   'Future perfect'
quan faràs 60 anys, ell ja s'haurà jubilat 'when you are 60, he will already have retired'
(3a)   Anterior-in-past   'Pluperfect'
va resultar que hi havien esmerçat molts diners 'it turned out they had invested a lot of money in it'
(3b)   'Past anterior'
no va callar fins que l'hi van haver explicat/hagueren explicat 'she didn't stop until they had explained it to her'
(4)   Anterior-in-prospective-in-past   'Conditional perfect'
va dir que quan faria 60 anys, ell ja s'hauria jubilat 'she said that when she was 60, he would already have retired'
(5)   Anterior non-finite
als vençuts, sempre els cou/coïa/courà la memòria d'haver perdut 'the defeated are always/were always/will always be resentful at the memory of having lost'

Of the two anterior-in-past indicative forms (3a, 3b in the chart) the first, much the commonest, consists of the past imperfective indicative of *haver* + participle; the second ('past anterior') consists of the past perfective indicative of *haver* + participle. The distinction in usage is not the aspectual one the forms might lead one to suppose. The 'past anterior', whose use is always optional, denotes immediate anteriority. The anterior-in-past, alone among the relative tenses, distinguishes a subjunctive: *hagués perdut*, etc. The anterior-in-prospective-in-past ('conditional perfect') is the only relative tense with two reference points. It is also used in the apodosis of impossible past conditional sentences, for example, *encara que ho haguéssim sabut, hauriem perdut* 'even if we had known, we would have lost'. The structure of the perfect aspectual paradigm, namely present of *haver* + participle, might suggest it should be included among the relative tenses as 'anterior-in-present', thereby unifying the *haver* + participle periphrases under the relative tense label anterior. Such an analysis, though morphologically attractive, betrays the semantics. In main clauses, at least, *ha*, etc. + participle, does not just express 'anterior relative to the present' — this is just what the past tense paradigms themselves convey. However, there is some justification for speaking of anterior-in-non-past when *haver* + participle is used in those subordinate clauses in which the present–future contrast is neutralised and the anterior-in-future ('future perfect') is excluded, e.g. *si ha arribat, trucarà* 'if she has arrived (now)/if she shall have arrived, she will knock'; *prefereixo que no l'hagis comprada abans que la vegi* 'I would prefer (literally 'do prefer') you not to have bought it before I see it'.

Aspect

Perfective and imperfective aspect are distinguished consistently only in the past indicative. A marked past perfective subjunctive is also used in certain syntactic contexts (see p. 203). The past perfective has two paradigms: a synthetic one (already by 1500 largely analogically reconstructed and replacing the forms derived from the Latin perfect), and an analytic one consisting of the *va-* auxiliary + infinitive. The structure of the synthetic past perfective is as follows. To the preterit stem is attached, in the first person singular, *-i* for all conjugation classes; in other persons the theme vowel (I /a/, II /e/, III /i/) is followed by Ø (3 sg.), otherwise by /re/ + person/number suffixes. The /re/ morph is originally only in the third person plural (*compraren* 'they bought', *perderen* 'they lost', *sentiren* 'they heard', etc.). Elsewhere it is analogical. The forms of the analytic past perfective auxiliary have been discussed above. The synthetic forms are in regular spontaneous spoken use only in central Valencian, though certain forms may be heard in other Valencian and in Balearic varieties. However, the synthetic forms are widely used in written Catalan, alongside the periphrastic forms, in all areas. The origin of these periphrastic forms is much debated. Europeanists generally expect collocations of 'go' + main verb to express future time (as in English, French, Spanish), and this pattern (*anar a* + infinitive) has existed also in Catalan, though not with any great strength.

Past imperfective forms consist of the verb root + (class I) theme /a/ + /v/ or (class II–III) theme /i/, + /a/ + person/number endings. (*Ser* 'be' has stem /er/ + /a/ + person/number endings.) All past paradigms (including relative past) have stress on the theme vowel if there is one — there almost always is — otherwise on the root. In the past imperfective indicative of class II verbs in root-final /j/ the theme vowel /i/ is absent and root stressing results. In contexts of neutralisation of aspectual contrasts the imperfective forms appear. These contexts are: in the protasis of unreal conditionals, for example *si venia* 'if I came', and in the auxiliary element *haver* of the anterior-in-past relative tense, e.g. *havia vingut* 'had come'. In the context of present, future, or relative tenses, or in past contexts where perfective–imperfective contrasts cannot be directly expressed, it is increasingly common to use the periphrastic *estar* + gerund 'progressive' to convey imperfective aspect.

The perfect aspect denotes 'past with present relevance', and is expressed by the present of *haver* + participle. Relevance to the present is, not surprisingly, a largely subjective matter. Catalans interpret the notion much as speakers of British English do, with the exception that any previous event 'today' is regarded as presently relevant, and unless imperfective in aspect, the perfect is obligatory; so, for example, *aquesta tarda he comprat dos rellotges* 'this afternoon I bought/have bought two watches'.

Mood
Subjunctive combines with two synthetic and three periphrastic tense/aspect categories to give: (1) non-past subjunctive; (2) past subjunctive; (3) present perfect/anterior non-past subjunctive (non-past subjunctive of *haver* + participle); (4) anterior-in-past subjunctive (past subjunctive of *haver* + participle); (5) past perfective subjunctive (subjunctive of *va*-auxiliary + infinitive). The inflections of the synthetic subjunctives (1) and (2) are notably innovative in standard Catalan, though more conservative in some other dialects, especially Valencian. The most striking innovation is an /i/ morph which appears in the singular and third person plural of the non-past subjunctive, in the plural and second person singular of the past subjunctive, and throughout the (non-past) subjunctive of *va*- and *haver*. The non-past subjunctive stem (i.e. with /g/, etc., for class IIa verbs) + subjunctive + /i/, as above, is followed by person/number endings. In the first and second person plural the non-past subjunctive stem is followed by theme vowels /ɛ/ or /i/, as in the indicative. Consequently in these persons, only verbs with a distinct non-past subjunctive stem contrast subjunctive with indicative. (Balearic is more consistent, retaining *-am*, *-au*

for class I first and second person plural indicative which contrast with *-em*, *-eu* subjunctive, and having developed first and second person plural subjunctive endings *-iguem, -igueu* for class III verbs.) The past subjunctive consists of the preterit stem + theme vowel (I–II /e/, III /i/) + /s/, which is separated from person/number endings, if any, by the subjunctive morph /i/, e.g. 1/3 sg. *vingués*, 2 sg. *vinguessis* 'come'. Spoken Valencian uses a different set of forms derived from the Latin pluperfect indicative: 1/3 sg. *vinguera*, 2 sg. *vingueres*, etc. (cf. the position in Spanish, p. 99). Except in the first and third person singular, these forms are identical with the synthetic past perfective indicative.

The second person singular positive imperative consists of present stem (+ theme vowel /a/ in class I) + Ø person/number inflection: *compra!* 'buy!', *tramet!* 'send!', *ofereix!* 'offer!'. The other imperative forms are identical with other present verb forms. The first person plural and third person forms are identical with non-past subjunctive forms, which are, of course, their origin. The second person plural imperative is the same as the second person plural indicative. Since in the case of most verbs first and second person plural subjunctive forms are identical to the indicative anyway, the above system in the first and second person plural imperative gives rise to substantial confusion in the case of those verbs where this is not so, with much pressure to construct the first and second person plural imperative in the same way. That is, instead of standard 1 pl. *prenguem!* 'let us take!', 2 pl. *preneu!* 'take!', we commonly find *prenguem, prengueu* or *prenem, preneu*. The negative imperative is expressed with *no* + non-past subjunctive, clitics being in their normal finite verb proclitic position.

4 Syntax

Noun Phrases

Determiners
Definite determiners are used in NPs without N heads, such as *la més lletja* 'the ugliest one', *les que preferim* 'the ones we prefer', *el de la meva dona* 'my wife's', literally 'the of the my wife'.

Adjectives
Adjectives may precede or follow nouns. Post-position is normal for identifying or defining adjectives (equivalent in function to restrictive relatives). Pre-position is possible in particular for adjectives used evaluatively. Typically, for instance, *dèbil* 'weak', *estrany* 'odd', *important* 'important', *senzill* 'simple', are so used. Pre-position may also occur with adjectives such as *diferent* 'different', *principal* 'major', which are perhaps assimilated to the class of indefinites/quantifiers which nearly always precede. *Mal* and

dolent 'bad' are in complementary distribution, the former occurring in prenominal position, the latter elsewhere. Some adjectives have fairly distinct interpretation according to whether they precede (evaluative/semi-indefinite/quantifier) or follow (specifying), e.g. *cert* 'certain', *mateix* 'same' and 'him/her/itself', *pobre* 'poor', *sol* 'only/just one' and 'alone', *trist* 'sad' (cf., for instance, French, p. 227).

Possessive adjectives likewise may either precede or follow nouns. If they precede, they must themselves (except for *llur*) be preceded by a determiner. If they follow, the phrase need not have a determiner, e.g. *un teu projecte* or *un projecte teu* 'one of your plans/a plan of yours', *el teu projecte* or *el projecte teu* 'your plan', *aquest teu projecte* or *aquest projecte teu* 'this plan of yours'. In predicative position, possessive adjectives (like other adjectives) are undetermined, for example, *aquelles joguines són meves* 'those toys are mine'. Possessive 'pronouns' (here in fact headless NPs) have the definite determiner: *aquelles joguines són les meves* 'those toys are my ones'.

Deictic adjectives may precede the noun, or, unusually in Romance, follow it with definite determiner: *aquest paper* = *el paper aquest* 'this paper'. The latter construction belongs only to informal style. Deictic adjectives, like adjectives generally, can be used pronominally.

Quantifiers, Indefinites, and Other Pronouns
Most degree adverbs (e.g. *molt* 'very', *mig* 'half', *bastant* 'quite', *gaire* '(not) much', *massa* 'too') can also be used as adjectives, and, like other adjectives, may be used pronominally with ellipsis of N heads. Some of them are marked for gender, and most of them for number, in such constructions; colloquial speech extends number marking to, for example, *prou* 'enough', *força* 'a lot', *massa* 'too many'. Most of them can also be followed by a PP complement with *de*, retaining gender and number marking, e.g. *poques de vegades* = *poques vegades* 'few times'. *Tot* 'all', as a degree adverb has the peculiarity of inflecting for gender and number in agreement with its AP head, as in *es banyaven tots nus* 'they went swimming stark naked'. Other quantifiers/indefinites are primarily adjectives (e.g. *algun* 'some', *quin* 'which?', *cap* 'any, no') of which a few, including *cap*, and *cada* 'each', take no gender or number inflection. A few, such as *cada*, *ambdós* 'both', *sengles* 'one each, respective', cannot be used 'pronominally'. Purely pronominal are, for example, *tothom* 'everyone', *res ~ re* 'anything, nothing'.

Prepositional Phrases
Another example of the overlap between *en* and *a* (cf. p. 182) is the fact that subcategorised or locative *en* is regularly replaced by *a* (occasionally by *de*) before an infinitive, e.g. *vacil.la en l'execució* 'hesitates in the execution'; *vacil.la a fer-ho* 'hesitates to do it'. (*En* readily appears before

infinitives in temporal adverbial phrases, such as *en entrar el rei, tots s'alçaren* 'when the king entered, they all rose'.) There is also a certain reluctance, by no means so marked, to maintain *amb* before an infinitive, *a* or *de* being preferred: *ens amenaçaren amb l'expulsió* 'they threatened us with expulsion'; *el vaig amenaçar de treure'l* 'I threatened to remove him'.

The expected collocation of the atonic prepositions with complementiser *que* + S is not found in the standard language (except for the literary compound conjunction *amb que* 'provided that'). *A, en,* and *de* disappear altogether before *que*; **per que* and **per a que* both appear as *perquè* 'because, in order that'. In this example the alternation of unstressed *que* with stressed *què* after a preposition is analogous to the regular alternation, in the relative pronoun system, of *que* with preposition + *què*: *a què* 'to which', *per què* 'by which', etc., are normal. Where **amb que* would be expected, both *Ø que* and *amb què* are found: *estic content que/content amb què hagis vingut* 'I am pleased you have come'. In non-standard Valencian, where the distinction between atonic *que* and tonic *qué* is by no means obvious, both *perqué* 'because' and *per a que* 'in order that' are retained. In non-standard spoken Catalan generally, unstressed *a que, de que, en que* are widely used, though this pattern is usually attributed to Spanish interference.

Quite common, though by no means universal, in the spoken language is the use, parallelled in Spanish (pp. 106-7), of *a* (non-standard variants *an, ana,* cf. p. 182) before definite direct object NPs referring to persons. The direct object clitics are unaffected. In the standard language this usage of *a* is obligatory before stressed personal pronouns, for example, *a, mi, no em convenç* literally 'to me, not me it-convinces', 'I'm not convinced'; *s'enganya a si mateixa* 'she deceives herself'. It is accepted before certain other pronouns referring to definite persons: *tothom* and *tots* 'everyone', *el qual* and *qui* 'whom', and when an object phrase referring to a possible agent directly follows the subject: *el perseguia com el gat a la rata* 'she pursued him like the cat (pursues) the rat'.

Verbal Group

Agreement
As expected, finite verbs show inflectional agreement with the person/number category of their grammatical subject. However, the question may arise of what the grammatical subject is, especially with 'impersonal' verbs such as *caldre* 'be necessary', *faltar* 'be lacking', with 'presentational' verbs like *haver-hi* 'there is', *passar* 'there passes, happens', *venir* 'there comes', or with 'impersonal reflexives', e.g. *es lloguen cadires* 'chairs for hire' (literally 'chairs hire themselves'). In the standard language these verbs show agreement with their traditional subject (i.e. with their surface NP argument), except in the case of *haver-hi*, which is constructed as a subjectless transitive verb: *hi ha moltes raons* 'there are many reasons'. Eastern

Catalan extends plural agreement here: *hi han moltes raons*. On the other hand there is a tendency — not all that strong, and condemned as Spanish interference by normative grammarians — to make the impersonal reflexive truly impersonal, treating the following NP as direct object: *no s'hi farà molts progressos* 'not a lot of progress will be made on it'. In western Catalonia this tendency is more widespread, affecting all types of verbs mentioned here, for example, *aquí hi fa falta més braços* 'here more hands are needed', literally 'here (it) makes need more arms'; *es cull moltes pomes* 'many apples are picked'; *aquí hi ve molts turistes* 'many tourists come here', literally 'here there comes many tourists'.

In Old Catalan the participle of the perfect/anterior paradigms of transitive verbs was active, and was inflected to agree with the direct object in number and gender. This usage is maintained, alongside more modern patterns, in Balearic, e.g. *la barca s'era allunyada* 'the boat had moved further off' (Balearic retains in some measure the older use of *esser* 'to be' as a perfect/anterior auxiliary with reflexive and certain intransitive verbs, as, for instance, in Occitan, p. 270); *havia trobada una olla plena d'or* 'had found a pot full of gold'. In the standard language and in many spoken varieties the participle still often agrees with a preceding third person direct object non-reflexive clitic, expecially if it is feminine, especially if it is singular. That is, agreement is more often found in *l'he trobada ~ trobat* 'I've found it' than in *les he trobades ~ trobat*; and more often here than in *els he trobat(s)*. Third person direct object here includes partitive *en*, so, for example, we find *d'aquelles maduixes, jo només n'he menjada una* 'of those strawberries, I've only eaten one'. Except in the perfect/anterior paradigm with *haver*, the participle is intransitive and inflects for number and gender in agreement with its subject if the finite verb is intransitive, and with its object if the verb is transitive. In absolute constructions an agreeing full NP follows. The participle is usually perfective in aspect, or it expresses the state resulting from an action: *la vam trobar dormida a la taula* 'we found her asleep at the table'; *vistes així les coses, sembla que teniu raó* '(when) things (are) looked at like that, it seems you are right'. Participles take no clitics; anaphoric indirect objects, partitive, locative and agentive expressions have to be expressed by stressed PPs, adverbs, etc., for example, *els elements trets d'aquell* 'the elements taken from it'; *els premis oferts a elles* 'the prizes offered to them'. Other verb + participle constructions are: *ser* 'be' + participle, which is the familiar passive, the agent being expressed by a PP with *per* (most agentive) or a PP with *de* (most instrumental), e.g. *les portes són obertes* 'the doors are opened'; *quedar* (and synonyms) 'remain' + participle, expressing 'resultative', e.g. *així les conversacions quedaven interrompudes* 'in that way the conversations got (and stayed) broken off'; and *estar* 'be/stay' + participle 'stative', e.g. *les portes estan obertes* 'the doors are open'.

Non-finite VPs
Clitics with infinitives are enclitic (except in North Catalan). The subject
NP, if present, normally follows, e.g. *en lloc d'anar-hi ells* 'instead of them
going there'.

Certain verbs regularly followed by non-finite VPs have some affinities
with the modal verbs of other languages. These show either or both of the
following characteristics: (a) no preposition before a following infinitive;
(b) clitic raising. In the latter case, the participle of the 'modal' verb, in a
perfect/anterior periphrasis, is likely to show agreement with a clitic which
is semantically the object of the infinitive, e.g. *no l'he sabuda agafar* 'I
haven't been able to catch it (f.)'. The commonest verbs showing the above
characteristics are: *anar a* 'be going to', *acabar de* 'have just', *acostumar
a/de* (and obsolescent *soler*) 'be accustomed to', *començar a/de* 'begin to',
deixar 'let', *deure* 'must (epistemic)', *fer* 'make', *gosar* 'dare', *haver de*
'have to, must (deontic)', *poder* 'can', *saber* 'know how to, manage to',
tornar a 'do again', *voler* 'want to'. The best case for modal status could be
made for those verbs which do not take NP objects (*gosar, poder, haver
de*), or whose sense outside the constructions mentioned here is markedly
different (*deixar* 'leave, lend', *deure* 'owe').

Gerunds are generally imperfective and active, that is, their subject is
controlled by that of the main verb. Clitic pronouns are enclitic; a subject
NP, if present, normally follows, and must follow if the gerund phrase is
used absolutely, as, for example *col.laborant tants, no el necessitem* 'with
so many cooperating, we don't need him'. A gerund may also have its subject controlled by the object of a verb of perception (e.g. *veure* 'see', *notar*
'note') or representation (e.g. *descriure* 'describe'). Here it functions like a
restrictive relative clause: *el reconegueren baixant de l'avió* 'they recognised
him descending the aircraft steps'; but note *el reconegueren, baixant de
l'avió* 'they recognised him, (as they were) descending the aircraft steps'. A
construction which is less grammaticalised than *haver* + participle, but
which has greatly extended its range recently is *estar* + gerund 'progressive'. Its use emphasises imperfective and/or durative aspect, and in
present and past imperfective paradigms corresponds quite closely to the
English present and past progressive, except that imperfective and durative
meanings are not excluded from the present and past imperfective paradigms of the corresponding simple verbs, for example, *estic llegint* 'I am
reading', *llegeixo* 'I read/am reading'; *estava llegint* 'I was reading', *llegia* 'I
used to read/was reading'; *vaig estar llegint* 'I was reading' (perfective +
durative). Until very recently *estar* + gerund 'progressive' did not combine
with *ser* + participle 'passive' or *haver* + participle 'perfect/anterior'.
These combinations can now be found, at least in journalistic prose influenced by Spanish (and directly or indirectly by English), for example, *el
debat està sent controlat pels organismes del partit* 'discussion is being controlled by the party organisations', *durant cinc anys he estat donant classes*

a estudiants de primer de carrera 'for five years I have been teaching first year undergraduates'. A related periphrasis consists of *anar* 'go' + gerund, expressing either (a) 'durative + motion', e.g. *anaren passejant-se amunt i avall* 'they were walking up and down'; or (b) 'durative + evolutive', e.g. *va acomiadant-se de tots* 'she is taking leave of them all one by one'; *es va posant bé* 'she is getting better'. The latter emphasises the development, unfolding, advancing, intensifying of an action in progress.

Clitics

The clitic *en* is anaphoric to (a) an indefinite or quantified NP, e.g. *ahir encara rajava vi; avui ja no en raja* 'yesterday wine was still flowing; today it is not flowing'; or (b) a PP with *de*, e.g. *en conec la dificultat* 'I know the difficulty (of it)'; *tornarà de la plaça? — ara en torna* 'will she come back from the square? — she's coming back (from it) now'. Note that a NP or PP cliticised by *en* may not be embedded within a PP: *hem passat per cinc pobles; encara *n'hem de passar per quatre* 'we've been through five towns; we still have four to go through'. Note also that *en* may be anaphoric to all or part of a subject NP: *surten autobusos avui? — sí que en surten* 'are there buses leaving today? — yes, there are'.

Clitic *hi* is anaphoric (a) to a PP other than one with *de* or a personal indirect object, for example, *parles sense pensar/amb el pare/amb sinceritat? — hi parlo* 'are you speaking without thinking/with father/with sincerity? — I am (doing so)'; (b) to a locative adverb phrase, e.g. *és allà dalt? — no hi és* 'is it up there? — no it isn't (there)'; (c) to a manner adverb phrase, e.g. *parles així/com un nen/bé. — hi parlo* 'you are speaking in this way/like a child/well. — I am (doing so)'; (d) marginally, to time adverbials — generally these have zero anaphora.

The nominal or adverbial complement of verbs of 'being, seeming, becoming', etc., can be represented by third person direct object pronouns (*el/la/els/les*), or by *ho, hi, en*. Which of these is appropriate depends both on the verb involved and on the category of the predicate phrase. With the verb *ser* 'be' and a definite NP predicate phrase, third person direct object pronouns are grammatical (if generally literary); *ho* is more spontaneous, for example, *creia que era la veïna de casa però no l'és/no ho és* 'I thought it was my next-door neighbour, but it isn't (her)'. With *ser* and other NP PredPs, and with *estar* 'be' or *semblar/parèixer* 'seem' and all NP and AP PredPs, we find *ho* (sometimes *en*): *està malalt? — sí que ho està* 'is he ill? — yes he is'. With all other verbs plus NP and AP PredPs, and with all verbs plus AdvP, the clitic is *hi*, e.g. *ho trobava fàcil; ara no l'hi trobo tant* 'I used to find it easy; now I don't find it so (easy)'. An alternative to *ho* or *hi* with adjectival or adverbial PredPs is *en*. This may reflect the fact that many adjectives and adverbs, being inherently gradable, are treated as implicitly quantified (in the following example this is explicit): *vas bé? — no en vaig gens* 'are you OK? — not at all'. In addition (perhaps an aspect of the same phenomenon), adjectives added as expansions or afterthoughts require *de* before them. The pronominalisation by *en* is consistent with this.

With respect to verb forms, the placing of clitics is straightforward: clitics follow positive imperatives, infinitives, and gerunds; otherwise they precede. Clitic movement, that is, attraction of clitics from their semantically expected position with a non-finite verb to the finite VP on which it depends, though always optional, is generally preferred in Catalan when the main verb is one of the quasi-modals mentioned above (p. 195), and also with, for instance, *venir a* 'come to', *sentir (a)* 'hear', *veure (a)* 'see'. The investigation of exactly which verbs allow clitic movement has yet to be done. As expected, if a non-finite verb has more than one clitic, either all are raised, or none are.

Sentences

Word Order, Topicalisation
Unmarked basic word order is: Frame PP/AdvP, subject, *no*, verb, short AdvP, direct object or PredP, indirect object, PP/AdvP; for example, *quant a la ràdio, els periodistes han donat avui un avis a la direcció sobre la vaga proposada per a dimecres* 'as far as the radio is concerned, the journalists have today given notice to the management about the strike planned for Wednesday'. A major variant of basic word order, with one-place verbs, has the subject following the verb, particularly when the subject carries most of the 'new' information. (These are sometimes referred to as 'presentational sentences'.) For example, *han pujat molts autocars* 'many coaches have come up'; *molts autocars han pujat, però fins ara pocs han baixat* approximately = *han pujat molts autocars, però han baixat pocs fins ara* 'many coaches have come up, but few have gone down so far'. Impersonal reflexives often follow this pattern. Badia claims a possible difference in meaning between VS order ('impersonal active') and SV order ('passive'), at least when a short subject phrase is involved: *s'ha proposat aquesta solució* 'people have suggested this solution', *aquesta solució s'ha proposat* 'this solution has been suggested'. The distinction is, admittedly, a subtle one. This variant order may rather reflect a form of heavy-NP shift. NPs have a tendency to be longer than verbs, and longer elements get shifted rightwards, to avoid ending with a short constituent. The same phenomenon may be at work in relative clauses in which the direct object has been *wh*-fronted, and the subject is placed after the verb in final position: *el temps que experimentem els del nord* 'the weather which those of us in the north experience'; *? el temps que els del nord experimentem.* As far as variation from basic word order in general is concerned, rightward movement of NP, PP, corresponds to heavy-NP shift, focus (on new information), or expansion or clarification, as in *alguns industrials han ofert al museu la major part de la col.lecció* 'some industrialists have offered the

museum the majority of the collection'; *no és cap collonada això de la Crida* 'it's no joke, that "Call" business'. Leftward movement corresponds to topicalisation, often with 'comma intonation' and generally, though not exclusively, with a resumptive clitic: *això no ho farà a les Balears* 'that, he won't do in the Balearics'; *al meu fill, no li ensenyen pas el català* 'my son doesn't get taught Catalan'; *allà, de moment, no els foten malbé les cabines* 'there, for the moment, they don't vandalise their telephone boxes'.

Questions
Basic question construction in Catalan is according to the traditional Romance pattern, namely: (P), (*wh*-word), V, (subject), (etc.). For example, *de qui són aquestes sabates?* 'whose shoes are these?'; *ha mort el conductor?* 'is the driver dead?'. However, V S DO sequences are heavily disfavoured in questions, and the most 'given' information is topicalised, or right-shifted, so as to avoid them: *els ciutadans, han contribuït molts diners a les despeses?* 'have the citizens contributed a lot of money to the expenses?'; ??*han contribuït els ciutadans molts diners a les despeses?*; *a què han contribuït molts diners, els ciutadans?* 'what have the citizens contributed a lot of money to?'; ?*a què han contribuït els ciutadans molts diners?*. If both subject and direct object are 'new', there is no easy escape, however. Clefting may serve: ?*a qui han ofert alguns industrials la major part de la col.lecció?* 'to whom have some industrialists offered the majority of the collection?'; *qui és a qui alguns industrials han ofert la major part de la col.lecció?* It is common, though frowned upon, to use resumptive clitics when PPs (including indirect object) are *wh*-fronted in questions, as also in topicalisation (see above), e.g. *a qui (li) heu donat el premi?* 'who have you given the prize to?'; *amb quantes persones (hi) compteu* 'how many people do you expect?'. The commonest tag question element (in Catalonia), for both positive and negative questions, is *oi*, probably derived from HOC 'this' (cf. Occ. *oc* 'yes'): *deuen ser les vuit, oi?* 'it must be about eight, mustn't it?'.

Negation
Catalan has a set of negative polarity items, comparable to those of English, whose occurrence is restricted to (a) negative sentences; (b) the scope of items like *sense* 'without', *a penes* 'hardly', *lluny* 'far', *dubtar* 'doubt', *repugnància* 'repugnance', *estrany* 'odd', *in-*, *des-*, indefinite relatives, comparatives, *fins que* 'until', *abans que* 'before'; (c) positive interrogative and conditional sentences. Group (b) is not easy to define semantically, but it evidently overlaps with that class of 'indefinite', 'doubtful', 'subjective' elements which require the subjunctive in a subordinate clause. The negative polarity items are *cap* 'any, no' (quantifier), *enlloc* 'anywhere, nowhere', *en ma (ta, sa) vida* 'ever, never in my (your, etc.) life', *gaire* '(not) much, (not) many', *gens* '(not) at all', *mai* 'ever, never', *ningú* 'anyone, no

one', *res* 'anything, nothing', *tampoc* 'either, neither', *ni* 'neither, nor'. The last two of these are not used in context (c) and only in the most clearly negative of contexts (b), e.g. *sense, dubtar.* In contexts (b) and (c) it can be seen that these elements are not in themselves negative, since the presence of *no* 'not' establishes a different meaning: *si hi trobeu cap defecte* 'if you find any defect in it' ≠ *si no hi trobeu cap defecte* 'if you don't find any defect in it'. However, in a sentence fragment (especially an answer to a question) all the elements except *gaire* can stand alone with purely negative meaning. In a negative sentence, if a negative polarity item follows the main verb, *no* must precede it. If a negative polarity item precedes the verb, *no* is optional, though preferred by normative grammar: *no l'hem trobat enlloc* = *enlloc (no) l'hem trobat* 'we haven't found it anywhere', **l'hem trobat enlloc*; likewise if only part of the proposition is negated: *s'ha posat una camisa (no) gens elegant* 'he has put on a shirt (which is) not at all smart'. In sentences containing *no*, with or without a negative polarity item, *pas*, placed after the verb, has the pragmatic function of emphasising the unexpectedness of the proposition negated, for example, *no dic pas que tot s'hagi fet malament* 'I'm not (in fact) saying it was all done badly'; *no té pas cap esquerda?* 'it hasn't got a crack in it, has it?', 'has it got crack in it, perhaps?'

Complex Sentences

Relatives
The next chart shows the relative pronouns, and, for comparison, the interrogative pronouns, in various functions in the standard language. The functions distinguished are: subject, direct object, atonic PP object, tonic or compound PP object or object of non-finite VP, NP complement, and time, place, or manner. Less common forms are in < >. Additional non-standard variants are *el* [± f., ± pl.] *que* as an alternative to *el qual*, and *lo que* for the neuter non-restrictive or free relative. Both of these are Spanish interference phenomena. Notable in the table are the overlaps between restrictive and non-restrictive relative forms, between non-restrictive and free relatives, and between free relatives and interrogatives. Note also that *qui* and *què* appear after weak prepositions in all functions except neuter free relative. *El que* is basically a neuter free relative construction; its spread into neuter non-restrictive relative, for example, *o, el que és pitjor, no en trobarem cap explicació* 'or, what is worse, we shan't find any explanation for it', is not always regarded as genuine. Grammars give as neuter free relative *això que, allò que* but these are no more than *això* 'this', *allò* 'that' as antecedents of *que* 'restrictive relative'. Similarly, *cosa que, la qual cosa* (neuter non-restrictive relatives) have a more basic analysis with *cosa* 'thing' as appositive head noun. *El qual* [± f., ± pl.] is essentially a relative adjective, whose NP head is generally omitted in the

Relative and Interrogative Pronouns

	Restrictive Relatives			Free Relatives	
	Animate	*Inanimate*	*Neuter*	*Animate*	*Inanimate/ Neuter*
Subject	que	} que	que	(tothom) qui, (tot) {aquell/el}{qui/que} [±f., ±pl.]	(tot) el que, ‹ço, que›
Dir. obj.	que, ‹al qual, a qui›				
Atonic P obj.	qui, el qual	què, el qual	què		
Tonic P obj.	el qual	el qual	{ què	?	?
NP compl.			{ —	—	—
Time		que			quan
Place		on			on, ‹on que›
Manner		que, com			com

	Non-Restrictive Relatives			Interrogatives	
	Animate	*Inanimate*	*Neuter*	*Animate*	*Inanimate/ Neuter*
Subject	que, el qual	} que, el qual	el que, cosa que	qui	} què
Dir. obj.	que, el/al qual		la qual cosa ‹ço, que›	(a) qui	
Atonic P obj.	qui, el qual	què, el qual	què, el que, la qual cosa		
Tonic P obj.	el qual	el qual	què, la qual cosa	qui	què
NP compl.	el qual	el qual	—		
Time		que, quan			quan
Place		on			on
Manner		?com			com

relative clause, though it need not be: *1.000 pessetes, la qual suma...* '1,000 pesetas, which sum ...'. Its fundamental role is as a non-restrictive relative, but it fills in for the restrictive relative especially in non-clause-initial positions. As an adjective it cannot play a true role in neuter relatives, which have by definition no possible N head. *Que* is basically the unmarked atonic relative. It must begin its clause (because it is atonic, or because it is not really distinct from the complementiser *que?*). Its appearance in relative time clauses is explained by the fact that adverbial time clauses may be formed by bare NPs such as *divendres* 'on Friday', *aquell dia* 'on that day', etc. In the animate free relatives *que*, preceded by *el* or *aquell*, is nowadays more common than *qui*. That is, the construction is not truly a distinct free relative one, but rather a restrictive relative whose pronominal antecedent is pragmatically interpreted as 'the (person) who, those (people) who'. NPs are not usually *wh*-fronted from within an NP or PP (or from a non-finite VP) without the rest of the phrase accompanying them. An NP complement with *de* may, grammatically, leave its head stranded (*llurs pares, dels quals també coneixem les motivacions de vinguda* 'their parents, whose motives for coming we also recognise') but this alternative is not generally preferred, and if it does occur, it seems not to allow *de qui, de què*, which we might otherwise expect at the front of a relative clause. In colloquial speech, in place of all the restrictive and non-restrictive relative clauses where the embedded clause function is other than subject or direct object, we find invariable *que* relative, with the relevant grammatical role expressed within the relative clause by clitics, possessives, etc., or both relative and resumptive pronouns together; for example, *en aquella urbanització que nosaltres hi teníem un solar* 'on that estate that we had a plot in'; *els seus pares, que coneixem les seves motivacions* 'their parents, whose motives we recognise'; *el porter que hi vas estar una estona enraonant ~ el porter amb qui hi vas estar ...* 'the concierge who you were talking to for a while'.

Conditionals
In typical protases, future/prospective tenses are excluded. The remaining indicative and subjunctive paradigms are thus somewhat ambiguous. In unreal conditions, aspect is not expressed, leading to further ambiguity.

Neutralisation of Tense and Aspect Distinctions in Conditional Protases

Tense/aspect distinctions in assertions	Conditional protasis possibilities	Gloss
vindrà		'if he comes' (future)
ve	si ve	'if he is coming' (present)
(ve)		'if he comes' (habitual)
haurà vingut	si ha vingut	'if he shall have come' (anterior-in-future)
ha vingut		'if he has come' (present perfect real)
venia		'if he was coming' (past imperfective real)
(venia)	si venia	'if he were coming' (imperfective unreal)
va venir		'if he came' (perfective unreal)
vindria		'if he were to come' (prospective-in-past unreal)
venia	si vingués	'if he were coming' (imperfective unreal)
va venir		'if he came' (perfective unreal)
va venir	si va venir	'if he came' (past perfective real)
havia vingut	si havia vingut	'if he had come' (anterior-in-past real)
hauria vingut		'if he had come' (unreal impossible)
hauria vingut	si hagués vingut	'if he had come' (unreal impossible)

Past indicative forms (e.g. *si venia, si havia vingut*) in unreal conditionals are always optional, and are currently less preferred in spontaneous usage.

Sentential Complements

Sentential subjects: these are most often subjects of intransitive or impersonal reflexive verbs, which they usually follow; for example, *convé que tothom ho sàpiga* 'it is appropriate that everyone should know'; *es diu que desembarcaran* 'it is said they will disembark'; *és una pena que no la puguem veure* 'it's a pity we can't see it'. Sentential subjects of transitive verbs appear in the usual initial subject position; they generally have their verb in the subjunctive: *que fossin molt amics no va impedir que se separessin* 'the fact that they were close friends didn't prevent them from separating'. The commonest kind of sentential complement is a direct object, e.g. *ja ens figuràvem que tot passaria igual* 'we guessed everything would stay the same'. Non-dependent sentences with initial *que* may be sentential objects with ellipsis of the main verb, or, what comes to another way of saying the same thing, main clauses permitted in pragmatically determined contexts: *que no ho saps?* '(do you mean) you don't know?'; *que votin!* 'let them vote!'. When the matrix verb is negated, the subordinate verb is typically subjunctive (p. 203).

Previously (p. 193) we have considered what happens to the preposition (and to *que*) when a sentential complement appears in certain PPs. What is semantically **per a que* + S appears on the surface as *perquè* + S with a verb in the subjunctive 'in order that', for example, *l'hem invitada perquè ens faci una conferència* 'we have invited her to give us a lecture'. But **per que* + S appears as *perquè* + S with a verb in the indicative 'because': *l'hem invitada perquè ens fa una conferència* 'we have invited her because she is giving us a lecture'. In the standard language a sentential complement appears without alteration as a NP complement or as an AP complement; the subjunctive of 'non-assertion' is quite usual. Spoken varieties are inclined to imitate Spanish and insert *de* here. For example, *la idea (de) que tots els homes siguin iguals* 'the idea that all men are equal'; *tinc por (de) que ens atrapin* 'I'm afraid that they'll catch us'; *està orgullós (de) que li hagi confiat els seus fills* 'he is proud you have entrusted your children to him'. Sentential complements also appear in 'consecutive clauses': *tant ... que* 'so many/much ... that', *tal ... que* 'such ... that', as in *hi ha tants alumnes que un s'hi perd* 'there are so many pupils that one gets lost', and in vaguely adverbial contexts, where the way in which the S is relevant is left free to the hearer to interpret, for example, *no l'escolto que no em faci riure* 'I can't listen to it without laughing'; *treballa que dóna gust* 'her work is a pleasure to see' (literally 'she-works that she-gives pleasure').

The majority of conjunctions introducing adverbial clauses consist of an adverb or a PP + *que*, e.g. *així que* 'as soon as' (literally 'thus that'), *encara que* 'although' (literally 'still that'), *sols que* 'if only, provided that' (literally 'only that'), *ja que* 'since' (literally 'already that'), *sempre que* 'as long as' (literally 'always that'), *de seguida que* 'as soon as' (literally 'immediately that').

Subjunctive Usage
The use of subjunctives in Catalan subordinate clauses is largely typical of Southern Romance. The following particular observations are, however, worth making. Subjunctives are not used in indirect questions or in indirect statements with positive main verbs, nor in the apodoses of conditionals. One of the most interesting contexts is the only one in which the past perfective subjunctive, a uniquely Catalan creation, can appear, that is, in subordinate clauses depending on negative expressions of propositional attitude ('I don't think that ...', 'it isn't likely that ...', 'they don't claim that ...'). Unfortunately these constructions have been inadequately investigated. Unlike most subordinate subjunctive environments, but like most reported speech environments, they are not subject to sequence of tense restrictions. The subjunctive is in any case not obligatory, but allows speakers to avoid commitment to the truth of the proposition in the subordinate clause, something which, when they are also the ones holding the negative propositional attitude, they are likely to want to do: *no crec que sigui veritat* 'I don't think it's true' (speaker = non-believer); *no creu que és/sigui veritat* 'she doesn't believe it's true' (speaker ≠ non-believer). My impression is that it is not so usual to replace future/prospective (conditional) tenses with subjunctive forms, unless to do so would not obscure relevant tense distinctions (e.g. when a time adverb or the pragmatic context clarifies the matter). Examples: *no crec que ho sabré* 'I don't think I'll find out'; *no crec que ho sàpiga fins massa tard* 'I don't think I'll find out until too late' (context rules out 'I don't think I know ...'); *no deia que el llegis* 'he didn't say he was reading/read it'; *no deia que el vagi llegir* 'he didn't say he read it'; *no deia que el va llegir* 'he didn't **say** he read it (but I guess he did)'.

Subjunctives may also appear in main clauses expressing wishes or exhortations, such as *facin el que vulguin* 'let them do whatever they want'; *ho haguessis dit abans* 'you should have said so before'; *tant de bo hagi guanyat* 'let's hope he's won'; *no m'ho diguin a mi* '(I hope) they don't say it to me', and, non-standardly, with adverbs of possibility, e.g. *potser, tal vegada* 'perhaps'; *tal vegada fos millor = tal vegada seria millor* 'perhaps it would be better'.

5   Lexis

Word Formation
We review here the main productive processes (excluding international

vocabulary). Except in the case of verb formation, derivation is almost entirely by suffixation. There are productive nominal 'prefixes', mostly of a pan-Romance kind like *inter-, ex-, pre-*. Their secondary stress, however, suggests that such derivations have rather the characteristics of compounds.

Suffixes

Of the suffixes common to nouns and adjectives, we may mention the affective ones: *-et* (diminutive), *-às* (augmentative), and *-ot* (despective), e.g. *cadireta* 'little chair', *cadirassa* 'great big chair', *cadirota* 'ugly old chair', *vellet/-a* 'little old', *grisot/-a* 'ugly grey'.

Other suffixes deriving nouns from nouns are:

Persons: *-er, -ista*, both 'professional concerned with *x*', e.g. *mainadera* 'child minder' (< *mainada* 'small children'), *taxista* 'taxi-driver'.

Places: *-ia*, e.g. *alcaldia* 'mayor's office', *rellotgeria* 'watch-maker's shop' (< *rellotger* 'watch-maker' < *rellotge* 'watch, clock').

Objects: *-er(a)*, e.g. *clauer* 'key-ring', *calaixera* 'chest of drawers' (< *calaix* 'drawer'); the suffix is particularly common in the names of plants/trees, e.g. *maduixera* 'strawberry plant'.

Collectives: *-ada*, e.g. *gentada* 'crowd of people'; collectives of plants: *-ar, -eda*, e.g. *tarongerar* 'orange grove' (< *taronger* 'orange tree' < *taronja* 'orange'), *roureda* 'oak wood'.

Abstract: *-ada* (1) 'blow with *x*', e.g. *banyada* 'wound from a horn'; (2) 'action typical of *x*', e.g. *pallassada* 'buffoonery' (< *pallasso* 'clown'); *-isme* 'practice of, or belief in, *x*', e.g. *ciclisme* 'cycling'.

Nouns from adjectives:

Abstract: *-esa*, e.g. *senzillesa* 'simplicity'; *-or*, e.g. *buidor* 'emptiness'; *-itat* (and variants), e.g. *suavitat* 'gentleness', *igualtat* 'equality'.

Nouns from verbs: *-dor(a)* 'agent, instrument, or location of *x*', e.g. *acomodador/-a* 'usher/-ette', *gronxador* 'swing', *escorxador* 'abattoir' (< *escorxar* 'slaughter').

Abstract: *-ment*, e.g. *penediment* 'repentance'; *-ció*, e.g. *recomanació* 'recommendation'; *-Ø*, e.g. *rebuig* 'rejection' (< *rebutjar* 'reject'); *-a*, e.g. *esmena* 'correction' (< *esmenar* 'correct').

Adjectives from nouns:

From place names: *-ès*, e.g. *vienès* 'Viennese'; *-i* /+in/, e.g. *gironi* 'from Girona'; *-enc*, e.g. *canadenc* 'Canadian'.

From proper names of various kinds *-(i)à* /+(i)an/, e.g. *danubià* 'Danubian', *wagnerià* 'Wagnerian'.

Others: *-ós* /+oz/, e.g. *polsós* 'dusty', *defectuós* 'defective'; *-al*, e.g. *genial* 'inspired' (< *geni* 'genius').

Adjectives from adjectives: -*enc* 'tending to colour *x*', e.g. *rosadenc* 'pinkish'; -*è* /+ɛn/ 'ordinal numeral', e.g. *quinzè* 'fifteenth'; *issim* 'extremely *x*', e.g. *amabilissim* 'most kind'.

Adjectives from verbs: -*ant/-ent*, e.g. *sufocant* 'suffocating', *sorprenent* 'surprising'; -*dor* (1) 'likely to *x*', e.g. *eixordador* 'deafening'; (2) 'likely to be *x*ed', e.g. *llegidor* 'readable'; -*dis* 'liable to *x*', e.g. *enyoradis* 'nostalgic' (< *enyorar* 'miss'); -*ble* '(li)able to be *x*ed', e.g. *exportable* 'exportable', *temible* 'awesome'.

Adverbs: -*ment* is added to the feminine form of an adjective, e.g. *arbitràriament* 'arbitrarily'. The retained secondary stress on the stem, together with the fact that -*ment* may be omitted in the second of a pair of conjoined adverbs, indicates that this type of adverb formation is still essentially phrasal, in which -*ment* functions as a feminine noun head.

Verbs: -*ejar* (generally intransitive) 'behave in a way connected with *x*', e.g. *ciutadejar* (of a town) 'affect to be a city', *fluixejar* 'be inclind to be weak' (< *fluix* 'thin, flimsy'); -*itzar*, e.g. *sistematitzar* 'systematise'.

Prefixes
The productive true, i.e. atonic, prefixes, are verbal:

Verbs from verbs: *re-* 'do *x* again', e.g. *reelegir* 'reelect', *repassar* 'go by again'.

Verbs from nouns or adjectives: *a-*, *en-*, e.g. *apressar-se* 'hurry' (< *pressa* 'haste'), *aprofundir* 'deepen', *embutxacar* 'pocket' (< *butxaca* 'pocket'), *embrutar* 'dirty', *emmalaltir* 'fall ill'; *es-* 'remove *x*', e.g. *espuntar* 'break (or otherwise remove) the point of'. There are 'parasynthetic' nouns and adjectives, which appear to be participles of derived verbs formed in the above way, but where the verb is unattested, e.g. *enfeinat* 'busy' (< *feina* 'work').

Compounds
Of the various types of compound, two seem noteworthy as productive. There are compound verbs with adverbial first elements, especially *mal* 'badly', *mig* 'half'. Word order shows that these are more closely bound than regular adverbs; e.g. *s'ha entestat a maleducar les seves filles* 'she has made up her mind to bring up her daughters badly'; *aquella masia, ja l'hem mig abandonada* 'we have more or less abandoned that farmhouse'. The other considerably more productive compounding process derives nouns from VPs, typically to name an instrument which has the purpose described, e.g. *para-xocs* 'bumper' (literally 'stops bumps'), *eixugamans*

'hand-towel' (literally 'dries hands'), *comptagotes* 'pipette' (literally 'counts drops').

Characterisation of Basic Vocabulary

Rather than attempt to discuss distinctive aspects of Catalan vocabulary as a whole, I shall concentrate on a basic vocabulary list of 800 words, established on the basis of frequency counts by J. Llobera. This will give a more practical impression of the vocabulary of everyday usage, and of possible difficulties for learners coming to Catalan via another Romance language. Of the 800 words in the basic vocabulary, some 155 (over 19 per cent) are etymologically distinct from their most likely Spanish translation. Note, of course, that this does not mean that a cognate cannot be found anywhere in Spanish for any of these 155, but only that the central or most obvious meaning would most probably be expressed by an unrelated word. Of these 155 words, 52 (6.5 per cent of the total 800) are etymologically distinct from their most likely gloss in Occitan, French and Italian also. These 52 items, listed below, are thus the ones which are a distinctively Catalan part of common vocabulary.

aixecar	raise	*groc*	yellow
ampolla	bottle	*llavor*	seed
amunt	up	*fer malbé*	damage, spoil
avi, àvia	grandfather, grandmother	*massa*	too (much)
aviat	soon	*menjador*	dining-room
barallar-se	argue	*mica*	bit
barret	hat	*mitjó*	sock
brut	dirty	*noi, noia*	boy, girl
butxaca	pocket	*només*	only
capellà	priest	*oi*	(tag question element)
cridar	call	*pagès*	peasant, farmer
dalt	above, upstairs	*paleta*	building worker
dolent	bad	*pujar*	go up
dur (v.)	bring	*raspall*	brush
eina	tool	*rentar*	wash
endur-se	take away	*ros*	fair(-complexioned)
enlloc	anywhere, nowhere	*soroll*	noise
enraonar	talk	*tancar*	shut
estimar	love	*tardor*	autumn
feina	work	*tou*	soft
forat	hole	*trencar*	break
fuster	carpenter	*treure*	take out, off
galleda	bucket	*vegada*	time (occasion)
ganivet	knife	*vermell*	red
gens	(not) at all	*vespre*	evening
gos	dog	*vora*	beside, edge

6 Conclusion

It is difficult to be confident about the prospects, whether favourable or unfavourable, for the health of Catalan. There are a number of negative factors: to a large extent Catalan is no longer being learnt as a first language in France or in Alghero — in both regions most native speakers are over 40 — and language shift is also taking place in the far south, in the city of Alacant (Alicante) and the surrounding region. Well engrained diglossic attitudes restrict the role of Catalan in daily use in the País Valencià, in Eivissa (Ibiza), and to some extent in the other Balearics. About half the population of Catalonia and the País Valencià is of immigrant origin; most of these people have passive knowledge of Catalan and some are fluent speakers. These are found particularly in those places where the proportion of Spanish-speaking population is small. Virtually all Catalan speakers in Spain are fluent in Spanish, the language which has the prestige associated with international culture and commerce (even when this is in fact calqued on English). Favourable factors include the mutual intelligibility of all dialects and the acceptance of standard Catalan by virtually all speakers — the Valencian opposition to this is promoted mostly by people who do not regularly use the language. An important development since 1975 has been the institutionalisation of Catalan as an official language, as a language of the mass media, and as a language of education. All of these have increased the social prestige of the language, while those who have themselves learnt to read and write Catalan, or have even had part of their education through the medium of Catalan, are much more confident of their competence, and of the value of their linguistic abilities, than an older, semi-literate generation. There is no real parallel situation, of a large, bilingual, European, non-state speech community, from which lessons can be drawn about the path Catalan may follow.

Bibliography

Alarcos Llorach, E. (1983) *Estudis de lingüística catalana.* Ariel, Barcelona.
Alcover, Antoni M. and Francesc de B. Moll (1930–62) *Diccionari Català-Valencià-Balear.* Moll, Mallorca.
Badia i Margarit, Antoni M. (1951) *Gramática histórica catalana.* Noguer, Barcelona.
—— (1962) *Gramática catalana* 2 vols. Gredos, Madrid.
Bonet, Sebastià, and Joan Solà (1986) *Sintaxi generativa catalana.* Enciclopèdia Catalana, Barcelona.
Calveras, Josep (1928) 'Variants de les preposicions *a, en, ab* en els dialectes catalans', *Anuari de l'Oficina Romànica de Lingüística i Literatura* 1: 151–78.
—— (1929–30) 'La forma 'que' del relatiu català', *Anuari de l'Oficina Romànica de Lingüística i Literatura* 2: 185–254; 3: 177–243.
Colon, Germà (1975) 'A propos du parfait périphrastique VADO + *infinitif* en català, en provençal et en français'. *Travaux de Linguistique et Littérature* 13:

31–66. Also, in Catalan, in Germà Colon, *La llengua catalana en els seus textos* Vol. 2, 131–74. Curial, Barcelona, 1978.

—— (1976) *El léxico catalán en la Romania.* Gredos, Madrid.

Comrie, Bernard (1985) *Tense.* Cambridge University Press, Cambridge.

Coromines, Joan (1971) *Lleures i converses d'un filòleg.* Club Editor, Barcelona.

—— (1976–7) *Entre dos llenguatges* 3 vols. Curial, Barcelona.

—— (1980–) *Diccionari etimològic i complementari de la llengua catalana.* Curial/'La Caixa', Barcelona.

Duarte i Montserrat, Carles, and Alex Alsina i Keith (1984–6) *Gramàtica històrica del català, 1–3.* Curial, Barcelona.

Fabra, Pompeu (1913–14) 'Els mots àtons en el parlar de Barcelona', *Butlletí de Dialectologia Catalana* 1: 1–17; 2: 1–6.

—— (1968) *Gramàtica catalana* 4th edn. Teide, Barcelona.

Llobera i Ramon, Josep (1968) *El català bàsic.* Teide, Barcelona.

López del Castillo, Lluís (1976) *Llengua standard i nivells de llenguatge.* Laia, Barcelona.

Moll, Francesc de B. (1982) *Gramàtica catalana, referida especialment a les Illes Balears* 5th edn. Moll, Mallorca.

Solà, Joan (1972–3) *Estudis de sintaxi catalana* 2 vols. Edicions 62, Barcelona.

Veny, Joan (1982) *Els parlars catalans. (Síntesi de dialectologia)* 3rd edn. Moll, Mallorca.

Wheeler, Max W. (1979) *Phonology of Catalan* (Publications of the Philological Society, 28). Blackwell, Oxford.

—— (forthcoming) 'L'estructura fonològica de la síl.laba i del mot en català', *Estudis de Llengua i Literatura Catalanes.* (Homenatge a Antoni M. Badia i Margarit.)

6 French

Martin Harris

1 Introduction

We have seen (pp. 13–14) that standard French is primarily derived from the dialect spoken originally in the Ile de France, that is, in more or less the geographical centre of the area covered by the northern group of dialects known collectively as the *langue d'oïl* (see Map V). Although as the national language developed, it absorbed certain elements, in particular lexical items, from other dialects — as indeed it did from other languages — it is overwhelmingly from Francien that French has developed, and it is accordingly the historical development of this dialect which underlies the synchronic description presented hereafter.

2 Phonology

One of the most immediately striking facts about French in comparison with its cognate languages is the radical nature of the phonological changes which the language has undergone, changes which clearly differentiate the *langue d'oïl*, and Francien in particular, from other forms of Romance. Four processes especially have contributed to this global effect: the evolution of the tonic vowel system and the very significant reduction of originally atonic vowels; a period of nasalisation and subsequent partial denasalisation of vowels preceding nasal consonants; the widespread palatalisation of many consonants in appropriate environments (which in turn affected the vowel system); and, more recently, the effacement of most unsupported final consonants and, for most speakers, of final /ə/ also.

Vowels

The vowel system of contemporary French is shown in Table 6.1. There are a number of points to be noted about this system. Firstly, of the pairs of higher mid and lower mid vowels, only the opposition between /o/ and /ɔ/ is clearly maintained (*saute* /sot/ 'jumps': *sotte* /sɔt/ 'foolish' (f.))

Table 6.1: Vowel Phonemes of French

Oral

i	y		u	
e	ø		o	
ɛ	(œ)		ɔ	
		ə		
	a		(ɑ)	

Nasal

ɛ̃	(œ̃)	ɔ̃
	ɑ̃	

Note: for those speakers for whom the opposition between /a/ and /ɑ/ is neutralised, the remaining phoneme is a low central vowel, with the result that the quadrilateral system shown here is in effect replaced by a triangular one, with /a/ *moyen* as its apex.

with /o/ having generalised in open final position. In the case of /ø ~ œ/, the higher variant has again generalised in open final position, but elsewhere the situation is much less clear, with analogical forces noticeably at work. In terms of classical minimal pairs, however, there are very few indeed (e.g. *jeune* /ʒœn/ 'young' vs *jeûne* /ʒøn/ 'fast'), and the distinction is certainly not made by all native speakers. It is for this reason that /œ/ as a phoneme is bracketed in Table 6.1. In the case of /e/ : /ɛ/, neutralisation might well have occurred (with [e] in open syllables and [ɛ] in closed), but for a concerted attempt, dating back to the seventeenth century, to retain [ɛ] also in open final position, and thus minimal pairs of the type *piqué* 'stung' : *piquait* 'was stinging' (/pike/ : /pikɛ/). Again, this distinction is not by any means consistently made: however, it seems that both /e/ and /ɛ/ should be retained within the inventory of phonemes for the time being. The phonological opposition between /ɑ/ and /a/ has already been lost in much of France, to the profit of /a/ or rather of a low central vowel between [a] and [ɑ]; /ɑ/, a relatively late addition to the inventory in certain very specific environments, is retained in the Parisian area only by older speakers and is also bracketed in Table 6.1. Of the four nasal monophthongs shown, one, /œ̃/, has a very low functional yield, and for many speakers is in the process of being absorbed by /ɛ̃/, the few oppositions such as that between *brin* 'sprig' /bʀɛ̃/ and *brun* 'brown' /bʀœ̃/ thus being lost. It is therefore bracketed, although it should be noted that for those speakers who do retain /œ̃/, it has a high frequency of occurrence because of the masculine singular indefinite article *un* /œ̃/. Various attempts to view nasal vowels as conditioned allophones of oral vowels in specifiable contexts do not appear convincing (see below), and their status as phonemes seems secure. All of the vowels shown may occur in tonic position, albeit in the case of one of them, /ə/, only rarely (e.g. *faites-le* 'do it'), where it may in the event be replaced by /ø/. There is also a wide range of complex vocalic nuclei, both oral and nasal, some of which emerged from early Romance diphthongs (p. 35) (e.g. *pied* [pje] 'foot' < PĔDEM, see below) while others have developed later in the history of the language in particular conditioning environments, for instance *feuille* /fœj/ 'leaf' from earlier /fœʎ/. All of these sequences in the contemporary language are best analysed as combinations of glide(s) (see below) plus monophthong; note too in this context three-element sequences such as /vjɛj/ *vieille* 'old' (f.), from earlier /viɛʎ/.

Various complex historical developments underlie the modern system. Of the seven tonic vowels inherited from late Latin (p. 33) by Gallo-Romance (GR), no fewer than five diphthongised, although exclusively in open syllables (contrast Spanish, pp. 35, 88); only /i/ remained essentially unchanged, while /u/ fronted to /y/ (as in Occitan: cf. p. 247). The most interesting development is the early passage of Latin /a/, probably via a diphthong, to a lower mid front vowel, a marked characteristic of the *langue d'oïl* (MATREM > *mère* /mɛʁ/ 'mother'). Of the four remaining diphthongs, two (/ue/ < GR /ɔ/ and /eu/ < GR /o/) monophthongised and merged as /ø ~ œ/ (see above), i.e. as a second front rounded vowel, a type of segment found within Romania only in Gallo-Romance. (Compare PŎTET ([ɔ]) 'can' > *peut* [pø] with NŌDUM ([o]) 'knot' > *nœud* [nø].) A third diphthong, OFr. /oi/ (< GR /e/), passed to [wɛ] and then split in a most unusual way, passing either to Mod. Fr. /wa/ or to /ɛ/, on no discernible phonetic or lexical basis: compare, for example, the nationality adjectives *français* 'French' and *anglais* 'English', with /ɛ/, and *danois* 'Danish' and *suédois* 'Swedish', with /wa/. The fourth diphthong, OFr. /ie/ (< GR /ɛ/), developed into a glide plus monophthong sequence, as noted in the case of PĔDEM > *pied*, above. Various other developments of tonic vowels in specific environments restored both lower mid and higher mid back and front vowels and a back high vowel to the system by the Middle French period, where they remain, albeit rather tenuously in a couple of cases, as we have already seen. The particular effect of the history of stress in French on atonic vowels is noted briefly below.

A special word is appropriate about the development of nasal vowels and vocalic sequences in French. (Compare the discussion of the phenomenon in Portuguese, p. 136, and Gallo-Italian, p. 282.) During the period from the tenth to the thirteenth centuries, all vowels and diphthongs occurring before any nasal consonant nasalised, the low vowels first, then the mid and finally the close vowels. This development took place regardless of whether the syllable concerned was closed or open and in many instances the resulting nasalised vowel was lowered; diphthongs tended to monophthongise. To give just one example, FĪNEM 'end' gave [fin], then [fĩn], then [fɛ̃n], now [fæ̃] (/fɛ̃/). During the latter part of the Middle French period, syllable structure became crucial, in that nasality was maintained only where the vowel and the relevant nasal consonant were in the same syllable; elsewhere, nasalisation was reversed, and the vowel became once again oral, sometimes before lowering (*FĪNAM > *fine* 'fine' (f.) /fi-nə/), sometimes afterwards (FĒMĬNAM > *femme* 'woman' /fa-mə/, not */fɛ-mə/). This left nasalised vowels only in closed syllables, where the nasal consonants ceased to be pronounced, as with /fɛ̃/ above: contrast *inconfortable* (initial vowel /ɛ̃/) and *inévitable* (initial vowel /i/). The net result of these changes was that nasalised vowels ceased to be conditioned allophones of oral vowels before a nasal consonant, and became, as indicated in Table 6.1, phonemes in their own right, the number of minimal pairs being greatly increased by the effacement of final /ə/ (see below) after denasalisation. Compare the development of the masculine and feminine forms of the adjective SANUM 'healthy': both nasalise, but only the latter denasalises, thus: (m.) SANUM > [sãin] > [sɛ̃n] > [sɛ̃] > [sæ̃]; (f.) SANAM > [sãinə] > [sɛnə] > [sɛn]; (/sɛ̃/ : /sɛn/).

Consonants

The consonant inventory of contemporary French is given in Table 6.2. Several points are worth noting. Firstly, French (like virtually all its cognate languages) makes use of the palatal place of articulation, absent from (Classical) Latin (cf. p. 29). A fourth member of this group, /ʎ/, was widely found until the seventeenth century (and still is in certain peripheral dialects) but was progressively lost in the standard language, becoming one source of the palatal glide /j/. (Recall the earlier discussion of *feuille*; for a comparable development in Spanish, cf. p. 84). Secondly, there were in Old French four affricates, /ts, dz, tʃ, dʒ/, all of which had resulted from palatalisation under many and varied circumstances. (One particular source of /tʃ/ was from /k/ before /a/, tonic or atonic, a development highly characteristic of Francien and unlike most other Romance dialects (but cf. Occitan, p. 250), thus CARUM > *cher* 'dear' (OFr. [tʃier]), CABĂLLUM > *cheval* 'horse' (OFr. [tʃəval]). /ts, dz/, originally alveolar, dentalised and later simplified, to merge with /s, z/, while /tʃ, dʒ/ also simplified to the palatal fricatives shown in Table 6.2; the class of affricates was thus once again lost to the language. /h/ survived in initial position in certain words of Germanic origin and was restored by analogy in a few words with Latin, Greek or Arabic etyma; it persisted until the Middle French period, but its loss was acknowledged as irreversible by the seventeenth century. One residual effect of the loss of [h], which had earlier been pronounced, is the absence of liaison in cases such as /la aʃ/ *la hache* 'axe'. ('h' was also restored purely orthographically in a number of words such as *heure* < HŌRAM, OFr. *eure*.) Finally, we should note that /ʁ/ is

Table 6.2: Consonant Phonemes of French

	Labial	Dental	Palatal	Velar	Uvular
Plosive	p b	t d		k g	
Fricative	f v	s z	ʃ ʒ		ʁ
Nasal	m	n	ɲ		
Lateral		l			

included in the table, since a uvular fricative is the normal urban pronunciation of what was etymologically the /r/ phoneme, at least in northern
French, although a uvular trill is not infrequent and a dental or alveolar trill is
still found, particularly in the south.

The development of final consonants in French is worthy of special note.
Consonants already in this position in Latin were widely effaced in earliest
French, /θ/ surviving until perhaps the mid-twelfth century, and only the
dentals /s, n, l, r/ in general persisting thereafter. A whole range of secondary final consonants was created in Old French, however, by the loss of
post-tonic syllables, discussed briefly below: PŎNTEM > *pont* 'bridge'
(OFr. [pɔnt]) is a case in point, as is CAPUT > *chef* 'chief' (OFr. [tʃief]). In
fact, the Old French final consonant system, which subsumed the four
earlier survivors mentioned above, consisted of twelve phonemes, involving
all the manners and places of articulation. Of these twelve, the fate of
nasals and of /ʎ/ has already been considered, while /l/ and to some
extent /ʁ/ have been maintained. The fate of final voiceless plosives and
fricatives, whether primary or the result of terminal devoicing, has, however, been more complex. The general tendency was for two or even three
distinct pronunciations to develop, one before a pause, one before a subsequent initial consonant and one before a subsequent initial vowel, a situation which has survived in some very few cases to the present day: an
obvious example is that of *dix* 'ten', pronounced as /dis/ in isolation, /di/
before a consonant (*dix femmes* 'ten women'), and /diz/ before a vowel
(*dix élèves* 'ten pupils'). It will be noted that the final consonant has been
lost completely before a following initial consonant, and it is in this
environment that the effacement of many final consonants appears to have
begun. By the middle of the seventeenth century, most final plosives and
fricatives — including /s/ even when the plural marker, a point discussed
later — had fallen silent, except in a number of monosyllables (where the
danger of homonymic clash is greatest) and except before a word beginning
with a vowel within the same sense group.

The modern phenomenon of liaison has its roots in this development.
According to the traditional rules, final consonants are pronounced if the
following word within the immediate sense unit begins with a vowel, an
otherwise voiceless fricative (though not a plosive) being voiced. Thus we

find *il faut y aller* /i(l)fotiale/ or *les enfants* /lezɑ̃fɑ̃/. It has to be said, however, that the principle of invariance exerts a strong pressure, and that even in careful speech, let alone more casual registers, liaison is often not made: in other words, the last vestiges of the secondary final plosives and fricatives are tending to be lost, thus *pas encore* 'not yet', often /paɑ̃kɔʁ/, or, in the case of the example above, /ifoiale/.

It might be thought that that would be the end of the story of final consonants. Not so, however. With the effacement of final /ə/ alluded to earlier, a range of tertiary final consonants has come into being, a range which includes in fact every one of the consonantal phonemes of the modern language, thus *vache* 'cow' /vaʃ/, *vigne* 'vine' /viɲ/ etc. These consonants show no sign whatever of weakening or loss: that particular stage in the language's history is over. Indeed, as will be noted in the discussion of English loan-words, closed monosyllables are currently very much a favoured word-type in French.

Glides

French has three glide phonemes, /j/, /w/ and /ɥ/. While these are clearly related historically to the three high vowels /i/, /u/ and /y/ respectively and may at times be in morphophonemic alternation with them, within contemporary syllable structure they behave more like consonants than vowels, for instance in precluding liaison, thus /lejɔt/ rather than */lezjɔt/ for *les yachts* 'the yachts'. Note also such pairs as /uj/ *houille* 'coal' and /wi/ *oui* 'yes'. As has already been noted, one or even two glides may combine with a vowel to form a complex vocalic nucleus, thus *vieille* /vjɛj/ discussed above. We may also contrast monosyllabic *pied* /pje/ 'foot' with disyllabic *piller* /pije/ 'to ravage', or *paye* /pɛj/ 'pays' with *pays* /pei/ 'country'.

Stress and Schwa

Finally in this section, one should note more explicitly the effects of stress on the overall shape of French words.

In the Latin of northern Gaul, the intensity of the stress accent grew, to the point where most tonic vowels lengthened and broke (i.e. diphthongised as noted above) and even more significantly, virtually all posttonic vowels except /ə/ (< Lat. /a/) were eventually lost. The effect of this was to create a fixed-stress language, with the stress either on the now final syllable or the penultimate syllable if the vowel of the final syllable was /ə/; subsequent effacement of final /ə/ in (standard) spoken French, noted in our discussion of nasalisation earlier, has further simplified the position, and the tendency for both verbal and nominal groups to function as ever more tightly bound units, discussed below, has meant that such units have increasingly borne only one stress. Essentially, therefore, we may say that modern French is a final-stress, phrase-stress language, with a very strong tendency, in non-learned words, towards monosyllabism. A clear example of the process can be seen by comparing the characteristic development of the trisyllabic Latin word PŌPULUM 'people' to a mono-syllabic *peuple* /pøpl/ (via [pœ-plə]) in French, compared with It. *popolo*, Sp. *pueblo* and Rum. *popor*.

This loss of schwa in word-final position is in fact part of a much more general tendency for it to be effaced in speech broadly speaking when its loss would not lead to unacceptable initial or medial consonant clusters. Given that words within a sense group function, as we have seen, very much like a single word, these rules apply across the phrase rather than to words in isolation. Thus *elle est petite* 'she is small' may well be pronounced /ɛ-lɛp-tit/, whereas *une petite femme* 'a small woman' is perhaps more likely to be /yn-pə-tit fam/ to avoid the sequence /npt/. Compare also *petite amie* 'little friend' /p(ə)-ti-ta-mi/ (initial [pt] being acceptable only in fairly rapid speech) with *ma petite amie* 'my little friend' /map-ti-ta-mi/ where the problem does not arise. Interestingly, in speech, /ə/ may actu-ally be introduced, for instance to avoid a three-consonant cluster, thus *Arc de Triomphe* /aʁ-k(ə)-də-tʁi-ɔ̃f/, *un ours blanc* /œ̃nuʁs(ə)blɑ̃/ 'a white bear'. The question of the phonemic status of [ə] is left open here. One acceptable way of viewing schwa in contemporary French certainly seems to be as an unstressed positional variant of [ø], this being the phonetic realisation in those rare instances where words such as *le* are stressed, e.g. *fais-le* 'do it'; at times, however [ə] is simply introduced in particular contexts in the way just described — hence, in part at least, such names as *ə-muet*, *ə-instable* and *ə-caduc*.

Orthography

To say that French orthography is less than ideal would be an understate-ment. When the first vernacular texts came to be written down, it was natural that the scribes should turn to the Latin alphabet, despite the obvious fact that it was already unsuitable for the representation of a lan-guage whose phonological system had by that time evolved considerably from that of Latin and which was to continue to develop rapidly. Neverthe-less, despite the difficulties, a relatively standardised and quasi-phonemic orthography was widely used during the eleventh, twelfth and thirteenth centuries, 'quasi-phonemic' in the sense that it relied in part on 'distrib-utional rules' (e.g. 'c' represents /k/ in certain environments (*cœur* 'heart') but /ts/ (later /s/) in others (*cent* 'hundred')) and in part on the use of one letter as a diacritic to indicate that an adjacent letter had a special value ('g' before 'n' marks the palatal nasal, thus 'gn' = /ɲ/; 'h' after 'c' marked first /tʃ/ and now marks /ʃ/). The shortcomings of vowel orthography, however, especially the need to use one symbol (e.g. 'e') with various values (i.e. /e/, /ɛ/, /ə/), could only be partially alleviated by the use of certain conventional digraphs (e.g. 'ez' for /e/).

During the following three centuries, two major developments occurred to overturn the relative stability just described. Firstly, there was a further period of very rapid and radical phonetic change (one particular consequence of which was the emergence of many monosyllabic homophones), and secondly, not unconnected, there was a marked increase in the use of quasi-etymological spellings, in which one or more letters appropriately present in a Latin etymon were reinserted in the corresponding French derivative, even though the sound they represented had been modified or lost in the interim, thus *doi(g)t* < DIGITUM 'finger' although the [g] had long been effaced and similarly *pie(d)* < PEDEM 'foot', *se(p)t* < SEPTEM 'seven'. (The label 'quasi-etymological' is used because recourse was not infrequently had to incorrect etyma: thus *poi(d)s* 'weight' does not come from PONDUS but from *PENSUM.) The sixteenth and seventeenth centuries saw various attempts at reform and in particular the acceptance of distinction between 'i' and 'j' and 'u' and 'v' and the use of the cedilla; the three principal accents were not finally accepted by the Academy until 1740. Some of the more extraordinary 'gothic' spellings (e.g. *sçapvoir* for *savoir* 'know', based partly on SCIRE and partly on SAPERE) have also been resimplified. The nineteenth and twentieth centuries have seen repeated attempts at reform, both unofficial and official, the best known of the latter being the reports of the two Beslais commissions, in 1952 and 1965. The second of these proposed a small number of sensible and limited reforms, such as the use of 's' as a standard plural marker (thus *bijous* for *bijoux* 'jewels'); the simplification of many unnecessary double consonants; the reduction of the Greek-derived digraphs 'ph' 'rh' and 'th', and the rationalisation of the use of accents (e.g. *è* for *é* as the second vowel in *événement* 'event'). However, nothing has in fact happened, and the situation remains more or less as it has been since the 1740 edition of the Academy dictionary.

3   Morphology

Nouns

As far as noun morphology is concerned, French has dramatically simplified the five-declension, five-case, three-gender system it inherited. The case system in fact survived longer in French, Occitan, and Rhaeto-Romance than anywhere else except Rumanian, to the extent that, for many nouns at least (mainly those of masculine gender), a nominative : oblique distinction was maintained in Old French, being progressively lost only during the thirteenth and fourteenth centuries to the profit in all but a few instances of the oblique form, which thus underlies almost all French nouns. (The Old French system was not unlike that described for seventeenth- and eighteenth-century Surselvan, pp. 364-5.) Thus, to take a particularly clear case, Latin INFANS (nom.) gave OFr. *enfes*, while

INFÁNTEM (acc.) gave *enfant.* (Compare this with the discussion of strong and weak verb forms, below.) It is *enfant* which has prevailed as the modern French form. In a handful of instances only, the subject form persisted, either alone (*prêtre* < PRESBYTER 'priest') or as well (*sire* < SE(N)IOR (nom.), *seigneur* < SENIOREM (acc.), literally 'elder'). One interesting such doublet is *on* 'one' < HOMO (nom.), discussed later, and *homme* 'man' from HOMINEM (acc.). In synchronic terms, however, such nouns are no longer in any way distinguished.

The functions of the various Latin case endings came to be marked in French in two ways. Nominal subjects and direct objects came increasingly to be distinguished by their ordering respectively before and after the finite verb: the question of word order in both literary and popular French is taken up again later. The other semantic and grammatical relationships marked in Latin by suffixed case morphemes were replaced by various prepositional syntagms, thus LIBRUM MARCO (dat.) DEDIT 'the book to Mark (he) gave' is replaced by *il a donné le livre à Marc.* It is interesting to note that nominals in the oblique case referred to above, particularly those with animate or personified referents, continued until well into the thirteenth century to be used without any preposition with both a genitive and to a lesser extent a dative function, thus OFr. *la nièce le duc* (where *le duc* is in the oblique case) 'the niece (of) the duke', or, from a twelfth-century text, *mon neveu erent delivrees/de ma terre trois cenz livrees* '(to) my nephew will be delivered of my land three hundred poundsworth'. One unusual survival of the former usage is *hôtel-Dieu* 'hospital', literally 'hostel (of) God': consider also the place name *Pont-L'Evêque,* literally 'bridge the bishop'. It seems worth drawing particular attention to the fact that the loss of distinctive case suffixes did not of itself necessitate, for some considerable time at least, the use of explicit prepositional structures to mark certain semantic or grammatical relationships.

The only survivor of Latin inflectional noun morphology lies in the almost universal use of *-s* (of which 'x' is an orthographic variant) as the marker of plurality; this derives directly from the *-s* of the Latin accusative plurals -AS, -OS and -ES, and thus generalised as oblique forms ousted nominatives. This final *-s,* however, is now purely orthographic in all but liaison contexts: plurality, like gender, which survives in the form of a binary masculine : feminine opposition, is actually dependent for overt marking in almost all instances on the form of the associated determiner (see section 4), thus *le père* 'father' (m. sg.) : *la mère* 'mother' (f. sg.) : *les pères* 'fathers' (m. pl.) : *les mères* 'mothers' (f. pl.) (/lə pɛʁ/ : /la mɛʁ/ : /le pɛʁ/: /le mɛʁ/). Oppositions such as *le cheval : les chevaux* (/lə ʃ(ə)val/: /le ʃ(ə)vo/), due to earlier phonetic changes (in this case the vocalisation of /l/ preconsonantally ([ls] > [us]) but not finally, i.e. in the plural *chevals* but not the singular *cheval*), are very much the exception in the modern language.

Adjectives and Adverbs

Adjective morphology is relatively simple. Adjectives vary according to the number and — less consistently — the gender of the noun with which they are collocated. In respect of number, the point just made applies: the distinction is orthographic rather than phonetic in most cases. Many feminine adjectives, however, are quite distinct from their masculine counterparts, in that the maintenance of post-tonic [ə] at the time final consonants were being effaced prevented their loss in feminine adjectives. Numerous pairs of adjectives are, therefore, distinguished orthographically by the presence or absence of a final −e, but phonetically by the presence or absence of a final consonant, thus m. *grand,* f. *grande* 'big' (/gʁɑ̃/ : /gʁɑ̃d/). One may view these consonants as underlyingly present and thus deleted from the masculine forms, or alternatively as inserted in the feminine forms, which are thus seen (traditionally) as derived. In other cases, that same [ə] prevented devoicing at an earlier stage in the language's history (m. *vif* /vif/ : f. *vive* /viv/ 'lively') or provoked denasalisation (see above), thus m. *plein* /plɛ̃/ : f. *pleine* /plɛn/ 'full'. In many instances, however, there is no phonetic distinction between masculine and feminine adjectives in contemporary French (e.g. m. and f. *rapide* 'rapid'). Adjectives derived from the Latin third declension frequently did not distinguish between masculine and feminine forms in Old French for etymological reasons: gradually, however, these came to be assimilated to the normal pattern, with the result that forms such as *Rochefort* and *grand-mère* 'grandmother' (for **Rocheforte* and **grande-mère*) are isolated relics.

Within the adjectival concord system, masculine forms serve, here as elsewhere in the language, as the unmarked form when the gender is unknown, unspecified or conflicting. In the most popular registers of French, there does seem to be some tendency for adjectival concord to weaken, particularly in predicative position, as in German: cf. (substandard) *elle est bien trop vieux (m.) pour se marier* 'she is much too old to get married' where the feminine form *vieille* would be expected; any such preference for a given adjective to be invariable inevitably also favours the masculine form. It is worth noting also by way of a historical footnote that the loss of the two-case system of Old French (p. 216) manifested itself particularly early in respect of predicative adjectives, which clearly 'escape' relatively easily from constraints which operate with greater strength within a unitary noun phrase.

Adverbs are generally formed in French by the addition of the suffix *-ment* (< Latin -MENTE, literally 'in a ... mind') to the feminine form of the adjective (*vivement, rapidement,* occasionally with minor changes, e.g. *évidemment* rather than **évidentement*). Certain adjectives, historically neuter but now indistinguishable from the masculine form, function also as adverbs, e.g. *dur* (*il travaille dur* 'he works hard'), not *durement,* this usage being relatively more common in certain written styles.

Finally, a word on the comparative and superlative of adjectives and adverbs. The history of French shows the advance of an analytic structure *plus aimable/le plus aimable* ('more/the more (=most) likable'), at the expense of synthetic forms (cf. p. 63–4). Of this latter group, among adjectives only the opaque *meilleur* 'better' (cf. *bon* 'good') seems secure, *pire* 'worse' being rivalled by *plus mauvais* (literally 'more bad') and *moindre* ('less(er), lower') (< MINOR) no longer functioning as a comparative of *petit* 'small'; we may note also, with adverbial function, *moins* (< MINUS) 'less' and *mieux* 'better' (not *plus bien* 'more well').

Pronouns

Among the various sets of pronouns, we shall note just four. Personal pronouns in French fall into two sets, conjunctive (i.e. those which can occur only immediately preceding a verb form) and disjunctive (i.e. those which can occur independently of a verb). (Special rules apply in relation to pronouns cooccurring with imperatives.) Conjunctive pronouns retain a nominative : oblique distinction in the first and second persons singular (*je* 'I', *me* 'me/to me') and a unique three-fold distinction in the third person (e.g. *il* 'he', *le* 'him', *lui* 'to him'): there is also a third person reflexive form *se* serving for both genders and both numbers. In the first and second persons plural, the nominative : oblique distinction is neutralised, as is indeed the conjunctive : disjunctive opposition, *nous* and *vous* serving with all values: elsewhere, the disjunctive pronoun is formally distinct, *moi*, for instance, in the case of the first person singular (cf. *je/me* above). We may, therefore, contrast singular *tu te lèves, toi?* (with three distinct forms) with plural *vous vous levez, vous?* ('are you getting up, you?').

Personal Pronouns

Second person singular				Third person singular masculine		
	Disjunctive	Conjunctive			Disjunctive	Conjunctive
Nominative	toi	tu		Nom.	lui	il
Oblique	toi	te		Acc.	lui	le
				Dat.	(à) lui	lui

The position in the third person is rather complex. A system in which the basic distinctions are gender and case is rivalled, at least in part, by one in which sex rather than gender is a crucially relevant parameter. Thus the conjunctive subject pronouns *il* and *elle* (and even more so the corresponding disjunctive pronouns *lui* and *elle*), ostensibly to be used for both males and masculines, females and feminines respectively, are increasingly restricted to animates, in particular to humans, to the profit of the originally 'neuter' *ce*, and the corresponding disjunctive form *ça*. Thus *il est beau, lui* 'he's good-looking, him' is naturally interpreted as referring to a man, the corresponding description of a non-human masculine referent frequently being *c'est beau, ça.* So far, however, *ce* has not entirely ousted *il* from another of its functions, that of 'unmarked' subject pronoun, a category necessary in French because of the absolute requirement for an overt subject even when none is semantically motivated, as for example with weather verbs, e.g. *il pleut* ('it is raining'), though here too, *ça pleut* 'that's raining' is not infrequent. A further complication is that the 'non-human' conjunctive set includes a so-called 'genitive' form *en* ('of it'/'from it', best interpreted as the pronominal equivalent of *de* + nominal) which has no human counterpart, so that *je m'en souviens* (literally, 'I remind myself of it', i.e. 'I remember it') cannot, according to the rules of prescriptive grammar, have a human referent, i.e. cannot be interpreted as 'I remember him/her'. In informal registers, however, this is a possible interpretation, which in turn disrupts the long-standing parallel distribution of *en* and the 'non-human' dative *y*. To cut a long story short, *y* (like *ci* in Italian, p. 291) is now encroaching on to the 'animate' territory of *lui* and *leur*, in parallel, as it were, with the advance of *en*, which is simply filling a *case vide*. One final point of interest is that *ça*, which we saw earlier as the appropriate non-human disjunctive form, can also be used with a human and even a plural referent, usually with a pejorative sense: *ça me dégoûte, les conservateurs* literally 'that disgusts me, the conservatives', i.e. 'they disgust me . . .'.

Table 6.3: Third Person Pronouns

	Masculine		*Feminine*		*Neuter*
Nom.	il		elle		ce/il
Acc.	le		la		le
	[+human]	[−human]	[+human]	[−human]	[−human]
Dat.	lui	y	lui	y	y
Gen.	—	en	—	en	en
Disj.	lui	(ça)	elle	(ça)	ça

tending to be replaced by

	Human		*Non-human*
	Male	Female	
Nom.	il	elle	(il): ce/ça
Acc.	le	la	le/la
Dat.	lui (y)	lui (y)	y
Gen.	(en)	(en)	en
Disj.	lui	elle	ça

Two other points deserve brief mention. We have already seen that the Latin nominative HOMO 'man' gave a form *on* alongside *homme* < HOMINEM. This form *on* has been wholly assimilated into the personal pronoun system as a conjunctive subject form, at first with an impersonal value (*on dit* 'people say'; cf. German *man sagt*), but later as an alternative to various other subject pronouns and in particular to *nous*, which it has largely ousted in this function from the popular spoken language (*on part en voyage* 'we're off on a trip'). Note that *on* has neither an oblique nor a disjunctive form; within the immediate verb phrase, the third person reflexive form *se* is used (*on se lève de bonne heure* 'we get up early'); elsewhere, the semantically appropriate form reappears, thus *nous, on va sortir avec nos amis* (literally, 'us, one is going to go out with our friends' — note also the first person plural possessive form *nos*, to the exclusion of the third person singular form *ses*).

The relationship between *tu* and *vous* is not a straightforward singular : plural one. Since the seventeenth century, it has been normal to use *vous* in the case of singular addressees to mark 'respect', *tu* being limited to intimate contexts (e.g. within a family), or to mark a superior–inferior relationship (e.g. master to servant). *Vous* used as a 'respectful' singular shows singular concord outside the immediate verb phrase: *vous êtes content, monsieur?* (not *contents*) 'are you satisfied, sir?'. French thus shows in a rudimentary way an address system of a kind much more highly developed in certain of the other Romance languages. In fact, however, as elsewhere, the 'intimate' forms are tending to gain ground in all but the most formal situations.

The demonstrative pronouns of French represent a twofold opposition of proximity, as do the corresponding determiners. In the contemporary language, this opposition is marked by the suffixes -*ci* and -*là* ('here' and 'there'), thus *celui-ci* : *celui-là* ('this', 'that', m. sg. pronouns) (cf. the corresponding determiners *cette femme-ci* : *cette femme-là* 'this woman' : 'that woman'). There is also a genderless pair of demonstrative pronouns *ceci* and *cela*, a reduced form of the latter yielding *ça* which we have already discussed as a 'personal pronoun' and which has lost its distal value. The suffixes -*ci* and -*là* may be omitted when proximity marking is not essential, principally when the identity of the referent is immediately made clear, thus *celui que j'ai trouvé* literally 'that which I have found', i.e. 'the one that I've found'; the omission of -*ci* and -*là* is relevant also to the discussions of determiners in French, below. It should be noted also that usage of the proximal and distal demonstratives heavily favours the latter, particularly in speech: *celui-là* may be used where there is no opposition of proximity (e.g. *celui-là de Jean* for *celui de Jean*) and also somewhat surprisingly for both 'this one' and 'that one' even in a context where they are juxtaposed, *celui-là-bas* 'that one over there' being used to disambiguate if absolutely necessary. Finally, it is worth pointing out that the marking of semantically relevant information suffixally in this instance is wholly exceptional to the very pronounced tendency for French to prefer pre- rather than post-position wherever possible.

Possessive pronouns and possessive adjectives derive from the same Latin etyma, with stress, as so often, the major factor leading to formal differentiation. Pronouns bear stress more often than determiners, and possibly as a result of this, the originally tonic forms have been grammaticalised as pronouns and originally atonic forms as determiners. Thus, for instance, Latin MEUM ('my, mine') gives both *mon* (atonic) and *mien* (tonic), this latter form, now accompanied by the definite article, being the masculine singular first person possessive pronoun in contemporary French, while *mon* is the determiner 'my'. A similar distinction is made in respect of the first and second person plural forms, where, for instance, *votre* ([vɔt(ʁ)]) 'your' is opposed to *le vôtre* ([votʁ]), whereas in the third person plural no distinct atonic form emerged, with the consequence that only the presence or absence of the definite article distinguishes *leur* 'their' from *le leur* 'theirs'.

There are two sets of relative pronouns in French; a monosyllabic set in everyday use (*qui, que, quoi*) and a more complex set (*lequel* etc.) found primarily in formal written registers, the first element of which is the definite article and which vary according to the gender and number of their antecedent (*les femmes* (f. pl.) *lesquelles* (f. pl.) *j'ai vues* (f. pl.) 'the women I have seen'). Relative *qui* has two main uses. Firstly, it is the normal form for a relative which is the subject of its own clause, regardless of the semantic characteristics of its antecedent (*l'homme qui est* .../*le livre qui est* ... 'the man who is .../the book which is ...'). Secondly, it is found post-prepositionally when its antecedent is human: *l'homme à qui j'ai donné*... 'the man to whom I have given ...'. *Que* on the other hand occurs clause-initially when it is functioning as a direct object in that clause (*l'homme/le livre que j'ai vu* 'the man/the book who(m)/which I saw'), whereas *quoi* occurs elsewhere with a non-human or indefinite referent (*le livre à quoi je me suis reporté* 'the book to which I referred'). The complex forms *lequel* etc. can be found with all these functions, but it is only post-prepositionally that they are at all frequent in the spoken language, particularly with non-human referents (*la religion dans laquelle j'ai été élevé* 'the religion in which I was brought up'). In so far as relative adjectives are found in modern French, these complex forms are used for the function also. Finally, we should mention *dont* (< Latin DE UNDE, literally 'of/from whence'), which can and does serve as an alternative to a sequence of *de* plus any of the relatives discussed above (except, of course, *que*), and is thus (with *en*) one of only two 'genitive' nominal elements in the language (*le livre dont* (or *duquel* or *de quoi*) *j'ai lu quelques pages* 'the book of which I have read several pages'). It is perhaps worth noting a tendency in the most popular registers for *que* (homophonous as we shall see (p. 238) with the unmarked subordinator) to gain ground from the other relatives, in particular from *dont* but even from *qui*: consider such (substandard) examples as *un homme que j'ai trouvé son nom* 'a man that I found his name', i.e. 'whose name I found' (*que... son = dont... le*), or *la jeune fille qu'il doit se marier avec* 'the girl that he is to marry with' i.e. *avec qui* 'with whom' (cf. p. 55).

Verbs

The verbal morphology of contemporary French is not particularly complex, especially in the spoken language. Superficially at least, the four conjugation types of Latin have been retained, as verbs in *-er* (*donner* 'give'), *-oir* (*voir* 'see'), *-re* (*rompre* 'break'), and *-ir* (*venir* 'come') respectively. In practice, however, the *-oir* and *-re* classes are closed in contemporary French, membership of the former group in particular being heavily restricted. Almost all new verbs in French enter the *-er* class, though the *-ir* class will admit new members if there is a strong analogical reason to do so (e.g. *alunir* 'to land on the moon': cf. *atterrir* 'to land', i.e. on earth). The *-ir* class in fact comprises three subtypes, those (the vast majority) which have incorporated an infix *-iss-* (originally inceptive in value, but now an empty morph, cf. Spanish, p. 101, or Italian, p. 294) into verbal paradigms based on the present stem ((*nous*) *fin-iss-ons* 'we finish' ← *fin-ir*), a much smaller group which do not ((*nous*) *ven-ons* 'we come' ← *ven-ir*), and an even smaller group (essentially *ouvrir* 'open', *couvrir* 'cover' and derivatives) which form their present tense like *-er* verbs.

French inherited a set of suffixed person markers which varied according to conjugation type and paradigm. The history of the language shows a marked tendency for the generalisation of a lesser number of variants, the clearest cases being in the plural where (with the sole exception of the preterit discussed below) the appropriate suffixes are now spelt 1 pl. *-ons*; 2 pl. *-ez*; 3 pl. *-nt*. In the singular, there are in effect three patterns in the written language, namely (i) 1 sg. *-e*; 2 sg. *-es*; 3 sg. *-e*; (ii) 1 sg. *-s*; 2 sg. *-s*; 3 sg. *-t*; and (iii) 1 sg. *-ai*; 2 sg. *-as*; 3 sg. *-a*, i.e. the present tense of *avoir* 'have' which, in the singular at least, has resisted analogical levelling. The first of these sets is associated primarily with the present indicative of *-er* verbs, and with the present (and imperfect) subjunctive of all verbs; the second set is associated with the present indicative of non-*er* verbs, and with the imperfect and conditional paradigms of all verbs (and compounds thereof); and the third set with the present perfect and future paradigms of all verbs, for reasons to be discussed hereafter. A heavily simplified tabulation of French verbs as they appear in the written language is thus as shown in the chart of verbal conjugation. Several things need to be noted about this tabulation. Firstly, the stress pattern inherited from Latin varied through the paradigm of the present indicative, thus DÓN-AT 'he gives' (a 'strong' form stressed on the root), but DON-ÁMUS 'we give' (a 'weak' form

French Verbal Conjugation

(a) Conjugation type and present indicative

donner	*rompre*	*voir*	*finir*	*venir*	*ouvrir*
donn-e	romp-s	voi-s	fini-s	vien-s	ouvr-e
donn-es	romp-s	voi-s	fini-s	vien-s	ouvr-es
donn-e	romp-t	voi-t	fini-t	vien-t	ouvr-e
donn-ons	romp-ons	voy-ons	fin-iss-ons	ven-ons	ouvr-ons
donn-ez	romp-ez	voy-ez	fin-iss-ez	ven-ez	ouvr-ez
donn-ent	romp-ent	voi-ent	fin-iss-ent	vienn-ent	ouvr-ent

(b) Imperfect of all verbs
donn-ais (cf. fin-iss-ais)
donn-ais
donn-ait
donn-ions
donn-iez
donn-aient

(c) Present subjunctive of all verbs
romp-e
romp-es
romp-e
romp-ions
romp-iez
romp-ent

(d) Future of all verbs
fini-r-ai
fini-r-as
fini-r-a
fini-r-ons
fini-r-ez
fini-r-ont

(e) Conditional of all verbs
fini-r-ais
fini-r-ais
fini-r-ait
fini-r-ions
fini-r-iez
fini-r-aient

(f) Past participle
donn-é, romp-u, v-u, fin-i, ven-u, ouv-ert

(g) Present participle/gerund
donn-ant, romp-ant, voy-ant, fin-iss-ant, ven-ant, ouvr-ant

stressed on the desinence). Given what we have already seen about the divergent development of tonic and atonic vowels in French, it is not surprising that paradigms with two stems frequently emerged, thus OFr. *aim-e* < ÁMAT 'he loves', but *am-ons* < AMÁMUS 'we love'. In general, the 'weak' form prevailed, thus for example the stem *treuv-e* (strong) ceded to *trouv-ons* (weak) during the sixteenth century: persistence of the strong stem *aim-* is accordingly exceptional. In a small number of cases, both stems have survived: *venir* in the chart of verbal conjugation (*vien-t* : *ven-ons*) is an instance of this. Additionally, four of the six personal endings whose orthographic representations have just been discussed are in fact silent (and hence of course homophonous) in modern French, only -*ons* ([ɔ̃]) and -*ez* ([e]) being pronounced. (Third plural future -*ont* is an exception to this generalisation.) How concord with the subject of the verb is actually marked in the contemporary spoken language is discussed below (pp. 231–2).

The chart omits the preterit. This paradigm, together with the related imperfect subjunctive paradigm, unlike those considered so far, is not morphologically based on the 'present' stem inherited from Latin, but on the so-called 'historic' stem, which, in the case of irregular verbs, may be significantly different. It has also resisted the analogical levelling of its personal suffixes. Both these paradigms have been ousted from normal spoken French (see below). Specimen paradigms are provided in the chart of preterits.

Preterits

(a) Regular
     donn-ai, donn-as, donn-a, donn-âmes, donn-âtes, donn-èrent
     (*donner*)
     fin-is, fin-is, fin-it, fin-îmes, fin-îtes, fin-irent
     (*finir*)
(b) Irregular
     vins, vins, vint, vînmes, vîntes, vinrent
     (*venir*)

The future tense of modern French derives from the infinitive (or occasionally a phonetically modified form thereof) followed by (a reduced form of) the present tense of *avoir* 'have' which has now completely fused with the stem (unlike Portuguese, p. 150), thus *fini-r-ai* '(I) shall finish' in the verbal conjugation chart. The conditional is formed in the same way, the suffixes deriving in this case from the imperfect of *avoir*. There is a full range of compound paradigms involving either or both of the two auxiliaries *avoir* 'have' and *être* 'be' with the past participle. Essentially, the former has always been used in contexts where the subject has an agentive or comparable function in the sentence (*j'ai écrit la lettre* 'I have written the letter', originally 'I have the letter written'), whereas the latter is appropriate in the case of passives, medio-passives (and hence reflexives used with such a value) and non-agentive intransitives. This essentially semantic patterning has been disturbed in modern French by a tendency for perfective active paradigms to use *avoir* at all times, although *être* is still totally secure, at least in metropolitan French, with a small number of common intransitives and their compounds (*je suis venu* 'I have come', literally 'I am come'), whereas the compound tenses of even the most 'agentive' of reflexive verbs are now formed with *être*. This increase in surface regularisation at the expense of isomorphy between meaning and form is by no means an uncommon occurrence in French, although the process in this instance has gone much further in, for example, Spanish (p. 102) and Portuguese (p. 162).

    Two further points should be noted briefly at this stage. Firstly, the combination of *être* with the past participle of a transitive verb is, out of context at least, ambiguous as between an 'action passive' and a 'resultant state' interpretation. In other words, *l'affiche était clouée à la porte* can either mean simply 'the notice was nailed to the door' or 'the notice was (= used to be) nailed to the door (by someone) (e.g. every time there was a problem)'. (Contrast the situation in Spanish, p. 102). Any consequential difficulties are largely resolved by the use of alternatives to the passive, discussed hereafter. Secondly, a rather unexpected set of 'double compound' tenses (*temps surcomposés*) of the type *j'ai eu fait* (literally 'I have had done', in a non-causative sense) is found in certain circumstances. These too are discussed below.

Two verbs only in contemporary French may be said to have a truly idiosyncratic morphology: *être* 'be' (combining forms of both late Lat. *ESSERE and STARE 'stand') and *aller* 'go' (combining forms of VADERE 'go, walk' (e.g. *va* '(he) goes'), IRE 'go' (e.g. *ira* '(he) will go') and *ALLARE (generally thought to be a reduced form of AMBULARE 'to walk' — cf. pp. 49–50).

4   Syntax

The Nominal Group

The morphosyntax of the nominal group can be dealt with fairly briefly. We have seen that there are no consistent markers of gender on nouns or adjectives in contemporary French (although gender is marked in the case of many adjectives) and that the sign of plurality, the suffix -*s*, is purely orthographic in the vast majority of instances. Gender and number — or, to be more accurate, gender or number — are nevertheless clearly phonologically indicated in the case of most noun phrases. The reason is simply that in most contexts nouns are accompanied by a determiner, and that these determiners are almost all grouped in sets of three which distinguish a masculine from a feminine in the singular and also a plural, thus *le, la, les* (the definite article), *un, une, des* (the indefinite article), *du, de la, des* (the partitive article), *ce, cette, ces* (demonstrative), *mon, ma, mes* (possessive), etc. It is true that nouns can occur without a determiner (for example, in fixed phrases, e.g. *avoir faim* 'to have hunger', i.e. 'to be hungry'), often after the preposition *en*, or in partitive constructions (e.g. *assez de lait* 'enough (of) milk'), or with a determiner that does not mark gender (*chaque* 'each', numerals) or even number (*beaucoup de fromage(s)* 'much cheese/many cheeses', given that final orthographic 's' is silent, reveals neither the gender nor the number of *fromage(s)*); nevertheless, the general pattern is that determiners do serve to mark gender and number.

In the vast majority of cases, of course, a determiner is pragmatically motivated, and nothing more needs to be said. There is, however, one important consequence of the strong tendency for nouns to need an accompanying determiner. In Old French, a zero determiner was readily tolerated when the reference of the noun in question was not to be specified in any precise way. In the contemporary language, however, this is no longer so, and the distribution of the indefinite article, of the partitive article (the greatly increased use of which is a characteristic of French; compare Sp. *compré vino* (p. 106) with Fr. *j'ai acheté du vin* 'I bought (some) wine') and in particular of the definite article has expanded to cover the ground where previously no determiner was required, with *le/la/les* coming to serve, *inter alia*, as the 'unmarked' carriers of gender/number within contemporary French noun phrases. One clear-cut consequence of this is that, out of context, *j'aime le fromage* can mean either 'I like the cheese' (the original meaning of the definite article) or 'I like cheese', a generic sense, previously marked by a zero determiner, being one of those gained by *le/la/les* during the evolution of the language. As so often, however, a solution is to hand, in that whereas *ce fromage-ci* and *ce fromage-là* (i.e. forms with an appropriate suffix) are utilised as demonstratives as we have seen, *ce fromage* without a suffix is often best translated as 'the (particular) cheese' rather than 'this' or 'that cheese'. Put in other words, in one, but only one, of the two senses mentioned above, that of the original definite article, *le fromage* can be and often is replaced by *ce fromage*. It may well be that, ultimately *ce/cette/ces* will emerge as the primary indicator of this value in French, leaving *le/la/les* as the unmarked or fall-back determiner used to indicate the gender and number of the relevant nominal and little else, a development not so far parallelled elsewhere in Romance.

Attributive adjectives in French normally follow the noun with which they are collocated, a situation not uncommon in SVO languages such as contemporary French is generally said to be (but cf. pp. 235–6). Most adjectives may however, precede the relevant noun, either on formal grounds (e.g. a short adjective with a longer noun, as *un bref résumé* 'a short summary'), or when the reference is to an inherent and hence non-defining quality (e.g. *la blanche neige* 'white snow'), or on stylistic grounds, to highlight the adjective for whatever reason, as in *un formidable appartement* 'an amazing flat'. It is often argued that adjectives tend to precede nouns when they are primarily evaluative (e.g. *une charmante soirée* 'a charming party') and to follow when they are 'defining', that is when they delimit in some way the reference of the noun (e.g. *un tapis vert* 'a green carpet', *une décision arbitraire* 'an arbitrary decision'). (For a discussion of the position in Italian, cf. p. 299.) A small group of frequently used adjectives normally precede the noun — *une petite maison* 'a small house', *le deuxième problème* 'the second problem' — and it is said that if these are postposed, similar stylistic effects can be obtained to preposing a more typical adjective; in practice, however, such postposing does not appear to be frequent. A third group of adjectives have a different semantic value depending on whether they precede or follow the noun, thus *un grand homme* 'a great man' versus *un homme grand* 'a tall man' or *le même homme* 'the same man' versus *l'homme même* 'the man himself'. Interesting to note also is the widespread use of the particle *de* (cf. p. 234) between a noun and a following adjective, as in *oui, on a une chambre de libre* (as opposed to *une chambre libre*), a distinction generally said to correspond to that in English between *yes, we have a room (which is) free* and *yes, we have a free room.* In similar vein, we may juxtapose *ma soeur malade,* roughly 'my ill sister' with *ma soeur de malade,* roughly 'my sister who's ill'. This use of *de* may be compared with that found in, for instance, *une beauté de femme,* literally 'a beauty of woman' as a stylistic alternative for *une belle femme* 'a beautiful woman', the result being the highlighting of the 'adjectival' notion 'beautiful'.

We noted earlier that a relationship between two nominal elements, which in Latin had been marked either by a case suffix or by a preposition, came ultimately (and despite considerable resistance in Old French) to be marked entirely in the second manner. In not every case, however, did one single preposition emerge as wholly dominant. In the case of the relationship of possession in particular, the rivalry between *de* and *à* (which goes back at least as far as a comparable rivalry between the genitive and dative cases in Latin) remains strong, in that whereas the literary language has in general preferred the former preposition, the spoken language makes frequent use of *à,* particularly in the case of animate referents (i.e. those where the zero possessive marking discussed above survived longest): thus one finds *le fils à Jean* literally 'the son to John', i.e. 'John's son'. This structure is normal to disambiguate possessives, e.g. *son livre à lui* literally 'his/her book to him', i.e. 'his book' as opposed to *son livre à elle* 'his/her book to her', i.e. 'her book'.

The Verbal System

The verbal system of French presents a number of interesting features. Within the indicative mood, the basic pattern is of four temporal possibilities on each of two time axes (a pattern familiar to speakers of English), with only one fully grammaticalised aspectual opposition, that between punctual and durative at the simultaneous point on the past axis. This may be represented as in Figure 6.1.

The reason that *a fait* appears on the table twice and that *fit* appears only in brackets is that the inherited aspectual distinction between *faisait* 'was doing'/'used to do' and *fit* 'did' is now maintained in all spoken and most written registers by the use of *a fait* for *fit,* the former paradigm having taken over the functions of the latter (while retaining its own of marking a past event with present relevance) during the seventeenth and eighteenth centuries; *fit* is now restricted in effect to formal written registers. (The loss of *fit* necessarily entailed the loss of *eut fait,* the 'past anterior', in the same circumstances and this was one reason for the creation of the double compound form *a eu fait,* discussed below.) The *a fait* paradigm thus corresponds both to English 'has done' and to 'did', while the original punctual : durative/habitual aspectual distinction is now main-

Figure 6.1: The Indicative Verbal System of French

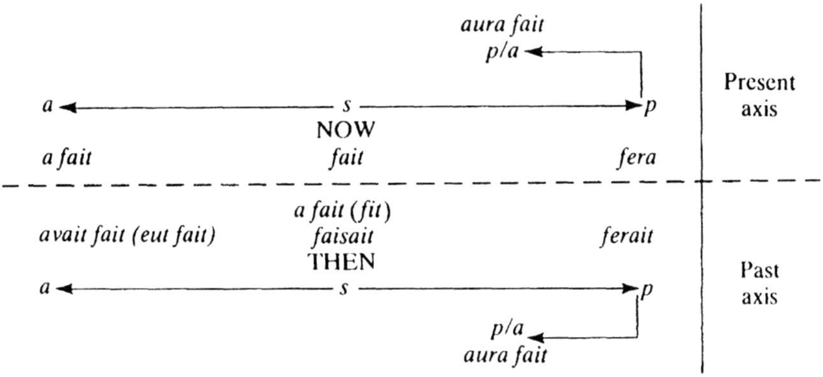

Note: *a*: anterior; *s*: simultaneous; *p*: posterior; *p/a*: posterior/anterior (i.e. earlier than some later time)

tained by *a fait* : *faisait*.

Synthetic forms, the 'future' (*fera*) and 'conditional' (*ferait*) paradigms, mark posterior time on each axis. However, these synthetic forms with future time reference are rivalled by analytic forms incorporating as an auxiliary the verb of motion *aller*, thus *va faire* 'is going to do' and *allait faire* 'was going to do' respectively. The present perfect *a fait* having lost its unambiguously 'present relevance' meaning, an alternative structure *vient de faire* (literally 'comes from doing', i.e. 'has just done') is available for use, but this has not been incorporated into the system to anything like the same extent as *va faire*. Finally within the indicative mood, we should note the use of the *temps surcomposés* ('double compound tenses') of the type *il a eu fait* (literally 'he has had done') (cf. p. 265 for Occitan). The primary use of this paradigm is in place of the past anterior (*après qu'il l'a eu fait, il a vu Pierre* 'after he had done it, he saw Peter') where *eut fait* has become *a eu fait* just as *vit* has become *a vu*. These forms are also used by some (but by no means all) native speakers as an optional marker of perfectivity (*quand il a eu payé...*' literally 'when he has had paid', the sense being 'as soon as he had finished paying'), thus restoring to the language the possibility of marking an aspectual distinction which had been central to the verbal system of Latin (p. 58). Such double compound tenses are attested — though in certain cases very infrequently — across the whole range of tense, mood and voice, and even when the primary auxiliary is *être*, thus *quand je me suis eu assis ...* (literally 'when I myself am had seated', i.e. 'as soon as I (had) sat down', or perhaps rather 'once I'd got myself a seat'). One more regionally localised use of the *parfait surcomposé* is in the sense of a truly perfective present perfect, thus *la vigne ça a eu payé, mais ça paye plus* i.e. 'vines have paid (in the past) but they don't pay any longer'.

It was noted earlier (p. 225) that the sequence *être* + past participle had several uses in French, in particular to mark the passive voice and the (active) perfect tenses of a number of intransitive verbs. In all of these cases, there is concord of number and gender between the subject of the verb and the relevant participle, as there would be with an adjective: thus *elles sont venues* (f. pl.) 'they are (=have) come'. The situation with the other category of verbs noted, those reflexive in appearance, is that these also generally display concord with the subject, either when the reflexive element is genuinely reflexive or reciprocal (*elles se sont lavées* (f. pl.) 'they (f. pl.) washed themselves/each other') or when it marks the medio-passive voice (see below) or is simply a permanent accompaniment of a verb (generally one with a more or less 'middle' value), as *elles se sont évanouies* (f. pl.) 'they (f. pl.) fainted'. In the former case, the subject is of course synonymous with the direct object, which in such cases precedes in the participle: this, therefore, overlaps with the only case of participial concord when the auxiliary verb is *avoir*, namely with preposed direct objects, as *je l'ai vue* (f. sg.) literally 'I her have seen' or *les femmes* (f. pl.) *que j'ai vues* (f. pl.) 'the women that I have seen'. When however the reflexive pronoun is the indirect object of the verb, then concord is precluded by the rules of prescriptive grammar, thus *elles se sont imaginé* (m. sg., i.e. unmarked) *que* ... 'they (f. pl.) imagined (to themselves) that ...'. However, since this particular subtype of reflexive verb is in effect the sole case of a syntagm involving *être* plus a past participle which does not show concord with the subject, it is not at all surprising to find the 'rule' breached frequently, even in the best authors. It is worth recalling finally that in any event, concord of both gender and number is in respect of most (though not all) verbs realised orthographically only: in the example cited above, *imaginé*, *imaginés* and *imaginées* are now all homophonous.

Mood

The subjunctive mood in contemporary French survives largely only as a conditioned variant in specifiable subordinate contexts, having been eliminated from main clauses in all but a handful of idioms (e.g. *advienne* (subj.) *que pourra* 'come what may') and the so-called 'jussive' structure (e.g. *qu'il le fasse* (subj.) literally 'that he may it do', i.e. 'let/have him do it'). The use of the subjunctive in dependent clauses is partly determined by the semantic class of the main verb or the conjunction (e.g. verbs of 'emotion', thus *je regrette qu'il le fasse* (subj.) 'I'm sorry he's doing so') and partly lexically (e.g. *vouloir* 'wish' requires the subjunctive but *espérer* 'hope' does not). In general, since no opposition with the indicative is possible in the vast majority of these contexts, we may doubt that the subjunctive mood is in any real sense meaningful, although a small number of minimal pairs may still be found (e.g. *de sorte que* 'so that' with the indicative marks result, and with the subjunctive, purpose). In spoken and informal written French, only the present and perfect subjunctive (*fasse, ait fait*) are still in use, the past and pluperfect (*fît, eût fait*) being restricted in the same way as the preterit. The virtual loss of semantic value by the subjunctive mood should not be taken to indicate the imminent demise of the two remaining paradigms as formal variants: they are learnt very early by children, for example colligated with *(il) faut que* 'it is necessary that', and the present subjunctive forms of the commonest irregular verbs are very distinctive (*soit, ait, fasse, vienne, aille, puisse, sache*: 'be', 'have', 'do', 'come', 'go', 'be able', 'know').

The modal nuances previously carried by the subjunctive mood have very largely passed to the *fera* and in particular the *ferait* paradigms, noted earlier (p. 229) as the markers of posterior time on the two temporal axes within the indicative mood. *Ferait* can be used in main clauses (*le roi serait mort* literally 'the king would be dead', i.e. 'the king is reputedly dead'), in apodoses (*il le ferait si ...* 'he would do it if ...') and in many subordinate clauses where the subjunctive is required by the rules of prescriptive grammar, thus *je cherche une maison qui aurait un jardin* 'I'm looking for a house that would have a garden', the precise identity or location of such a house being at present unknown (cf. p. 239). The most obvious use of the future paradigm with a modal value is in cases such as *ce sera Pierre* 'that'll (probably) be Peter'. Other indicative paradigms, particularly the imperfect (p. 240), can also be used with modal value, in contexts which preclude a straightforwardly temporal or aspectual interpretation: cf., for instance, the discussion of conditional sentences hereafter.

Subject Clitics

One of the most interesting developments in the verbal system of at least popular spoken registers of French has been the change in status of the conjunctive subject pronouns discussed earlier. It will be recalled that four of the person-marking suffixes are homophonous in contemporary speech. Given the progressive replacement of *nous* in the role of conjunctive first plural subject pronoun by *on* 'one', which is grammatically third person singular (i.e. the replacement of *nous donnons* by *on donne* /dɔn/), only -*ez* (/e/), the second plural suffix, is now distinctive, and the effective suffixal marking of the subjects of finite verbs in the case of most paradigms still in current use is a dead letter. This has not, however, resulted in the loss of person and number marking; rather, the appropriate conjunctive pronouns, which had become obligatory where there was no other subject by the end of the Middle French period (probably as a result of a phase in while French was a strongly 'verb-second' language in main clauses — for a description of this phenomenon in detail in Rhaeto-Romance, cf. pp. 368–9), have become steadily more tightly bound to the verb of which they are subject, to the extent that they are found not only when a disjunctive pronoun of equivalent value is also present (*moi je pense*... literally 'me I think ...') but, in popular speech, increasingly even when there is an overt nominal subject (*mon père il dit que* ... literally 'my father he says that ...'). The virtual elimination of the preverbal negative element *ne* (p. 237) and the widespread avoidance of inversion in interrogatives (p. 237) have facilitated the tendency for the sequence 'conjunctive subject pronoun + finite verb' to become indivisible, and for these pronouns to be reanalysed as bound prefixes with their semantic value unchanged. Put at its simplest, we may regard French *ils aiment* /izɛm/ 'they love' as one polymorphemic word (subject-prefix + stem) in exactly the same way as one regards Latin AMANT or OFr. *aiment* as one polymorphemic word (stem + subject-suffix). Parallel developments in the case of non-subject pronouns, and the interaction of all of these changes with sentential word order are discussed later.

Verb Phrases and Noun Phrases

It is interesting to observe at this point the striking parallelism between verb phrases and noun phrases in contemporary French, a parallelism, what is more, which reflects a complete reversal of the initial situation in Latin. In verb phrases, particularly in the spoken language, much relevant grammatical information is carried by auxiliary verbs and by clitic pronouns (bound affixes) which precede the verbal stem (and not by suffixes); in noun phrases, almost all relevant grammatical information is carried by determiners and by prepositions which precede the nominal stem (and not by suffixes): the -*ci* and -*là* of the demonstratives (pp. 221–2) are the only significant exception. Personal pronouns and determiners are both virtually obligatory, with the result that 'unmarked' forms (chosen from a historically identical source) are needed when no pronoun or determiner is semantically motivated. The evolution and present-day structure of noun phrases and verb phrases are quite astonishingly similar.

Voice

One final word on the finite verb. There exists a passive structure of a familiar kind, which permits both subject deletion (*il a été écrasé* 'he has been crushed') and subject demotion (*il a été écrasé par la voiture* 'he has been crushed by the car'). When the underlying agent is human but cannot be or is not to be specified, the pronoun *on*, already discussed as an alternative to *nous* 'we', is very frequently pressed into service, the voice of the verb remaining active (*on a ouvert la porte* 'someone has opened the door/the door has been opened'). Another strategy when the object is not human, used less than in Italian or Spanish but nevertheless not uncommon, is the pseudo-reflexive structure, that is, the use of the active forms of a verb reflexive in appearance but with *se* actually serving as a morphological marker of the fact that the phrase is to be interpreted in a 'passive' sense (*les fleurs se vendent ici le dimanche* literally 'flowers sell themselves ...', i.e. 'flowers are sold here on Sundays'). The original object may, as here, be promoted to subject, with appropriate verbal concord, or not (particularly in more formal registers), in which case an impersonal pseudo-reflexive structure is found, thus *il se pense toujours beaucoup plus de choses qu'il ne s'en dit* literally 'it thinks itself always many more things than it speaks itself of them', i.e. 'many more things are always thought than are said'. (Note the unmarked third person singular verb because no subject has been promoted and also the empty subject pronoun *il* necessary to prevent the 'subject' slot from being left empty.) In the contemporary language, all of these structures are available in the case of subject deletion, whereas only the first, the passive, permits the use of an agentive phrase. When such a phrase is present, the ambiguity of the *être* + past participle sequence noted earlier (p. 225) can, in many cases at least, be reduced or eliminated because of a fairly clear tendency — though this is by no means an absolute rule — for truly agentive phrases to make use of the preposition *par* ('by'), whereas phrases which are in effect circumstantial complements modifying a participle used in a quasi-adjectival way are introduced by *de*. Thus we may compare *l'arbre a été renversé par le vent* ('the tree was blown down by the wind') with *la rue était decorée de riches boutiques* ('the street was adorned with rich shops').

Non-finite Verbs
An examination of the non-finite parts of the verb reveals a number of points of interest. As far as the infinitive is concerned, usage is in some ways more restricted than at earlier periods of the language, when a full range of nominal functions with determiners, with prepositions, marked for plurality and the like was possible. As a legacy of this phase, a number of infinitives, while retaining their original function, have also become fully nominalised (e.g. *le déjeuner* 'lunch'/ *déjeuner* 'to have lunch'; *le coucher* 'bed-time'/ *coucher* 'to go to bed'). The infinitive, used now without a determiner, may still serve as the subject or complement of a verb (*penser n'est pas difficile* 'to think/thinking isn't difficult'), although a particle *de*, discussed below, is not uncommon in such instances (*de penser à toi me soutiendra* 'to think/thinking of you will sustain me'): a cleft construction, in which this *de* is obligatory, is certainly much more frequent (*il n'est pas difficile de penser*).

Perhaps most interesting has been the changing use of the infinitive as the complement of a matrix verb. This has always been possible when the subject of both verbs is identical (Lat. VOLO CANTARE (cf. p. 66), Fr. *je veux chanter* 'I want to sing'), where the infinitive may of course be interpreted simply as the direct object of 'want'. Here too the particle *de* is not unknown, as with *essayer* 'to try' (*j'ai essayé de chanter* 'I have tried to sing'). The infinitive spread in late Latin and Romance to a whole range of contexts in which the matrix verb had a nominal complement also, which was in effect the semantic subject of the infinitive as well, thus *je lui ai demandé de le faire* ('I asked him to do it'). (Note again the particle *de*.) 'Bare' infinitives are found, for example, with verbs of perception (*je le vois venir* 'I can see him (acc.) com(ing)') or with the causative verb *faire*, where the form of the nominal complement depends on whether or not the infinitive itself has a direct object. (Contrast *personne ne le fera venir* 'no-one will make him come' with *personne ne lui fera résoudre ce problème* 'no-one will make him solve this problem', where *le* and *lui* are 'accusative' and 'dative' respectively; see also Italian, p. 307).

In many cases, as we have seen, the use of an infinitive, even in absolute initial position, now requires the use also of an infinitive particle *de*. At the risk of oversimplifying a very complex area of syntax, we may say that a particle *de* homophonous with a preposition *de* 'of, from' seems to have emerged as an unmarked infinitival subordinator, rather like 'to' in English, but that some matrix verbs continue to permit the earlier zero marker (as with verbs of perception and causatives just exemplified). Neither is this *de* found when there is a preposition preceding the infinitive (all prepositions except one collocating with this form of the verb), a fact which explains its absence when the matrix verb requires use of the preposition *à* before a following infinitive, a situation found (broadly speaking) with verbs indicating effort, aims, goals, tendencies and the like. In one or two cases, such as *commencer* 'begin', usage vacillates between this preposition *à* and the particle *de*. Whether *à* or *de* is found, the nominal complement may be accusative or dative, this being lexically determined by the matrix verb: thus we may compare *je l'ai aidé à le faire* 'I helped him (acc.) to do it' with *je lui ai appris à le faire* 'I taught him (dat.) to do it'. Finally, we should remember that the 'true' preposition *de* can also collocate with an infinitive: thus *Jean est certain de revenir* 'John is certain to return' may be compared with *Jean en est certain*, where *en* 'of it', which we saw earlier (p. 220) to be the pronominal equivalent of a prepositional phrase introduced by *de*, is in this case coreferential with *de revenir* (literally 'Jean is certain of it', in this case 'John is certain to do it'.) This prepositional usage of *de* must not of course be confused with the particle *de* discussed earlier, which seems rather to be equatable with the *de* of *une chambre de libre* (p. 228), as a kind of unmarked link for items other than tensed clauses (where the unmarked subordinator is of course *que* (p. 238 and, more generally, p. 69))).

We noted earlier that all French prepositions except one collocate with the infinitive; the exception is *en* ('in, while, by'), which alone is found with a form in -*ant*, to which we shall now turn. Synchronically speaking, this form represents the merger of three separate elements in Latin: the gerundive, the gerund and the present participle. Essentially, we may say that when the form is being used in a way which is wholly nominal or adjectival — functions found only with certain lexical items — then the normal rules of concord apply, thus *les passants* (m. pl.) 'passers-by', (*des*) *feuilles tremblantes* (f. pl.) 'trembling leaves'. This adjectival usage has extended in some unexpected ways: consider *billets payants* ('tickets which must be paid for'), *couleur voyante* ('colour that can readily be seen', i.e. 'loud'), *rue passante* ('street where many pass', i.e. 'busy') and many others. (*Thé dansant* 'tea dance' is of this type.) When, however, the form is being used in any way verbally (except at times with a preceding adverb) then it is invariable. This subsumes both the structure with *en* referred to above (*je l'ai résolu en ouvrant la fenêtre* 'I solved it by opening the window') and the more straightforward participial structures such as *j'ai vu les collines environnant la ville* 'I saw the hills surrounding the town'. The -*ant* form was used with various auxiliaries in earlier periods of the language to form a durative aspect supplementing that marked by the opposition between *faisait* and *fit/a fait* mentioned above (p. 228); such a structure with *être* is now rare to the point of ungrammaticality, but with *aller* is still well attested, at least in writing (i.e. *le mal va croissant* 'the illness is (lit. 'goes') getting worse').

The Sentence

As far as the syntax of main clauses is concerned, we shall glance briefly at two topics: sentential word order, and interrogative and negative structures. As far as the order of basic constituents is concerned, standard literary French is often said to be a canonical SVO language, that is, the subject (which is obligatory) precedes the verb which precedes the complement(s) in positive, declarative utterances. This situation has come about only since Middle French, after a period in which the language was strongly 'verb-second', that is, the finite verb followed immediately after one (and only one) preceding element, whether or not this was the subject (cf. main clauses in modern German). A few survivors of this V2 structure can be found in formal styles, for instance, *peut-être vient-il demain* literally 'perhaps comes he tomorrow', i.e. 'perhaps he's coming tomorrow', but essentially SVO came to be overwhelmingly preferred, even to the extent of strongly inhibiting the use of a variant order in interrogative sentences (see below). Note that exceptionally when the complement is a conjunctive personal pronoun, it precedes the finite verb.

Alongside this SVO order, however, there is a wide variety of other possible orders, involving the dislocation of one or more of the nominal elements associated with a verb to the left and/or to the right of the core sentence. Thus alongside SVO *je déteste Marie* ('I loathe Mary'), we find, in appropriate pragmatic circumstances, *moi, je déteste Marie*; *je déteste Marie, moi*; *Marie, je la déteste*; *je la déteste, Marie*, and even double dislocations to the right, to the left, or both (e.g. *je la déteste, moi, Marie*);

treble dislocations of the type *je le lui ai donné, moi, le livre, à Pierre* (literally 'I gave it to him, me, the book, to Peter') are not unknown. (The commas are conventional: the question of intonation is discussed below.) From these examples, it will be noted that not only is the subject clitic *je* retained even if *moi* is present elsewhere in the sentence but that there is in addition a clitic coreferential with the direct object when this constituent is displaced (e.g. *je la déteste, Marie* literally 'I her loathe, Mary') and even with the indirect object, thus *lui* = *à Pierre* in the example of treble dislocation given above. In other words, the 'true' subject and/or complements can be placed, in either order relative to each other, before or after the core sentence, which remains grammatically complete because of the clitic pronouns, while the sentence as a whole normally remains unambiguous because these coreferential clitics, now effectively prefixes bound to the finite verb, make the function of each nominal clear. In this way, *je l'aime, moi, Marie* (S before O) and *je l'aime, Marie, moi* (O before S) both mean 'I love Mary', the 'verb' being *je l'aime*. Of course, so long as these structures remain dislocated — that is, so long as the commas correspond to a genuine intonation break — then the original word order of the core sentence is unaffected. As soon, however, as the nominal groups are felt to be reabsorbed into the core sentence, and the intonation break is lost, then we must speak of an alternative sentential word order. This is a most complex area, but in essence it seems that left-dislocated nominals generally remain outside the core sentence serving as a familiar kind of topic slot (*Marie, je la déteste*, in other words, is not (yet) an object-initial sentence), but right-dislocated nominals frequently are assimilated, so *on y va nous à Paris* (literally 'one there goes, us, to Paris', i.e 'we're off to Paris') can be analysed as V (*on-y-va*) S Adv. (Note the absence of commas on this occasion.) Be that as it may, we can certainly agree that popular spoken French has a highly flexible word order of the kind often called 'free', and that the device which all such languages necessarily have to avoid ambiguity is in the case of French not a set of nominal case affixes as in Latin but a complex system of preverbal affixes derived from earlier conjunctive personal pronouns. It is also worth observing finally the results of recent work indicating that 'classic' SVO sentences are extremely rare in spoken French, and that as well as the alternative structures noted in this paragraph, considerable use is made of presentative cleft structures of the type *(Il) y a Jean qui l'a fait* literally '(there) is John who has done it', i.e. 'John has done it', the effect being to ensure that the transitive verb *faire* does not in the event have two lexical arguments within a single clause.

Interrogation

As far as interrogative sentences are concerned, Old French made use of the fact that there were heavy restrictions on the initial placement of verbs in declarative sentences, in unmarked contexts at least, to grammaticalise

SV inversion as a principal mode of question-forming. This structure still survives when the subject is a conjunctive pronoun (*vient-il?* 'comes he?', i.e. 'is he coming?') and in written French, in a construction known as *fausse inversion*, also when the subject is a noun, thus *le président vient-il?* literally 'the president comes he?'. In practice, alongside the rise of SVO as the normal order in declarative sentences, interrogative inversion was progressively ousted from spoken French, questions being marked either by the use of intonation alone, or by the use of an element *est-ce que*, originally a phrase meaning 'is it (a fact) that?' but now better analysed as /ɛsk(ə)/, a question-forming particle (*est-ce que le président vient?*). When there is an interrogative word present, fronting involves inversion in the literary language (*où vas-tu?* literally 'where go you?'): in speech, however, this can be avoided in at least four ways (*où est-ce que tu vas?, où que tu vas?, où tu vas?, tu vas où?*). One interesting development in this area is that of the particle /ti/, (written *ti, ty, t'y*, etc.) found in structures such as *tu viens-ti?* Still very much regarded as substandard, this particle arose through a reanalysis of forms such as *vient-il?* /vjɛ̃ti/ as stem (/vjɛ̃/) and interrogative marker (/ti/): thus also with *aime-t-il?* (/ɛmti/). The particle gradually detached itself from the third person, and became usable in principle with any form of the verb, thus *j'puis-t'y entrer?* 'can I come in?'.

Negation

The history of negation in French shows a constant see-saw between one- and two-word patterns. The literary language currently utilises an embracing structure, requiring *ne* between subject clitic and the following constituent, and another element — pronoun, adverb or simply 'reinforcer' — after the finite verb, thus *il ne vient pas* literally 'he not comes step', i.e. 'he isn't coming', or *il ne l'a jamais fait* 'he not it has (n)ever done', i.e. 'he has never done it'. These postverbal elements were (with one or two exceptions) originally positive in value, thus *ne ... rien* 'not ... a thing', *ne ... personne* 'not ... a person', *ne ... pas* 'not ... a step'. *Pas* has generalised in contexts where no more specific negative element was needed, though *point* is also still found in certain circumstances.

The constant collocation of words such as *rien* with *ne* has led to them becoming themselves negative in value, so that *rien, personne, jamais* and the like now carry the values 'nothing', 'nobody', 'never' (*qui est là? — personne.* 'who's there? — nobody'). (For a similar process in Spanish, see p. 116). One interesting and rather awkward side effect of this is that *plus* sometimes has the value '(some) more' and sometimes the negative value 'no more'. Furthermore, the preverbal particle *ne* is now frequently omitted in spoken French, including educated speech, formal *je ne sais pas* 'I don't know' being rendered /ʃsɛpɑ/, i.e. *j'sais pas.* We can therefore safely argue that alongside the embracing construction, there exists an alternative structure in which the postverbal elements, whether *pas* or a more specific item, alone carry the negative value. From this position, *pas* has become the everyday negator in virtually all other environments: thus an original *non moi* 'not me' has passed, via *non pas moi*, to *pas moi* in all but the most formal registers. Interestingly, double negation has in effect returned in the most popular registers, *je ne sais rien* passing, via *je sais rien* (see above) to *je sais pas rien*, though this is certainly regarded as substandard (cf. *je connais pas aucun homme*, literally 'I know not no man'). The loss of *ne* from the position between conjunctive pronoun subject and finite verb removes the only element (apart from other conjunctive pronouns) which hindered the total fusing of subject pronoun + verb as a single 'word' consisting of prefix and stem, a process discussed above (p. 232), and this same factor may have speeded the loss of the so-called 'pleonastic *ne*' from structures such as *avant qu'il (ne) vienne* 'before he comes', where the underlying assumption is of course that he has not yet come.

Subordination

Finally, within the domain of syntax, we shall look briefly at certain salient features of subordinate clauses. A tensed clause may have a nominal, adjectival or adverbial function within a matrix sentence. In the first case, we find that, according to the rules of normative grammar, when a nominal clause is fronted, its own verb is required, on purely syntactic grounds, to be in the subjunctive mood, whether the clause in question is the subject of the main verb (*que le problème soit* (subj.) *politique est hors de doute* 'that the problem is political is beyond doubt') or not (*que tu sois* (subj.) *sage, j'en suis certain* 'that you are sensible, I am certain of it'). Of course in practice such a clause is generally postposed, even where this requires clefting, and in all such cases the mood in the nominal clause, as we have seen earlier, will be semantically or lexically governed, thus *il est hors de doute que le problème est* (ind.) *politique* ('it (empty subject) is beyond doubt that the problem is political'). In more straightforward cases where the nominal clause is simply the complement of a matrix verb, we normally find the unmarked subordinator *que* (never omissible in French), the appropriate mood dependent, as we have seen, on the semantic class and/or precise identity of that matrix verb. It is worth noting that indirect statements, marked in Latin by a special 'accusative and infinitive' construction, were early assimilated to the favoured *que* + indicative structure, thus *j'ai dit qu'il allait venir* ('I said that he was going to come'), without the opposition of mood possible in, for example, Italian (p. 303) to mark the speaker's attitude to the truth or otherwise of the supposed coming. Indirect commands can be conveyed (in the case of most relevant verbs) either by a clause with a subjunctive verb (*je défends qu'ils fassent telle chose* 'I forbid them to do such a thing') or by the infinitive complement structure noted earlier (*je leur* (dat.) *défends de faire telle chose*). Certain verbs (such as *dire* 'say, tell') govern both statements and commands, with consequential minimal pairs (*je lui ai dit qu'il vient* (ind.) 'I told him that he is coming', *je lui ai dit qu'il vienne* (subj.) (or *je lui ai dit de venir*) 'I told him to come'). As regards indirect questions, French shows the polysemy, frequent elsewhere in Romance and more widely, between the relevant subordinator, and the principal marker of conditions, namely *si* ('if, whether'). Despite the fact that such clauses often express predicates which are less than certain, the indicative mood has been normal since the earliest times (*je ne sais pas s'il vient* 'I do not know whether/if he is coming').

In the case of adjectival (relative) clauses, a modal opposition is maintained, in more formal registers at least, between the indicative, where the antecedent is known or definite (*je cherche un livre que je veux* (ind.) *acheter* 'I'm looking for a book that I want to buy', i.e. one which I have identified in advance) and the subjunctive, where the antecedent is unknown or indeterminate (*je cherche un livre que je puisse* (subj.) *acheter* 'I'm looking for a book that I might buy'). By this same token, the subjunctive is required when the antecedent is negative or indefinite, as in *je ne vois personne qui sache* (subj.) *le faire* 'I can't see anyone who knows how to do it'.

Finally in this section, we shall look at a small subset of the various adverbial clauses in the language. As far as time clauses are concerned, the most frequent conjunction, *quand*, is used with the indicative mood, the future tense being used for future time reference, thus *quand il viendra* ... literally 'when he will come ...', i.e. 'when he comes ...'. In respect of the majority of temporal conjunctions, however, there is a long-standing tendency for a class pattern to override an earlier semantic distinction in respect of the indicative : subjunctive opposition. Thus whereas *avant que* 'before' and *jusqu'à ce que* 'until' might be expected on general semantic grounds to colligate as they do with a mood indicating events etc. which are less than certain, the converse is true with *après que* 'after', which of course frequently refers to events which have actually occurred and which therefore governed, at least in the eyes of prescriptive grammarians, the indicative mood. In practice, however, the subjunctive mood has long been found with *après que* also, no doubt as a result of surface analogical pressures, with the interesting consequence that when the marking of modality is really called for on semantic grounds, then the conditional — as our earlier discussions would lead us to expect — is pressed into service (*après que nous aurions* (cond.) *fait ce voyage, notre expérience serait grande* 'after we (would) have made this journey (if we make it), our experience would be great').

It is interesting to note in passing that this particular set of conjunctions illustrates particularly transparently the relationship between prepositions and conjunctions: the former (*avant* 'before', *après* 'after') govern nominals, while the latter, with the addition of the unmarked subordinator *que*, govern tensed clauses. Only a very small number of the most frequently used inherited conjunctions — such as *quand*, noted above, or *si* 'if', discussed below — do not incorporate this overt subordinator.

Reverting now to our principal theme, we may note briefly the concessive conjunctions *bien que* and *quoique* 'although'. In Latin, the two principal conjunctions in this semantic field patterned with the indicative and the subjunctive mood respectively, whereas in French both are said to require the subjunctive mood. In fact, however, a concessive clause may well relate a fact ('although he came ...'), so a meaningful opposition between moods would logically require a semantically governed choice: in any event, while the subjunctive is certainly the majority usage, the indicative has been fairly frequent at all periods in the language's history, and today the conditional is very frequent, once again, when genuine modality is to be marked. Interestingly in the light of the earlier discussion of *avant* and *avant que*, there exists a third concessive conjunction, *malgré que*, very common in popular speech, modelled on the concessive preposition *malgré* 'in spite of'.

Conditional clauses represent one of the major syntactic domains from which the subjunctive mood has retreated. In Latin, all doubtful or counterfactual hypotheses were marked by the use of the subjunctive mood (p. 72), with the same mood — and usually the same paradigm of that mood — in the corresponding apodosis. This was the situation also in Old French, although the commonest structure, involving the use of the imperfect subjunctive in both clauses, was multiply ambiguous. In the apodosis of such sentences, in a usage going back ultimately to Latin, the conditional and conditional perfect gradually rivalled the subjunctive, a development found also in Spanish and Italian. Indeed it seems highly likely that this was one of the principal contexts in which these paradigms came to be so heavily tinged with the modal value which we have seen to be so much a feature of the contemporary language. Unlike (standard) Spanish and Italian, however, French has ousted the subjunctive mood from non-factual protases also, thus *s'il venait* (imperf. ind.), *je le verrais* (cond.) 'if he came, I would see him'. Note this modal use of the imperfect indicative paradigm *venait*, in a context where the 'past' value which it normally carries is precluded: compare **il venait demain* (*'he came tomorrow') with *s'il venait demain* ... ('if he came tomorrow ...'). In substandard and regional French, as elsewhere in Romance, the conditional, or conditional perfect, is found in both clauses, to the despair of purists: cf. *je l'aurais pas fait si j'aurais su* literally 'I wouldn't have done it if I would have known', i.e. 'if I had known'.

It is idle to speculate whether this retreat by the subjunctive mood from an archetypally modal context was a cause of, or a result of, the loss of semantic distinctiveness by the subjunctive mood which we have noted on several occasions: that the developments are related seems beyond dispute.

We may certainly, by way of conclusion to this brief survey of subordination in French, reiterate the view hinted at earlier, that the use of the subjunctive mood is now governed almost entirely by grammatical rules and by the appearance of certain classes of words, or individual lexical items as the governing matrix verb or the conjunction, as appropriate. In only a very small number of cases is there a meaningful opposition between indicative and subjunctive moods, and even these are scarcely the stuff of everyday conversation: there, certain indicative paradigms have assumed the role of modality markers, in particular the conditional, to the point that the question has been raised on more than one occasion as to whether this paradigm (with or without its sister paradigm, the future) should not be regarded as a mood in its own right.

5   Lexis

The core vocabulary of French derives in very large measure from the Latin spoken in Gaul, the lexical items in question having in general undergone all the phonetic changes discussed briefly earlier which so often distinguish a French word so sharply from its cognates elsewhere in Romance. This Latin stock incorporated, before the linguistic fragmentation of the Romance-speaking area, a number of words from other sources, the subsequent development of which has been indistinguishable from that of their indigenous counterparts. We might mention Greek (e.g. COLAPHUM > *coup* 'blow', CHORDAM > *corde* 'rope', PETRAM > *pierre* 'stone'), particularly important as the source towards the end of the Empire of much specifically Christian vocabulary, some of which later greatly expanded its meaning (ECCLESIAM > *église* 'church', PRESBYTER > *prêtre* 'priest' (p. 217), but PARABOLAM 'parable', now > *parole* 'word'). Equally, among the earliest people whose territory was overrun by the Romans were the Celts, and some Celtic words — recognisable by their widespread distribution — were borrowed and assimilated into Latin very early: these included, for instance, CAMISIAM > *chemise* 'shirt', CABALLUM > *cheval* 'horse' and, more surprisingly, a very common verb CAMBIARE > *changer* 'to change'. The Celtic word CARRUM 'cart' underlies not only standard French *char* and (with a diminutive suffix) *charrette* 'cart', but also Norman French *carre*, whence English 'car', a word which has prospered not only in English but once again in French in the sense of '(motor) coach' (cf. p. 118). More specifically French, however, are the words, generally agreed to be approaching 200, which passed into the language from the local form of Celtic, Gaulish, many of them representing the names of plants, birds or other rural objects: one thinks, for instance, of *chêne* 'oak tree', *if* 'yew-tree', *alou-ette* 'lark', *soc* 'ploughshare' and *raie* 'furrow'. The word *grève*, in the sense of 'sandy river bank' is Celtic in origin: on one such bank of the Seine, unemployed workmen gathered, *en grève* thus coming to mean 'out of work' and later 'on strike'. A Celtic vigesimal counting system survives in *quatre-vingts* 'four score', i.e. 'eighty' (*huitante* and similar forms are found in many dialects: cf. *huit* 'eight').

The Roman occupation of Gaul was ended by the Germanic invasions. Although the conquerors eventually came to be French-speaking, they made a very significant impression on the language. Not only is the development of a strong stress accent, with such radical consequences on the phonological evolution of Latin words in northern Gaul, frequently attributed to Germanic influence, but so too very generally are syntactic features such as the prolonged preference for a V2 word order (p. 235) or the use of *on* as an alternative to the passive (p. 232). While none of these claims is wholly beyond dispute, what is certain is that many words in contemporary French can be traced back either to Frankish or to less specific Germanic sources: of the 1,000 most frequently used words in contemporary French, some 35 are from this source, whether found also in other Romance languages (e.g. *guerre* 'war', *franc* 'free', *riche* 'rich', *blanc* 'white', *jardin* 'garden') or more specifically French (e.g. *bleu* 'blue', *joue* 'cheek'). The fact that so many of these words have a direct cognate in English, itself of course a Germanic language, is readily apparent.

Much the biggest influence on the French lexicon, however, is from a perhaps unexpected source, namely Latin itself (with a not insignificant admixture from Greek). This is because, from the time of the very earliest texts and even more so during and after the Renaissance, the core vocabulary inherited directly via the spoken tradition proved inadequate for the new demands made of it. This process of enrichment has yielded a very large number of 'learned' words in modern French, many of them now 'learned' only in the technical sense that they have not undergone the phonetic changes that would have affected truly 'popular' words, thus *nature, facile* 'easy', *imaginer*. Often indeed one finds doublets in modern French, that is, a 'popular' and a 'learned' derivative of the same word: consider, for example, *loyal/légal* (< LEGALEM), *peser* 'weigh'/*penser* 'weigh up mentally', i.e. 'think' (< PENSARE) or *frêle/fragile* 'breakable'. This last pair, both derived from FRAGILEM, shows particularly clearly how much closer phonetically the 'learned' word will often be to its etymon (cf. Eng. *frail* and *fragile*).

By far the most significant present-day source of loan words other than Latin/Greek is English, reflecting at times a genuine cultural or technical innovation, but at times simply a change of fashion. During the eighteenth century, many political and legal terms (*budget, vote, jury, parlement*) were borrowed, reflecting admiration in France for the form of government in Britain at that time. (Note that many of these had themselves earlier been absorbed into English from (Norman) French, including all of those listed above.) During the nineteenth century, various kinds of sport were emulated, giving words such as *sport, golf, jockey, turf* 'racecourse, horseracing', *boxe* 'boxing', etc., whereas words reflecting England's lead in the Industrial Revolution were also borrowed, particularly in the domain of the railway and textile industries. (Again, many words such as *ticket, tunnel, sport* had themselves earlier passed from French to English.) The twentieth century has seen many borrowings which meet a need in this way, but also many which merely reflect either the belief on the part of advertisers and others that an English name or slogan will enhance sales (*le drink pour les men* is somehow superior to *la boisson pour les hommes*) or simply the willingness of those such as pressmen constantly engaged with material in both English and French to use an English word that is readily to hand. (*Pipeline* is a much-quoted example, with the indigenous *oléoduc* now strongly favoured in its place.) Many of the borrowings take the form of closed monosyllables (p. 214), a particularly favoured phonological type in modern French, as we have seen (*cross* 'cross-country race', *test, pull* ('pullover'), *spot* 'spot-light', *star*, etc.), or of polysyllables ending in *-ing* (*parking* 'car park', *dumping*) or *-man* (*rugbyman*). It is important, however, to keep the question of English influence in perspective. One notes, for instance, that of the list of 1,445 words drawn up largely on the basis of frequency counts for the introductory teaching programme *Le français fondamental*, there are, leaving aside 'international' words such as *radio* and *taxi*, only two words (*film* (1889) and *sport* (1828)) and one sense (*train* as in 'railway train' (1827) — the word itself is found as early as the twelfth century and is itself the etymon of the English word) borrowed relatively recently from English.

Just as there has always been an exceptionally high degree of interest among educationalists and the French public more generally in the niceties of grammar, so too the present wave of Anglicisms has not passed unnoticed. Efforts have been made to staunch the inflow of such borrowings, both where they are clearly unnecessary and, more importantly, in a wide range of specialist areas where, given a little thought, a perfectly acceptable French word could become widely used and accepted. The *Office du vocabulaire français*, founded in 1957, surveys all aspects of the contemporary vocabulary, especially but not exclusively loan words, and makes recommendations which, if promulgated in the *Journal officiel*, may at times carry the force of law, at least in respect of the written language.

The fact that the preceding paragraphs have focused attention on the borrowing of words from other languages should not be allowed to obscure the fact that French has many productive means of word formation of its own. Verbs — overwhelmingly *-er* verbs, cf. p. 223 — can readily be formed from nouns (e.g. *américaniser*), while there is a whole range of suffixes, both learned and popular, to derive one type of noun from another. One very much used suffix of this type is *-ier*, as in *fermier* 'farmer' (cf. *ferme* 'farm'), a suffix whose precise value is in many cases opaque (cf. *cendrier* 'ash-tray', from *cendre* 'ash'). Various foreign suffixes have had brief heydays: -*man*, for example, noted earlier in respect of *rugbyman*, is found in various (now largely obsolescent) derivatives such as *yachtman* [*sic*], *crossman* ('cross-country runner') or *wattman* '(electric) tram driver', the English equivalents of which are attested rarely, if at all, in the language from which the component elements have undubitably come. Prefixes too play an important role in enhancing the lexical possibilities of the language. Finally, we might note a noticeably increasing tendency simply to juxtapose two otherwise free-standing words, a process long familiar to speakers of English, thus *station service* 'service station', *mot-clé* 'key word', *assurance-incendie* 'fire insurance' and the like.

6 Conclusion

French, then, is a language still evolving rapidly in all its aspects, particularly in respect of its lexis, and of its grammatical system (where the gap between the classical model which is prescribed and what even educated speakers actually do is at times quite extraordinarily wide). In phonology, too, the position has not yet fully stabilised, although the eventual outcome of the various unresolved questions discussed in section 2 is in most cases now tolerably clear. As a world language, French is holding its own surprisingly well in the face of constant competition from English, although only time will tell how long this can be sustained.

Bibliography

Brunot, F. and Ch. Bruneau (1969) *Précis de grammaire historique de la langue française.* Masson, Paris.

Centre National de la Recherche Scientifique (1973) *Les dialectes romans de France à la lumière des atlas régionaux.* CNRS, Paris.

Fouché, P. (1959) *Traité de prononciation française.* Klincksieck, Paris.

Grevisse, M. (1980) *Le Bon Usage.* Duculot, Paris-Gembloux.

Harmer, L.C. (1979) (ed. P. Rickard and T.G.S. Combe) *Uncertainties in French Grammar.* Cambridge University Press, Cambridge.

Harris, M. (1978) *The Evolution of French Syntax: a Comparative Approach.* Longman, London.

Herslund, M., O. Mørdrup, and F. Sørensen (1983) *Analyses grammaticales du français.* Etudes Romanes de l'Université de Copenhague, Revue romane no. spécial 24. Akademisk Forlag, Copenhagen.

Judge, A. and F.G. Healey (1983) *A Reference Grammar of Modern French.* Arnold, London.

Lucci, V. (1983) *Etude phonétique du français contemporain à travers la variation situationnelle.* Publications de l'Université des Langues et Lettres de Grenoble, Grenoble.

Rickard, P. (1974) *A History of the French Language.* Hutchinson, London.

Ruwet, N. (1972) *Théorie syntaxique et syntaxe du français.* Editions du Seuil, Paris.

—— (1982) *Grammaire des insultes et autres études.* Seuil, Paris.

Thody, P. and H. Evans (1985) *Faux Amis and Key Words*. Athlone Press, London.
Thomas, A.V. (1956) *Dictionnaire des difficultés de la langue française* rev. edn. Larousse, Paris.
Togeby, K. (1982–5) *Grammaire française* 5 vols. (= special nos. *Revue romane*). Akademisk Forlag, København.
Tranel, B. (1981) *Concreteness in Generative Phonology: Evidence from French*. University of California Press, Berkeley and Los Angeles.
Valdman, A. (1976) *Introduction to French Phonology and Morphology*. Newbury House, Rowley, Mass.
—— (1979) *Le Français hors de France*. Champion, Paris.
Wall, K. (1980) *L'inversion dans la subordonnée en français contemporain*. Uppsala University Press, Uppsala.
Walker, D.C. (1981) *An Introduction to Old French Morphophonology*. Studia Phonetica 19. Didier, Paris.
Walter, H. (1982) *Enquête phonologique et variétés régionales du français*. Presses Universitaires de France, Paris.

7 Occitan

Max W. Wheeler

1 Introduction

The geographical area of modern Occitan is discussed on p. 16. The language shows a wide range of dialect variation; the distribution of the major dialects is shown in Map VI. They can be divided into two basic groups: a northeastern group consisting of Lemosin, Auvernhat, Alpin and Provençal; and a southwestern group consisting of Lengadocian and Gascon. The northeastern group is on the whole more innovative phonologically (especially northern Lemosin and northern Auvernhat), with isoglosses linking these varieties with adjacent French dialects. There are also closer syntactic parallels with French. Gascon diverged at a very early stage in both phonology and morphology. Probably only its copresence within the French cultural sphere has kept it from being regarded as a separate language. Franco-Provençal, which is not considered here (but see p. 17), has generally been regarded as a separate language, though it is probably not more divergent from Occitan overall than Gascon is. Lengadocian is generally the most conservative dialect and is the basis of modern standard Occitan. In fact, there are two standard orthographies, with their associated grammars, in current use. The Felibrige standard (cf. p. 17), which avoids the term 'Occitan', is based on the Rhone variety of Provençal, as used by such major writers as Frederi Mistral. Its orthography is largely phonemic, and when applied to other dialects emphasises the differences between them. Occitan as promoted by the Institut d'Estudis Occitans returns approximately to the medieval orthography, which is morphophonemic and is avowedly pan-Occitan in scope. It is this orthography which is followed here. There are also major ideological differences associated with the two orthographies. Only the Institut d'Estudis Occitans proposes a standardised morphology and lexis, which is referred to as *occitan referencial.*

2 Phonology

In what follows, we adopt a basically diasystemic, and somewhat abstract,

approach to the phonological system. This is intended as a key to understanding what is going on in Occitan as a whole, rather than as a strict
phonological analysis of any one dialect, which, considered on its own, may
differ markedly from the rest.

Vowels
The vowel systems are set out in Table 7.1. These somewhat unusual vowel
systems have arisen through unconditioned sound changes, /u/ > /y/ and
/o/ > /u/, which have affected all dialects, giving, e.g. *luna* ['lyno]
'moon', *comun* [ku'myn] 'common', *musica* [my'ziko] 'music', *ora* ['uro]
'hour', *vòlon* ['vɔlun] 'they want'. Pretonic vowel reduction of a pan-
Romance type gives rise to neutralisation of /ɛ/ and /e/ as /e/, as, for
example, in *pèl* [pɛl] 'skin', *pelar* [pe'la] 'to skin', *pel* [pel] 'hair', *pelós*
[pe'lus] 'hairy'; *lèvas* ['lɛvos] 'you raise (2 sg.)', *levatz* [le'vats] 'you raise (2
pl.)'; and of /u/ and /ɔ/ as /u/, as in *sola* ['sulo] 'alone (f.)', *soleta*
[su'leto] 'alone (diminutive)', *sòla* ['sɔlo] 'sole of foot', *soleta* [su'leto] 'sole
of shoe', *pòrtas* ['pɔrtos] 'you bring (2 sg.)', *portatz* [pur'tats] 'you bring (2
pl.)'. In unstressed final syllables, PWR /o/ and /e/ merged as Occitan
/e/ after consonant groups which could not stand as syllable codas (e.g.
paire 'father', *pòble* 'people', *sòrre* 'sister') and were generally deleted elsewhere. Consequently post-tonic /u/ is largely restricted to third person
plural verb forms such as *lièjon* 'they read' (together with first singular in
the Alpin dialect: *pòrto* 'I bring'). PWR /a/ in atonic final syllables has a
wide range of realisations in modern Occitan: [a], [o], [u], [ə], of which [o]
predominates. Post-tonic /i/ is found in examples like *òli* 'oil', *glòria*
['glɔri] 'glory', and has an important role in the inflectional morphology of
many dialects.

Table 7.1: Vowel Systems

Tonic			Pretonic			Post-tonic	
i y		u	i y		u	i	u
e			e			e	o
	ɛ ɔ						
	a			a			

The opposition between /e/ and /ɛ/ is to a large extent neutralised in
the northeastern dialect group, with [e] and [ɛ] realisations being conditioned by the environment. Characteristic of most dialects to this day is
the retention of the Latin falling diphthong /aw/ as in *causa* 'thing', *ausir*
'to hear'.

Medieval Occitan derived rising diphthongs from PWR /ɛ/ and /ɔ/
before palatal or velar consonants, giving rise to modern forms like *vielha*
'old (f.)', *fiera* 'fair', *mieg* 'half', *ieu* 'I', *siegre* 'to follow', *fuòlha* 'leaf',

cuòissa 'thigh', *nuòch* 'night', *buòu* 'ox', *fuòc* 'fire'. The diphthong [jɛ] from this or other sources has largely remained unaltered in modern Occitan, but [wɔ] has undergone a divergence of realisations, most of which involve fronting: [ɥɔ], [ɥɛ], [wɛ], [jɔ], [jɛ], [jø], [jy], [ɛ], [ø], [y]. Rising diphthongs also develop from -ĀRĪUM, -ĀRĬAM, e.g. *primier*, *primie(i)ra* 'first', *carrie(i)ra* 'street'; and PWR /i/ or /u/ preceding /l/ or /w/, such as *anguila ~ anguiala* 'eel', *estiu ~ estieu* 'summer', *mula ~ muòla* 'mule', *cuòl* 'arse'. In most of Provence, and in some other areas, all other /ɔ/ is subject to a more recent diphthongisation, in which the glide remains labial as in *pòrta* ['pwɔrto] ~ ['pwarto] ~ ['pwɛrto] 'door'. Rising diphthongs also develop generally from /i/ + V, that is, with stress shift if the /i/ was stressed, for example, *paciéncia* [pa'sjensi] ~ [pa'sjensjo] 'patience', *foliá* [fu'ljɔ] ~ [fu'ljɛ] 'madness'.

Consonants
Table 7.2 presents the consonant phonemes of a diasystem of standardised Occitan. The parenthesised elements are phonemically marginal, or are absent in some dialects — /ʃ/ and /ŋ/ are clear phonemes only in Gascon.

Table 7.2: Consonant Phonemes

	Labial	Dental/ alveolar	Prepalatal	Palatal	Velar	Uvular
Stop						
[−voice]	p	t	(ts) ʧ		k	
[+voice]	b	d	ʤ		ɡ	
Fricative						
[−voice]	f	s	(ʃ)			
[+voice]	(v)	z				
Nasal	m	n		ɲ	(ŋ)	
Lateral		l		ʎ		
Trill		r				(ʀ)
Glide	(ɥ)			j	w	

The following observations outline the realisations of these phonemes in various phonological contexts, or in various dialects. The voiced stops /b, d, ɡ/ may be realised as fricatives in Lengadocian and Gascon, when they occur between continuants. The sibilants /s, z/ may be apico-alveolar; in certain regions, especially of Auvernhat and Lemosin, they are prepalatal [ʃ, ʒ]. This realisation is usually accompanied by depalatalised realisations of /ʧ, ʤ/. As a phoneme distinct from /t/ + /s/ or from /ʧ/, the dental/ alveolar affricate /ts/ is extremely marginal. It really only corresponds to the morphophonemic alternation [ts] ~ [z], e.g. *crotz* 'cross' ~ *crosar* 'to cross', *dètz* 'ten' ~ *desena* 'tenth'. The affricate diaphonemes /ʧ, ʤ/ are variously realised. In a northern area (Lemosin, Auvernhat, and northern Lengadocian) they have been depalatalised, generally to [ts, dz], but in the northernmost part of this area to [s, z]. A good part of Lengadocian merges the voiced affricate with the voiceless (and also has /dz/ → [ts], e.g. *dotze* [dutse] 'twelve'). Or /ʤ/ may be realised as [ʒ] (the rest of Lengadocian) or as [ʝ ~ j] (most of Gascon); in these areas /ddʒ/ < /-t'k-/, /-d'k-/, remains distinct from /ʤ/, e.g. *viatge* 'journey', *jutjar* 'to judge', which contain [ddʒ] or [tʃ] or [ʝʝ]. A characteristic of the South-western dialect group is the loss of /v/, which has merged with /b/ (or with /w/ intervocalically, in Gascon). This is an areal feature common to Basque, Spanish, Galician and most of Catalan.

In syllable codas /n/ is realised in Provençal as a homorganic nasal or [ŋ], but typically only in Auvernhat do we find loss of syllable-final /n/ with nasalisation of the preceding vowel, as in French. In Lengadocian, Lemosin and Auvernhat, Proto-Occitan word-final /n/ is deleted. Except in Gascon and adjacent areas, word-final /m/, /ɲ/, /nt/ are neutralised as /n/. A distinctive feature of Gascon is the loss of intervocalic /-n-/ (cf. Basque), while /-nd-/ > /n/ (cf. Catalan, p. 172) and /-mb-/ > /m/ (as in Spanish), e.g. Gascon *cama* 'leg', *enténer* 'to understand'.

Nasals

				Gascon	Lengadocian	Provençal
BALNEUM	>	banh	'bath'	/baɲ/	/ban/	[baŋ]
FŪMUM	>	fum	'smoke'	/hym/	/fyn/	[fyŋ]
*FANT	>	fan	'do (3 pl.)'	/hɛn/	/fan/	[faŋ]
DĒNTEM	>	dent	'tooth'	/den(t)/	/den/	[dɛŋ]
HĂBĒMUS	>	avèm	'we have'	/a'wɛm/	/a'bɛn/	[a'vɛŋ]
VĪNUM	>	vin	'wine'	/biŋ/	/bi/	[viŋ]
ANNUM	>	an	'year'	/an/	/an/	[aŋ]
CAMPUM	>	camp	'field'	/kam(p)/	/kan/ ~ /kam(p)/	[kaŋ]
LŎNGUM	>	long	'long'	/luŋ(g)/	/lun/	[luŋ]
LUNAM	>	luna	'moon'	/'lyo/	/'lyno/	['lyno]

Of the liquids, /l/ is generally dental, but velarised variants occur, and were doubtless once widespread, in syllable codas at least. For, except in Lengadocian, original Latin /-l-/ has become [w] in codas, e.g. *auba* 'dawn', *cau* 'is necessary' < CĂLET, *faus* 'false'. (Within Lengadocian some varieties show /l/ > [w] only before dentals, while others show /l/ > [w] except before dentals, and the remainder have no /l/ > [w].) In intervocalic position the palatal lateral /ʎ/ survives as such in a consider-able part of Occitania (excluding Provence, where it has merged with /j/). In word-final position /ʎ/ is retained in Gascon; depalatalisation to [l] is typical of Lengadocian, while other dialects show a mixture of [j] and [w]. The latter seems to have originated in nominal plurals, where [ʎs] > [ls] > [ws], for example, *genolh* 'knee' Leng. [dʒe'nul], Prov. [dʒe'nuj]; *filh* 'son' Leng. [fil], Prov. [fjew]. Original geminate /-ll-/ has in some varieties followed the path of /-l-/, in others, that of /-ʎ-/: bèl < BELLUM ELeng. [bɛl] 'fine', cf. ELeng. sal [saw] < *SALEM 'salt'. Prototypical Gascon is distinguished by a separate development of /-ll-/, which became /r/ in onsets (era pora < ILLAM PULLAM 'the chicken'), but /c/ in codas. This latter palatal plosive, spelt -th, has subsequently diverged lexically into /t/ and /tʃ/; for example, eth vedèth /et be'dɛt/ 'the calf', poth /putʃ/ 'cock'.

The phoneme /r/ seems originally to have had an allophonic distribution of alveolar variants comparable to that found in Spanish and Catalan, namely, a tap [ɾ] within words between vowels or glides and word-finally, otherwise a strongly trilled [r] in syllable-initial position, including /-rr-/, and a weakly trilled [r̆] (two or three beats) adjacent to a consonant. The conservative west largely retains this distribution. In other varieties, frequently [r], often [r̆], and sometimes [ɾ] too, have been replaced by a uvular [ʀ], on the French model. Except in Alpin, Proto-Occitan word-final [r] is deleted in suffixes, and often in stems as well.

The phonemic status of /j/ in contrast to /i/ is well established (e.g. trairà /traj'ra/ 'will pull out' vs traïrà /trai'ra/ 'will betray'). The status of /w/ is less firm. It occurs rarely in syllable onsets (but note oelha /'weʎo/ 'sheep', coard /kwart/ 'coward'), and in codas [w] represents, morphophonemically at least, /l/ or /ʎ/ or /v/, e.g. cau 'is necessary' ~ calià 'was necessary', filh [fjew] 'son' ~ filha [fi(j)o] 'daughter', nòu (m.) ~ nòva (f.) 'new'. The phonemic status of /ɥ/ is very dubious; [ɥ] occurs only in prenuclear position and appears not to contrast with /y/. Its position in the diasystem represents the raised element of diphthongs deriving from Proto-Occitan */ɔ/, variously realised as [ɥ], [w], [j], etc. The sequences /iw/ and /ju/, e.g. violeta 'violet', passion 'passion', are not consistently distinguished, nor are /yj/ and /ɥi/. Gascon alone retains /kw/ and /gw/, e.g. quatre 'four', Gasc. /kwate/, other dialects /katre/; guaire '(not) much', Gasc. /gwajre/, other dialects /gajre/.

Other Consonant Changes
Also distinctive of Gascon is the unconditioned change /f/ > /h/. Corresponding to Common Occitan filha 'daughter', farina 'flour', flor 'flower', fred 'cold', calfar 'to warm', Gascon has hilha, haria, hlor, hred, cauhar. This h- is now silent in hlor, hred, etc. or has been replaced by Common Occ. /f/; in some Gascon varieties /h/ > Ø is general. (For a comparable development in Spanish, cf. p. 92.) Gascon has also developed a prosthetic vowel before initial /r/ (cf. Basque errege 'king' < RĒGEM), for example, arradim 'grapes', arròda, 'wheel', arriu 'river'.

Northern dialects (Lemosin, Auvernhat, northern Alpin) share with French (p. 212) the palatalisation of Latin velar stops before /a/. That is, /k/ becomes /tʃ/; chabra ~ cabra 'goat', vacha ~ vaca 'cow', blancha ~ blanca 'white (f.)', while /g/ becomes /dʒ/ initially and after a consonant (*jalina* ~ *galina* 'hen', *lonja* ~ *longa* 'long (f.)'), and becomes /j/ after a vowel (*braias* ~ *bragas* 'breeches', *paiar* ~ *pagar* 'to pay'). Latin /-kt-/ becomes /jt/ in Gascon, western Lengadocian, northern Auvernhat and Alpin (cf. in French, Catalan, Portuguese), but elsewhere it becomes /ʧ/ (cf. Spanish): *fait* ~ *fach* 'done', *nuòit* ~ *nuòch* 'night'. Both of these dialect divergences are attested from earliest Occitan, and are reflected in standard orthography.

Original Latin intervocalic /-d-/, /-c-/, /-s-/ result, in standard Occitan, in /z/, for example, *ausir* 'to hear', *susar* 'to sweat', *rasim* 'grapes', *disèm* 'we say', *causa* 'thing', *camisa* 'shirt'. Other dialects have /d/ for the first of these, or for the first and second, e.g. Gascon *sudar* 'to sweat', *arradim* 'grapes'. Much of Provençal has lost intervocalic /z/, giving, with consequential changes, the forms *cauva* 'thing', *camiá* 'shirt', *diam* 'we say'. And much of Provençal, together with Alpin and Auvernhat, has lost intervocalic /d/ < /-t-/ also, e.g. *polida* 'pretty' Alpin [purˈje], *amada* 'loved (f.)' variously [amˈaː], [aˈmaja].

Preconsonantal /s/ is subject to weakening, as it has been in French, in adjacent dialect areas of Lemosin, northern Auvernhat, northern Alpin. The outcome is variously [x], [h], [j], vowel lengthening, or zero, e.g. *escòla* 'school' [ehˈkɔlo] ~ [ejˈkɔlo] ~ [eˈkɔlo], etc. This process is most widespread, and [j] the most likely result, before sonorants, with voiced consonants being the next most favouring environment. For comparable but much more widespread changes affecting word-final /s/, see p. 252 below.

Stress

Except in Nice and varieties in Italy where, e.g. *mànega* 'sleeve', *diménegue* 'Sunday', ˈ*parla-li* 'speak to him', are to be found, Occitan shuns proparoxytones, and shifts stress to a following syllable, to give, for example, paroxytonic *lagrema* 'tear', *persegue* 'peach', *silaba* 'syllable', *classica* 'classical (f.)', *credula* 'credulous (f.)'. Unless a final consonant is an inflectional morpheme (e.g. *joves* 'young people', *dison* 'they say', *cantàvam* 'we sang') consonant-final paroxytones are rare. Many have become vowel-final through elision of the final consonant, as in *conóisser* 'to recognise', *Antibol* 'Antibes', *àngel* 'angel', *crèdit* 'credit'; while masculine nominals have undergone stress shift by analogy with the related feminine forms, e.g. *classic* 'classical (m.)', *credul* 'credulous (m.)', *contemporanèu* 'contemporary (m.)', *filològ* 'philologist (m.)'. Post-clitic pronouns are now stressed: ˌ*parla*-ˈ*li* 'speak to him', *do*ˈ*natz*-ˌ*me* 'give me'.

Sandhi Processes

A general phonological characteristic of Occitan (especially of dialects other than Gascon) has been and is the weakness of consonants in syllable codas. This weakness is reflected in loss of distinctions in voice and place of articulation, in weakening of manner of articulation along a strength hierarchy (obstruent stop – fricative – sonorant – glide – vowel), and in simple deletion. We shall assume here that Occitan orthography represents underlying forms, though many of the processes involved here (especially word-internal ones) are more strictly sound changes now completed. Phonological restructuring of lexical entries on the basis of sandhi variants has been widespread.

In all dialects voice is neutralised in obstruents in syllable codas. In utterance-final position they are realised as voiceless. In word-final position before vowels plosives are voiceless, fricatives voiced, while /ʧ/ may be either, e.g. *nuech e jorn* 'night and day' Prov. [njøʧ e ʤur], *puech agut* 'pointed hill' Leng. [pɛʤ aˈgyt]. Obstruents agree in voicing with following consonants. Also, as we have seen, /v/ is realised as [w] in codas, as is /l/ in a large proportion of dialects including otherwise conservative Gascon. Only Gascon and adjacent Lengadocian varieties maintain the place of articulation contrasts between sonorants in utterance-final, or in word-final prevocalic, position, that is, contrasting /ʎ/ and /l/ (Lengadocian); /m, n, ɲ, (ŋ)/. Place contrasts between final obstruent stops /p, t, ʧ, k/ are maintained before vowels, in addition, in most of Lengadocian and in Alpin. Virtually everywhere, however, place of articulation contrasts are not maintained before a following consonant (except for the contrast between /s/ and /f/ which survives wherever the former remains in codas). The examples which follow are conservative Lengadocian: *còps* [kɔts] 'blows', *ròcs* [rɔts] 'rocks', *Occitan* [utsiˈta], *escapçar* [eskaˈtsa] 'to cut the end off', *acte* [ˈatte] 'act', *lums* [lyns] 'lights'; *nap gelat* [naddʒeˈlat] 'frozen turnip', *rat grèule* [rag ˈgriwle] 'dormouse', *avètz jogat* [aˈbɛddʒuˈgat] 'you have played'. Final stops, where they are retained at all, assimilate in manner to [−continuant] sonorants, as in *mieg nut* [mjɛn nyt] 'half naked', *tap long* [tal lun] 'long cork', *ròc mòl* [rɔm mɔl] 'wet rock'. Consonants between consonants are omitted: *camps* [kans] 'fields', *cauds* [kaws] 'hot (m. pl.)', *tòrts* [tɔrs] 'wrongs', *forns* [furs] 'ovens', *taps longs* [tal luns] 'long corks', *bèls miralhs* [bɛl miˈrals] 'nice mirrors', *pòrcs negres* [pɔr ˈnegres] 'black pigs'.

In Lengadocian, word-final /s/, unless already deleted by previously mentioned processes, becomes [j] before consonants other than voiceless stops; so, for example, *las claus* [las klaws] 'the keys', but *los buòus* [luj bjɔws] 'the oxen', *bonas sègas* [ˈbunoj ˈsɛgos] 'good harvests', *bonis vins* [ˈbuni bis] 'good wines', *los anhèls* [luz aˈɲɛls] 'the lambs', *còs nut* [kɔj nyt] 'bare body', *es mòrt* [ej mɔr(t)] 'is dead', *las femnas* [laj ˈfennos] 'the women'.

The modifications exemplified above give rise to many cases of omission of stem-final consonants. If we bear in mind also that many dialects have simplified to [s] final /ts/, which may correspond to /ts/ or /t+s/, /p+s/,

/k+s/, and that many do not accept geminate consonants at all, the generalised final-obstruent deletion characteristic of Provençal, Lemosin and Auvernhat becomes understandable. Provençal, for example, retains only /s/ after a stressed vowel (and in second person singular verb forms), and a few other obstruents before vowels in close liaison environments. The consequence of these processes is that in 'advanced' dialects only the following consonants (no consonant groups) are admitted in codas (or indeed word-finally before vowels where they are onsets): /j/, /w/, /r/, /N/ (homorganic nasal), /s/ and, rarely, /f/. The most 'advanced' dialects exclude /s/ altogether and substitute a nasalised vowel for a vowel + /N/.

Other Phonological Points
Two other phonological processes are worth mentioning: the first, because of distant parallels to it elsewhere in Romance; the second, because of its rarity in Romance in general. Neither is standard or reflected in the orthography. The first concerns a weakening of /l/. In Alpin dialects /l/ > [r] before labial consonants, e.g. *balma* ['barmo] 'cave', and intervocalically, e.g. *pala* ['paro] 'shovel'. In southern Auvernhat intervocalic /l/ is replaced by a velar or labio-velar consonant, or even /v/: *pala* [pawo ~ pago ~ pavo]. The second phenomenon, restricted to Auvernhat and contiguous parts of Lemosin, is palatalisation especially of dental/alveolars, but also of labials, especially before /j/ and /i/, but also before /y/, /e/, and /ø/.

The following passage from the parable of the Prodigal Son illustrates this range of phonetic realisations and other dialect differences. The versions are taken, with modifications, from the work of P. Bec.

Occitan Referencial (Lengadocian)
Un òme aviá pas que dos dròlles. Lo pus jove diguèt a son   paire:
yn 'ɔme a'bjɔ pas ke duj 'drɔlles lu py 'dʒube di'gɛt a sum 'pajre

'Es ora per ieu de me governar sol e d'aver
ez 'uro per jew de me guber'na sul e da'be

d'argent: me cal poder partir e véser de país.
dar'dʒen me kal pu'de par'ti e 'beze de pa'is

Despartissètz lo vòstre ben e donatz-me çò que devi aver.'
desparti'sɛdz lu 'bɔstre be e du'naj me sɔ ke 'debi a'be

'O mon filh,' diguèt lo paire, 'coma voldràs tu; siás un
ɔ mu fil   di'gɛl lu 'pajre 'kumo bul'dras ty sjɔz ym

marrit e seràs castigat.' Apuei dubriguèt una tireta,
ma'rit e se'ras kasti'gat a'pej dybri'gɛt 'yno ti'reto

despartiguèt lo sieu ben e ne faguèt doas parts.
desparti'gɛl lu sjew be e ne fa'gɛd dɔs pars

Gascon. (Valence/Baïse, Gers.)
Un òme n'avèva pas que dus hilhs. Lo mès joent digoc a son
yn 'ɔme na'wɛwo pa ke ðys hils   lu mɛ ʒwen di'ɣuk a sum

pair : 'Qu'e temps que siái mon mèste e qu'àujai argent;
paj   ke   tens ke sjɔj mum 'mɛste e 'kawʒoj ar'ʒen

que cau que póiscai me'n anar e que véigai païs.
ke   kaw ke 'puʃkoj men a'na e ke 'βejɣoj pa'is

Partatjatz   vòste ben e balhatz -me çò que divi aver.'
partaʃ'ʃadz 'bɔste βeŋ e βaʎ'ʎam me sɔ ke 'ðiwi a'we

'Que òc, mon hilh,' digoc lo pair, 'coma volhes; qu'ès un
  ʧɔ   muŋ hiʎ di'ɣug lu paj 'kumo 'βuʎes k ɛz ym

maishant e que seràs punit.' La-vetz daureiscoc un tiroèr, que
ma'ʃan e ke se'ras py'nit   la βedz dawreʃ'kuk yn ti'rwɛɾ ke

partatgèc son ben e que'n hascoc duas porcions.
partaʃ'ʃɛk sum beŋ e keŋ   has'kug 'dyos pur'sjus

Provençal
Un òme aviá ren que dos fius. Lo pus joine   diguèt a son
yn 'ɔme a'vje ʀeŋ ke dus fjew lu py 'dzujne di'gɛ a sum

paire: 'Ei temps que fugue mon   mèstre e qu'ague de sòus;
'pajɾe ej teŋ   ke 'fyge mum 'mɛstʀe c 'k age   de sɔw

fau que pòsque me'n anar e que vegue de païs. Partatjatz
fɔw ke 'pɔske men a'na e ke 'vege de pa'is paʀta'dza

vòste ben e donatz-me çò que duve aguer.' 'O mon fiu,'
'vɔste beŋ e du'na me sɔ ke 'dyve a'ge   ɔ mum fjew

faguèt lo paire, 'come voudràs; siás un marrit e saràs
fa'gɛ lu 'pajɾe 'kume vu'dʀas sjez ym ma'ʀi e sa'ras

punit.' E puei durbiguèt un tirador, partatgèt son ben e
py'ni   e pjɛj dyʀbi'gɛ yn tira'du paʀta'dzɛ sum beŋ e

ne'n faguèt doas parts.
nem fa'gɛ dɔs paʀ

Southeastern Lemosin
Un òme aviá mas dos filhs. Lo pus jòune dissèt a son
œn 'ɔme ɒ'vjɒ ma dɔw fiɾ   lu py 'zɒwne ʃi'ʃe ɒ ʃũ

pair: 'Es temps qu'iòu siá mon mèstre e qu'age de
pɛj ej tẽ   kjɒw ʃjɒ mũ 'mɛhtʀe e 'kaze   de

l'argent; chau que puesche me'n anar e que vege del païs.
laʀ'zẽ   sɔw ke 'pœse   men ɒ'na e ke 'veze dɛʀ pɒ'ji

Partissètz vòstre ben e donatz-me çò que devi aver.' 'O mon
paʀciˈʃe ˈvɒhtʀe be e duˈna me ʃɒ ke ˈdeɣi ɒˈve ɔ mũ

filh,' dissèt lo pair, 'coma voudràs; sès un maichent e
ʃiʀ ɟiˈʃe lu pɛj ˈkumɒ vuˈdʀa ʃeʒ œ mejˈsɛ̃ e

siràs punit.' Puei drubiguèt una tireta, partiguèt son ben e
ʃiˈʀa pyˈɲi pɛj dʀyɓiˈɡe ˈynɒ ciˈʀetɒ paʀciˈge ʃũ be e

ne'n faguèt doàs parts.
nɛ̃ fɒˈɡe dwa paʀ

Southern Auvernhat. (Saugues, Haute-Loire.)
Un òme aviá mas dos garçons. Lo pus joine diguèt a son
en ˈɔme aˈbjɛ ma duj ɡaʀˈsu lu ʀy ˈdzɯjne ɟiˈɡe a sum

paire: 'Lo moment es vengut que siáie mon mèstre è que
ˈpajʀe lu muˈmɛ̃ ij benˈɟy ke ˈʃɛje mum ˈmɛstʀe ɛ ke

age d'argent; chal que puesche me'n anar è que vege de
ˈaʒe daʀˈʒɛ̃ tsa ke ˈpœʃe men aˈna ɛ ke ˈbeʒe de

païs. Partajatz voste ben e bailatz-me çò que duve avèdre.'
paˈjis paʀtaˈdza ˈbuste bɛ̃ ɛ beˈla me sɔ ke ˈɟybe aˈbɛdʀe

'O mon garçon,' diguèt lo paire, 'coma voudràs; siás un
ɔ muŋ ɡaʀˈsu ɟiˈɡe lu ˈpajʀe ˈkuma buˈdʀas ʃɛz em

maissant è saràs punit.' E pueissa badèt un tirador, partagèt
meˈʃɔ ɛ saˈʀas pyˈɲi ɛ ˈpœjsa baˈdɛ en ciʀaˈdu paʀtaˈdzɛ

son ben è ne'n faguèt dos morsèls.
sum bɛ̃ ɛ nem faˈge duj muʀˈsɛj

Gloss
'A man had only two sons. The younger said to his father, "It is time for me to be my own master and to have some money. I need to be able to go out and see the world. Divide your fortune and give me what I should have." "O my son," said the father, "you're a bad lad and you'll be punished." Then he opened a drawer and divided his fortune, making it into two parts.'

3 Morphology

Nominal Categories

Gender
Gender is inherent in NPs with noun heads (explicit or not). The main gender suffixes are -*e* (m.) and -*a* (f.); zero suffix is also typical of masculine nominals, but Occitan shows a marked tendency to extend the range of -*e* and -*a*, or to reassign gender according to such endings already present.

Given the weakness of word-final consonants, the extension of *-e* and *-a* has as much a phonological function — to preserve or restore the phonological transparency of stems — as a grammatical one. Traditionally, surnames are marked for feminine gender with *-a*.

Gender Marking

	Masculine	Feminine	
Nouns	vendeire	vendeira	'seller'
	Durand	Duranda	(surname)
	poète (non-standard form)		'poet (m.)'
		cauma	'stuffy heat' (originally m.)
	revenge		'revenge'
		frasa	'phrase'
Adjectives	grand	granda	'large'
	mortal	mortala	'mortal'
	alègre	alègra	'cheerful'
	roge	roja	'red'
	comòde	comòda	'convenient'

Verb phrases and clauses, and the pronouns *çò, aiçò* 'this', *aquò* 'that' are pronominalised by the 'neuter' clitic *o*. The demonstrative *çò* also has considerable use as a neuter definite determiner (cf. Sp. *lo*, p. 94) alongside the masculine article *lo* in the same function, e.g. *çò pus bèl de l'afar* 'the best part/aspect of the matter', *çò nòstre* 'what is ours', *çò meteis* 'the same thing'.

Number

The traditional system of plural formation, with /+s/ suffixed to each element of the NP, survives in phonologically conservative dialects. In these, syllabic /+es/ or /+is/ is added to stems ending in sibilants or groups containing a sibilant, for example, *nis : nises* 'nest', *fach : faches* 'fact', *bòsc : bòsques* 'wood', *crotz : croses* 'cross'. Stems ending in a stressed vowel or in /l/, /n/, /nt/ or /wt/ are liable to have 'double plurals' in /+ses/ which are non-standard, e.g. *pe : pès ~ pèses* 'foot', *ostal : ostals ~ ostalses* 'house', *molin : molins ~ molisses* 'mill', *malaut : malauts ~ malausses* 'ill (m.)'. These syllabic plurals are not generally used in Gascon, nor currently (though they once were) in those dialects (Provençal, Auvernhat, Lemosin) which delete /s/ after a consonant or an unstressed vowel; such syllabic plurals help to explain the origin of plural marking in Provençal. Here plurality in NPs is marked (as in French, p. 226) only in the definite determiner and other prenominal elements (demonstratives, quantifiers, adjectives). Atonic *-os, -as, -es* have regularly become *-ei* [ej] ~ [i] before consonants: e.g. Prov. *lei* 'the', *aquestei* 'these', *autrei* 'other', *quauquei* 'some', *polidei* 'pretty (f.)', *richei* 'rich'. Though *los, las,* *aquestes, aquestas* would originally have been retained before vowels, these forms have been replaced by analogical *leis, aquesteis* there. Provençal plural nominal phrases may be illustrated as follows: *de bèus jorns* [de bɛw dzuʀ] 'fine days', *mei bèus amics* [mej bɛwz a'mi] 'my good friends', *aquestei polidei raubas* [a'kestej pu'lidej 'ʀawbo] 'these pretty dresses', *quauquei marrideis èrbas* ['kawkej ma'ʀidejz 'ɛʀbo] 'some weeds'.

Note that non-syllabic (i.e. generally unmarked) plurals are retained for consonant-final masculine adjectives, but masculine determiners etc. usually use the *-ei(s)* ending, e.g. *toteis aquelei dròlles* 'all those boys', and may extend its use to phrase-final position, e.g. *me'n vau ambe leis autrei/ autres/autras* 'I'm going with the others'. Lemosin and Auvernhat retain some distinct nominal plurals as a result of vowel changes conditioned by /s/ which is now lost, e.g. Lem. *òme* 'man', *òmei* 'men'; *autre*, pl. *autrei* 'other'; Auv. *fraire*, pl. *frairi* 'brother'. More radically, in quite wide areas of Auvernhat and Lemosin, feminine plural /+as/ has become [a:], attracting stress, and giving rise to vowel alternations of the following kinds: Lem. *ala* ['alo], *alas* [ɔ'la:] 'wing'; *chausa* ['tsawzo], *chausas* [tsɔw'za:] 'thing'; *aiga* ['ajgo], *aigas* [ej'ga:] 'water'; Auv. *autra* ['ɔtro], *autras* [y:'tra:] 'other'. Stem-vowel alternations without stress shift are also to be found in certain Lemosin and Auvernhat varieties, e.g. Lem. *terra* ['tjaro], *terras* ['tjera:] 'land'; *brava* ['bravo], *bravas* ['brova:] 'good'; Auv. *chabra* ['tʃabro], *chabras* ['tʃɔbræ] 'goat'. These are hard to explain historically except in terms of stress shift, followed by vowel reduction, followed by stress retraction. Stress retraction is attested by other evidence.

We have referred above to number marking in adjectives in Provençal (p. 256), where prenominal *-es, -as* have become *-ei*. A superficially similar development is found in western Lengadocian and southeastern Gascon, where prenominal masculine elements only have a suffix *-i/-es/-is* in the plural, for example, *pichonis passes* 'small steps', *vielhis mòts* 'old words'. This has the effect of maintaining some plural marking in consonant-final adjectives where /+s/ would be liable to sandhi deletion before consonants. Ronjat presents some evidence that this suffix (originally /+i/) spread from the Old Occitan nominative plural masculine definite determiner *li*, but a contributory source is likely to have been original *-es* plurals (e.g. *vòstres* 'your') and analogical *-es* plurals after sibilants (e.g. *gròsses* 'big', *aquestes* 'these') with *-es* > *-ei* > *-i* regularly before consonants other than voiceless stops. Such plurals are sometimes, if variably, found in non-prenominal position too, especially, it seems, in participles, e.g. *de plus gausats s'èron anadis enjocar* 'bolder ones had gone to roost'.

Case, Person
The personal pronouns are displayed in the next chart. Direct and indirect object cases are distinguished in the third person non-reflexive clitics only: dir. obj. *lo, la, los, las*; ind. obj. *li, lor*. Of the tonic personal pronouns, *se*

third person reflexive/reciprocal is 'oblique' case only, and may be replaced by the non-reflexive forms, as in Catalan (p. 000); otherwise, there are no distinct prepositional object forms. The second person singular pronoun of address for a superior (non-reciprocal usage), or for non-solidarity, is *vos*, which is grammatically second plural. Of the tonic pronouns, *elis* (m. pl.) shows the analogical syllabic masculine plural ending (see above), which is widely used even in those dialects where /-Cs/ would often survive phonologically.

Personal Pronouns and Case Forms

	Tonic	Non-subj. clitic	Ind. obj. clitic	Possessive (±f. ±pl.) Atonic	Tonic
1 sg.	ieu	me		mon	mieu
2 sg. (fam.)	tu	te		ton	tieu
3 refl.	se	se			
3 sg. m.	el	lo	} li	} son	sieu
3 sg. f.	ela	la			
3 sg. n.	çò	o	i		
1 pl.	nosautres/-as	nos		nòst(r)e	nòstre
2 pl.	vosautres/-as	} vos		vòst(r)e	vòstre
2 sg. (pol.)	vos				
3 pl. m.	els ~ elis	los	} lor	son ~ lor	sieu ~ lor
3 pl. f.	elas	las			

Most varieties of Occitan are 'pro-drop' languages but subject pronoun usage is commoner as one moves towards the French dialect boundary, and obligatory in the northernmost varieties. In many varieties the indirect object clitics are not distinguished as shown; *lor* may not be used, and either *i* or *li* may be used interchangeably in all of the functions (cf. p. 220 for French and p. 291 for Italian). There is a wide range of feminine forms of the tonic possessives, e.g., corresponding to *tieu* (m.): *tieu* (f.), *tia*, *tua*, *tieua*, *tieva*, *tieuna*, with further variants of the stem vowels. The standard third person plural possessive *lor* is marked for number but not for gender; many dialects use *son/sieu* etc. instead for both singular and plural possessors. The clitic forms displayed in the chart of deictic elements are the ones found in preconsonantal environments: *me, te, se, lo, la*, and the adverbial *ne*, reduce to *m', t', s', l', n',* before vowels. In Old Occitan most of the atonic pronouns had an enclitic variant as well when a vowel preceded: *'m, 't, 's, 'l, 'lh (li), 'ns, 'us, 'ls, 'n*. Gascon retains most of these (though not *'lh*, since Gascon no longer distinguishes a pronominal indirect object at all). Only *'l, 'ls* and *'n* survive in other dialects, where they are used, optionally, after *me, te* and *se*. The neuter clitics *o* and *i* (=adverbial *i*) are often adapted to the CV structure of the other singular clitics, to give, e.g. *lo, li,* (i.e. resulting in syncretism with masculine forms) or, e.g. [go] ~ [va], [je] ~ [zi]. As far as the order of clitics is concerned, second person precedes first; *ne* (variants *en*, *'n*) must follow all clitics except *i*. Otherwise all orderings may be found, though each dialect prefers one type, so, for example, *lo nos an raubat* ~ *nos l'an raubat* 'they have stolen it from us', *te o dirai* ~ *o te dirai* 'I'll tell you (it)'. A substantial area uses *se* as first person plural reflexive instead of *nos*: *s'endormirem* ~ *nos endormirem* 'we'll fall asleep' (cf. Milanese, p. 291). In most dialects clitics precede verb forms except for positive imperatives, but Gascon still puts clitics after infinitives as well, e.g. *entà parlà'u* = Occ. *per li parlar* 'to speak to him'.

Deixis
The three-term, person-oriented, system of deictic adjectives, pronouns and adverbs (see the chart of deictic elements) presented in normative grammars seems to have broken down (except perhaps in Gascon) and to have been replaced by a system more like the French one (p. 221), which has many terms unmarked for relative proximity. Just as the third person pronouns *el*, *çò*, *lo*, *o*, *li*, *i*, are unmarked for remoteness, so are generally the adjective *aquel* 'this/that', the pronoun *aquò* 'this/that', and the adverb *aquí* 'here/there'. Where a contrast is intended, *aqueste* 'this' is distinguished from *aquel* 'that', and similarly *aiçò* 'this' contrasts with *aquò* 'that', and *aicí* 'here' with *ailà* 'there'. The elements *çai* 'here', *lai* 'there' are also available and function rather like French -*ci* and -*là*. And the adjectives and pronouns may combine with the adverbs for further precision, e.g. *aquel-d'aquí* refers to a person or object which is distant, but nearer to the speaker than to the addressee. But not all possible combinations are well formed.

Deictic Elements

	Adjective	Neuter pronoun	Locative adverb
1 person	aiceste [±f. ±pl.]	aiçò	aicí
2 person	aqueste [±f. ±pl.]	aquò	aquí
3 person	aquel [±f. ±pl.]	ailò	ailì ~ ailà

Determiners
The definite determiner is *lo* m. sg., *la* f. sg., *l'* sg. prevocalic, *los* m. pl., *las* f. pl. Provençal has a common plural *lei(s)*. The masculine articles contract with atonic prepositions, e.g. *a* + *lo* > *al* ~ *au*, *de* + *los* > *dels* [des], and may contract with other monosyllabic prepositions too, e.g. *jos* + *lo* > *jol* 'under the'. Southwestern Lengadocian and Eastern Gascon retain the masculine determiners *le*, *les*, of which the former, at least, has been current since earliest times (< ILLE). The masculine plural form *li* of some

dialects may also survive from the Old Occitan nominative plural *li* < ILLI, rather than being merely a preconsonantal allomorph of *los*. The characteristic Gascon forms, used now only towards the Pyrenees, are *eth* m. sg., *ets* m. pl., *era* f. sg., *eras* f. pl.; these feminine forms are unusual in Romance for retaining two syllables.

To mark indefinite NPs only the singular or dual 'count' determiner *un/una* was well established in the medieval language, and survives in e.g. *una femna m'a dich* 'a woman has told me', *unis esclòps* '(a pair of) clogs'. Indefinite plural and mass NPs had no obligatory determiner. This usage, which is also that of Ibero-Romance, survives regularly in Gascon and adjacent regions of Lengadocian, and is not unknown elsewhere; for example *minjar habas* (Bearn) 'to eat beans', *aquí se vénden libres* (Foix) 'books are sold here', *tirar lausa* (Alpin) 'to quarry slate'; it is still common in idioms such as *passar bona nuech* 'to spend a good night', *portar esfrai* 'to inspire terror'. One development is to extend the use of plural *unis/unas* beyond duals, as in *unis caçaires* '(some) huntsmen', *unis vuech jorns* 'a week or so'. Most common, currently, is the use of *de* with indefinite plural or mass NPs, e.g. *de pans se son cremats* 'some loaves have burnt', *donatz-li d'argent* 'give him (some) money', *se'n es anat amb de bèls libres* 'he's gone off with some nice books'. Unless one were to take these phrases, superficially PPs, as complements of zero NPs, it seems inevitable to regard *de* as an indefinite determiner. Northern dialects have the French pattern, with *de* + definite determiner in these constructions; for example *vòli del pan* 'I want bread', *as plan de la rason* 'you are quite right'. These indefinite NP patterns are all illustrated in the transcribed texts on pp. 253–5.

Adjectives
A characteristic of Occitan is the marking of all adjectives for feminine gender (/+a/), the only exceptions being those few already ending in /-a/, e.g. *ipocrita* 'hypocritical', and, in the standard language, *jove* 'young' and the synthetic comparatives derived from Old Occitan nominative case forms, viz *màger* 'greater' (< MAIOR), *pièger* 'worse' (< PEIOR), *mendre* 'lesser' (< MINOR). Colloquially these too have distinct feminine forms: *jova, maja, pieja, mendra*. Comparison of adjectives and adverbs is expressed with either *mai* or *p(l)us* 'more'. When such an AP is definite and follows a noun, the definite determiner may be repeated as in French: *l'ostau (lo) mai aut de la carriera* 'the highest house in the street'. Only *bon* 'good', *marrit* 'bad' have synthetic comparatives (*melhor, pièger* or the Gallicism *pire*) in regular use, and even these are optional, as are the corresponding adverbs *mielhs, pieis*.

Verbs
The paradigms in the chart are those of *pèrdre* 'to lose', a regular conjugation II verb, in standard Occitan, based on Lengadocian usage. The

Paradigms of a Regular Verb (Conjugation II)

Present indicative
pèrdi, pèrdes, pèrd, perdèm, perdètz, pèrdon
Non-past subjunctive
pèrda, pèrdas, pèrda, perdam, perdatz, pèrdan
Future
perdrai, perdràs, perdrà, perdrem, perdretz, perdran
Prospective-in-past/conditional
perdriá, perdriás, perdriá, perdriam, perdriatz, perdrián
Past imperfective indicative
perdiá, perdiás, perdiá, perdiam, perdiatz, perdián
Past perfective indicative
perdèri, perdères, perdèt, perdèrem, perdèretz, perdèron
Past subjunctive
perdèssi, perdèsses, perdès(se), perdèssem, perdèssetz, perdèsson
Positive imperative
pèrd, perdam, perdètz
Present perfect/anterior relative tenses
paradigms of aver 'have' + perdut
'Temps sobrecompausats'
Perfect/anterior of aver + perdut

Infinitive	*Gerund/present participle*	*Past participle*
pèrdre	perdent	perdut [±f. ±pl.]

next chart attempts to systematise the various sets of person and number endings, some of which also involve, completely or in part, exponence of tense, aspect and mood categories. Analogy has already worked widely to derive these forms which, with the variation indicated, are typical of a large central area (Lengadocian and Provençal). Most other possible combinations of these elements, together with many not mentioned here, are attested in dialects. Gascon has markedly different paradigms. The letters on the left of the chart of person/number inflections identify the sets of forms for the chart of verb inflection, which presents the structure of verb inflection in the various tense, aspect and mood combinations with the conjugation classes. Occitan verbs are assigned to three conjugation classes, of which class III has two substantial variants. Class IIIa consists of verbs with no stem extension in the present, past imperfective, or gerund (e.g. *sentir* 'to feel'). Class IIIb consists of verbs which have an infix /-is-/ ~ /-isk-/ in these forms. The stem of class IIIb is thus always extended with /+i+C+/: +is+, +isk+, +ir+, +ig+, +id+. As a result of sound changes and various analogical developments, several of them very ancient, the conjugation classes are not well distinguished in finite forms, but are somewhat more so in the non-finite forms and those that depend on them, viz the future and prospective-in-past/conditional. In general, classes II and III are hardly distinguished at all except as just mentioned, and class I is not different in the past perfective, past subjunctive or, in many varieties, in the non-past subjunctive either. A typical element in classes II and III is a

Combinations of Theme Vowels with Person/Number Inflections

	1 sg.	2 sg.	3 sg.	1 pl.	2 pl.	3 pl.
A1	-i/-e/-o	-as	-a	-'am	-'atz	-an/-on
A2	-a	-as	-a	-'am	-'atz	-an/-on
B	-i/-e/-o	-es	-e/Ø	-èm	-ètz	-on
C	-i/-e/-o	-es	-e	-'em	-'etz	-en/-an
D	-'ai	-às	-à	-'em	-'etz	-'an
E	-iá/-iái/-iáu	-iás	-iá	-'iam	-'iatz	-ián
F	-i/-e/-o	-es	-Ø	-em/-'iam	-etz/-'iatz	-on
G	-i/-e/-o	-es	-e/Ø	-em/-'iam	-etz/-'iatz	-en/-on
H	-i/-e/-o/-a	-as	-a	-am/-em/-'iam	-atz/-etz/-'iatz	-an/-on
J		=3 sg. pres. ind.		=1 pl. non-past subj.	=2 pl. pres. ind.	

Structure of Verb Inflection

Conjugation	I	II	IIIa	IIIb
Pres. ind.	A1	B	B	is+B
Non-past subj.	C	A2 ~ C	A2 ~ C	isk+A2 ~ is/ig+C
Future	Inf. +D	Inf. +D	Inf. +D	Inf. +D
P.-in-p./cond.	Inf. +E	Inf. +E	Inf. +E	Inf. +E
Past imperf.	av+H	E	E	is+E
Past perf.	'er+F	pret. stem+'er+F	pret. stem+'er+F	pret. stem+'er+F
Past subj.	'es+G	pret. stem+'es+G	pret. stem+'es+G	pret. stem+'es+G
Pos. imp.	J	J	J	J
Inf.	a+r	(e)r(e)	i+r	i+r
Gerund	a+nt	e+nt	i/e+nt	is+e+nt
Ptcp.	a+d	u+d	i+d	i+d

preterit stem variant in /+g/ ~ /+eg/ ~ /+ig/ (cf. Catalan, p. 184) which in many varieties is extended to all verbs of these classes. It is found in the past perfective indicative and the past subjunctive, and has made extensive inroads into the participle, non-past subjunctive and gerund, and a few sorties into the infinitive (not into the future or prospective-in-past/ conditional, though). The source of this /+g/ element is twofold: one source is the Latin /-wi-/ preterit element after consonant stems, e.g. DEBUIT > OOcc. *dec*, DEBUISSET > *deguès*. The other is in Latin verbs with stem-final /k/ or /g/, which regularly survives in Occitan as /g/ only in the non-past subjunctive, e.g. IMPINGAT > *empenga* 'push', ADDUCAT > *aduga* 'bring'. Irregular verbs are mainly of class II. Several which were once irregular class IIIa are transferred to regular IIIb, as indeed have been many IIIa verbs anyway, e.g. *ausir* 'hear', *colhir* 'pick', *lusir* 'shine'. Irregularity (exemplified in the chart below) consists largely of stem-final consonant alternations, which were originally conditioned by following front vs back vowels or by position in codas. Athematic participles also contribute to irregularity. Stem-vowel alternations are found corresponding to the productive vowel-reduction processes, but also to original diphthongisation of stressed half-open vowels. The tendency here is to unify the stem, by extension of either of the variants, e.g. *cuelhi* > *culhi/colhi* 'I pick', *colhir/ culhir* > *cuelhir* 'to pick'.

Stem-final Consonant Alternations in Verbs

z ~ ts ~ g ~ j	e.g. adusèm, adutz, aduga, aduire, aduch 'bring'
ɲ ~ ŋg ~ etc.	e.g. astrenhèm, astrenga, astrench 'squeeze'
v ~ dʒ ~ g	e.g. avèm, aja, aguèri 'have'
v ~ w ~ g	e.g. bevèm, beure, bega 'drink'
b ~ wp ~ pj	e.g. cabent, caupèri, càpia 'fit'
js ~ sk ~ g	e.g. conoissèm, conoscam, conoguèri 'know'

Person and Number
The first person singular endings -*i*, -*e*, -*o*, are all analogical. Their source appears to be in support vowels after consonant groups, e.g. *dòbre/dòbri* 'I open', or perhaps in Lat. /-j-/ after 'non-absorbing' consonant groups, e.g. *dòrmi* < DORMIO 'I sleep'. Of the alternative forms, -*i*, which is attested in early texts, is now typically Lengadocian; -*e* is typically Provençal but spreads much wider; -*o* is characteristically Alpin. Set A2 has no distinct first person singular morph, a fact which doubtless contributes to the obsolescence of the set. Type E was originally subject to the same problem (cf. Ibero-Romance), but it has developed -*iái*, which adopts the 1 sg. -*i* of the other sets with the model of D in particular support. The form -*iáu* [-jew] is a Provençal variant. In this dialect [-'i.a] > [-'je] is regular, and [-jew] doubtless echoes the subject pronoun *ieu* 'I'. The second person singular inflection is /+s/, except in the positive imperative, where the traditional forms are, e.g. I *canta* 'sing', II *adutz* 'bring', IIIa *sent* 'feel', IIIb *bastis* 'build'. Nowadays -*e* or -*i* is frequently added to the class II and III forms, in accord with the general tendency not to leave stem-final consonants in word-final position. Similarly in the second person singular Latin /-es/, /-is/, would regularly give -*s*, but this has been replaced by -*es* throughout Occitan in the post-troubadour period, i.e. since 1200. Final /-Cs/ was even more subject to opacifying sound change than final /-C/ alone. Innovations in the third person singular likewise illustrate the tendency to avoid /-C/ endings. The introduction of -*e* in the past subjunctive (set G) follows that in the non-past subjunctive (set C). In the present indicative of classes II and III -*e* is typical of Provençal. The past perfective suffix /+ɛr/ has the allomorph /+ɛt/ in the third singular. This is all that directly remains of the late Lat. -DEDI preterits on which the whole of the past perfective was originally constructed. (Gascon and some other dialects retain /+k/ in the third person singular past perfective form < /-wit/.) The first and second person plural endings are stressed in the

present and future paradigms. The past (including prospective-in-past/ conditional) forms -*iam*, -*iatz*, have also retained final stress. (The vowels of [-ˈjan], [-ˈjats], show that this is so, rather than, e.g. /-eˈ(b)atis/ > /-ˈiats/ > *[-ˈiɔts] > *[-jɔts].) After glide formation, stress retraction in these forms on the pattern of other past paradigms would have given rise to -ˈVCjVC#, which was doubtless felt to be phonotactically anomalous. Stress retraction is the norm in other past forms, with the effect that stress falls on the same post-stem syllable throughout the paradigm, as in Spanish and Catalan. By contrast, the typically Provençal spread into all past paradigms of -*iam*, -*iatz* (which somewhat recalls that of French -*ions*, -*iez*) restores a paradigm stress pattern typical of the present system. In the third person plural the distribution of -*an*, -*en*, -*on*, no longer corresponds to the etymology. In OOcc. -*on* had already expanded into the sphere of -*an*, and especially of -*en*. The current distribution is such that the vowels involved serve no semantic or thematic function at all.

Substantial use is made of *aver* + participle and *èsser* + participle to express present perfect aspect and the anterior relative tenses, together with the *temps sobrecompausats* (cf. the French *temps surcomposés*, p. 229). As expected, *èsser* + participle also expresses the passive. The selection of *aver* or *èsser* for the perfect and anterior paradigms is governed partly syntactically and partly lexically. Reflexive constructions, whatever the 'case' of the reflexive pronoun, require *èsser*, e.g. *s'èron taisats* 'they had fallen silent', *me soi copat lo dit* 'I've cut my finger'; and certain intransitive verbs require *èsser*, viz. *anar* 'go', *arribar* 'arrive', *davalar* ~ *descendre* 'go down', *èsser* 'be', *intrar* 'go in', *montar* ~ *pojar* 'go up', *morir* 'die', *nàisser* 'be born', *tornar* 'return', *venir* 'come'; and variably *caire* ~ *tombar* 'fall', *demorar* 'stay', *espelir* 'hatch, open', *partir* 'leave', and perhaps some others. The *temps sobrecompausats* are a characteristic pattern of Occitan. They consist, as it were, of perfect + perfect, that is of *aver agut* + participle or *èsser estat* + participle, according as the main verb is conjugated with *aver* or *èsser*. (Note that the *sobrecompausat* of *èsser* itself is *es agut estat* or *es estat agut*, etc. not **es estat estat* as might be expected.) The use of this construction is explained below (p. 265).

Non-finite Forms

The gerund/participle consists of the suffix -*nt* added to the present stem + thematic vowel (generally with -*iss*- in class IIIb verbs), e.g. *cantant* 'singing', *cresent* 'believing', *sentint/sentent* 'feeling', *fenissent* 'finishing'. Some dialects construct the gerund on the preterit or non-past subjunctive stem, giving *aguent* or *agent* 'having'. Its use is generally adverbial, with imperfective aspect; the gerund is typically preceded by *en* or *tot* or *tot en*, as in *partiguèron de lor païs (tot) en menant amb elis lor bestial* 'they left their country taking their flocks with them'. As 'participles', i.e. qualifying a noun, we find either lexicalised adjectives with gender and number agreement (*ametlas amargantas* 'bitter almonds'), or, occasionally, with a verb complement in the French manner functioning as a relative clause, as, for example, *una societat avent son sèti a Marselha* 'a society with its headquarters in Marseille'. This pattern is regarded as an archaism or as a Gallicism.

Original allomorphy in the suffix of the class II infinitive, namely, stressed *-er* (*valer*), unstressed *-er* (*plànher*), *-r* (*dir*), *-re* (*beure*), has given rise to widespread dialect variation, with extension particularly of the unstressed *-er* variant, e.g. *veire* ~ *véser* 'to see', *dòldre* ~ *dòler* 'to grieve', *far* ~ *faire* ~ *fàser* 'to do', *voler* ~ *vòl(d)re* 'to want'.

Tense
Tense usage, both of primary and relative tenses, is generally that of conservative Romance (cf. Catalan, p. 187). The future and the prospective-in-past/conditional are also used in an inferential sense, e.g. *l'auran perdut* 'they must have lost it', *auretz dejà comprés que ...* '(I expect) you will already have gathered that ...'; French shows similar usage, cf. p. 231. The characteristic *temps sobrecompausats* have two main uses. Firstly, related to the speaker's present, the *sobrecompausat* expresses present relevance of an event remote in time, in contrast to the present perfect, which expresses present relevance of a recently past event/state; for example, *ai agut vist* *'Le Dernier Tango à Paris'* 'I have seen "Last Tango in Paris" (i.e. already/once upon a time/several times in the past)' vs *ai vist 'Le Dernier Tango à Paris'* 'I have seen "Last Tango in Paris" (i.e. recently/this week)'; *i siatz aguda estada en Arle, vos?* 'have you ever been to Arles?'. Secondly, in anterior relative time contexts, it allows the retention of the expression of perfect aspect, which in other Romance languages is neutralised in this context; e.g. *quand a agut ausit aquò, es sortida de l'ostal* 'when(ever) she has heard that she has left the house', *quand aguèt agut ausit aquò, sortiguèt de l'ostal* 'when she had heard that, she left the house', *si aguès agut ausit aquò, seriá sortida de l'ostal* 'if she had (just) heard that, she would have left the house'. These characteristic constructions should be further investigated while there are still native speakers available.

Aspect
The aspectual contrasts of Occitan are also the traditional Romance ones. Imperfective and perfective aspects are distinguished in the past indicative, and this distinction is, apparently, retained in the past relative tenses so that, for example, *aviá vist* 'had seen' (imperfective) is contrasted with *aguèt vist* 'had seen' (perfective). The inflections expressing past imperfective are generally those of traditional southwestern Romance, namely, *-ava-* in conjugation I and *-ia* in the other conjugations, though inherited stress alternations have been ironed out so that the first vowel of *-ava-* is

stressed throughout, e.g. *cantavi, cantaves, cantava, cantàvem, cantàvetz, cantàvan* (the *-e*'s here are analogical). In contrast the second vowel of *-ia-* is stressed (cf. the chart of regular verb paradigms, p. 262). The 'inchoative' class IIIb includes *-iss-* here generally, e.g. *causissiá* 'he chose'. Gascon offers some interesting alternative patterns. Its conjugation I past imperfective is even more conservative than the pattern given for *cantar* above. In the other conjugations we may find a transparent theme vowel + *-va-*, e.g. *vedèvas* 'you (2 sg.) saw', *dromívan* 'they slept'. Though at first glance this looks like an archaism (< VIDEBAS, DORMIBANT), it is possibly to be interpreted, as are parallel forms in Aragonese and standard Italian, as an analogical recreation on the model of conjugation I. Another Gascon conjugation II pattern is: *vedí, vedès, vedè, vedèm, vedètz, vedèn*. Except in the first person singular, these endings are those found in Gascon in the past perfective of conjugation I (*cantès, cantè,* etc., see below). These conjugation II imperfective suffixes are also used in the prospective-in-past/ conditional in the same dialects: *cantarí, cantarès,* etc. It is likely, therefore, that they go back to *-ia, -ias,* etc., though the details of this development are not clear.

The use of the past perfective indicative is maintained throughout Occitan with little competing pressure from the present perfect. Since the earliest times, however, its forms have been subject to radical and dialectally varied analogical re-formations, in which the most productive elements can be traced back to the Lat. -DEDI preterits, to the /-g-/ affix arising out of Latin consonant + /-wi-/ preterits (e.g. HABUIT > OOcc. *ac*), and to the /-r-/ element of the Latin third person plural preterit. In the classical troubadour period the -DEDI form provided the only 'weak' past perfective paradigm for conjugations I and II, e.g. *perdèi, perdèst, perdèt, perdèm/-em, perdètz, perdèron*. From the 'strong' /-wi-/-type third person singular *-c* was soon attracted to weak types: *cantèc, perdèc, sentic.* The /-r-/ from the third person plural or the /-g-/ from the third person singular (conjugations II and III), or both, form the basis of most past perfectives outside Gascony. The standard language favours the following forms (conjugation II has the same endings as I): *cantèri/-e/-o, cantères, cantèt, cantèrem/canteriam, cantèretz/canteriatz, cantèron*; conjugation IIIa: *sentèri,* etc. or *sentiguèri,* etc.; conjugation IIIb: *causissèri,* etc. or *causiguèri,* etc. Other common types in conjugation II are, e.g. *batègui, batègues, batèc, batèguem, batèguetz, batèguen*; or *bateguèri, bateguères, bateguèt, bateguèrem, bateguèretz, bateguèron*. Gascon varieties have again followed a divergent path, avoiding disyllabic suffixes in the past perfective, and maintaining or reintroducing thematic vowels which distinguish the conjugations. Typical forms are: *cantèi, cantès, cantè(c), cantèm, cantètz, cantèn; vedoi, vedós, vedó(c), vedom, vedotz, vedon; sentii, sentis, senti(c), sentim, sentitz, sentin*. The models seem to be again the OOcc. -DEDI type and the inherited 'weak' conjugation III pattern. But the source of /-u-/ in

conjugation II is not obvious; can it be from forms of the verb 'to be', viz *fo*
< FUIT, *fom* < FUIMUS, etc.?

Mood
The past subjunctive in -*ss*- survives in regular usage. In Gascon (particularly in Bearn) there is also a 'past subjunctive' in /-r-/, whose origin is
probably mainly the Latin pluperfect indicative (cf. Spanish, p. 99). Its
main use seems to be to express relative tense, viz prospective-in-past, in
subordinate clauses, e.g. *qu'avè dit que bastira ogan* 'he had said he would
build this year', *non credèm pas que venóratz* 'we didn't think you would
come', *lo trobar clus ont arrés qu'eths medishs non vedora ne lutz ne halha*
'"trobar clus" which no one but themselves could make head nor tail of',
literally ... 'where no one but themselves would see light nor torch'. Main
clause examples seem comparable, e.g. *qué'vs calora de mèi?* 'what else
would/will you need?'.

4   Syntax
Some scholars at the turn of the century claimed that Occitan had no syntax of its own, but was, in effect, French with different words. Though this
view is clearly incorrect, and was soon enough denounced by native
grammarians, it does perhaps reflect the fact that there are few constructions typical of French which cannot be parallelled somewhere among
the wide variety attested in Occitania. This variety corresponds as much to
the retention of what are archaisms from the Gallo-Romance point of view
as to the development of new patterns. In addition to variety, a characteristic of Occitan syntax is flexibility, especially as compared with standard
French. Part of the reason for this, at least, is the absence of normative
pressure, which in other European languages has given prestige to a Latinising style, or has even stigmatised popular patterns as incorrect.

Noun Phrases

Determiners
Of the use of the definite determiner, one may note particularly its absence
with the names of rivers and peaks, e.g. *Ròse* 'the Rhone', *Ventor*
'Ventoux', and also from various PPs, e.g. *sota terra* 'underground', *signe
de crotz* 'sign of the cross'; the definite determiner with *en* 'in' is always
ungrammatical. It is used with vocative nouns: *de qué disètz, l'ancian?*
'what are you saying, old man?', and familiarly, with personal names: *lo
Pèire, la Bernadeta, lo Bòsc, la Bòsca.*

Order
The unmarked order in NPs is N A. Only demonstratives, indefinites and

quantifiers generally precede. Adjectives used to evaluate rather than to specify may do so. Typically these are *bon* 'good', *marrit* 'bad', *bèl* 'fine', *polit* 'pretty', *grand* 'big', *pichon* 'small', *paure* 'poor' *vielh* 'old', e.g. *una paura lenga rufa de pastres* 'a poor, harsh, shepherds' language', **una rufa lenga paura de pastres*. Preposing of adjectives seems less favoured than in Spanish or Catalan, and much less so than in French; there is nothing corresponding to the lexicalised contrast of preposed vs postposed *grand* or *pauvre* in French (p. 227). The tonic possessives have regular adjective syntax, that is, they may be definite or indefinite, attributive or predicative, prenominal or postnominal, headed or headless. The atonic possessives are proclitic and inherently definite.

Quantifiers, Indefinites, and Other Pronouns

Most degree adverbs (e.g. *quant* 'how much', *tot* 'all', *mai*, 'more', *trop* 'too') can also be used as adjectives, and like other adjectives may be used 'pronominally' with ellipsis of their N heads, as, for example, *gaire(s) se'n trachan* 'not many take notice of it'. Colloquially they may be marked for both gender and number in such constructions, though this is standard only in a few cases (those which were adjectives also in Latin). Most of them can also be followed by PP complements (with *de*), with possible gender and number agreement as in the adjectival use, e.g. *tròp de carn/tròpa carn/ tròpa de carn* 'too much meat'. *Tot* 'all' and *mieg* 'half' as degree adverbs have the peculiarity of being inflected for gender and number in agreement with their AP heads, to give, e.g. *èra tota vestida de blanc* 'she was dressed completely in white'. Other quantifiers/indefinites are primarily adjectives: e.g. *qualque* 'some', *cada* 'each', *meteis ~ meme* (Gallicism) 'same', *(ai)tal* 'such', *autre* 'other', *qual ~ quin ~ quan* 'which', *quin que ((se) siá(n))* 'whichever'. Most, but not *cada*, inflect for gender and number. A few quantifiers are apparently NPs which take *de* + NP complements, e.g. *aviá nòu caps e atretant de coas* 'it had nine heads and as many tails'. Purely pronominal elements are, for example, *degun* 'no one', *res ~ ren* 'nothing', *quaucòm ~ quaucaren* 'something', *als ~ aure* 'something else', *dont* 'whose, of which'.

Prepositions

The atonic prepositions are *a, de, en, per* and *amb*. *A* has non-standard prevocalic variants *az, an*. Its range of functions is very wide; locative (including 'time at which ...'), allative, circumstantial, function, indirect object, personal direct object in some contexts, subject of a non-finite VP which is the object of a transitive verb: *van a Marselha* 'they go to Marseille', *son a Marselha* 'they are in Marseille', *me vau passejar a ser* 'I am going for a walk in the evening', *es a morir* 'he is to die/is dying', *es polit a sa mòda* 'it is pretty in its way', *filat a peisses* 'fishing net', *ela me paga a ieu* 'she pays me', *n'ages paur qu'el non t'aime aitant qu'a Miramonda* 'don't be afraid that he doesn't love you as much as he does Miramonda', *aquò que ausi dire a l'aucèl* 'what I hear the bird say'. *De* has the expected wide range of functions: unspecified complement of NP (including function, cf. *a*), ablative, 'time within which ...', circumstance, purpose: *molin d'aura* 'windmill', *molin d'òli* 'oil press', *lo gat de la coa copada* 'the cat with the docked tail', *d'ivèrn coma d'estiu* 'in winter as in summer', *es de creire* 'it is to be believed'. Both *a* and *de* are widely used introducing non-finite VPs, the choice between them being lexical, dialectal, or free. Compound prepositions nearly all consist of an adverb or a PP + *de*, e.g. *luenh de* 'far from', *ran de* 'near', *daval de* 'below', and most tonic prepositions may be followed by *de*, e.g. *sens (de)* 'without', *segon (de)* 'according to', *pròp (de)* 'near'. *En* 'in (locative, temporal)', as mentioned above, is not used before a definite determiner, where *dins* substitutes; *es en preson* 'he's in prison', **es en la preson*; *en temps de semenar* 'at sowing time', *camina en cantant* 'he walks singing'. Some uses of *en* suggest it is a variant of *a* in locative, indirect object or other senses, preferred especially before vowel-initial NPs, as in *en Arle = a Arle* 'in Arles', *te fises en el = te fises a el* 'you trust him', but also in *en qué servis aquò?* 'what is that for?', *es en cantar = es a cantar* 'is singing'. *Per* covers largely the range of French *par* and *pour*, without always being clearly distinguishable semantically from *a, en, de*. As well as 'place or time through which ...', *per* expresses vague locative or temporal senses, and also the senses of 'instrument', 'in exchange for', 'for the benefit of', 'on the point of', 'as regards', 'because of', and 'agent': *es tombada per sòl* 'she fell to the ground', *per meisson* 'at harvest time', *o aprenguèri per mon paire* 'I learnt it from my father', *a donat son ostal per pas res* 'he has given away his house for nothing', *per deman, veirem* 'tomorrow we shall see'. *Amb* 'with' takes a variety of forms in the dialects (*damb, an, emé*, and most permutations of these) but has a much more specific semantic range than the other atonic prepositions: 'comitative', 'instrumental', 'circumstantial', e.g. *es venguda amb son fraire* 'she has come with her brother', *arribar amb lo batèl* 'to arrive by boat', *ont vas amb la plueja que tomba?* 'where are you going in this rain?'

Verbal Group

Agreement
In third person constructions where verb precedes subject, number agreement may be absent, as in *pica tres oras* 'three o'clock strikes', *existís qualques adjectius irregulars* 'there are several irregular adjectives', though plural forms are equally good. The whole range of Romance ways of expressing impersonal verbs is found in Occitan: third person plural, e.g. *li dison Pèire* 'he is called P'; *(l')òm*, as in *l'òm a seis idèas* 'one has one's own ideas'; *un* ('one'), as in *un di* 'it is said'; *vos* ('you'), e.g. *es de causas que vos disètz e que non lei diriatz ais autres* 'there are things you say to

yourself you wouldn't say to other people'; and, not least, the impersonal reflexive, in which number agreement with the logical object has been optional (cf. Spanish, p. 110) since the sixteenth century at least; e.g. *se bastiguèt una glèisa* 'a church was built', *se ditz de causas falsas* 'untrue things are said', *despuei d'ans que non se nombra* 'after countless years'.

Number and gender agreement in participles in perfect/anterior constructions is well maintained in most varieties. If the auxiliary verb is *èsser* agreement is with the subject, e.g. *me som facha mal* 'I (f.) have hurt myself', *ela s'es copada lo braç* 'she has cut her arm', though object agreement is possible if the verb is transitive: *Castelà s'es facha una glòria* 'C. has turned into a wonder'. When the auxiliary is *aver*, participles nearly always agree with preceding objects, and very often with following objects, even objects of dependent non-finite VPs, provided participle and infinitive are not separated: *la n'ai volguda far sortir* 'I wanted to make her go out', *an pas tornadas trobar sas amigas* 'they haven't found their friends again', **a pas volgudas las veire* 'she hasn't wished to see them'. Note that Occitan is much more conservative than French or Catalan here.

Non-finite VPs
Infinitives are widely used in adverbial, non-finite VP, constructions introduced by prepositions, or preposition + determiner *al*. The subject need not be the same as that of the main verb: *se plorava dempuei tres jorns sens degun lo poder consolar* 'he wept for three days without anyone being able to console him', *al tocar la pòrta, lo gos se botèt a jaupar* 'when somebody knocked at the door, the dog began to bark', *on as tu demorat despuei non t'aver vista?* 'where have you been since I last saw you?'

Modern Occitan does not make a great deal of use of verbal periphrases, that is, of lexicalised collocations of inflected and non-finite verb. The *anar* + gerund pattern, which Occitan shares with Catalan (p. 196), is less common now than previously. *Anar* + infinitive has been used as an expression of perfective aspect (as in Catalan), e.g. *tot en un còp van entreveire Lagalanta* 'suddenly they caught sight of L.', but the modern preference, supported by French, is to use this collocation to express immediate future. Other verb (+P) + infinitive collocations in use are *tornar* + infinitive 'to do *x* again', *voler* + infinitive 'to be going to,' e.g. *vòl nevar* 'it's going to rain', *èsser per* + infinitive 'to be about to', *èsser de* + infinitive 'is to be *x*-ed', *èsser a* + infinitive = progressive, e.g. *èra a se passejar* 'she was taking a walk', *venir de* + infinitive 'to have just *x*-ed'. One periphrasis exceptionally contains V + *de* + participle: *téner de* + participle 'to keep *x*-ing', e.g. *lo ten de velhat* 'she keeps watching him'.

Quasi-modals
Like other Romance languages, Occitan has no well defined class of modal verbs, but several characteristics may combine to distinguish an elastic

grouping of quasi-modals from other 'normal' verbs in V + non-finite VP collocations. These are: clitic raising, absence of preposition before non-finite VP, participle agreement with the object of the non-finite verb, choice of perfect/anterior auxiliary determined by the non-finite verb, finite verb used only in V + non-finite VP construction, or used there with a different sense from elsewhere. For example, *es pas pogut venir* 'he hasn't been able to come', *l'ai pas poguda trobar* 'I haven't been able to find her', and cf. sentences with *voler* and *tornar* (p. 270). Verbs which show several of these characteristics are *acabar de* 'finish', *(s')acostumar a/de* 'get used to', *anar* 'be going to', *cercar a/de* 'try', *començar a/de* 'begin', *contunhar a/de* 'continue', *daissar* 'let', *deure* 'ought', *far* 'make', *gausar* 'dare', *mancar* 'fail to', *poder* 'be able', *saber* 'know how to', *venir de* 'have just', *voler* 'want to'.

Clitics

A good deal of Occitan's syntactic flexibility comes down to the ability to express succinctly a wide range of concepts and relations within the verbal group; these expressions may not, however, have a simple relation to logical form. Indirect object clitics may express, for example, 'ethic dative', e.g. *m'avetz rendut un servici que lo vos oblidarai pas* 'you've done me a service which I won't forget (literally: to you)'; or 'possessive', e.g. *lor ai cremat lo covent* 'I have burnt their convent' (literally 'I have burnt to them the convent'); or prepositional object, e.g. *li tombèt dessobre* 'he fell on him'. 'Vague reflexive' clitics, e.g. *se demoràvam muts* 'we remained silent', are perhaps similar to ethic datives. The original role of *i* was to pronominalise locatives and other inanimate objects of the preposition *a*, but in many dialects, as a result of syncretism with *li* and *lor* (p. 258), it now corresponds to all types of *a* PP; and it may be used particularly in indirect object function with zero direct object clitic (cf. Portuguese, p. 158), as in *i as donada?* 'have you given (it (f.)) to him?'; note here the agreement of the participle with the unexpressed feminine singular direct object. Adjective or indefinite noun predicate phrases, among other things, may be pronominalised by *o*, e.g. *si jamai es estat ferme, cresètz que o serà per vos* 'if he has ever been firm, believe that he will be for you'. Definite predicate phrases are pronominalised by 'direct object' pronouns: *siatz lei mandadors de l'emperaire? — lei siam* 'are you the emperor's representatives? — we are'; and in Provençal adjective predicate phrases may be likewise, e.g. *a fòrça de creire que son malauts, lei son* 'as a result of believing they are ill, they are'.

It is not uncommon to cliticise phrases which are explicit elsewhere, not only with (leftward) topicalisation, as in *mas tu, Joaneta, la lenga d'òc la legissiás pas* 'but you, J., couldn't read Occitan', but also with phrases in their normal position, for example, *los sauvatges i créson pas a l'autre monde* 'savages don't believe in the other world', *te la metrem la testa dins lo sac* 'we'll put your head in the bag'.

Clitic climbing is the rule for the objects of non-finite VPs depending on *far* 'make', *daissar* 'let', *mandar* 'send', *menar* 'bring', *veire* 'see', *ausir* 'hear', *sentir* 'perceive' and their synonyms; e.g. *nos mandàvan quèrre* 'they sent for us' (literally 'they sent us to look for'), *los entendi parlar* 'I hear them talking'. It is also current with the quasi-modals, e.g. *o saupràs faire?* 'will you be able to do it?', *nos la cal cercar* 'we must look for her'.

Sentences

Word Order, Topicalisation, etc.
Occitan retains the relative freedom in word order typical of Southern Romance in general. One respect in which Occitan basic word order resembles French rather than, say, Ibero-Romance, is in its preference for short adverbials to be placed between an auxiliary (or quasi-modal) and a non-finite verb, as in, *vos siatz ren facha mau?* 'have you hurt yourself (at all)?', *anem-los un pauc veire* 'let's go and see them for a while'. Typical deviations from SVO PP order in affirmative sentences are: VS order in presentational sentences, e.g. *seguís un chapitre sus la metatèsi* 'there follows a chapter on metathesis'; VS order in relative clauses, e.g. *A vinhon, que i deviá renàisser un jorn lo Gai Saber* 'Avignon, where Lo Gai Saber was one day to be reborn' — but this is probably generally a case of heavy NP shift, for one would probably say *A vinhon, que lo Gai Saber i deviá renàisser un jorn de sei cendres* '... be reborn from its ashes'. There are two patterns of topicalisation, or leftward movement of NP/PP. In the first, there is typically a comma separating the leftmost shifted element from another preverbal phrase, and often a resumptive clitic; e.g. *la lumiera, Dieu veguèt qu'èra bona* literally 'the light, God saw that it was good', *de ieu, tot autre es lo vejaire* literally 'of me, quite other is the opinion' — note double topicalisation here — *a cò de mon fraire i serai* literally 'at my brother's I shall be'. The other pattern has *que* between the topicalised element and the rest, e.g. *cinc sòus que mos esclòps costèron* literally 'five sous that my clogs cost'. This pattern seems to be a variant of clefting, in which the topicalised element is presented with 'it is ...', 'look at ...', 'there is ...', etc. as, for example, *es aquel libre que vòle* 'it's that book I want', *tèn lo gos que se'n vai* 'there's the dog running off', *aquò's el que vesèm* 'it's him we can see'.

Questions
The traditional pattern, with the order (*wh*-word) V X, survives well, reinforced in many dialects with a postverbal interrogative particle *-ti*, as, for example, *me caldrà-ti prene las armas?* 'will I have to take arms?', *de qué me vòles-ti?* 'what do you want (from me)?', *lo paire, es-ti a l'ostau?* 'is father at home?'. Some have claimed that this element is just French *-t-il?*,

with an extended use as in popular French (cf. p. 237); others that it is a
variant of atonic *tu* ~ *ti* 'you', occurring originally as in the second
example above. Possibly both sources combine. The positive answer to a
positive alternative question is, of course, *òc* 'yes', whence the name of the
language (cf. p. 13); this is extended to *òc-ben*, used particularly to a person addressed as *vos*. We have also *non* 'no', and *si* to answer 'yes' to a
negative question.

Negation
For simple negation, preverbal *non* alone (conditioned variants *no'*, *'on*,
n'), as in Medieval Occitan, survives in idioms and proverbs, such as *qui
non mòstra non vend* 'he who doesn't show doesn't sell', and in certain subordinate clauses (e.g. after a negative, comparative or dubitative main
clause, cf. French *ne*, p. 238), for example, *ne dison mai que non i a* 'there's
more talk about it than fact'. The first development of this, adding *pas* after
the finite verb to *non*, is standard in Gascon, e.g. *no'i volèva pas créder* 'he
didn't want to believe it', and is current in some other dialects. Most of
Occitan, like popular French, p. 237, now uses postverbal *pas* alone: *i voliá
pas creire* 'he didn't want to believe it'. Other negative elements are *cap*
'not at all' or 'not any' according to dialect, *degun* 'no one', *enluòc* 'not
anywhere', *gaire* 'not much/many', *ges* 'not at all', *jamai* 'never', *ni*
'neither nor', *niu* 'not at all' < NIL, *pus* 'no more', *que* ~ *ren que* ~ *son
que* ~ *mai que* ~ *(no)màs* 'only', *ren* 'nothing', *res* 'no one' or 'nothing'
according to dialect. These elements may be used (a) with *non*, e.g. *non
siás qu'un pauràs* 'you're only a poor old thing'; (b) with *non ... pas*, e.g.
non s'avisèt pas de res 'he didn't realise anything'; (c) with *pas* alone —
favoured in the west, e.g. *aviá pas que paur de poder pas* 'she was only
afraid of not being able to', *pas jamai s'ausiá de chamalha* 'one never heard
any argument'; (d) on their own, e.g. *s'ausissiá cap de bruch* 'no noise
could be heard', *ai ges d'amic* 'I have no friend at all'. These negative
polarity items may still to some extent be used in a non-negative sense in
interrogative and conditional contexts, eg. *se jamai i vau, t'avertirai* 'if ever
I go there, I'll let you know', Gasc. *cercatz arren?* 'are you looking for anything?', *si'u trobatz enlòc ...* 'if you find it anywhere ...'.

Positive Particles: *Enonciatius*
A notable feature of Gascon syntax is the presence in most positive main
clauses of one of a small set of preverbal particles. The Gascon text transcribed on p. 254 illustrates the use of one of these, *que*, which is the
commonest and is unmarked relative to the other two, *be* and *ja*. In the
Gascon heartland of Bearn the presence of one of these in positive,
affirmative, main clauses is obligatory. They are not used in imperative sentences; there is usually some particle too (one of the above, or *se* or *e*) in
an alternative question. The particles may also be found in subordinate

clauses, at least in sentential complements. Medieval Occitan made quite substantial use of a positive preverbal particle *si* < SIC, e.g. *lo reis d'Englaterra si la tòlc per moiller* 'the king of England took her to wife', but this had died out by the sixteenth century before the Gascon *enonciatius* became established. (*Que* is attested in the fourteenth century, but became regular only in the eighteenth.) Here is another example of a normal sentence in modern Gascon: *lo men frair que't voleré parlar* 'my brother would like to talk to you'; and a subordinate S example: *quan credó que la mort que tustava au portau ...* 'when he thought death was knocking at the door ...'. It is likely that this *que* is indeed the complementiser *que*, and that, in effect, subordinate clauses have become main clauses, though the shift of *que* from clause-initial to preverbal position needs explaining. The other particles, *be* — now a distinct element from its source *ben* 'well' — and *ja*, originally 'already', are more emphatic, e.g. *tot-un, d'autas nacions be's son reviscoladas* 'even so, other nations have (indeed) revived', *j'ac pensi* 'I (should) think so'; cf. Sp. *ya lo creo*. In questions we find, e.g. *qu'i vas entà la hèira?* 'are you going to the fair?', *s'ei grèva, la malautia deu vòste pair?* 'is it serious, your father's illness?', *e l'as entenut?* 'have you heard him?'. As for *que* here, parallels in other Romance languages make it very likely that this is indeed the complementiser; *se* is surely the same as the indirect question particle 'whether'. The particle *e* [e] seems to have diverged from *e* [ɛ] 'and'.

Since the nineteenth century *e* [e] has been attested in affirmative clauses with a rather different distribution from the other affirmative particles. In one of its uses, perhaps the original one, it precedes a main verb after an incision of some kind, e.g. '*volètz-ve carar?' e responó la mainada* '"will you shut up?" the girl replied', *se veniva, e vederé* 'if she came she would see'; *e* also occurs in subordinate clauses where *que* might appear in a main clause, e.g. *que cau que l'un de nosauts e se'n ane* 'one of us must go', *quan lo caperan e demandava aus nòvis ...* 'when the priest asked the bride and groom ...'; *l'airolet qui matin e ser e jumpa las huelhas* 'the breeze which, morning and evening, rocks the leaves'; *la harga on los mainatges deu vilatge, las vrespadas de mai, e venguèvan guaitar son pair* 'the forge where the children from the village, on May evenings, used to come and watch his father' — note incisions as well as subordination in the last two examples. Recently, at least, *e* seems to have become a stylistic variant of *que*, e.g. *en despieit d'eth, Gasconha e vencerà* 'in spite of him, Gascony will win'. *E* is not excluded from negative sentences, however, and can occur alongside *que* and *be* in questions (*e que poderi entrar?* 'could I come in?') and wishes (*e b'i posquiatz tornar* 'if only you could start again').

Relative Clauses
Perhaps the most distinctive aspect of the syntax of Occitan as a whole is

the construction of relative clauses. It has gone further than other Romance languages except Rumanian (cf. p. 409) in accepting the popular tendency to use a relative particle (here = complementiser *que*) with normal pronominalisation and no *wh*-movement, in preference to moved *wh*-relative pronouns. When the relativised NP is subject of its clause, of course, as in *la dròlla que canta* 'the girl who is singing' or *l'aiga que raja* 'the water that flows', either interpretation of *que* is possible. With the relativised NP as direct object in its clause, the traditional movement construction, e.g. *l'ostal que cercatz*, and the 'unmoved' *l'ostal que lo cercatz* 'the house you are looking for', are both current, though the former is still preponderant. But in indirect object or other PP functions the unmoved pattern is preferred, e.g. *vos naisserà un enfant que li donaretz lo nom de Jesús* 'a child shall be born to you to whom you shall give the name Jesus'; *un vielh potz que lei tropèus i anavan beure* 'an old well which the flocks went to drink at', *ieu, que mon educacion linguistica s'es facha un pauc a l'aventura* 'I, whose linguistic education came about somewhat by chance'. The traditional, fronted, pattern can still be found, especially in writing; it involves *dont* 'of which, whose', *ont* 'where', or preposition + *qui ~ qual* 'who', *qué* 'what', *lo qual* [±f., ±pl.] 'which'. For example, *la dralha ont mon passat se pèrd* 'the path on which my past gets lost', *la facilitat amb la quala fas tos vèrses* 'the facility with which you compose your verses'. *Qui ~ qual* and *qué* are used in free relative constructions too. It is also possible for the precise role of the NP in the relative clause not to be expressed at all, especially with locative phrases; for example, *als temps que parle* 'at the time I'm speaking (of)', *la lana que vòli far lo drap* 'the wool I want to make the cloth (of)', *la vila que soi nascut* 'the town I was born (in)'.

Subjunctive Usage
Occitan usage is, again, largely on the traditional Southern Romance pattern. In the southwestern dialect group the subjunctive is preferred in indefinite clauses (as in Hispano-Romance, including most spoken Catalan): *tanlèu que pòsca* 'as soon as she can', *quan las ovelhas àujan hèit los anhèths* 'when the ewes have produced their lambs', *çò que volgatz* 'what(ever) you like', *d'esclòps malaisits que l'aguèsson empachada de córrer* 'ill-fitting clogs such as to have prevented her from running'. Dialects in the northeastern group use, like French (p. 231), the future and prospective-in-past/conditional in these constructions. The protasis of unreal conditionals may have either the past subjunctive, e.g. *s'aguèssi gausat, l'auriá seguit* 'if I had dared, I would have followed her'; *se l'ase foguèsse un aucèu, l'èr seriá plen de musica* 'if the ass were a bird, the air would be full of music'; or the past imperfective indicative, e.g. *s'èra arribat per aquèu trin, seriá a l'ostau* 'if he had arrived on that train, he would be at home'. The indicative is currently preferred here except when the finite verb is *aver* or *èsser*.

The subjunctive is quite widely used in complement clauses depending on verbs (not only negated ones) of propositional attitude ('believe', 'think', 'say') when the speaker wishes to avoid commitment to the truth of the proposition the complement clause expresses, e.g. *totis cresián qu'aguèssi fait fortuna* 'they all believed I had made a fortune'; *cresegueriam que la granda sala esclatèsse* 'we thought the great room was exploding' (cf. Italian, p. 303). Non-past subjunctive in main clauses is used for negative commands, as in *regardatz ben e toquetz ren* 'look closely and don't touch'; past subjunctive for wishes, e.g. *saupessiatz coma la nuech es sorna* 'if only you know how dark the night is'.

5 Lexis

One of the difficulties in establishing a standard Occitan lies in the very substantial lexical variation between the dialects; this is evident enough in the texts transcribed on pp. 253–5. Occitan has never been the language of a political unity or a centralised culture; there has been virtually no brake on natural divergence of lexical choice and creation. More recently variety has been increased by the introduction of Gallicisms, but of different ones in different places. There follow some examples in each word class, plucked from the pages of Bec and Nouvel, but excluding Gascon variants. Nouns: *viet-d'ase ~ aubergina ~ merinjana* 'aubergine', *mameta ~ menina ~ granda* 'grandmother', *ostal ~ maison ~ casa* 'house', *bòria ~ mas ~ granja* 'farm', *paròt ~ aret ~ marre* 'ram', *auton ~ tardor* 'autumn', *cap ~ testa* 'head', *talent ~ fam* 'hunger', *vèspre ~ ser* 'evening', *padena ~ sartan* 'frying pan', *balaja ~ engraniera ~ escoba* 'broom', *calças ~ bragas* 'trousers'. Adjectives: *petit ~ pichòt ~ pichon* 'small', *qual ~ quin ~ quan* 'which', *marrit ~ maissant ~ dolent ~ mal* 'bad'. Verbs: *achaptar ~ crompar* 'buy', *faler ~ caler* 'must', *balhar ~ donar* 'give', *ausir ~ entendre* 'hear', *se taire ~ se calar* 'be quiet', *acampar ~ amassar* 'collect', *agachar ~ mirar* 'look', *quèrre ~ cercar* 'look for', *aturar ~ arrestar ~ estancar* 'stop', *tombar ~ caire* 'fall', *tampar ~ barrar* 'shut', *atudar ~ amortar ~ escantir* 'put out (fire)'. Prepositions: *demest ~ entre ~ abarreja* 'among', *fins ~ d'aqui a ~ entrò* 'as far as', *sus ~ sobre* 'on', *sot(a) ~ jos* 'under'. Pronouns and quantifiers: *quaucaren ~ quicòm* 'something', *beucòp ~ fòrça* 'a lot', *mai ~ p(l)us* 'more', *qual ~ qui ~ cu* 'who'. Adverbs: *çaiquelai ~ pasmens ~ pr'aquò* 'even so', *benlèu ~ saique ~ tanplan ~ bensai* 'perhaps', *lèu ~ aviat ~ redde* 'soon, quickly', *alavetz ~ alara* 'then', *totjorn ~ sempre* 'always'. Among these alternatives one often notices one lexical type cognate with the French word, while another is cognate with Spanish.

Even when the stem is the same, the affix may be different, e.g. *frescor ~ frescura ~ frescum ~ frescada* 'freshness', *postada ~ postat ~ postam* 'floor', *sornariá ~ sorniera ~ sornura* 'darkness', *pauruc ~ paurós* 'fearful', *penós ~ penible ~ peniu* 'painful', *sègre ~ seguir* 'to follow', *brandir ~ brandar* 'to shake', *contristar ~ atristar ~ entristesir* 'to sadden'.

Occitan retains a number of freely usable suffixes such as the diminutive/ affectives, *-et, -òt, -on, -èl,* e.g. *castelòt* 'a little castle', *lasson* 'a little tired'; these may be doubled: *gatonèl* 'little kitten'. The favourite augmentative/ pejorative is *-às/-assa,* as in *galinassa* 'great big hen'; it may combine with a diminutive, e.g. *lapinonàs* 'quite-a-fat-dear-little-rabbit' vs *lapinasson* 'a-great-fat-rabbit-that's-quite-nice-really', *potonasson* 'great big kiss'. Agentive nominals are formed with *-aire/-eire,* e.g. *jogaire* 'player, playful', *legeira* 'reader (f.)'. Frequentative/pejorative verbs are formed with *-ejar,* e.g. *potonejar* 'kiss often', *trabalhejar* 'work ineffectively', *caravanejar* 'go caravanning in an unenjoyable way'.

6 Conclusion

It is hard to be optimistic about the survival of Occitan as a living language into the twenty-first century. Recent times have, it is true, seen a few positive developments. The French Government now proclaims that the cultural and linguistic diversity of France is a matter of pride, deserving official protection, but, even with effective government action, which is by no means assured, it will take a long time to overcome the effect of having proclaimed the opposite for over 400 years. Significant, though not large, numbers of young people study Occitan at school. Occitan is the vehicle of a good deal of regional popular song, which has helped to reawaken a sense of cultural distinctiveness and of southern unity. And the hostility between Occitanist and Felibrige literary traditions and othography is waning. The difficulties remain very serious. The major negative factor must be the small number of fluent active native speakers under the age of 40. Such as there are are widely dispersed, almost without exception in rural areas. Most of those who study Occitan at school come with at best a passive knowledge. Dialect diversity is very great, as has been evident throughout this chapter, and though mutual intelligibility between distant spoken dialects can be achieved, it requires effort — for most it is easier to switch to French for interdialectal communication. Much written material cannot travel far without notes and glossary. Even recent pro-Occitan feeling is strongly diglossic; there are few social situations in which using Occitan, even alongside French, is regarded as appropriate. Institutional support for, or promotion of, Occitan is minimal. In several respects the position of Occitan resembles that of Irish, but without that measure of official support which at least makes it possible in Ireland for interested individuals to pursue the goal of second-language competence realistically.

Bibliography

Alibert, Loïs (1935) *Gramatica occitana segón los parlars lengadocians.* Societat d'Estudis Occitans, Tolosa.

Bec, Pierre (1967) *La langue occitane* 2nd edn. Presses Universitaires de France, Paris.

—— (1973) *Manuel pratique d'occitan moderne.* Picard, Paris.

Coustenoble, Hélène N. (1945) *La Phonétique du provençal moderne en Terre d'Arles.* Stephen Austin and Sons, Hertford.

Fourvières, Xavier de (1966) *Grammaire provençale,* rev. edn. Aubanel, Avignon.

Grammaire du provençal rhodanien et maritime (graphie classique). Comitat Sestian d'Estudis Occitans, Éguilles, 1983.

Grandgent, C.H. (1905) *An Outline of the Phonology and Morphology of Old Provençal.* Heath, Boston.

Kremnitz, Georg (1974) *Versuche zur Kodizifierung des Okzitanischen seit dem 19. Jh. und ihre Annahme durch die Sprecher.* Narr, Tübingen.

—— (1981) *Das Okzitanische. Sprachgeschichte und Soziologie.* Narr, Tübingen.

Lafont, Robert (1967) *La phrase occitane. Essai d'analyse systématique.* Presses Universitaires de France, Montpellier.

—— (1972) *L'ortografia occitana. Lo provençau.* Universitat de Montpellier III. Centre d'Estudis Occitans.

Mistral, Frédéric (1878–86) *Lou tresor dóu Felibrige, ou dictionnaire provençal-français* 2 vols. Veuve Remondet-Aubin, etc., Aix-en-Provence.

Nouvel, Alain (1975) *L'occitan sans peine.* Assimil, Chennevières-sur-Marne.

Ronjat, Jules (1930–41) *Grammaire istorique des parlers provençaux modernes* 4 vols. Société des Langues Romanes, Montpellier.

Smith, Nathaniel B., and Thomas G. Bergin (1984) *An Old Provençal Primer.* Garland, New York.

Taupiac, Jacme (1977) *Pichon diccionari francés–occitan.* Institut d'Estudis Occitans, Tolosa.

8 Italian

Nigel Vincent

1 Introduction

For reasons which have already been set out (pp. 18–19), Italian evinces less homogeneity than any other Romance vernacular that has achieved the status of a national language. Correspondingly, dialects and regional varieties still play a significant role in the linguistic life of the peninsula (see Map VII). The extent of variation, however, differs according to the level of linguistic structure. Most speakers betray their geographical origin to some degree in their accent and often, too, in their vocabulary. Morphology, on the other hand, exhibits very little variation. Syntax and morphosyntax occupy an intermediate position, with the major patterns of word order, relativisation and complementation being fairly uniform up and down the country, but with geographically definable differences emerging clearly in tense, mood and aspect usage.

In the separate sections, therefore, of the present chapter, we will begin in each case by examining the structure of the educated norm and the routes by which this has developed from Latin, shading off our description into regional and dialectal usage as circumstances dictate. It should be clear, however, that there will not be space to offer even a partial conspectus of the structures and histories of individual dialects, which will be dealt with only in so far as they impinge on, or provide interesting contrasts with, the standard language.

2 Phonology

Consonants

The chequered linguistic and political history of the peninsula has meant that at the phonetic and phonological level there has been even less uniformity of usage than at other levels. The conventional starting point for any treatment of Italian phonology is the speech of educated Florentines. Table 8.1 sets out the consonant phonemes usually recognised in such a

Table 8.1: Italian Consonant Phonemes

	Bilabial	Labiodental	Dental	Alveolar	Palato-alveolar	Palatal	Velar
Stop	p b		t d				k g
Affricate				ts dz	tʃ dʒ		
Fricative		f v		s (z)	ʃ		
Nasal	m			n		ɲ	
Lateral				l		ʎ	
Trill				r			

system. Some comments on points of detail are in order. First, note that for the vast majority of speakers [s] and [z] do not contrast: in initial position before a vowel all speakers have [s], including after an internal boundary as in *ri*[s]*aputo* 'well known' — cf. [s]*aputo* 'known'; [s]*taccato*[s]*i* 'having detached onself' — cf. [s]*taccare* 'to detach' and [s]*i* 'third person reflexive pronoun'. Preconsonantally the sibilant takes on the value for voicing of the following segment, hence [s]*tanco* 'tired', [s]*figurare* 'to lose face', but [z]*bagliare* 'to make a mistake', [zʤ]*elo* 'thaw', [z]*litta* 'sledge', [z]*nello* 'slim', etc. Intervocalically, when no boundary is present, the pronunciation of *s* is one of the clearest indicators of regional origin, northern speakers having only [z] and southern speakers only [s]. In parts of Tuscany, including Florence, on the other hand, it is possible to find minimal pairs: *chie*[s]*e* 'he asked' vs *chie*[z]*e* 'churches'; *fu*[s]*o* 'spindle' vs *fu*[z]*o* 'melted'; *ingle*[s]*e* 'English' vs *france*[z]*e* 'French'.

The opposition between /ts/ and /dz/ is also somewhat shaky. In initial position, although both are found in standard pronunciation — /ts/ in *zio* 'uncle', *zucchero* 'sugar', and /dz/ in *zona* 'zone', *zero* 'zero', there is an increasing tendency due to northern influence for /dz/ to be used in all words. Medially, the two sounds continue to exist side by side, and a few genuine minimal pairs can be found, e.g. *ra*[tts]*a* 'race' vs *ra*[ddz]*a* 'ray fish'. In post-consonantal position, many central and southern speakers exhibit an incipient merger of affricates and fricatives, the latter being pronounced with a more or less perceptible plosive onset: thus, *falso* 'false', *senso* 'sense' become [fal'so, sen'so] or even [faltso, sentso]. For a more restricted number of (generally more southern) speakers, this affrication has spread to the labials: e.g. *tonfo* 'thud' [tonᵖfo] or [tompfo], *inverno* 'winter' [imᵇvɛrno] or [imbvɛrno]. /ts, dz/ share with /ʃ, ɲ, ʎ/ the property of always occurring long intervocalically, an environment in which for all other consonants there is an opposition between short and long (or single and double): e.g. *copia* 'copy' vs *coppia* 'couple'; *beve* 'he drinks' vs *bevve* 'he drank'; *grato* 'grateful' vs *gratto* 'I scratch'; *vano* 'vain' vs *vanno* 'they go'; *serata* 'evening' vs *serrata* 'lock-out' etc.

Vowels
The vowel system is displayed below:

/i, u/ have allophones [j, w] in non-nuclear position in the syllable: *più* ['pju] 'more', *può* ['pwɔ] 'he can'. The oppositions /e ~ ɛ/ and /o ~ ɔ/ are neutralised outside stress, but even allowing for this their status is problematic, since, although most speakers have four sounds, the lexical classes and phonological rules which govern their distribution vary widely.

Another type of neutralisation in Italian phonology is that which affects nasals before consonants and ensures that the whole cluster is homorganic. This is only reflected orthographically in the case of bilabials — hence *campo* 'field', *impossibile* 'impossible', etc., while labiodentals, dentals, etc. are always spelt *nc*: *inferno* [im'fɛrno] 'hell', *indocile* [iɲ'dɔtʃile] 'unmanageable', *incauto* [iŋ'kauto] 'incautious'. The same process also operates across word boundaries in a fully productive manner: *con Paolo* [..mp..] 'with Paul' vs *con Carlo* [..ŋk..], etc. This constraint of homorganicity in -NC- clusters, typical of all central and southern speech forms, is coupled in a number of Calabrian and Sicilian dialects with the loss of initial unstressed vowels, thereby producing the word-initial sequences /mp, nt/ etc.: e.g. Cal *mpicari* 'to hang' (cf. It. *impiccare*), *mpannu* 'afloat', *ndudda* 'kind of sausage', *ncrinu* [ŋk ...] 'slope'. Phonetically these are often realised by an apparently very un-Romance sound type, a series of prenasalised stops. Beside this we may set the tendency of northern dialects to exhibit velarisation of syllable final nasals. Thus, Pied. *sinsent* [siŋsɛŋt] 'five hundred', *kamp* [kaŋp] 'field'. This phenomenon is now almost the norm among many, even non-dialectophone, speakers of Italian north of the Appennines, and contributes to the phonetic quality of the northern standard pronunciation which some commentators see (hear?) emerging in the current climate of social and economic prestige which attaches to prosperous commercial centres such as Turin, Milan, Genoa and Bologna. In the dialects of this region there is often also loss of final vowels, leading to forms like *pan* [paŋ] 'bread'. Subsequently, the nasal consonant may be absorbed into the vowel — e.g. Mil. *pan* [pã], *kanp* [kãp], as of course has standardly happened in French (pp. 211–12) and Portuguese (p. 136).

A morphophonemic process can be observed in the synchronic residue of Romance palatalisation (pp. 39–40), which is revealed in alternations such as *amico* 'friend (m. sg.)', where *c* = /k/, and *amici* 'friends (m. pl.)', where *c* = /tʃ/, and similarly in the voiced series: *antropolo*[g]*o*, *antropolo*[dʒ]*i* 'anthropologist(s)'. Hence we find verbal alternations such as:

di[k]o	'I say'	vol[g]o	'I turn'
di[tʃ]i	'you say'	vol[dʒ]i	'you turn'
di[tʃ]e	'he/she says'	vol[dʒ]e	'he/she turns'
di[k]a	'say (subjunctive)'	vol[g]a	'turn (subjunctive)'
di[tʃ]eva	'he/she was saying'	vol[dʒ]eva	'he/she was turning'

In the case of verb morphology, a verb may either alternate or not, but if it does alternate, then the process is triggered by both /i/ and /e/. Masculine nouns are also either alternating — cf. *amico* above — or not — cf. *bu*[k]*o* 'hole', *bu*[k]*i* 'holes'. Feminine nouns, however, never exhibit the effects of palatalisation: e.g. *ami*[k]*a* 'friend (f. sg.)', *ami*[k]*e* 'friends (f. pl.)'. The diachronic explanation is straightforward in that the nominal suffix for feminine plural derives from Latin /ai/, where the non-front onset of the diphthong inhibited palatalisation of the preceding velar whereas verbal -*e* always derives from Latin /i/ or /e/, precisely the triggering environment for the sound change. Synchronically, however, the situation requires the analyst to recognise a degree of morphologically and lexically conditioned arbitrariness.

A further synchronic residue is observable in what are traditionally called *dittonghi mobili* 'movable diphthongs', as in *buono* 'good' but *bontà* 'goodness', *viene* 'he comes' but *venire* 'to come'. They are the result of the diphthongisation of Latin /ĕ, ŏ/ in stressed open syllables (pp. 34–6), but the pattern of alternation is now being eroded away by analogical generalisations in both directons: e.g. *suono* 'I play' had a past participle *sonato* (cf. *sonata* literally 'something played'), but now one more commonly finds *suonato*, whereas *provo* 'I try' has replaced an earlier *pruovo*.

Italian words may consist of one or more syllables and are subject to a general constraint that they be vowel-final. Exceptions to this are certain loan words (*sport, boom, slip, camion*, etc.), a handful of Latinisms (*lapis* 'pencil', *ribes* 'blackcurrant'), and an increasing number of acronyms (*Agip, Fiat*). Some grammatical words — e.g. the masculine singular of the definite article *il*, the prepositions *in, con, per*, the negative particle *non* — have final consonants, but the rules of the syntax will never allow them to appear in sentence- or phrase-final position. Hence they are best treated as proclitics rather than independent phonological words. Similarly, there is a vowel truncation rule which deletes final /e/ after /l, r, n/, but only between words in a close syntactic nexus: *volere dire* 'to mean' (literally 'to want to say') may become *voler dire* but not *volere dir*, even though the latter sequence is possible with a different constituency, e.g. *volere* (*dir bene di qualcuno*) 'to want to speak well of someone'.

Words may begin with either a consonant or a vowel. A word-initial single consonant may be any of those given in Table 8.1, though initial /ɲ/ is rare (*gnomo* 'gnome', *gnocco* 'a kind of dumpling', and a few others) and initial /ʎ/ is non-existent in lexical words. However, since the form *gli* [ʎi] occurs both as the masculine plural of the definite article before vowel-initial nouns (*gli amici* 'the friends' cf. pp. 289–90) and as the masculine singular dative unstressed pronoun (*gli dissi* 'I said to him' cf. p. 291), /ʎ/ in utterance-initial position is very common. Apart from in borrowings and in technical terms, two-member initial clusters are limited to the following types:

(i)   /p b t d k g f/ + r
(ii) /p b k g f/ + l
(iii) s + /p b t d k g ʃ dʒ f v l r m n/

(It should be stated that purists do not admit [sʧ], but it is regularly heard in words where there is a clear morphemic boundary, e.g. *scentrato* 'off centre'.) Note too that of these clusters, types (i) and (ii) are pan-Romance, although in some languages (including Italian) type (ii) is limited to learned and borrowed forms.

Three-member clusters can only consist of /s/ plus any of the possible two-member clusters under (i) or (ii). A non-final syllable may end in /l, r, s/ or a nasal. Examples of intervocalic clusters can be created productively by juxtaposing forms such as *il, per, bis* and *in* with a noun or an adjective, although only a subset of the possible clusters generated in this fashion are attested internally in existing lexical items. An intervocalic cluster may also consist of a geminate consonant, with a syllable boundary between the two: *piop-po* 'poplar', *gof-fo* 'clumsy', *cad-de* 'he fell', *bel-lo* 'beautiful'. Indeed, the evidence of syllable division is one of the principal reasons for treating them as geminates rather than long consonants. Note that in such groups, if the first member is a stop or affricate, it is unreleased, hence such transcriptions as [pat-tso] for *pazzo* 'mad', [fat-ʧa] for *faccia* 'face'.

Tautosyllabic vowel sequences all conform to the pattern of a nuclear vowel followed or preceded, or both, by [j] or [w]: *piano* ['pjano] 'flat', *sai* ['saj] 'you know', *buono* ['bwɔno] 'good', *quei* [kwej] 'those (m. pl.)'. Otherwise, vowel sequences involve a hiatus between two syllables: *teatro* 'theatre', *poeta* 'poet'. We have both in *laurea* 'university degree' ['law-re-a].

Primary or lexical stress is not predictable on phonological grounds alone, hence such minimal pairs as *principi* (plural of *principio* 'principle') and *principi* (plural of *principe* 'prince'), or *capito* 'I turn up', *capito* 'understood', *capitò*, 'he turned up'. (For a discussion of comparable sets in Spanish, cf. p. 87.) There are, however, a number of morphological cues to stress. A third person singular preterit verb form is always final-stressed, while all second person plural forms are penultimately stressed. Such patterns are best described by distinguishing in the morphology between stress-neutral and stress-attracting suffixes. The lexical bases which receive these suffixes may be either penultimately or antepenultimately stressed: *canta* 'sing' vs *fabbrica* 'make'. A stress-neutral suffix attached to the latter produces stress four syllables from the end: *fabbricano* 'they make'. If clitics are attached postverbally, stress may be made to appear even farther from the end of the word: *fabbricalo* 'make it', *fabbricamelo* 'make it for me', *fabbricamicelo* 'make it for me there'. Underived words, however, can only have stress on one of the last three syllables: *anima* 'soul', *lèttera* 'letter', *periodo* 'period'; *radice* 'root', *divino* 'divine', *profondo* 'deep'; *virtù* 'virtue', *caffè* 'coffee', *velleità* 'wish'. Final-stressed words are either loan words, often from French, or the results of a diachronic truncation: *virtù* < Old It. *virtude* < Latin VĪRTŪTEM. Secondary stress is not in general contrastive, but is assigned rhythmically in such a way as to ensure that (a) the first syllable, if possible, is stressed; (b) there are never more than two unstressed syllables in sequence; (c) there are never two adjacent stressed syllables. Minimal pairs can, on the other hand, be adduced in cases of compound stress such as: *àuto-reattóre* 'auto-reactor' vs *autòre-attóre* 'author-actor' (contrasting position of secondary stress); *procùra* 'he procures' vs *pròcúra* 'fore-care' (two stresses vs one).

Stress interacts with vowel length and the distribution of geminate consonants. Vowels are always short if not primarily stressed, or if followed by a consonant in the same syllable. They are long, therefore, in stressed, open syllables: *ànima* ['a:-ni-ma], *lèttera* ['lɛt-te-ra], *divìno* [di-'vi:-no], *profòndo* [pro-'fon-do]. Final vowels are always short, so that if stressed and in close nexus with a following word, they ought to create a violation of our previously stated principle. Such a situation, however, is avoided by so-called *raddoppiamento sintattico* 'syntactic doubling', whereby the initial consonant of the following word is geminated: *parlò chiaro* 'he spoke clearly' [par-'lɔk-'kja:-ro]. The double consonant here also seems to act as sufficient barrier to permit two adjacent main stresses. It has recently been pointed out that in the north, where the doubling effect is not found, the first of the two stresses is retracted instead. This doubling also takes place after a number of words which have lost the final consonants they had in Latin: *tre* 'three' < Lat. TRĒS, *a* 'to' < Lat. AD, though again this effect is only found south of the La Spezia–Rimini line (p. 18). *Raddoppiamento*, then, is typical of central and southern speech, and the failure of northern speakers to adopt it mirrors its absence from their own dialects. Their habit of pronouncing only those geminates which the orthography indicates is yet another aspect of the emergence of a kind of standardised spelling pronunciation based on the interaction of northern phonetic habits and an orthography which reflects the Florentine origin of the standard.

Orthography
The Italian spelling system exhibits a fairly regular pattern of phoneme–grapheme correspondences, with the following consonant letters having more or less their IPA values: *p, t, d, f, v, m, n, l, r*. The letter *s* represents either [s] or [z] according to the principles outlined above (p. 281), but *z* corresponds unpredictably to either /ts/ or /dz/. Note that *z* is always pronounced long in intervocalic position, even in words like *grazie* 'thank you' where only one letter is used. In all other cases, single vs double letters marks a phonemic contrast. The letters *h* and *i* interact with *(s)c* and *g* as set out in the following chart:

Orthography	Context	Pronunciation

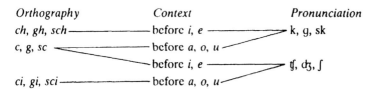

The only other function of *h* is as a kind of silent 'morphographeme' in the stem-stressed forms of the present indicative of *avere*, viz *ho, hai, ha, hanno*, though at earlier stages etymological spellings like *honore* 'honour' for modern *onore* were frequently attested.

The combinations *gn* and *gli* spell respectively /ɲ, ʎ/. The letters *j, k, w, x, y* now only figure in the spelling of foreign words and names, though *j* and *x* were once used in old-fashioned spelling.

Among the vowels, *i, u, a* have close to cardinal values, although *i* and *u* also represent [j] and [w] respectively in prevocalic position. Spelling reformers have often lamented the fact that *e* and *o* each correspond to two vowel phonemes, /e, ɛ/ and /o, ɔ/, so that *legge* 'he reads' (with /ɛ/) and *legge* 'law' (with /e/) are pronounced differently but spelt the same, as are *torta* 'twisted' (with /ɔ/) and *torta* 'cake' (with /o/). However, the number of minimal pairs is so small and regional differences so great that there is a strong functional argument for retaining the orthographic *status quo* in this respect. Perhaps the biggest defect in Italian orthography consists in the failure to mark the location of stress, except when it falls on the final syllable (*parlò* 'he spoke', *caffè* (*è* = /ɛ/) 'coffee', *perché* (*é* = /e/) 'why'), even though it is not in general predictable. An accent mark is also used to distinguish orthographically certain homophonous monosyllables: e.g. *dà* 'he gives' vs *da* 'from'; *sé* 'himself' vs *se* 'if' and *se* 'third singular reflexive clitic'.

Diachronic Phonology

In regard to the phonological structure of the word, standard Italian exhibits many features which must also have been characteristic of the later stages of Latin: stress ranges freely and contrastively over the last three syllables of the word; immediately pre- and post-tonic vowels have remained intact to a greater extent than elsewhere (It. *frassino* 'ashtree', *manica* 'sleeve' vs Fr. *frêne, manche*; Sp. *fresno, manga*); original final consonants have been lost and secondary ones have not emerged (It. *mese* 'month' vs Fr. *mois*, Sp. *mes*); and vowel and consonant length are in complementary distribution in the tonic syllable. Segmentally, too, we may note the conservativeness of the Italian seven-vowel system when set beside what we have called the Proto-Western-Romance system (p. 33), and of the consonantal inventory, which has undergone the effects of palatalisation but not, for the most part anyway, of lenition (p. 39). Nevertheless, a number of points are worth noting.

In particular, although the interaction of vowel and consonant length must reflect an early stage in Romance phonological development, Italian long or geminate consonants derive from a number of different sources. Some, of course, are direct inheritances from Latin, e.g. *fossa* 'ditch', *mille* 'thousand', *ferro* 'iron', including many compounds with AD, SUB, etc.: e.g. *apprendere* 'to learn' (< APPREHENDERE < *AD+PREHENDERE) *succedere* 'to happen' (< SŬCCĒDĔRE < *SUB+CEDERE). Others are the result of later assimilations, such as *sasso* 'stone' (< SAXUM), *nozze* 'marriage' (< NŪPTĬAE), *vittima* 'victim' (< VĪCTĬMAM). Yet others betray the effect of a compensatory lengthening of the consonant which took place after an original short (or shortened) vowel in proparoxytonic words: *femmina* 'woman' (< FĒMĬNAM), *attimo* 'moment' (< ĂTŎMUM). Likewise, oxytones give rise to gemination of the initial consonant of following words, hence the so-called *raddoppiamento sintattico* (p. 285), whereas paroxytones undergo lengthening of the vowel (CĂNEM gives *cane* and not *canne). Finally, the liquids and glides /j, w, l, r/ cause gemination of consonants in intervocalic clusters: *faccia* 'face' < FĂCIAM, *acqua* 'water' < ĂQUAM, *pubblico* 'public' < PŪBLĬCUM, *febbre* 'fever' < FĔBREM. In regard to the last two examples, it should be noted that there is in any case a strong tendency to geminate intervocalic (and even initial) /b/ and /m/ in central and southern speech, hence such frequent misspellings as *libbro*, *gommito* for standard *libro* 'book', *gomito* 'elbow'.

The preservation, and indeed expansion, of double consonants is often argued to be linked to the retention of intervocalic voiceless stops, since the majority of Romance dialects — including those spoken in Italy north of the La Spezia–Rimini line — exhibit the opposite pairing: no geminates and voicing (and often eventual loss) of intervocalic stops. Thus, contrast It. *saputo* 'known', *fatto* 'done' with Ven. *savuo*, *fato*. Nevertheless, a number of words in Italian show the effects of lenition: e.g. *luogo* 'place' (< LŎCUM) but *fuoco* 'fire' (< FŎCUM), *lago* 'lake' (< LĂCUM), *padre* 'father', *madre* 'mother' (< PĂTREM, MĀTREM) but *fratello* 'brother' (< FRĀTĔLLUM). Such instances are commonly explained as being due to dialect mixture, but there seems no obvious reason why the words for 'lake' and 'place' should be northern except the purely circular one that they have northern forms. Alternatively, we may have here a case of lexical diffusion, with different residues in different dialects.

Another kind of intervocalic weakening is to be found in Tuscany where Latin /p t k/ develop into aspirates or fricatives — the so-called *gorgia toscana* ('Tuscan throat') — hence such common regional pronunciations as [kɔhahɔla] for *Coca Cola*, [statʰo] or [staθo] for *stato* 'been', [pipʰa] or [piɸa] for *pipa* 'pipe'. In the same area the affricates /ʧ, ʤ/ are realised as [ʃ, ʒ] intervocalically. Note that these changes do not entail any concomitant weakening of the geminates.

The effects of palatalisation of stops in Italian can easily be seen in the following chart of correspondences:

Latin	Initial	Intervocalic		Post-consonantal	
tj	—		tts	ts	ʧ
dj	ʤ	ddʒ	ddz	dz	
kj	—	tʧ	tts	ts	ʧ
gj	—	ddʒ			

The absence of examples for initial position is not surprising in view of the absence of the necessary clusters in Latin. Note indeed that the classic example for /dj/ > /dʒ/ is a special case of the derived adjective DIŪRNUM 'daily' > giorno 'day'. In the other positions the problem is the frequent dual outcomes: e.g. the suffix -ACEUM yields both -accio and -azzo; the masculine form CĂLCĔUM gives calcio 'kick' and the feminine CĂLCĔAM gives calza 'stocking'; the noun INĬTĬUM gives inizio 'beginning' but the compound CŎMĬN(I)TĬĀRE gives cominciare 'to begin'; from *RŎTĔŎLĀRE we have ruzzolare 'to tumble' but the compound *ĔXDĒRĊTĔŎLĀRE yields sdrucciolare 'to slither'. Again the usual explanation involves dialect mixture: /tj/ would then give /ts/ everywhere, /kj/ develops as /ts/ in the north and /tʃ/ in Tuscany. Aberrant forms are due to interdialectal borrowing and/or hypercorrection. The same pattern does not extend so easily to the voiced series, however, and a unified solution is still to be found. Note finally that in many dialects palatalisation also affects clusters with labial + j, so that, for example, from Lat. SĂPĬO 'I know' we get the widespread southernism saccio (cf. standard faccio 'I do' < FĂCĬO), or northern dialect forms such as Ligurian ciü 'more', giancu 'white', sciama 'flame' beside standard più, bianco, fiamma (< PLŪS, *BLĂNKUM, FLĂMMAM).

A special case is Lat. /skj/, which gives It. /ʃ/, hence the morphophonemic alternations in verbs such as cono[sk]o 'I know' vs cono[ʃʃ]i 'you know', where the original cluster may be seen as the source of the obligatory length of intervocalic /ʃ/ in Italian (p. 281). /ʃ/ might also be expected to be the outcome of /sj/, but curiously we find /tʃ/: BĀSĬUM > bacio 'kiss', CĂMĬSĬAM > camicia 'shirt'. This is usually explained as a non-Tuscan hypercorrection occasioned by the Tuscan habit of pronouncing /tʃ/ as [ʃ] intervocalically.

Other cases of Cj have both multiple inputs and multiple outcomes. Thus, Latin /gl/ may on the one hand be treated as heterosyllabic, with consequent development of g > j, whence the cluster [jl] gives /ʎ/ exactly as the cluster [lj] does: VĬG(I)LĀRE > vegliare 'to keep watch' and FĪLĬAM > figlia 'daughter'. In the same way /ɲ/ may derive either from [jn] — DĬGNUM > degno 'worthy' — or from [nj] — VĪNĔAM > vigna 'vineyard'. (Note again the survival of the obligatory length in It. /ɲ, ʎ/.) Alternatively, the group /gl/ may be treated as syllable-initial, in which case /l/ gives /j/ (cf. PLĀNUM > piano 'flat', *GLĂCĬUM > ghiaccio 'ice') and gemination produces /ggj/: e.g. the now antiquated vegghiare also from VĬGILĀRE. Latin /rj/ has /j/ as its reflex in Tuscany, and thus in the standard language — -ARIUM > -aio 'agentive suffix', *MŎRĬO > muoio 'I die', but /r/ elsewhere: e.g. JĂNŬĀRĬUM yields standard gennaio 'January' but Gennaro as the name of the patron saint of Naples. Indeed, this particular isogloss is often taken as one of the diagnostic phonological features of Tuscan, together with the gorgia, the absence of metaphony (pp. 35–6), and the rentention of four vowels /i e a o/ in unstressed final position.

3 Morphology

In morphology Italian inherits from Latin the clear separation of verbal and nominal inflection, the latter also encompassing pronouns, articles and adjectives.

The Noun

Nouns inflect for gender — masculine and feminine — and number — singular and plural — according to the following patterns:

Singular	Plural	Gender	
-o	-i	m.	*libro* 'book'; exception *mano* (f.) 'hand' (< Lat. MANUM (f.))
-a	-e	f.	*casa* 'house', *donna* 'woman'
-e	-i	m. or f.	*monte* (m.) 'mountain', *mente* (f.) 'mind'
-a	-i	m.	*problema* 'problem' and other words of Gk. (*sistema, programma*, etc.) or Lat. (*artista, poeta*, etc.) origin

Such a system of plural by vowel alternation rather than by suffixing of -*s* is one of the features which marks Italian (and Rumanian — pp. 398–9) off from Western Romance languages such as French or Portuguese; for the position in some forms of Spanish, cf. p. 85. Nouns which in the singular end in -*i*, e.g. *crisi* 'crisis', in stressed vowels, e.g. *città* 'town', *tribù* 'tribe', and in consonants, e.g. *sport, camion* 'lorry', are unchanged in the plural. A small class of nouns — e.g. *dito* 'finger', *uovo* 'egg', *lenzuolo* 'sheet' — distinguish between a collective and a non-collective plural: *osso* 'bone', *le ossa* 'bones (together, as in a skeleton)', *gli ossi* 'bones (scattered)'. The synchronically unusual -*a* in the collective plural is a residue of the Latin neuter plural. Note that articles and adjectives accompanying such nouns are masculine in the singular and feminine in the plural.

Adjectives and Determiners

Adjectives fall into two principal classes, having either four forms: *buono, -i, -a, -e* 'good' or two: *felice, -i* 'happy' (with a few like *rosa* 'pink', originally nouns, that are uninflected), which reflects the structure of the developing Latin declension system discussed above (p. 42). The four-form pattern also shows up in the third person clitic pronoun series *lo/la/li/le*. In Old Italian these were also the forms of the definite article, but the modern language has a more irregular pattern whereby the masculine singular and masculine plural forms vary according to whether the following word begins with a consonant (column 1 in the chart below) or with /ʃ ʎ ɲ/, /s/ + C, or certain non-native initial clusters such as /pn-/, /ks-/, etc.

(column II in the chart). Other items which follow the same pattern are the indefinite article, the distal demonstrative *quello* (< ECCU+ILLUM), the word *santo* when used as the title 'Saint' and the prenominal adjective *bello* 'beautiful':

	M. sg. I	M. sg. II	M. pl. I	M. pl. II	F. sg.	F. pl.
Indef. art.	un	uno	–	–	una	–
Def. art.	il	lo	i	gli	la	le
'this'	quel	quello	quei	quegli	quella	quelle
'beautiful'	bel	bello	bei	begli	bella	belle
'saint'	san	santo	santi	santi	santa	sante

When the above words occur before a vowel-initial word, the column II form is used, but with deletion of the final vowel in the singular. This vowel truncation effect is optionally shared by the proximal demonstrative *questo* (< ECCU+ISTUM) and the clitic pronouns.

For the syntax of adjectives and determiners within the nominal group, see pp. 298–9.

Personal Pronouns

Italian first and second person pronouns have three forms, viz:

	1st person Sg.	1st person Pl.	2nd person Sg.	2nd person Pl.
Stressed subject	io	noi	tu	voi
Clitic object	mi	ci	ti	vi
Stressed/prep. object	me	noi	te	voi

Italian is a pro-drop language (p. 334), and has no clitic subject form parallel, for example, to French *je*. A number of (particularly northern) dialects do have such forms — e.g. Ven. *ti dizi* 'you say' — though the conditions which govern their appearance vary both according to grammatical person and to dialect (cf. p. 385). The overt subject forms are therefore used when stressed (*chi vuol venire? – io* 'who wants to come? – me'), and *me* and *te* are limited to oblique environments (contrast the distribution of French *moi*, *toi* as discussed on p. 219). Note too that, unlike in French and Spanish, so-called clitic-doubling is not normal in Italian, hence *ha visto me* 'he has seen ME', though examples with indirect objects such as *a me mi piace* 'I like it' (literally 'to me it pleases me') are widespread in colloquial usage.

The plural clitic forms *ci* and *vi* are of interest in that they derive from Lat. HIC 'here' and IBI 'there' respectively, and in the modern language do double duty as personal and locative pronouns, having supplanted the earlier reduced forms *no* (< NOS) and *vo* (< VOS).

The first and second person non-subject forms are also used in reflexive constructions, for which there is a third person pair *si* and *se* with parallel distribution. Note that in some northern dialects, the form *si* has extended its usage so that it has become a general reflexive marker with no indication of person: Mil. *mi se acorgi* vs It. *io mi accorgo* 'I realise'. In the south, on the other hand, we often find *si* replaced by *ci*, as indeed happens in the standard language when a reflexive and an impersonal combine: *si lava* 'one washes' or '(he) washes himself' but *ci si lava* 'one washes oneself'. For further discussion of the grammar of reflexives and impersonals, see below, pp. 302–3.

The situation in the third person non-reflexive is more complex. In everyday Italian, the (optional) subject forms are m. sg. *lui*, f. sg. *lei*, pl. *loro*, forms derived from Latin oblique cases which have generalised to subject position. Once again a number of northern and central dialects show clitic subject forms, even in impersonal constructions: Mil. *on omm el gh'aveva duu fioeu* literally 'a man he to him had two sons', *el pioeuv* 'it is raining'. For oblique uses two forms are standardly distinguished, an accusative (*lo/la/li/le*) and a dative (m. sg. *gli*, f. sg. *le*, pl. *loro*) series. Of these, *loro* is unique in that it follows even finite verb forms: *ho detto loro* 'I said to them', and in colloquial usage even by educated speakers it is regularly replaced by *gli*. In its other use as a plural possessive — *il loro libro* 'their book' — it is also anomalous in not indicating gender, and it is commonly replaced in substandard usage by the singular possessive *suo* 'his, her' (cf. Sp. *su*, Port. *seu* and contrast Fr. *leur*, Rum. *lor*). The form *loro* has therefore virtually disappeared from popular registers of the language. *Le* seems to be following it, in so far as it is standardly replaced in clitic clusters by its masculine congener, hence, for example, *gliene* 'of it to him/her', and even in isolation *gli* for *le* is attested with increasing frequency although the usage is still felt to be substandard. In *italiano popolare* (p. 312) and in many dialects, as in most popular registers of French (p. 220), the whole system *gli/le/loro* merges with neuter *ci*, which thus becomes an omni-purpose indirect object clitic.

The chart below sets out the relative order of clitic pronouns when they occur in clusters:

1 sg.	3 sg. (dat.)	2 pl.	2 sg.	1 pl.	Refl.	3 sg./pl. (acc.)	Impers.	Partitive
mi	*gli* (m.)	*vi*	*ti*	*ci*	*si*	*lo* (m. sg.)	*si*	*ne*
	le (f.)					*la* (f. sg.)		
						li (m. pl.)		
						le (f. pl.)		

Note, however, that combinations of *ne* and the third person accusative forms are rare, and when they do occur, *ne* precedes: *ne la ringrazierò* 'I'll thank her for it'. In clusters there is a morphophonemic adjustment of /i/

to /e/ before sonorants, hence *me lo, te ne,* etc. Clusters of three pronouns are relatively uncommon, though by no means structurally impossible: *gli se ne parlerà* 'one will speak to him about it'. There are a number of cases where a clitic cluster has become fossilised as part of an idiom: *prendersela con qualcuno* 'to take it out on someone', *andarsene* 'to go away'.

A curious historical point is the shift of clitic order in about the fourteenth century, so that where the Italian of Dante had the sequences *lo mi, la ti,* etc. the modern language requires the reverse order. These and a number of other diachronic fluctuations in clitic combinations have not yet been satisfactorily explained, but in all probability they are related to the more general change in the rules governing clitic position. Old Italian was characterised by the so-called Tobler–Mussafia law, which prevented a clitic from taking initial position in a sentence or clause: thus, *quando mi disse* 'when he said to me' but *dissemi* 'he said to me'. This has given way to the modern principle whereby clitics precede finite verb forms but follow non-finite ones: *me lo darà* 'he will give it to me', *per darmelo* 'in order to give it to me', *avendomelo dato* 'having given it to me'. Certain verbs, however, which take a dependent infinitive allow the latter's clitics to 'climb' and attach to the governing verb: *vuole parlarti* or *ti vuole parlare* 'he wants to speak to you', *volendo parlarti* or *volendoti parlare* 'wanting to speak to you'.

Finally in this section, mention must be made of the system of address. Like many languages, standard Italian distinguishes between a familiar and a polite style. The former is expressed through the use of the second person singular forms *tu, ti, tuo* and the imperatives *canta, temi, senti.* The latter requires the deferential third person pronoun *Lei* (the capital letter is used in formal writing — cf. also clitic forms *La, Le* and possessive *Suo* but curiously not with the reflexive *si*), while the present subjunctives *canti, tema, senta* are used in lieu of the imperatives. The use of *Lei* goes back to late Latin, and became widespread apparently as a result of Spanish influence in the Renaissance. Until quite recently the same distinction could be regularly maintained in the plural with *voi, vi, vostro* for familiar usage and *Loro* (literally 'they') as the polite form. The latter form is becoming increasingly rare in this usage as in others, and is now only used in the most formal circumstances — otherwise *voi* serves both functions. *Voi* as a polite singular, reminiscent but apparently independent of French (p. 221), on the other hand, is still common in parts of southern Italy, particularly amongst older speakers, and used to be a more widespread popular deferential form in contrast to the in origin upper and middle class *Lei.*

The Verb

The chart of finite forms represents the paradigmatic structure of three typical regular verbs exemplifying the three traditional conjugations, each of which is marked by a characteristic thematic vowel, *a, e* or *i*. A typical

Finite Forms of Italian Regular Verbs

	1	2	3	4	5	6
Present indicative	{cant, tem, sent} -o	-i	canta {tem, sent} -e	{cant, tem, sent} -iamo	{canta, teme, senti} -te	canta-no {tem, sent} -ono
Imperfect	canta {teme, senti} -v -o	-i	{canta, teme, senti} -va -Ø	-mo	-te	-no
Present subjunctive	cant -i {tem, sent} -a	-i	-a	{cant, tem, sent} -iamo	-iate	cant -i {tem, sent} -a -no
Preterit	{canta, teme, senti} -i	-sti	cantò, temè, sentì	{canta, teme, senti} -mmo	-ste	-rono
Past subjunctive	{canta, teme, senti} -ss -i	-i	-e	-imo	{canta, teme, senti} -ste	-ro
Future	{canter, temer, sentir} -ò	-ai	-à	-emo	-ete	-anno
Conditional	-ei	-esti	-ebbe	-emmo	-este	-ebbero

verb form contains four classes of elements: stem, thematic vowel, tense/ aspect/mood markers, and person/number markers, whose linear relations are stated in the formula: stem + TV + (T/A/M) + P/N. This entails that a form such as, for example, the second person plural imperfect indicative of *temere* 'to fear' would be segmented thus: *tem+e+va+te*. In the chart, on the other hand, we have used curly brackets in an attempt at an alternative analysis which highlights some of the patterns of overlap between the traditional conjugations (albeit at the expense of some non-traditional segmentations). The numbers here and throughout this section refer to the six grammatical persons, three singular and three plural. However, a classification of this kind is inadequate in two apparently contradictory respects. On the one hand, it does not allow for a number of further classes which seem to be necessary, for instance, to distinguish between two types of *e*-verb according to whether they have stem or ending stress in the infinitive: *credere* 'to believe' and *vedere* 'to see' do not rhyme. Historically, in fact, the stem-stressed verbs have in some cases even undergone loss of the theme vowel in the infinitive with attendant consonant deletion or assimilation: Lat. PONERE, DICERE, BIBERE > It. *porre, dire, bere.* We also need to recognise two types of *i*-verb, one with the originally inceptive stem augment *-isc-* in persons 1/2/3/6 of the present and one without: *capisco* 'I understand' but *servo* 'I serve', and *partisco* 'I divide' as against *parto* 'I leave'. (For the same phenomenon in French, cf. p. 223.) These latter two verbs have a number of homophonous forms elsewhere in the paradigm: *partiamo, partire, partivo,* etc. On the other hand, a basically tripartite classification fails to capture the generalisation that *e*- and *i*-verbs are a good deal more similar to each other morphologically than either is to *a*-verbs (which constitutes the main open class for new coinings and borrowings — e.g. *allunare* 'to land on the moon', *ammarare* 'to splash down', *zumare* 'to zoom (of a camera)'). This relationship is particularly noticeable in forms 3/6 of the present indicative, and in the reversal effect whereby the present subjunctive vowel is *-i-* for *a*-verbs and *-a-* for *i/e*-verbs. Hence a better representation of Italian conjugational structure might be that given in Figure 8.1. In addition to these finite forms, each verb has a past participle (*cant-a-to, tem-u-to, sent-i-to*) and a gerund (*cant-a-ndo, tem/sent-e-ndo*), which are used both independently and in a number of verbal periphrases (see section 4 for details of these and of the functions and values of the various finite forms). The present participle formation (*-a/e/ie-nte*) is of more equivocal status since its use is in practice limited to very formal registers, or else the forms in question have become reanalysed as nouns (*cantante* 'singer', *dirigente* 'manager') or adjectives (*sorridente* 'smiling', *brillante* 'brilliant').

There are, of course, a number of verbs which fail to conform to the schemata established above, but it would be neither possible nor helpful in the present context to list all such idiosyncrasies. It is, however, of interest

Figure 8.1: A Model of Italian Conjugation Structure

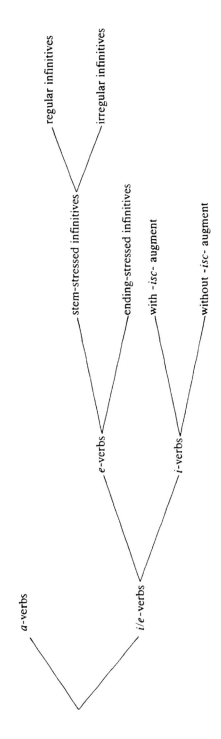

to note the ways in which patterns of irregularity intersect with the regular verb paradigms. For example, no verb has any anomalous formations in the imperfect (except *essere* 'to be', which seems to stand outside all such generalisations), and, again excluding *essere*, only *dare* 'to give' and *stare* 'to be, stand' have irregular past subjunctives (*dessi, stessi* for the expected **dassi, *stassi*). Discrepancies in the future and the conditional (and no verb is irregular in one without having the same irregularity in the other) are due either to the verb already having an exceptional infinitive — *porrò, dirò, farò* — or to the historical effects of syncope on the periphrases from which they derive: VENIRE + HABEO > *verrò*, VOLERE + HABUIT > *vorrebbe*, etc.

By far the largest number of exceptions, however, are to be found in three parts of the paradigm: the present (indicative and subjunctive), the preterit and the past participle. Of these, the latter two are closely related: very few verbs have an irregular preterit and a regular past participle, and even fewer have an irregular past participle and regular preterit. The characteristic perturbation in both cases is a reduced stem, which appears in persons 1/3/6 and the participle: e.g. for *prendere* 'to take', we have *preso* (pp.), and *presi* (1), *prese* (3), *presero* (6) vs *prendesti* (2), *prendemmo* (4), *prendeste* (5). Historically, the -s- in the preterit forms represents the Latin (and ultimately Indo-European) sigmatic marker, which was not original with all verbs in this class — cf. the Latin perfect PREHENDI — but which spread in the course of time into the stem-stressed forms of a large class of verbs (p. 51) — hence **PRE(HE)NDSI* but **PRE(HE)NDISTIS* — and thereby created consonant clusters which underwent various processes of reduction and assimilation. The -s- of the past participle, by contrast, is original — PREHENSUM — and represents the dissimilatory product of an earlier sequence **PREHEND+TOM* (cf. **DIVIDTOM* > DIVISSUM > DIVISUM 'divided'). Synchronically, there seems little reason not to treat the -s- in *presi* and *preso* as the same formative, but the history helps to explain the relative paucity of 'sigmatic' participles in Italian. Note too in the same vein the interesting case of It. *risposto* 'replied' from **RESPONSTUM*, where the -s- is the reflex of the Indo-European -*tom* formation and the -T- is due to the late Latin analogical extension of the same formative. If the vowel is not present the regular -*to* suffix (< -TUM) will trigger the same effects: e.g. *assumere* 'to take on', *assumesti* (2), but *assunsi* (1) and *assunto* (pp.). In other instances the irregular preterit base is due to the Latin -U- [u ~ w] perfect marker. Subsequent sound changes then produce a geminate consonant from the earlier [Cw] sequence: VOLUI > *volli* (1) 'I wanted' (cf. *volesti* (2)), **CADUIT* > *cadde* (3) 'he fell' (cf. *cademmo* (4)), **COGNOVUERUNT* > *conobbero* (6) 'they knew' (cf. *conosceste* (5)). Such verbs also have participles in -*u*-: *avuto, caduto, conosciuto*. Although this participial -*u*- is etymologically from a different source, namely verbs in -UO such as BATTUO 'I beat', it extended its range considerably in late Latin (p.

51) (cf. the classical forms HABITUM, CASUM, COGNITUM), suggesting that it had been morphologically reanalysed as being the same element as perfective -U- (cf. the conflation of the two sigmatic elements discussed above). Finally, in this connection, we may note the form *vissuto* 'lived' < *VIXUTUM, which represents the extension of the -UTUM suffix to the already sigmatic Latin perfect from VIXI. The original Latin participle VIC-TUM survives instead in the word *vitto* 'food'.

There are perhaps 200 verbs whose only irregular formations are in the preterit and the past participle, almost without exception members of the class of *e*-verbs. Interestingly, in southern dialects where the use of the preterit is more extensive than in the centre and north, many of these irregularities have been analogised away: e.g. Sic. *persuadei, volette, vivuto, dipenduto* beside standard *persuasi* 'I persuaded', *volle* 'he wanted', *vissuto* 'lived', *dipeso* 'depended'. When it comes to the present tense, there are less than 50 irregular verbs, spread throughout the conjugation classes. We cannot characterise all the patterns here, but once again it is worth noting how the incidence of stress was one of the principal determining factors diachronically for these alternations. (For a full discussion of the processes involved in one language, see the treatment of parallel phenomena in Spanish pp. 99–101.) In the chart below, the forms have been set out deliberately to show how for different types of alternation — including even suppletion in the case of *andare* — the grouping of forms reflects the original (and present) location of stress rather than any natural grouping on morphological grounds. (Accent marks have been added here for clarity, although, as already noted, the normal orthography does not use them.)

	uscire 'to go out'	*andàre* 'to go'	*morire* 'to die'	*sedère* 'to sit'
1	èsco	vàdo	muòio	sièdo
2	èsci	vài	muòri	sièdi
3	èsce	và	muòre	siède
6	èscono	vànno	muòiono	sièdono
Subj.	èsca(no)	vàda(no)	muòia(no)	sièda(no)
4	usciàmo	andiàmo	moriàmo	sediàmo
5	uscìte	andàte	morìte	sedète
Imperf.	uscìvo	andàvo	morìvo	sedèvo
Pret.	uscìi	andài	morìi	sedètti

This chart should not, of course, be taken to imply that all irregular verbs conform to this distribution. For example, the epenthetic -*g*- in *salgo* 'I go up' (contrast the infinitive *salire*) only occurs in forms 1, 6 and the present subjunctive. Our point is simply that although the content of the alternations may be very different in the individual cases, there are some intriguing recurrent patterns in their distribution through the paradigm, and it is not unreasonable to suggest that these patterns may have come to serve as a kind of morphological template conditioning the range of irregularity within the language.

One verb that seems to defy all generalisation is *essere*, whose paradigm we list below:

Present: 1 *sono*   2 *sei*   3 *è*   4 *siamo*   5 *siete*   6 *sono*
Imperf. :   1 *ero*   2 *eri*   3 *era*   4 *eravamo*   5 *eravate*   6 *erano*
Pres. subj.:   *sia(no)*
Future: *sarò, sarai,* etc.
Conditional: *sarei, saresti,* etc.
Preterit: 1 *fui*   2 *fosti*   3 *fu*   4 *fummo*   5 *foste*   6 *furono*
Past subj.:   1/2 *fossi*   3 *fosse*   4 *fossimo*   5 *foste*   6 *fossero*
Past part.:   *stato*
Gerund: *essendo*

4 Syntax

The Nominal Group

Nouns in Italian may be accompanied by articles, definite or indefinite, numerals and quantifiers, demonstratives, possessives and objectives. Of these, demonstratives and articles have parallel distribution and may be united in a single class of determiners. It is worth noting that only a two-term deictic opposition survives in modern usage, proximal *questo* vs distal *quello.* The often cited third term, *codesto* 'that by you' (cf. Sp. *ese,* p. 95), is now limited to Tuscany, and is obsolescent even there. Many southern dialects, however, have an active third term — e.g. Nap. *chisso* (< ECCU+IPSE) 'that by you'. Possessives behave distributionally more like adjectives than determiners, occurring either before or after the noun. In the former circumstance, except in the case of nouns for close members of the family, the possessive must be accompanied by a determiner: *mio zio* 'my uncle', *la mia macchina* 'my car', *un tuo cugino* 'one of your cousins' (literally 'a your cousin'), *questi suoi libri* 'these books of his' (literally 'these his books'), *nella mia vita/in vita mia* 'in my life'. Quantifiers such as *alcuni* 'some', *parecchi* 'several', *pochi* 'few' may also precede the possessive: *parecchi nostri amici* 'several (of) our friends'. Some items which, to judge by their pre-possessive position, must count as quantifiers and not adjectives, may also occur in the regular post-nominal adjective position, though with clearly distinguishable meanings: thus, *certe persone* 'a certain number of people' and *certi miei colleghi* 'some (of) my colleagues', but *persone certe* 'people who are certain'; *diversi tuoi professori* 'several (of) your teachers' but *due caratteri diversi* 'two different characters'.

Examples such as these point directly to one of the central issues of the syntax of the noun phrase in Italian: the function and position of the adjective. It is clear that there are independent pre- and post-nominal positions: *una breve visita* 'a short visit', *una visita turistica* 'a sightseeing visit', *una breve visita turistica* 'a short sightseeing visit'. Three questions arise: are there any constraints on how the two positions may be filled? Can a systematic meaning be attached to each position? Is one position dominant, such that it would make sense to say that Italian has noun–adjective order, say, in the way that typological classification seems to require? Note first that although there is a small class of adjectives where a change of position corresponds to a quite discernible change of meaning (cf. the above examples and others: *un semplice soldato* 'a mere soldier' vs *un soldato semplice* 'a private soldier', *numerose famiglie* 'many families' vs *famiglie numerose* 'large families'), most adjectives can occur in either position. Nor is length a decisive factor: the heptasyllabic *interessantissimo* 'very interesting' frequently precedes the noun in the speech of the more gushing interviewers and journalists! What differentiates the two positions rather is the function of the adjective: if it is used in a distinguishing or restrictive sense, it follows; if the use is descriptive, rhetorical, emphatic or metaphorical, it precedes. *Pietre preziose* are 'precious stones' as opposed to ordinary ones, but one would refer to *i preziosi gioielli della contessa* 'the countess's precious jewels', where the value is taken for granted. Similarly, courtesy would require one to thank a friend for *il suo prezioso aiuto* 'his valuable help'. Hence, whether an adjective precedes or follows will depend on how easily its inherent meaning lends itself to one or other or both types of use. Adjectives of place and nationality are normally contrastive and therefore tend to follow: *i turisti inglesi* 'English tourists', *l'industria settentrionale* 'northern industry'. To distinguish Florentine literature from that of Rome or Venice one would talk of *la letteratura fiorentina*, but since everybody knows that 'The Divine Comedy' is by a Florentine, the adjective has a more rhetorical function and precedes in *la fiorentina Divina Commedia*. A postposed adjective would suggest that Dante had a rival elsewhere!

We are, then, required to say that Italian has two equal but different adjective positions. The opposition being thus grammaticalised, the typological parameter of adjective–noun order is rendered irrelevant. Note too that there is strong evidence that rather similar principles governed the distribution of adjectives in Latin, so that what changes there have been relate to the gradual rigidification of order which we have already discussed (pp. 60ff), and to the occasional semantic shifts induced by repeated use in one position: e.g. *diverso* 'several' from Latin DIVERSUS 'different'.

The Verbal Group
In addition to the inflectional forms listed in the chart (p. 293), it is impossible to discuss the morphosyntax of the Italian verb without making reference to two periphrastic constructions. The first of these is formed

from the auxiliary *avere* or *essere* plus the past participle and is referred to variously as the perfect, the compound past or, in native terminology, the *passato prossimo* ('near past') — e.g. *ho mangiato* 'I have eaten', *siamo caduti* 'we have fallen'. The second periphrasis is formed with *essere* (and occasionally other auxiliaries) plus the past participle and is one of the means of expressing the passive — e.g. *fu trascurato* 'it was neglected', *sarà criticata* 'she will be criticised'. Since *essere* as a perfect auxiliary only occurs with a subclass of intransitives, and since passives are (in Italian, anyway) only formed from transitive verbs, there is no danger of overlap. Indeed, the two may cooccur as in *è stato promosso* 'he has been promoted' (note that *essere* in Italian takes *essere* as its auxiliary — contrast It. *sono stato* and Fr. *j'ai été* 'I have been'). For discussion of the historical origin of these constructions, see pp. 56ff, and for their usage in contemporary Italian, see below. Another group of periphrases, somewhat less closely integrated into the verbal system, are formed from *stare* 'to be, stand', *andare* 'to go' or *venire* 'to come' plus the gerund. These express various shades of progressive meaning: *gli stavano parlando* 'they were talking to him', *la situazione è andata complicandosi* 'the situation has been getting complicated', *si viene stampando un vocabolario* 'a dictionary is being published'. A formal correlate of the less fused nature of these periphrases is the fact that, as the examples show, the clitic pronouns may either precede or follow, whereas a clitic may only attach to a past participle when the auxiliary is not present: *ci è arrivato* 'he has arrived there', *è arrivatoci but *arrivatoci* 'having arrived there'.

The interrelation of the periphrastic *ha cantato* and the inflectional *cantò* and *cantava* is perhaps the central issue in the analysis of aspect in Italian. The conventional view is that the last of these — the so-called imperfect — expresses an incomplete or habitual action ('he was singing' or 'he used to sing'), while the former two refer instead to single completed actions. The difference between them in turn involves the recentness of the events described and their relevance to the current situation. Hence, the native term *passato remoto* ('remote past') for *cantò* parallel to the already cited *passato prossimo* ('near past') for *ha cantato*. However, the imperfect is often found, particularly with verbs of mental state — *non sapeva cosa dirmi ieri* 'he didn't know what to say to me yesterday' — and in journalism and less formal writing where traditional usage might require one of the other two forms. Thus, it has recently been argued that the imperfect is the unmarked past tense, deriving its precise value from the context, whereas both the perfect and the preterit have an inbuilt aspectual value. One advantage of this view is that it more easily accommodates the common, though by no means obligatory, progressive periphrasis *stava cantando* 'he was singing'. In the case of the preterit and the present perfect, the issue is further complicated by the fact that spoken usage varies considerably up and down the peninsula. Northern speakers rarely utter the preterit, so the perfect subsumes both the completed past and the current relevance senses (as generally in French, p. 228), while southern speakers often use only the preterit, and reserve the reflex of the Latin HABEO + past participle for a sense more like that in English 'I have the letter written' or Spanish *tengo preparada la cena* (p. 102). The traditional distinction lives on in central Italian (including Florentine and Roman) speech, but northern influence is strong even here and may eventually come to predominate.

One question not treated in the preceding discussion concerns the choice of auxiliary verb in constructing the perfect periphrasis. There are four possibilities: (a) some verbs always take *avere* — e.g. *ho pensato* 'I have thought', *ha viaggiato* 'he has travelled', *abbiamo letto il libro* 'we have read the book'; (b) others always take *essere* — *è uscita* 'she has (lit. is) gone out', *è morto* 'he has died'; (c) some take either auxiliary, but with more or less discernible differences of sense — *hanno aumentato il prezzo* 'they have increased the price', but *è aumentato il prezzo* 'the price has gone up'; *ha corso* 'he has run (= done some running)' vs *è corso* 'he has run (= gone by running)'; (d) a very small number of verbs, particularly weather verbs, take either auxiliary with no difference of meaning — *è/ha piovuto* 'it has rained'. Crucial to an understanding of the process of auxiliary selection is an appreciation of the semantic relation between the subject and the verb. If the subject is the agent or the experiencer (for a verb of mental state), then the auxiliary is *avere*; hence type (a) regardless of whether the verb is transitive or intransitive. If the subject is more neutrally involved in the activity or state defined by the verb — in traditional terms a patient — then the auxiliary is *essere*. Such verbs will by definition be intransitive — *andare* 'to go', *salire* 'to go up', *morire* 'to die', *ingiallire* 'to turn yellow, wither' (contrast *nuotare* 'to swim', *viaggiare* 'to travel' with *avere*). If a verb can take two different types of subject — *aumentare* 'to increase', *correre* 'to run', *crescere* 'to grow', *procedere* 'to proceed' (with patient subject and *essere*) vs *procedere* 'to behave' (with agent subject and *avere*), then it can take both auxiliaries. If the distinction between agent and patient is not valid for certain types of activity/state, then either auxiliary may be chosen indifferently — *piovere* 'to rain', *vivere* 'to live'. A final point to note here is that if the infinitive following a modal verb (*dovere* 'to have to', *potere* 'to be able', or *volere* 'to want') would independently take *essere*, then by a process of auxiliary attraction the modal itself, which would normally take *avere*, may take *essere*: either *ho dovuto uscirne* or *sono dovuto uscirne* 'I had to go out of there'. If the clitics precede the modal, then this process of auxiliary attraction becomes obligatory: *ci sono potuto andare* 'I could go there' and not **ci ho potuto andare*. Both the clitic movement and the auxiliary change suggest, therefore, that such sentences have been, to use the recently coined term, 'restructured' and contain a single complex verb rather than two separate verbal elements. In other words they behave more like auxiliary + verb

combinations such as *ho mangiato* 'I have eaten' than verb + verb groups
like *decise di farlo* 'he decided to do it'.

Patient as subject not only identifies *essere*-taking verbs but is of course
the time-honoured way of characterising the passive voice, and it is not
coincidental that *essere* is also the auxiliary in the passive construction: *gli
svedesi vinceranno la battaglia* 'the Swedes will win the battle', *la battaglia
sarà vinta dagli svedesi* 'the battle will be won by the Swedes'. In fact, if we
regard the subject of *essere* as itself being a patient (i.e. having a neutral
role as the person/thing/etc. about which predications are made), then we
can achieve a unified explanation of why (a) it takes *essere* as its own
auxiliary; (b) it is the active auxiliary of the appropriate subclass of intransitives and the passive auxiliary of all transitives; (c) the other two verbs
which enter into passive periphrases are also patient subject verbs. The first
of these is *venire* 'to come', which may be regularly substituted for *essere* to
distinguish an 'action' from a 'state' passive. Thus, *la bandiera veniva/era
issata all'alba* 'the flag was hoisted at dawn', but only *essere* in *in quel
periodo la bandiera era issata per tutta la giornata* 'at that time the flag was
hoisted (i.e. remained aloft) all day' (cf. Rhaeto-Romance where *vegni* 'to
come' is the normal and often only passive auxiliary, see p. 364). The
second is *andare* 'to go', which combines with the past participle to express
the meaning 'must be V-ed', e.g. *questo problema va risolto subito* 'this
problem must be solved at once'. One interesting morphosyntactic
restriction is that neither *andare* nor *venire* can occur in these functions in
their compound forms, whereas *essere* of course can. Curiously, *andare*
does occur as a compound auxiliary in *la casa è andata distrutta* 'the house
was (lit. is gone) destroyed', but then there is no sense of obligation and the
construction is limited to verbs of loss and destruction.

Essere is also the auxiliary for all reflexives: *Maria si è criticata* 'Mary
criticised herself'. Since a reflexive is only a transitive verb where agent and
patient happen to be identical, one might expect to find *avere*, as indeed
one sometimes does in Old Italian and in some, notably southern, dialects.
However, another very frequent use of the reflexive construction is as a
kind of passive. Thus, in *le finestre si sono rotte* 'the windows got broken
(lit. broke themselves)' the sentence is formally reflexive but the subject is
patient rather than agent (contrast the non-reflexive in *Giorgio ha rotto le
finestre* 'George has broken the windows'). Furthermore, since patient subject verbs and constructions in Italian frequently have post-verbal subjects
(see below), we also have the possibility of *si sono rotte le finestre*, a
structure which is susceptible to an alternative analysis, viz: *si* (su.) V *le
finestre* (obj.). Evidence that such a reanalysis has taken place comes from
the fact that, colloquially at least, such sentences often have a singular verb:
si parla diverse lingue in quel negozio 'several languages are spoken in that
shop', and from the extension of the construction to intransitive verbs of all
kinds: *si parte domani* 'one is leaving tomorrow', *si dorme bene in cam-*

pagna 'one sleeps well in the country'. Indeed, it is even possible, quite unlike in the apparently parallel construction in Spanish (p. 110), to have the so-called impersonal *si* in combination with a reflexive verb: *ci si lava(no) le mani prima di mangiare* 'one washes one's hands before eating' (where *ci* is a morphophonemic variant of *si* before *si*).

These two *si*'s (impersonal and reflexive) take different positions in clitic sequences (cf. the chart on p. 291): *lo si dice* 'one says it', *se lo dice* 'he says it to himself', and hence with both present we find *ce lo si dice* 'one says it to oneself'. Notice too that if *si* in impersonal constructions is taken as subject, then examples like *si rilegano libri* 'one binds books' have to be construed as involving object agreement on the verb. Subject *si* is also unusual in that in predicative constructions while the verb is singular, following adjectives, participles and predicate nominals are plural: *si è ricchi* (m. pl.) 'one is rich', *si è usciti* 'one has gone out', *quando si è attrici* (f. pl.) 'when one is an actress'. That this is more generally a characteristic of indefinite subjects rather than specifically a property of *si* can be seen from examples with impersonal verbs like *bisogna essere sicuri* 'it is necessary to be sure'. When impersonal *si* is found with a verb which normally requires *avere*, the auxiliary becomes *essere*, as with reflexive *si*, but the past participle does not agree: *si è partiti* 'one has left' vs *si è detto* 'one has said'.

Object agreement is obligatory with third person clitics but not, in the modern language at least, with full NPs: *ho trovato Maria* 'I've found Mary' vs *l'ho trovata* 'I've found her'. Examples like *ho vista la dama* 'I saw the lady' abound in earlier periods. The partitive clitic *ne* also triggers agreement: *ne hanno mangiati tre* 'they have eaten three of them (m. pl.)' (contrast French *en*). With first and second person pronouns, usage varies; either *ci ha visto* or *ci ha visti* 'he saw us' is acceptable.

The last verbal category which we shall treat is that of mood. The Italian subjunctive has retained from Latin not only clear formal marking (see section 3), but also substantial semantic motivation. Note first pairs such as the following which were also typical of Latin and which find ready analogues in the other Romance languages: *Pietro vuole sposare una ragazza che ha* (ind.)/ *abbia* (subj.) *studiato l'astrofisica* 'Peter wants to marry a girl who has (ind./subj.) studied astrophysics'. The indicative tells us there is a particular girl, one of whose attributes is that she has studied astrophysics; with the subjunctive we know only what Peter considers to be the desirable quality in a future wife, but not whether such a person exists. These bring out most clearly the function of the subjunctive as denying, putting in doubt or suspending judgement on the independent existence of the state of affairs referred to in the relevant proposition. Italian, unlike a number of the other Romance languages, has retained this role for the subjunctive in all its uses. Thus, compare *si dice che sia morto il re* 'they say the king is (subj.) dead' and *il ministro ha annunciato che è morto il re* 'the minister has announced that the king is (ind.) dead'. The subjunctive, then, is mandatory in complement clauses of verbs which express attitudes towards possible, desired, feared, etc. situations rather than assert that such situations actually obtain: *voglio/temo/spero che il treno sia in ritardo* 'I want/fear/hope that the train is late'. With other verbs a contrast emerges: *se pensi che ha soltanto dodici anni* 'if you think (= bear in mind) that he is only twelve' vs *se pensi che abbia soltanto dodici anni* 'if you think (= believe) that he is only twelve'. Likewise the subjunctive is appropriate after a negated verb: *capisco perché l'ha fatto* 'I understand why he did it' but *non capisco perché l'abbia fatto* 'I don't understand why he did it'; and after conjunctions that introduce an element of doubt or futurity: *prima che il gallo canti* 'before the cock crows', *benché Giorgio sia partito* 'although George has left', *lavora sodo perché lo si paga bene* 'he works hard because they pay him well' vs *lavora sodo perché lo si paghi bene* 'he works hard so that they pay him well' Similarly in conditionals, subjunctives are used in unlikely or impossible conditions: *se le elezioni si tenessero oggi ...* 'if the elections were held today ...', *se avesse potuto sarebbe scappato la sera stessa* 'if he had been able to, he would have escaped that very evening'.

The foregoing should suffice to demonstrate that the subjunctive is a semantically productive category in modern Italian. However, it is undoubtedly used less widely in colloquial registers, where it tends to be replaced by the conditional. Examples like *se verrebbero ci aiuterebbero* 'if they came (lit. would come) they would help us' are commonly heard, though generally regarded as substandard. Interestingly, in Sicilian and some other southern dialects where a conditional verb form has not emerged historically, the converse pattern of two past subjunctives is found, as it had been in Latin: Sic. *vivissi si ci fussi acqua* 'I would drink if there was any water'. Indeed, in such dialects subjunctives regularly take the place of simple main clause uses of the conditional: Campano *chi l'essə mai ditto?* 'who would have said it?' *mə facissi nu piacerə?* 'would you do me a favour?'.

Particularly surprising, given the usual semantics of such verb forms, is the originally popular and dialectal but now entirely acceptable use of two imperfect indicatives in impossible conditionals of the form: *se mi lasciavi lassù, era tanto meglio* 'if you had left me up there, it would have been a lot better'.

The Sentence

In this section we shall be concerned with two principal topics: word order in the simple sentence and the structure of complementation. As regards the former, if we assume a traditional division of the sentence, we find both the orders subject + predicate and predicate + subject attested: *Pietro fumava una sigaretta* 'Peter was smoking a cigarette' and *è arrivato il treno* 'the train has arrived'. To understand what distinguishes the two we need to adduce the concepts of theme (= what is being talked about) and rheme (= what is being said about the theme), and a general ordering principle for Italian to the effect that the theme precedes the rheme. In the unmarked case, a subject which identifies the agent/experiencer of the activity/state expressed by the verb will constitute the theme, and will accordingly come first. The rheme will consist of the verb plus, where appropriate, an object whose interpretation follows directly from the meaning of the verb, what we have earlier called a patient. Thus, SV(O) is a natural order for sentences with any transitive and some intransitive verbs in Italian. This generalisation will hold for most complex sentences if, as seems reasonable, we extend the notion object to include the sentential and infinitival complements of the verb, again where appropriate. If, however, the subject is rhematic with respect to the verb, as it will be if its semantic verb is patient, then it will normally follow. Hence, the characteristic post-verbal subjects in the *essere*-taking constructions discussed above: *verrà Giorgio* 'George will come' (taking the 'mover' as patient with a verb of motion), *domani saranno riaperti il porto e l'aeroporto* 'tomorrow the docks and the airport will be reopened', *si svolgeva il dibattito* 'the debate took place'. In suitable circumstances and with suitable intonation the basic patterns can be reversed, but that does not alter the fact that the position of the subject in Italian is not fixed but depends on its semantic relation to the verb (cf. the discussion of Latin word order, pp. 61–2). Moving the object from its post-verbal position is, by contrast, less easy and normally requires a pronominal copy: *quel libro non lo legge nessuno* 'that book nobody reads'. Similarly, it is rare and decidedly rhetorical for the subject to be interposed between verb and object. Adverbs and subcategorised adjectives, on the other hand, regularly separate verb and noun: *parla bene l'italiano* 'he speaks Italian well', *il professore ha fatto felici tutti gli studenti* 'the teacher made all the students happy'.

   The possibility of post-verbal subjects with *essere*-taking verbs and the general optionality of pronominal subjects have been linked in the recent generative literature with another detail of Italian syntax, namely the fact that sentences such as *chi credi che verrà?* 'who do you think will come?' are grammatical (contrast the ungrammaticality of the literal English rendering *who do you think that will come?*). If such an example was derived from an intermediate (in a synchronic sense) structure like *credi che verrà chi?*, then Italian and English both agree in being able to extract from a post-verbal position (cf. English *who do you think that Fred saw?*), but differ in what may occupy that position. Specifically, English puts all its subjects before their respective verbs and so the accessible category for questions is only objects of transitive verbs, whereas Italian locates all patients post-verbally and therefore what are accessible are objects of transitives and subjects of the relevant type of intransitives. Within the broader spectrum of Romance, French seems to behave rather (but not completely) like English, while many northern Italian dialects behave in the same way as standard Italian, even when they have clitic pronouns in subject position. In addition to suggesting some interesting hypotheses for future research about the evolution of the category clitic in Romance and its grammatical function, observations of this kind make it clear that the so-called null-subject or pro-drop parameter which distinguishes English and French on the one hand from Italian, Piedmontese, Rhaeto-Romance, etc. on the other has to be seen as a cluster of putatively related syntactic properties rather than as a simple choice between languages which have overt subjects and those which do not (cf. also p. 384). Other diagnostics of null-subject languages include rightward agreement of the copula (*sono io* 'it's me' — contrast Fr. *c'est moi*), so-called 'long' *wh*-movement of the subject (*l'uomo che mi domando chi abbia visto* 'the man that I wonder who he saw' — cf. the ungrammaticality of the English gloss) and the possibility of an empty resumptive pronoun in embedded clauses (*ecco la ragazza che mi domando chi crede che vincerà* vs Eng. **there's the girl that I wonder who believes that she will win*). We may confidently expect the further development of ideas such as these to shed considerable light on the many understudied areas of diachronic and dialectal Italian syntax (cf. Chapter 10, section 4).

Turning our attention now to complementation structures, we begin by noting that in Italian, as in most other Romance languages — Rumanian is the notable exception (p. 441) — these may be classified into two general types: finite, involving the complementiser *che* plus a tensed clause, with a further choice of subjunctive vs indicative dictated by considerations already discussed (pp. 303–4), and infinitival, with again subclasses depending on whether the infinitive is introduced by *di*, *a* or zero: *il professore voleva promuovere tutti gli studenti* 'the teacher wanted to pass all the students', *Paolo ha deciso di venire* 'Paul has decided to come', *mi sono azzardato a parlare* 'I dared to speak'. These patterns yield in part to an analysis in terms of grammatical relations. Where the infinitive clause is the subject of the matrix predicate, no linking particle is required: *è necessario tornare presto* 'it is necessary to come back early', *mi piace bere il vino* 'I like drinking wine' (literally 'to drink wine pleases me'). When the (unexpressed) subject of the infinitive (often labelled PRO) is coreferential to the subject, object or indirect object of the controlling verb, the two are linked by either *di* or *a*. The rationale for the choice of particle is not always easy to discern, but some tendencies can be stated. For example, *di* is generally found with verbs of assertion, belief, etc.: e.g. *dire* 'to say', *ammettere* 'to admit', *ricordare* 'to remember', *sapere* 'to know that' (contrast *sapere* + infinitive 'to know how to'), *credere* 'to believe', *promettere* 'to promise', *sperare* 'to hope', *pretendere* 'to claim', etc. In general, with such verbs, *di* + infinitive and an unexpressed subject is in complementary distribution with *che* + a full sentence with an overt subject: e.g. *sa che pioverà* 'he knows it's going to rain' vs *sa di aver sbagliato* 'he knows he's made a mistake'. The alternation between *di* and *che* is parallel to that found with certain adverbs and prepositions: e.g. *prima di venire* 'before coming', *prima che tu venga* 'before you come'. On the other hand, *a* is usually found when the matrix verb expresses an action that is preliminary or preparatory to that expressed by the dependent infinitive: *forzare* 'to force', *apprestarsi* 'to get ready', *incoraggiare* 'to encourage', *invitare* 'to invite', *convincere* 'to persuade', *aspirare* 'to aspire', *mandare* 'to send', etc. As one might expect, if a matrix verb can be construed in both ways, then minimal pairs with *di* and *a* result: e.g. *lo ha persuaso a dimettersi* 'they persuaded him to resign' (the persuasion precedes the resignation) but *lo hanno persuaso di essere innocenti* 'they persuaded him that they were innocent' (cf. *hanno detto di essere innocenti* 'they said they were innocent') and *lo hanno persuaso che Giorgio era innocente* 'they persuaded him that George was innocent'. (See pp. 68–9 for a discussion of the Latin background to these patterns.) A slightly different type of minimal contrast can be seen in the following: *Paolo sembra aver capito* 'Paul seems to have understood', *sembra a Paolo di aver capito* 'it seems to Paul that he has understood', *sembra a Paolo che Maria abbia capito* 'it seems to Paul that Mary has understood'. We may note again the alternation between *di* + infinitive and *che* + S, but this time the third structure involves a 'raising' verb in which *Paolo* is the grammatical subject of *sembra* but only contracts a semantic relation with the infinitive *aver capito*. Although the foregoing cannot for obvious reasons of space claim to be a full treatment of Italian complement structures, and despite the existence of occasional difficult cases — e.g. *provare a fare* roughly equivalent to Eng. 'to try doing' but *cercare di fare* close to Eng. 'to try to do', there is every reason to believe that the vast majority of infinitival complementation patterns can be brought within the scope of a set of semantico-syntactic rules of the kind just sketched.

In addition to the cases already mentioned, the 'bare' infinitive also occurs after modal verbs such as *dovere* 'to have to', *volere* 'to want' and *potere* 'to be able to', and a handful of others such as *preferire* 'to prefer', *osare* 'to dare'. One special case is the combination of verb plus infinitive in the causative construction: e.g. *la crisi fece cadere il governo* 'the crisis caused the government to fall'. Here *fare* adds its own subject, the 'causer', to the arguments of the infinitive to produce a complex verb. What would have been the subject of the verb in the infinitive — *il governo* in the example given — thus becomes object. If the infinitive already has an object then the subject becomes indirect object: *abbiamo fatto chiudere la porta allo studente* 'we made the student close the door' (literally 'we made close the door to the student'). Evidence that we are dealing with a complex verb rather than two separate ones comes from the fact that if the arguments are pronominal rather than full NPs they must attach to *fare*. Hence, for the two examples already cited: *lo fece cadere* and *gliela abbiamo fatto chiudere*. This process of clitic 'climbing' takes place even if it formally converts the causative into a reflexive and provokes an attendant auxiliary change: *si è fatto dare un aumento di stipendio* 'he got himself given a rise'. This absolute prohibition on clitics attached to the infinitive distinguishes the Italian causative from the apparently similar construction found elsewhere in Romance, as does the fact that the causative complex may be directly passivised: *lo fecero entrare* 'they made him go in' and *fu fatto entrare* 'he was made to go in'. (On the historical origin of the causative, see pp. 69–70.)

5   Lexis

It might seem the most self-evident of truths to say that, with due allowance for neologisms and borrowings, the bulk of the vocabulary of Italian derives from Latin. There are, however, a variety of routes by which words of Latin origin may join the lexical stock of modern Italian. First and most obvious are the cases of direct continuity, where the standard Latin word for a given concept persists, the vicissitudes of phonological and morphological change apart, until the present day. Thus, Lat. CORPUS 'body' may change gender and declension class and undergo phonetic shifts but it is recognisably the same item with the same meaning that we find in It. *corpo* (and also in Fr. *corps*, Sp. *cuerpo*, Port. *corpo*, Sard. *korpus*, etc.). Other common terms of direct descent, and general Romance cognateness, are: *mano* 'hand', *legge* 'law', *piovere* 'to rain', *pugno* 'fist', *scrivere* 'to write', *venire* 'to come'. Examples of words that have survived directly from Latin, but where most or all of the other languages have innovated are: *faccia* 'face (body-part)', *vicolo* 'alley', *ogni* 'every', *chiudere* 'to close'. A different kind of direct inheritance is involved in the case of Lat. TESTA 'pot', which survives as It. *testa* 'head'. The formal continuity is clear, but the meaning testifies to a semantic development in colloquial Latin (cf. Fr. *tête*, and for the same semantic relation between cognates, Eng. *cup* vs German *Kopf* 'head'). Already the complexity of the Italian situation emerges. On the one hand, the Latin word for the body part, CAPUT, still survives in the sense of 'senior person', e.g. *capostazione* 'station-master', *capo* 'boss', and with the meaning of beginning, as in the musical term *da capo*. Note, however, that other transferred senses require *testa*: e.g. *in testa a* 'on top of (a list or league-table)', *intestazione* 'letterhead'. On the other hand, *capo* is the normal anatomical term in most dialects of southern Italy and Sicily (cf. also Cat., Occ., Rum. *cap*), and this creates the possibility that southerners, even when clearly speaking Italian and not dialect, may transfer the dialect meaning to the standard form. Such cases, known as semantic regionalisms, considerably complicate the task of describing Italian vocabulary. Some further examples are set out opposite:

Lexical item	Standard meaning	Regional meaning	
catenaccio	bolt	padlock	(Sicily)
spingere	to push	to lift	(Sicily)
esperto	skilled	shrewd	(Sicily)
cascare	to fall	to happen	(Bologna)
bagaglio	luggage	gadget	(Bologna)
addobbare	to decorate	to satisfy	(Calabria)
spandere	to spread	to drip	(Calabria)
chiamare	to call	to ask	(Piedmont)
arrivare	to arrive	to happen	(Piedmont)
osso	bone	(fruit)stone	(Veneto)

Another Calabrianism, *imbattere* 'to happen', provides an interesting extra complication in that the standard language only has the reflexive *imbattersi* 'to meet by chance, to come across'. The regionalism therefore fits a sort of natural gap in the language.

Dialects may also serve to pass words to the standard language by the more familiar mechanism of borrowing. The nowadays international word *ciao* derives from the Venetian form of the salutation (*vostro*) *schiavo* 'your servant' (the palatalisation by secondary /i/ and the loss of the inter-vocalic consonant are typical Venetian sound changes). Likewise the verb referring to handbag-snatching by thieves mounted on scooters, *scippare*, derives from a southern dialectalism meaning 'to pull'. Others such include *teppista* 'thug, hooligan' (from Milanese), *grana* 'generic name for hard cheeses of the parmesan type' (from Lombardy), *cafone* 'yob' (from Abruzzi), *largo* 'small square' (from Naples).

Of course, in one sense all Italian words might be considered dialect-alisms, since the standard language is fundamentally Tuscan, or more specifically, Florentine, in origin (see pp. 18–19). It is worth noting, therefore, some of the many cases where the contemporary Tuscan term bears a markedly regional or archaic flavour, and where the more usual word in national usage, e.g. in the media, has a different source. Thus, *formaggio* 'cheese' is in origin northern (cf. Fr. *fromage*), while the more directly inherited and increasingly less used *cacio* (< CASEUM) is the indigenous term south of the Appennines. Other instances are:

	Standard	Tuscan
manure	letame	concio
to divide	dividere	partire
crust (of bread)	crosta	corteccia
to pick up	raccogliere	raccattare
to hire/rent	affittare	appigionare

A curious case is the Tuscan word *pigliare* 'to take', which is nowadays used throughout Italy as a colloquial equivalent to *prendere*, but which also has the ring of a literary archaism in early prose and poetry.

The foregoing discussion presupposes that it is both feasible and reasonable to identify certain items as belonging to the standard language, implying that, within limits, if one were to attempt to elicit say the word for the concept 'run' from speakers from Turin to Taranto and from Trieste to Trapani, the answer would always be *correre* (due allowance being made for regional phonetics). While this does not seem intuitively implausible in many cases, on the one occasion on which an empirical study of this kind was carried out, by Rüegg in the early '50s, only one of the 242 concepts investigated, 'strong black coffee served in a bar', had a common designation for the 124 informants from 54 provinces, namely *espresso*! It can, of course, hardly be the case that there is no other common vocabulary in the whole of the pensinsula, but what this result does highlight is the fact that for many everyday items there may indeed be no nationally available term. For example, the kind of bread roll that many Italians eat with their *espresso* at breakfast time is called a *brioche* in the northern half of the pensinsula and a *cornetto* from Rome southwards. The number of different names for a plumber is legendary: *idraulico* is probably the nearest to a national term, but we also find *fontaniere, lattoniere, lanternaio, trombaio, stagnaio, stagnaro, stagnino*. To put variation of this kind, which is only the tip of an iceberg, in perspective, it is worth recording that a recent dictionary of Calabrian dialects listed 91 words for 'see-saw', while the standard term *altalena* is ambiguous, meaning both 'see-saw' and 'swing'!

Apart from through the complex interaction of regional and national forms that we have just described, Latin words may enter Italian as a result of borrowing from external sources. There are three possibilities, the first of which is direct borrowing from Latin itself, as the international vehicle of learning and religion, from the Middle Ages on. Such borrowings, often dubbed learned forms, can usually be identified by their failure to undergo many of the normal sound changes, though, as with all loan words, there is generally some concession to the different phonetic restrictions of the receiving language. Some examples are set out below:

Latin	Inherited ('popular') form	Borrowed ('learned') form
AUGUSTUS	agosto 'August'	augusto 'noble'
CAUSA	cosa 'thing'	causa 'cause'
FRIGIDUS	freddo 'cold'	frigido 'frigid'
PLATEA	piazza 'square'	platea 'stall (in a theatre)'
VITIUM	vezzo 'habit'	vizio 'vice'

A second possibility is that Latin words may come to Italian as loan words from other Romance languages, in particular French and Spanish. French has influenced Italian over a long period, either because of cultural contacts and prestige or because of military presence in the peninsula, and French loans range from the everyday (*mangiare* 'to eat', *giallo* 'yellow', *mestiere* 'job') to the technical (*destriere* 'charger', *chilogrammo, omelette*), from the early (*viaggio* 'journey', *conte* 'count', *bandiera* 'flag', all from before the fourteenth century) down the centuries (*approccio* 'approach' sixteenth century, *parrucca* in the sense of 'wig' seventeenth century, *toilette* eighteenth century, *burocratico* nineteenth century) to the modern (*roulotte* 'caravan', *boutique*). Of course, not all of these and other such items are Latin in origin, and some which are were actually learned forms in French (*appello* 'roll-call', *ambulanza* 'ambulance'). In the case of Spanish loans, we find a variety of words referring principally to cultural and social practices (*bolero, toreador, sussiego* 'hautiness', *etichetta* 'etiquette', and perhaps under this heading too *compleanno*, the usual Italian word for 'birthday'). A more recent kind of Spanish cultural prestige is testified to in the term for a prolific goal scorer in football, *goleador*.

The final way a Latin form might add itself to the lexical resources of Italian would be as a borrowing from a non-Romance language. There are many of these from English in the eighteenth and nineteenth centuries, such as *conformismo, radicale*, etc. English loans, of Latin or other origin, have been particularly frequent in the twentieth century, though many were removed as a result of government censorship in the Fascist period — thus football terms like *corner* and *goal* have largely been replaced by calques such as *calcio d'angolo* and *rete* 'net'. Where they have survived, they have often shown some more or less surprising semantic twists: *golf* means 'pullover', *night* 'nightclub', *box* 'garage' and *speaker* 'announcer'. English influence may also be traced in what might be called semantic Anglicisms such as *premio* in the sense of 'insurance premium' besides its inherited meaning 'prize'.

Other influential types of loans in Italian include Germanisms, especially in the late Latin period (see p. 76) and Arabisms such as *dogana* 'customs', *zecca* 'mint', *ragazzo* 'boy' (originally 'stable-lad'), *albicocco* 'apricot', *sciroppo* 'syrup'. Naturally these are more extensive in dialects spoken in the areas of greatest historical contact — Sicily and southern Italy for Arabic, Lombardy and the Veneto for Germanic, Piedmont for French, but documentation of these possibilities would take us too far afield.

Suffixes
We cannot conclude this section without mentioning the extensive use Italian makes, in the matter of word formation, of affective suffixes relating to the size and to the speaker's (dis)approval of the object in question. Thus, from *ragazzo* 'boy', we have *ragazzino, ragazzetto, ragazzuccio* 'little boy', *ragazzone* 'big lad', *ragazzaccio* 'nasty boy, lout', *ragazzotto* 'sturdy lad'. The chief analytical problem is that not all suffixes combine with all nouns, yet no clear rules are discernible for predicting the possible combinations: *-ello* is a diminutive but **ragazzello* cannot be used for 'little boy'. Sometimes too a noun plus suffix has acquired independent status as a lexical item: *pane* 'bread', *panetto* 'a small loaf', *panino* 'a bread roll' and

panettone (etymologically containing two contradictory suffixes *-ett-* 'small' and *-one* 'large') refers to a special kind of fruit cake eaten at Christmas. This process is reminiscent of the way certain items of Italian vocabulary are derived from Latin diminutives — e.g. Lat. FRATER 'brother', but It. *fratello* < FRATELLUM (see p. 74). These suffixes are most commonly attached to nouns, but can also be used with other categories: adjectives — *facile* 'easy', *facilino* 'quite easy', *caro* 'dear', *caruccio* 'quite expensive' (but note *carino* 'pretty'); adverbs — *bene* 'well', *benone* 'very well', *benino* 'quite well'; verbs — *dormire* 'to sleep', *dormicchiare* 'to snooze', *sputare* 'to spit', *sputacchiare* 'to splutter'.

Suffixes too may enter into many of the forms of borrowing and regional influence discussed above with respect to fully fledged lexical items. Thus, Sicilianisms such as *piattini* 'cymbals', *affumare* 'to smoke (meat, fish, etc.)', stand in local usage beside the more usual standard forms *piatti* and *affumicare*. In other instances, a single Latin suffix may have two different regional forms, as when -ACEUM, -UCEUM gives *-azzo, -uzzo* in the north and *-accio, -uccio* in the south, or -ARIUM becomes *-aio* in Tuscany and *-aro* elsewhere. The same suffix may also have a learned and a non-learned form, hence *-ezza* from Lat. -ITIAM in words of direct inheritance (*tristezza* 'sadness', *ebbrezza* 'drunkenness') and *-izia* in Latin borrowings (*avarizia* 'greed', *astuzia* 'astuteness'). Finally, a suffix may increase its range through borrowing from a cognate language as with the many French loans in *-aggio, -iere* (*coraggio* 'courage', *omaggio* 'homage', *cavaliere* 'knight', *scudiere* 'squire') and with the Provençalisms in early poetry in *-e/anza* (*doglienza* 'suffering', *intendanza* 'understanding', *rimembranza* 'remembering').

6 Conclusion

Italian, then, although in one sense a national language on a par with French, Spanish, Portuguese and Rumanian, has a rather special status vis-à-vis the dialects of the peninsula because of the lateness of political, and thence linguistic, unification. Some scholars, however, have been led to recognise a new type of national language, so-called *italiano popolare* 'popular Italian', a kind of nationwide substandard, a language which is neither the literary norm traditionally inculcated by the educational system nor yet a dialect tied to a particular town or region. Among the features which characterise it are: the extension of *gli* 'to him' to replace *le* 'to her' and *loro* 'to them' and the extension of *ci* to replace all three, and, relatedly, of *suo* 'his/her' to include 'their'; a reduction in the use of the subjunctive in complement clauses, where it is replaced by the indicative, and in conditional protases, where it is replaced by the conditional or the imperfect indicative; the use of *che* 'that' as a general marker or subordination; plural instead of singular verbs after nouns like *gente* 'people'. Not surprisingly these traits are all (morpho-)syntactic: regionally inspired variation is still strong at the lexical and phonological levels, though it is by no means absent in (morpho-)syntax as well. Some of these uses — e.g. *gli* for *loro*, the reduction in the use of the subjunctive, and the use of the imperfect in irrealis conditionals — have also begun to penetrate upwards into educated colloquial usage, and it is likely that forces for linguistic unification such as the media, conscription and the effects of industrialisation will spread other emergent patterns in due course. Meanwhile dialects, though recessive in many areas, are by no means moribund, and their developing relations with the standard — one of the subthemes of this chapter — will certainly be a fascinating topic for future study.

Bibliography

Albano Leoni, F. (ed.) (1979) *I dialetti e le lingue delle minoranze di fronte all'italiano* 2 vols. Bulzoni, Rome.
Bertinetto, P.M. (1981) *Strutture prosodiche dell'italiano*. Accademia della Crusca, Florence.
—— (1986) *Tempo, aspetto e azione nel verbo italiano*. Accademia della Crusca, Florence.
Brunet, J. (1978-) *Grammaire critique de l'italien*. (8 vols. of projected 12 published to date.) Université de Paris VII, Vincennes.
Burzio, L. (1986) *Italian Syntax*. Reidel, Dordrecht.
Chapallaz, M. (1979) *The Pronunciation of Italian*. Bell and Hyman, London.
Cortelazzo, M. (1969-) *Avviamento alla dialettologia italiana*. (2 vols of projected 4 to date.) Pacini, Pisa.
—— and P. Zolli (1979-) *Dizionario etimologico della lingua italiana*. (4 vols. of projected 5 — reaching letter R — published to date.) Zanichelli, Bologna.
De Mauro, T. (1983) *Storia linguistica dell' Italia unita* 8th edn. Laterza, Bari.
Devoto, G. (1968) *Avviamento alla etimologia italiana*. Le Monnier, Florence.
Fogarasi, M. (1983) *Grammatica italiana del Novecento* 2nd edn. Bulzoni, Rome.
Lepschy, A.L. and G.C. Lepschy (1977) *The Italian Language Today*. Hutchinson, London. Revised Italian version: *La lingua italiana*. Bompiani, Milan, 1981.
Migliorini, B and T.G. Griffith (1984) *The Italian Language* 2nd edn. Faber and Faber, London. English translation/adaptation of B. Migliorini, *Storia della lingua italiana*. Sansoni, Florence, 1960.
Muljačić, Z. (1972) *Fonologia della lingua italiana*. il Mulino, Bologna.
—— (1982) *Introduzione allo studio della lingua italiana* 2nd edn. Einaudi, Turin.
Rizzi, L. (1982) *Issues in Italian Syntax*. Foris, Dordrecht.
Rohlfs, G. (1966-9) *Grammatica storica della lingua italiana e dei suoi dialetti* 3 vols. Einaudi, Turin.
Schwarze, C. (ed.) (1983-) *Bausteine für eine italienische Grammatik*. (2 vols. of projected 3 published to date.) Gunter Narr Verlag, Tübingen.
Tekavčić, P. (1980) *Grammatica storica della lingua italiana* 2nd edn, 3 vols. il Mulino, Bologna.
Zingarelli, N. (1983) *Vocabolario della lingua italiana* 11th edn. Zanichelli, Bologna.

9 Sardinian

Michael Jones

1 Introduction

Sardinian can be defined, roughly, as the language spoken by the indigenous inhabitants of the island of Sardinia. However, there are two main provisos which must be appended to this definition.

Firstly, although Sardinian is not spoken outside Sardinia (except by emigrants), there are areas which do not share the linguistic traditions of the rest of the island — notably Alghero on the north-west coast (where Catalan is spoken) and the offshore communities of Carloforte and Calasetta off the south-west coast (Ligurian) (cf. pp. 20, 315). Also the dialects of Gallura and Sassari (spoken along the northern coast) can be classified as varieties of Italian, though they show some affinities with Sardinian. Gallurese is a variety of Southern Corsican whereas Sassarese is a hybrid dialect which evolved during the Middle Ages as a result of the close contact between the native Sardinian population of Sassari and the maritime powers of Pisa and Genoa. The above-mentioned dialects are not dealt with in this account.

Secondly, although the dialects of Sardinia (other than those mentioned above) are sufficiently distinct from the other Romance languages to warrant the status of a separate language, there are significant differences among them (particularly with respect to phonology and morphology). Moreover, there is no single dialect which is recognised as a standard form of the language and there is no standard orthography. Sardinian has not enjoyed any official status since the Middle Ages, a privilege currently held within the island by Italian and, previously, by Catalan and Spanish. There are few written texts in contemporary Sardinian (apart from dialect poetry, whose language tends to be rather artificial), the language being used mainly for informal oral communication.

Sardinian is generally acknowledged to be the most conservative of the Romance languages. This conservatism is reflected in two ways: the preservation of many archaic features of Latin which are not found in other Romance languages and the absence of any significant influence from non-Romance languages.

The first of these characteristics can be attributed to the fact that Sardinia was one of the first areas outside the Italian peninsula to be colonised by the Romans (238 BC) and to its early isolation from the rest of the Romance-speaking community. Although it is an established historical fact that Roman dominion over Sardinia lasted until the fifth century, it has been argued, on purely linguistic grounds, that linguistic contact with Rome ceased much earlier than this, possibly as early as the first century BC.

Following the collapse of the Roman Empire, Sardinia was exposed to various influences from outside the Romance-speaking world (Vandal occupation during the latter half of the fifth century and the beginning of the sixth century, Byzantine administration in the eighth and ninth centuries, periodic Arab incursions which lasted until the eleventh century), but these had little linguistic impact. Most non-Romance elements in Sardinian were either transmitted via other Romance languages or can be attributed to substratal influence.

Evidence from early manuscripts suggests that the language spoken throughout Sardinia (and indeed Corsica) at the end of the Dark Ages was fairly uniform and not very different from the dialects spoken today in the central (Nuorese) areas. The dialectal diversity of modern Sardinian is due largely to the influence of other Romance languages: initially Tuscan and Ligurian dialects and, later, Catalan and Spanish.

During the early Middle Ages (eleventh to fourteenth century) much of Sardinia came under Pisan or Genoan control, the principal centres being Sassari in the north and Cagliari in the south. The influence of Tuscan and Ligurian (predominantly the former) spread outwards from these centres, becoming weaker in the more remote areas, with the result that the central-eastern areas were relatively unaffected. Moreover, the innovations which were adopted in the south are significantly different from those found in the northern dialects.

Of the two languages introduced into Sardinia during the period of Hispanic rule (1326–1718), Catalan was the more influential, particularly in the south. The influence of Catalan and Spanish is most apparent in the domain of lexis (see p. 347), but may also have played a role in consolidating some phonological and morphological trends initially due to Tuscan influence (e.g. lenition of intervocalic consonants and, in the south, palatalisation of velar stops before front vowels and the decline of the imperfect subjunctive in favour of forms derived from the Latin pluperfect subjunctive).

For the purposes of this account, the dialects of Sardinian proper are divided into three major areas (see Map IX): Campidanese (spoken in the southern half of the island), Nuorese (central-eastern area) and Logudorese (northern-western area, except Gallura, Sassari and Alghero). The most radical differences are those which distinguish Campidanese from

Logudorese and Nuorese; indeed, some linguists classify the Nuorese dialects as subvarieties of Logudorese. It must be emphasised that these dialectal divisions are approximate. The various isoglosses in terms of which
the dialects are defined do not coincide exactly and there are others which
cut across the major divisions. Moreover, there are many subdivisions
within each of these areas. Consequently, references to dialect areas should
be taken as indicating that the phenomenon in question is concentrated
within the area specified, but not necessarily that it is wholly contained
within or spread throughout this area.

In order to reconcile the problem of dialectal variation with the need to
base synchronic analysis on a reasonably homogeneous linguistic system,
the following policy is adopted in this chapter. Section 2 gives a general
overview of the major phonological developments which characterise the
language as a whole with brief indications of the dialects in which they
occur. This section concludes with a study of the phonological system of a
single local dialect, a variety of Nuorese (as spoken in the village of Lula)
which is a fairly typical example of a conservative, rural dialect. The subsequent sections (morphology, syntax and lexis) are based primarily on the
Lula dialect, with brief comments on significant dialectal variations.

In the section on phonology, all examples are given in a broad phonetic
transcription, unless otherwise indicated. In the subsequent sections, in the
absence of a standard system of spelling, we have chosen to cite examples
in an orthography which corresponds broadly to the phonemic system of
the Lula dialect (as outlined at the end of section 2) but which ignores certain features which are not typical of Nuorese as a whole (e.g. elision of
initial /f/). In unclear cases, the choice of spelling is determined by etymology. An acute accent is used to indicate word-stress when this falls on a
syllable other than the penultimate and an apostrophe is used to indicate
that segments have been elided.

2   Phonology

The dialectal divisions illustrated in Map IX are based mainly on phonological criteria. The Logudorese and Nuorese dialects share many features
which distinguish them from Campidanese, particularly: maintenance of a
five-vowel system in all positions, absence of palatalisation of /k/ and /g/
before front vowels and partial neutralisation of /r/ and /s/ in word-final
position. They also differ from Campidanese in terms of the evolution of
glides and in the distribution of prothetic vowels. On the other hand, the
Nuorese dialects differ from both Campidanese and Logudorese with
respect to lenition or elision of intervocalic consonants.

Vowels
At the phonemic level, the Logudorese–Nuorese dialects have a classic

five-vowel system, with three levels of aperture and a front–back distinction for high and mid vowels, as shown in Table 9.1(a). All five vowels occur in all positions. Historically, this system results from the simple neutralisation of the Latin length distinction (p. 32). The mid vowels /ɛ/ and /ɔ/ are subject to a process of metaphony, whereby they raise to [e], [o] when the vowel of the following syllable is high (/i/ or /u/): /ˈsolu/ (< SŌLUM) 'alone' (m.), /ˈbeni/ (< VĒNI) 'come' but /ˈsɔla/ (< SŌLAM) 'alone' (f.), /ˈbɛnɛ/ (< BĔNE) 'well'. In the Logudorese–Nuorese dialects, the close and open variants of mid vowels are not phonemically distinct, the alternation between the two variants being conditioned entirely by the following vowel.

Table 9.1: Vowel Systems of Sardinian

(a) Logudorese–Nuorese (all positions)		(b) Campidanese (non-final syllables)		(c) Campidanese (final syllables)	
/i/	/u/	/i/	/u/	/i/	/u/
		/e/	/o/		
/ɛ/	/ɔ/				
		/ɛ/	/ɔ/		
	/a/		/a/		/a/

The same process occurs in the Campidanese dialects, but in some cases the conditioning factor is obscured, at the surface level, by neutralisation of mid and high vowels in final syllables. In Campidanese /ɛ/ and /ɔ/ are raised to /i/ and /u/ respectively in final syllables. However, this raising process does not give rise to mutation of the preceding vowel. Thus, in Campidanese we find /ˈbeni/ (< VĒNI) 'come', /ˈsolu/ (< SŌLUM) 'alone' but /ˈbɛni/ (< BĔNE) 'well', /ˈsɔli/ (< SŌLEM) 'sun'. Consequently, according to distributional criteria we can postulate seven vowel phonemes in Campidanese, reduced to a three-way contrast in final syllables, as shown in Table 9.1(b) and (c).

In all dialects, raising of mid vowels to high vowels (/ɛ/ > /i/, /ɔ/ > /u/) is frequent, though not systematic, in pretonic position: /griˈnuku/ (< GENŪCŬLUM) 'knee', /kunˈtɛntu/ (< CONTĔNTUM) 'happy'. The effects of this process are particularly apparent in the paradigms of certain verbs where displacement of stress leads to a change in the stem vowel: /ˈkɔkɔ/ vs /kuˈkimus/ (< CŎQUĔRE) 'I/we cook', /ˈɛssɔ/ vs /isˈsimus/ (< EXĪRE) 'I/we go out'.

Raising of /ɛ/ also occurs immediately before vowels, yielding /e/ in Logudorese–Nuorese but /i/ in Campidanese. Thus, the first person singular possessive forms (< MEUM, MEAM) are realised as /ˈmeu/, /ˈmea/ in Logudorese–Nuorese, /ˈmiu/, /ˈmia/ in Campidanese. Frequently, Lat. /o/ is raised to /u/ when preceded by a labial consonant or followed by /nd/: /ˈpustis/ (< PŎST) 'after', /ˈtundɛrɛ/ (< TŎNDĒRE) 'to shear', /funˈtana/ (< FONTĀNAM) 'fountain'.

Apart from the cases mentioned above, atonic vowels in Logudorese-Nuorese generally have the same quality as in Latin. However, in Campidanese atonic vowels are much less stable, giving rise to frequent cases of assimilation or dissimilation with much local (even idiolectal) variation: CĒNA PŪRA > (Log.-Nuor.) /kɛ'napura/, (Camp.) /ʧɛ'naβara/, /ʧa'naβra/ 'Friday'; CĔRĔBĔLLUM > (Log.-Nuor.) /kɛr'veḍḍu/, (Camp.) /ʧɛr'beḍḍu/, /ʧɔr'beḍḍu/ 'brain'. Generally, Latin atonic vowels, are retained in Sardinian, though syncopation occurs frequently before and after liquids (/l/ and /r/), as in the examples just cited, provided that the resulting consonant cluster conforms to normal phonotactic patterns (see below p. 326).

Diphthongs arise only as a result of elision of an intervocalic consonant: /'faula/ (< FABŬLAM) 'lie', /mei'kina/ (< MĔDĬCĪNAM) 'medicine'. There is no diphthongisation in words such as /'peðɛ/ (< PĔDEM) 'foot' and /'novu/ (< NŌVUM) 'new' — compare Italian *piede, nuovo*, p. 35. By the same token, the Latin diphthongs /ai/, /oi/ are reduced to /ɛ/, and /au/ to /a/: /'kelu/ (< CAELUM) 'sky', /'pɛna/ (< POENAM) 'punishment', /'paku/ (< PAUCUM) 'little, few'. Occasionally /au/ > /ɔ/, with /u/ as a variant in pretonic position: /o'rikra/, /u'rikra/ (> AURĬCULUM) 'ear'.

Nasal vowels occur in some varieties of Campidanese where intervocalic /n/ is elided (Western Campidanese) or replaced by a glottal stop (Villaputzu area) with compensatory nasalisation of the preceding vowel: /'bĩ(ʔ)u/ (< VĪNUM) 'wine', /'lũ(ʔ)a/ (< LŪNAM) 'moon'. Since these dialects also exhibit elision or glottalisation of other, non-nasal consonants in intervocalic position, the nasal/oral vowel distinction can be considered phonemic.

Consonants and Glides
Table 9.2 presents the consonant phonemes of the Lula variety of Nuorese whose phonological system is discussed at the end of this section (pp. 327–8). Parentheses indicate segments which occur only in loan words (mainly from Italian).

The Nuorese dialects as a whole have basically the same inventory except for the phoneme /v/ which occurs only in certain local dialects. Campidanese and Logudorese lack the phoneme /θ/, but have a set of voiced fricatives /β, ð, ɣ/ which function as lenis variants of /p, t, k/ but which nevertheless contrast with these voiceless stops for reasons which will be discussed below. In addition to such differences in the inventory of phonemes, there are many cases where a given phoneme occurs in all dialects but as a result of different historical processes, thus leading to different lexical distributions according to dialect. For example, the palato-alveolar affricates /ʧ/ and /ʤ/, which are restricted to loan words in Logudorese-Nuorese, occur in indigenous words in Campidanese: as palatalised variants of /k/ and /g/ and also as derivatives of certain Latin

Table 9.2: Consonant Phonemes

	Bilabial	Labiodental	Dental	Alveolar	Retroflex	Palato-alveolar	Palatal	Velar
Stops	p b		t d		ɖ			k g
Affricates				ts dz		(tʃ dʒ)		
Fricatives		f v	θ	s				
Nasals	m		n				(ɲ)	
Liquids				l r				
Glides	(w)						j	

consonant + glide sequences realised variously as /t/, /θ/, /dz/ or /j/ in Logudorese–Nuorese (see p. 324 for details). Moreover, there are many significant dialectal differences with respect to contextually governed phenomena such as elision, allophonic variation and partial neutralisation of phonemic oppositions.

In intervocalic position, stops and fricatives (except /θ/) undergo a process of lenition leading, in some cases, to elision. The general effects of this process in Sardinian are as follows:

(a) voiceless stop > voiced fricative;
(b) voiced stop > voiced fricative > Ø;
(c) voiceless fricative > voiced fricative.

It might appear that these would lead to large-scale neutralisations in intervocalic position since all three processes can yield voiced fricatives as their output. In practice this does not happen. Firstly, the dialects which show only the first stage of process (b) (fricativisation of voiced stops) do not allow process (a); conversely, the dialects which have process (a) typically exhibit the full extent (elision) of process (b). Thus within each of these dialect types the outputs of processes (a) and (b) are distinct. Secondly, stops are distinguished from fricatives in terms of their place of articulation, a distinction which is normally maintained under lenition. Thus /v/ and /z/ are lenis forms of fricatives (/f/ and /s/) whereas the lenis forms of underlying stops (voiced or voiceless according to dialect) are /β/, /ð/ and /ɣ/, though in some dialects /v/ functions as a lenis form of /b/. (Nuorese has a third voiceless fricative /θ/, but this consonant, as indicated earlier, never undergoes lenition and is thus ignored here; see p. 324).

Process (a) is restricted to Campidanese and Logudorese, where /p/ > /β/, /t/ > /ð/, /k/ > /ɣ/: /'aβε/ (< APEM) 'bee', /'luðu/ (< LŪTUM) 'mud', /'paɣu/ (< PAUCUM) 'little, few'. In Nuorese, voiceless stops are retained in intervocalic position: /'apε/, /'lutu/, /'paku/. In the dialect of Cagliari (a variety of Campidanese), intervocalic /t/ > /ɾ/ (alveolar flap): /nɛ'βɔɾi/ (< NEPŌTEM) 'nephew'.

Process (b) occurs in all dialects, though to different degrees. In Campidanese and Logudorese, elision is the norm, whereas in Nuorese intervocalic /b/, /d/ and /g/ are typically realised as fricatives: CABĂLLUM > Camp.–Log. /'kaɖɖu/, Nuor. /ka'βaɖɖu/ 'horse'; PĔDEM > Camp.–Log. /'pε(i)/, Nuor. /'pεðε/ 'foot'; SŪGERE > Camp. /'suiri/, Log. /'suεɾε/, Nuor. /'suɣεɾε/ 'to suck'. This generalisation is not absolute, however. In Campidanese and Logudorese a few words show fricativisation rather than elision: /'nuðu/ < NŪDUM 'naked', /'niðu/ < NĪDUM 'nest'. Conversely, in some Nuorese dialects elision of intervocalic voiced stops occurs in many words: /'nuε/ < NŪBEM 'cloud', /mei'kina/ <

MĔDĪCĪNAM 'medicine', /'jeo/ < ĒGO 'I'.

Process (c) applies in all dialects: TRĪFŎLIUM > Log.–Nuor. /tri'vudzu/, Camp. /tri'vullu/ 'clover'; RŎSAM > Log.–Nuor. /'rɔza/, Camp. /ar'rɔza/ 'rose'.

Stops and fricatives derived from Latin geminates or clusters do not undergo the processes described above. Thus, there is no lenition or elision in cases such as /'abba/ (< AQUAM) 'water', /'nuḍḍa/ (< NŪLLAM) 'nothing' and /'issa/ (< IPSAM) 'her'. Similarly, in Campidanese and Logudorese the voiceless stops are retained in words such as /'latɛ, -i/ (< LACTEM) 'milk' and /'baka/ (< VACCAM) 'cow'. The distinction between geminate and simple consonants in the Sardinian transcriptions given above is largely notational. In the first set of examples, /bb/, /ḍḍ/ and /ss/ are transcribed as geminates on the grounds that they appear to have a characteristically 'long' pronunciation, though this is difficult to establish with certainty since the effects of lenition/elision preclude direct comparison with the corresponding etymologically simple consonants in the same contexts. Consequently, their apparent geminate status may simply be a reflection of their failure to undergo lenition. On the other hand, the voiceless stops in the second set of examples do not appear to be phonetically geminate. In Nuorese, where direct comparison with etymologically simple segments is possible because of the inapplicability of process (a), intervocalic voiceless stops have the same pronunciation regardless of etymology; e.g. the /t/ in /'latɛ/ (< LACTEM) 'milk' is identical to the /t/ in /'latu/ (< LATUM) 'side' (Camp.-Log. /'laðu/).

The same processes apply, with the same dialectal variation, across word boundaries: e.g. in Campidanese and Logudorese we find /su 'βorku/, /sa 'ðɛrra/, /su 'ɣanɛ, -i/ (where /su/ and /sa/ are definite articles) corresponding to /'porku/ (< PŎRCUM) 'pig', /'tɛrra/ (< TĔRRAM) 'land', /'kanɛ, -i/ (< CANEM) 'dog', whereas in Nuorese initial voiceless stops are unchanged: /su 'porku/, /sa 'tɛrra/, /su 'kanɛ/. In the same contexts, initial voiced stops are elided in Campidanese and Logudorese, but typically fricativised in Nuorese: /'boɛ, -i/ (< BŎVEM) 'ox', Camp.-Log. /su 'ɔɛ, -i/, Nuor. /su 'βɔɛ/ or /su 'vɔɛ/; /'dɔmɔ, -u/ (< DŎMO ablative) 'house', Camp.-Log. /sa 'ɔmɔ, -u/, Nuor. /sa 'ðɔmɔ/; /'gatu/ (< GATTUM/CATTUM) 'cat', Camp.-Log. /su 'atu/, Nuor. /su 'ɣatu/. In some Nuorese dialects elision of initial /b/ occurs in certain words: /'buka/ (< BUCCAM) 'mouth', /sa 'uka/. Elision of initial voiced stops has given rise to many analogical forms involving insertion or substitution of an anetymological consonant, particularly in Logudorese where /b/ has supplanted initial /g/ in almost all indigenous words: /bɛs'sirɛ/ (< EXĪRE) 'to go out', /'batu/ (< GATTUM) 'cat'. The initial /d/ in /'dɛu/, /'dɛɣo/ (< ĔGO) and /'donzi/ (< It. ogni) 'every' may be due to a similar process. Elision or lenition of initial voiced stops does not apply to loan words: /su bi'zondzu/ (< It. bisogno) 'need', /sa 'gana/ (Cat., Sp. gana) 'hunger, desire'. Also, initial /b/ derived from Latin /kw/ (see p. 324), as in /'bator/ (< QUATTUOR) 'four', never undergoes elision or lenition. Voicing of initial /s/ and /f/ is common to all dialects (though elision of initial /f/ also occurs in some Nuorese dialects, see p. 328): /'sɔlɛ/ (< SŌLEM) 'sun', /su 'zɔlɛ/; /'fidzu/ (< FĪLIUM) 'son', /su 'vidzu/.

Initial consonants do not undergo lenition/elision when the intervocalic context is created by deletion of the final consonant of the preceding word (see p. 326). On the contrary, there is a general tendency for all consonants in this position to have a 'reinforced' or geminate pronunciation, as in the following examples where deleted consonants are given in parentheses: /ki(n) ssu 'pɛðɛ/ 'with the foot', /'mandika(t) ssu 'kazu/ '(s)he eats the cheese', /'kɛrɛ(t) ddor'mirɛ/ '(s)he wants to sleep' (compare: /prɔ zu 'pɛðɛ/ 'for the foot', /'mandika zu 'kazu/ 'eat the cheese!' (imperative), /'kɛljɔ 'ðor'mirɛ/ 'I want to sleep'). The same phenomenon occurs after certain vowel-final prepositions and connectives which have lost a final consonant as a result of historical processes; e.g. /a/ (< AD or AUT), /ɛ/ (< ĒT) and /nɛ/ (< NĒC) /a d'dɔmɔ/ '(to) home', /ɛ ssu 'ɣatu/ 'and the cat', /nɛ ss 'unu nɛ ss 'ateru/ 'neither one nor the other'.

A feature of the consonant system of Sardinian which is particularly distinctive within Romance as a whole is the failure of velar stops to undergo palatalisation before front vowels, at least in Logudorese–Nuorese: /'kentu/ (< CĔNTUM) 'hundred', /'kidzu/ (< CĪLIUM) 'eyebrow', /'gɛneru/ (< GĔNĔRUM) 'son-in-law'. Palatalisation does occur in Campidanese, however, where /k/ > /ʧ/ and /g/ > /ʤ/, as in Italian: /'ʧentu/, /'ʧillu/, /'ʤɛneru/. In Italian loan words, Logudorese–Nuorese generally has /ts/, /dz/ corresponding to the palatal affricates /ʧ/, /ʤ/: /'tsertu/ (< It. certo) 'certain', /'dzɛntɛ/ (< It. gente) 'people'.

Turning now to the liquid consonants, two phonemes can be postulated; /l/ and /r/. In Logudorese–Nuorese the opposition between these two phonemes is consistently maintained in initial and intervocalic position. Essentially the same is true of Campidanese, but with some complications. Firstly, in Campidanese initial /r/ is always geminate and is preceded by a prothetic vowel, usually /a/: /ar'riu/ (< RĪVUM) 'bank', /ar'raiɣa/ (< RADĪCAM) 'root'. Secondly, intervocalic /r/ in infinitive endings is deleted systematically with -are verbs and optionally with -ere and -ire verbs: /an'dai/ (< *ANDARE) 'to go'; /'timi/, /'timiri/ (< TĬMĒRE) 'to fear'; /bes'si/, /bes'siri/ (< EXĪRE) 'to go out'. Thirdly, in Campidanese intervocalic /l/ has a variety of realisations according to local dialect; /l/, /β/, /ʀ/ and /ʔ/: SŌLEM > Log.–Nuor. /'sɔlɛ/, Camp. /'sɔli/, /'sɔβi/, /'sɔʀi/, /'sɔʔi/ 'sun'.

In all dialects there is a strong tendency towards neutralisation of /l/ and /r/ before and after consonants, typically in favour of /r/: (/'artu/ (< ALTUM) 'high', /'fɔrtɛ/ (< FŎRTEM) 'strong', /'prenu/ (< PLĒNUM) 'full', /'kraɛ/ (< CLAVEM) 'key'. However, some varieties of Logudorese and Campidanese show neutralisation in favour of /l/ before consonants; /ˈaltu/, /ˈfɔltɛ/. In some Northern Logudorese dialects, /l/ and /r/ (also /s/) are assimilated to the following consonant (see p. 325). The same dialects show palatalisation of /l/ after consonants (as in Italian), with /kl/ > /dʒ/: /ˈpjenu/ (< PLĒNUM) 'full', /ˈfjama/ (< FLAMMAM) 'flame', /ˈdʒaru/ (< CLARUM) 'clear'.

Frequently the position of /r/ (including /r/ < /l/) is affected by processes of metathesis, particularly in Campidanese where preconsonantal /r/ is often inverted with the preceding vowel (with lenition/elision of the consonant): Camp. /brɛˈβɛi/ (< VĔRVĔCEM) 'sheep', /droˈmiri/ (< DŌRMĪRE) 'to sleep'. This process may be phonotactically motivated in so far as it serves to create open syllables. However, in some cases it also yields aberrant initial clusters as in /ˈmraku/ (= /ˈmarku/ 'Mark', proper name). Moreover, in Campidanese, clusters of the form /t/ + /r/ are often inverted (with lenition of /t/ to /ð/), yielding a closed syllable: /ˈpɛrða/ (< PĔTRAM) 'stone', /ˈbirðiu/ (< VĪTR(E)UM) 'glass'. A similar phenomenon characteristic of Nuorese is attraction of post-consonantal /r/ to the first syllable of the word, provided that the resulting consonant cluster is phonotactically well formed: /ˈprɛta/ (< PĔTRAM) 'stone', /preˈðuku/, /priˈuku/ (< PĒDĪCŪLUM) 'louse', /britsiˈkɛta/ (< It. bicicletta) 'bicycle'.

In Logudorese-Nuorese there is partial neutralisation of /r/ and /s/ in word-final position. Final /r/ > /s/ before a voiceless consonant (except /f/ or /θ/): /ˈbatɔr aˈmikɔs/, /ˈbatɔr ˈgatɔs/, /ˈbatɔs ˈkanɛs/ 'four friends/cats/dogs'. Conversely, final /s/ is realised as /r/ (sometimes /l/ as a free variant) before a voiced consonant (and /f/ and /θ/) and as /z/ before a vowel: /sos ˈkanɛs/, /sɔz aˈmikɔs/, /sɔr ˈgatɔs/ 'the dogs/friends/cats'.

Sardinian has two nasal consonants, /m/ and /n/, in indigenous words. Palatal /ɲ/ occurs in some loan words, such as /ˈbaɲu/ (< It. bagno) 'bath', but has marginal status and is frequently changed to /ndz/ (Log.-Nuor.) or /ndʒ/ (Camp.) or, occasionally, to /nn/. In initial and intervocalic position, the opposition between /m/ and /n/ is maintained except in the varieties of Campidanese where intervocalic /n/ is realised in terms of nasalisation of the preceding vowel (see p. 318). In preconsonantal position (word-internally and -externally), nasals are homorganic with the following consonant: /ˈkɔŋka/ (< CŎNCHAM) 'head', /imˈbɛssɛ/ (< INVĔRSE) 'wrong way', /im ˈbuka/ 'in mouth', /iŋˈgula / 'in throat'.

Within Sardinian as a whole, two glides /j/ and /w/ can be postulated, though /j/ has marginal status in Campidanese as does /w/ in Logudorese-Nuorese. The following discussion is confined to glides in prevocalic position, the off-glides in words such as /ˈfaula/ (< FABŬLAM) 'lie', /fraiˈkarɛ/ (< FABRĪCĀRE) 'to build' and /ˈfaɛɖˈɖarɛ/ (< FABĔLLĀRE) 'to speak' being treated here as reduced forms of vowels.

In Logudorese-Nuorese the Latin palatal glide /j/ is generally maintained in initial position, with /dz/ as a variant: /jɔˈkarɛ/, /dzɔˈkarɛ/ (<

JŌCĀRE) 'to play'; /juˈrarɛ/, /dzuˈrarɛ/ (< JURĀRE) 'to swear'. To some extent this is a fortis–lenis distinction, with /j/ occurring predominantly after vowels and /dz/ after consonants (overt or deleted), though there is some degree of free variation particularly in absolute initial position. In some words, such as /ˈjanna/ (< JĀNUAM) 'door', initial /j/ appears regardless of preceding context. In Campidanese, initial /j/ > /ʤ/, with mutation of following /a/ to /ɛ/: /ˈʤɔβia/ (< *JŌVIAM) 'Thursday', /ˈʤɛnna/ (< JĀNUAM) 'door'. When the preceding word ends in a vowel, /ʤ/ is often elided: /sa ˈʤɛnna/ > /s ˈɛnna/. Intervocalic /j/ is typically retained in Logudorese–Nuorese, but is usually elided in Campidanese: Log.–Nuor. /ˈmaju/, Camp. /ˈmau/ (but sometimes /ˈmaju/) (< MAJUM) 'May'.

The bilabial glide /w/ of Classical Latin merges with /b/ in most dialects or is transformed to /v/. This glide is retained in Campidanese in sequences of the form /kw/, /gw/, but not in Logudorese–Nuorese, where /kw/ and /gw/ are typically transformed to /b/ or /bb/, though /kw/ > /k/ is also common in initial position (see the chart of consonant + glide sequences for examples). Consequently, /w/ does not occur in Logudorese–Nuorese except, marginally, in loan words such as /kwinˈtalɛ/ (< It. *quintale*) 'quintal'.

The evolution of Latin consonant + glide combinations is given in the

Evolution of Consonant + Glide Sequences

/dj/	> Log.–Nuor. /j/ or /dz/: /ˈjossu/, /ˈdzossu/ (<DEŌRSUM) 'down', /ˈɔjɛ/ (< HŌDIE) 'today'
	> Camp. /ʤ/ (Ø in intervocalic position: /ˈʤossu/, /ˈoi/
/kj, tj/	> Nuor. /θ/: /ˈpeθa/ (<*PĔTTIAM) 'meat'
	> Log. /t/: /ˈpeta/
	> Camp. /ts/: /ˈpetsa/
/sj/	> /z/: /ˈkazu/ (< CĀSEUM) 'cheese'
/lj/	> Log.–Nuor. /dz/: /muˈdzɛrɛ/ (< MŬLIEREM) 'wife'
	> Camp. /ll/: /mulˈleri/
/nj/	> Log.–Nuor. /ndz/: /ˈbɛndzɔ/ (< VĔNIO) 'I come'
	> Camp. /nʤ/: /ˈbɛnʤu/
/nw/	> /nn/: /ˈjanna/, /ˈʤɛnna/ (< JĀNUAM) 'door'
/kw, gw/	> Log.–Nuor. /b/ or /bb/: /ˈbatɔr/ (< QUATTUOR) 'four', /ˈabba/ (< AQUAM) 'water', /ˈlimba/ (< LINGUAM) 'tongue'
	> Camp. /kw/, /gw/: /ˈkwatɔr/, /ˈakwa/, /ˈlingwa/
/kw-/	> /k-/ (some words): /ˈkalɛ / (< QUĀLEM) 'which', /ˈkimbɛ/ (< QUĪNQUE) 'five

Evolution of Consonant Clusters and Geminates

/rs/   >   /ss/: /'jɔssɔ/, /'dʒɔssɔ/ (< DEÒRSUM) 'down'

/ps/   >   /ss/: /'issa/ (< ĪPSAM) 'her'

/ks/   >   /ss/: /las'sarɛ/ (< LAXĀRE) 'to leave, let'

/ns/   >   /z/: /'mɛza/ (< MĒNSAM) 'table'

/ɲn, mn/ >   /nn/: /'mannu/ (< MAGNUM) 'large', /'sonnu/ (< SŎMNUM) 'sleep'

/kt, pt/ >   /t/: /'fatu/ (< FACTUM) 'made', /'sɛtɛ/ (< SĔPTUM) 'seven'

/rn/   >   /rr/: /'korru/ (< CŎRNUM) 'horn'

/nd/   >   /nn/ (some Nuor. only): /an'narɛ/ (< ANDÁRE) 'to go'

/rb/   >   /rv/: /'ɛrva/ (< HĚRBAM) 'grass'

/nv/   >   /mb/: /im'bɛssɛ/ (< INVĚRSE) 'wrong way'

/ll/   >   /ɖɖ/ (retroflex): /'nuɖɖa/ (< NŪLLAM) 'nothing'

first chart. The evolution of /dj/ is essentially the same as that of /j/ described above, with the same dialectal variations. The derivatives of Latin /kj/, /tj/ (/θ/, /t/ and /ts/), which also occur as initial segments in many words of pre-Romanic origin (see p. 345), do not undergo the lenition processes normally applicable to initial stops and fricatives.

The evolution of Latin consonant clusters and geminates is outlined in the next chart. Apart from the change /ll/ > /ɖɖ/ (retroflex), which is also attested in many southern Italian dialects, Latin geminates remain unchanged, though as noted earlier (p. 321) the synchronic distinction between simple and geminate obstruents is somewhat problematic. However, /nn/ and /rr/ are distinct from /n/ and /r/ in all dialects: /'mannu/ (< MAGNUM) 'large' vs /'manu/ (< MANUM) 'hand', /'korru/ (< CŎRNUM) 'horn' vs /'kɔru/ (< CŎR) 'heart'. In Campidanese, /ll/ (< /lj/) is generally distinct from /l/, though this distinction is obscured somewhat by variations in the pronunciation of intervocalic /l/ in some local dialects (see p. 322). The same distinction is made in other dialects which maintain /ll/ in loan words: /'bɛllu/ (< It. *bello*) 'beautiful' vs /'kelu/ (< CAELUM) 'sky'.

With regard to clusters, the changes outlined in the chart of consonant clusters and geminates are fairly uniform across dialects, with the exception of northern Logudorese dialects which show a distinctive evolution of clusters of the form /l,r,s/ + consonant:

/l,r,s/+/t/ > /ɬt/ or /ɬɬ/ (/ɬ/ = voiceless lateral fricative): /'mɔɬtu/, /'mɔɬɬu/ (< MORT(U)UM) 'dead', /'pɔɬta/, /'pɔɬɬa/ (< POS(I)TAM) 'put' (pp.).

/l,r,s/+/d/ > /ɖɖ/ or /ɖɖ/ (/ɖ/ = voiced lateral fricative): /'saɖɖu/, /'saɖɖu/
    (< SARDUM) 'Sardinian'
/l,r,s/+/k/ > /xx/: /'pixxɛ/ (< PĬSCEM) 'fish'
/l,r,s/+/g/ > /ɣɣ/: /'muɣɣɛɾɛ/ (< MŬLGĒRE) 'to milk'
/l,r,s/+/p/ > /pp/: /'kuppa/ (< CŬLPAM) 'fault'
/l,r,s/+/b/ > /vv/: /'ɛvva/ (< HĔRBAM) 'grass'

In these dialects, the above changes also apply across word boundaries:
/sɔx 'xanɛs/ 'the dogs', /sɔɣ 'ɣatɔs/ 'the cats', /'batɔx 'xanɛs/, /'batɔɣ 'ɣatɔs/ 'four dogs/cats', etc.

Syllable Structure and Word-stress

In all dialects there is a strong preference for open syllables. In word-final position, a maximum of one consonant from a restricted set (/s/, /t/, /r/ and /n/) is permitted. However, in absolute final position an epenthetic vowel (identical to the preceding vowel) is added to create an open syllable: /'batɔr/, /'batɔrɔ/ (< QUATTUOR) 'four'; /'tempus/, /'tempuzu/ (< TĔMPUS) 'time'; /lɛ'tamɛn/, /lɛ'tamɛnɛ/ (< LAETĀMEN) 'manure'; /'kantat/, /'kantata/ (< CANTAT) 'he sings'. Note that the presence of this epenthetic vowel does not affect word-stress.

Final /t/ (third person singular verb forms) is elided before all consonants, with reinforcement or gemination of the latter as described on p. 322. The final /n/ of /in/ 'in', /kin/ 'with' and /nɔn/ 'not' is elided before fricatives and liquids: /i l'letu/ 'in bed', /nɔ r'ridɛzɛ/ 'do not laugh'. The final /n/ of /nɔn/ is also elided before vowels: /nɔ 'andɛzɛ/ 'do not go'. Before the indefinite article /unu/, /una/, intrusive /ɖ/ appears after /in/ and /kin/: /in ɖ unu 'libru/ 'in a book', /kin ɖ una 'prɛta/ 'with a stone'. Final /s/ and /r/ are not normally elided but in Logudorese–Nuorese undergo the processes described on p. 323.

In word-initial position, Logudorese–Nuorese dialects allow only clusters of the form obstruent + liquid (where the liquid is normally /r/). Campidanese also allows initial clusters of the form /s/ + obstruent (+ liquid), whereas in Logudorese–Nuorese a prothetic vowel /i/ is added in such cases to allow the /s/ to act as the final consonant of the initial syllable: Camp. /'skri-tu/, Log.–Nuor. /is-'kri-tu/ (< SCRĪPTUM) 'written'.

Within the word, the structure of the syllable follows the Logudorese–Nuorese pattern outlined above. Thus a maximum of three consonants can be concatenated of which the first must be a possible final consonant (/s/, /t/, /r/ or /n/, with /n/ > /m/ before /p/ or /b/), the second an obstruent and the third a liquid: /kos-'trin-gɛrɛ/ (< CONSTRĬNGĔRE) 'to constrain', /kum-'prɛn-dɛ-rɛ/ (< COMPRĔHĔNDĔRE) 'to understand'.

The final vowels of articles and clitics are systematically elided before another vowel except, normally, when an initial consonant in the following word has been deleted: /s 'ominɛ/ 'the man', but Log. /su 'atu/ 'the cat'.

Also, the final vowel in infinitives of the type /ˈ...ɛrɛ/ is normally elided except in absolute final position, suggesting perhaps that it should be treated as an epenthetic vowel on a par with that found in /ˈbatɔr(ɔ)/, /ˈkantat(a)/, etc. (see above).

Word-stress normally falls on the penultimate or antepenultimate syllable. Stress on final syllables is generally avoided in Sardinian. Indeed, a final epenthetic vowel is added to Latin monosyllables to yield paroxytonic forms. When the Latin base ends in a consonant, the epenthetic vowel takes its quality from the stem vowel (with raising of mid vowels in Campidanese): CŎR > /ˈkɔrɔ/, /ˈkɔru/ 'heart'; MĔL > /ˈmɛlɛ/, /ˈmɛli/ 'honey'. When the Latin base ends in a vowel, the epenthetic vowel is /ɛ/ (/i/ in Campidanese): TU > /ˈtuɛ/, /ˈtui/ 'you' (sg.). However, oxytonic forms do arise, mainly in Campidanese and Logudorese, as a result of elision of an intervocalic consonant: Log. /ˈpɛ/ (< PĔDEM) 'foot', Camp. /droˈmi/ (< DŎRMĪRE) 'to sleep'. A further process which yields final stress is truncation of the post-tonic sequence in vocative uses of nouns (particularly proper names and diminutives) and certain imperatives: /juˈa/ (← /juˈanne/ 'John'), /pitsinˈne/ (← /pitsinˈneḍḍu, -a/ 'little boy/ girl'), /aˈba/ (← /aˈbarra/ 'stay'), /ˈtɛ/ (← /ˈtɛnɛ/ 'hold').

When a verb (e.g. an imperative) is followed by a single clitic, the verb retains its normal stress pattern. However, if two or more clitics are added, the stress may (optionally) be shifted to the penultimate syllable of the whole sequence: /ˈnarami/ 'tell me', /ˈnaramilu/, /naraˈmilu/ 'tell me it'.

Phonemic Structure of a Sample Dialect

The purpose of the following account is to illustrate briefly the effects of the various phonological processes described above within a single local dialect, the dialect of Lula (a variety of Nuorese). This dialect is used as a basis for the discussion of morphology and syntax in the following sections.

The vowel system conforms to the standard Logudorese–Nuorese pattern (see Table 9.1(a) and discussion, p. 317) with [e] and [o] as allophones of /ɛ/ and /ɔ/.

The inventory of consonant phonemes is as in Table 9.2. The behaviour of consonants follows the Nuorese pattern in most respects. The voiceless stops /p/, /t/ and /k/ show no lenition in intervocalic position and /d/, /g/ and /s/ have the lenis forms [ð], [ɣ] and [z]. However, /b/ departs from the usual Nuorese pattern in having [v] (rather than [β]) as its lenis form, though in many cases intervocalic /b/ is elided (as in Logudorese): /ˈnuɛ/ (< NŪBEM) 'cloud', /sa ˈuka/ (< BUCCAM) 'mouth'. In this dialect /v/ exists as a separate phoneme deriving from CLat. [w] (unlike most other dialects where CLat. [w] > /b/). However, /v/ also has /b/ as a fortis variant which typically occurs after consonants (overt or deleted), with the result that the phonemic opposition between /b/ and /v/ (e.g. /ˈbiɛrɛ/ (< BĬBĔRE) 'to drink' vs /ˈvɛnnɛrɛ/ (< VĔNĪRE) 'to come') is obscured in many contexts (and indeed is often uncertain even in absolute initial position): /'keljɔ 'viɛrɛ/, /'keljɔ 'vɛnnɛrɛ/ 'I want to drink/come'; /'kɛrɛ(t) 'biɛrɛ/, /'kɛrɛ(t) 'bɛnnɛrɛ/ '(s)he wants to drink/come'. Moreover, /v/ (like /b/) is often elided in intervocalic position: ('vɛstɛ/ (< VĚSTEM) 'clothes', /sa 'ɛstɛ/. Nevertheless, there are many words in which the contrast between initial /b/ and /v/ is maintained in all contexts (particularly where /b/ < /kʷ/ and in loan words): /'bindiki/ (< QUĪNDĚCIM) 'fifteen', /'bellu/ (< It. *bello*) 'beautiful', /'vita/ (< VĪTAM) 'life'.

The dental fricative /θ / (< /kj/, /tj/) never undergoes lenition. Retroflex /ḍ/ occurs as a geminate intervocalically (/'nuḍḍa/ < NŪLLAM 'nothing') and epenthetically as described on p. 326.

In the Lula dialect, initial /f/ is freely deletable before a vowel except in loan words: /'(f)aula/ (< FABŬLAM) 'lie', /'(f)emina/ (< FĒMĬNAM) 'woman'. A similar phenomenon occurs in many other Nuorese dialects, though typically it is conditioned by the presence of a preceding vowel. In the Lula dialect the determining factor appears to be register rather than phonological context, retention of initial /f/ being characteristic of more formal speech, sometimes resulting in hypercorrect forms such as /'(f)ominɛ/ (< HŎMĬNEM) 'man', /(f)is'sirɛ/ (< EXĪRE) 'to go out'. Voicing of initial /f/ is frequent in loan words (/va'milja/ < It. *famiglia* 'family') and occurs systematically before /r/: /'vratɛ/ (< FRATREM) 'brother'.

The liquids /l/ and /r/ contrast only in initial and intervocalic position, with only /r/ occurring before or after consonants (see p. 322). In final position the opposition between /r/ and /s/ is neutralised when the following word begins with a consonant, as in most other Logudorese-Nuorese dialects (see p. 323).

With regard to nasals, the only distinctive feature of the Lula dialect (and some other varieties of Nuorese) is the use of /nn/ corresponding to Latin /nd/: /'kannɔ/ (< QUANDO) 'when'.

In initial position /dz/ and /j/ (< /j/, /dj/) are interchangeable in many words, with /dz/ typically as the fortis variant. Word-internally they function as distinct phonemes with /dz/ < /lj/, and /j/ < /j/, /dj/: /'adzu/ (< ĀLIUM) 'garlic', /'ojɛ/ (< HŎDIE) 'today'. The alveolar affricates /ts/ and /dz/ also correspond to Italian /tʃ/ and /dʒ/ in loan words.

3 Morphology

The following account is based primarily on Nuorese forms as attested in the Lula dialect with brief notes on significant dialectal variants other than those which are directly attributable to phonological differences of the type outlined in the previous section.

Nominal Elements

Sardinian has two genders: masculine and feminine. Latin masculine and feminine nouns normally retain their gender, whereas neuter nouns become masculine (cf. pp. 33–4).

The majority of nouns are derived from Latin accusative forms by deletion of -*m*:

- -*a*: feminine (from Latin first declension).
- -*u*: mainly masculine (from Latin second declension), but includes some feminine nouns of fourth declension: *manu* (f.) 'hand' < MANUM; also *domo* (f.) 'house' < DOMO (ablative of DOMUS).
- -*e*: masculine and feminine nouns of third and fifth declensions: *frate* (m.) 'brother' < FRATREM, *nue* (f.) 'cloud' < NUBEM, *die* (f.) 'day' < DIEM.

Neuter nouns of the third declension whose Latin accusative form ends in a consonant other than -*m* conserve this consonant and become masculine: *tempus* (m.) 'time' < TEMPUS, *letamen* (m.) 'manure' < LAETAMEN.

Plurals are formed by adding -*s*, with change of -*u* to -*o* (except in Campidanese): *gatu, gatos* 'cat(s)'; *manu, manos* 'hand(s)'; *mesa, mesas* 'table(s)'; *nue, nues* 'cloud(s)'.

Diminutives are productively formed by adding -*eddu* (m.), -*edda* (f.) to the noun or adjective stem (plural forms: -*eddos*, -*eddas*): *kaneddu* 'little dog', *domedda* 'little house', *mesedda* 'little table', *minoreddu* 'very small'. Iteration of the diminutive affix is occasionally attested: *minoreddeddu* 'very, very small'. (Note that here and throughout the graphy *dd* represents /ḍḍ/.)

Adjectives follow the nominal pattern of inflection giving two inflectional types:

(i)   -*u*, -*a*, -*os*, -*as*:   *mortu, -a, -os, -as* (< MORTUM, etc.) 'dead';

(ii)   -*e*, -*es*:   *forte, -es* (< FORTEM) 'strong'.

Adjectives agree in number and gender with the modified noun, though the gender distinction is not overt with type (ii) adjectives.

The definite articles are derived from IPSUM, IPSAM: *su* (m.), *sa* (f.). In Logudorese–Nuorese the plural forms are *sos* (m.), *sas* (f.), whereas Campidanese has a common form *is* for both genders. The indefinite articles are *unu* (m.) and *una* (f.) in all dialects.

Demonstrative determiners and pronouns show a three-way deictic contrast which can be defined approximately as follows: *kustu* (close to speaker), *kussu* (close to addressee), *kuddu* (remote from both speaker and addressee). These forms inflect for number and gender in the same way as type (i) adjectives.

The possessive modifiers are: *meu, tuo, suo, nostru, vostru, issoro*. With the exception of the third person plural *issoro* (invariable), these forms inflect for number and gender (endings: -*a*, -*os*, -*as*) but show no gender distinction with respect to the possessor.

There are two types of personal pronoun; disjunctive (or tonic) pronouns which occur in the same syntactic positions as full noun phrases and always have animate (typically human) reference, and clitic (or atonic) pronouns which are always attached to the verb and may have inanimate reference in the third person forms.

The disjunctive pronoun forms are listed in the next chart. In the first and second person singular there is a four-way case distinction: nominative (for subjects), accusative–dative (for direct and indirect objects introduced by *a*), comitative (for complements of *kin* 'with') and oblique (for complements of other prepositions). Disjunctive pronouns functioning as direct objects are always preceded by the preposition *a* (the 'prepositional accusative', see p. 336). Dialectal variants of the forms given in the chart include: *dego, deo* (for *jeo*), *mime, tibe* (for *mie, tie*), *se, issu* (for *isse*). Campidanese has a single form *tui* for all cases of the second person singular. An honorific form *bosté* (which takes third person singular verb inflection) is used when addressing persons of superior rank. The second person plural form *vois* (and its possessive and clitic counterparts) is also used as a polite form with singular reference.

Disjunctive Pronouns

	Singular				Plural			
	1	2	3		1	2	3	
			m.	*f.*			*m.*	*f.*
Nominative	jeo	tue						
Acc./Dat.	mie	tie	isse	issa	nois	vois	issos	issas
Comitative	mekus	tekus						
Oblique	me	te						

The clitic pronoun forms are listed in the next chart. The third person, non-reflexive clitics show an accusative/dative contrast, with a gender distinction in the accusative. The first and second person forms, which can function as reflexives, and the third person reflexive are invariable. In Campidanese the third person non-reflexive forms are: (acc.) *ddu, dda, ddus, ddas*; (dat.) *ddi, ddis*. Also in Campidanese *si* is used as a suppletive form of the third person dative before an accusative clitic and, sometimes, as a first person plural form.

Clitic Pronouns

	Singular					Plural				
	1	2	3			1	2	3		
			m.	*f.*	*refl.*			*m.*	*f.*	*refl.*
Accusative			lu	la				los	las	
	mi	ti			si	nos	bos			si
Dative			li					lis		

There are also three 'adverbial' clitics: *nde* (< INDE), *-nke* (< HINC) and *bi* (< IBI) (Camp. *ßi* < It. *ci*). The form *-nke* (which cannot occur in absolute initial position) is used to indicate the source from which an entity is moved. *Nde* can have the same function, but is also used to represent an indefinite or partitive direct object or inverted subject (see p. 340): *nde apo vistu meta* 'I have seen many (of them)', *nde vio* 'I will drink some', *nde son vénnitos trese* 'there came three of them'. *Bi* is primarily a locative or adessive particle, but it also has various pleonastic uses; e.g. as an existential operator with *áere* 'have' and *éssere* 'be', as a means of expressing capacity with respect to an action (*bi lu fákese?* 'can you manage it?' vs *lu fákese?* 'do you do it?'). It normally accompanies *áere* when used possessively (*bi nd'apo* 'I have some') and the impersonal uses of *kérrere* and *mankare* (see p. 340). It is also used as a pronominal substitute for inanimate complements of *a* (*bi pesso* 'I think of it') and (in Logudorese–Nuorese) as a suppletive form of the dative pronoun before an accusative clitic (*narrabilu* 'tell him it').

Verbs
There are three regular conjugations distinguished by the form of the infinitive: (i) *-are*; (ii) *'-ere* (stress on preceding syllable); (iii) *-ire* (Campidanese: (i) *-ai*, (ii) *'-i(ri)*; (iii) *-i(ri)*). Class (i) corresponds to·the Latin first conjugation (-ARE); class (ii) to the second and third conjugations (-ĒRE, -ĔRE); and class (iii) to the fourth conjugation (-IRE). The normal person inflections are:

	1st	*2nd*	*3rd*
Sg.	-o (-e, -a)	-s	-t
Pl.	-mus	-tes (-dzis)	-n

An epenthetic vowel is added to forms ending in a consonant in absolute final position and typically to monosyllabic forms in all contexts. In Campidanese the third person plural ending is *-nt* + paragogic vowel (determined by the theme vowel and pronounced in all contexts).

Most dialects have just two inflectional tenses: present and imperfect (with indicative and subjunctive paradigms). In general, the Latin perfective has not survived, although some North Logudorese dialects do have a paradigm derived from that source, albeit via Tuscan (*-ezi, -esti, -ezit, -emus, -edzis, -edzin*). Other indigenous perfective forms survive in some dialects (e.g. *kerfit* < *QUAERUIT 'sought', *bóffidi* < VOLUIT 'wanted') but these are generally confined to literary style (e.g. dialect poetry). There is no synthetic future or conditional paradigm.

The following chart gives full paradigms for regular verbs of each conjugation, using *kantare* 'sing', *timere* 'fear' and *pulire* 'clean' as representative examples.

The present indicative forms given in the chart are valid for most

Regular Verb Paradigms

(i)	(ii)	(iii)	(i)	(ii)	(iii)
Present indicative			*Present subjunctive*		
kánto	tímo	púlo	kánte	tíma	púla
kántas	tímes	púlis	kántes	tímas	púlas
kántat	tímet	púlit	kántet	tímat	púlat
kantámus	timímus	pulímus	kantémas	timémas	pulémas
kantátcs	timítes	pulítes	kantétas	timétas	pulétas
kántan	tímen	púlin	kánten	tíman	púlan

Imperfect indicative			*Imperfect subjunctive*		
kantaío	timío	pulío	kantárepo	timerépo	pulírepo
kantaías	timías	pulías	kantáres	tímeres	pulíres
kantaíat	timíat	pulíat	kantáret	tímeret	pulíret
kantaíamus	timíamus	pulíamus	kantáremus	timerémus	pulíremus
kantaíadzis	timíadzis	pulíadzis	kantáredzis	timerédzis	pulíredzis
kantaían	timían	pulían	kantáren	tímeren	pulíren

Past participle			*Imperative*		
kantátu	tímitu	pulítu	kánta	tíme	púli
			kantáte	timíte	pulíte

Present participle
kantánde   timénde   pulínde

Logudorese–Nuorese dialects. In the first singular forms of some class (ii) verbs the theme vowel -e- is realised as a glide or by a change in the final consonant of the stem: *abeljo* 'I open' (from *abérrere*), *pondzo* 'I put' (from *pónnere*). Campidanese has the plural forms *kantaus, kantais, kántanta*; *timeus, timeis, tíminti*; *puleus, puleis, púlinti* (with elision of -m- and -t- in the first and second person forms).

The imperfect indicative paradigm varies considerably according to dialect. Some Nuorese dialects have a class (i) paradigm *kantabo, -bas, -bat, -bamus, -bates, -ban* and, in classes (ii) and (iii), the first and second plural forms *timiabamus, -bates*; *puliabamus, -bates*. A similar paradigm occurs in Campidanese with elision of -b- (*kantabat > kantát*) and mutation of the theme vowel in the first and second plural forms in classes (ii) and (iii) (*timiabamus > timemus*). Also many Campidanese dialects have the first singular endings -*amu* (class (i)) and -*emu* (classes (ii) and (iii)). In many dialects (various areas), -*a* (< -AM) is retained as the first singular desinence in preference to -*o* (formed by analogy with the present indicative).

The present subjunctive is characterised by change of the theme vowel to -*e*- in class (i) and to -*a*- in classes (ii) and (iii), with some variation in the first and second plural forms. Sometimes the stem vowel undergoes mutation: *lesset* = *lasset* (from *lassare* 'let').

The survival of the Latin imperfect subjunctive paradigm (used primarily as an inflected form of the infinitive) is often cited as a distinctive feature of Sardinian, though it has become obsolete in many dialects. Stress patterns sometimes vary from those indicated in the chart of verbal paradigms, with penultimate stress throughout the paradigm in some dialects. In some Logudorese dialects the theme vowel is generalised to -e- in all classes. In Campidanese the corresponding forms are derived from the Latin pluperfect subjunctive with endings of the type -essi in all classes.

The imperative forms are derived by deletion of the final -s of the second person present indicative (singular and plural). They are used only in positive commands; in negative commands the present subjunctive is used.

Past participles inflect for number and gender, with the same endings as class (i) adjectives (p. 329), under the conditions outlined on p. 334. In many dialects (mainly Campidanese) the -t- of the endings is elided when the preceding and following vowels are distinct: *kantau, timiu, puliu*, etc. The past participle forms listed in the chart of verbal paradigms are regular weak forms. Strong Latin participles (mainly class (ii) verbs) are generally preserved, with minor phonological changes: *postu* (< POSTUM) 'put', *fatu* (< FACTUM) 'made, did', *lintu* (< LINCTUM) 'licked'.

Present participles are invariable. In Campidanese–Logudorese the form -*ende* is generalised to all three conjugations: *kantende, timende, pulende*.

Apart from the regular conjugations described above, there are many verbs whose paradigms are irregular, at least in part. Some of the principal cases are listed below. Only irregular forms, as attested in the Lula dialect, are cited. Where partial paradigms are given (third person singular and second person plural), the other person endings are as shown on p. 332.

(a) *éssere* 'be'. Pres. ind.: *so(e), ses, es(t), semus, sedzis, sun.* Imperf. ind.: *fipo, fis, fit, fimus, fidzis, fin.* Pres. subj.: *siat, siadzis.* Imperf. subj.: *ésseret, esseredzis.* Suppletive forms from *istare* are used for the imperative and past participle: *ista, istate; istatu.*

(b) *áere* 'have'. Pres. ind.: *apo, as, at, amus, adzis, an.* Imperf. ind.: *aiat, aiadzis.* Pres. subj.: *apat, apadzis.* Past participle: *ápitu.* (no imperative).

(c) *nárrere* 'say, tell'. The infinitive is class (ii), but inflected forms are basically those of class (i), with reduced forms in many cases. Pres. ind.: *naro, naras/nas, narat/nat, namus, nadzis, naran/nan.* Imperf. ind.: *naiat, naiadzis.* Pres. subj.: *naret/niet, naradzis/niedzis.* Imperative: *nara, nadzi.* Past participle: *natu.* Pres. participle: *nande.*

(d) *dare* 'give'. Pres. subj.: *diet, diedzis* (with -a as alternative theme vowel). Imperative: *dae, dadzi.*

(e) *abérrere* 'open', *mórrere* 'die', *vénnere* 'come'. Inflected forms follow the class (iii) pattern, e.g. pres. ind.: *aberit, aberites; morit, morites; venit, venites.*

(f) *kérrere* 'want', *dólere* 'hurt'. Past participle: *kérfitu, dórfitu.*

(g) *andare* 'go'. Alongside the regular imperatives *anda, andate*, there are suppletive forms *vae, vadzi* (< VADERE).

In addition to the synthetic tense forms illustrated above, there are a number of periphrastic constructions which have a temporal or aspectual value.

Perfect and pluperfect are expressed respectively by the present and imperfect of *áere/éssere* + past participle, with *áere* as the unmarked auxiliary. *Éssere* is used with certain intransitive verbs expressing motion, existence, appearance and disappearance, and also with verbs accompanied by a reflexive clitic (except when the reflexive is dative and the verb has a direct object). With *éssere* the participle agrees in number and gender with the (understood) subject, but when the auxiliary is *áere* the participle agrees only with an accusative clitic in the third person.

Áere is also used with the infinitive preceded by *a* to express future time. Alternatively, future can be expressed by *dévere* 'must' with a bare infinitive. The simple present can also be used with future reference.

Éssere is used (in both present and imperfect) with the present participle to express progressive aspect. This construction is extremely common and is often used in preference to the simple present or imperfect when describing actual (rather than typical or habitual) situations in the present or past, sometimes even with stative verbs: *non ti so kredende* 'I do not believe you'.

4   Syntax

Unlike the phonology and morphology, the syntax of Sardinian is reasonably uniform. Thus, although examples are based on the Lula variety of Nuorese (with the orthographic conventions outlined on p. 316), the points which they illustrate can be taken as valid for all dialects unless otherwise specified.

Structure of the Clause

The canonical order of elements within the simple clause is: subject – (auxiliary) – verb – complement(s), though a variety of other orders are permitted (see pp. 338–40). Like most of the other Romance languages (except French and some varieties of Rhaeto-Romance), Sardinian is a 'pro-drop' language; i.e. the subject can be omitted in finite clauses when the inflection of the verb is sufficient to establish intended reference.

Noun Phrases

Within the noun phrase articles, quantifiers, numerals and other elements which have a 'specifier' function normally precede the head noun, whereas complements and modifiers of a descriptive type (e.g. adjectives, relative clauses and preposition phrases) normally follow the head noun.

Possessives (*meu, tuo*, etc.) always follow the head noun, and in this respect can be classed as adjectives. Nouns modified by a possessive are introduced by a definite article except (optionally) when they denote a kinship relation or are used as terms of endearment: *su libru meu* 'my book', *(su) frate meu* 'my brother', *(su) koro meu* 'my darling' (literally 'my heart'). Indefinite articles may also occur with the possessive, or a partitive construction with *de* may be used: *unu libru meu, unu de sos libros meos* 'a book of mine/one of my books'.

Plural and non-count nouns may appear without an article or quantifier when indefinite: *apo kumpratu kasu* 'I have bought cheese'. However, the definite article is used when such nouns are used generically: *sos sórrikes mándikan su kasu* 'mice eat cheese'. Some singular, count nouns (e.g. *domo* 'house') may occur without an article, particularly when introduced by a preposition: *in domo* 'at home', *in domo sua* 'in his/her house'.

The quantifier *totu* 'all' normally precedes the definite or demonstrative article and is invariable. However, when *totu* quantifies the subject NP, it can be placed after the auxiliary: *totu sas ervekes sun giratas, sas ervekes sun totu giratas* 'all the sheep have returned'. In this position *totu* can also quantify a direct object clitic: *los apo totu mandikatos* 'I have eaten them all'.

Other quantifiers (e.g. *kada, donzi* 'every', *karki* 'some', *meta* 'many, much', *paku* 'few, little') and cardinal numerals occur without an article and precede the noun, though *meta* and *paku* can also follow the noun: *b' amus meta vinu, b' amus vinu meta* 'we have a lot of wine'.

Ordinal numerals and certain adjectives which have a specifier function precede the noun and are introduced by an article when the NP is definite: *primu* 'first', *sikundu* 'second', *úrtimu* 'last', *áteru* 'other', *matessi* (invariable) 'same'. Attributive adjectives always follow the noun except for some 'affective' adjectives such as *bellu* 'beautiful' and *bonu* 'good' which can also occur prenominally: *una pitsinna bella, una bella pitsinna* 'a beautiful girl'.

The definite article can be used without a head noun when followed by a relative clause or a prepositional phrase introduced by *de*: *su ki keljo* 'what I want', *sos de Bitti* 'the ones from Bitti'. Also many common adjectives can be used as nouns with specific reference: *su mannu* 'the big one', *unu vetsu* 'an old one, an old man', *s' áteru* 'the other one', etc.

Adjective and Adverb Phrases

The order of elements within adjective and adverb phrases is similar to that found in noun phrases, in that degree modifiers typically precede the head whereas complements follow the head.

The degree modifiers *adziku* 'rather', *gai* 'so', *meta* 'very', *totu* 'completely' and *paku* 'not very' are invariable and normally precede the adjective or adverb, though *meta* can also occur post-adjectivally (just as it can occur after the noun in its use as a quantifier, see above). Also, *mannu* (normally an adjective 'large, great'), used as an intensifier with some adjectives, always follows the adjective and agrees with it in number and gender: *issa es' kuntenta manna* 'she is very happy'. Iteration of the adjective or adverb is common as a means of expressing intensity: *tostu tostu* 'very hard', *abell' abellu* 'very gently'. Iteration is also used to form adverbs from other parts of speech: *note note* 'all night', *kurrende kurrende* 'in a hurry' (literally 'running running').

Comparison is expressed by *prus* + adjective/adverb, except for *bonu/bene* 'good/well' and *malu/male* 'bad/badly' which have comparative forms *medzus* and *peus* (invariable). The comparative of inferiority is expressed by *prus paku* (literally 'more few') + adjective/adverb. The superlative is formed by adding the definite article. The complement of the comparative can take either of two forms:

(a) *de* + NP, where NP is the term of comparison: *Juanne es' prus mannu de Maria* 'John is taller than Mary'.

(b) *ki* + *non* + X, where X can be construed as a clause parallel to the main clause but in which redundant elements are omitted: *semus prus kuntentos oje ki non eris* 'we are happier today than (we were) yesterday', *es' prus riku ki no' est intellidzente* 'he is more rich than (he is) intelligent'.

In comparatives of equality, the complement is introduced by *ke, kantu* or *komente*. With *ke* the following noun usually lacks an article and has non-specific reference: *istraku ke poleddu* 'as tired as a donkey'. When the complement has definite human reference, it takes the prepositional accusative form (with *a*, see below) just as in direct object position: *mannu koment'/kant' a tie* 'as tall as you'.

Verb Phrases
In sentences of the canonical type, auxiliaries precede the main verb and complements (other than clitics) follow the verb, with the unmarked order: direct object – indirect object – complement clause.

A notable feature of the Sardinian verb phrase is the 'prepositional accusative' phenomenon referred to above. Essentially, when the direct object has human reference and is definite, it must be prefixed by the preposition *a*, which is also used to introduce dative complements (cf. Spanish, pp. 106–7). Direct objects introduced by *a* function as noun phrases (rather than prepositional phrases); e.g. they can be conjoined with non-prepositional direct objects: *apo vistu su kane e a su pastore* 'I saw the dog and the shepherd'. The prepositional accusative is also used when animals are referred to by means of a proper name or a disjunctive pronoun. The use of the prepositional accusative is not restricted to direct objects in postverbal position; e.g. it is obligatory with preposed interrogative pronouns and with dislocated direct objects: *a kie as vistu?* 'who(m) did you see?', *a Maria l' apo inkontrata* 'Mary, I have met her'.

Clitics

Clitic pronouns are used in preference to disjunctive forms except when emphasis is placed on the pronoun or when the use of a clitic is precluded for syntactic reasons (e.g. the pronoun is conjoined with another phrase or governed by a preposition for which there is no corresponding clitic, or when the utterance is an elliptical construction lacking a verb).

Clitics always precede finite and infinitival forms of the verb but follow present participles and imperatives: *lu piko* 'I take it', *provo de lu fákere* 'I try to do it', *fakéndelu gai, non bi risessis* 'doing it like that, you will not succeed', *pikalu* 'take it'. In progressive constructions with *éssere* and the present participle, clitics are usually placed before the auxiliary, but encliticisation to the participle is also possible: *lu so fakende, so fakéndelu* 'I am doing it'. Clitics cannot be adjoined to past participles; e.g. in perfective and passive constructions clitics are always attached to the (first) auxiliary: *l' apo fatu* 'I have done it', *kustu regalu m' est istatu prumissu* 'this gift was promised to me'. Clitic-climbing is obligatory with modal and causative verbs which take a 'bare' infinitive: *lu keljo pikare* 'I want to take it', *l' apo fatu mandikare a su kane* 'I made the dog eat it'. However, in other infinitival constructions the clitic is adjoined to the verb of which it is a complement.

Order of Clitic Pronouns

I	*II*	*III*	*IV*	*V*
mi				
				lu
ti				
		nde	li	la
si	bi			
		-nke	lis	los
nos				
				las
bos				

The order of clitics, both pre- and post-verbally, is indicated in the chart. Sequences of clitics from class I and combinations of classes I and IV, though possible, tend to be avoided. In such cases, the dative pronoun is realised as a disjunctive form introduced by *a*: *mi so presentatu a isse* 'I introduced myself to him'. Combinations of classes IV and V are not generally possible, though the strategies for avoiding such sequences vary according to dialect. In many dialects (including the Lula dialect) the locative clitic *bi* replaces the datives *li* and *lis* in such cases: *bi lu dao* vs *li dao su libru* 'I give it/the book to him'. (For a comparable use of locative *y* in popular French, cf. p. 220.) In Campidanese (as in Spanish, p. 110), the reflexive *si* is used as the suppletive dative form. Some dialects have composite forms for dative + accusative combinations: *liu* (=*li(s)* + *lu*), *lia*, *lios*, *lias*.

Constituent Order Variations

In addition to the canonical SVO order, Sardinian allows a wide range of alternative orders. These can be described in terms of the following processes: dislocation (placement of a constituent at the beginning or end of a sentence with a resumptive pronominal element to indicate its grammatical function), fronting (placement of a constituent in sentence-initial position without a resumptive pronoun) and inversion of the subject with the verb.

Dislocation of NPs and PPs to the left (LD) or right (RD) of the sentence is common in colloquial speech. Dislocated phrases are normally separated from the rest of the sentence by a break in the intonation contour (represented here by a comma), though this effect is less marked in cases of right-dislocation. Dislocated phrases have a 'topic' or 'non-focal' interpretation and, for this reason, are usually definite. However, indefinite direct objects consisting of a plural or non-count noun may be dislocated with *nde* as the resumptive clitic. In such cases, the noun can be alone in left-dislocated position but must be introduced by *de* when right-dislocated: *non apo kumpratu pane* 'I have not bought bread' → (LD) *pane, non nd' apo kumpratu*, (RD) *non nd' apo kumpratu de pane*. Definite subjects of finite clauses can also be dislocated with the null subject (or personal inflection on the verb) functioning as the resumptive pronominal element: *kredo ki Gavinu bi venit krasa* 'I think Gavin is coming tomorrow' → (LD) *Gavinu, kredo ki bi venit krasa*, (RD) *kredo ki bi venit krasa, Gavinu.*

Fronting of a constituent (without a resumptive pronoun) has a strong focusing effect similar to that of clefting in English; i.e. the fronted element expresses information which is new or deemed to be particularly noteworthy: *kustu libru apo lessu* 'it is this book that I have read'. Fronting can apply to a wide range of complements: *semus girande a domo* → *a domo semus girande* 'we are returning home', *ses kuntentu* → *kuntentu sese* 'you are happy', *es' diventatu sordatu* → *sordatu es' diventatu* 'he became a soldier', *apo bitu meta vinu* → *meta nd' apo bitu de vinu* 'I have drunk a lot of wine' (fronting of the quantifier *meta* with right-dislocation of the quantified phrase). Fronting can also apply to participles or infinitives dependent on an auxiliary or modal verb: *as mandikatu* → *mandikatu asa* 'you have eaten', *ses dorminde* → *dorminde sese* 'you are sleeping', *keljo issire* → *issire keljo* 'I want to go out'. However, finite or infinitival complement clauses (except for infinitives dependent on modal verbs) cannot undergo fronting: *provo de andare* → **de andare provo* 'I try to go', *kredo* *ki so amitu* → **ki so amitu kredo* 'I think I am hungry'. When the fronted participle or infinitive has a non-prepositional direct object, this object must either be fronted along with the verb or, more usually, it must be dislocated, with a resumptive pronoun prefixed to the auxiliary or modal: *as tunkatu su barkone* 'you have shut the window → (fronting of VP) *tunkatu su barkone asa,* (with LD) *su barkone, tunkatu l' asa,* (with RD) *tunkatu l' asa, su barkone,* but not **tunkatu asa su barkone.* However, this restriction does not apply to prepositional complements, including prepositional accusatives: *apo vistu a Juanne* → *vistu apo a Juanne* 'I have seen John'. Note that when fronting and left-dislocation cooccur, the left-dislocated item must appear first, as in *su barkone, tunkatu l'asa* where *su barkone* is a left-dislocated NP and *tunkatu* a fronted participle (but not **tunkatu, su barkone, l'asa*).

Fronting, particularly of predicative categories such as adjectives or verbs, occurs predominantly, but not exclusively, in yes-no questions and in answers to questions. Thus examples such as *kuntentu sese* and *dorminde sese* would be typically interpreted as questions ('are you happy?', 'are you sleeping?') and *issire keljo* would be typically used as an answer to a question of the type 'what do you want to do?'.

An important syntactic restriction on fronting is that the canonical subject position must be empty; i.e. when an element is fronted the subject either remains unspecified or must be dislocated or inverted with the verb. Thus, fronting of the direct object in *Juanne a' tunkatu su barkone* can yield *su barkone a' tunkatu (Juanne)* or, with left-dislocation of the subject, *Juanne, su barkone a' tunkatu,* but not **su barkone Juanne a' tunkatu.* This restriction does not apply to left-dislocated elements: *su barkone, Juanne l' a' tunkatu.*

The third reordering process, inversion, has an effect similar to that of right-dislocation of the subject. However, there are three important syntactic differences between these two processes. Firstly, inversion applies readily to indefinite NPs: *karkunu est arrivatu* 'someone has arrived' → *est arrivatu karkunu.* Secondly, unlike left-dislocation, inversion is inhibited by the presence of a postverbal complement. Thus the subject cannot be inverted in examples like *karkunu a' tunkatu su barkone* 'someone has shut the window': **a' tunkatu karkunu su barkone,* **a' tunkatu su barkone karkunu* (compare the dislocated construction with definite subject: *a' tunkatu su barkone, Juanne*). Thirdly, inversion cannot occur when a participle or infinitive is fronted: **arrivatu es' karkunu* (compare the dislocated example *arrivatu este, Juanne*).

Inversion of the subject is frequent with verbs of existence, arrival, disappearance, etc.: *bi sun metas ervekes inoke* 'there are a lot of sheep here', *sun vénnitos tres ómines* 'three men came'. Inversion is also usual with verbs such as *piágere* 'please', *kumbénnere* 'suit, be convenient', *bastare* 'suffice', which take a non-agentive subject and a dative object denoting an animate 'experiencer', provided that the dative object is removed from the postverbal position (e.g. by fronting or dislocation): *su kasu piaget a sos sórrikes* 'mice like cheese' (literally 'cheese pleases mice') → *a sos sórrikes piaget su kasu* or *lis piaget su kasu, a sos sórrikes*, but not **piaget su kasu a sos sórrikes*. A further function of inversion is to permit pronominalisation by *nde* of a subject governed by an indefinite quantifier or numeral: *nde sun arrivatos meta/duos* 'many/two of them arrived' vs **meta/duos nde sun arrivatos*.

Note that in all of the above cases the verb agrees in number and person with the inverted subject. Some verbs (typically introduced by pleonastic *bi*) are used in an impersonal construction which resembles the inverted construction except that there is no agreement with the accompanying NP; i.e. the verb always has third person singular inflection. Typical examples are *bi + kérrere* 'be necessary' and *bi + mankare* 'be lacking, be missing': *bi keret/*keren duos ovos* 'two eggs are required', *bi mankat/*mankan duos butones* 'two buttons are missing'. With these verbs, *bi* can be replaced by a dative clitic denoting an 'interested person': *mi mankat duas dentes* 'I have two teeth missing'. By the agreement criterion, the existential predicate *bi + áere* qualifies as an impersonal verb (in contrast to *bi + éssere* which normally occurs in the inverted construction, see above p. 339): *b' at/*an metas ervekes inoke* 'there are many sheep here' (vs *bi sun/ *es' metas ervekes ...*). In the impersonal construction, the accompanying NP may occur in preverbal position, but does not determine verb inflection, thus suggesting that it is a fronted constituent (in the sense described above, p. 338) rather than a syntactic subject: *duos ovos bi keret, metas ervekes b' ata*.

Voice

An analytic passive construction with *éssere* + past participle exists in Sardinian, but it is rarely used in colloquial speech and is regarded by some grammarians as an innovation due to Italian influence. The subject in this construction corresponds to the direct object of the active verb and the agent can be specified (optionally) by an NP introduced by *dae* 'from': *kusta domo est istata fraikata dae un Italianu* 'this house was built by an Italian'. The past participle is often used with a passive function after *kérrere* (with the meaning 'need') and after the preposition *kene* 'without': *kusta kamisa keret lavata* 'this shirt needs (to be) washed', *sa peθa es' kene mandikata* 'the meat has not been eaten' (literally 'the meat is without eaten').

The effect of the passive is more commonly achieved by means of the pronominal verb construction with the reflexive clitic *si*. Apart from its use as a reflexive pronoun, *si* can be prefixed to a verb to assign generic reference to the understood subject: *no' si dormit in kustu letu* 'one cannot sleep in this bed'. When the verb is transitive, the understood direct object assumes the status of syntactic subject (determining the inflection of the verb), though it may occur in postverbal position as a result of inversion: *kussas kosas no' si faken, no' si faken kussas kosas* 'one does not do such things'.

The clitic *si* is also used to indicate the intransitive use (with patient as subject) of certain verbs which can also be used transitively: *sa janna s' est aberta* 'the door opened' (vs *apo abertu sa janna* 'I opened the door'). The reflexive clitics (including first and second person forms) are adjoined to verbs of motion when the 'source' is indicated by -*nke*: *sink' est andatu* 'he has gone away (from here)', *sinke son rutos* 'they fell down (from there)'. Pleonastic *si* often occurs with -*nke* before certain transitive verbs: *Juanne sink' a mandikatu su pane* 'John has eaten the bread'.

Negation

Simple negation is expressed by placing *non* in front of the verb (before any clitic pronouns which may be present). Syntactically *non* is a proclitic and, as such, can be prefixed only to verb forms which allow proclitic pronouns; i.e. to finite verbs (including auxiliaries) and most infinitives, but not to participles, imperatives or bare infinitives governed by a modal or causative verb.

When the sentence contains a negative pronoun, quantifier or adverb (e.g. *neune* 'nobody', *nudda* 'nothing', *ne...ne* 'neither...nor', *mai* 'never', *a/in nedue* 'nowhere', etc.) in postverbal position, *non* must be prefixed to the verb: *no' apo vistu a neune* 'I have not seen anyone', *non bi so mai andatu* 'I have never gone there'. Similarly, *non* must occur when the negative element is an inverted subject: *no' es' vénnitu neune* 'nobody came'. However, *non* does not occur when the negative pronoun, quantifier or adverb precedes the verb (e.g. in the canonical subject position or as a fronted element): *neune es' vennitu, mai bi so andatu*.

Interrogative Constructions

Simple yes-no questions are distinguished from corresponding statements primarily by intonation (questions lack the full descent in pitch on the item bearing main sentence-stress, which is characteristic of declaratives). Although fronting of a constituent (particularly a predicative element) is common in yes-no questions, as remarked above (p. 339), this is not specifically a question formation process. Sardinian has an interrogative particle *a* (< AUT) which can be placed at the beginning of a yes-no question. When *a* is present the canonical subject position must be empty, though a dislocated or inverted subject may appear: **a Juanne venit?, a venit (Juanne)?* 'is John coming?'.

In specific questions, the interrogative pronoun, adverb or quantifier (e.g. *kie* 'who', *ite* 'what', *kale* 'which', *kantu* 'how much/many', *komente* 'how', *proite* 'why', *kando* 'when', *inuve* 'where') or the phrase containing it is normally placed in sentence-initial position. Fronting of interrogative items is subject to constraints similar to those which govern the general fronting process described earlier (pp. 338–9). In particular, when the interrogative item is fronted, the subject must be omitted, inverted or dislocated: *ite Maria a' mandikatu?, ite a' mandikatu (Maria)? 'what did Mary eat?'. Left-dislocated phrases must precede the fronted interrogative item: su vinu, proite l'as vitu? 'the wine, why did you drink it?'. Also, fronting of the interrogative item precludes fronting of any other constituent: kando e' vénnitu?, *kando vénnitu este? 'when did he come?'.

Complement and Adverb Clauses

Finite complement clauses (indicative or subjunctive) are always introduced by the complementiser ki. Infinitival complements are introduced by de or a (according to the governing verb or adjective), except for the complements of certain modal and causative verbs which take a 'bare' infinitive. The complementisers ki and de also occur after the adverb or subordinating conjunction in most types of adverb clauses. However, the complementiser does not occur in finite clauses introduced by kando 'when', ka 'because', si 'if' and mankari 'although', or in infinitive clauses introduced by kene 'without' and pro 'for'.

The subjunctive is used in finite complements of verbs expressing desires, orders, affective relations, etc.: keljo ki bi venat isse 'I want him to come', narabilu ki bi venat krasa 'tell him to come tomorrow', mi piaget ki kantes tue 'it pleases me for you to sing'. Verbs of belief or assertion can also take the subjunctive when negated: non kredo ki Juanne siat inoke 'I do not think that John is here'. The subjunctive is also used in the following types of adverbial clauses:

(a) purposive clauses: apo vautu sa kitarra pro ki kantes tue 'I have brought the guitar so that you can sing';

(b) clauses introduced by imbetses 'instead': imbetses ki kantes tue, kanto jeo 'instead of you singing, I will sing';

(c) concessive clauses introduced by mankari, vinas 'although, even if', and basta 'as long as': mankari grides, non ti lasso andare 'even if you shout, I will not let you go', vinas ki siat vetsa es' meta bella 'although she may be old, she is very beautiful', potes jokare, basta ki non grides 'you can play, as long as you do not shout';

(d) time clauses introduced by prima 'before' (other time expressions take the indicative): devo intrare prima ki proat 'I must go in before it rains'.

In all of the above cases the infinitive is generally used, whenever possible, in preference to the subjunctive.

The so-called 'imperfect subjunctive' is used as a past tense form of the subjunctive only with the verbs *áere* and *éssere* (as main verbs and auxiliaries). With other verbs it functions as an inflected form of the infinitive and is introduced by the infinitival complementiser *de* rather than *ki*: *keljo de bi vénneret isse* 'I want him to come', *imbetses de kantares tue, ...* 'instead of you singing, ...' (compare examples above with the present subjunctive).

In conditional constructions the indicative is normally used, with identity of tenses in both the condition and consequent clauses. When the condition clause denotes a situation which is potentially realisable in the future, present tense is used: *si divento riku, kompro una bella domo* 'if I become rich, I will buy a beautiful house'. When the condition is hypothetical or counterfactual, the imperfect or pluperfect is used: *si fipo riku, kompraio una bella domo; si fipo istatu riku, aio kumpratu una bella domo* 'if I were/ had been rich, I would buy/have bought a beautiful house'. The imperfect subjunctive of *áere* and *éssere* is sometimes used in the condition clause (often with suppression of the consequent) to give an optative effect: *si aerepo jutu sas alas a volare, (fipo volatu a ti videre)* 'if only I had wings to fly, (I would fly to see you)'.

Relative clauses normally require the indicative: *s' ómine ki es' vénnitu* 'the man who came', *su libru ki so legende* 'the book which I am reading'. However, the subjunctive is sometimes used when describing an entity whose existence is hypothetical: *no' apo akatatu mank' una kratea ki siat kómoda* 'I have not found a single chair which is comfortable'. The item *ki* in the above examples can be regarded as the complementiser which introduces most types of finite subordinate clauses rather than a relative pronoun. Indeed, Sardinian does not have a distinct class of relative pronouns. When the modified noun corresponds to the subject or direct object of the relative clause, as in the examples above, there is no element referring back to the modified noun. In other cases, a personal pronoun or possessive item is normally used to refer back to the modified noun, though resumptive dative or adverbial clitics are sometimes omitted in casual speech: *s' ómine ki (li) dao sa krae* 'the man to whom I give the key' (literally 'the man that I give the key (to him)'), *s' istrada ki (bi) kolat su postale* 'the road where the bus passes' (literally 'the road that the bus passes (there)'), *s' ómine ki semus andatos a domo sua* 'the man whose house we went to' (literally 'the man that we went to his house'). However, in locative relatives *inuve* 'where' is sometimes used as a relative pronoun replacing *ki*: *s' istrada inuve kolat su postale.*

The infinitive is typically used in complement and adverb clauses when the understood subject is identical to some participant in the main clause: *so provande de dormire* 'I am trying to sleep', *apo natu a Juanne de andare* 'I told John to go', *so issitu pro fákere s' ispesa* 'I went out to do the shopping'. However, although infinitives (including the personal infinitive/ imperfect subjunctive) never allow an overt subject in the canonical preverbal position, some verbs and subordinating conjunctions permit the following infinitive to take an overt postverbal subject which is not co-referential with an element in the matrix clause and which has nominative case (as shown when it is a first or second person singular pronoun): *non keren de vénnere jeo* 'they do not want me to come', *kredo de éssere andatu isse* 'I believe him to have gone', *imbetses de bi vénnere tue b' es' vénnitu Juanne* 'instead of you coming John came'. Under favourable pragmatic circumstances, this subject may be omitted while still preserving its independent reference: *non keljo de mi madzare* 'I do not want you/them/ anyone to hit me'. In such cases, the use of the personal infinitive is often preferred: *non keljo de mi madzares/madzaren* etc., *prima de andarémus, kántanos una kaθone* 'before we go, sing us a song'. The personal infinitive can also be used when the subject is overtly specified or, less frequently, when it is controlled by an element in the main clause: *keljo de andares tue* 'I want you to go', *amus ditsisu de nonk' andáremus* 'we decided to go away' (*nonk'* = pleonastic *nos + nke*).

When the verb *kérrere* 'want' takes an infinitive whose subject has independent reference, as in the above examples, the infinitive is always introduced by the complementiser *de* (or, in some dialects, *a*). However, when the subject of the infinitive is controlled by the subject of *kérrere*, no complementiser is present: *keljo kantare* 'I want to sing'. Certain other 'modal' verbs (*dévere* 'must', *iskire* 'know (how to)', and *pótere* 'can') also require a bare infinitive: *devo/isko/poto kantare*. The modal verbs in these constructions have a number of 'auxiliary-like' properties which distinguish them from other verbs (e.g. *provare* 'try') which take an infinitival complement. Firstly, clitic-climbing is obligatory in these constructions: *lu keljo mandikare*, **keljo lu mandikare* 'I want to eat it' vs **lu provo de mandikare, provo de lu mandikare*. Similarly, the infinitive cannot be prefixed by the negative particle *non*: *non devo rúgere, *devo no' rúgere* 'I must not fall' vs *provo de no' rúgere*. Like participles dependent on an aspectual auxiliary, but unlike complement clauses in general, the infinitive governed by a modal can be fronted: *dormire keres?* 'do you want to sleep?' vs **de dormire provas?*. Moreover, modals are transparent with respect to choice of perfective auxiliary, i.e. the choice between *áere* and *éssere* is determined according to the lexical properties of the following infinitive: *apo kérfitu mandikare* 'I wanted to eat', *so kérfitu andare* 'I wanted to go' vs. *apo provatu de mandikare, apo provatu de andare*.

Infinitival causative constructions with *fákere* 'make, cause' and *lassare* 'let' follow the familiar Romance pattern. The dependent infinitive lacks a complementiser and its subject is expressed as a direct or indirect (dative) object according to whether the infinitive is intransitive or transitive, though this distinction is obscured by the effects of the prepositional accusative phenomenon (see p. 336) when the subject of the infinitive is human and definite: *apo fatu/lassatu dormire sos gatos* 'I made/let the cats sleep', *apo fatu/lassatu dormire a sos pitsinnos* 'I made/let the boys sleep', *su mere a fatu/lassatu múrgere sas ervekes a sos θerakos* 'the master made/let the servants milk the sheep'. However, the accusative/dative distinction is shown clearly when a third person clitic is used to represent the subject of the infinitive: *los apo fatu/lassatu dormire, lis apo fatu/lassatu múrgere sas ervekes*. When the infinitive is transitive, its subject can be omitted or introduced by *dae*, especially when this entity is construed as being instrumental in the realisation of the event described: *a' fatu/lassatu múrgere sas ervekes (dae sos θerakos)* 'he had the sheep milked (by the servants)'. Clitic-climbing is obligatory, except with reflexive clitics referring to the subject of the infinitive, which are always adjoined to the infinitive: *los a' fatu/lassatu múrgere a/dae sos θerakos* 'he had/let the servants milk them', *apo fatu/ lassatu si vestire a su pitsinnu* 'I made/let the boy dress himself'.

5 Lexis

The lexical stock of Sardinian is composed almost entirely of words of Latin origin, either derived directly from Latin or imported from other Romance languages (particularly Catalan, Spanish and Italian).

Little is known for certain about the language spoken in Sardinia prior to the Roman occupation, though there has been much speculation on the matter. A number of words of presumed pre-Roman origin survive in local dialects particularly terms related to fauna, flora and geomorphic features. Among such words there are a few which show affinities to Basque: *sekaju* 'year-old lamb' (Basque *segaila* 'year-old goat'), *kóstike* 'variety of maple' (Basque *gastigar* 'maple'), Campidanese *dʒágaru* 'hunting dog' (Basque *tsakurr* 'dog'). A further example is *kúkuru* 'top' (Basque *kukur* 'summit'); although the meaning of the Sardinian term has been extended (in expressions such as *prenu a kúkuru* 'full to overflowing', *kúkur' in kulu* 'upside-down', *kukurumbeddu* 'somersault'), the geomorphic sense of the Basque term is preserved in the diminutive *kukureddu* 'pinnacle, mound'.

An intriguing feature of primitive lexical items is the frequency of common nouns with the initial segment /θ/ (dialectal variants /ts/ and /t/) which some linguists have analysed as the vestige of a pre-Roman article, possibly related to Berber. Support for this hypothesis (though not necessarily the link with Berber) is provided by cases where /θ/ (+ vowel) has been prefixed to a Latin base: *θilikerta* 'lizard' (< *θi* + LACERTAM), *θruku* 'neck' (variants *tsugu*, *θúgulu*) (< *θ* + JUGULUM), *θulungrone*, *tsilingru* 'worm' (< *θ* + *LUMBRICUM 'earthworm'), *tuntunnu*, *túnniu* 'mushroom' (< *θ* + FUNGUM).

A few words of Punic origin survive in Campidanese (dating from Phoenician settlements in southern and western areas during the three centuries or so prior to the Roman occupation): *tsipiri* 'rosemary', *tsikiria* 'dill', *tsingorra* 'type of small eel', *mitsa* 'spring'.

The central core of the vocabulary of Sardinian consists of words derived directly from Latin. Although many words of Latin origin have cognates in other Romance languages which subsequently influenced Sardinian, the independence of the Sardinian lexical heritage is evidenced by many words in common usage which do not occur in these languages (except with specialised meanings or as lexical formatives): *domo* 'house' (< DOMO (ablative)), *emmo* 'yes' (< IMMO), *iskire* 'know' (< SCIRE), *janna* 'door' (< JANUAM), *krasa* 'tomorrow' (< CRAS), *mannu* 'large' (< MAGNUM), *nárrere* 'say, tell' (< NARRARE). Particularly noteworthy in this respect is the survival of many archaic Latin words: *ákina* 'grapes' (collective noun, < *ACINAM), *juljare* 'call' (< *JUBILARE), *peθa* 'meat' (< *PETTIAM), *viskidu* 'sour' (< *VISCIDUM).

Some Latin words of an abstract nature have assumed more specialised, concrete meanings in Sardinian: *apeddare* 'bark' (< APELLARE 'call'), *turvare* 'to herd (sheep, cattle etc.)' (< TURBARE 'disturb'), *berbu* 'spell, incantation' (< VERBUM 'word') (also *berbare* 'to cast a spell', *abbaberbata* 'water endowed with magic healing powers by means of incantation'). Similarly, in many dialects, *bonu* (< BONUM 'good') tends to be used only with the sense 'good to eat or drink'. A few words have undergone more radical changes in meaning. The word *konka* (< CONCHAM 'shell, vessel shaped like a shell') is adopted as the normal word for 'head'. The common noun *jana* 'fairy, sprite' is derived from the proper name DIANA, goddess of the moon and of hunting. The quantifier or degree modifier *meta* 'much, many, very' derives from METAM, which in Classical Latin denotes a conical or pyramid-shaped form, but may have had an earlier meaning 'heap'. The noun *kita* 'week' can be traced back to ACCITUM, -AM (past participle of ACCIRE 'summon') via the medieval practice of summoning citizens for guard-duty according to a weekly roster.

Germanic influence on the vocabulary of Sardinian is negligible. Although much of the island was subject to Vandal incursions during the latter half of the fifth century and the beginning of the sixth century, these left no linguistic traces. The few Germanic words which do occur are items which had either been adopted in late Latin or were transmitted to Sardinian via other Romance languages. Some common words of this type are: *frisku* 'fresh, cool', *iskina* 'back, spine', *brundu* 'blond', *bianku* 'white', *anka* 'leg'.

A number of words of Greek–Byzantine origin were introduced during the period of Byzantine rule (seventh to ninth centuries). Many of these are judicial or ecclesiastical terms which have since become obsolete: *kondaki* 'record of legal transactions' (< Gk.-Byz. *kontakion*), *munisteri*, *muristeri* (< Gk.-Byz. *monasteri*), *éniu* 'without heir' (< Gk.-Byz. *annegguos*). A more lasting example of this type is *(d)inari* 'money' which is claimed to derive from Greek *dinarion* rather than from Latin DENARIUM. There are also a number of non-specialist words in current usage which can be traced to or, at least, related to Greek: *lepa, liputsu* 'knife' (Gk. *lepos* 'blade'), *kasku, kaskare* 'yawn (noun and verb)' (Gk. *khasku* 'yawn'). The term *θeraku* 'servant' (also used to mean 'young man' in early texts) may be cognate with Greek *therapon* 'servant', though other etymologies have been proposed. It is not clear whether words of this type are derived directly from Greek (either during the Byzantine period or as a result of Greek settlements in the pre-Romanic era) or whether such items are derived in parallel from some more remote common source.

Sardinian has adopted a considerable number of words of Spanish or Catalan origin (dating from the period of Hispanic rule 1326-1718). Many of these words represent artefacts, activities and concepts which were introduced during, or as a result of, the Hispanic occupation. The following lists indicate some of the main spheres of Spanish and Catalan influence with representative examples of words which have gained general currency.

Clothing and fashion: *babutsa* 'slipper' (< Cat. *babutxa*, Sp. *babucha*, originally from Arabic *babux*), *bonete* 'hat' (< Cat. *bonet*), *butsaka* 'pocket' (< Cat. *butxaca*), *gapote* 'coat' (< Cat. *capot*), *midza* 'sock' (< Cat. *mitja*), *mukadore* 'kerchief' (< Cat. *mocador*), *randa* 'lace' (< Sp. *randa*), *sabata* 'shoe' (< Cat. *sabata*).

Household artefacts: *kalassu* 'drawer' (< Cat. *calaix*), *manta* 'blanket, bed-cover' (< Sp. *manta*), *prantsa* 'smoothing-iron' (< Cat. *planxa*, Sp. *plancha*), *saffata* 'tray' (< Cat. *safata*), *tassa* 'drinking-glass' (< Cat. *tassa*, Sp. *taza*), *tsikera* 'cup' (< Cat. *xicra*).

Food and drink: *abbardente* 'brandy, liquor' (< Sp. *aguardiente*), *irmudzare* 'take breakfast' (< Cat. *esmorzar*), *kassola* 'type of stew' (< Cat. *cassola*), *sindria* 'water-melon' (< Cat. *síndria*), *tamata* 'tomato' (< Sp. *tomate*), *vábrika* 'basil' (< Cat. *alfàbrega*).

At the same time there are many words of Catalan or Spanish origin which do not reflect particular cultural influences *baratu* 'cheap' (< Cat. *barat*, Sp. *barato*), *ditsosu* 'fortunate' (< Sp. *dichoso*), *gana* 'hunger, desire' (< Cat., Sp. *gana*), *kaente* 'warm' (< Sp. *caliente*), *lástima* 'shame, waste' (< Cat. *llastima*), *brinkare* 'to jump' (< Sp. *brincar*), *istimare* 'to love' (< Cat. *estimar*), *kusire* 'to sew' (< Cat. *cosir*), *travallare* 'to work' (< Cat. *treballar*). Included in this class are a few function words: Camp. *kini* 'who' (< Cat. *quin*), *bosté* 'you' honorific form (< Cat. *vosté*), Log.-Nuor. *matessi* 'same' (< Cat. *mateix*).

The richest source of loan words is Italian. The first influx of Italian words occurred from the eleventh to the fourteenth century when the maritime powers of Pisa and Genoa exerted strong commercial and political influence over much of Sardinia. Borrowings of this period include: *betsu* 'old' (< It. *vecchio*), *bianku* 'white' (< It. *bianco*), *(b)irgondza* 'shame' (< It. *vergogna*), *póveru* 'poor' (< It. *póvero*), *tsitate* 'city, town' (< Olt. *cittade*), *riku* 'rich' (< It. *ricco*). Many words borrowed during this period are adaptations of Tuscan dialect forms: *abbaitare* 'look' (< Tusc.

aguaitare), *fortsis* 'perhaps' (< Tusc. *forsi*), *galu* 'yet, still' (< Tusc. *aguale*), *massaju* 'peasant' (< Tusc. *massaio*).

A number of Piedmontese dialect words, introduced during the period when Sardinia was part of the Kingdom of Savoy (1718–1861), survive in common usage: *baɲa* 'sauce' (< Pied. *bagna*), *barkone* 'window' (< Pied. *balcone*), *lavandinu* 'kitchen-sink' (< Pied. *lavandin*), *istantsia* 'room' (< Pied. *stanssia*).

Recent borrowings from standard Italian are innumerable. Given the widespread diffusion of Italian (now spoken by almost all Sardinians), the vocabulary of Italian has assumed the status of an ancillary lexicon which is not perceived as being foreign and can be readily exploited without impeding comprehension. Almost all words relating to aspects of modern culture are Italian words, usually adapted to Sardinian phonology and morphology, as in the following Nuorese examples: *britsiketa* 'bicycle' (< It. *bicicletta*), *dziradisku* 'record-player' (< It. *giradisco*), *ispatsola* 'brush' (< It. *spazzola*), *otsales* 'spectacles' (< It. *occhiale*), *tanadzas* 'pliers' (< It. *tanaglie*). However, there are some terms denoting modern concepts which are not current in standard Italian: *postale* 'motor-coach, bus', *franku* 'lira' (unit of currency).

A number of Italian function-words have gained general currency in Sardinian: *dopo* 'after' (which has largely supplanted the indigenous item *pustis*), *karki* 'some' (< It. *qualche*), *ma* 'but', *mai* 'never', *però* 'however', *tra* 'between, among'.

6 Conclusion

As was pointed out in section 1, Sardinian owes its distinctiveness to its early and prolonged isolation from the rest of Romance. Although later contact with Tuscan, Catalan and Spanish gave rise to significant innovations in certain dialects, these dialects (except Sassarese and Gallurese) still preserved their essentially Sardinian character — they did not become transformed into local varieties of Tuscan, Catalan or Spanish. Moreover, these languages do not appear to have posed any serious threat to Sardinian as the medium of communication among the native inhabitants, though they deprived Sardinian of its role as an 'official' language, possibly thwarting any tendency which may have existed towards the establishment of a standard form of Sardinian.

In the modern period, Italian has proved to be a much more formidable rival. Universal education, the media and contact with the Italian mainland have ensured the diffusion of Italian throughout the island and at every social level to the extent that almost all speakers of Sardinian can converse fluently in Italian, though the converse is by no means true. Little effort has been made to promote the use of Sardinian. On the contrary, even the token recognition afforded to other 'minority' languages in Italy (e.g.

French in the Aosta valley, German in the southern Tirol and, indeed, Catalan in Alghero) does not extend to Sardinian, which tends to be regarded as a degenerate variety of Italian whose use is to be discouraged. Moreover, on a purely practical level, increased migration within the island and improved communications between communities have favoured the use of Italian for informal social purposes quite simply because speakers from different areas find it easier to converse in Italian than in their own local dialects. As a result, many children nowadays are brought up to speak only Italian.

We have already commented on the lexical influence of modern Italian on Sardinian (see pp. 348) which has to some extent eroded the distinctive character of Sardinian, though arguably no more so than earlier borrowings from other Romance languages. However, another consequence of the widespread diffusion of Italian is the emergence of a regional variety of Italian which is heavily influenced by Sardinian: e.g. in phonology, neutralisation of the opposition between open and close mid vowels, failure to distinguish between geminate and simple voiceless stops; in syntax, the use of the prepositional accusative, fronting of constituents to achieve a focusing effect, a preference for progressive aspect where standard Italian would require a simple tense form; at the lexical level, a tendency to use Italian words in accordance with conditions which govern their Sardinian cognates rather than according to accepted Italian usage. Thus, although 'authentic' Sardinian and standard Italian are still, quite clearly, different languages which have evolved independently from their common Latin source, the distinction between the two languages as they are actually used in Sardinia has become rather blurred — a situation which is perhaps not very different from that which obtained in Sassari in the Middle Ages and which gave rise to the local 'hybrid' dialect. If present trends continue, it is possible that within a few generations the regional variety of Italian will supplant Sardinian as the popular idiom and that linguists of the future will be obliged to refer to Sardinian as a substratal influence which has shaped a regional dialect of Italian rather than as a living language descended directly from early Latin.

Bibliography

Atzori, M.T. (1963) 'Varianti fonetiche nel dialetto sardo-campidanese', *Orbis* 12: 408–42.
—— (1975) *Glossario di sardo antico*. STEM — Mucci, Modena.
—— (1982) *Sardegna. Profilo dei dialetti italiani*. Pacini, Pisa.
Blasco-Ferrer, E. (1984) 'Sull'italianità linguistica del gallurese e del sassarese', *Revue Roumaine de Linguistique* 29: 399–412.
—— (1984) *Storia linguistica della Sardegna*. Max Niemeyer, Tübingen.
—— (1986) *La lingua sarda contemporanea*. Edizioni della Torre, Cagliari.

Contini, M. (1970) 'Résistance et passivité de sujets logoudoriens face à l'italian-isation de leur langue', *Revue de Linguistique Romane* 34: 366–76.
—— (1985) *Etude de géographie phonétique et de phonétique instrumentale du sarde*. Edizioni dell'Orso, Alessandria.
Corda, F. (1979) *Una lingua per i sardi*. Trois 3T, Cagliari.
—— (1983) *Saggio di grammatica gallurese*. Trois 3T, Cagliari.
de Dardel, R. (1985) 'Le sarde représente-t-il un état précoce du roman commun?', *Revue de Linguistique Romane* 49: 263–9.
Loi Corvetto, I. (1983) *L'italiano regionale di Sardegna*. Zanichelli, Bologna.
Lorinczi, M. (1971) 'Appunti sulla struttura sillabica di una parlata sarda campidanese (Guasila)', *Revue Roumaine de Linguistique* 16: 423–30.
Lüdtke, H. (1953) 'Il sistema consonantico del sardo logudorese', *Orbis* 2: 411–22.
Paulis, G. (1983) *Lingua e cultura nella Sardegna bizantina: Testimonianze dell' influsso greco*. L'Asfedolo, Cagliari.
Pittau, M. (1972) *Grammatica del sardo-nuorese*. Pàtron, Bologna.
—— (1981) *La lingua dei sardi nuraghici e degli etruschi*. Dessi, Sassari.
Porru, V.R. (1975) *Saggio di grammatica sul sardo meridionale*. Cagliari, 1811; reprinted by Dessi, Sassari.
Sanna, A. (1975) *Il dialetto di Sassari e altri saggi*. Trois 3T, Cagliari.
Senes, A. (1971) *Curiosità del vocabolario sardo*. Fossataro, Cagliari.
Spano, G. (1966) *Vocabolario sardo-italiano e italiano-sardo* 2 vols. Cagliari, 1851; reprinted by Arnaldo Forni, Bologna.
Virdis, M. (1978) *Fonetica del dialetto sardo campidanese*. Della Torre, Cagliari.
Wagner, M.L. (1951) *La lingua sarda. Storia, spirito e forma*. Francke, Berne.
—— (1960-4) *Dizionario etimologico sardo*. C. Winter, Heidelberg.
—— (1984) *Fonetica storica del sardo*. Introduction, translation and appendix by G. Paulis. Trois, Cagliari.

10 Rhaeto-Romance

John Haiman

1 Introduction

The linguistic unity of the heterogeneous dialects comprising Rhaeto-Romance has been recognised for over a hundred years, but the relatively few distinguishing features of Rhaeto-Romance serve less to characterise a unique branch of Romance than to separate this group of dialects from Italian. Among these features is the retention of inherited consonant + /l/ clusters, the palatalisation of velars before inherited /a/, an -s plural for nouns, an -s second person singular verbal ending, and a virtual 'three-syllable rule' which militates against antepenultimate stress. Other peculiarities are characteristic of some dialects, rather than of Rhaeto-Romance as a whole. Among these are the retention of an inherited dative case in third person singular pronouns and in the definite article (an archaism apparently confined to Surmeiran in Switzerland, and both the major Italian dialects), and the correlation between a fairly rigid verb-second order and the requirement that all clauses have surface subjects (confined apparently to the Swiss dialects). (For this last point in respect of French, cf. p. 231.)

Even the most cursory investigation of Rhaeto-Romance must recognise the existence of three major dialect groups: Swiss Rhaeto-Romance, with about 40,000 speakers, spoken in the canton of Graubünden in south-eastern Switzerland; Ladin Rhaeto-Romance, with something over 10,000 speakers in the Alto Adige (Südtirol) of northern Italy; and Friulan Rhaeto-Romance, with some 400,000 to 500,000 speakers in the Friulan plain around Udine, in northeastern Italy. (See Map X.)

A description of Rhaeto-Romance which focused on its conservative features would enumerate those properties which unite the language with Old French (for example, the retention of consonant + *l* clusters), and we could say little about what makes Rhaeto-Romance unique. On the other hand, a description which focused on its innovations would impel us to recognise a major break between the Swiss and the Italian forms of Rhaeto-Romance. Swiss dialects are characterised by massive borrowing from Swiss German (for example, the verb-second constraint), while the Italian dialects have borrowed equally heavily from northern Italian dialects (for example, in the distribution of clitic pronouns, Ladin and Friulan are very similar to Zeneyze and Trentino). Again, there is nothing we can say about defining properties of Rhaeto-Romance as a whole. This is a natural consequence of the fact noted earlier (p. 21) that Rhaeto-Romance corresponds to no political entity, and that there are probably no monolingual speakers of any Rhaeto-Romance dialect in the world today.

This chaotic state of affairs will force us to recognise no fewer than seven distinct dialects at various points in the following description. Five of these are Swiss, all canonised by language planners and having literary traditions dating back as far as the sixteenth century. From west to east, they are Surselvan, Sutselvan, Surmeiran, Puter, and Vallader. The last two, spoken in the upper and the lower Engadine valley respectively, differ minimally, and mutual comprehensibility among all Swiss dialects is high. Nevertheless, even in Switzerland, where these dialects, under the generic name Romantsch, have had the status of a national language since 1938, attempts to create a single 'Romontsch fusionau' have failed. No similar standardising influence has been exerted on any of the Ladin or Friulan dialects, and from a phonetic standpoint at least, we can do no better than to follow the pioneering descriptions of scholars like Ascoli and Gartner and recognise as many dialects as there are villages and communities. We will therefore select as 'standard' dialects of Ladin and Friulan those for which the most exhaustive and careful descriptions exist.

2   Phonology

Every dialect has its own phonemic inventory, but the following general observations may be made. Every Rhaeto-Romance dialect has a vowel system of at least seven vowels identical with, but not necessarily directly inherited from, PWR /i, e, ɛ, a, ɔ, o, u/. The only diphthongs common to all dialects are /aj/ and /aw/. There is in addition a maximally unspecified vowel /V/ which surfaces as schwa in syllables with reduced stress, and as the second element of diphthongs whose conventional orthographic representation (in the Swiss dialects) is *ie* or *uo*. All the dialects have phonologised a series of palatals, including the stops /c, ɟ/, the affricates /ʧ, ʤ/, the fricatives /ʃ, ʒ/, and the sonorants /ɲ, ʎ/. Although the velar nasal [ŋ] occurs in most dialects, its status in most of them seems to be that of a subphonemic (syllable-final) variant of /n/. In their phonological development, the Italian Rhaeto-Romance dialects (Ladin and Friulan) seem to have been more conservative than the Swiss, as the following cursory sketch may indicate.

Inherited Lat. /i/ is retained in the Italian dialects and in Vallader in all environments. It is retained in open syllables in all dialects. In syllables closed by /r/, Surmeiran and Puter exhibit the peculiar diphthongisation known as *Verschärfung* 'sharpening' whereby inherited /i/ becomes [ik] or [ɛk], possibly via ?[ij]. Thus DŌRMĪRE becomes [durmɛkr] 'to sleep'. That this change is subphonemic is reflected in the fact that it is not indicated in the standard orthography of either dialect, and is apparently stigmatised by speakers as 'uncouth'. In syllables closed by a cluster, or by a nasal consonant, both Surselvan and Surmeiran lower /i/ to /ɛ/. Thus PRĪMUM, DĪCTUM become /(ɛm)prɛm/ 'first', /dɛc/ 'said', respectively.

Inherited Lat. /u/ again is retained in the Italian dialects. In all the Swiss dialects (as in French, p. 211), it is fronted to /y/, and in the westernmost Swiss dialects (Surselvan, Sutselvan, and Surmeiran) this resulting vowel is unrounded to /i/. The latter change seems to have preceded the lowering of inherited /i/ to /ɛ/, viz Surselvan /flɛm/ 'river' < FLŪMEN. Surmeiran and Puter once again exhibit *Verschärfung* in syllables closed by /r/. Thus DŪRUM becomes Puter /dykr/, Surmeiran /dɛkr/.

Inherited Lat. /e/ underwent diphthongisation to /aj/ in all Rhaeto-Romance dialects, but this general process was either inhibited or reversed in many environments. Friulan has restored /e/ almost everywhere; Ladin has /ɛj/ or /aj/ in open syllables, /e/ in closed; Vallader, here the most conservative dialect, seems to have retained /aj/ regularly; Puter (whose orthography still indicates /aj/) has very recently restored /e/; Surmeiran exhibits *Verschärfung*, particularly in syllables closed by /r/; Sutselvan has /aj/ or /oj/ before nasals, but has elsewhere restored /e/; and Surselvan has restored /e/ almost everywhere. The range of variation is exemplified in the second conjugation infinitival endings: Lat. -ĒRE > Surselvan /e/, Surmeiran /ɛkr/, Puter /er/, Vallader /ajr/, Ladin /aj/, and Friulan /e(j)/.

Inherited Lat. /o/ is preserved in the Italian dialects, while in the Swiss dialects the vowel was diphthongised to /uV/ before /l/+ consonant or consonant +/l/ or syllable-final /l/, and simply raised to /u/ elsewhere. Thus CŪLPA becomes /kuVlpa/ in all the Swiss dialects. Surmeiran diphthongises /u/ to [uk] before all oral consonants: LŪPUM 'wolf' > Italian R-R /lo(w)f/ and Swiss R-R /luf/, phonetically [lukf] in Surmeiran.

Inherited /ɛ/ throughout Rhaeto-Romance diphthongised to /ɛa/ (still attested in spoken Sutselvan, and in si˙teenth-century Surselvan and Engadine orthography). In all dialects except Sutselvan (here the most conservative), this diphthong became /ja/ or /je/ or /jɛ/, which is what Surselvan and the Italian dialects now have. In the Engadine dialects, /ja/ has very recently undergone remonophthongisation to /ɛ/. Thus, Lat. BĔLLA 'beautiful (f. sg.)' > Surselvan /bjala/, Sutselvan /bɛala/, Engadine /bɛla/, Ladin /bjela/, and Friulan /bjɛla/.

Inherited /ɔ/ was originally diphthongised to *wɔ/ throughout Rhaeto-Romance, but this diphthong is not retained in a single dialect today. In the Swiss dialects, it has been remonophthongised to /o/ except before 'umlauting environments', which include not only /-Ci/, but also the inherited masculine singular accusative, or neuter singular -UM. Before these environments, we encounter Surselvan /iV/, Sutselvan /ja/ and Engadine /yV/. This umlauted diphthong in turn is retained only before liquid clusters (/l+C/ or /C+l/), giving way elsewhere to the monophthong /ø/ in the Engadine dialects, or to a number of other nuclei in Surselvan and Sutselvan. In Ladin, inherited /ɔ/ remonophthongised to either /o/ or /ɔ/ except in umlauting environments, where it seems to have become /e/. Friulan appears to be the only Rhaeto-Romance dialect not to exhibit a peculiar reflex of /ɔ/ in umlauting environments, having instead the diphthong /wa/ before liquid clusters, and /o/ (alternating with /we/ or /u/) elsewhere. For an example of the range of possibilities in an umlauting environment, FŎCUM 'fire' > Surselvan /fjuɡ/, Sutselvan /fjak/, Engadine /fø/, Ladin /fek/, and Friulan /fuk/ ~ /fok/.

Inherited /a/ is regularly retained in Friulan. In Ladin, it is retained in final position and before nasals, but is elsewhere raised to /e/. The Swiss dialects innovated in diphthongising /a/ to /aw/ before nasals. The resulting diphthong was retained before syllable-final /n/ which was also word-final, and before syllable-initial /n/, but it was monophthongised to /ɔ/ before /m/ and before syllable-final /n/ which was not word-final. Further complex innovations occurred in the central Swiss dialects (Sutselvan, Surmeiran and Puter). The following correspondence illustrates the vicissitudes of inherited /a/ before word- and syllable-final /n/: Lat. CANEM 'dog' > Surselvan /cawn/ (phonetically [cɔwn]), central Swiss /cɛm/, Vallader /can/ (phonetically [caŋ]), Ladin /tʃan/ (phonetically [tʃaŋ]), and Friulan /can/ (phonetically [caŋ]).

Inherited /aw/ (from Latin /au/ and syllable-final /al/) was monophthongised to /o/ at some time after the palatalisation of velars before inherited /a/. There has been a tendency throughout Rhaeto-Romance to reestablish the original /aw/ diphthong or /al/, a tendency which has resulted in a number of hypercorrections which have 'restored' an etymologically unjustified /l/: examples include Surmeiran [galdɛkr] < GAUDĒRE 'rejoice', Vallader /(d)alda/ < AUDIT 'hears (3 sg.)', Ladin /(l)alda/ < LAUDAT 'praises (3 sg.)' and Friulan /polsa/ < PAUSAT 'stops (3 sg.)'.

Turning now to the development of unstressed vowels, there seems to be only one perfectly general Rhaeto-Romance process: the loss of all final unstressed vowels other than /a/.

Two functionally related developments 'conspired' to eliminate antepenultimate stress in Rhaeto-Romance, namely:

$$\begin{bmatrix} V \\ V \\ -low \end{bmatrix} \begin{array}{l} > \emptyset / \#C\acute{V}C\_\_CVC \# \quad \text{(e.g. DŎMĬNA} > /\text{d\'onna}/\text{)} \\ > \emptyset / \#C\grave{V}C\_\_C\acute{V}C \# \quad \text{(e.g. TĪTŬLARE} > /\text{tɛdlár}/ \text{ 'listen').} \end{array}$$

But there is a distinction between the Swiss and the Italian dialects here: in general there are more exceptions to both of these rules in the Italian dialects, which as a consequence are much more tolerant of violations of the stricture against antepenultimate stress, cf. Ladin /fɔ́mɛna/ 'woman', /píʧola/ 'little girl'. That this distinction is dynamic may be seen from the differing treatments of clitics in verb + clitic combinations in the various dialects. In general, the Swiss dialects reduce these clitics in conformity with the principle that only final and penultimate stress are allowed, but the Italian dialects do not, and verb + clitic combinations in general are a productive source of words with antepenultimate (or even earlier) stress. (A morphosyntactic distinction between the Swiss and the Italian dialects which is compatible with — though probably not a direct consequence of — this phonetic distinction is the constraint on the number of object clitics that may occur before or after the same verb. The Swiss dialects in general allow only one such object clitic while the Italian dialects of Rhaeto-Romance allow several.)

A qualitative distinction between stressed and unstressed vowels is preserved in verb-stem alternations which occur (though subject to different degrees of levelling) in all the Rhaeto-Romance dialects. Originally phonetically motivated, these alternations are no longer productive, and attempts to predict their nature by assigning abstract 'underlying' vowels to the verb stems which display alternation are probably misconceived. Generally speaking, the set of vowels occurring in unstressed syllables is smaller, and contains fewer marked members, than the set of vowels occurring in stressed syllables. (Typically, the verb stem is stressed in all persons and numbers of the present indicative except the first and second person plural.) Examples are Surselvan and Valloder /dórm/ ~ /durm/ 'sleep', Ladin /lav/ ~ /lév/ 'wash' and Friulan /dwár/ ~ /durm/ 'sleep'. The dialect which seems to preserve the richest system of alternations (including alternations in both vowels of certain bisyllabic stems) is Surselvan, which in this one respect deserves to be called the most conservative dialect of Rhaeto-Romance.

While vocalic developments typically distinguish the various dialects from one another, there are at least two features of the consonantal system which characterise the Rhaeto-Romance dialects as a group. The first, a retention, is the preservation of /C+l/ clusters. The second, an innovation, is the palatalisation of velars before inherited /a/. Each of these features sets Rhaeto-Romance apart from Italian and puts it together with French and Northern Occitan. The retention of /C+l/ is not entirely general: in Ladin, as in Italian (p. 228), original /C+l/ has become /Cj/, although there is strong evidence that this change in Ladin occurred only within the last hundred years or so. Latin CLAVEM 'key' thus yields French /kle/, common R-R /klaf/, Ladin /kjef/, and standard Italian /kjave/.

The palatalisation of velars before inherited /a/ may have occurred originally only in stressed syllables. Thus Surselvan and Sutselvan distinguish between /cawn/ 'dog' (with palatalisation, < CANEM) and /kaváʎ/ (without palatalisation, < CABĂLLUM). In all dialects to the east of Sutselvan, however, palatalisation of inherited /k/ occurred before both stressed and unstressed /a/ equally.

Velars also palatalised before inherited front vowels, the outcome of this (almost certainly earlier) palatalisation being the affricates /ʧ/ and /ʤ/. In the Swiss dialects, the outcomes of the two palatalisations are unambiguously two distinct sets of phonemes: thus CĬRCAT 'searches' > /ʧerca/. In the Italian dialects, a merger seems to be underway. Although several explicitly phonemic descriptions of both Ladin and Friulan recognise a phonemic contrast between palatal stops and affricates, other more phonetically oriented descriptions of these dialects seem to show the two palatals in free variation in many cases. Thus Elwert's classic description of Fassa Ladin had both /c/ and /ʧ/ before inherited /a/: [ʧantá] 'to sing' and [cánte] 'I sing'. On the other hand, he consistently recorded only the affricate /ʧ/ before inherited front vowels.

Inherited /s/ was palatalised before inherited /i/ and before any consonant. The latter change, which gives Rhaeto-Romance a German phonetic flavour, may perhaps be added to the list of peculiarly Rhaeto-Romance innovations. Obscuring of the conditioning environment in the first case has led to the phonologisation of a new phoneme /ʃ/. Throughout Rhaeto-Romance, inherited /gn/, and inherited /n/ before /i/ and /y/ (the latter from Latin /u/, cf. p. 353 above) became /ɲ/.

The development of the inherited cluster /kt/ split Rhaeto-Romance into two major areas. In the western Swiss dialects (Surselvan, Sutselvan and Surmeiran), this cluster yielded /c/, /t/, or /ts/. In the Italian dialects, the cluster was simplified to /t/. Finally, in the eastern dialects of Switzerland, spoken in the Engadine valley, most /kt/ became /t/, while a handful became /c/.

Intervocalic stops in all dialects were subject to lenition. The phenomenon of strengthening, which followed the apocope of final syllables (cf. p. 354, above) provides evidence for at least two separate stages of lenition. Given an original CVCV form, we may posit:

First lenition: CVCV > CV*c*V (/*c*/ here representing a more sonorous lenited consonant);
Apocope: CV*c*a > CV*c*a (final /a/ does not undergo apocope);
                   CV*c*V > CV*c* (all other final vowels do undergo apocope);
Further changes: CV*c*a > CVʔa (intervocalic /*c*/ undergoes further lenition or disappears);
                   CV*c* > CVC (final /*c*/ is strengthened, usually by devoicing).

For the contrast between full and partially reversed lenition, consider the development of inherited /p/ in PĪPER and LŬPUM. In the former, no apocope occurs and lenition converts /p/ to /v/, as in /pɛjvVr/ 'pepper'. In the latter, final -UM eventually disappears, and /p/ becomes /f/, as in /lof/. Like the palatalisation of velars before inherited /a/, primary lenition must have occurred before the monophthongisation of /aw/, that is, at a time when /aw/ still functioned as a VC sequence. Note the contrast between MATŪRUM, in which /t/ is lenited to /d/ in all Rhaeto-Romance dialects (Italian R-R /madur/, Engadine /madyr/, Surselvan /madir/), and AUTŬMNUM in which /t/ remains unaffected by lenition (Swiss R-R /uton/ ~ /atun/).

Finally, inherited initial /j/ was strengthened in all dialects: Latin JŬVĚNEM > Surselvan /ɟuvVn/, Ladin /ʒown/, Friulan /ʒevin/ 'young'.

3 Morphology

Verbal Categories
It is convenient to distinguish between synthetic and analytic constructions, where by the former we mean the system of verbal affixes, and by the latter, auxiliary verb constructions. All verbal categories in Rhaeto-Romance except the future, the perfect and the passive, are expressed by affixes.

The Synthetic Forms
All verbs in Rhaeto-Romance consist of a root followed by a number of suffixes. Finite verbs are those in which the final (perhaps the only) suffixes are subject agreement markers, while non-finite verbs are those in which there are no agreement marking suffixes. Vestiges of the inherited four-conjugation system of Latin are preserved, if at all, only in the suffix immediately following the verb stem. The system of four conjugations is retained only in the infinitive in Rhaeto-Romance: in all other verbal categories, there is some conflation.

The basic split in verbal suffixes is between agreement markers and all others. The agreement markers may be subcategorised in terms of the following three parameters:

(a) their proximity to the verb stem;
(b) whether they retain some vestiges of the four-conjugation system;
(c) whether they exhibit movable stress.

Generally, only desinences which are adjacent to the verb stem have properties (b) and (c) but this covariation is not absolute. Thus, for example, the subjunctive desinences in the Engadine dialects are adjacent to the root but exhibit no conjugation class allomorphy or movable stress.

Conversely, the imperfect desinences in Ladin are not proximate to the root but exhibit movable stress.

Non-personal desinences may be divided into those which are non-finite (and cannot be followed by agreement markers), and those which are finite (and must be followed by agreement markers). The non-finite desinences are the infinitive, the perfect participle, the gerund and the present participle. The finite desinences are the augment, the imperfect, the imperfect subjunctive, the future, the past definite and the counterfactual conditional.

The first chart given here presents the non-finite non-personal desinences in the two major Swiss dialects, Ladin and Friulan: it will be noted that Ladin has no gerund. Finally, the present participle is a productive verbal form in Surselvan only.

Non-finite Verb Endings

Infinitival Endings

		Surselvan	Vallader	Ladin	Friulan
Conj.	I	-a	-ar	-ar	-a
	II	-e	-ajr	-er	-e
	III	'-er	'-er	'-er	'-i
	IV	-i	-ir	-ir	-i

Perfect Participial Endings

	Surselvan	Vallader	Ladin	Friulan
I	-aw	-a	-a	-at
II	-iw	-ü	-u	-ut
III	-iw	-ü	-u	-ut
IV	-iw	-ü	-i	-it

Gerund Endings

	Surselvan	Vallader	Friulan
I	-ond	-ond	-ant
II–IV	-end	-ind	-int

Present Participle (Surselvan only)

I	-ont
II–IV	-ent

Finite non-personal desinences may be divided into strictly meaningless morphemes like the augment, and the suffixes indicating tense, aspect and mood.

Reflexes of the (originally inchoative) augment -ISC- are found with fourth conjugation verbs in all Rhaeto-Romance dialects: Surselvan /ɛs/, all other dialects /is/. In the Swiss dialects, the augment has been generalised to a number of first conjugation verbs, and in the Engadine dialects there is a distinction betweeen I /ɛʃ/, IV /iʃ/. The paradigmatic distribution of the augment is the same as in French (p. 223) and Italian (p. 294): always stressed, it follows (and thus destresses) the verb stem, unless the verb stem is followed by a stressed (first or second person plural) personal desinence. In effect, this eliminates vocalic alternations between stressed and unstressed verb stems.

The next charts present the imperfect indicative suffixes (from Latin -ĀB-, -ĒB-, -ĪB-) and the past subjunctive suffixes (from Latin -ASS-, -ESS-, -ISS-). The imperfect indicative suffix is consistently stressed except in Ladin, where following first and second plural personal desinences are stressed. Preceding these, the suffix /e/ becomes /a/: /cantéa/ 'was singing (3 sg.)', but /cantaáne/ 'we were singing'.

Imperfect Indicative

	Surselvan	Vallader	Ladin	Triulan
I	av	ev	e	av
II, III	ev	cv	e	ev
IV	ev	iv	i	iv

Past Subjunctive

	Surselvan	Vallader	Ladin	Triulan
I	as	es	as	as
II, III	es	es	es	es
IV	es	is	is	is

The future as a bound or synthetic morpheme is totally absent in Surselvan, and perhaps not an indigenous phenomenon in any of the Swiss dialects. The Engadine and Ladin future suffixes are I–III /ar/, IV /ir/, while Friulan has /ar/ throughout. A peculiarity of Friulan is that fourth conjugation verbs in /is/ retain this (now unstressed) augment before the future suffix (and no other non-personal suffix): /partisaraj/ 'I will leave', etc. (Personal future desinences, as elsewhere in Romance, are stressed throughout the paradigm.)

In Puter, Ladin and Friulan, the future occurs as the first morpheme in one of two complex tense/mood suffix compounds. The first of these, which I call the 'suppositive future', seems to occur only in Puter, and consists of /ar/ + /eɟ/ (etymology unclear): /pud-ar-eɟ-ans/ 'we will probably be able', /ɲ-ar-eɟ-a/ 'I would come', contrasting with the simple future /pud-ar-ans/ 'we will be able', /ɲ-ar-o/ 'I will come'. The second compound form, the counterfactual conditional, occurs only in the Italian dialects, and consists of /ar/ followed by the invariable imperfect subjunctive /es/. As the future in Friulan may occur with the /is/ augment, so also may the compound derived from it: /part-is-ar-és/ 'I would leave'. (The counterfactual conditional in the Swiss dialects is expressed by the past subjunctive, cf. p. 304.)

The past definite, a clear Italianism, is established only in Friulan, where, as in Italian, it is impossible to separate the suffix from the personal

desinences: 1 sg. /aj/, 2 sg. /áris/, 3 sg. /a/, 1 pl. /árin/, 2 pl. /áris/, 3 pl.
/árin/. In written Vallader, the paradigm has been restructured (as in
Occitan) around the inherited third person singular. The suffixes are I–III
conjugation /et/, IV /it/, and are invariably stressed.

Personal desinences may be classified as either primary or secondary,
where primary desinences are defined as those which display conjugational
allomorphy and stress shift in the first and second person plural. Secondary
desinences exhibit neither feature. A possibly defining feature of the Ladin
dialects is the existence of a hybrid set of personal desinences which have
stress shift but no conjugational allomorphy.

The present indicative and imperative are primary in all Rhaeto-
Romance dialects; the past subjunctive and the future are secondary. The
present subjunctive is primary except in the Engadine dialects. The imperfect
indicative personal desinences are secondary in all dialects except Ladin,
where they are 'hybrid' (cf. p. 359).

The present indicative, as one would expect, exhibits the richest system
of personal desinences. With the exception of Ladin (where 3 sg. = 3 pl. by
virtue of the apocope of final 3 pl. /n/ under Lombardic influence), all
Rhaeto-Romance dialects distinguish three persons in both the singular
and the plural. All retain vestiges of conjugational allomorphy in the
second person plural; all but Friulan do so in the first plural; both Ladin
and Friulan distinguish conjugations in the third singular; and Friulan does
so in the first singular. The relevant data are presented in the chart of
present indicative agreement markers. (The remarkable conservatism of
Friulan in maintaining a three-way distinction in the second person plural is
confined to the westernmost dialects. In Udine Friulan I=III /es/.)

Present Indicative Agreement Markers

	Surselvan		Vallader	Ladin	Friulan	
Singular						
1	el		Ø	e	I	e
					II–IV	Ø
2	as		aʃ(t)	es	is	
3	a		a	I	a	c
				II–IV Ø ~ e	Ø	
Plural						
1	I–III	éjn	ájn	ón	ín	
	IV	ín	ín	jón		
2	I–III	éjs	ájvat	éde	I	ájs
	IV	ís	ívat	íde	II–III	éjs
					IV	ís
3	an		an	(=3 sg.)	in	

The positive imperative is an inflectional category of the verb, while the negative imperative is almost always expressed by some periphrastic construction. The forms of the positive imperative desinences are given in the chart.

Positive Imperative Agreement Markers

	Surselvan	Vallader	Ladin		Friulan	
Sg.	a	a	I	a	e ~	a
			II–IV	Ø	Ø	
Pl.	I–III éj	áj	I	á	ájt	
	IV í	í	II–III	é	éjt	
			IV	í	ít	

In the expression of the negative imperative we observe a fundamental split between two constructions:

Western: /buka ~ betj/ (negative *word*) # positive imperative
Eastern: /no ~ nu/ (negative *proclitic*) + infinitive (plural)

Surselvan and Sutselvan have only the western form; the Engadine dialects, Latin and Friulan, only the eastern form; and Surmeiran has both. It is noteworthy that the eastern construction is available for both singular and plural, thus e.g. Vallader /nu cant-ár/ 'don't sing! (sg.)' and /nu cant-ar-áj/ 'don't sing! (pl.)'. The polite pronoun in all Rhaeto-Romance dialects but those of the Engadine valley is the second plural, and the polite imperative is thus the same as the plural imperative. In the Engadine dialects, the polite pronoun is third singular, and the polite imperative is the subjunctive, introduced by the complementiser /ca/.

The hortatory imperative in all Rhaeto-Romance dialects but Surselvan is the same as the first person plural indicative. In Surselvan, it consists of /lejn/ followed by the infinitive, where /lejn/ is the first person plural of /(vu)ler/ 'to want': /lejn ir/ 'let's go!'.

Imperfect Indicative Agreement Markers

	Surselvan	Vallader	Ladin	Friulan	
Singular					
1	el	a	e	i	
2	as	ast	es	is	
3	a	a	a	e ~	a
Plural					
1	an	an	áne	in	
2	as	at	éde	is	
3	an	an	a	in	

The imperfect indicative agreement markers occur exclusively with the imperfect suffix. Except in the Ladin dialects, they are typically secondary desinences, without conjugational allomorphy and without shifting stress. A peculiar usage of the imperfect, confined apparently to Surselvan, is to express a counterfactual imperative. No language (to my knowledge) has a separate form for the counterfactual imperative, but whereas English uses a periphrastic construction involving *should*, Surselvan uses the imperfect indicative:

```
pag - av     - as    tes  déjvɛts
pay (imperf.) 2 sg. your debts
'You should have paid your debts.'
```

The present subjunctive desinences, as noted, are primary in all Rhaeto-Romance dialects except those of the Engadine valley. They immediately follow the verb stem, and are commonly used to express indirect speech. Surselvan alone among the Rhaeto-Romance dialects has innovated in allowing these desinences to follow two verbal suffixes: the imperfect indicative and the past subjunctive. (Following a suffix, the subjunctive desinences become secondary, 1 pl. (invariably) /jɛn/, 2 pl. (invariably) /jɛs/.) Thus /kant-éjɛn/ '(we) are said to sing', /kant-áv-jɛn/ '(we) were said to be singing', /kant-ás-jɛn/ 'it was said (we) would sing'.

Present Subjunctive Agreement Markers

		Surselvan	Ladin	Friulan		(Vallader)
Singular						
1		i	e	i ~ ∅		a
2		jɛs	es	is		ast
3		i	e	i		a
Plural						
1	I–III	éjɛn	óna	ín		an
	IV	íɛn				
2	I–III	éjɛs	éjda	I	ájs	at
	IV	íɛs	ída	II–III	éjs	
				IV	ís	
3		iVn	e	in		an

The past subjunctive desinences in all dialects occur exclusively after the past subjunctive suffix *as ~ es ~ is*. The Vallader forms are identical to the present subjunctive desinences given in the chart except in the first and third person singular (and it is this set of forms which have been pressed into service for the past definite). Like the imperfect indicative desinences, these are secondary in all dialects but Ladin, and hybrid in Ladin.

Past Subjunctive Agreement Markers

	Surselvan	Vallader	Ladin	Friulan
Singular				
1	Ø	Ø	c	Ø
2	es	aʃt	es	is
3	Ø	Ø	a	Ø
Plural				
1	en	an	áne	in
2	es	at	éde	is
3	en	an	a	in

Future personal desinences in Vallader are identical with those of the present subjunctive but invariably stressed. The forms of the Italian dialects are given in the chart.

Future Personal Desinences

	Ladin	Friulan
Singular		
1	c	aj
2	s	as
3	a	a
Plural		
1	on	in
2	de	ejs
3	a	an

The Analytic Verbal Forms: a Sketch of the Auxiliary Verb System

The major periphrastic or analytic auxiliary constructions in Rhaeto-Romance are the future, the perfect and the passive, which combine in that order. Thus, in Surselvan:

/jaw veɲVl   ad ésVr veɲíws   klamáws/
1   fut.-1 sg. to to-be come-pp. called-pp.
'I will have been called.'

The aspectual, temporal and modal categories discussed in the immediately preceding section can be expressed only on the first auxiliary verb of an Aux + Verb complex. In the example above, therefore, the first auxiliary is marked as present indicative and first person.

An analytic future in (a reflex of) VENIRE AD + infinitive is found throughout Rhaeto-Romance, and, as noted above (p. 359) is the only possible future in Surselvan. There is considerable variation in the pre-position used, and even in the auxiliary verb. For example, Friulan allows not only /veɲír/ 'come', but also /avájr/ 'have' and (possibly only in the dialects described by Iliescu, spoken in Rumania under Rumanian influence) /voj/ 'I want'. In both the passive and the perfect, the auxiliary verb is followed by the perfect participle, which is inflected for number and gender. The passive auxiliary is /ɲir/ 'come' (Surselvan) and either /vɛɲir/ 'come' or /ɛsVr/ 'be' in all dialects to the east of Surselvan. Subject to individual dialect variation, the rule of use seems to be that 'come' is preferred when the passive is the only auxiliary, 'be' when the passive auxiliary follows another auxiliary. Thus Vallader /ɛw vɛɲ inɟoná/ 'I am tricked', but /ɛw sun ʃtat inɟoná/ 'I have been tricked'. The perfect auxiliary is either /ɛ́sVr/ 'be' or /avájr/ 'have'. The former auxiliary occurs with a subset of intransitive verbs, including the basic verbs of motion. For reflexive verbs, the perfect auxiliary in the Engadine dialects and Ladin (which we might call the central Rhaeto-Romance dialects) is invariably 'have'. Surselvan and Friulan have both 'have' and 'be', and the factors which control variation, especially in the latter dialect, are obscure.

In general, the perfect participle agrees with the subject in number and gender when the auxiliary is 'come' or 'be', and fails to agree when the auxiliary is 'have.' In the Engadine dialects, however, the reflexive perfect occurs with /avájr/ 'have', but the perfect participle nevertheless agrees with the subject. Thus Vallader /ɛla s a lavá-da/ 'she washed herself' contrasts with /ɛl s a lavá/ 'he washed himself'. Agreement is presumably with the subject rather than the preposed object, which exhibits no gender or number marking in the third person.

Nominal Categories
The term 'nominal' will be used to identify those parts of speech which mark gender (and sometimes case) as inflectional categories: included are nouns, pronouns, demonstratives, adjectives, numerals and participles. Notable peculiarities are:

(a) the retention of a plural marker in -s;
(b) the retention of an inherited dative case in -i (with at least historical attestation in all but the Engadine dialects);
(c) the retention of an inherited nominative/accusative distinction in the masculine singular;
(d) the retention of a distinctive neuter gender (only in Surselvan).

Nouns
Almost all common nouns in Rhaeto-Romance in the singular represent reflexes of an inherited oblique (probably accusative) case. Given the loss of almost all singular gender and case markings, the evidence for this is largely indirect. In Surselvan, final -UM but not -US was an umlauting environment (contrast, for example, /buns/ 'good (m. sg.)' < BONUS with

/biVn/ 'good (n. sg.)' < BONUM); therefore, Old Surselvan /ciVrf/ 'crow'
derived from CORVUM rather than CORVUS. On the other hand, there are a
handful of doublets, most notably the name of the deity, in which a productive oblique case /diw/ contrasts with a fixed formulaic /diws/, and the
reflexes of the actual nominative and accusative case endings are still
present.

The plural marker -s continues the inherited accusative plural, and is
exceptionless in the Swiss dialects. In the Italian dialects, however, some
nouns take (reflexes of) an inherited -i nominative plural (cf. p. 63). In both
Ladin and Friulan, the -s plural is found on both feminine nouns in final /a/
and on masculine nouns ending in a consonant (Ladin /lɛnges/ 'tongues',
Friulan /ʒambas/ 'legs'; Ladin /dɛnts/ 'teeth', Friulan /klafs/ 'keys'). In
Ladin, some consonant-final masculine stems form their plural in -i, while
in Friulan some vowel-final masculine stems do (Ladin /neʃ/ 'noses' <
*nes-i contrasts with /nes/ 'nose', and Friulan /ʒaline/ 'hens' contrasts
with /ʒalina/ 'hen').

Definite Articles
The basic paradigm in Rhaeto-Romance is of four contrasting forms marking number and gender, but not case. Typical is Surselvan il/la 'singular',
ils/las 'plural'. The dative and other oblique cases are marked by prepositions. In modern Surmeiran, however, there still exists a pair of definite
articles li/lis, which continue inherited ILLI, ILLIS: /li feʎ/ 'to the son' contrasts with /il feʎ/ 'the son' (cf. the position in Rumanian, pp. 398–9).

Personal Pronouns
All Rhaeto-Romance dialects with the exception of Surselvan have two
sets of personal pronouns: a disjunctive stressed set (which is all that
Surselvan has), and a reduced clitic set. This contrast exists in the
paradigms for subject, object and reflexive pronouns, which will be treated
separately.

In all dialects but those of the Engadine valley, both stressed and clitic
object pronouns distinguish a dative from an accusative case, at least in
some persons and numbers. Thus, for example, the first person singular
disjunctive (a) mi 'dative' contrasts with the first singular disjunctive me
'accusative' in Surselvan, Ladin and Friulan. On the other hand, Vallader
maj and Puter me '1 sg. disjunctive' are distinguished only by the prepositions with which they cooccur.

As in French (p. 291) a distinction is maintained between nominative
and oblique cases for all pronouns except the first and second person
plural.

All the Swiss dialects retain a distinct third person singular neuter pronoun which functions as 'ambient it' with impersonal predicates, and
occurs only as a dummy subject. For example /ej túna/ 'it thunders, there

is thunder' contrasts with /ɛl túna/ 'he thunders'. The Swiss dialects also have a common gender third plural form distinct from the third plural masculine or feminine pronouns: formally, this is identical with the third person singular neuter, but takes plural verb agreement, and refers exclusively to human agents. Thus Surselvan /ej tséjvran núVrsas/ '3 pl. common gender shear-3 pl. sheep-pl.' is probably best translated by a passive or a similar construction in English which backgrounds the identity of the agent, and contrasts with /ɛls ~ ɛlas tsejvran nu Vras/ 'they (m. or f.) shear sheep'.

The syntax of clitic subject pronouns distinguishes the Swiss dialects from the Italian in two ways: first, in the Swiss dialects subject clitics occur only post-verbally, while in the Italian dialects, they occur both as verbal prefixes and suffixes; second, in the Swiss dialects it is quite rare for subject clitics to co-occur with full noun phrase subjects, while in the Italian dialects (as in popular French, cf. p. 232) such co-occurrence is common.

Surselvan, which has no atonic pronouns at all, has no enclisis; the central and eastern Swiss dialects, which have both subject and object clitic pronouns, but rarely permit the former, have more; while the Italian dialects, in which atonic pronouns are well on the way to becoming agreement markers, have carried enclisis the furthest.

Reflexive pronouns manifest reduction in various ways: morphologically, in the reduction of formal oppositions of person and number in the reflexive paradigm; and syntactically, in cliticisation and concomitant fixity of word order.

Surselvan, which has no clitic set of pronouns, has gone further than any other Rhaeto-Romance dialect in reducing reflexive pronouns: not to a set of clitics, but to an invariably inseparable verbal prefix *se*. In all other dialects, the reflexive pronoun marks person and number, may occur either before or after the verb (depending on whether the mood of the verb is indicative, infinitive or imperative) and is separated from the verb by the perfective auxiliary, if one is present. In other words, only in Surselvan does the reflexive pronoun not behave like other object pronouns (cf. p. 291).

Adjectives

This class includes perfect participles, possessive pronominal adjectives and what we may call 'true adjectives' like 'big'. In the modern dialects, all of these are inflected for number and gender and agree with the head noun in a nominal syntagm (as attributive adjectives) and with the subject noun phrase (as predicate adjectives).

In earlier Rhaeto-Romance, a stage attested in seventeenth- and eighteenth-century Surselvan, masculine adjectives at least were also inflected for case. Schematically, the case oppositions were as set out in the chart provided here (where the left column for each category is Latin, while the right-hand column represents Old Surselvan). The same suffix -*s* functioned as both a plural marker and a masculine nominative case marker. In accordance with Kuryłowicz's fourth law, the relatively peripheral case distinction was given up in favour of the more basic number distinction — but not completely, and not in the same way in all the Rhaeto-Romance dialects. (For a similar development in French, cf. pp. 216–17).

Case Marking of Masculine Adjectives in Latin and Old Surselvan

	Possessive		Participles		True adjectives	
Singular						
Nom.	MEUS	mes	LAUDATUS	ludaws	SANUS	sawns
Acc.	MEUM	miw	LAUDATUM	ludaw	SANUM	sawn
Plural						
Nom.	MEI	mej	LAUDATI	ludaj	SANI	sawni
Acc.	MEOS	mes	LAUDATOS	ludaws	SANOS	sawns

In the plural, all dialects have eliminated the case distinction. Surselvan has generalised the acc. pl. -s for possessive pronominal adjectives and true adjectives, but the nom. pl. -i for participles; the Engadine dialects and Friulan generalised -s for all adjectives, while Ladin generalised -i.

In the singular also, the inherited case distinction was transformed in all dialects but Surselvan. Puter generalised acc. (i.e. a null desinence) -Ø for all adjectives, as did Ladin and Friulan. Vallader generalised the accusative for true adjectives and perfect participles but innovated in the possessive pronominal adjectives: nom. -s is used in the attributive function, while acc. -Ø is used in the predicative (possessive pronoun) function: /mes riʃpli/ 'my pencil', but /il riʃpli ajs miw/ 'the pencil is mine'.

The reinterpretation of an inherited case distinction as an attributive/ predicative distinction, confined in Vallader to the possessive pronominal adjectives, was totally productive in Surselvan. What is notable is that in the latter dialect, it was the accusative which became attributive, while the nominative became predicative, the precise opposite of what happened in Vallader.

/miw kudiʃ/ 'my book', but /il kudiʃ ej mes/ 'the book is mine';
/in biVn um/ 'a good man', but /il um ej buns/ 'the man is good';
/in cawn ɛmblidaw/ 'a forgotten dog', but /il cawn vɛɲɛmblidaws/ 'the dog is forgotten'.

In both Surselvan and Vallader, the only two dialects which transformed the inherited case opposition into an attributive/predicative contrast, the suffix -s continues to mark both masculine singular and masculine plural, thus retaining its ambiguous double function.

Demonstrative Pronouns

All Rhaeto-Romance dialects have reflexes of ECCU ISTE and ECCU ILLE, while some have a third series deriving from ECCE ILLE. As in Occitan and Ibero-Romance, the definite article has some of the privileges of occurrence of the demonstrative and may, if followed by an NP complement, occur without a head noun: Surselvan /ils de flɛm/ 'the people of Flem', Vallader /ils da gwarda/ 'the people of Guarda' are parallel to (Surselvan) /kwɛl de las kornas/ 'the one with the horns', i.e. 'the devil'.

The interrogative pronouns are morphologically and phonetically heterogeneous, the only common Rhaeto-Romance form being /ko/ 'how'; the Ladin forms for 'who' and 'what' are /ki/ and /ke/; in all other dialects, the velar is palatalised (Swiss /ci/, /ce/; Friulan /t͡ʃi/, /t͡ʃe/); 'when' in Swiss Rhaeto-Romance is a reflex of QUA HORA (as in Occitan), and in Italian Rhaeto-Romance of QUANDO (as in French, Spanish and Italian).

Relative Pronouns

In all Rhaeto-Romance dialects except those of the Engadine valley, the relative pronoun is invariable, and identical with the complementiser (Surselvan, Ladin /ke/, Friulan /ka/ ~ /ke/). In Puter and Vallader a contrast exists between the accusative relative pronoun /ca/ (identical with the complementiser), and the nominative relative pronoun /ci/, which is identical with interrogative 'who'.

The subordinate conjunctions 'when', 'where', etc., generally consist of the interrogative pronoun followed by the complementiser: thus, Vallader /kura ca/ 'when', /inʲo ca/ 'where', /ko ca/ 'how', and so on.

4   Syntax

The following discussion is limited to the following major features of Rhaeto-Romance syntax:

(a) word order in both principal and subordinate clauses;
(b) the status and relative order of constituents within noun phrases and in the verbal complex;
(c) the syntax of the 'predicate case' in Surselvan;
(d) the status of the Rhaeto-Romance dialects with respect to what has been called (by David Perlmutter) the 'type A constraint' and (by Noam Chomsky) the 'pro-drop parameter' (cf. p. 334).

Word Order

In the Swiss dialects, almost certainly under massive and prolonged German influence, word order in principal assertive clauses is verb-second. The rule is explicitly asserted in some of the normative pedagogical grammars, and is hardly ever violated. Very occasional examples of verb-third order are attested in both Surmeiran and Puter:

Surmeiran: ad en unfawnt malpardert ins ʃto dar seʎ   ciʎ
            to a child   rude   one must give on-the rear
            'Rude children should be given a kick up the backside.'
Puter: il di zieva il sulaʎ s   alvet il   tʃel
            the day after the sun refl. raised in-the sky
            'The next day, the sun rose in the sky.'

But these are hardly systematic.

Not surprisingly, there seems to be no corresponding verb-second rule in the Italian dialects, since the major external influence they fall under is that of the northern Italian dialects. While both Ladin and Friulan are SVO dialects, word order in them is relatively free and one frequently encounters sentences with word order that would be impossible in Swiss Rhaeto-Romance. To illustrate verb-initial order it will be necessary to say a few words about the status of subject pronoun clitics in Ladin and Friulan. There is evidence in these dialects (as in popular French) that these clitics are syntactically a part of the verbal complex, rather than being in construction with, and thus preceding, it. That is, there is a contrast between the two structures:

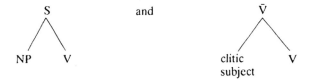

The principal criterion for placing full NPs outside the verbal complex, and the clitics within it, is the position of the two subject morphemes relative to the negative particle *no*, itself prefixed to the verb. Full NPs (including disjunctive pronouns) precede the negative particle, while both subject and object clitics follow it. Thus, for example, the Ladin sentence

εl no l se   fida
he not he refl. trusts
'He does not dare'.

is, by this hypothesis, assigned the syntactic structure

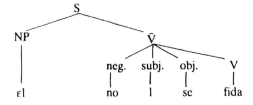

The following, then, are examples of verb-initial order from Ladin and Friulan:

(Ladin)   no n   troarede   sori n awtrɔ
not partitive you-will-find (pl.) such an other
'You will not find another like her.'

se koŋ ʃtɛr   da ite
refl. must to-stay of inside
'It is necessary to stay inside.'

te   l dage
to-you it I-give
'I (will) give it to you.'

la ɟe a fat petʃa
she her has made pity
'She felt sorry for her.'

no i   la maj pju vedudɔ
not they her ever more have-seen (f. sg.)
'They never saw her again.'

(Friulan) soj viɲút   kun una makina
I-am come (pp. m. sg.) with a   car

l aj   ritʃevút
it I-have received

era   palta granda
was-3 sg. mud great
'There was a lot of mud.'

l era   una ploja in kel di
it was-3 sg. a rain in that day
'There was rain that day.'

e tornada   la riʃpoʃta
is returned (f. sg.) the answer
'There came back the answer.'

l e reʃtat   numa kel pluj picul
he is stayed (m. sg.) only that more small
'There remained only the smallest.'

Note in the Friulan examples that the subject pronoun clitic is sometimes present and sometimes absent, but that *ex hypothesi*, verb-initial order is consistently maintained in all of these examples.

There are also many examples of verb-second order (both SVO and TVX) which are so frequent and unexceptionable as to require no exemplification. But we do need to show that verb-third order is also common and far from being a deviation, as it is in Swiss Rhaeto-Romance.

(Ladin)   dapɔ da sera la vaces i   se   pɛrla
          after at night the cows they refl. talk
          'Afterwards, at night, the cows talk to each other.'

          indomaŋ   el patron l   era mɔrt
          next morning the boss   he was dead (m. sg.)
          'The next morning the master was dead.'

          kɛla valɛnta   sia mɛre   no la la podea   veder
          that good (f. sg.) her mother not she her could-3 sg. see
          'The worthy one, her mother couldn't stand'.

(Friulan) kwant al e partit   luj   al a   ʃkomeŋʧat   a maŋʒa
          when he is left (m. sg.) he   he has   begun to to-eat
          'When he left, he began to eat.'

          alora luj il e ʒut   a fa   gwardja aj   purtʃej
          then he he is gone (m. sg.) to make guard to-the (m. pl.) pigs
          'Then he went to watch over the pigs.'

This relatively free word order is probably the inherited one for Rhaeto-Romance, and we can still see it preserved in subordinate clauses in all the dialects. (In view of the relative homogeneity of the dialects, we will allow one of them, Puter, to serve for purposes of illustration of relative clauses and conditionals, and another, Surselvan, to illustrate gerundive and absolutive clauses.)

Relative and Complement Clauses

What the word order is in any relative clause depends on the syntactic position of the relative pronoun, that is, on whether it is reckoned to be inside or outside the clause. Whatever the analysis we adopt, word order within the relative clause will be found to vary. If the relative pronoun is viewed as being a constituent within the relative clause, then there are no instances of verb-initial order, but plenty of examples of everything else; if, on the other hand, the relative pronoun is viewed as a complementiser in construction with the relative clause, then all orders are possible and attested. In other words, there is no pressure to maintain either consistent verb-second or verb-final order. Arbitrarily, we will assume that the relative pronoun has the status of extra-sentential complementiser in the following Puter examples. Note that we find verb-first (V1), verb-second (V2) and verb-third (V3) orders, irrespective of whether *ca* introduces a relative or a complement clause.

Cases of V1:
yn kudaʃin ca purtɛvans   a nos ɟɛnituors
a booklet that we-carried to our parents

kwant   gro   ca ʃtuvɛns al savajr
how-much gratitude that we-must him know
'How grateful we must be to him!'

il   myr ci   tsirkundeʃa la   baselɟa
the wall that surrounds   the church

jorɟa   ci   o   abanduno la   kloʃtra
Georgia who has abandoned the cloister

ʃku ca   s - vetsa dals   eksempVls
as   that refl. sees   from-the (m. pl.) examples
'as can be seen from the examples'

ca   tʃernins   la   via   komoda
that we-choose the road easy

ca   nun era   py   priVvəl;
that not was-3 sg. more danger
'that there was no more danger'

kur   ca   saro   ɲida   la   dumɛnɟa fiksɛda
when that will-be-3 sg. come (f. sg.) the Sunday   determined
'when the determined Sunday arrives'

(ɛla laʃa   las tjosas inua) ca   sun
she leaves the things where that they-are

ʃabajn   ca   sun   kreʃiws
although that they-are grown (m. pl.)

Cases of V2:
yna lingwa   c(a) ɛ inklej
a   language that I I-understand

kwɛl ci   al   prym mel   plɛndza sia sɔrt
he   who at-the first   misfortune bewails his lot

(bjers krajan) ca   pel   tjɛm saja   tuot   bun avuonda
(many believe) that for-the (m. sg.) dog   be-3 sg. subj. everything good enough
'Many believe that anything is good enough for a dog.'

apajna c(a) ɛ fyt   lo
hardly that I I-was there
'as soon as I got there'

Cases of V3:
(tmajvan) ca   er   ʃa l - amalo as   desidɛs   da s-   laʃɛr operɛr il
(they fear) that even if the sick   refl. decide-past. subj. of refl.   let   operate the
miedi   arivɛs   mɛma tart
doctor arrive-past. subj.   too   late
'They fear that even if the patient allowed himself to be operated upon, the doctor
may arrive too late.'

il   kudaʃin c(a) ils   ʃkolars   il   prɔsim di   purtɛvan   a lur   djɛnituors
the booklet that the scholars the next   day they-carried-imperf. to their parents

Conditional Clauses
One syntactic feature of conditional clauses in Rhaeto-Romance that sets
this language apart from both standard French and standard northern and

central Italian is the morphological symmetry of the verb in protasis and apodosis clauses: counterfactual conditionals exhibit the past subjunctive in both protasis and apodosis (cf. p. 304). From the point of view of word order, conditional protases merit separate treatment from other subordinate clauses only because they are introduced by a different complementiser, /ʃa/ 'if'. This difference, however, makes no difference to the word order possibilities in protases, which parallel those in *ci* and *ca* clauses.

Cases of V1
(a plova) ʃku ʃa nu vulɛs   py   ʎivrɛr
(it rains) as if not want-imperf. subj. more to-stop
'It's raining as if it would never end.'

ʃa ns dajs   kwalcosa (ʃi   diw as bɛnɛdɛʃa)
if us you-give something (then God you bless)

ʃa nu fys   la mama (ʃi   fys kwe   yn dɛʃuordɔn komplɛt)
if not be-past subj. the mama (then be-past. subj. a disorder   complete)
'If it were not for mama, there would be utter disorder.'

Cases of V2:
ʃa ty ɛʃt   dabzøɲ d yn mantəl
if you have-2 sg. need   of a coat

(ɛ nu fys ko)   ʃa yna cɛvra nu m - avɛs   salvo la vita
(I would not be here) if a goat not me-have-past subj. saved the life
'I would not be here if a goat hadn't saved my life.'

ʃa nun c   caritɛd (ʃi nun am ɟyda kwe tuot ynguota)
if I not have-1 sg. charity (then not me help that all   none)
'If I have not charity it profiteth me nothing.'

Cases of V3:
ʃa ty   zieva yn tɛmp ʃtuvɛsaʃt   darco turnɛr   in kwarta
if you after a time had-2 sg. past subj. again to-return in fourth
'If after a time you had to return to fourth grade'

ʃa ɛl kun una bɔka maʎa (ʃto taʃajr   ɛl pɛr intɛnt)
if he with one mouth eats (must be-silent he for the-meantime)

Gerundive and Absolute Clauses
These are clauses without finite verbs. The gerund in - *Vnd* is used for concomitant activity, the perfect participle for prior activity. Both are almost always same-subject constructions with elided subjects, hence VX order: but occasionally, especially with the past participle, they are different-subject constructions. Very probably on the model of the verb-initial subjectless clauses, different-subject absolute clauses are also verb-initial, and rigidly display VXS order. The examples below are culled from Surselvan:

veɲɛnd l   awtra damɛwn il   padɔr gwardjan ɛn la   kɔmbrɛta fuva   il
coming the other morning the father guardian in the chamber   was-3 sg. the
kavrer   mɔrts
goatherd dead-m. sg.
'When the Father Superior came into the chamber the next day, the goatherd was
dead.'

s- aproksimɔnd il   tɛmps da karga veɲ   kwej purun   in di tiɔr la
refl.-nearing   the time of to-load comes this   peasant-aug. one day to the
viwa
widow
'When the time came to seize (the property), the landowner came to the widow.'

faca   la lavur turnejn   nus a kasa
done-f. sg. the work return-1 pl. we to house
'When the work is done, we go back home.'

vargada   la ʧejna van   ils   dus kumpoɲs de viadi   a lec
finished-f. sg. the feast go-3 pl. the-m. pl. two comrades of voyage to bed
'After supper, the two fellow travellers went to bed.'

Although I believe the class of subordinate clauses to be in many
respects a heterogeneous one, the subordinate clause types described above
share a number of properties. The first, reviewed here, is their word order,
in contrast with the relatively rigid V2 order in principal clauses. The
second is that they are incorporated into the matrix sentence where they
occur. If they stand at the beginning of this sentence, the verb must follow
them immediately in order to satisfy the verb-second constraint.

Word Order within Major Constituents
Rhaeto-Romance is a fairly typical VO language, and the order of constituents within the NP is not surprising. The order of pronominal and other
clitics within the verbal complex, on the other hand, shows considerable
dialect variation.

Order of Elements within NP
Generally, adjectives and participles follow the noun they modify (unlike
numerals, possessive pronominal adjectives and demonstratives). A small
group of extremely common adjectives may precede the head noun. For
example, in Puter, these include /juven/ 'young', /veʎ/ 'old', /grand/
'big'. /piʧen/ 'small', /bɛl/ 'beautiful', /trid/ 'ugly', /bun/ 'good' /nuʃ/
'bad', /cer/ 'dear', /lung/ 'long', /kuVrt/ 'short', /larg/ 'wide', and a
greater or lesser subset of these are found in prenominal position in the
other Rhaeto-Romance dialects.
Prenominal position may be an index of incorporation. Speaking in
favour of this hypothesis is not only the fact that it is the most common
adjectives which typically occur prenominally, but also the fact that where
both orders are possible, it is the postnominal position which is used for the
literal, and the prenominal position which is used for the metaphorical

meaning. Thus, as in French and Spanish, the etymon for 'poor' in both Surselvan and Friulan means 'impoverished' postnominally, but 'pitiable' prenominally.

Finally, as in Spanish (p. 105), even those adjectives which typically occur prenominally must appear postnominally when they are in focus (in their specifying, rather than their evaluative, function).

The correlation between incorporation and preposing is more transparent in the case of object pronouns in Rhaeto-Romance. Disjunctive pronouns, like full NPs, follow the verb, while clitic pronouns precede it.

Order of Elements within the Verbal Complex
By the verbal complex I mean the combination of the verb and its clitic satellites. Three categories of these clitics are to be recognised:

(a) subject pronouns;
(b) object pronouns (dative, accusative and partitive);
(c) the negative particle *no ~ nu ~ nun*.

A fairly sharp distinction exists between Surselvan and all the other Rhaeto-Romance dialects here. Modern Surselvan has virtually no clitics in any of the three categories above. The exceptions may be dealt with quickly.

Subject pronouns exhibit no reduced forms except in the second person (singular and plural), where the pronoun in inverted word order may surface as phonetic zero:

cej   pudejs   (vus)   far?
what can-2 pl. you-all to-do
nua   vas   (ti)?
where go-2 sg. you

The clitic form of the second person pronoun in all Rhaeto-Romance dialects is zero: but it is uncertain whether this is not better treated as a syntactic deletion than as a phonetic reduction. A better candidate for status as a clitic subject pronoun may be 3 sg. neuter *i*, the postverbal form of *i ~ ej* (cf. p. 365 above).

The only clitic object pronoun is the invariable reflexive prefix *se*, briefly discussed above (p. 366). All other object pronouns are postverbal: in fact, unlike object pronouns in German they follow the entire auxiliary + verb complex, as in

nus vejn klamaw tej
we have called you

The absence of object clitic pronouns in Surselvan seems to have been a recent development. As late as the seventeenth and eighteenth centuries, object pronouns in this dialect are recorded preverbally. That this was not a reflection of a canonical SOV order can be inferred from the fact that object nouns followed the verb, and from the fact that, although verb-second order was established, the structure subject + pronoun object + verb does not seem to have counted as an exception to this (nor does it in modern Engadine dialects).

The negative particle *buka* follows the finite verb, and may either precede or follow the imperative. Again, Old Surselvan, like the other modern Rhaeto-Romance dialects, had a preverbal particle *nun*, still preserved in some formulaic expressions (e.g. /ci ke obɛdɛʃa nun falɛʃa/ 'who obeys does not go wrong'). The inherited form may have been a discontinuous *nun…buka*, which occurs in Surmeiran as *na … bec.*

The remaining Swiss dialects cliticise all three categories of morphemes, subject to two general restrictions:

(a) subject pronouns are phonetically reduced or deleted in inverted word order only (that is, postverbally). Inversion occurs in questions and in TVX constructions where the initial constituent in the clause is something other than the subject;

(b) only a single object pronoun may be cliticised.

There are, however, some exceptions to the second of these constraints. In Puter, dative + accusative clitic combinations occur, as in

vus ans ilas tsedis
you to-us them yield-2 pl.
'You yield them to us.'

This construction, however, is being marginalised by others which avoid a piling up of object clitics, either by leaving one of the objects as a full NP, or by expressing the indirect object as a (postverbal) prepositional phrase.

A more general exception to constraint (b) in the Swiss dialects is the toleration of accusative + reflexive object clitics (but perhaps only where the reflexive morpheme is the expression of an unspecified agent). Thus Surmeiran:

la sandet as ʃtem i pir kur c(a) i la s o pɛrsa
the health refl. values the most when *pro* it refl. has lost
'Good health is valued most when one has lost it.'

(Compare Italian *il diavolo non è così brutto come lo si dipinge* 'the devil is not as black as he's painted'.)

The Italian Rhaeto-Romance dialects, like other northern Italian dialects, are characterised by a massive piling up of clitics of all three categories. The following discussion, which focuses on the relative order of clitics within the verbal complex, is most important for these. In order to do justice to each of the dialects, we will treat them separately, beginning with the westernmost.

In Surmeiran, the negative particle *bec* follows the verb, except in the imperative mood, where it precedes. Thus

i na viɲ   bec da plover
it not comes not of to-rain
'It will not rain.'

but, in the imperative

bec sera la faneʃtra
not close the window
'Do not close the window.'

The syntax of reflexive object pronouns differs in two respects from that of other object pronouns.

First, while object pronouns invariably precede the (auxiliary) verb in the indicative, reflexive pronouns may either precede or follow the perfective auxiliary 'have':

ia ma   va   trac   ajnt   *or* la va ma trac ajnt
I myself have-1 sg. drawn (m. sg.) in
'I have dressed.'

The former construction is standard for all Rhaeto-Romance dialects spoken to the east of Surmeiran, while the latter, as we have seen, is characteristic of Surselvan. As it happens, it is the latter which is by far the most common in Surmeiran.

Second, while object pronouns follow the verb in all persons and numbers of the imperative, the reflexive object pronoun follows the imperative only in the second person singular imperative.

	Object pronouns			*Reflexive pronouns*	
2 sg.	do-m	'give me!'	*but*	téjra-t ajnt	'get dressed!'
1 pl.	daɲ-iʌs	'let's give them'		ans tiráɲ ajnt	'let's get dressed'
2 pl.	de-m	'give me!'		ats tiré ajnt	'get dressed!'

In Puter, object clitics may cooccur, although this usage, as we have noted above (p. 376) is disappearing particularly in the spoken language. Where object clitics cooccur, dative precedes accusative (the standard order in the Italain dialects), and the reflexive (whether dative or impersonal) precedes the object. Object pronouns (including the reflexive) precede the (auxiliary) verb except in the imperative. In the negative imperative, object pronouns may either precede or follow the verb:

nu t   laʃer (vɛndzɛr dal   mɛl)
not you let-inf. conquer-inf. of-the (m. sg.) evil
'Don't let yourself (be conquered by evil.'

nu konfurmé -   s   (a kwiʃt muond)
not conform-2 pl. you-pl. (to this world)
'Do not conform (with this world).'

In Vallader, there is no morphological distinction between dative and
accusative object pronouns, which may not cooccur, but a syntactic difference is that the perfect participle agrees obligatorily with the accusative,
and only optionally with the dative object pronoun:

ty ans aʃt   invida -   ts
you us have-2 sg. forgotten - m. pl.
'You have forgotten us.'

but

ɛl tila a   dit /   dita   ses   parajr
he her has told (m. sg.)/told (f. sg.) his (m.) opinion
'He told her his opinion.'

(It will be seen from this that the masculine singular is the unmarked form
for purposes of agreement.)

Object pronouns, including the reflexive, precede the (auxiliary) verb
except in the second person of the affirmative imperative:

kufórta-t   'Console yourself!'
ʃkrivá-m   'You (pl.) write to me!'

but

nu t   ʃtramantar
not you to-torment
'Don't worry!'

ans kufortajn
us we-comfort
'Let's take heart!'

In all the Swiss dialects, the syntax of subject pronoun clitics is straightforward. Subject pronoun clitics occur only in inverted word order
(questions, and sentences where T ≠ subject) and only immediately after
the verb. Thus, where they cooccur with object pronoun clitics, the object
pronouns precede, and the subject pronouns follow, the verb:

(Puter)   at   lod   - i
          you praise - I
          'Do I praise you?'

In the Italian dialects, subject pronoun clitics occur preverbally. The relative order of subject and object pronouns where both precede the verb is
subject–object:

(Fassa Ladin)   ɛl no l se fida
he not he self trusts
'He doesn't dare.'

(Friulan)   Tu tu ti viodis
you you you see
'You see yourself.'

(It seems evident from examples such as these that subject clitics in the Italian dialects are copies of the 'full' subject pronouns, with which they cooccur. We return to this below, p. 380.) Among object clitics, the relative orders are:

(a) dative $\begin{cases} \text{accusative} \\ \text{partitive} \end{cases}$

(b) reflexive object

(Fassa Ladin)   te l dage
you it I-give
'I give it to you.'

di ʝe   lo
say to-her it
'Tell it to her.'

daʒe   ne ne
give-pl. us some
'Give us some.'

(Friulan)   si   ju sint
refl. her hears
'*pro* hears her; she is heard.'

si   lu puarte
refl. it carries
'*pro* carries it; it is carried.'

puarti ma l
carry me it
'Bring it to me!'

Object pronouns precede the (auxiliary) verb except:

(a) in Ladin, in the affirmative imperative (as in the Engadine dialects);
(b) in Friulan, in the non-finite moods and the imperative (as in standard Italian).

As we have seen, the Swiss dialects tend to avoid an agglomeration of clitics on the verb by leaving some object pronouns in the full form. We see the effects of a similar tendency even in Friulan.

First, the sequence reflexive–object–verb may be optionally transformed into reflexive–verb–object: *si-lu-puarte*, but also *si-puarti-le* 'it is carried'.

Second, the sequence subject–object–verb reduces optionally to object–verb except where the subject is second person singular:

jo o mi viot   *but also* jo mi viot
I I me see-1 sg.
'I see myself.'

Finally, the sequence negative–subject–verb reduces optionally to negative–verb except where the subject is second or third person singular:

jo no o saj   *but also* jo no saj
I not I know-1 sg.
'I don't know.'

The status of pronominal clitics in the Italian dialects is apparently very different from that of the clitics in the Swiss dialects. In the Swiss dialects, clitics are in complementary distribution with full NPs, and there is little reason to suspect that they are anything other than autonomous grammatical items. In the Italian dialects, on the other hand, it is clear that subject clitics may cooccur with full subject NPs or pronouns (see the examples on p. 379). There is even a tendency in colloquial speech to allow object pronoun clitics to cooccur with full NP objects (see above, and cf. p. 291):

jɛ   dise a so fradi
to-him I-said to his brother
'I told his brother.'

tjali - mi me
look me me
'Look at me!'

This suggests an entirely different categorial status for pronominal clitics in the Italian dialects, perhaps as agreement markers.

In fact, the distinction between the Swiss and the Italian Rhaeto-Romance dialects is not quite so clear-cut. In the first place, even in the Swiss dialects, clitic and full pronouns may cooccur. The full disjunctive pronoun is required for focus or contrastive stress, as in the Vallader example:

las troklas piʎajn - a no
the bags   take-1 pl. we we
'As for the bags. we'll take them.'

Second, clitic pronouns, even in Friulan, betray their syntactic links with full NPs in undergoing subject–verb inversion in questions. In this, they contrast with full pronouns, whose dislocated status is reflected in their movability from the leftmost margin of the sentence to the rightmost and in their optionality. In the examples below, from Friulan, the disjunctive pronouns are indicated in brackets. Note that they are optional, and not subject to subject–verb inversion triggered by the interrogative mood:

Assertive	*Interrogative*
(jo) o feveli	(jo) feveli - o
I I-speak	I I-speak I
o feveli (jo)	fevili - o (jo)
I I-speak I	I-speak I I

Most probably the Swiss and Italian Rhaeto-Romance dialects are now at different points on a well-worn and familiar diachronic progression, whereby unstressed pronouns are reduced to affixes, and reinforced by disjunctive pronouns (which in their turn will also be reduced).

The Syntax of the 'Predicate Case' in Surselvan

The survival and the transformation of the -US/-UM distinction in Surselvan, alone of all the Rhaeto-Romance dialects, is of interest to general linguistics in providing a diagnostic for predicative (as opposed to attributive) adjectives, and for subject (as opposed to non-subject) noun phrases.

In the unmarked case, the -*s* predicate adjective suffix occurs in the frame [NP Copula Adjective]$_S$, where the subject NP is masculine singular. The contrasting attributive adjective suffix -Ø (null) occurs in the frame [Noun Adjective]$_{NP}$, where the head noun again is masculine singular.

il   hotel ej vɛɲiw - s   natsionalizaw - s
the hotel is become (pred.) nationalised   (pred.)
'The hotel has been nationalised.'

il   hotel natsionalizaw - Ø
the hotel nationalised   (attr.)
'the nationalised hotel'

There are two constructions where the form of the adjective is not entirely predictable on *a priori* principles: where the adjective is appositional and where the adjective is a superlative.

By appositional adjectives I mean a (perhaps heterogeneous) class of constructions exemplified in English by sentences like:

Miserable and discouraged, they finally gave up.
He made them aware of the danger.
She always works alone.

In all of these, the adjective in Surselvan is treated as a predicate adjective and occurs with the final -*s* (where gender and number of the head noun permit):

iʎ   um   ʃiʃeva malsawn - s   in lec
the man lay   ill   (pred.) in bed

εls fan atεnt - s   εl sil   prigVl
they make aware (pred.) him on-the danger
'They make him aware of the danger.'

εl mejna persul - s   omisdus hotεls
he manages alone (pred.) both   hotels

The peculiar status of superlative adjectives is illustrated by the following paradigm:

kwej regal ej kuʃtejvVl - s
this present is costly   (pred.)

kwej regal ej pli kuʃtejvVl - s
this present is more costly   (pred.)

Predicate superlative adjectives (unlike positive and comparative predicate adjectives) are treated as though they were attributive adjectives, appearing without the predicate suffix -s. This is not surprising, given the universal status of the 'superlative adjective' as an actual referential form, whose suppressed head noun is something like 'one'. The nominal status of the superlative, syntactically attested by its ability to assume any NP role in a sentence, is simply confirmed by the morphological evidence of Surselvan:

kwej regal ej il pli kuʃtejvVl - Ø
this present is the most costly   (attr.)

In his pioneering treatment of predicate -s in Surselvan more than a hundred years ago, Böhmer observed that there are no neuter lexical nouns in Surselvan. Therefore, the only subject NP which could compel neuter singular predicate adjective agreement (with suffix Ø) are the neuter pronouns kwej 'this, that', iʎ 'it', tut 'everything', nuVt 'nothing', and a handful of others. Therefore, neuter singular predicate adjective agreement is exactly what we expect to find where any of these serves as the actual or dummy subject.

kwej ej ʃtaw - Ø   fεrm tubak
that is been (n. sg.) strong tobacco
'That was strong tobacco.'

The neuter singular pronoun iʎ serves as a dummy subject in existential sentences, impersonal passives, sentences with extraposed sentential subjects and presentative sentences. Preverbally, before a consonant, it is /ej/, before a vowel, it is /iʎ/; postverbally, it is /i/:

ej veɲ priw - Ø   ina kolεkta
it comes taken (n. sg.) a   collection
'There is taken a collection.'

iʎ ej veɲiw - ∅   priw - ∅   numerusas mesiras
it is come (n. sg.) taken (n. sg.) numerous measures
'There were taken numerous measures.'

kwɛʃt jamna ej   - s -   i vɛɲiw - ∅   debataw — ∅   vehementamejn
this week is (hiatus breaker) it come (n. sg.) debated (n. sg.) vehemently
'This week there was vehement debate.'

Corresponding to sentences with postverbal /i/, there are others in which the dummy pronoun is entirely absent. (It is as if the dummy pronoun were present only in order to keep the verb in second position, and could otherwise be omitted.) What is problematic about these sentences is that the predicate adjectives still manifest neuter singular 'agreement':

ɛn ɛmprɛm linja ej _ vɛɲíw - ∅   ɛksaminaw - ∅   il   ʃtat tɛknik   dils
in first   line is   come (n. sg.) examined (n. sg.) the state technical of-the
vehikVls
vehicle
'First, the technical condition of the vehicles was examined.'

tiVr   nof pɛrsunas ej_ vɛɲíw   - ∅   ordinaw - ∅   ina kontrola dil   sawn
among nine persons is   come (n. sg.) ordered (n. sg.) a   checkup of-the health
'For nine people a medical checkup was ordered.'

plinavon ej_ vɛɲíw   - ∅   retrac ∅   sil   plats sjat pɛrmisiuns da kará
moreover is   come (n. sg.) withdrawn (n. sg.) on-the spot seven driving licences
'Moreover, there were seven driving licences withdrawn on the spot.'

impurtont - ∅   ej_ kɛ kwej biVn uzit   véɲi   kontinuaw -s
important (n. sg.) is   that this good custom come-3 sg. subj. continued (pred.)
'Important is that this good custom should be continued.'

In all of the above sentences, the dummy pronoun is possible in the position indicated by the blank. The question is, with what, if anything, does the neuter predicate adjective agree in these sentences? Clearly, not with the presentative postposed subject, which (in the examples above) is masculine singular, feminine singular, feminine plural and neuter singular. The minimal hypothesis is that the adjective agrees with a preceding subject: where the only subject in the sentence follows (and perhaps is not a 'real' subject at all), the neuter singular form as the maximally unmarked form appears because there is nothing for the adjective to agree with. More problematic is a set of sentences in which lexical noun phrases without articles stand in sentence-initial position and apparently take neuter singular predicate adjective concord (in spite of the important fact noted by Böhmer that all lexical nouns in Surselvan are either masculine or feminine).

kaʃiVl ej biVn - ∅   (not bun-s)
cheese is good (n. sg.)   good (m. sg.)

mo ɛkstrɛms ej buka sanadejvVl- Ø   (*not* sanadejvVl-s)
only extremes is not   healthy (n. sg.)   healthy (m. pl.)
'Extremes are unhealthy.'

tsigarɛtas ej nuʃejvVl — Ø   (*not* nuʃejvl-as)
cigarettes is harmful (n. sg.)   harmful (f. pl.)
'Cigarettes are harmful.'

Note that it is not only the predicate adjective which fails to manifest (gender and number) agreement, but the copula verb (which is invariably third person singular irrespective of the person and number of the supposed subject). It seems likely that a paraphrase is possible for each of the above sentences in which the apparent subject is actually a part of a complement clause of some kind. It is this clause ('to eat cheese', 'to go to extremes', 'to smoke cigarettes') which is functioning as the actual subject of the sentence and taking neuter singular predicate adjective agreement. Further complications (which a brief study such as this must pass over) serve to confirm that Surselvan predicate -s is a diagnostic for a rather deep notion of 'subjecthood', treating as subjects the subjects of infinitives (as in *make him (to be) aware*), and disregarding a number of low-level 'subject-creating' rules (among them fronting and clause reduction) which put NPs into canonical subject position and award subject status in languages like English.

Rhaeto-Romance and the Appearance of Expletive Pronoun Subjects
Like most of the Germanic languages, like French, and like practically no other language on earth, Swiss Rhaeto-Romance seems to be what David Perlmutter has called a 'type A' language, in which:

(a) personal pronoun subjects cannot in general be omitted, even when the person and number of the subject is unambiguously indicated in the personal desinence on the verb;

(b) impersonal verbs (including impersonal passives and reflexives) require a non-referential dummy subject like *it* or *there*;

(c) verbs with extraposed sentential subjects require a similar pronoun subject;

(d) verbs with presentative 'subjects' in sentence-final position do likewise; and

(e) a special pronoun (cf. French *on*, German *man*) exists to denote unspecified agents.

It seems probable that all 'type A' languages are or once were verb-second languages, and that the requirements enumerated above existed originally for no other reason than to keep the verb in the second position in the sentence. (For a similar stage in the history of French, cf. p. 235).

The Rhaeto-Romance dialects provide a good empirical test for the hypothesis that word order and expletive pronoun subjects are related in this way. In the first place, even in Swiss Rhaeto-Romance, the V2 constraint does not exist in subordinate clauses. If the word order correlation is solid, we might expect to find differences between principal and subordinate clauses with respect to requirements (a)–(e) listed above. In the second place, the V2 constraint does not exist at all in the Italian dialects. Once again, if the correlation is a strong one, we should expect to find that neither Ladin nor Friulan are 'type A' languages.

To anticipate the results of the following presentation, we will find that there is some evidence in Rhaeto-Romance that expletive pronoun subjects appear to satisfy the exigencies of the verb-second constraint. But the evidence is by no means as clear-cut as we might wish.

Personal Pronoun Subjects

In the Swiss dialects, personal pronoun subjects can hardly ever be omitted. But the subject pronoun is frequently omitted in subordinate clauses with verb-initial order (cf. pp. 371 ff above); and in inverted word order second person pronoun subjects are typically deleted.

In the Italian Rhaeto-Romance dialects, as in Italian (cf. p. 290), full personal pronoun subjects are omitted unless they are in focus. Clitic pronoun subjects are frequently present (for some examples, cf. p. 378 and p. 380 above), but since these clitic pronouns are not immediate constituents of the sentence (p. 369), their distribution, *ex hypothesi*, will be independent of word order: and this does seem to be the case.

Dummy Pronouns with Impersonal Passives and Reflexives

As noted earlier (p. 383), the dummy pronoun in Surselvan may be absent in inverted word order, where some constituent other than the subject stands in sentence-initial position. In the Engadine dialects, the corresponding dummy pronoun is always mandatory where its absence would lead to a violation of the verb-second constraint, but it is always mandatory in normal word order in subordinate clauses as well (where this constraint does not apply). (In all of the examples below the dummy pronoun /id ~ i/ (preverbal), /a/ (postverbal) will be glossed as *pro* representing the unspecified agent.)

i s po kwintar kun yna subvɛntsiun canunɛla
pro refl. can reckon with a subsidy cantonal
'A cantonal subsidy can be depended on.'
... davo c(a) id era kumparyda la plata kula cantsun
after that *pro* was compared (f. sg.) the record with-the song
'after the record was compared with the song'

(The last example is interesting in showing that in Vallader, unlike Surselvan (cf. pp. 382–3 above) the perfect participle agrees even with a postposed 'subject'.)

Where the verb-second constraint is satisfied by some other constituent, the dummy pronoun occurs postverbally, and, apparently, optionally, just as it does in Surselvan:

davo evnas m - e - s -　　　　a　ɲy dit ca . . . . . .
after weeks me is (hiatus breaker) *pro* come said that
'After several weeks, I was told that . . .'

in konsks　　kuɲ la　surfabrikatsiun in Avant Muʎins es - Ø ɲy　inʃkrit
in connection with the construction　in A.M.　　　　is　　come legislated
yn drɛt da pasaɟi publik pɛr pedruns
a right of passage public for pedestrians
'In connection with the construction at A.M., a bill was passed guaranteeing the right of free public passage for pedestrians.'

In the Ladin dialects, the preferred construction instead of impersonal passives and reflexives seems to be a third person plural verb with common gender subject.

In Friulan, the impersonal reflexive occurs without a dummy subject, irrespective of the position of the verb:

a caval regalat　no si cale in boce
to horse presented not refl. looks in mouth
'Never look a gift horse in the mouth.'

no si a　nie　par nie
not refl. gives nothing for nothing
'You can't get anything for nothing.'

Dummy Pronouns with Presentative Verbs
In the Swiss Rhaeto-Romance dialects, the dummy pronoun is always present irrespective of word order, in both principal and subordinate clauses, as illustrated with the following examples from Vallader:

i ns ʃtan　　er a dispozitsiun plys løs　pɛr kwiʃt tsɛntVr
it us they-stand also at disposal　more places for this centre
'There are also at our disposal more places for locating this centre.'

pro nus nu da - j -　a yn titVl adɛkwat
for us not gives (hiatus) it a title adequate
'We have no adequate title for it.'

The Italian dialects also have a dummy subject for presentative verbs, one which is morphologically identical with the third singular masculine personal pronoun. It seems never to be omitted in Ladin, but may be omitted in Friulan. Hence the Friulan sentence:

(al) era una volta una fameja
it was one time a family
'Once there was a family.'

(Whether the difference between Ladin and Friulan is significant, rather than an accidental consequence of incomplete materials at my disposal, is doubtful.)

Dummy Pronouns with 'Weather' Verbs

In the Swiss dialects, the dummy meteorological pronoun seems to be required irrespective of word order, as in Surselvan:

ej plova
it rains

ʃa diw vut,   plova-i sentsa   niblas
if God wants rains it without clouds
'If God wishes it, it rains even when there are no clouds.'

In Ladin, there is no evidence that the dummy pronoun can ever be omitted. In Friulan, meteorological impersonal verbs require a dummy subject, but it seems that transitive impersonal verbs do not. Witness the contrast (which may not be significant) between:

l a   lampat
it has lightened
'There was lightning.'

riʃi   ti   se __ te   ʃpisa
scratch yourself if   you itches
'Scratch if it itches you.'

Extraposition

Sentences with extraposed sentential subjects require a dummy pronoun in all Rhaeto-Romance dialects, and I have no evidence that this pronoun can ever be omitted in any of them under any circumstances. The following illustrative sentences are from Vallader:

id es pusib Vl da reajir ply   ʃvelt
it is possible of to-react more quick
'It is possible to react more quickly.'

lura es-a bun ʃ(a) i pon   ir   dats   kumands klers
then is it good if   it can-3 pl. come given (m. pl.) commands clear (m. pl.)
'Then it is good if clear commands can be given.'

Unspecified Agent Pronouns

The western Swiss dialects (from Surselvan to Surmeiran) have a special pronoun *ins* (presumably from UNUS, note the nominative -*s*), which corresponds almost exactly to French *on*. As far as I am aware, it can never be omitted. Nothing comparable exists in the Engadine dialects, which employ the impersonal reflexive. Ladin has a special unspecified agent pronoun /aŋ/, but far more frequently employs the third person plural common gender subject for unspecified agents, while Friulan, the standard Italian, uses the impersonal reflexive (invariably without a dummy subject).

5 Lexis

Over three quarters of the common Rhaeto-Romance vocabulary is Latinate, and almost all of the rest is German. Of the relatively few words occurring throughout Rhaeto-Romance which do not also occur in Italian, one of the most striking is /tVliVr/ 'plate', from the German *Teller*. The highest concentration of characteristically Rhaeto-Romance words occurs in the Swiss dialect area, and within this area, the lexically most conservative dialects are Surselvan and Sutselvan. Some almost exclusively Swiss Rhaeto-Romance words are /ferm/ < FIRMUM, /kudiʃ/ < CODICEM, /alf/ < ALBUM, /vawt/ < German *Wald*, and /ʃto/ < STUPET. Quintessentially Rhaeto-Romance words occurring only within the most conservative Swiss dialects are /kuVlm/ < German *Kulmen* 'hill', /tserkladur/ 'June' < SARCULARE + ATOREM and /fenadur/ 'July' < FENU + ATOREM. A smaller number of Rhaeto-Romance words are restricted to the various Italian dialects, among them Ladin /foʃk/ 'black' < FUSCUM, and Friulan /frut/ 'child' < FRUCTUM. Predictably, there are several dozen words that are restricted to 'contiguous' dialect areas within Rhaeto-Romance. For example, Swiss Rhaeto-Romance and Ladin share /aʃ/ 'bitter' < ACIDUM, /meza/ 'table' < MENSAM, /kocen/ 'red' < COCCINUM, and /buɉén/ ~ /guɉén/ 'gladly' < VOLIENDO. Ladin and Friulan, on the other hand, share /canel/ 'corn crib' < CANALEM, and /fral/ 'decayed' < FRACTUM. There are also a small number of Rhaeto-Romance words that are confined to the 'peripheral areas', namely Swiss Rhaeto-Romance and Friulan, and do not appear in Ladin. Among these is /krap/ ~ /klap/ 'stone', whose etymology is obscure.

6 Conclusion

Over a hundred years ago, the great Romanist Theoder Gartner predicted the ultimate demise of Rhaeto-Romance within several decades. If he were alive, he would probably make the same prediction today, since the linguistic situation is still pretty much as he described it, at least in Italy. In Switzerland, the Romantsch dialects have been self-consciously maintained, standardised and given official recognition, and it is probably safe to say that they will continue to be spoken for the foreseeable future.

A Note on Sources

Standard pedagogical grammars of the Swiss dialects are Nay (1965) (Surselvan), Thöni (1969) (Surmeiran), Ganzoni (1977) and Scheitlin (1980) (Puter), Arquint (1964) and Ganzoni (1983) (Vallader). For Ladin, I have relied heavily on Elwert (1943) — a classic grammar — and Gartner (1892). For Friulan, basic sources are Francescato (1966), Marchetti (1967), and Iliescu (1972).

There is no dearth of painstaking analyses of the historical phonetics of individual Rhaeto-Romance dialects. The greatest of these is Lutta's magnificent description of the dialect of Bergün (a Surmeiran dialect), Lutta (1923). Explicitly phonemic analyses of two Ladin dialects are Plangg (1973) and Politzer (1967); of Friulan, Bender *et al.* (1952). Notable morphological studies are Grisch (1939) (contrasting Surmeiran with other Swiss dialects), Prader-Schucany (1970) (contrasting Surselvan with Italian dialects spoken in the canton of Ticino), Tekavčić (1972–4) (Surselvan), Benincà and Vanelli (1976) (Friulan), and Iliescu (1982) (Friulan).

There has been very little written on Rhaeto-Romance syntax. A notable exception is Böhmer (1871), on Surselvan predicate -*s*. Two further studies on the same topic are Stimm (1976) (with very rich data) and Linder (1982). Haiman (1974) proposes the correlation between word order and the presence of expletive pronoun subjects using some data from Surselvan.

Classic overviews of Rhaeto-Romance as a separate language are Ascoli (1873; 1883), Gartner (1883; 1910), and most recently, Rohlfs (1975).

Anthologies of texts in Surselvan and Friulan are included in Gregor (1975, 1982).

All examples cited, except in Surselvan, Puter and Vallader, derive exclusively from these sources. For the latter dialects, I have had access to the *Gasetta Romontscha* (a Surselvan weekly newspaper), and *Fögl Ladin* (another weekly in Puter and Vallader), and used my own field notes.

Bibliography

Arquint, J. (1964). *Vierv Ladin.* Lia Rumantscha, Tusan.
Ascoli, G.I. (1873) *Saggi Ladini* (=*Archivo Glottologico Italiano* 1). Loescher Rome/Florence, Turin.
—— (1883) *Saggi di morfologia i lessicologia soprasilvana. AGI,* 7.
Bender, B.W., G. Francescato and Z. Salzman (1952) 'Friulan Phonology', *Word* 8: 216–23.
Benincà, P. and L. Vanelli (1976) 'Morfologia del verbo friulano: il presente indicativo', *Lingua e contesto* 1: 1–62.
Böhmer, E. (1871) 'Prädicatscasus im Rätoromanischen', *Romanische Studien* 2: 210–26.
Elwert, W.Th. (1943) *Die Mundart des Fassa-Tals.* (Wörter and Sachen, NF Beiheft 2). Carl Winter, Heidelberg.
Francescato, G. (1966) *Dialettologia friulana.* Società Filologica Friulana, Udine.
Ganzoni, G. (1977) *Grammatica Ladina (d'Engiadin' Ota).* Lia Rumantscha, Samedan.
—— (1983) *Grammatica Ladina (d'Engiadina Bassa).* Lia Rumantscha, Samedan.
Gartner, Th. (1883) *Rätoromanische Grammatik.* Henniger, Heilbronn.
—— (1892) 'Die Mundart von Erto', *ZRPh* 16: 183–209, 308–71.

—— (1910) *Handbuch der rätoromanischen Sprache und Literatur.* Niemeyer, Halle.

Gregor, D. (1975) *Friulan. Language and Literature.* Oleander Press, Cambridge/New York.

—— (1982) *Romontsch. Language and Literature.* Oleander Press, Cambridge/New York.

Grisch, M. (1939) *Die Mundart von Surmeir.* (Romania Helvetica 12.) Droz, Paris.

Haiman, J. (1974) *Targets and Syntactic Change.* Mouton, The Hague.

Heinz, S. and U. Wandruszka (eds.) (1982) *Fakten und Theorien.* Gunter Narr, Tübingen.

Iliescu, M. (1972) *Le Friulan.* Mouton, The Hague.

—— (1982) 'Typologie du verbe frioulan', in Heinz and Wandruszka, pp. 193–204.

Linder, K. (1982) 'Die Nichtübereinstimmung von finitem Verb und nachgestelltem Subjekt bei (Genus und) Numerus im Rätoromanisch in Graubünden', in Heinz and Wandruszka, pp. 147–62.

Lutta, M. (1923) *Der Dialekt von Bergün und seine Stellung innerhalb der rätoromanischer Mundarten Graubündens.* (Zeitschrift für romanische Philologie, Beiheft 71). Niemeyer, Halle.

Luzi, J. (1904) 'Die sutselvische Dialekte: lautlehre', *Romanische Forschungen* 16: 757–846.

Marchetti, G. (1967) *Linearmenti di grammatica friulana* 2nd edn. Società filologica Friulana, Udine.

Nay, S. (1965) *Lehrbuch der rätoromanischen Sprache* 3rd edn. Lia Rumantscha, Disentis.

Perlmutter, D. (1971) *Deep and Surface Structure Constraints in Syntax.* Holt, Reinhart and Winston, New York.

Plangg, G. (1973) *Sprachgestalt als Folge und Fügung.* (Zeitschrift für romanische Philologie, Beiheft 133). Niemeyer, Tübingen.

Politzer, R. (1967) *Beitrag zur Phonologie der Nonsberger Mundart.* (Romanica Aenipontana, 2). Leopold-Franzens Universität, Innsbruck.

Prader-Schucany, S. (1970) *Romanisch Bunden als selbstständige Sprachlandschaft.* (Romania Helvetica, 60). Francke, Bern.

Rohlfs, G. (1975) *Rätoromanisch.* Beck, München.

Scheitlin, W. (1980) *Il pled Puter* 3rd edn. Uniun dals Grischs, Samedan.

Stimm, H. (1976) 'Zu einigen syntaktischen Eigenheiten des Surselvischen', in W.Th. Elwert (ed.), *Rätoromanisches Colloquium, Mainz.* (Romanica Aenipontana, 10.) Leopold-Franzens Universität, Innsbruck, pp. 31–58.

Tekavčić, P. (1972–4) 'Abbozzo del sistema morfosintattico del soprasilvano odierno', *Studia Romanica et Anglica Zagrabiensa* 33–6: 359–488; 37: 5–134.

Thöni, G. (1969) *Rumantsch-Surmeir.* Lia Rumantscha, Chur.

11 *Rumanian*

Graham Mallinson

1 Introduction

As we have already seen (p. 22 and Map XI), Balkan Romance is represented by four variants, Daco-Rumanian (DR), the national language of
Rumania, being the main one. Dialects vary in their degree of conservatism
depending largely on the influence of other Balkan languages, and it is the
Wallachian subdialect of Daco-Rumanian which has been most subject to
change. As the variant that for political and geographical reasons became
the standard language, it more than any other came into contact with
French and Italian during the early to mid-nineteenth century (pp. 415–
16). It thus became the medium through which Western Romance innovations entered Daco-Rumanian as a whole.

Standard Rumanian, centred on Bucharest, is the form of Balkan
Romance that this chapter is primarily concerned with, though there will be
some reference to other Balkan Romance variants, Arumanian (AR) in
particular. Daco-Rumanian forms are given in the standard orthography,
Arumanian in IPA.

2 Phonology

Since current Rumanian orthography is little more than a century old, it
has not had time to diverge markedly from the spoken language. For this
reason, normal orthography will be used rather than IPA for citation forms.
Table 11.1 gives the phoneme equivalents of orthographic symbols, together
with some comments on problem items.

Vowels

As in the rest of the Romance-speaking area, the length-based vowel
system of Classical Latin (pp. 29ff) gave way in Balkan Romance to one
based on quality. The seven stressed simple vowels of the standard language are as follows:

Table 11.1: Rumanian Orthography

a	/a/	h	/h/ or /χ/	r	/r/
ă	/ə/	i	/i/*	s	/s/
b	/b/	î/â	/i/	ş	/ʃ/
c (+h)	/k/	j	/ʒ/	t	/t/
c (+i/e)	/tʃ/	k	/k/	ţ	/ts/
d	/d/	l	/l/	u	/u/
e	/e/	m	/m/	v	/v/
f	/f/	n	/n/	x	/ks/
g (+h)	/g/	o	/o/	z	/z/
g (+i/e)	/dʒ/	p	/p/		

Note: *k* and *ch* are equivalent, the former only being used for common international words, e.g. *kilo-*;
*i has the following values when not a stressed vowel:
(1) word-final: represents palatalisation of the preceding consonant (but CC clusters where the second C is a liquid cause it to be a full vowel, e.g. *tigri* /tigri/ 'tigers').
(2) before any other vowel: represents a palatal semi-vowel, e.g. *iad* /jad/ 'hell', *ied* /jed/ 'kid'. A small number of words beginning with *e-* also are pronounced /ye/, e.g. *este* /jeste/ 'is'. This gives rise to occasional homonyms, e.g. *era* /jerá/ 'was', *era* /éra/ 'the era'.
Stress is unmarked in Rumanian, and can be phonemic,
e.g. *cíntă* 'he sings'   *cintắ* 'he sang'
   acéle 'those'   *ácele* 'the needles'
Only where it is relevant to the discussion is stress represented in the text.

Of these, /u/ and /o/ are rounded, the remainder unrounded. In addition, there are the two rising diphthongs /eá/ and /oá/ (e.g. *neam* 'people', *oare* 'perhaps'). Some linguists list /eo/ (e.g. *deodată* 'suddenly') as a third diphthong, but it is more realistically treated as a sequence of simple vowels. Examples of words containing the seven simple and two compound vowels are as follows, along with their Latin etyma:

Vowel	DR word	Translation	Latin origin
/i/	zi	'day'	DĬEM
/e/	meu	'my'	MĔUM
/a/	lat	'wide'	LĀTUM
/o/	nod	'knot'	NŌDUM
/u/	gură	'mouth'	GŬLAM
/ɨ/	cînt	'I sing'	CANTO
/ə/	păr	'hair'	PĬLUM
/ea/	beată	'drunk (f.)'	BĬBĬTAM
/oa/	coamă	'mane'	CŎMAM

The Latin sources of these examples to a large degree confirm the standard claim for the mixed nature of a late Balkan Latin stressed vowel pattern — combining the western pattern for front vowels and the

Sardinian system for back vowels (p. 33).

Departing from the Latin six-vowel pattern, modern standard Rumanian has developed two central vowels not found in other standard Romance language stressed vowel systems: /ə/ and /i/. The second of these is considered by most Rumanian linguists to have arisen in Daco-Rumanian since the Common Rumanian period, whose vowel pattern has been reconstructed as lacking the higher of the two central vowels that are today found in both Daco-Rumanian and southern variants such as Arumanian. In these latter forms of Balkan Romance /i/ usually occurs only in free variation with, or as an allophone of, /ə/. Its phonemic status in Daco-Rumanian is confirmed by minimal pairs such as *vîr* 'I thrust'; *văr* 'cousin'.

The higher of these central vowels appears to be a Slavic borrowing, entering the language via words such as *ris* 'lynx' < Sl. *rysĭ.* A limited number of such Slavic items can be found (e.g. *jupîn* 'boyar, master'; *stînă* 'sheep pen'; *smîntînă* 'sour cream'), but the functional load of the phoneme increased as Latin items were also affected. Like the last three words illustrated, many such items developed /i/ in the environment of a following nasal (CAMPUM > *cîmp* 'field'; CANTO > *cînt* 'I sing'; LĀNAM > *lînă* 'wool'). This is not, however, a watertight rule, so that sometimes the /a/ + nasal sequence failed to produce /i/ (ĂNĬMAM > *inimă* 'heart'; ANNUM > *an* 'year'). Nevertheless, other vowels in Latin ended up as high central vowels in Daco-Rumanian, again normally in the environment of a following nasal (VĒNAM > *vînă* 'vein'; SĬNUM > *sîn* 'breast'; VĔNTUM > *vînt* 'wind'; but MĔNTEM > *minte* 'mind'). /i/ now accounts for something like four per cent frequency compared with five to eleven per cent for the other vowels.

Although more normally the result of weakening of unstressed /a/ in Latin (e.g. COMPĂRAT > *cumpără* 'he buys'), /ə/ does occur as a stressed vowel in the modern language. Alongside *păr* cited earlier, stressed examples include CANTĀMUS > *cîntăm* 'we sing' and DA > *dă* 'give!'

Other Latin vowels also gave rise to /ə/, both stressed and unstressed (RĔUM > *rău* 'bad'; SEPTĬMĀNA > *săptămînă* 'week'; FŎRAS > *fără* 'without'), a pattern also reflected in the treatment of Slavic vocabulary (*nărod* 'people' < Sl. *nerodŭ*) and Greek (*cărămidă* 'brick' < Gk. κεραμίδα).

The two diphthongs form a symmetrical pattern in the modern language, and the examples given earlier show how each has undergone the assimilating influence of /a/ in the following syllable. As *soare* and *floare* in the examples below show, /oa/ can arise when it precedes /e/ (CĒRAM > *ceară* 'wax'; SĒRAM > *seară* 'evening'; PŎRTAM > *poartă* 'gate'; SŌLEM > *soare* 'sun'; FLŌREM > *floare* 'flower'). The same treatment was given to Slavic words (*četa* > *ceată* 'throng'; *mrena* > *mreană* 'barbel'; *kosa* > *coasă* 'scythe'; *raskola* > *răscoală* 'uprising').

A Latin word resisting diphthongisation is VŌCEM, which in the standard language gives *voce* 'voice'. However, in regional Daco-

Rumanian and in Arumanian, the process follows its normal path to give *boace*.

Despite appearances, the *au* sequence in Rumanian does not represent a continuation of the Latin /au/ diphthong, but is a two-vowel sequence: e.g. *caut* 'I seek', *laud* 'I praise'.

Latin unstressed vowels either reduced to /ə/ or frequently disappeared altogether, as in /eks/ > /s/ (EXPŌNĔRE > *spune* 'say'; EXVŌLARE > *zbura* 'fly') or between consonants (DŎMĬNUM > *domn* 'Mr'; VĔTĔRĀNUS > *bătrîn* 'old').

Consonants

Table 11.2 shows the consonant system of modern standard Daco-Rumanian. The table includes two semi-vowels in addition to 20 true consonants. Some analyses of Rumanian present a larger number of diphthongs by treating these semi-vowels as vowel units (thus /ja/ would under such a system be regarded as a diphthong, rather than the CV sequence it is treated as here — e.g. *iapă* /jap/ 'mare' < ĔQUAM). Also, the consonant inventory would be increased if a palatalised set was recognised. A common singular–plural alternation for masculine nouns is by palatalisation of the final consonant, e.g. *lup* /lup/ 'wolf' → *lupi* /lupʲ/ 'wolves'.

The tendency to palatalisation (cf. pp. 39–40) has played an important role in the history of Balkan Romance. In particular, velar stops, both voiced and voiceless, were fronted before front vowels to give the modern-day post-alveolar affricates (GĔMO > *gem* 'I groan'; CĔNAM > *cină* 'dinner'). However, this complementary distribution did not survive intact and examples of post-alveolar affricates before back vowels include: *giulgiu* 'shroud'; *gionate* 'legs'; *ciudat* 'strange'; *ciocan* 'hammer'. Velar stops before front vowels are found, for example, in *ghetou* 'ghetto'; *ghid* 'guide'; *chinez* 'chinese'; *chenzină* 'fortnightly salary'. In many such instances, this is the result of lexical borrowing after the palatalising development had taken place within words directly inherited from Latin. However, Latin /kl/ also developed into a slightly fronted velar /kʲ/ (CLĀMARE > *chema* 'call'; AURĬCŬLAM > *ureche* 'ear'). A similar process applied to the voiced version (VĬGĬLARE > *veghea* 'be awake'; GLACĬEM > *gheață* 'ice'). Slavic /gl/ sequences were usually unaffected by this development (*glezna* 'ankle'; *oglindă* 'mirror').

In some instances, fronting was advanced enough to give dental affricates, though perhaps this development reflects the already more fronted nature of velar stops in Latin before /i/: SŎCĬUM > *soț* 'spouse'; GLACĬEM > *gheață* 'ice'). In Arumanian this more advanced fronting is even more common. Compare the development of Latin *CĬNUSĬA as DR *cenuşă* and AR /tsənusə/ 'ash'.

Within Daco-Rumanian there is an asymmetry to the affricate pattern,

Table 11.2: Standard Daco-Rumanian Consonant System

	Bilabial		Labiodental		Dental		Post-alveolar		Palatal		Velar		Glottal	
	−V	+V	−V	+V	−V	+V	−V	+V	−V	+V	−V	+V	−V	+V
Stops	p	b			t	d					k	g		
Affricates					ts		tʃ	dʒ						
Fricatives			f	v	s	z	ʃ	ʒ			[h]		h	
Nasals		m				n								
Laterals						l								
Flaps						r								
Semi-vowels		w								j		[w]		

/dz/ not occurring within the standard dialect. However, it does occur regionally, and is the norm in Arumanian. The origin is usually Latin /di/ (DĬEM > DR zi, AR /dzuə/ 'day'; VĬRĬDĬA > DR varză, AR /vardzə/ 'cabbage'; PRANDĬUM > DR prînz, AR /prindzu/ 'lunch').

Contact with Slavic added to the Rumanian consonant system. Words of Slavic origin such as zăpadă 'snow' augmented the /z/ deriving directly from Latin sources. Post-alveolar /ʒ/ also had two sources: Latin (ADIŬNGIT > ajunge 'arrives' (AR /adzundʒe/); IŎCAT > joacă 'plays' (AR /adzwakə/)) and Slavic (zali > jale 'woe': grazdi > grajd 'stable'). The voiceless equivalent /ʃ/ also arose in a great number of words of Latin origin, through attraction to following front vowels (SĔPTEM > şapte 'seven'; SĪC > şi 'and'; CĀSĔUM > caş 'cheese'). It also occurs when part of a cluster where the second element has been palatalised (trist 'sad (sg.)' → trişti 'sad (pl.)'). This also extends to plurals where /ʃ/ is separated from the final front vowel by two consonants (nostru 'our (sg.)' → noştri /noʃtri/ 'our (pl.)').

Before front vowels, there was also a tendency for Latin /l/ to palatalise and to become a mere palatal glide or disappear completely, though in Arumanian the palatalised lateral remains (LĔPŎREM > DR iepure 'hare', AR /ʎepure/; LĪBERTARE > ierta 'forgive'; LĪNUM > in 'flax'). This loss of /l/ also occurred word-medially in words of Latin origin (MŬLĬEREM > muiere 'woman'; FĪLĬUM > fiu 'son') and in Slavic loans too (poljana > poiană 'glade'; nevolja > nevoie 'need'). The same fate also awaited some instances of Latin /-g-/ (MĂGĬS > mai 'more'; QUADRĀGĒSĬMA > păresimi 'Lent').

The liquids also underwent changes, /l/ often becoming /r/ (MŎLAM > moară 'mill'; ANGELUM > înger 'angel'; DŎLUM > dor 'longing'; CAELUM > cer 'sky').

The labiodental voiced fricative often became a bilabial stop (VĔRVĒCEM > berbece 'ram'; CORVUM > corb 'raven'; VĔTĔRĀNUM > bătrîn 'old').

Assumed to be of Slavic origin is the laryngeal/velar fricative /h/. Whether or not this represents the reintroduction of a phoneme independent of the Latin /h/ which had long since disappeared, it was certainly augmented substantially by Slavic loans, now occurring in Rumanian in positions /h/ did not occupy in Latin (duh 'spirit'; hrană 'food'). Some Slavic sources of /h/ underwent a change to the voiceless labiodental fricative (Sl. prahŭ > praf 'dust'; vrahŭ > vraf 'heap'). This occurs also in words of Hungarian origin (marha > marfă 'merchandise'). The rather late timing of this development is suggested by its failure to occur in Istro-Rumanian (DR flămînd 'hungry', IR hlamund: DR foame 'hunger', IR home).

The development of h into f nevertheless does not involve a change in the consonant inventory of Rumanian, merely a redistribution of the existing consonant pattern. This was also the case with other developments. Thus, Latin /kt/ frequently gave rise to Rumanian -*pt*- (cf. p. 38) (*COCTORĬUM > *cuptor* 'furnace'; FACTUM > *fapt* 'fact'; NŎCTEM > *noapte* 'night'; LACTEM > *lapte* 'milk'; DĪRĒCTUM > *drept* 'true, straight'). /gn/ became -*mn*- (SĪGNUM > *semn* 'sign'; LĬGNUM > *lemn* 'wood'; COGNĀTUM > *cumnat* 'brother-in-law').

Some Latin CC clusters were reduced to single consonants: /pt/ often became *t* (BAPTĪZARE > *boteza* 'baptize'); /kt/ similarly became *t* (VICTĬMARE > *vătăma* 'injure'); /rs/ and /ns/ followed the common Romance development of reducing to *s* (DĒORSUM > *jos* 'down'; MĒNSAM > *masă* 'table' — note also AR *mes* 'month' < MĒNSEM, cf. below, p. 414).

Yet, despite such reduction, Rumanian does exhibit a wide range of consonant clusters, some of which do not occur in Western Romance and can be attributed to contact with other Balkan languages. Table 11.3 illustrates the range of two- and three-consonant clusters (all of those shown can occur word-initially).

Table 11.3: Consonant Clusters

CCC

spl	ʃpl		
spr	ʃpr		
str	ʃtr	zdr	
skl		zgl	
skr		zgr	

CC

sp	ʃp	zb		
sk		zg	ʒg	
st	ʃt		ʒd	
sf	ʃf	zv		
sm	ʃm	zm		
sn	ʃn		ʒn	
sl	ʃl	zl		
	ʃr			
tr		dr		
kl		gl		
kr		gr		
pl		bl		
pr		br		
hr				
hl				
		ml		
		mr		
		mn		
ks				
kt				

3 Morphology

Nominal Morphology

The chart of noun declensions gives a representative set of paradigms for the three genders, two cases, singular and plural, definite and indefinite forms.

Rumanian Noun Declensions

Representative masculine nouns

(i) *lup* 'wolf'

		Sg.	Pl.
Nom./Acc.	−def	lup	lupi
	+def	lupul	lupii
Gen./Dat.	−def	lup	lupi
	+def	lupului	lupilor

(ii) *arbore* 'tree'

Nom./Acc.	−def	arbore	arbori
	+def	arborele	arborii
Gen./Dat.	−def	arbore	arbori
	+def	arborelui	arborilor

(iii) *codru* 'forest'

Nom./Acc.	−def	codru	codri
	+def	codrul	codrii
Gen./Dat.	−def	codru	codri
	+def	codrului	codrilor

Representative feminine nouns

(i) *casă* 'house'

		Sg.	Pl.
Nom./Acc.	−def	casă	case
	+def	casa	casele
Gen./Dat.	−def	case	case
	+def	casei	caselor

(ii) *stea* 'star'

Nom./Acc.	−def	stea	stele
	+def	steaua	stelele
Gen./Dat.	−def	stele	stele
	+def	stelei	stelelor

(iii) *cîmpie* 'plain'

Nom./Acc.	−def	cîmpie	cîmpii
	+def	cîmpia	cîmpiile
Gen./Dat.	−def	cîmpii	cîmpii
	+def	cîmpiei	cîmpiilor

(iv) *învăţătoare* 'teacher'

Nom./Acc.	−def	învăţătoare	învăţătoare
	+def	învăţătoarea	învăţătoarele
Gen./Dat.	−def	învăţătoare	învăţătoare
	+def	învăţătoarei	învăţătoarelor

Representative 'neuter' nouns

(i) *studiu* 'study(ing)'

Nom./Acc.	−def	studiu	studii
	+def	studiul	studiile
Gen./Dat.	−def	studiu	studii
	+def	studiului	studiilor

(ii) *oraş* 'town'

Nom./Acc.	−def	oraş	oraşe
	+def	oraşul	oraşele
Gen./Dat.	−def	oraş	oraşe
	+def	oraşului	oraşele

(iii) *deal* 'hill'

Nom./Acc.	−def	deal	dealuri
	+def	dealul	dealurile
Gen./Dat.	−def	deal	dealuri
	+def	dealului	dealurilor

As can be seen, the Latin noun declension system has fared better within Balkan Romance than elsewhere in the Romance area. The sample given in this chart is fairly representative, but the following singular/plural alternations can be added:

Masculine	Sg.	Pl.	
	om	oameni	'man'
	împărat	împăraţi	'emperor'
	băiat	băieţi	'boy'
	cal	cai	'horse'
	fiu	fii	'son'
	brad	brazi	'fir tree'

Feminine			
	basma	basmale	'kerchief'
	viaţă	vieţi	'life'
	carte	cărţi	'book'
	fată	fete	'girl'
	dovadă	dovezi	'proof'
	bară	beri	'bar'
	bere	beri	'beer'

Neuter			
	tablou	tablouri	'picture'
	nume	nume	'name'
	templu	temple	'temple'

The most noticeable characteristic is the tendency for a change in termination to a front vowel resulting in palatalisation of the preceding consonant(s) and/or assimilation of the last vowel of the stem.

The conservative nature of the Rumanian declension system is, in part at least, a result of the development of suffixal determiners, a clear Balkan feature. Thus, to take a classic example, HOMO ILLE gave rise to *omul* (*om* + *ul*) 'the man' (forms of such nouns in Arumanian, e.g. /om^u/, and the definite forms of masculine nouns in -*e* in Daco-Rumanian, e.g. *fratele* 'brother', suggest that in *omul* -*u*- is historically part of the noun stem rather than of the definite suffix, but synchronically the division given above is more realistic). This phenomenon has served to maintain a morphological distinction between the nominative/accusative case form and the genitive/dative case form in the singular of masculine nouns, and the plural of all nouns, which would otherwise be lacking. As can be seen from the chart, it is only in the singular of feminine nouns that such a distinction is apparent in the unarticulated noun itself. Generally speaking, the unarticulated genitive/dative singular form of feminine nouns coincides with the two plural forms (this is true of three of the four examples of feminine nouns given in the chart — this pattern is not apparent with nouns like *învăţătoare* since they have no distinct unarticulated plural forms) whereas the masculine nouns always have identical forms for unarticulated nominative/accusative and genitive/dative forms. However, the retention of a nominative/accusative–genitive/dative morphological distinction within the indefinite article system serves to differentiate noun phrases in which the actual nouns have neutralised the distinction (the forms of the indefinite article are given in the discussion of numerals later in this section). Augmenting this regular and productive two-case system, there is a defective set of vocative case forms — defective first in that not all nouns show a vocative (as might be expected, their occurrence is restricted to items high on the animacy hierarchy) but also in that the system is gradually decaying. The plural vocative is always identical with the genitive/ dative articulated plural (e.g. *oameni* 'men' → *oamenilor*; *fete* 'girls' → *fetelor*), while in the singular, masculine nouns add -*e* to the articulated form (*om* 'man' → *omule*), but kin terms involve an unarticulated form, normally the same as the nominative (e.g. *frate* 'brother' → *frate*; *tată* 'father' → *tată*), though it is sometimes affected by assimilation (e.g. *cumătru* 'godfather' → *cumetre*). The vocative singular of feminine nouns also either coincides with the nominative (e.g. *fată* 'girl' → *fată*) or has a separate form, often in -*o* (e.g. *soră* 'sister' → *soro*). With proper names, whether or not an articulated form of the vocative is used depends on the stem termination (e.g. *Radu* → *Radule*; *Gheorghe* → *Gheorghe* (**Gheorghele*); *Ana* → *Ana, Anǎ* or *Ano*). Such forms in -*o* are a Slavic legacy, and there is little doubt that the richer case systems of the southern Slavic languages that Rumanian came into contact with either continued or reinforced the distinct Latin vocative case.

Also doubtless a result of Slavic contact is the existence of a so-called neuter gender in Rumanian. Whether the third group of nouns in the declension chart deserve the label 'neuter' is a matter I take up in section 4, but there is no doubt that morphologically it includes many of the nouns which in Latin came under the neuter heading. As a result of phonetic attrition, the singulars of second and third declension neuter nouns fell together with masculine singulars, while the plurals of such nouns fell together with feminine plurals (SCAMNUM (II n. sg.) > *scaun(ul)* 'chair' *but* SCAMNA (II n. pl.) > *scaune(le)* 'chairs'; TEMPUS (III n. sg.) > *timp(ul)* 'time' but TEMPORA (III n. pl.) > *timpuri(le)* 'times'). These form the nucleus of a large set of nouns in Rumanian that have masculine forms in the singular and feminine forms in the plural, a set that has been increased substantially by assigning imported words to the 'neuter' category.

Despite the high frequency of neuters with *-uri* plurals, there has been a tendency since the nineteenth century to replace this ending with *-e*. For example, *niveluri* 'levels' is now commonly found as *nivele*, though this is a feature of written rather than spoken language. The sociolinguistic basis for this development appears to be an awareness that *-e* endings derive in many instances from Western Romance loans, and as such have higher status. Frequently the original gender of French will govern which gender a word takes, with singular nouns spelt in *-e* becoming feminine in Rumanian. However, many such words borrowed during the nineteenth century have also ended up as neuters, apparently because they came to Rumanian via Russian, where the silent *-e* caused them to be treated as masculines. Once the feminine link was thus broken, neuter was a more likely categorisation in Rumanian because of the inanimate meaning of the items involved, e.g. *vals* 'waltz' and *garderob* 'wardrobe' (the latter has now gone out of use, though the direct loan *garderobă*, which recreates the mute *-e* of French, is used for 'cloakroom').

Adjectives

A representative set of adjectives is given in the chart of adjective morphology. Typically, adjectives (e.g. *bun* 'good') follow a similar pattern to nouns, with feminine genitive/dative singulars matching feminine plurals. Forms for *drept* 'straight, correct' are given to illustrate palatalisation and diphthongisation patterns. As can be seen from adjectives like *mare* 'big', there is some neutralisation between masculine and feminine adjectives in both singular and plural ranges (e.g. *mare* (m./f. sg.) – *mari* (m./f. pl.) 'big') — though note that the feminine genitive/dative singular *mari* without the suffixed article coincides with the plural forms (masculine: *mare*) consistent with the pattern of most nouns and most other adjectives. The forms for *verde* 'green' are given to illustrate palatalisation.

Adjective Morphology

	m./n. sg.	m. pl.	f. sg.	f./n. pl.
bun 'good'				
Nom./Acc.	bun	buni	bună	bune
Gen./Dat.	bun	buni	bune	bune
drept 'straight'				
Nom./Acc.	drept	drepţi	dreaptă	drepte
Gen./Dat.	drept	drepţi	drepte	drepte
mare 'big'				
Nom./Acc.	mare	mari	mare	mari
Gen./Dat.	mare	mari	mari	mari
verde 'green'				
Nom./Acc.	verde	verzi	verde	verzi
Gen./Dat.	verde	verzi	verzi	verzi

Demonstratives

These agree with their heads in person, number and gender, but morphologically they are augmented by an articulated set, used when the demonstrative either follows its head or is used pronominally. A representative set is given in the chart of demonstratives.

Demonstratives

		m./n. sg.	m. pl.	f. sg.	f./n. pl.
acest 'this' (< ECCE + IST-)					
Nom./Acc.	−def	acest	aceşti	această	aceste
	+def	acesta	aceştia	aceasta	acestea
Gen./Dat.	−def	acestui	acestor	acestei	acestor
	+def	acestuia	acestora	acesteia	acestora
acel 'that' (< ECCE + ILL-)					
Nom./Acc.	−def	acel	acei	acea	acele
	+def	acela	aceia	aceea	acelea
Gen./Dat.	−def	acelui	acelor	acelei	acelor
	+def	aceluia	acelora	aceleia	acelora

Pronouns

The pronoun system also retains case distinctions, and the chart demonstrates the forms of clitic and free personal pronouns, including possessives (in the form of adjectives agreeing with their heads in gender, person and number). Note the preposition *pe*, which acts as an accusative marker for pronouns in general, and is also used to mark some NPs as direct objects. This point is discussed in section 4.

Personal Pronouns

		1st sg.	2nd sg.	3rd sg. (m.)	3rd sg. (f.)	1st pl.	2nd pl.	3rd pl. (m.)	3rd pl. (f.)
Nominative	Cliticised								
	Free	eu	tu	el	ea	noi	voi	ei	ele
Accusative	Cliticised	mă	te	îl	o	ne	vă	îl	le
	Free (pe +)	mine	tine	el	ea	noi	voi	ei	ele
Dative	Cliticised	îmi	îţi	îi	îi	ni	vi	le	le
	Free	mie	ţie	lui	ei	nouă	vouă	lor	lor

Adjectival and Pronominal Forms of Possessive Pronouns

1/Sg.

	m./n. sg.	f. sg.	m. pl.	f./n. pl.
Nom./Acc.	(al) meu	(a) mea	(ai) mei	(ale) mele
Gen./Dat.	meu	mele	mei	mele

2/Sg.

	m./n. sg.	f. sg.	m. pl.	f./n. pl.
Nom./Acc.	(al) tău	(a) ta	(ai) tăi	(ale) tale
Gen./Dat.	tău	tale	tăi	tale

3/Sg.

	m./n. sg.	f. sg.	m. pl.	f./n. pl.
Nom./Acc.	(al, ai, a, ale) lui/ei			
Gen./Dat.	lui/ei			
Nom. Acc.	(al) său	(a) sa	(ai) săi	(ale) sale
Gen./Dat.	său	sale	săi	sale

1/Pl.

	m./n. sg.	m. pl.	f. sg.	f./n. pl.
Nom./Acc.	(al) nostru	(ai) noştri	(a) noastră	(ale) noastre
Gen./Dat.	nostru	noştri	noastre	noastre

2/Pl.

	m./n. sg.	m. pl.	f. sg.	f./n. pl.
Nom./Acc.	(al) vostru	(ai) voştri	(a) voastră	(ale) voastre
Gen./Dat.	vostru	voştri	voastre	voastre

3/Pl.

Nom./Acc.	(al, ai, a, ale) lor			
Gen./Dat.	lor			

Note: The forms above are used to represent the genitive of the personal pronouns. For first and second person, singular and plural, they take the form of adjectives, agreeing in person and number with the **possessed**. In the third person, the free dative forms of the personal pronouns are used, the number and gender forms of which reflect the **possessor**. There does exist an adjectival form *său* which follows the first and second person agreement pattern by reflecting the possessed, but its use is waning. Elements in parentheses make the forms pronominal.

Numerals

The cardinal numbers from one to ten demonstrate the clear Latin heritage of the system.

Classical Latin	Daco-Rumanian
UNUS	unu
DUO	doi (m.)/două (f.)
TRES	trei
QUATTUOR	patru
QUINQUE	cinci
SEX	şase
SEPTEM	şapte
OCTO	opt
NOVEM	nouă
DECEM	zece

The forms of *unu* as the indefinite article are given below:

	m./n. sg.	*m. pl.*	*f.sg.*	*f./n. pl.*
Nom./Acc.	un	unii	o	unele
Gen./Dat.	unui	unor	unei	unor

Numbers eleven–nineteen are modelled on a Slavic pattern, though using Romance morphemes. Thus, UNUS SUPER DECEM 'one on ten', etc.:

unsprezece	'eleven'
douăsprezece	'twelve'
treisprezece	'thirteen'
paisprezece	'fourteen'
cincisprezece	'fifteen'
şaisprezece	'sixteen'
şaptesprezece	'seventeen'
optsprezece	'eighteen'
nouăsprezece	'nineteen'

Multiples of ten are represented by 'two tens', 'three tens' etc., again a Slavic calque:

douăzeci	'twenty'
treizeci	'thirty'
patruzeci	'forty'
cinzeci	'fifty'
şaizeci	'sixty'
şaptezeci	'seventy'
optzeci	'eighty'
nouăzeci	'ninety'

'Thirty-one', 'thirty-two', 'forty-one' etc., are 'thirty and one', 'thirty and two' etc., e.g. *treizeci şi unu* 'thirty-one'. The same pattern is used in Daco-Rumanian 'twenty-one' to 'twenty-nine', e.g. *douăzeci şi unu* 'twenty-one', but Arumanian has extended the Slavic system for 'eleven' to 'nineteen' into the 'twenty-one' to 'twenty-nine' pattern — though unlike Daco-Rumanian it retains the Latin for 'twenty' (/jingits/ < VĪGINTI), e.g. /ʃaispreyjingits/ 'twenty-six' (literally 'six on twenty').

Finally, 'one hundred' is Slavic: *sută* (< *suto*) but 'one thousand' is Romance: *mie* (< MILLE).

Verb Morphology
The chart of verb morphology gives the present tense forms for all regular verb declensions, with the two major irregulars 'have' and 'be'. The categorisation into conjugations used here is not a division followed by all linguists concerned with Rumanian morphology. It follows the pattern directly inherited from Latin, but can be justified synchronically in terms of the following features.

Vowel Alternations
The root vowel of type 1(a) is -*a*, alternating with the third person subjunctive in -*e*, and maintained within the -*ez* pattern of type 1(b). Of all types, 1(b) appears to be the most productive in the language today. The root vowels for types 4 and 5 are -*i* and -*î* respectively, alternating with subjunctives in -*a* (though 5(a) could just as well be categorised with type 1 on these grounds). Both types 2 and 3 follow the -*e* indicative/-*a* subjunctive pattern.

Distribution of Person/Number Forms
All verbs exhibit complete homophony between singular and plural present subjunctive forms in third person (all other persons/numbers being identical with the indicative). With type 1 and type 5(a) verbs, this merely continues the neutralisation between singular and plural indicative forms of the third person. With all other verb types the subjunctive causes a change in the neutralisation pattern. As can be seen, it is the first singular and third plural forms that are identical in the indicative for these.

Infinitive Form
Types 2 and 3 continue the Latin distinction between conjugations II and III (VIDERE > *vedea*; FACERE > *face*). However, this distinction is unlikely to stay reliable since there is apparently a tendency among some present-day speakers to re-form type 2 infinitives as type 3 (e.g. *putea* 'be able' → *poate*).

Stress
In all verbs except type 3, stress in present tense forms is on the final

Rumanian Verb Morphology

Type 1 (a)

cînta 'sing'

Inf.			
1 sg.	cînt	1 pl.	cîntăm
2 sg.	cînți	2 pl.	cîntați
3 sg.	cîntă	3 pl.	cîntă
subj.	să cînte	pp.	cîntat

Type 2

vedea 'see'

Inf.			
1 sg.	văd	1 pl.	vedem
2 sg.	vezi	2 pl.	vedeți
3 sg.	vede	3 pl.	văd
subj.	să vadă	pp.	văzut

Type 4 (a)

dormi 'sleep'

Inf.			
1 sg.	dorm	1 pl.	dormim
2 sg.	dormi	2 pl.	dormiți
3 sg.	doarme	3 pl.	dorm
subj.	să doarmă	pp.	dormit

Type 5 (a)

omorî 'kill'

Inf.			
1 sg.	omor	1 pl.	omorîm
2 sg.	omori	2 pl.	omorîți
3 sg.	omoară	3 pl.	omoară
subj.	să omoare	pp.	omorît

Type 1 (b)

lucra 'work'

Inf.			
1 sg.	lucrez	1 pl.	lucrăm
2 sg.	lucrezi	2 pl.	lucrați
3 sg.	lucrează	3 pl.	lucrează
subj.	să lucreze	pp.	lucrat

Type 3

face 'do, make'

Inf.			
1 sg.	fac	1 pl.	facem
2 sg.	faci	2 pl.	faceți
3 sg.	face	3 pl.	fac
subj.	să facă	pp.	făcut

Type 4 (b)

zidi 'build'

Inf.			
1 sg.	zidesc	1 pl.	zidim
2 sg.	zidești	2 pl.	zidiți
3 sg.	zidește	3 pl.	zidesc
subj.	să zidească	pp.	zidit

Type 5 (b)

urî 'hate'

Inf.			
1 sg.	urăsc	1 pl.	urîm
2 sg.	urăști	2 pl.	urîți
3 sg.	urăște	3 pl.	urăsc
subj.	să urască	pp.	urît

Irregular A

fi 'be'

Present Indicative

Inf.			
1 sg.	sînt	1 pl.	sîntem
2 sg.	ești	2 pl.	sînteți
3 sg.	e(ste)	3 pl.	sînt
		pp.	fost

Present Subjunctive

1 sg. să	fiu	1 pl. să	fim
2 sg. să	fii	2 pl. să	fiți
3 sg. să	fie	3 pl. să	fie

Irregular B

avea 'have'

Inf.			
1 sg.	am	1 pl.	avem
2 sg.	ai	2 pl.	aveți
3 sg.	are	3 pl.	au
subj.	să aibă	pp.	avut

Note: This chart assumes a division into five conjugations, of which three have two subtypes each. The grouping is based on the morphological structure of the verb system of modern standard Rumanian, rather than on the traditional conjugation system of the Latin from which it basically derives. For each representative verb, six forms of the present indicative are given, together with the third person present subjunctive, the infinitive and the past participle. All other forms (but see the text for discussion of the gerundive and imperative) are predictable. The chart also includes relevant forms of the two major irregular verbs *fi* 'be' and *avea* 'have'.

syllable of the stem except for first and second plural (e.g. *omoáră* but *omorîm*; *lucrézi* but *lucráți* — for this pattern to work, the -*ez*, -*esc* and -*ăsc* forms should be seen as part of the stem, a part that disappears in first and second plural). This pattern also applies to type 2 (*véde* but *vedém*) but not to type 3 — thus *fáce* but *fácem, fáceți*. Arumanian does not have this distinction between type 3 and the rest and the following is the present tense pattern for the equivalent verb in that variant:

/fák°/   /fitʃém°/
/fátʃ/   /fitʃéts/
/fátʃi/   /fák°/   subj. /fákə/

Tense and Mood
The imperfect endings are a direct development from Latin forms in -BAM. The forms for *cînta* 'sing' are: *cîntám, cîntái, cîntá, cîntám, cîntáți, cîntáu.* The -*a* root of the imperfect terminations matches the -*a* root of type 1(a) verbs and leads to neutralisation between some forms (second plural present and second plural imperfect), whereas this is avoided in other verb types, e.g. *vedéți → vedeáți.*

   Also deriving directly from Latin (< CANTAVI) is the simple perfect: *cîntái, cîntáși, cîntắ, cîntárăm, cîntáráți, cîntáră.* However, this is normal only in some areas of Daco-Rumanian (in particular, in Oltenia, in the west of the Muntenian region), and the standard language uses a periphrastic past. On the other hand, standard Rumanian does have a synthetic plu-perfect, deriving from the Latin pluperfect subjunctive (CANTAVISSEM): *cîntásem, cîtáseși, cîntáse, cîntáserăm, cîntáseráți, cîntásera.* Precisely the opposite development for perfect and pluperfect took place in Arumanian. Here, the pluperfect is periphrastic and the perfect is synthetic (a pattern that can be attributed to contact with Greek): AR /kintáj/ 'I sang' but /avjam kintátə/ 'I had sung'. In standard Daco-Rumanian, the peri-phrastic past is made up of the past participle preceded by auxiliary forms of *avea* 'have': *am cîntát, ai cîntát, a cîntát, am cîntát, a cîntát, au cîntát.*

   The future is also periphrastic, the standard form being the infinitive preceded by the auxiliary verb *voi* (*voi, vei, va, vem, veți, vor cînta*). This appears to derive from some development of Latin VELLE, later *VOLERE 'wish' (cf. p. 57). Arumanian has fully complied with the Balkan trend of replacing infinitives with subjunctives and forms its future by an invariable third person present indicative form of 'wish' + the variable sub-junctive: /va mi duk/ 'I will go'; /va i dukə/ 'he will go' (compare Greek θα πάω). A similar pattern is also found in Daco-Rumanian: *o să mă duc* 'I will go'; *o să se ducă* 'he will go'.

   The conditional in Rumanian is periphrastic (*aș, ai, ar, am, ați, ar cînta*). This involves an auxiliary plus the infinitive but appears to have developed from a synthetic form *cîntareaş*, etc., still used in eighteenth century texts and resembling more closely the pattern of Western Romance conditionals. Separation of the two parts allowed reduction of the *-re* infinitive in line with the reduction of all infinitives, a point that is discussed in section 4.

The gerundive in *-înd* is a development of Latin forms in -ANDU(M). All conjugations except type 4 follow this pattern. (*cîntînd, făcînd*), though with some palatalisation of final root consonants (*trimite → trimiţînd* 'sending'; *vedea → văzînd* 'seeing'). Type 4 verbs take the form *-ind*, (*dormi → dormind* 'sleeping'). The gerundive is used in a variety of ways (see section 4), and is also the basis of a periphrastic verb form expressing probability: *va fi venind* 'he'll be coming (I imagine)'.

Finally, imperatives continue the Latin pattern. Plural forms are identical with the second plural indicative (*cîntaţi* 'sing!/you are singing'). Singular forms sometimes coincide with the second singular indicative (*vezi* 'see!/you see'), sometimes with the third singular (*lucrează* 'work!/he is working'), depending on the morphological relationship between the original Latin imperative and these personal forms. In addition, some irregulars have been carried over from Latin (DIC > *zi* 'say!'; DUC > *du* 'carry!'; FAC > *fă* 'do!').

4 Syntax

The basic SOV constituent order of Classical Latin gave way to the essentially SVO order of modern Rumanian. Even though there are a variety of circumstances in which the language deviates from this order, it nevertheless exhibits a number of characteristics normally associated with the SVO language type. Within the NP, genitives follow the head (*soţia lui Ion e sora regelui* 'Ion's wife is the king's sister'). Adjectives normally follow their head (*copilul bucuros a furat cărţile scumpe* 'the happy child stole the expensive books'), though enough of the SOV heritage remains for adjectives to be able to occur before their heads, where they may even take the definite suffix (*bunul om* 'the good man'). Relative clauses follow their head (*Radu a cumpărat casa pe care am construit-o* 'Radu bought the house that I built'). Prepositions are used, rather than postpositions (*am pus cartea pe masă cu grijă* 'I placed the book on the table with care').

With its prepositions, Rumanian has developed an odd minor rule. When governed by all but one or two of these (*cu* 'with' is an exception), a definite-marked noun loses its suffix unless it is further modified. Note the alternation between [+def] and [−def] in the form of *teatru* 'theatre' in the following: *m-am dus la teatru* 'I went to the theatre'; *m-am dus la teatrul nou* 'I went to the new theatre'. This rule also serves as a syntactic criterion for distinguishing restrictive and non-restrictive relative clauses. *Casă* alternates with *casa* in the next two examples, since the restrictive relative in the second modifies its head more intimately than the non-restrictive clause in the first: *Radu a intrat în casă, pe care am construit-o* 'Radu entered the house, which I built'; *Radu a intrat în casa pe care am construit-o* 'Radu entered the house which I built'.

The relatively conservative nature of the Rumanian case marking system has led to some freedom of word order, but in some sentence types word order is fixed. Yes-no questions normally have the same order as statements, but in *wh*-questions the fronted *wh*-word leads to subject–verb inversion (*cînd a venit Ion?* 'when did Ion come?').

To balance complex sentences, heavy subjects can be moved into sentence-final position, as in the following example, containing a lexically headed subject complement clause (*merită să fie notate încercările scriitorului de a găsi un echivalent sunetelor ă și î* 'there deserve to be noted the attempts of the writer to find an equivalent for the sounds *ă* and *î*').

Rumanian also tolerates an OVS pattern, the availability of case marking for distinguishing subjects and objects allowing topicalisation strategies like those available in other Balkan languages, such as Modern Greek (*pe Maria a văzut-o Ana* 'Ana saw Maria'); consider also the position in Spanish (p. 115). The object marker *pe* (< PER) occurs more frequently the higher one goes up the animacy hierarchy. It is regularly found marking proper names and pronouns, irrespective of their position in relation to the verb (*l-am văzut pe el* 'I saw him'; *am văzut-o pe Maria* 'I saw Maria'). With personal names, many speakers can dispense with *pe*, but not when the object inverts with the subject, as in the first example in this paragraph, where it is *pe* alone which distinguishes object from subject.

In each of the last three examples it will be noticed that there are added clitics, a feature shared both within the Balkan *Sprachbund* and also to varying degrees by a number of other Romance languages (cf., for instance, p. 107, p. 235). In Rumanian the clitics serve to strengthen the object marking, something that the relatively free word order sometimes necessitates. Nevertheless, both *pe*-marking and resumptive clitics can occur redundantly. In the following example, either *pe* or the masculine object clitic is redundant, since each alone is sufficient to mark *Radu* as object: *pe Radu l-a văzut Maria* 'Maria saw Radu'.

Thus, Rumanian has clearly institutionalised the use of resumptive pronouns — that is, they are used according to rule and not merely selected when ambiguity would otherwise ensue. This is clearly the case with the resumptive pronouns found obligatorily in relative clauses. In the following example, the object marker *pe* on the relative marker *care* shows it is the direct object of 'bought'. Yet the resumptive feminine object marker cliticised to the past participle is obligatory even though *carte* 'book' is low on the animacy hierarchy: *aceasta e cartea pe care am cumpărat-o* 'this is the book that I bought'. The resumptive pronoun system also extends to indirect objects, as illustrated by the simple sentence: *Radu i-a dat Anei trei cărţi* 'Radu gave Ana three books'; or by the relative clause in: *aceasta e fata căreia i-am dat cartea ieri* 'this is the girl that I gave the book to yesterday'.

Rumanian often drops subject pronouns, there being adequate variation in verb forms to make them redundant. They are retained only for emphasis or contrast, and free object and indirect object pronouns are added for the same purpose. In the following example there is no subject: *ai plecat?* 'did you leave?'; in the following there are free pronouns representing subject and indirect object, in addition to accusative and dative clitics: *eu i-am dat-o-lui* 'I gave it to him'. As can be seen from these examples, most direct and indirect object clitics precede the verb (or auxiliary), but an exception is the feminine singular object marker *o*, which is suffixed to gerundives and past participles, as in the last example. In common with most other Romance languages, clitic pronouns follow imperative forms of the verb. When both accusative and dative clitics precede the verb, the dative comes first: *mi l-a dat* 'he gave it to me' and the same order is used after imperatives: *dă-mi-l* 'give it to me'.

As mentioned at the end of section 3, modern Rumanian imperatives are a direct development of the Latin system. When negative, the plural is again identical with the indicative: *nu plecaţi* 'you are leaving/don't leave!'. In the singular, the infinitive form is found: *nu pleca!* 'don't leave!', though some speakers retain the irregulars even under these circumstances, so that either of the following is possible: *nu zi!/ nu zice!* 'don't say!'. Notice also that, as, for instance, in Spanish (p. 116), negatives in Rumanian are of the double variety: *n-am venit niciodată* 'I never came'.

In addition to verb inflection, noun inflection, prepositions and resumptive pronouns, Rumanian is also fairly rich in agreement as an aid to identifying case relations. Adjectives and demonstratives agree with their heads and predicative adjectives also agree with the subject of the sentence: *fetele sînt frumoase* 'the girls are pretty'; *caii sînt puternici* 'the horses are strong'. The occurrence of such agreement has enabled the Rumanian Academy to offer proof of the existence of a neuter category of nouns. It will be recalled (p. 401 above) that these nouns have forms coinciding in the singular with masculine nouns and in the plural with feminine nouns, attributive agreement of adjectives and demonstratives following the same pattern, as does predicative agreement: *scaunul e negru* 'the chair is black'; *scaunele sînt negre* 'the chairs are black'. When two 'neuter' singulars are conjoined, agreement is 'neuter' plural, as might be expected: *scaunul şi gardul sînt negre* 'the chair and the fence are black'. However, when a masculine singular and a neuter singular are conjoined in this way, the Academy claims an agreement pattern like the following: *peretele şi gardul sînt negre* 'the wall and the fence are black'. Although *perete* is masculine and *gard* is 'neuter', the neuter agreement overrides the default rule that combinations of nouns of different genders attract masculine plural agreement when one of the nouns is masculine. This suggests that the notion of inanimacy is dominant, the agreement in this last example reflecting a neuter (i.e. inanimate) interpretation. In fact, few if any speakers follow the Academy rule and the question of whether the third type of noun in Rumanian should be labelled 'neuter', 'ambigeneric' or something innocuous, like 'type III', is likely to remain unresolved. Despite contact with Slavic, there is no hard evidence that Rumanian reinstituted a semantically neuter gender.

Multiple-clause Sentences
Conjoining is not, however, restricted to NPs, and Rumanian also allows the conjoining of sentences: *Ion a furat cartea şi Radu a furat carnetul* 'Ion stole the book and Radu stole the notebook'; of VPs: *Radu a plecat de acasă şi a furat maşina* 'Radu left home and stole the car'; but normally not of minor constituents, though prepositions are amenable: *rîndunica a zburat prin şi peste pomi* 'the swallow flew through and over the trees'. A certain amount of elision is possible, so that one finds instances of gapping. The first example in this paragraph can be reduced in this way to give: *Ion a furat cartea şi Radu carnetul* 'Ion stole the book and Radu the notebook'.

Of the other complex sentence types, relative clauses have already been illustrated, but it is within the complement system that Rumanian has acquired important Balkan features. One Balkan development was the replacement of the infinitive by a subjunctive paradigm as a marker of complement clauses. This phenomenon is complete in Arumanian, but Daco-Rumanian, situated much further from the centre of the *Sprachbund,* has resisted it to a greater extent. Both infinitive and subjunctive marking are possible in some circumstances, including sentences where a subject clause has been extraposed: *e suficient să dormi/a dormi trei ore pe noapte* 'it is sufficient to sleep three hours per night'. Even more common is the infinitive after prepositions: *în loc de a citi, m-am uitat la televizor* 'instead of reading, I watched television'. The existence of what appears to be an infinitive after the semi-modal *putea* 'be able' seems to suggest that an extension in the use of the subjunctive has met another barrier: *pot veni* 'I can come'. However, the subjunctive is still an alternative: *pot să viu,* and the best analysis treats the 'infinitive' here as a stem. It is not preceded by the particle *a,* which usually marks the infinitive, and 'be able' clearly falls into the range of verbs with a modal value. *Pot veni* can be treated as an auxiliary + stem construction.

Most references so far have been to the short infinitive, a truncated form lacking the final *-re.* The process by which true infinitives lost this clearly Latin termination was almost complete at the time of the earliest extant texts, but forms in *-re* do still occur and very productively in Daco-Rumanian, with a value similar to that of gerunds or derived nominals in English. That is, the *-re* form is more nominal than verbal, as demonstrated by the definite suffix and adjectival agreement it attracts: *plecarea lui a fost neaşteptată* 'his departure was unexpected'. In Arumanian too these survive, also with some nominal value, and are indeed the only trace of an original infinitive.

Other non-finite forms include a descendant of the Latin supine, again having both nominal and verbal characteristics: *fumatul oprit* 'smoking prohibited'; *e de mirat cum trăieşte* 'it's amazing how he lives'. The gerundive is used as a subordinate marker after verbs of perception: *l-am văzut pe Radu venind spre oraş* 'I saw Radu coming towards the town'; and sometimes as the verbal element in participial relative clauses: *bărbatul venind spre oraş e Radu* 'the man coming towards the town is Radu'; occasionally crystallising (though not productively) as a pure adjective: *mîini tremurînde* 'trembling hands'.

Nevertheless, it is the subjunctive which has taken on the lion's share of the work in marking subordinate clauses (p. 407 above). Furthermore, in addition to those instances where it has replaced the infinitive, it also continues the Latin jussive subjunctive, occurring without a superordinate clause: *să vii!* 'come!'. Finally, it is used, as widely elsewhere in Romance, to mark relative clauses where no particular referent has been established and may indeed not exist: *caut o bicicletă care să fie roşie* 'I'm looking for a bicycle that's red'.

5 Lexis

As was pointed out in section 1, some (sub)dialects of Balkan Romance are more innovative, others more conservative, and this particularly applies to lexis. The Maramureş region of northern Rumania produced some of the oldest extant Rumanian texts (sixteenth century), and these are noted for their rhotacising of intervocalic nasals. This feature is also found in modern day Istro-Rumanian (DR *albină* 'bee' but IR *albiră*; DR *cineva* 'someone' but IR *cireva*; DR *vineri* 'Friday' but IR *vireri*) and supports the claim that this westernmost form of Balkan Romance represents a fairly late breaking away from Daco-Rumanian, rather than a direct product of the breakup of Common Rumanian much earlier. Among more conservative features of the Maramureş subdialect are lexical items such as *gint* 'people' (< GENTEM) and *arină* 'sand' (< ARENAM) — compare the standard language *popor* (< POPULUM) and *nisip* (< Sl. *nasip*) respectively. At the same time, the geographical position of Maramureş has allowed greater influence from Hungarian, which is also reflected to some extent in Istro-Rumanian.

There follows a more structured discussion of the lexical development of Balkan Romance, divided into the main sources of innovation.

Dacian

There appears to have been very little substrate influence on the Latin of

Dacia. Greek lexicographers of the period before the Roman occupation list fewer than a hundred words of Dacian, most of these being plant names, so that a direct historical comparison is not possible. Given the uncertain grouping of Dacian, Thracian and Illyrian within Indo-European, it is questionable whether Albanian and Rumanian shared a substrate language, though the existence of cognate lexical items of non-Latin origin might be taken as evidence of some common substrate influence on the two languages. Such items include:

Rumanian	Albanian	Translation
abure	avull	steam
mînz	mës	colt
pîrîu	përrua	brook
scrum	shkrump	ash
vatră	vatrë	hearth

However, such cognates do not prove a common Thraco-Illyrian substratum any more than the fact that Albanian has many Latin loans cognate with Rumanian means the two languages share a Latin heritage.

Slavic
Much more substantial than the Germanic adstrate in the Western Romance languages (cf. p. 76) is the Slavic adstrate in Balkan Romance. From around the middle of the first millennium there must have been considerable contact between southern Slavic and what was to become Rumanian. Initially of a popular nature, lexical influence was later also religious and political, resulting in a very substantial Slavic percentage of the total word stock of Rumanian (though the figures have been exaggerated).

The oldest Slavic elements in Rumanian are popular and have Bulgarian characteristics. Later it was through the medium of Old Church Slavonic that vocabulary of a more learned nature entered Rumanian, this being the liturgical language of Orthodox christianity in the Balkans. In early Daco-Rumanian texts, primarily of a religious content, it is hardly surprising that many terms are either straight loans or calques from Slavic. There are a number of doublets in Rumanian of Slavic words borrowed at different periods — compare popular a sfîrşi with more learned a săvîrşi, both being derived ultimately from Old Slavic sŭvŭrşiti 'finish, complete'. Later, vocabulary from other neighbouring Slavic languages made its mark on Rumanian. Such influence was more local in character, there being more Serbian vocabulary borrowed in the Banat, for example, and more Ukrainian in northern Moldavia. In fact, these neighbouring languages also themselves borrowed from Rumanian. Vatră 'hearth', for instance, given earlier as a possible Thraco-Illyrian substratum item, is found in Ukrainian. Istro-Rumanian has accommodated a good deal of Croatian vocabulary, and much of this is very basic. *Miset* 'month' derives from Croatian, while the word for 'moon' has stayed Romance (*lură*, cf. DR *lună*, 'moon' and 'month'; AR /lunə/ 'moon' but /mes/ 'month' < MENSEM).

The fate of Slavic vocabulary in Balkan Romance as a whole was very mixed. Everyday terms that became established at an early date were more likely to survive than later learned vocabulary. Thus *prag* 'threshold' was an early enough loan to occur both in Daco-Rumanian and Arumanian (/pragᵘ/), where it thrives today. even some kin terms are Slavic, e.g. *nevastă* 'wife' (cf. AR /nevʲastə/ 'daughter-in-law'). On the other hand, administrative terminology such as *dragoman* or *postelnic*, both political ranks, while common in texts of the sixteenth to eighteenth centuries are, not surprisingly, unused in the modern language. Yet *rai* 'heaven, paradise' and *blagoslovire* 'blessing', do survive (the latter albeit with a somewhat limited distribution). *Hrănilniță* 'larder' does not appear to have survived, while *a hrăni* 'to feed, nourish' has. Finally, of interest too are calques from Slavic. On the basis of Slavic *světŭ* 'world' and 'light', LUMEN/LUMINEM survives in Rumanian as *lume* 'world' and *lumină* 'light'.

Greek

Though the influence of Ancient Greek on Balkan Romance is minimal (other than those items which found their way there via Latin itself), Byzantine and Modern Greek have had quite an important effect on Rumanian. Up to the eighteenth century, Greek influence was primarily through the medium of Old Church Slavonic. Thus, the religious term *chilie* 'cell' derives via Old Church Slavonic from Greek κελλιον, and the same path was taken by *arhimandrit* 'archimandrite', *călugăr* 'monk' and *psaltire* 'psalter'. More basic Greek vocabulary also entered Rumanian via Slavic, though not necessarily through the religious language: e.g. *sfeclă* 'beetroot', *drum* 'road' and *busuioc* 'basil'. It has been estimated that of nearly 300 Greek terms borrowed by Rumanian between the seventh and fifteenth centuries, only 20 or so were direct loans. On the other hand, more than 1,200 Greek loans entered Rumanian during the Phanariot period of 1711 to 1821, though of these perhaps only 150 were everyday items and no more than 100 would still be in use today. These include *stridie* 'oyster' and *nostim* 'pleasant' (the latter referring to personality or appearance; compare AR /nostim/, which preserves the sense of Greek νόστιμος 'pleasant-tasting').

Turkish and Hungarian

It was mainly during the eighteenth and early nineteenth centuries, when the principalities of Moldavia and Muntenia were administered for the Ottoman Empire by Phanariot princes, that Turkish vocabulary found its way into Rumanian. Alongside military and administrative vocabulary (*aga* 'aga', *ciohdar* 'Pasha's servant' and *stanbol* 'a type of gold coin'), Turkish

material found in texts of the time includes the slightly pejorative suffixes
-*giu* and -*lic* (*scandalagiu* 'scandalous (person)'; *avocatlic* 'lawyer') and
more basic vocabulary, some of which has survived today: *chel* 'bald' and
duşman 'enemy'. Once again, influence was often localised. There was substantial Turkish influence in Moldavia and Muntenia but relatively little in
Transylvania, which was until 1919 a part of the Austro-Hungarian
Empire. It is here, in this largest of the provinces of modern Rumania, that
Hungarian influence was at its greatest. Some very basic Rumanian
vocabulary is Hungarian in origin — including *gînd* 'thought', *făgădui* 'to
promise', *fel* 'way, method' and *viclean* 'cunning'. The widespread bi-
lingualism in the province today has not only given the Hungarian of
Transylvania a flavour not shared by 'mainland' Hungarian, but has also
given Transylvanian Rumanian terms not in normal use in the rest of
Rumania.

Romance and Other Western Sources
Although the phonological and grammatical structure of the modern
language had become more or less fixed by the late eighteenth century, the
lexical stock of the standard language has undergone quite significant
development in the last 200 years. With the political isolation of Transylvania from the two principalities, it is not surprising that there should
come from here the first nationalist movement to develop the language
artificially. Members of the Transylvanian School of the late eighteenth and
early nineteenth centuries were at pains to demonstrate the Latin origins of
the language. This involved early attempts to develop a Roman writing
system to replace the Cyrillic, something that was not finally achieved until
the late nineteenth century, with the political union of Moldavia and
Wallachia. The writing system proposed in these early days was doomed to
failure. It was formulated only partly on a phonetic basis, and was intended
to reflect the etymology of words. Thus modern *om* 'man' was rendered by
homu (to capture the etymon HOMO), *fîntînă* by *fontana* (< FONT-), *vînt*
'wind' by *ventu* (< VENTUM) and *ţară* 'land, country' by *tierra* (<
TERRAM). This approach was extended to verbs: on the basis of Latin
HAB-, the modern Rumanian, *am, ai, are, avem, aveţi, au* (present tense
forms of 'have') were rendered by *abiu, abi, abe, abemu, abeti, abu.* Such
an approach was surely always going to meet consumer resistance from the
very people it was intended to educate. Its proponents also engaged in
something of a witch hunt against Slavic words, attempting to replace them
entirely by others of Latin origin. In the process they managed to attribute
a Slavic origin to words that were clearly Romance — for example, they
attempted to proscribe *şi* 'and' though it derives from SIC. They created
many portmanteau words from Slavic and Latin, e.g. Slavic-based *război*
'war' + BELLUM → *războl.* While this died a speedy death (and *război* is
still the normal word), other examples were more successful: Slavic-based

năravuri 'customs' and Latin MORES were combined to give *moravuri*, in common use today. Not content with merely introducing Latin vocabulary, members of the School even 'translated' them into Rumanian. For example, the linguistic term in modern Rumanian *propoziţie* 'clause' was rendered by *spunere* (< *a spune* 'say'). Other, less esoteric, vocabulary was meddled with and many new terms again failed to catch on: *dracone* failed to replace *zmeu* 'dragon' and *granditate* failed as an alternative to *măreţie* 'greatness'.

Less eccentric, and perhaps for that reason more successful, were writers of the nineteenth century in the other two regions and especially Muntenia (where the major city Bucharest became the capital of the united principalities). They too made conscious efforts to add a fuller Romance flavour to Rumanian, importing large numbers of words from Italian and, to an even greater extent, from French (France being taken both then and now as a cultural model). Unlike the new vocabulary introduced by their Transylvanian forerunners, the material introduced by people such as Ion Heliade Rădulescu was largely successful. They too introduced both straight loans and loan translations: *masculin* and *feminin*, as labels for masculine and feminine genders, have survived: *bărbătesc* (< *bărbat* 'man') and *femeiesc* (< *femeie* 'woman') have not. *Futur* and *pasat* died, with the homespun terms *viitor* ('about to come') and *trecut* ('having passed') now being the normal terms for 'future' and 'past' within both grammatical and ordinary language.

Developments were fairly rapid in this period. In a second edition in 1847 of his 1828 grammar of the language, Rădulescu was scathing about his own earlier use of *strămutătoare* (an adjective from *strămuta* 'to change') for the full loan *tranzitiv* 'transitive'. The negative form of this *nestrămutătoare* 'intransitive' also gave way to *netranzitiv* (but this in turn has given way to the direct loan *intranzitiv*). The same tendency was present in this period as in the Transylvanian school, though to a more limited degree — adapting new Romance loans to the form they might have taken had they always been in the language. Modern *naţiune* 'nation' had to fight against the now defunct *năciune* but the latter died. It is during this period that there arose many of the Romance doublets that characterise the modern language, as words from Western Romance were imported alongside cognates directly inherited from Latin:

Recent Romance loan		Native Latin word	
monument	'monument'	mormînt	'tomb'
celest	'celestial'	ceresc	'heavenly'
sentiment	'sentiment'	simţămînt	'feeling'
direct	'direct'	drept	'straight, true, direct'

Twentieth-century Rumanian Vocabulary

Despite its prolonged period of isolation from the west, and the various influences on it from languages it has come into contact with in the Balkans, Rumanian vocabulary still retains a high proportion of Latin-based items. The proportion of Romance to non-Romance material is difficult to quantify because of a number of variables: which dialect or sub-dialect is taken as representative (the standard dialect has been open to more influence from international vocabulary than others); whether spoken or written language, learned or popular is taken as the norm; which elements are inherited from Latin and which borrowed from Romance. The last point is particularly troublesome — while we can pick out clear doublets like those just shown, some vocabulary may have been artificially accommodated within Rumanian to make it seem basic and inherited.

Most Rumanian linguists maintain that basic core vocabulary is, and always has been, Latin. A figure of as much as 40 per cent has been bandied around for the Slavic content, as against 20 per cent Latin and 20 per cent Turkish. However, these figures appear to be based on dictionaries such as that by Cihac in the 1870s, containing fewer than 6,000 entries. One linguist has examined the 1958 *Dicţionarul Limbii Romîne Moderne*, containing more than 48,000 entries and gives the following figures: 20 per cent Latin, 14 per cent Slavic and an enormous 35 per cent French. If one counts other Romance sources, the overall Latin-based content comes to around 85 per cent. The actual use of Romance vocabulary in, for example, a modern newspaper also comes to around 80 per cent of the text, and a comparable figure of 70–80 per cent is said to hold for the work of Rumania's most venerated poet, Mihai Eminescu, who wrote in the nineteenth century. If one considers the usual 200 or so items of truly basic vocabulary, Latin achieves an even higher percentage in standard Rumanian.

A survey of the Arumanian spoken in several villages of Thessaly in northern Greece shows that here too there is a high Romance content. There are indeed differences, not only between Rumanian and Arumanian, but also between different Arumanian-speaking villages. Because of direct and prolonged contact with Greek, a number of terms from the national language have been taken over, e.g. /anas/ 'breath' from Greek ανάσα — compare Rumanian *respiraţie*, itself a French loan. Slavic terms may occur in Arumanian that have either been borrowed since the breakup of Common Rumanian or been lost in Rumanian; for instance, AR /pravdə/ '(farm) animal' does not occur in Rumanian. Or Arumanian has retained a Latin term that has been eased out of standard Rumanian but still remains in subdialects of Daco-Rumanian, e.g. *negru* 'black' in Daco-Rumanian but /laj/ in Arumanian. Or both have a Latin term but a different one, thus DR *muşc* 'I bite' < *MUCCICARE but AR /kisku/ < *PICCICARE (though a village ten miles away has /musku/).

The number of imported words from French has begun to ease of late, now perhaps being surpassed by international vocabulary, much of it

English (*miting, ofsaid*). Yet, the importance of French as a source cannot be dismissed — so many words that are originally English have been imported via French, where they were also loans (*dumping, smoching*). And even loans from English may contain originally Romance material, such as the first syllable of Rumanian *biftec* (Rumanian < French < English < French *boeuf*).

Thus, all in all, modern Rumanian has attained, if not necessarily retained, a high level of Romance vocabulary, though raw lexical statistics fail to give an adequate picture of precisely how much a Romance language it really is.

6   Conclusion

Although one would expect a language to develop most rapidly through contact at the lexical level, there are some syntactic features that demonstrate how Rumanian is gradually returning to the Romance fold. Some linguists have claimed there is a gradual weakening of the case marking system, so that the preposition *la* 'to' can be used instead of a dative inflection and there are also instances of *de* taking over from the genitive where it is not strictly possession that is involved. Certainly in Arumanian the dative marking on nouns has been replaced by a prepositional marking. However this is not Western Romance influence, but the influence of Greek, where the dative has disappeared as a separate case form for full nominals.

Clearly of Romance origin is the resurgence of the short (i.e. true) infinitive in standard Daco-Rumanian, particularly in bureaucratic language, with French very much the model (though the position of Daco-Rumanian on the northern extremity of the Balkan region meant that the infinitive was less subject to replacement by the subjunctive than in other Balkan Romance variants).

And finally, at risk also is the reflexive passive. Undoubtedly because of Slavic influence, the reflexive as a whole flourished in Balkan Romance. In addition to normal reflexive usage: *Ion se spală* 'Ion washes himself', the reflexive pronoun crystallised as an intransitive marker: *mă duc* 'I am going' and in the third person became an impersonal passive: *se spune că* ...' 'it is said that ...'; *aici se vînd cărțile* 'books are sold here'. Far more common now than it was before French influence started to take hold in the nineteenth century is the analytical passive. A pattern like the following will perhaps eventually become the norm, completely ousting the reflexive passive: *cartea a fost furată* 'the book was stolen'.

Precisely how far this re-Romancing tendency can go is unclear, but what is clear is that, despite its Balkan features, Rumanian in its various forms retains enough of its Latin heritage at all linguistic levels to qualify for membership of the Romance family in its own right.

Bibliography

Agard, F.B. (1958) *Structural Sketch of Rumanian.* Linguistic Society of America Monograph No. 26. Baltimore

Caragiu Marioţeanu, M., Ş. Giosu, I. Ionescu-Ruxăndoiu, and R. Todoran (1977) *Dialectologie română.* Editura didactică şi pedagogică, Bucharest.

Close, E. (1974) *The Development of Modern Rumanian — Linguistic Theory and Practice in Muntenia 1821–1838.* Oxford University Press, Oxford.

Graur, Al. (1963) *Gramatica Limbii Romíne.* 2 volumes, 2nd edn. Editura academiei, Bucharest.

—— (1968) *Tendinţele actuale ale limbii române.* Editura ştiinţifică, Bucharest.

Grosu, Al. and G. Mallinson (in preparation) *Island Constraints in Rumanian.*

Iordan, I. and V. Robu (1978) *Limba română contemporană.* Editura didactică şi pedagogică, Bucharest.

Juilland, A. (1978) *Transformational and Structural Morphology.* Anma Libri, Saratoga.

Lombard, A. (1974) *La langue roumaine — une présentation.* Klincksieck, Paris.

Mallinson, G. (1984) 'Problems, Pseudo-problems and Hard Evidence — Another Look at the Rumanian Neuter', *Folia Linguistica* 18: 439–51.

—— (1986) *Rumanian.* Croom Helm, London.

Rădulescu, I.H. (1828/1847) *Gramatică românească.* Reprinted 1980, Editura Eminescu, Bucharest, with notes by V. Guţu Romalo.

Rosetti, Al. (1968) *Istoria limbii române de la origini pînă în secolul al XVII-lea.* Editura pentru literatură, Bucharest.

Ruhlen, M. (1974) 'Two Rival Approaches to Rumanian Grammar: Classical Structuralism vs. Transformational Analysis', *Romance Philology* 28: 178–90.

Russu, I.L. (1970) *Elemente autohtone în limba română. Substratul comun româno-albanez.* Editura academiei, Bucharest.

Vasiliu, E. (1968) *Fonologia istorică a dialectelor dacoromâne.* Editura academiei, Bucharest.

—— and S. Golopenţia-Eretescu (1969) *Sintaxa transformaţională a limbii române.* Editura academiei, Bucharest. Also published as: *The Transformational Syntax of Romanian.* Mouton, The Hague, 1972.

12 Romance Creoles

John N. Green

1 Introduction

The aim of this chapter is to present a schematic comparison of the modern creoles whose vocabulary is derived from Romance (for their geographical location and speaker statistics, see Chapter 1). The creoles, unlike the majority of Romance varieties described in earlier chapters, have not been fully standardised and most have no universally recognised norm or orthography. Most geographical labels for creoles in fact subsume a number of varieties, which may be dialectally related, but which more commonly range along a sociolectal continuum whose length is determined by the degree and intensity of historical contacts with the model language. In extreme cases, a considerable linguistic distance separates the basilect ('bush taak', 'habla bozal', and so on) from the acrolect (in effect, standard Romance with an identifiable local pronunciation). As the relationship among sociolects is often covertly historical, we shall need to make quite frequent reference to diachronic factors, even though our primary focus is synchronic.

Creole linguistics, which has a pedigree of more than a century, has only recently begun to make a significant impact on general linguistic theory, and some of the challenging new concepts it has produced — such as the 'bioprogram' or blueprint for language learning — are still being evaluated. Also unresolved are a number of older controversies, chiefly concerning the genetic origins of creoles and their relationship to the lexifier languages. Accordingly, before moving on to the main description, we shall devote some space to the important issues where consensus has not yet been established, and which cannot therefore be presented in a theoretically neutral manner.

2 Creoles and Linguistic Theory

The term 'creole' is usually reserved for languages that have evolved from an earlier pidgin. Pidgins are minimal communication systems negotiated into existence by adults who have no shared language but who need to communicate for a particular, limited purpose. The typical linguistic characteristics of a pidgin are: simplified phonology, extremely restricted lexis, invariant morphology, and a syntax virtually restricted to the relations actant–action–recipient. Since pidgins are generally used to further a mutually agreed purpose, such as bartering produce or services, contextual inference plays a major role in the transmission of meaning. Indeed, in the immediate context of a transaction, gesture and mimetic and iconic improvisation may be the primary means of communication, with the properly linguistic elements acting only as secondary reinforcements. Although some pidgins are known to have persisted in relatively stable form over long periods of time, more often they are both transient and subject to considerable linguistic instability. A creole develops when children acquire a pidgin as their first language; or, seen from a different perspective, a creole can be defined as a pidgin which has acquired native speakers.

Such a change of status is almost invariably the consequence or concomitant of a major social upheaval (it is hard to imagine a linguistically stable community freely choosing to force the next generation to invent a new language). To create a language able to serve the full range of their needs, speakers of the emergent creole must now put into reverse the pidginisation process: they must massively expand the vocabulary and greatly develop the rudimentary system of grammatical relations. Recomplication of the phonology and the invention of new morphology will not be consciously sought but, as we shall see below, can be early by-products of other processes. The expansion of vocabulary on the required scale cannot be achieved by applying compositional or derivational mechanisms to the meagre existing stock, and so takes the form of wholesale absorption (with due phonological adjustment) from one of the contact languages, known in consequence as the 'lexifier'.

The social conditions necessary to set in train the creolisation of an existing pidgin were created between the late fifteenth and eighteenth centuries by European colonisation of newly discovered territories and the emergence of plantation economies dependent on imported slave labour. The enslavement and mass transportation to new colonies of large African populations, allied to a deliberate policy of breaking down family and linguistic ties, ensured the rapid development of pidgins as essential means of communication not only between slaves and captors but also among slaves from differing ethnic and linguistic groups. Under such extreme circumstances, it is scarcely surprising that the dominant European languages should have provided both the core vocabulary during pidginisation and its wholesale expansion during subsequent creolisation. Together with English and Dutch, three Romance languages played a significant role as lexifiers: French, Portuguese and Spanish. This affiliation, however, is no longer equally apparent in the modern creoles. Whilst lexical material originating from French usually remains quite clearly recognisable, Spanish and Portuguese etymologies are often harder to disentangle, especially in a creole like Papiamentu where early Portuguese influence was later overlaid by layers of Spanish (see p. 463).

Types of Linguistic Change

The recent expansion of creole studies has led to a tendency to apply the terms 'creole' and 'creolisation' more widely than the above definition seems to warrant. It has, for instance, been suggested that the period with which we are concerned was closely paralleled by the early development of Romance from Latin, which also went hand in hand with colonial expansion, slavery and enforced population movements. While some historical parallels are undeniable, in the case of Latin the linguistic consequences seem to have been different, perhaps because the languages in contact were typologically much more similar. For present purposes, we shall operate with the more restricted definition of creoles. This entails an important corollary for linguistic theory, namely that 'normal' evolutionary change, characteristic of all linguistic communities over time, can and should be distinguished from the sudden or 'catastrophic' change implied by pidginisation and creolisation. The difference, in other words, is of kind not of degree.

This is not to deny that creoles, after the initial phase of catastrophic reduction and rebuilding, become subject to normal evolutionary change. Two examples will suffice. In Haitian, the originally invariant postposed determiner /-la/ now has five allomorphs /a, ã, la, lã, nã/ in a predictable but complicated phonological distribution which has arisen through weakening of intervocalic /l/, its assimilation to a preceding nasal consonant, and progressive nasal vowel harmony — all commonly attested phonological changes. Hence, /kaj+la/ 'the house' > [kaj la], but /põ+la/ 'the bridge' > [põ ã], and /lalin+la/ 'the moon' > [lalin nã]. In Mauritian, the completive marker /fin/ is now often contracted to /in/ or /n/, which in turn may become homorganic with a following consonant; hence, /mo+fin+aste/ 'I have bought' > [mo naste], and /li+fin+kud+li/ 'she has sewn it' > [liŋ kud li]. Both could be cited as classic examples of the creation of allomorphy through the application of 'blind' sound laws.

Adopting, as we have done, the narrower definition of creole, but at the same time admitting that creoles once in existence are subject to the same kinds of gradual evolution as 'normal' languages, must call into question the validity of 'creole' as an identifiable synchronic category. If the original linguistic distinctiveness of creoles is subsequently eroded by general evolutionary processes, the time must come when they can no longer be usefully distinguished from other languages. Has that time now come? Some creolists have indeed suggested so, pointing out that all the varieties we have defined as creoles have been in existence for at least two centuries, most of them longer, and that in some cases the preceding pidgins must have sprung up over 500 years ago. True; and in the intervening period sociopolitical conditions have changed out of all recognition. But evolutionary linguistic change does not always proceed so quickly, and even a half millennium's development would not normally erase the traces of a complete morphosyntactic reorganisation. Since such traces are not only still present in the modern Romance creoles but are also instantiated by typological features not generally present in other Romance languages, we shall adhere to the more traditional view that creoles do exhibit sufficient synchronic distinctiveness to justify their treatment as an independent category.

Let us summarise so far. In the context of Romance linguistics, the term 'creole' is best reserved for the varieties which came into existence in conditions of great social inequality, in the European colonies dependent on imported slave labour, between the sixteenth and eighteenth centuries. The creoles are believed to have been preceded by pidgins, which may have sprung up in the colonies themselves as a means of communication between overseers and slaves and among slaves of differing linguistic backgrounds, but which more probably had already been in use during transportation to the colonies and earlier in the slave assembly stations principally sited in the Gulf of Guinea. The linguistic simplification entailed by the creation of a pidgin, especially when the languages in contact are structurally dissimilar, and the expansion and reanalysis implied by the acquisition of a pidgin as a mother tongue, together amount to catastrophic change of the linguistic system. Once in existence, the creole is subject to gradual change which can eventually be expected to remove the evidence of its atypical history. The Romance creoles have not yet reached this stage. The decision to treat them as a synchronic group is to be justified on comparative grounds: they have in common a number of features either totally absent from other Romance languages or only marginally represented there.

Are Creoles 'Romance'?

The thorny question we have not so far broached is whether this group of creoles should be described as 'Romance' at all. The question has political, as well as linguistic, dimensions. Creole politicians and intellectuals, understandably wishing to raise the social status of their language, have reacted angrily to the assumption that what they speak is 'French' creole, or 'Portuguese', or 'Spanish', and have condemned such unthinking linguistic annexation as neo-colonialist. Descriptors of this kind, it is argued, undermine the hard-won linguistic independence of the creoles as symbols of autonomous nations, quite aside from belittling the non-European contribution, both linguistic and cultural, to their make-up. Creolists sensitive to these views tend in consequence to refer to 'French-lexicon creoles' and so on, achieving a somewhat pedantic accuracy at the expense of euphony. For the present chapter, the descriptor 'Romance', which is not the designation of any other language or independent nation, has been chosen as more neutral and politically less tendentious. The choice does not altogether meet the objections of those seeking greater recognition for the non-European components of creoles, but this is at least a matter of linguistic judgement, to which we shall return in the concluding section.

The suitability of 'Romance' as a linguistic label, however, raises in acute form the problem that has long plagued advocates of typological classification, namely: how should contradictory evidence from different linguistic levels be interpreted and hierarchised? If lexical affinity is taken as paramount, the Romance classification of the creoles is beyond dispute. (Note that this does not automatically follow from the fact that the original lexifiers were Romance; two or more centuries of evolutionary change could have resulted in widespread lexical differentiation through borrowing, but this has not in fact happened.) If, on the other hand, precedence is accorded to inflectional morphology, the creoles cannot be grouped with Romance, nor indeed with Indo-European in general. In the ensuing sections, we shall try to determine the extent of similarities and differences at other levels of analysis, and whether or not the lexical affinities are so strong that they should be allowed to overrule discrepancies at other points in the system.

Explanations of Creole Structures

The single most controversial issue in creole linguistics has been how to account, not for the existence of similarities between each creole and its lexifier (which has, perhaps misguidedly, often been taken as self-evident), but rather for the undoubted structural similarities between far-flung creoles whose direct contact can never have been great.

The early focus within Romance linguistics on the historical development of creoles from Romance languages inevitably tended to obscure rather than illuminate the reasons for their synchronic affinities. Historical explanations were formulated in terms of ingredients to language mixing, or of substrates and overlays. Typical of the conclusions reached were: that the chief European component of 'French' creoles was not standard French but a western dialect, probably Norman; and that the creoles in general should be viewed as Romance overlaid on an African substrate. Both undeniably contain an element of truth, but uncritical reliance on such inadequate generalisations long hindered the elaboration of a more satisfactory general framework for the investigation of creolisation. Ethnolinguistic explanations, for instance, which must be founded on the most meticulous analysis of shipping logs, were attempted at a time when such research was at a rudimentary stage. Moreover, advances in sociolinguistics have now revealed difficulties of interpretation that were not originally anticipated: knowing the domicile and port of embarcation of early settlers does not tell us their level of education, whether they habitually spoke patois or standard local Romance, their motivation to retain or modify their previous speech patterns, nor how they might accommodate to speakers of other regional varieties. Though great progress has been made over the years in the mapping of population movements, the gain in purely linguistic terms has been relatively modest, enabling some wilder hypotheses to be rejected rather than providing the elusive key to the creolisation process.

It was substrate explanations, however, whose inadequacy in a creole context was most clearly exposed. In European dialectology, the substrate had been invoked, quite uncontroversially, to account for lexical residues and also, but less consensually, for phonological changes; it had rarely been advanced, or needed, for morphosyntactic innovations. Attempts to extend a similar explanation to creoles quickly revealed that the substrate was essentially a spatial concept, presupposing a homogeneous linguistic area, and therefore quite inappropriate for contexts where the original linguistic communities had been effectively destroyed. As an explanation for lexical borrowing from non-European sources, the substrate is superfluous; and in phonology and syntax it is either irrelevant or makes incorrect predictions. For example, Haitian and Seychellois can hardly be supposed to share an identical substrate, but they diverge from French phonology in often very similar ways: both un-round French front rounded vowels, so that 'street' is /lari/ < /la + ʁy/ and 'fire' is /dife/ < /dy + fø/ in both. Likewise, Papiamentu and Chabacano have evolved similar tense–aspect systems, quite unlike those of European Romance, despite having substrates (in so far as these can be identified at all) belonging to discrete linguistic families. In neither instance does the parallel trajectory seem to have been inherited from Romance nor initiated by a shared substrate.

A redirection of focus onto the structural parallels among creoles gave rise to the theory of monogenesis, once well supported but now increasingly discounted. It shifts the burden of proof by returning to an older model of historical change — gradual divergence from a common ancestor — in which shared features are presumed to have been inherited from the proto-language and therefore not to require explanation. Advocates of monogenesis claim that the ancestor language was a widely used Portuguese trading pidgin which was later 'relexified' and spread even further afield. Such a pidgin would be comparable to the *lingua franca*, also a Romance pidgin, which was widely employed from the thirteenth century onwards as a means of communication among traders, crusaders and other travellers to the eastern Mediterranean. The existence of *lingua franca* is well documented; but it is very sparsely attested and we have little idea of its linguistic characteristics or precise origin. It is entirely plausible that in the fifteenth and sixteenth centuries Portuguese sailors should have evolved a similar pidgin in their contacts along the African coast and points east. There are, indeed, literary attestations, dating from as early as 1455, of a form of pidginised Portuguese apparently evolved in Portugal itself by West Africans recruited for training as interpreters for subsequent trading missions. But the widespread use among sailors of a Portuguese pidgin is not directly attested, and its existence can only be inferred from indirect evidence which is both scant and difficult to interpret.

In any event, proof of the existence of the supposed ancestor pidgin does not of itself validate the monogenetic theory. The crucial concept of relexification, invoked to explain how British, Dutch, French and other users of the Portuguese pidgin later endowed it with completely different vocabularies while maintaining its structure intact, has never been adequately elaborated, nor shown to be plausible. It is not immediately apparent that European traders and adventurers would elect to learn a pidgin propagated by their Portuguese rivals. Nor is it clear why the latecomers could not have negotiated into existence new pidgins based on their own languages by making use of the same talents and mechanisms the Portuguese had earlier employed. Even the wide distribution of a few putatively Portuguese words like *savvy* 'know' is inconclusive: they could just as well be normal lexical borrowings — perhaps vogue words in nautical jargon — as vestigial traces of the Portuguese substrate in the newly relexified pidgin.

Probably the most telling criticism levelled at the monogenetic theory is that it aims to explain the distribution of certain structural features of creoles when it should be explaining their function. It rests on the misconception that these characteristics (like the preverbal tense–aspect markers; see p. 450 below) are so unusual that they can only have arisen randomly and been propagated from a single source. In fact, we now know that they are not unusual, but quite common in West African languages and elsewhere. It is perfectly plausible for pidgins arising from contact between European and African languages to develop independently into creoles sharing similar features. Polygenesis along these lines is now invoked as an explanation not only for the Romance creoles with which we are immediately concerned, but more crucially for instances of parallel evolution where the relevant features are absent from all known contributor languages, and where patterns of contact and isolation exclude any possibility of relexification of a pre-existing pidgin.

Polygenesis has recently received a major boost from the 'bioprogram' hypothesis. This relates the creation of a creole to more general language acquisition processes, stressing that first language acquisition, even in a stable and relatively homogeneous speech community, is discontinuous and requires the child to recreate the community language from observed data and interaction. Innate language learning mechanisms always guide and inform this process, but they take a much more active steering role when, as in the case of first-generation learners of a pidgin, the input data is grossly deficient. The bioprogram, in other words, acts only as a facilitator when the child is presented with adequate samples of a well developed grammatical system; when there is no such system available, it prompts the creation of a coherent grammatical structure while leaving unspecified the material of the lexical cloak. The bioprogram is thus claimed to explain the similarities in grammatical organisation among creoles with widely differing genetic inputs. The hypothesis is still being evaluated, but it has generally been well received and indeed hailed as a major advance, even by those who feel that in its present form it underestimates the child's awareness of the need to create a viable social identity and to manipulate (albeit at an unconscious level) the acquisition process towards this goal.

To conclude this section, we may say that linguists of many persuasions have been convinced of the need to account for structural similarities among creoles. Traditional approaches to historical change have not proved very helpful in this respect. The monogenetic theory can be seen as an ingenious attempt to tackle new questions by reformulating them in a manner accessible to old answers, but its crucial intermediate stage of 'relexification' is inadequately specified and inherently implausible. At the opposite extreme, polygenetic approaches based on social interaction theories, while plausible in general terms, have lacked linguistic rigour. The bioprogram is, to date, the most promising and comprehensive proposal, but it remains largely untested, especially on Romance data. If the evaluation proves satisfactory, the bioprogram will still require supplementation from more conventional historical and ethnolinguistic methods to explain areal patterns of similarity and divergence among creoles of the same linguistic affiliation.

3   Phonology

A well known feature of most creoles is their phonological variability. This was portrayed in some early accounts as unsystematic and unstable, but has now been shown to be conditioned in most cases by a complex interplay of factors, in which focusing towards perceived regional and sociolinguistic norms may complement or counteract such intra-linguistic mechanisms as shifts of register and tempo. In the present section we can give no more than a schematic outline of phonological inventories and processes, together with a sample of phonetic detail. A brief comparison is nevertheless useful in highlighting structural features which are present throughout the Romance creoles and which in some ways are more striking than the synchronic relationships between individual creoles and their lexifiers.

Vowel Systems
With only minor deviations, the basilectal vowel systems of the Romance

creoles can be assigned to one of four types, which in turn may be characterised by two parameters: a five-term versus seven-term oral system,
and presence versus absence of phonemic nasality (almost all creoles show
phonetic nasalisation; see p. 430). The rarest combination, a large oral
inventory with no phonemic nasality, is only documented in the creole of
Guinea-Bissau. As can be seen from Table 12.1, the largest inventories are
found in São Tomense and in the maximal system of Haitian, the smallest
in Chabacano and most varieties of Papiamentu, with Mauritian and
Seychellois exemplifying the happy medium. The creoles for which Spanish
is the chief lexifier have the smallest vowel systems, but the other synchronic types cut across any diachronic correlation with French and Portuguese.

Table 12.1: Sample Vowel Systems

The Vowel System of São Tomense and Haitian (Maximal)

	Oral			Nasal	
High	i		u	ĩ	ũ
Higher mid	e		o		
Lower mid		ɛ	ɔ	ẽ	õ
Low		a		ã	

The Vowel System of Mauritian and Seychellois

	Oral		Nasal	
High	i	u		
Mid	e	o	ẽ	õ
Low	a		ã	

The Vowel System of Chabacano and Papiamentu (Basilectal)

	Oral	
High	i	u
Mid	e	o
Low	a	

All the basilectal systems share two salient characteristics: perfect
symmetry and maximal spread. The articulation of simple nuclei in tonic
syllables is usually tense, with no diphthongal off-glide and very little
tendency to laxing or centralisation. Laxer variants of high and mid vowels

have been observed in closed syllables, but these environments, for reasons we shall explore later, are relatively uncommon. Few Romance creoles make systematic use of phonemic length (an example of compensatory lengthening is discussed below), but tonic vowels can be prolonged to double or even triple their normal length, again without laxing, for emphasis or other stylistic effect. In atonic syllables, most creoles operate with a reduced inventory usually favouring lower vowels (though Chabacano and Palenquero both prefer raising; see p. 436).

Minimal pairs and more extensive contrasting sets are for the most part easily found in the creoles relying on a five-term oral sysem. By way of illustration we will quote just one complete series from Seychellois, some of whose members are themselves homophonous — /si/ 'if' : /se/ 'presentative particle' : /sẽ/ 'holy, healthy' : /sa/ 'that' : /sã/ 'without, hundred' : /so/ 'hot' : /sõ/ 'peal' : /su/ 'cabbage'. Two problem areas where the evidence is less clear-cut and which have consequently proved more contentious, are the analysis of nasals and the status of mid vowels.

In seven-term systems, it is not difficult to elicit contrastive pairs of mid vowels in citation forms, as in Haitian /ke/ 'tail' : /kɛ/ 'heart', /ne/ 'knot' : /nɛ/ 'nerve', /pe/ 'peace, be quiet!' : /pɛ/ 'priest, fear', /ve/ 'wish' : /vɛ/ 'glass, green', /fo/ 'false' : /fɔ/ 'strong', /po/ 'skin, vase' : /pɔ/ 'harbour'. Such distinctions, however, are not always maintained in discourse, particularly at rapid tempo, owing to a combination of sandhi and prosodic factors. Since the second member of each pair has a French cognate ending in /-ʁ/, and the distribution of higher and lower mid vowels in French is largely predictable from syllable structure (see p. 209), the most plausible historical explanation for the Haitian contrasts would be the loss of a post-vocalic /-r/, leading to the phonemicisation of what was formerly a conditioned alternation. The same mechanism has been responsible for comparable pairs in São Tomense, witness /'petu/ 'chest' : /'pɛtu/ 'clever', /'sotʃi/ 'blow' : /'sɔtʃi/ 'luck'. This historical change has left few if any alternations of /-r/ and /-∅/ in the basilect, and should thus arguably be discounted in a synchronic treatment. Nevertheless, a more abstract analysis recognising underlying /-r/ has been championed on the twin grounds that basilects lacking /-r/ are usually in contact with acrolects maintaining it (Haitian /fɔ/ ~ /forti'tid, forti'fjã/), and that notwithstanding the loss of /-r/, creoles can remain mutually intelligible with others in which it is preserved.

A related problem, amenable to similar reasoning, is that of vowel length in some eastern Caribbean creoles, notably Dominican and St Lucian. The long vowels occur at the site of a former post-vocalic /-r/, where the loss remains marked by compensatory lengthening of the preceding vowel — [nɛf] 'nine' : [nɛːf] 'nerve', [sɔt] 'foolish' : [sɔːt] 'go out'. Should length be treated as phonemic in such cases? Despite the surface contrast, most analysts have resisted this conclusion, chiefly because length would only be phonemic for a subset of vowels whose delimitation could no longer be phonologically motivated. The counter-proposal is to postulate an underlying segment always realised on the surface as vowel length. Support for this solution can be found in the more conservative Indian Ocean creoles, where post-vocalic /-r/ is rarely lost outright but is regularly weakened to an approximant [-ɣ] or to an r-coloured off-glide [ɚ], which in turn can lengthen the preceding vowel. At the same time, it must be recognised that the mildly abstract and theoretically neat analyses advanced for Haitian and Dominican are motivated not within their respective basilects but essentially by diasystemic — and by implication diachronic — considerations.

Similar reductionism has been attempted with respect to nasality, with arguments adduced both for dislodging individual sounds from the phonemic inventory and for a more sweeping reanalysis of all nasal vowels as surface representations of underlying /V + N/ sequences. The suspect individuals are /ĩ/ and /ũ/. In the creoles lexically related to Portuguese, once a nasal category has been recognised, there can be no grounds for excluding the high vowels, since they participate in a full range of lexical oppositions, as in STo. /fita/ 'ribbon' : /fĩta/ ' collection', /fudu/ 'clean' : /fũdu/ 'deep'. In Haitian, on the other hand, though phonetic [ĩ] and [ũ] are quite frequent, they seem to be distinctive — if at all — in a different lexical stratum from the other nasal vowels. Formerly, they were common in words of African etymology, but such vocabulary is now fast disappearing from the basilect, with the exception of a series of terms associated with voodoo rites: /vodũ/ itself, /ũfɔ/ 'temple', /ũgã/ 'priest', and /ũsĩ/ 'female assistant'. These and related items are subject to heavy nasalisation and aspiration, [w̃ũgã, ɦ̃ũŋgã], perhaps for emotive effect. Though syntagmatic oppositions can be constructed, as in /ũsĩ/ : /usi/ < /u + si/ 'you are sure', these words do not enter into paradigmatic contrasts. It therefore seems best to treat [ĩ] and [ũ] as marginal to the vowel system and possibly the product of prosodic nasality.

Scepticism about the independent status of any nasal vowel is mainly associated with abstract generative phonology and is nowadays rarely indulged. The reductionist and explanatory aims of /V + N/ analyses are obvious, but proliferating synchronic rules tend to outweigh other advantages, particularly in a language like French, where vowel lowering, syllable adjustment and denasalisation processes have created highly complex alternations (see p. 212). At first sight the creoles, with a much lower incidence of alternation, should be better candidates for reanalysis. In practice, this is not so: stating the environments for nasal assimilation is far from straightforward, and defining the conditions for nasal consonant deletion is impossible without resort to lexical stratification, for which there is little independent evidence.

Phonetic nasality can be both progressive and anticipatory; it occurs regularly before tautosyllabic nasals, frequently before heterosyllabics and, in rapid delivery, often across a word boundary, hence: Pal. [pa'lẽŋge] 'stockade', [ku'sīna] 'kitchen', Hai. [pũ'mwẽ] < /pu+mwẽ/ 'for me'. Some instances of progressive nasality seem to have undergone lexical restructuring: Sey. /konẽ/ 'know', /māmā/ 'mother', /zamẽ/ 'never'. The creoles differ in their degree of restructuring, and in their constraints on assimilation. For instance, nasalisation is permitted across the site of a former /-r/ in Haitian, as in ['fɛ̃mẽ] 'close' and ['dɔ̃mĩ] 'sleep', but blocked in most eastern Caribbean creoles, especially where there is a long vowel — Dom. [mɔːn] 'dreary', not *[mɔ̃ːn].

The major argument against an analysis without underlying nasals is the presence of many tautosyllabic nasal consonants which may cause anticipatory nasal assimilation on their preceding vowel, but show no sign of disappearing. So., Hai.,Mau., Sey. /fõ/ 'bottom' contrasts with /fon/ 'melt' which may be pronounced [fɔn] or [fɔ̃n] but not *[fɔ̃]; Sey. /lasãm/ 'room' contrasts with /lasãn/ 'ash', neither of which can be reduced to *[la'sã]; Hai. /ʃã/ 'field' contrasts with both /ʃãm/ 'room' and /ʃam/ 'magic spell'; and STo. /fudu/ 'clean' contrasts with both /fũdu/ 'deep' and /fundu/ 'burn', which may be pronounced ['fũndu] but not *['fũdu]. Clearly, if ['fũdu] meaning 'deep' were to be derived from underlying /fundu/ by nasal assimilation and consonant deletion, only an unmotivated exception feature could prevent coalescence with 'to burn'. Likewise, if ['mũtu] 'much' were derived from underlying /muntu/, an arbitrary constraint would be needed to prevent the transformation of /punta/ 'ask' into *['pũta]. All told, more is lost than gained by refusing to recognise underlying nasal vowels.

Consonants and Glides

All Romance creoles have at least two glides, /j/ and /w/, forming a bridge between the vowel and consonant systems. Although they are in partial complementary distribution with the vowels /i/ and /u/ respectively, there are sufficient distributional irregularities to justify their independent phonemic status. Treating the glides as allophonic would unnecessarily complicate the statement of syllable structure (a point amplified below, p. 435) and would imply that their surface exponents were semi-vocalic, whereas the balance of evidence, in the majority of creoles, favours a semi-consonantal designation. Two other consonantal segments, /ɲ/ and /r/, which are articulated as weak approximants in several creoles, have also been classified as glides, /ɲ/ then being retranscribed as / j̃/. We shall return to this suggestion after examining the sounds that are unequivocally consonants.

As can be seen from Table 12.2, the creole consonants form less compact and economical systems than the corresponding vowels, with most varieties defining a number of contrasts that are under-utilised. In addition

Table 12.2: Sample Consonant Systems

The Maximal Consonant System of Haitian Contrasted with Basilectal Mauritian/Seychellois

	Labial	Dental	Palatal	Velar	Glottal	Labial	Dental	Palatal	Velar	Glottal
Oral stops	p b	t d		k g		p b	t d		k g	
Affricates			tʃ dʒ							
Fricatives	f v	s z	ʃ ʒ			f v	s z			
Nasal stops	m	n		ŋ		m	n		ŋ	
Lateral		l					l			
Approximants	w		j j̃	r	h	w		j j̃	r	h

The Consonant System of Chabacano Contrasted with Papiamentu

	Labial	Dental	Palatal	Velar	Glottal	Labial	Dental	Palatal	Velar	Glottal
Oral stops	p b	t d		k g		p b	t d		k g	ʔ
Affricates			tʃ					tʃ (dʒ)		
Fricatives		s				f	s	ʃ		h
Nasal stops	m	n		ŋ		m	n		ŋ	
Lateral		l					l			
Approximants	w	r	j			w	r	j		

The Consonant System of São Tomense

	Labial	Dental	Palatal	Velar	Glottal
Oral stops	p b	t d		k g	
Affricates			tʃ dʒ		
Fricatives	f v	s z	ʃ ʒ		
Nasal stops	m	n			
Lateral		l			
Approximants	w		j j̃		

to the glides /j, w/, all Romance creoles share the six oral stops /p, b, t, d, k, g/, the two nasal stops /m, n/, and the lateral /l/. Also universal are: a velar nasal [ŋ] whose phonemic status is often marginal, and a voiceless sibilant, transcribed /s/, which is certainly phonemic within each creole, but which operates as a member of such diverse fricative sets that its diasystemic comparability must be seriously in doubt. Aside from the fricatives, the principal structural divergences are to be found in the palatal column and among the approximants.

The voiceless stops are generally articulated as unaspirated plosives, their counterparts being fully voiced, sometimes with prenasalisation. In the west African creoles, especially those in direct contact with Kwa languages, prenasalisation of oral stops and lengthening of initial nasal consonants are conspicuous features. So too are the labiovelar consonants retained in a few lexical items of African origin (Pri. [iɡ͡be'ɡ͡be] 'snail', STo. ['ŋ͡wini-'ŋ͡wini] 'ideophone for smallness') and the regularly implosive pronunciation of /b/ and /d/, as in STo. /dodo/ ['ɗoɗo] 'mad', /bɔ'dõ/ [bɔ'ɗõ] 'cudgel'. Likewise almost certainly assimilated from a contact language, in this case Tagalog, is the Chabacano glottal stop, which is phonetically salient in words like ['hɛnde?] 'person, someone'; but it is confined to word-final position and may not be contrastive.

In all the creoles, the non-labial stops, voiced and voiceless alike, are subject to palatalisation before /i, j/, with results varying between slight allophonic affrication and full palatality capable in turn of phonemicisation or merger with existing palatal consonants. Where phonemic affricates occur, their distribution pattern generally differs from that of oral stops. Since the extent of palatalisation has sociolinguistic implications, we shall postpone further discussion to a later section (p. 439), except to note that palatalising tendencies are partly responsible for the striking diversity in the inventories of fricatives. But a more obvious correlation, clearly visible in Table 12.2, can be drawn between the absence of a voiced fricative series and lexical relationship to Spanish, which alone among the European Romance languages also lacks phonemic voiced fricatives (see p. 81). The /h/ phoneme recorded among the fricatives for Chabacano and Papiamentu, corresponds to Spanish /x/ in the weakened articulation characteristic of Mexico and Central America. Chabacano, in its early form, further reduced the set of fricatives by assimilating etymological [f] to /p/, as in /pilipinas/ 'Philippines', /pwelte/ 'strong'.

The phoneme /r/ occurs in most, but not all, Romance creoles, often with a range of allophonic variants that suggest ongoing linguistic change. There is no /r/ in the basilectal forms of either São Tomense or Annobonese, though some speakers of the former now use a uvular fricative [ʀ] in recent borrowings from European Portuguese, and an alveolar vibrant [r] has been introduced into Annobonese in borrowings from Spanish — the official language of Equatorial Guinea. To describe the distribution of /r/ and its allophones in other creoles, we must distinguish prevocalic occurrences from post-vocalic. Most basilectal Romance creoles, regardless of lexical affiliation, have no post-vocalic /-r/, as can be seen in Hai., Gua., Mar., Dom., SLu. [fɛ] 'do', [le, lɛ] 'hour, when', [pati] 'leave', cognate with Fr. *faire, l'heure, partir* respectively; and in Pri. [buka], Cha. [buska, buskaʔ] 'look for', cognate with Port., Sp. *buscar*. The more conservative creoles which preserve post-vocalic /-r/ nevertheless distinguish between the two environments, using noticeably weaker articulations in post-vocalic position: Réu., Mau., Sey. [fɛːˣ, fɛːˠ, fɛˀ], [paːˠti, paˀti], as opposed to prevocalic [ʀɑ̃t, ʀɑ̃tʀe] 'return' and [tʀuv] 'find'. As we saw above (p. 429), an intermediate stage is illustrated by the Caribbean varieties with compensatory lengthening at the site of a former post-vocalic /-r/. In prevocalic position, Papiamentu and Chabacano use an alveolar approximant [ɹ], the Indian ocean group uses a uvular or velar fricative [ʀ, ɣ], but the Caribbean varieties divide into two subgroups, opposing Lou., Hai. [ʀɑ̃tʀe] 'return', [teʀib] 'terrible', to Gua., Mar., Dom., SLu. [wɑ̃twe], [tewib]. Whether or not this second group should be classified as r-less is disputed, since the merger of /r/ with /w/ does not seem to be complete for all speakers, and occasional forms with initial and intervocalic [ʀ] are recorded. The main dialects of Haitian appear to be transitional, using [ɣʷ ~ w] before rounded vowels or glides and [ʀ] elsewhere: [twɔ] 'too much' [kwɛ] 'believe' but [ʀesi] 'succeed'.

The recent evolution of /r/ is only one of a series of historical processes still in train, which are combining to affect the whole class of approximants. In terms of absolute frequency, /w/ is gaining, /j/ and /ĵ/ seem stable, and /r/ and /h/ are both losing ground. Now virtually extinct in Haitian, /h/ maintains a precarious independence in the eastern Caribbean. It is restricted to word-initial position and, except in a tiny handful of words like /haʃ/ 'axe' and /hɛn/ 'hatred' (cognate with formerly aspirated items in dialectal French), alternates freely with /r/. Historically, the /r/ phoneme has gained at the expense of /h/, no doubt because of the similarity of their articulation; witness Hai. /rad/ 'clothes', /roma/ 'lobster', /rotɛ/ 'height'. But /r/, as we have seen, has been eliminated without trace from some contexts, and has elsewhere lost membership to /w/ via labialisation. In the more remote past, /j/ benefited from depalatalisation of /ʎ/ (comparable to Spanish *yeísmo*; see p. 84) and, in Haitian, from palatalisation of final /-z/, as in Hai. /kaj/ 'house', /ʃoj/ 'thing' versus Mau. /lakaz/, /soz/. Similarly, lax articulation of /ɲ/ gave rise to /ĵ/, as in Hai. /pēĵ/ 'comb', Mau. /gɑ̃j/ 'get', Ann. /iĵa/ 'finger nail', cognate with Fr. *peigne, gagner*, and Port. *unha* respectively. But whereas /ĵ/ has maintained its ground and seems to be successfully resisting merger with /j/ — even though /j/ is subject to prosodic nasalisation when adjacent to a nasal vowel — /j/ itself has been depleted by its major contribution to the creation of new palatal consonants, as in: Dom., SLu.

[t͡ʃěbe] 'grasp', Pap. [ʃɛnto] 'hundred', cognate with Fr. *tiens bien* and Sp. *ciento*.

From this complex of shifting alliances, it seems clear that approximants form a natural class in all the Romance creoles, and that their diachronic adventures more often ally them with the consonants than with the vowels.

Phonotactic and Prosodic Structure

Creoles are often loosely described as 'CV languages' — a statement which, without further qualification, would not be true of any contemporary Romance creole. They all accept consonant clusters, sometimes quite complex, as syllable onsets, and most permit CVC syllables, albeit with a restricted set of consonantal codas. Many creoles do, however, show a marked preference for open syllables in all positions, and a weaker but still perceptible preference for consonantal onsets in word-initial position. Provided it is understood in this way, the label 'CV' is therefore not inappropriate.

Sequences of open syllables interspersed with a few consonant clusters have obvious implications for rhythmic and prosodic structure. Syllable-timed rhythms are the norm, together with a low incidence of complex syllable nuclei, and a tendency towards vowel harmony. Such languages are often also tonal. The Romance creoles, as a group, show many of these characteristics, though not always systematically. Only Saramaccan has so far been shown to be tonal, though potential instances of phonemic tone have also been detected in Papiamentu and Palenquero. Neither of these languages has a strong dynamic stress, with the result that high tone is the principal distinguishing feature in some minimal pairs which are differentiated by stress in cognate languages; witness Pal. /kūsinā/ 'kitchen' : /kūsinā/ 'to cook' < Sp. /ko'sina/ : /kosi'na(r)/. Creole intonation patterns have not been well studied and we can therefore draw few generalisations, but all creoles use intonation contrastively, and many analysts have commented on the occurrence of rapid 'stepping' tones and the semi-syntactic use of extended high pitch for emphasis, as in STo. /kět͡ʃi::::/ 'it's sizzling hot!'.

Whether or not Romance creoles permit complex vocalic nuclei is partly a matter of definition. What have elsewhere been classified as diphthongs almost always consist of nucleic monophthongs preceded or, much less commonly, followed by /j/ or /w/. Our earlier decision to treat the glides /j, w/ as 'semi-consonantal' (p. 431), necessarily alters the status of glide + vowel sequences, reducing the possible incidence of 'diphthongs' and entailing a different view of syllable structure. In support of this interpretation we may cite the following observations: some Romance creoles disallow any syllable nucleus but a simple vowel; few regularly permit vowels to have both on- and off-glides; none makes systematic use of vowels in hiatus or combinations of non-high vowels; and none makes productive use of diphthongisation in inflection or derivation.

Vowel harmony is now increasingly being accepted as an explanation for certain historical developments in Romance creoles, but its synchronic operation is not well understood. The clearest examples are to be found in those creoles that restructured lexical items by epenthesis: STo. /bi'li/ 'to open' < *abrir*, /fɔ'gõ/ 'stove' < *fogão*, Pri. /'mili/ 'thousand' < *mil*, /'sulu/ 'south' < *sul*. Full harmony of pretonics is also well attested in Papiamentu: /kus'tumbra/ 'custom' < *costumbra*, /ros'ponde/ 'answer' < *responder*, /no'gosi/ 'business' < *negocio*. Moreover, partial harmony may be a better explanation for what has been described as 'vowel raising' in atonic syllables in both Papiamentu and Chabacano: Pap./'midi/ 'measure' < *medir*, /'sigi/ 'follow' < *seguir*; Cha. /ku'mida/ 'meal' < *comida*, /pu'di/ 'be able' < *poder*, /vi'ni/ 'come' < *venir*, /vi'sino/ 'neighbour' < *vecino*. Less clearly, harmony may have influenced the re-interpretation of French schwa [ə]: *debout* 'upright' > Hai., Gua., Mar., Dom., SLu. /debut/, Guy., Mau., Sey. /dibut/; and *venir* 'come' > /vini/ almost universally. An instance of synchronic harmonisation is also documented in Haitian, where the pronoun or possessive particle /wu/ 'you, your' often loses its glide and adjusts to the height of an immediately preceding vowel, as in /mãʒe+wu/ [mãʒe o] 'your food', /frɛ+wu/ [frɛɔ] 'your brother', but /avɛk+wu/ [avɛk u] 'with you'.

The Romance creole whose phonology most nearly approximates to a CVCV pattern is Principense, though several other west African creoles, together with Palenquero, conform to a slightly more liberal definition of 'CV'. In Palenquero, the preferred syllable types are CV, CVC, V and CVN; there are no complex nuclei; closed syllables may only end in /-n/ or, word-medially, in a nasal homorganic with the following consonant; and practically all words end in a vowel. In Principense, the effect is more marked because almost all etymological CVN syllables have been reanalysed as CṼ, and in basilectal forms only stop + glide sequences are permissible as initial clusters. Some CVCV examples, together with their Portuguese cognates, are: /ka'so/ 'dog' < *cachorro*, /po'sã/ 'town' < *povoação*, /su'pe/ 'mirror' < *espelho*, /kẽ'se/ 'forget' < *esquecer*, /la'ta/ 'get up' < *levantar*, /sẽ'de/ 'stretch' < *estender*. Historical change has usually been reductive, often drastically so: /be/ 'also' < *também*, /bi/ 'open' < *abrir*, /sã/ 'woman' < *senhora*; but target syllable structures have also been achieved by epenthesis and metathesis: /'dosu/ 'two' < *dois*, /piʃi'kelo/ 'fisherman' < *pesqueiro*, /ki'rja/ 'bring up' < *criar*. Unlike Principense, São Tomense accepts medial CVN syllables, /'sumbu/ 'lead' < *chumbo*, and a few complex onsets, including the unusual combinations /ʃtl-, ʃkl-/, as in /ʃtlɛ'ka/ 'surround' < *cercar*, /ʃkle've/ 'write' < *escrever*, but despite these minor infractions the preponderance of CV syllables remains overwhelming. Such examples are legion, indicating beyond reasonable doubt that during the formative period of these creoles

open-syllable phonology was an irresistible target for adaptive change.
Such a conclusion cannot be so readily accepted for the creoles lexified
from French, which currently have an incidence of open syllables not so
different from that of European Romance. In terms of phonological targets, the historical tendencies seem contradictory. The early reanalysis of a
large number of nouns to incorporate particles that were etymologically
determiners and liaison consonants, whatever its motivation, has the clear
phonological effect of avoiding word-initial vowels and creating many new
CV onsets. Typical examples from Seychellois are: /dile/ 'milk' < *du lait*,
/delo/ 'water' < *de l'eau*, /diri/ 'rice' < *du riz*, /laso/ 'lime' < *la chaux*,
/lizje/ 'eye' < *les yeux* (Hai. /ʒe/), /zãfã/ 'child' < *S + enfants*, /zeɡwij/
'needle' < *S + aiguilles*, /zwa/ 'goose' < *S + oies*. More recently, the
incidence of open syllables, both medial and final, has been greatly
increased by the elimination of post-vocalic /-r/ that we examined earlier
(p. 429). Against all this, we should note that the original lexical stock,
quite unlike that of the creoles lexified from Spanish or Portuguese, contained large numbers of words with CVC final syllables, including many
newly restructured forms: Hai. /bat/ 'hit' < *battre*, /ʃif/ 'number' <
chiffre, /dezɔd/ 'rowdy' < *désordre*, /latus/ 'cough' < *la toux ~ tousser*,
/vɛp/ 'evensong' < *vêpres*, /zɛb/ 'grass' < *S + herbes*, /zõɡ/ 'finger nail'
< *S + ongles*. Words of (-)CVC# structure in the original lexical stock
have proved remarkably resistant to change. Again more recently, syllable
structure has been complicated by morphophonemic changes, which have
swelled the numbers of closed syllables and seem to have created some
syllabic consonants. Firstly, many verbs which were formerly disyllabic
later developed alternants without the final vowel: Hai. {rete, ret} 'stay' <
rester, {soti, sot} 'go out' < *sortir*, Mau. {ale, al} 'go' < *aller*, {mãze, mãz}
'eat' < *manger*; of these pairs, it is the shorter CVC or VC form which is
now preferred in all contexts save predicate-final. Secondly, Haitian subject
pronouns when proclitic to a verb optionally lose their vowel, producing a
CV onset to verbs normally beginning with a vowel, but a syllabic consonant if the verb begins with a consonant; witness, /m(wẽ) + ale/ [ma'le]
'I go', /n(u) + ale/ [na'le] 'we go', but /m(wẽ) + pale/ [m̩pa'le] 'I speak',
/n(u) + domi/ [n̩dõ'mĩ] 'we sleep'.

Similar changes have occurred, though usually on a much smaller scale,
in the creoles lexified from Portuguese and Spanish. In Papiamentu, for
instance, strong prosodic nasality has indirectly increased the frequency of
medial closed syllables, because many words have been reanalysed as con-
· taining a non-etymological nasal consonant: /frumiNga/ [fɹu'mĩŋga] 'ant'
< Port., Osp. *formiga*, /neN'ga/ [nẽŋ'ga] 'deny' < *negar*, /primiN'ti/
[pɹimĩn'ti] 'promise' < *prometer*. Syllabic consonants, too, have been
created following vowel loss in Principense and Crioulo, as in Pri. /ŋ'ga/
'deceive' < *enganar*, GBi. / ŋkan'ta/ 'delight' < *encantar*.

To sum up, we may say that a few Romance creoles are almost literally

CV in their phonology, and several more show a very strong preference for open syllables and for relatively simple consonantal onsets. Basilectal words in such creoles seem to have been adjusted to a phonological template quite different from that of their European cognates. Since most of the relevant features are widespread in west African languages, we cannot be certain whether their presence in Romance creoles is a direct survival from a contributor language, or whether CV phonology is regularly induced by a bioprogram mechanism during pidginisation. We can, on the other hand, demonstrate that the modern creoles vary quite considerably in their adherence to 'CV' principles, and that those lexified from French are the least consistent in their syllabic structure. While some increase in the frequency of closed syllables can be ascribed to gradual historical change, it is clear that numerous French (-)CVC# roots were assimilated into the original basilectal stock and have since been preserved intact. The persistence of such roots, in cognate but widely separated creoles, is proof that structural characteristics of the lexifier language can survive pidginisation, and that, in appropriate circumstances, any bioprogrammatic predisposition towards CV phonology can be overridden.

Diachronic and Sociolinguistic Processes
Of the Romance creoles so far mentioned, all are subject to variation within linguistically stable limits and only a small minority have achieved a recognised degree of standardisation. Most creoles are spoken in multilingual communities and many, though not all, are in regular contact with their lexifier language. These factors can combine to present a bewildering array of choices to the language learner seeking to establish a social identity. For historico-political reasons, approximation to a European standard is not often sought, except as part of the conscious learning of a second language, though local acrolects, whether established by a plantocracy or by the more recent focusing of educated usage, often differ from the lexifier language only in fairly superficial aspects of phonology and lexis. Since the synchronic spectrum from basilect to acrolect can be so broad, almost any phonetic variation or innovation may, and often does, become invested with sociolinguistic significance. We cannot treat this vast topic in detail and will therefore consider just two typical cases — vowel rounding and palatalisation.

In commenting earlier on Table 12.1, we noted that no basilectal Romance creole has phonemic secondary or central vowels. If the synchronic creole systems are compared with those of their respective lexifiers (for French, see p. 210; for Portuguese, p. 132; for Spanish, p. 85), it is immediately apparent that the creolisation process required differing degrees of phonological adaptation. In particular, any Portuguese words containing diphthongs, and any French items embodying the front rounded vowels /y, ø, œ/, would require reanalysis.

In almost all cases, the adaptation of French words containing /y, ø, œ/ has been achieved by unrounding the vowels to [i, e, ɛ]. Accordingly, six vowel phonemes of the maximal system of French are merged into three, or even two in those creoles that have eliminated the /e : ɛ/ opposition, though this reduction is less drastic than the comparison implies, since some of the French contrasts carry only a small functional load (see p. 210). In Haitian, which is typical in this respect: /di/ 'hard', /ʒiʒ/ 'judge', /limjɛ/ 'light' are cognate with Fr. /y/ in *dur, juge, lumière* respectively; /kre/ 'hollow', /ve/ 'wish', with Fr. /ø/ in *creux, voeu*; and /mɛb/ 'furniture', /vɛv/ 'widow', with Fr. /œ/ as in *meuble, veuve*. In a small number of words, thought to be among the earliest assimilated, etymological /y/ is backed to /u/, as in Hai. /bule/ 'burn' < Fr. *brûler* and /su/ 'on' < *sur*. More recent borrowings, however, all follow the unrounding process, which seems still to be operative: Sey. /lẽsertitid/ 'uncertainty' < Fr. *l'incertitude* and /medjater/ 'mediator' < *médiateur*. In most of the creoles in regular contact with standard French, the front rounded (etymological) pronunciation of these vowels is spreading in the acrolect and has become sociolinguistically marked throughout the community. This 'decreolisation' feature is not only prestigious in its own right, but a powerful index of literacy and education. Since the diachronic change involved merger, its reversal exposes upwardly aspiring speakers who are not fully literate in French to misidentification of the front vowels which need labiality. In a word like /sertitid/ 'certainty' < Fr. *certitude*, hypercorrect and inconsistent pronunciations like *[sœrtityd] and *[sœrtitid] risk provoking amusement if not ridicule.

Palatalisation is another process that is difficult to reverse for speakers not fully conversant with the lexifier language. As we saw above (p. 433), nearly all Romance creoles show evidence of the palatalisation of /t, d, k, g/ before /i, j/ and, less commonly, /e/. But the general process has led to very diverse outcomes depending on whether the system already contained palatal consonants, whether, if so, there was partial or complete merger, and whether any front rounded vowels or glides were also sites for palatalisation. In Haitian and Mauritian, for instance, /t, d/ are palatalised respectively as [tˢ, dʲ], [ṭ, ḍ] and, with rare exceptions, remain separate from fully palatal consonants; whereas in Dominican and most other eastern Caribbean creoles new palatal affricates have been created: /tʃebe/ 'grasp' < Fr. *tiens bien*, /tʃwe/ 'kill' < *tuer*, /dʒɔl/ 'mouth' < *gueule* (compare STo. /tʃa/ 'aunt' < Port. *tia*, /'ŋglãdʒi/ 'big' < *grande*). In the Indian Ocean creoles, however, phonetic palatalisation of /t, d/ went hand in hand with depalatalisation of etymological /ʃ, ʒ/ to [s, z], as in Mau., Sey. /lasas/ 'hunt' < Fr. *la + chasse*, /ziz/ 'judge' < *juge*. In these creoles, depalatalisation led to the unconditioned merger of /ʃ, ʒ/ with the phonemes /s, z/. The palatal consonants, however, figure prominently in acrolectal pronunciation and have now acquired strong sociolinguistic significance. Once again, it is very difficult for a non-acrolectal speaker who is not literate in French to identify the instances of /s, z/ which should be repalatalised to conform to more prestigious usage, with a consequent risk of inconsistency and hypercorrection. At the same time, palatality provides a good example of the divergence of the local acrolect from a European standard, since phonetic palatalisation of /t, d/ is not stigmatised. A high status Mauritian who felt superior to one who pronounced 'Thursday' as [ze'ɖi] < Fr. *jeudi*, would nevertheless quite happily pronounce it [ʒø'ɖi].

Orthography
Orthography is a contentious issue in many creole-speaking communities, but for reasons that are historical and political rather than linguistic. In purely linguistic terms, Romance creoles are well suited to alphabetic representation, having relatively small phonemic inventories and little morphophonemic variation. The design and propagation of such a writing system would certainly be hampered in some varieties by the absence of a recognised standard, but this is not an insuperable obstacle (elsewhere, indeed, the availability of a unified orthography has done much to promote language standardisation). The essential problem is that most Romance creoles have been written — not necessarily by native speakers, but often for long periods — in improvised and unsuitable orthographies that have now acquired the authority of tradition. The issue is thus not the creation of a writing system so much as spelling reform.

In a developing country, the formulation of a policy of spelling reform (aside from the practical and economic difficulties of its implementation) requires fundamental political decisions. The early missionaries, travellers and administrators who first attempted to write creole, however well intentioned, simply assumed that they were dealing with an exotic version of the relevant European language, and accordingly adapted, as best they could, the writing system of that language. In a newly independent creole-speaking country seeking to promote its language as a symbol of national unity, such an assumption is no longer appropriate. Opinion thus tends to polarise between those wishing to emancipate the creole from any unwelcome colonial associations and those wishing to preserve the traditional linguistic links, with, in the middle, cautious pragmatists anxious not to undermine the level of literacy already achieved. This is not the place to develop further the political arguments. We should nevertheless make the linguistic observation that just as a major spelling reform of French would destroy its visual relatedness to other Romance languages (see p. 215), so the design of new and individual writing systems for the creoles will certainly obscure their etymological relationship to the lexifier languages and may also conceal the links between cognate creoles.

4 Morphosyntax

Creoles are universally agreed to be non-inflecting languages — a synchronic property reflecting the drastic restructuring that took place during pidginisation. Since the Romance creoles show no systematic inflection for number, gender, case, person, tense, voice or mood, their grammatical organisation is necessarily very different from that of their respective lexifiers. They also differ in having a much lower incidence of stem alternation, which can be quite striking when verb forms are compared in, say, Papiamentu and Spanish. But the lack of both inflection and stem allomorphy does not entail — as has sometimes been assumed — either invariant morphology or fully analytic syntax. Most creoles have now undergone sufficient gradual change to have developed morphophonemic alternants of their own, especially among the grammatical particles; all have some productive derivational processes; and some have inherited complex forms, like the Papiamentu 'participles' in /-Vndo/, which in the lexifier would be called inflectional but which, being now sporadic and unsystematic, are best treated as derivational. We shall mention morphophonemic alternation, as appropriate, in this section, and postpone discussion of derivation to section 5.

Grammatical Categories

All Romance creoles are SVO in their grammatical organisation, and the syntactic role of word order is so important that there is little freedom for stylistic manoeuvre within basic constituents. As syncretism, even among grammatical particles, is by no means unknown, the polyvalency of individual forms can often only be resolved by reference to sentential position. This characteristic in turn has prompted some analysts to question whether the traditional grammatical categories can properly be applied to creoles. Such features as [+noun], [+verb], which for European Romance we assume to be inherently specified in lexical representations, are arguably redundant in a system where propositional meaning is a function of the relative positioning of constituents. More seriously, procrustean analyses which impose discrete categories on creoles, may distort syntactic relationships and understate the extent of polyvalency. In Haitian, for instance, there is a clear difference of propositional meaning between /jo mãʒe/ 'they eat' and /mãʒe jo/ 'their food'; and between /lɛ m-rive/ 'when I get there' and /li pa kɔn lɛ/ 'he can't tell the time' or /lɛ mwɛ̃ rete/ 'my watch has stopped'. What should we conclude about the status of the sequences /mãʒe/ and /lɛ/? To say, without more ado, that /mãʒe/ has two distinct lexical representations, one marked [+verb], the other [+noun], and that /lɛ/ has at least two representations distinguished by the features [+conj.] : [+noun], conveniently disregards the fact that the items are in complementary syntactic distribution and consequently not prone to the kind of ambiguity that can arise with 'accidental' homophones. It is, however, very hard to know whether the synchronic distribution remains transparent to Haitian speakers, or whether it is of purely etymological significance. On the answer to this question must depend the extent of categorial tolerance in the current system. If, as seems intuitively probable, Haitian speakers now treat /mãʒe/ as a single, bivalent lexical entry, but /lɛ/ as two discrete items, one a 'conjunction' and the other a polysemous 'noun', we may draw the twin inferences that the total categorial fluidity characteristic of the early phase of creolisation has been significantly restricted, and secondly, that the creole now operates with two major classes — functors and contentives — allowing some syntactic freedom within each class but not normally across the boundary.

Despite these reservations as to the theoretical validity of traditional 'parts of speech' for the analysis of creoles, the remainder of this section has been organised along conventional lines in order to facilitate comparisons with the Romance languages described in earlier chapters. We shall note explicitly any categorial mismatches between cognates, but elsewhere terms like 'noun', 'verb' and 'adjective' should be understood as if enclosed in inverted commas.

Noun Morphology

'Nouns' in Romance creoles are not marked for grammatical gender or case, nor necessarily for number or definiteness. The absence of overt marking is probably due to different factors in three of these four instances. Number and definiteness (further discussed below) are certainly valid categories in creole, but as both can often be inferred from the general context, grammatical marking is rarely obligatory. Case, in the sense of thematic role, is expressed by sentential position or by preposition; no Romance creole marks case directly on nouns, whether by inflection or any other morphological device, but some do have alternating sets of pronominal forms which could be described as case suppletives (we return to this point below). Grammatical gender is quite simply not a category of any Romance creole. Its elimination, however, has left isolated residues in pairs like GBi. /neto, neta/ 'nephew, niece' where natural gender is still overtly marked by derivational suffixes inherited from the lexifier and now of very limited productivity (see p. 468).

The doubt we earlier raised as to the validity of a noun class, could of course be allayed if creole 'nouns' were distinguished by canonical structure or by some other overt identification. Here, the evidence varies greatly between creoles and is not easy to interpret. Many creole nouns, when compared with their cognates in the lexifier languages, are seen to have undergone more or less extensive restructuring. We treated some aspects of this topic under the rubric of phonology (see p. 436), but it is by no means clear whether the original motivation for restructuring was phonological, morphological or a combination of the two. Conceivably, indeed, a phonologically motivated process gave rise to sufficient numbers of convergent forms for a succeeding generation to reinterpret them as morphologically regular or semi-regular.

Probably the nearest approximation among Romance creoles to canonical structuring of form classes is found in the west African group — adjacent to, and sometimes in direct contact with, language families well known for this characteristic. In Principense, by far the most common template for nouns is CVCV, a result usually achieved by syllable loss and cluster simplification, but also occasionally by vowel epenthesis. As examples of reduction (additional to those listed on p. 436), we may cite: /ˈbigu/ 'navel' < Port. *umbigo*, /ˈminu/ 'child' < *menino*, /paˈgɛ/ 'parrot' < *papagaio*, /kaˈra/ 'crab' < *carangueijo*, /ˈgeza/ 'church' < *igreja*; and as instances of lengthening: /ˈmeze/ 'month' < *mes*, /ˈvese/ 'occasion' < *vez*. There are, however, significant numbers of verbs and adjectives which have been similarly restructured: /koˈse/ 'to repair' < *consertar*, /fɛˈga/ 'to rub' < *esfregar*, /ˈdetu/ 'straight' < *direito*, /ˈgavi/ 'pretty' < *agradavel*. If, therefore, CVCV structure is to be posited as canonical in Principense morphology, rather than representing a favoured phonological pattern, it must operate across all contentives and not single out nouns as a special class.

The evidence for demarcative structure is even more tentative in the creoles lexically related to French. These have all restructured nouns by incorporating elements that were etymologically determiners and plural markers; but the effects are not uniform (see pp. 437 and 466). The word for 'bird' is variously /zwazo, zwezo, zozo/, but the initial /z-/ is universal. 'Water' has a large number of variants, including /delo, dilo, dolo, dlo, dljo, djo, glo, gjo/, but all begin with a consonant that can be reconstructed as /d-/. Almost universal are: /zõjõ/ 'onion', /lete/ 'summer', /livɛ, liver/ 'winter' and /dife/ 'fire'. Thereafter, the creoles diverge noticeably, the lowest incidence of agglutination being in Haitian and the highest in the Indian Ocean group, though even this generalisation is infringed by individual items, witness Hai. /ʃu/, Mau. /lasu/, but Sey. /su/ 'cabbage'. Variant forms are also attested within one creole, as in Hai. /izin, lizin/ 'refinery', Sey. /sãs, lasãs/ 'luck', but most of these are clearly affected by contact with the acrolect and may not be in free variation for individual speakers. It seems, then, that for most creoles, agglutination is the result of historical misanalysis rather than reanalysis directed towards any morphological goal. For Mauritian, the most we could say is that: very few nouns begin with a vowel; a large proportion, for reasons that can easily be traced to the lexifier, begin with a coronal consonant; and those with initial /l-/ mainly correlate with the feature [+count], while those with initial /di-/ often signal [+mass]. Such generalisations, and their exceptions, may be of interest to linguists but are unlikely to be psychologically real for Mauritian speakers.

The Nominal Group

The minimal creole noun phrase, whether subject or object in function, consists of a single pronoun or noun. In this respect, there is no distinction between proper and common nouns. A bare noun can be interpreted as generic or, in discourse where the topic has already been established, as definite: Cha. /sal diriti na agwa/ 'salt dissolves in water', Mau. /lulu tje li/ 'the wolf kills her'. All creoles also accept bare nouns as plurals in object position: Hai. /l ap aʃte zabriko/ 'she is buying apricots ' (note that *zabriko* is a restructured form). But they differ in their tolerance of unmarked plural subjects, such structures, where acceptable, often being ambiguous between specific plural and generic readings; compare Mau. /timun ti ule zwe/ 'the children wanted to play' and /timun kõtã zwe/ 'the children like to play' or 'children like to play, a child likes to play'.

In other respects, the creole nominal group is less open to generalisations, especially in the often complex interaction of deictic, number and personal attribution markers. All Romance creoles have an indefinite article, which precedes the nominal, and is related historically and usually also synchronically to the numeral 'one'; sample forms are: Cha., Pap., GBi. /un/, STo. /ũa/, Hai. /ju, jun, un, õ, jõ/, Gua., Dom., SLu. /jõ, õ/, Mar. /ã/, Réu., Sey. /ẽ/, Mau. /en/. All can indicate plurality by means of a numeral or quantifier, again preposed. Allowing for phonological adjustment, the lower numerals are all recognisably Romance, but in the higher reaches the syntax of compounding can differ, as in STo. /kwatlu dɛʃi ki oto/ 'forty-eight', literally 'four tens with eight'. The quantifiers /tu ~ tudu ~ tur/ 'all' and /ʃak ~ sak ~ kada/ 'each' are widely distributed, but there are numerous other expressions of quantity that have been reanalysed from former nominal periphrases, like Hai. /ɛnpil/, Sey. /ẽbõpe/, Sey., Mau. /ẽpake, enpake/, all meaning 'many', as in Mau. /enpake timun/ 'a bunch of kids'.

Aside from the marking of singularity by an indefinite article and plurality by a lexical quantifier, the treatment of number falls into one of three broad types. Some basilectal creoles have no other morphological signal of number. Palenquero, Guinea-Bissau Crioulo and some variants of Chabacano fall into this group, witness GBi. /tudu kil bu libru largu/ 'all those long books of yours'. (In these and other creoles lexified from Spanish and Portuguese, the morphological structure lends itself to the importation of an inflectional {-s}; but inflected plurals are reportedly uncommon and often regarded as affected or hypercorrect.) The second type of plural marking inserts an invariant free particle before the nominal head. Chabacano uses a form /mana ~ maŋga/, which may be borrowed from Tagalog, as in /el maŋga visino/ 'the neighbours'; and Indian Ocean creoles use a form reanalysed from Fr. *bande,* hence Réu. /lɔ bãn frãse/ 'the French (people)', Mau. /ku ban mulõdo/ 'with (the) water melons', and even /kot ban dipõ/ 'at the Duponts' house'. The third and most widespread type manifests two distinct order patterns. It employs the pronoun 'they', normally a free form, as a nominal clitic, preposed in some creoles — STo. /nẽ mwala/ 'the women', Pri. /nẽ ipĩ/ 'the thorns'; and postposed in others — Hai. /rekẽ jo/ 'the sharks', Pap. /tur e kabaj nan/ 'all the horses'. The Indian Ocean creoles also have a construction, used with parts of the body, that resembles a dual. Mau. /mo lipe fin ãfle/ is ambiguous, perhaps inconveniently so, between 'my foot has swollen' and 'my feet have swollen'; so to indicate that both are afflicted, one says /mo de lipe .../, literally 'my two feet ...'; but in this fairly common structure /de/ seems to have been partly grammaticalised, with the concomitant loss of its purely numerical value.

Turning now to determiners and deictics, we find an often bewildering array of systems. All the Romance creoles seem able to mark referentiality by means of particles cognate with definite articles or weak demonstratives in European Romance. A few have preposed definite articles which, if we disregard their invariant shape, match the distribution of their European counterparts: Cha. /el pwelko, el luna/ 'the pig, the moon', Pap. /e forki i e kuʧu nan/ 'the fork and the knives'. The majority pattern, uniform among the creoles lexified from French, employs a postposed determiner, as in Hai. /ʃat la/, Sey. /sat la/ 'the cat'. The particle /la/ (which is subject to considerable morphophonemic variation in Haitian and other Caribbean creoles, see p. 422) transparently derives from the French deictic suffix /-la/ and is probably better described as a referential marker than as a definite article, since it often cooccurs with a demonstrative: Hai. /ʃat sa la/, Sey. /sa sat la/ 'that cat'. São Tomense likewise lacks a definite article, but has a single, quasi-demonstrative particle /sɛ/, which is always postposed and seems to have both referential and weak deictic functions: STo. /piʃi sɛ/ 'this fish' or 'the fish (I'm talking about)'.

Deixis can differ in intensity, but no basilectal creole uses a distal system of more than two terms. Crioulo, for instance, which lacks a definite article, has a two-term demonstrative system with optional intensifying deictic particles: GBi. /es mindʒer, kil omi/ 'this woman, that man', but /es mindʒer li, kil omi la/ 'THIS woman, THAT man'. The creoles lexified from French have only one demonstrative /sa/, but they divide into two subgroups according to whether the particle is preposed (Guyanais and the Indian Ocean group) or postposed (in Louisiana and the Caribbean). There is also a minor cross-current in so far as some have optional intensifiers on the Crioulo pattern: Guy. /sa ʃat isi la/ 'this cat here' versus /sa ʃat la la/ 'that cat there'. The last pair of examples graphically illustrates the problems of intercomprehensibility and linguistic description posed by sets of particles that are homophonous or nearly identical in shape, and distinguished only by relative position. Other difficulties of description are caused by the interaction of markers for referentiality, deixis, possession and plurality, which are all post-nominal in some creoles: Hai. /ʃat mwẽ sa jo/ 'those cats of mine'. Although these markers are semantically compatible, by no means all combinations are acceptable or pragmatically interpretable. Nor are the constraints on combinations all negative. An unusual positive requirement is found in some eastern Caribbean creoles, where plural marking is optional but, if selected, must be accompanied by referential marking; hence, Dom., SLu. /pul/ 'hen, hens', /pul la/ 'the hen', /se pul la/ 'the hens' (= plural + hen + reference), but not */se pul/.

Before passing on to personal pronouns, let us sketch the bare outlines of noun phrase structure in Romance creoles. The minimal noun phrase consists of a single noun, unmarked for number and undifferentiated for subject or object function. It may be expanded by the addition of various determiners, and qualified by one or more adjectives or relative clauses (see p. 461). Attributive adjectives in most creoles follow the nominal head, often obligatorily so — STo. /kɛ ŋglãdʒi/ 'the big house', not */ŋglãdʒi kɛ/ — but in those lexified from French a small set of adjectives may immediately precede the noun, giving word order patterns very reminiscent of metropolitan French — Mau. /en zoli ti fler zon/ ≃ *une jolie petite fleur jaune* 'a pretty little yellow flower'. In all creoles, a universal or numerical quantifier, including the indefinite article, occupies the initial position of the group (quantifier 'floating' is not attested). Considerable variety characterises the other markers, both in their positions relative to the nominal head and to one another, and in their patterns of syncretism.

Personal Pronouns and Possessives
Some idea of the diversity of creole pronominal and possessive systems can be gained from the comparative perspective afforded by the chart given here, which omits minor morphophonemic alternations. Whilst most individual creoles, with the prominent exception of Crioulo, have relatively simple systems — certainly simpler than those of the respective lexifier languages — scarcely any pair of them is precisely congruent, and few generalisations are universally valid. The majority of the forms themselves are of Romance origin, though sometimes barely recognisable as a result of local phonological change and restructuring. More interesting from a typological viewpoint is the proliferation of fairly minor systemic differences, some of them historical residues, but others representing divergent innovations. The possessive markers, for instance, precede or follow their head noun in patterns which may have been determined by one of the original contact languages, but which now cut across both areal groupings and relations with the respective lexifiers.

The grammatical categories implied by the chart are: three persons, two numbers, and three functional differentiations or 'cases'. Discounting morphophonemic alternants, no creole has the eighteen distinct forms needed to maintain all oppositions; most have half or fewer. Syncretism on this

Pronoun and Possessive Systems

		Pal.	Pap.	STo.	GBi.	Hai.	Mau.
1	S	i	mi	N—/ami	N—/ami	mwẽ/m	mo
	O	mi	mi	mũ/ami	—n/mi	mwẽ/m	mwa
	P	+mi	mi+	+mũ	ɲa+	+mwẽ/m	mo+
2	S	bo	bo	bo	bu/abo	u	to/u
	O	bo	bo	bo	—u/bo	u	twa/u
	P	+si	bo+	+bo	bu+	+u	to/u+
3	S	ele	ele/el/e	e/e'le	i/el	li/l/i	li
	O	e	ele/e	e/e'le	—l/el/sil	li/l/i	li
	P	+ele	su+	+d—e	si+	+li	so+
4	S	suto	nos	nõ	no/anos	nu/n	nu
	O	suto	nos	nõ	—nu/nos	nu/n	nu
	P	+suto	nos+	+nõ	no+	+nu	nu+
5	S	utere	boso(nan)	inãse	bo/abos	zot/nu	zot
	O	utere	boso(nan)	nãse	bos	zot/nu	zot
	P	+utere	boso(nan)+	+nãse	bo+	+zot/nu	zot+
6	S	a'ne	nan	i'nẽ	e/elis	jo/j	zot
	O	a'ne	nan	i'nẽ	elis/selis	jo/j	zot
	P	+a'ne	nan+	+d—i'nẽ	se+	+jo	zot+

Notes: N is a homorganic nasal consonant; — indicates a semi-clitic form; + shows position of possessive in relation to head noun. S = subject, O = object, P = possessive.

scale must again cast doubt on the synchronic validity of the categories. By far the best maintained is that of number: the oppositions of singular and plural are morphologically distinct in almost every instance. Person is clearly a three-term system for most creoles, but some maintain a distinction between familiar and polite forms of address, and others, in the plural, give priority to the dimensions of inclusion and exclusion over strict parallelism with the singular. Hence, Hai. /nu/ embraces a group that does not specifically exclude the speaker, while Mau. /zot/ < Fr. S + *autres* covers any group in which the speaker is not specifically included. By far the least stable category is 'case' which, as we said above, is not marked on nouns and can usually be inferred from sentential position or immediate collocation. Most of the 'case' oppositions visible in the chart can be traced directly to suppletive forms in the lexifier. Tenacious though they are in the first person singular, they appear to be yielding slowly to analogical levelling.

Judged in purely grammatical terms, Haitian has the simplest system, in numbers of both forms and surface oppositions. Papiamentu is likewise simple, despite one suppletive possessive and a vestigial form of familiar address /tu/, now reserved for deliberate insults. Most of the eastern Caribbean creoles closely resemble Haitian, except that a phonological reduction of /li/ to /i/, in preverbal position only, has created an apparent case opposition in the third person singular. Unusually, this central Caribbean group contrasts with all other creoles lexified from French. Of the very scattered latter group, only Seychellois fails to distinguish familiar from polite address, and only Guyanais lacks 'case' distinctions.

Two unrelated creoles have more complicated systems that deserve special mention. Crioulo distinguishes up to five sets of forms: disjunctive or emphatic subject, neutral subject, post-verbal clitic, post-prepositional, and possessive. Their respective representations are: /aˈmi ~ N ~ -n ~ mi ~ ɲa/ for 'first person singular', /aˈbo ~ bu ~ -u ~ bo ~ bu/ for 'second singular', and /el ~ i ~ -l ~ sil ~ si/ for 'third'. Even allowing for productive morphophonological processes, this system is by far the most complex of the creoles we have so far examined and, for historical reasons which remain obscure, one of the closest to European Romance. Réunionnais, too, has a system more reminiscent of some varieties of popular French than of its Indian Ocean neighbours. It distinguishes objects from subjects quite systematically by means of the preposition /a/, as in /mwẽ : a mwẽ/ 'I : me'. (Such 'prepositional accusatives' are of course widespread in southern European Romance — see p. 106; and a similar structure using /kon/ is documented in one variety of Chabacano). Réunionnais also opposes familiar and polite forms of address, and, uniquely among the creoles lexified from French, has a series of possessives systematically distinct from the corresponding pronouns: /mwẽ : mõ/ 'I : my', /twe : tõ/ 'you : your (familiar)', /nu : nut/ 'we : our'. The resemblance to French, as we see again below, is unmistakable.

Verb Morphology
The most conspicuous morphological differences between Romance creoles and their lexifiers lie in the verb system. The creole verb entirely dispenses with the synthetic paradigms characteristic of European Romance, and instead conveys relations of tense and aspect by means of grammatical particles juxtaposed to a stem which is inflectionally neutral. The stems themselves normally derive from the infinitive or the third person of the present indicative. By virtue of their etymology, they sometimes embody traces of their former conjugation membership, as in Hai. /rive/ 'arrive' < Fr. *arriver*, /kuri/ 'run' < *courir*, /vãn/ 'sell' < *vend(re)*; GBi. /kansa/ 'tire' < Port. *cansa(r)*, /minti/ 'tell lies', < *mentir ~ mente*. Nevertheless, conjugation has nowhere survived as a synchronically valid or productive category.

Creole verb stems, though morphologically simple, are by no means always invariable. Some intriguing questions are raised by the interpretation of a large class of verbs, all in creoles lexified from French, that have bi-allomorphic stems. In Mauritian, for instance, it has been estimated that around 70 per cent of verbs have two forms, as in /asper ~ aspere/ 'wait', /gut ~ gute/ 'taste', /lav ~ lave/ 'wash', /res ~ reste/ 'stay', /tom ~ tõbe/ 'fall'. Of these, the longer form occurs in predicate-final position or before a time adverbial, and the short form in all other contexts. Their synchronic distribution and precise morphophonological relationship have so far eluded definitive explanation, as indeed has their historical origin. One suggestion is that the longer forms may be remnants of the Romance imperfect paradigm (which survives as a reanalysed marker in several creoles; see below). At first sight, the 'imperfect' etymology may appear to explain why bare verbs can often convey past meaning. But the past sense is not confined to the longer of the two forms, so that derivation from the imperfect would explain neither their synchronic distribution, nor all of the morphological alternations — witness /sort ~ sorti/ 'leave', /vin ~ vini/ 'come', but not */sorte/, */vine/.

On the assumption that the two forms are still related by a productive rule, it is much easier to derive the short from the long than vice versa, despite the fact that the short form is now clearly the unmarked one. In most instances, the derivation would consist merely of deleting the final vowel, but occasionally additional processes such as denasalisation and epenthesis of a nasal consonant would be required, as in: /ran ~ rãde/ 'give back', /tan ~ tãde/ 'hear', /van ~ vãde/ 'sell'. Notice that the combined effect of the adjustments is to make the overwhelming majority of verb stems conform to a (-)CVC# pattern. This cannot be accidental. Moreover, the direction of historical change seems to favour the eventual elimination of the longer form. But before concluding that Mauritian and similar creoles have evolved a canonical structure for verb stems since the creolisation phase, we should recall that these creoles are the very ones in which many noun stems have survived in (-)CVC# form (p. 437). Once again, it seems that a uniform pattern is being promoted for contentives, while a potential subcategorisation delimiting nouns from verbs is being actively blurred.

The extent to which creoles now possess morphologically complex verbs depends partly on definition, since the dividing line between concatenation of free forms and agglutination is often exceedingly fine. From an etymological standpoint, we may say that complex verb forms have survived only sporadically, and those whose cognates in European Romance would be classified as inflectional can usually be explained by some other mechanism in creole. Participles are a case in point. Basilectal creoles rarely use items that can be equated with European present participles or gerundives, though such forms are easily grafted onto creole structure and can certainly be found in acrolectal usage. Papiamentu has quite a large set of forms in /-Vndo/ which serve to introduce subordinate clauses but cannot be combined with an auxiliary particle to form progressive tenses.

Though historically inflectional, these are now best treated as derivational, both because the pattern is no longer fully productive (/baj/ 'go' and /wordu/ 'become' < Dutch *worden* have no associated 'participles') and because in certain pairs the relationship is clearly suppletive, witness /por ~ pudjendo/ 'can, being able'. The trade pidgin of Piñaguero Panare, as recorded in the late 1940s, made extensive use of /-Vndo/ forms; but these were not alternants, having apparently been adopted as unanalysed verb stems: /jo sabjendo el/ 'I knew her', /tu pagando fwerte/ 'you'll have to pay a lot'. An etymological past participle in /-do/ occurs in Chabacano, but only with adjectival functions. Likewise, São Tomense and Crioulo have a regular form in /-du/, used as a predicate with stative or resultative value, as in STo. /inẽ sa maladu/ 'they are tied up' (< Port. *amarrado*); but since /du/ is invariable, it can equally be analysed as a postposed passive marker. A rare example of borrowed inflection is found in Crioulo, where a causative infix /-nD-/ is fully productive with intransitive verbs: /dʒusta ~ dʒustanda/ 'be sufficient, make sufficient', /fria ~ frianta/ 'be cold, cool', /tʃiga ~ tʃiganta/ 'arrive, bring near', /subi ~ subinti/ 'go up, lead up'.

The Verbal Group

The next chart shows, in somewhat simplified form, a selection of creole tense–aspect systems and their associated markers. These ubiquitous particles, more than any other grammatical feature, serve to highlight the linguistic distance separating creoles from their European lexifiers. Patently, constructions like Mau. /nu pa ti pu rãtre/ 'we would not have returned' or Sey. /i ti n fek sorti/ 'he had only just gone out', can neither be directly equated with Fr. *nous ne serions pas rentrés, il ne venait que de sortir*, nor easily explained as reanalyses of grammatical periphrases in the lexifier. Awareness of the systemic parallels among creoles, however, should not blind us to some notable divergences of detail, in both underlying distinctions and their instantiations.

The markers themselves are of diverse origins. Several are transparently Romance, such as /tava, taba/ < *estava, estaba*. A few are non-Romance borrowings; for example STo. /kja/ is cognate with Bini /xiã/. Yet others may be blends, like the past marker /te, ti/ which, though often assumed to be derived from Fr. *était, été*, closely echoes the functions of the Yoruba past prefix /ti-/. In the majority of creoles, tense–aspect particles always precede the verb, but Crioulo and Chabacano both use post-verbal position for certain past markers, and the Papiamentu prospective /lo/ < Port. *logo* 'then, next', perhaps as a vestige of its etymology, most unusually precedes not only the verb but also the subject pronoun, as in /lo bo drumi/ 'you will sleep'. All creoles admit combinations of two markers, and several accept more complex sequences of three or four, together with a negative particle if appropriate (see p. 459). Combinations often give rise to

Tense–Aspect Systems (Simplified)

Time (± Past)	Aspect Perfective	Neutral	Imperfective	Prospective
Guy.				
−P	Ø (soti)	Ø	ka	ke
+P	te	te	te ka	te ke
Mau.				
−P	fin (fek)	Ø	pe	pu (a)
+P	ti fin	ti	ti pe	ti pu (ti a)
STo.				
−P	Ø (fi'ka, bi'la)	Ø	sa ka, ka →	ka, ke (ka bi)
+P	tava	tava	tava ka	te, kja
GBi.				
−P	Ø, +dʒa	Ø	na → ta →	na (na bin) ta
+P	+ba dʒa	+ba	na_+ba, ta_+ba	ta_+ba
Pap.				
−P	a kaba (bira)	Ø	ta	lo
+P	a	a	tabata	lo a
Cha.				
−P	Ø (ka'ba ja)	Ø	ta	de
+P	ja_(+ja)	ja	ta_+ja	de ka'ba, de_+ja

morphophonemic alternation, so fusing particles into clitics and blurring the morph-for-morpheme segmentation offered by citation forms; witness STo. /e+sa+ka+landa/ [e ʃka landa] 'he is swimming', Hai. /jo+te+a+vle+li/ [jo ta vlel] 'they wanted him', SLu. /mwẽn+kaj+we+i/ [ŋaj wej] 'I'll see her'.

Most creole verb systems give precedence to aspectual over strictly temporal relations. Few recognise more than one time opposition, [± past], and some indeed could be argued to function entirely on aspectual distinctions. The four aspects shown in the chart of tense–aspect systems are widely distributed and not always mutually exclusive (the labels have been chosen to maximise similarities to European Romance, but are not optimal in every case). A comparison of the first two columns reveals that the unmarked category is perfective, also known as 'completive'. Actions taking place in the present or envisaged for the future almost always require positive marking. Conversely, the meaning of a bare verb may need to be determined by reference to its inherent semantic properties. Hence, an unmarked verb which is inherently stative may be taken to refer to present time, whereas a dynamic verb will be assumed to signal the completed action; compare Mau. /mo malad/ 'I am ill' with /mo truv zot/ 'I found them'. Bare verbs are a well known feature of creole narratives, and it has sometimes been assumed that they represent a 'historic present' consciously exploited for dramatic effect. This interpretation is, however, grammatically suspect: most narratives in fact contain an explicit past marker in the opening sequence, which may in turn establish the time reference of all that follows, as in Sey. /ẽn zur ti ana ẽn ljev ki Ø kapa sãte/ 'once upon a time there was a hare who could sing'.

An action or event just completed but still relevant at the moment of speaking can usually be encoded by means of a preverbal element whose status is ambiguous between semi-auxiliary and fully integrated aspect marker. These 'pre-verbs' often echo popular constructions in European Romance: Mau. /li fek rive/ 'he's just arrived' ≃ Fr. *il ne fait qu'arriver.* Their function is, however, not uniform across all creoles: /soti, fek/ focus on the recent completion of an inherently dynamic action or state, whereas /fika, bila ~ bira/ < Port. *fica(r), vira(r)*, indicate resultant states, as in STo. /e fika kãsadu/ 'he has got tired' ≡ Mau. /li fin fatige/, but */li fek fatige/ is not possible, except perhaps in a transitive context — ?/li fek fatige so lisjẽ/ 'he's tired his dog out'. Among creoles lexified from French, Mauritian has a particularly rich system, having oppositions between completed and recent past, and between immediate and non-specific future, as in /nu pu aste en lakaz/ 'we're (on the point of) buying a house' versus /nu a lwe en loto/ '(maybe) we'll hire a car.'

As in European Romance, the creole imperfective category usually subsumes progressive and habitual, these being distinguished when necessary by means of explicit adverbs. Haitian is one of the few creoles to endow bare verbs with habitual meaning, so that Hai. /mwẽ pa travaj le samdi/ 'I don't work on Saturdays' would have to be rendered in most eastern Caribbean varieties as /mo pa ka travaj/, and in Mauritian as /mo pa pe travaj/. By contrast, some creoles of the west African group distinguish formally between progressive and habitual, but not always between imperfective and prospective: GBi. /e na baj (amaɲa)/ 'they are going (tomorrow)', /e ta ʧiga sedu/ 'they (always) arrive early, they'll arrive early'. Crioulo and São Tomense do, however, have a means of indicating more specific futurity by adding a reinforcing particle to the progressive marker, hence GBi. /na bin/, STo. /ka bi/. The prospectives themselves vary in complexity from a single particle only able to colligate with the past marker, as in Guyanais and Papiamentu, to configurations of up to five items distinguishing various hypothetical and volitive nuances in addition to the opposition between immediate and non-specific futurity. This potential complexity should not surprise us if we recall that no creole has separate morphology for a subjunctive or optative mood; all such meanings have to be expressed either by semi-auxiliaries or within the prospective category.

The marker system also serves to convey some types of modality. STo. /bo ka bi fla ku e/ 'you will speak to him' also carries a deontic sense 'you must speak to him', and /bo kia fla ku e/ 'you were about to speak to him' also has an epistemic reading, '(I infer that) you nearly spoke to him'.

Occasionally, creoles have special markers of modality that belong neither with the tense–aspect system nor with the auxiliary verbs. One such is STo. /sɛˈla/ 'must', which is preposed to the entire clause, and could therefore be analysed as a sentential extraposition: /sɛˈla (pa) bo fla ku e/ 'you must speak to him' (literally 'must (for) you speak with him'). More often, modal nuances are expressed by V + V sequences, as in European Romance, though creoles are not usually regarded as having a separate class of modal verbs. Papiamentu, for example, indicates possibility by /por/, necessity by /mester ~ meste/, and volition by /kjer ~ kje/, as in /bo por a bin mira nan/ 'you could have (come to) see them', /mi meste mira nan/ 'I must see them'. The comparable forms in the creoles lexified from French are: /kapav ~ kapa/, /dwe ~ divet/, /bezwɛ̃ ~ bizen/, and /vle ~ ule/, all of which may be colligated as appropriate with tense–aspect markers — Mau. /li pa ti kapav fer sa/ 'he couldn't do that', Hai. /mo te bezwɛ̃ fɛ l/ 'I had to do it', Mau. /li a ule zwan zot/ 'he'll want to meet you'. Such V + V constructions are frequent in creoles and by no means confined to modal contexts. Some have led to grammaticalisation of the first verb, as a habitual marker in Hai. /u kon ba m legim/ 'you used to give me vegetables' (< Fr. connaître) or Pal. /bo ase kuˈme kane ↑/ 'do you eat meat?' (< Sp. hacer); as an inchoative in Hai. /li tɔbe ʃate/ or Guy. /li prà ʃate/ 'he began to sing' (< Fr. tomber, prendre); and as a continuative in Pap. /e tabata sigi bende pisˈka/ 'he went on selling fish' (< Sp., Port. seguir).

Creoles are often claimed not to possess passives. The truth of the assertion depends very much on definition. As we noted earlier, few creoles have anything that could be analysed as passive morphology, and several have no equivalent of passive structures featuring overt agentives, on the model of *Rome was destroyed by the barbarians*. Many, however, admit intransitive constructions that could be analysed as stative or resultative passives, or alternatively as ergatives: STo. /e pleˈde/ 'she lost (her way), she got lost', /e biˈʃi/ 'she dressed (herself), she got dressed', Cha. /ele ta pastidiˈa ja/ 'he was getting annoyed', Mau. /dizef-la fin kase/ 'the egg's broken'. Widespread among the Indian Ocean group is a construction using the verb /ɡaɲ/ 'have, win, get', that behaves much more like a conventional passive, as in Sey. /zot pa ti ɡaɲ ɛvite/ 'they didn't get invited', /zot pu ɡaɲ peje par ɡuvernmà/ 'they'll get paid by the government'. It is, however, Crioulo that most clearly confounds the alleged non-existence of passives. Crioulo not only has a frequent acrolectal passive with an overt auxiliary, as in /ɡeriʎa jera alimentadu pa populaˈson/ 'the guerrillas were fed by the (local) people'; it also has a fully productive basilectal passive using the /-du/ inflection, but unlike any found in European Romance, as in /bu ʧiɡa la, bo koziɲadu komida/ 'no sooner had you arrived than your food was cooked' (literally 'you arrived there, your cooked food').

Most creoles also have serial verbs, which express complex semantic notions by juxtaposing, without coordination, what appear to be two main verbs: Guy. /li maʃe bwete/ 'he stumbled along' (literally 'he walked limped'), STo. /inẽ sa tasondu ka le/ 'they are sitting reading' (literally 'they −past seated +imperf. read'). Serial constructions can also lead to the grammaticalisation of one of the verbs, but this time the second member of the pair: in Guy. /pote vini mo rob a/ 'fetch me the dress' (literally 'carry come me dress the'), and /ãnu menẽ vire to mamã/ 'let's bring your mother back' (literally 'let's lead turn-round your mother'), the verbs /vini, vire/ function rather like the English adverb *back*, and neither has the full semantic value that would be associated with main-verb usage.

Another notable example of serial-type construction serves to express comparisons of inequality in the more conservative creoles, where the standard is introduced by a verb meaning 'surpass': Hai. /li pov pase m/ 'he is poorer than I am' (literally 'he poor surpass me'), Mar. /gasõ mwẽ grã pase fi mwẽ/ 'my son is older than my daughter' (literally 'boy my big surpass girl my'), Gua. /i pli sot pase u/ 'he's stupider than you', Pri. /rima mɛ maʃi fɔrti pasa mi/ 'my brother is stronger than I am'. Notice that some creoles use an unmarked adjectival predicate, while others mark the comparative with /pli ~ maʃi/. When a mark is present, the construction very easily lends itself to syntactic reanalysis whereby the former verb /pase ~ pasa/ is interpreted as a conjunction and, in acrolectal usage, is just as easily replaced by a particle like /ki ~ ke/ taken over from the lexifier. Similar reanalyses and substitutions are occurring quite rapidly in some creoles, so reducing the frequency of serial verbs to the point where their long-term survival must be in doubt.

The Status of the Copula

A convenient, but also contentious, bridge between the verbal group and sentence structure, is provided by the copula, whose precise grammatical status is a vexed question in several creoles. Among certain creolists, it has become almost an article of faith that basilectal creoles have no copula, and that such examples as do occur must be explained as 'contaminations' from the acrolect. The opposite view, that all creole lects have copulas, tends to be espoused by two very different groups of analysts: those whose approach is essentially historical, and those whose linguistic model distinguishes underlying from surface structure. It is not simply a Swiftian quarrel of Big and Little Enders. At the extreme, if the absence of an overt copula from certain constructions is viewed as criterial, then some of the varieties we have so far accepted without question as creoles will have to be reclassified. On a more practical descriptive plane, the answers we give on the status of the copula have far-reaching implications for the analysis of the tense–aspect markers, for the definition of grammatical categories, and for the grouping of syntactic structures. In many creoles, it is difficult both to give a neutral account of the facts, and to find a firm point of reference from which analytic solutions can be proposed that are not vitiated by logically circular definitions.

We should start by acknowledging that the term 'copula' is used in several different ways. In the narrow sense, a copula is a purely grammatical link between the subject and a nominal or adjectival predicate. But when, as in most of European Romance, the lexical item performing this function happens to be used in presentative and existential structures, and also as an auxiliary, there is a tendency to refer to the item itself as 'the copula', regardless of its contextual function. In French, for instance, *est* can be loosely referred to as the copula in all the following frames: *il est grand* 'he is tall', *il est médecin* 'he is a doctor', *il est fatigué* 'he is tired', *il est arrivé* 'he arrived', *c'est Jean* 'it is John', and *je ne sais pas où il est* 'I don't know where he is'.

In transferring the concept to creoles, we shall need to separate out the various functions. All Romance creoles use an overt particle to mark presentative and existential constructions: Guy. /sa bõ, a mo/ 'it is good, it is me', Mau. /se mwa (sa), en fwa ti ena .../ 'it is me, once upon a time there was ...', GBi. /i kin ↑/ 'who is it?' (literally 'is who?'), STo. /piʃi sẽ/ 'there is fish', Pap. /el a wetu ku tabata un larejna/ 'he saw that it was a queen', Hai. /m pa kon ola li je/ 'I don't know where he is'. (With the exception of Pap. /tabata/, all the particles just quoted differ formally from those used to mark tense and aspect.) Most creoles also require a marker, often identical to the presentative, before nominal predicates, as in /ʒã se (jun) bulãʒe/ 'John is a baker' (valid, with minor phonological adjustments, in Louisiana, Haïti and most of the eastern Caribbean). Whereas the presentative can be distinguished without difficulty from a copula in the earlier examples, this latter type is more problematic for analysts who wish to avoid recognising a copula. Their strongest argument is that /se/ does not behave like a conventional verb: it admits only a subset of tense–aspect markers and not in the same collocations; 'John was a baker' is rendered /ʒã se te (jun) bulãʒe/ not */ʒã te se .../ as we might expect. A possible analysis would be to treat /ʒã/ as an extraposed subject, in effect /ʒã, se .../, thus maintaining /se/ as a presentative in all its manifestations.

Let us now turn to one very widespread construction that lacks an overt copula. The following examples all represent equative predicates: Hai. /li gwo, li bjè, li malad/ 'he (is) fat, he (is) fine, he (is) ill', Cha. /el hente de sjudad bjen bugalon/ 'city folk (are) pretty stuck-up', Pri. /rima mɛ fɔrti/ 'my brother (is) strong', Mau. /laplim la dã so pos, li larejõ/ 'the pen (is) in her pocket, she (is in) Réunion'. In terms of surface representation, these are quite uncontentious: the meanings of all the morphemes are agreed and no item remains that could conceivably be analysed as a copula. It seems, therefore, that we have a straight choice between claiming that the creole has no copula at any level, or that an underlying copula is obligatorily deleted on the surface. The decision taken on this narrow issue necessarily

affects the structure of the predicate as a whole. The deletion hypothesis
favours the recognition of a set of adjectival predicates and hence of 'adjective' as an independent grammatical category; whereas the no-copula
analysis implies that the predicates are essentially verbal, so undermining
the case for an adjectival category.

The preceding examples are all neutral in time reference. Suppose we
now change this by means of the marker system, as in: Hai. /li te gwo/ 'he
was fat', Mau. /li ti fin malad/ 'he had been ill', Pri. /rima mɛ tava fɔrti/
'my brother was strong', Pap. /nan tabata maʃa pober/ 'they were
extremely poor'. Immediately we introduce a new item into the surface
structure we also open up a new series of analytic choices. If, for instance,
we had previously regarded /gwo/, /malad/, /fɔrti/ and /pober/ as verbal predicates, we should be confirmed in that belief on discovering that
they have the same privilege of occurrence with the tense–aspect markers
as other verbs. But the argument can be stood on its head: if the predicates
are classified as adjectives, this in turn invites us to reclassify the item that
we have so far assumed to be a tense–aspect marker, as a tensed copula.
Moreover, if /te, tava/ are regarded as copulas in predicative constructions, so that Hai. /li gwo/ is analysed as equivalent to Fr. *il était
gros* in synchronic structure as well as etymology, then /te, tava/ in other
contexts can be viewed as auxiliaries, precisely as the copula has auxiliary
functions in European Romance. In this way, an apparently limited debate
on the status of copula suddenly widens to embrace the entire verb system.

We cannot examine all of the ramifications of the debate here. The polar
positions are stark: /li te gwo/ is to be represented in the 'no-copula'
analysis as $_S[_{NP}[li]$ $_{VP}[past +$ $_V[gwo]]]$, in which case the creole has
'adjectival verbs' but no separate category of adjective; or alternatively, in
the 'etymological' analysis, as $_S[_{NP}[li]$ $_{VP}[$ $_{Vcop}[te]$ $_{ADJ}[gwo]]]$, in which case
the creole has independent adjectives and an auxiliary system similar in
function if not in form to that of the lexifier. For linguists seeking an
intermediate position (we have so far adopted the 'radical restructuring'
view of the tense–aspect markers while still recognising the independence
of adjectives), the difficulty lies in disentangling intrasystemic from sociolinguistic considerations. A basilectal creole that at present functions on the
radically restructured underlying system, nevertheless has a surface manifestation which lends itself to the importation of overt copula constructions
from the acrolect. The systematic spread of overt copulas in predicative
structures might well be enough, within a single generation, to reverse the
earlier restructuring and give the etymological analysis new currency. Such
'decreolisation' does indeed seem to have affected, for instance, Caboverdiano, which employs an overt copula in precisely those constructions
where Principense has no marker: Cab. /mjɛ irmõ e fɔrt/ 'my brother is
strong'. Most varieties of Caboverdiano likewise have a past-tense copula
on the Portuguese model: compare Cab. /ʃ el ɛra bõn amigu/ 'if he were a

good friend' with STo. /ʃ e ka sa bwa migu/. Such relatively minor surface discrepancies probably betoken major differences in underlying systems.

What should now be clear is that only the most procrustean of theoretical models could make all Romance creoles appear to share an identical verb system. To conclude this section, we shall briefly contrast two neighbouring creoles with divergent systems, Mauritian and Réunionnais. Mauritian, as we said earlier, has an especially well developed set of tense-aspect markers, and a presentative particle /se/ which does not impinge on their operation. Mauritian differs crucially from the Caribbean creoles like Haitian in accepting nominal equative predicates with no overt copula or presentative, hence /zã bulãze/ 'John (is a) baker'. (Such predicates nevertheless remain distinguishable from conventional verbs because they do not admit the full range of markers: /zã ti bulãze/ 'John was (a) baker', but not /*fek, *fin, *pe bulãze/.) In Réunionnais, on the other hand, a form /le/ < Fr. *(i)l + est*, is used in all three of the contexts we have identified as criterial: before predicative adjectives — /mõ frer le malad/ 'my brother is ill', before equative nouns — /mõ frer le bulãze/ 'my brother is a baker', and in predicate-final position — /usa li le#/ 'where he is'. There is no persuasive reason for not analysing /le/ as a copula. Moreover, when we also note that Réunionnais has an alternative future inflection /-ra/, as in /s(o)ra/ < Fr. *sera*, and, uniquely among the creoles lexified from French, traces of a conditional, a recent past marker /vjẽd/ < Fr. *vient de*, and a negative /pa/ which follows the verb stem, we should be justified in concluding that in the structure of its verbal group it is more similar to popular French than to the neighbouring Indian Ocean creoles. Whether Réunionnais has always had this structure (perhaps as a consequence of its settlement history), or has evolved it as a result of decreolisation towards the metropolitan norm, is a hotly contested issue on which we cannot pronounce here. In the eyes of most analysts, Réunionnais — like Cabo-verdiano — is still sufficiently distinct from its European lexifier to be grouped among the creoles. But we should recognise that this classification entails some relaxing of previous typological definitions.

Sentence Structure
Minimal declarative sentences in Romance creoles fall into two basic types: presentative and pivotal. Presentatives consist of a particle plus a contentive, usually in that order, and are used to assert the existence of a single underlying argument, as in Hai. /se mwẽ/, GBi. /i aˈmi/ 'it's me', Mau. /ena duri/, STo. /losu sẽ/ 'there's rice' (see also p. 455). Pivotal structures consist of two underlying arguments, best viewed pragmatically as a topic and comment, and in most creoles always appearing on the surface in that order: Guy. /mo dãˈse/ 'I danced', STo. /e taˈsõ/ 'he sat down', Hai. /kaj-la pwɔp/ 'the house is clean', GBi. /kasa kema/ 'the house is on fire'. Since no Romance creole is a 'PRO-drop' language, a declarative utterance

cannot consist of a bare verb, as would be possible in most southern varieties of European Romance (see, for instance, p. 93), although bare verbs do occur in all creoles as imperatives.

Transitive constructions are represented usually — and in some creoles obligatorily — by SVO patterns. (Chabacano is the only Romance creole regularly to permit subject–verb inversion, for the most part limited to personal pronouns and probably under the influence of Spanish; see p. 116.) The rigidity of word order can be mainly ascribed to the absence of inflection, which has removed any overt marking of subject–verb concord, just as in earlier Romance it led to a loss of distinctiveness between subjects and objects. (Chabacano and Réunionnais are both exceptional in using prepositional accusatives, see pp. 106 and 448.) Most creoles also fail to distinguish overtly between direct and indirect objects: Dom. /u ʒa di Ø madam mwĕ listwer sa/ 'you've already told my wife that story', GBi. /buska Ø alɡin ɡera/ 'to declare war on someone'. Moreover, several use no preposition to mark adnominal possessives or partitives: Hai. /pɔt Ø kaj Ø frɛ mwẽ/ 'the door of my brother's house', /bwat Ø alimɛt/ 'box of matches', Mau. /en po Ø diber/ 'a pot of butter' (*diber* is a restructured noun). Occasionally, even locatives are unmarked, as in Hai. /li Ø lekɔl/ 'she's at school', Mau. /li Ø larejõ/ 'she's in Réunion', GBi. /i baj Ø fera/ 'he went to market'; but more commonly they require a preposition, as in Lou. /jɛ parti kuri dã bwa/ 'they ran off into the wood' (literally 'they departed ran in wood'), Cha. /ja sa'li ele na kusina/ 'she went into the kitchen' (literally 'past went-out she in kitchen'). In practice, most catenated noun phrases are disambiguated by context or by word order conventions: the thing possessed always precedes the possessor, and indirect objects usually precede direct, probably as a result of a more general preference for ordering animates before inanimates: Dom. /ba mwĕ i/ 'give it to me' (literally 'give me it').

Perhaps the most salient difference in sentence structure between European Romance and creoles lies in the treatment of pronominal objects. In creole, these follow the verb and have the same privilege of occurrence as full object noun phrases, witness Pap. /mi ta mira bo, ... bo tata/ 'I see you, ... your father' (literally 'I imperf. see you'), SLu. /u kaj ale we jo, ... we kuzin jo/ 'you'll go and see them, ... their cousin' (literally 'you pros. go see them'). Like nominal objects, pronouns can also be directly co-ordinated with other noun phrases, as in Hai. /mwĕ te kõnĕ jo epi kamwad jo/ 'I knew (both) them and their friends'. Although pronouns are phonetically insubstantial and liable to morphophonemic reduction making them enclitic on the verb, as in Hai. /jo wɛ-n/ 'they saw us', GBi. /no odʒa-l/ 'we saw him' (see also p. 451), they are in principle free forms, and therefore no creole has an obligatory rule of clitic doubling.

The absence of preverbal clitic objects also means that creoles have no morphological category of reflexive verbs, those that are inherently reflexive in European Romance being reanalysed in creole either as simple stems or, more rarely, as serial verbs: Hai. /ʃita/, STo. /taˈsõ/ 'sit down', versus Pap. /kaj sinti/ literally 'fall sit'. When a sentence is semantically reflexive, most creoles require either a pronoun reinforced by /mes ~ mem/ 'self' or an overt lexical item which is more or less grammaticalised: Pap. /e tabata laba su mes/ 'he was washing himself', Hai. /li tuje tɛt li/, GBi. /li mata si kabesa/ 'he killed himself' (literally 'his head'), Hai. /jo rɛ̃mɛ̃ kadav jo/ 'they are vain' (literally 'they love body their'), Mau. /li-n zet so lekor dã dilo/ 'he flung himself (his body) into the sea', Sey. /mõ pa ti konɛ̃ ki mõ pu fer avek mõ lekor/ 'I didn't know what to do with myself (my body)'. Similarly, some creoles have lexical means of expressing reciprocity, one fully grammaticalised example being Sey. /kamarad/ 'friend(ly)' as in /zot kõtã kamarad/ 'they love each other'. Occasionally, too, reflexives and reciprocals are functionally differentiated in ways not immediately transparent, witness Guy. /je ɡade je kɔ/ 'they looked at themselves (their bodies)' versus /je ɡade je/ 'they looked at each other'.

Sentential negation is effected in most creoles by inserting a negative particle between the subject and the entire predicate phrase including the tense–aspect markers. The particle itself usually derives from Fr. /pa/, Port. /não/ or Sp. /no/, though /ka/ < nunca 'never' also has a wide currency in the west African group. By far the most common pattern, in which negation has only forward scope, is illustrated by: Pap. /bo no a vini/ 'you didn't come' (literally 'you neg. past come'), /mi-n tin nada di hasi/ 'I've nothing to do', Cha. /el vjeha no pwede dolˈmi/ 'the old woman can't sleep', SLu. /mwɛ̃ pa te kaj vle vini/ 'I shouldn't have liked to come', Mau. /li pa pu dir narjɛ̃/ 'he won't say anything', GBi. /kil ka na atraza ninɡin/ 'that didn't attract anyone', Cab. /mãˈɲã n-ka ta ba saˈi/ 'tomorrow I shan't go out'. By contrast, Palenquero marks negation by predicate-final /nu/, as in /i miˈna bo nu/ 'I didn't see you' (literally 'I saw you not'), /bo e ri aki nu/ 'you're not from here', /aˈne pule aˈbla ku bo nu/ 'they can't speak to you'. An apparently identical pattern is found in Principense, using a marker /fa/, of uncertain origin; but this distribution may be the result of recent reductive change since neighbouring São Tomense uses an 'embracing' structure /na fa/, as in /n-na ka ʃe amãˈɲã fa/ 'I shan't go out tomorrow' (note that STo. /ka/ is an imperfective marker, not a negative!). The most complicated distribution is found in Réunionnais. Here, the marker /pa/ follows a bare verb, but precedes any object, as in /li mãz pa sel/ 'he doesn't eat salt'. It also follows certain tense–aspect markers while preceding others, as in /li va pa travaj/ 'he won't work' versus /nu le pa dormir/ 'we won't sleep', or /li lete pa ãtrɛd dormir/ 'he wasn't sleeping'. If, however, we give /va, le, lete/ their etymological values as auxiliaries (see p. 457), then once again the affinity of Réunionnais to popular French, and its eccentricity in comparison with the other creoles, stand out quite unmistakably.

Turning now to interrogatives, we find that all creoles make contrastive use of rising intonation to differentiate yes-no questions from statements, as in Mau. /li pa vo lapen ↑/ 'isn't it worthwhile?' versus /li pa vo lapen ↓/ 'it's not worthwhile'. Various alternative patterns are attested, the two most frequent being an invariable interrogative marker in sentence-initial position and a 'tag' particle occurring in final position. Among the creoles lexified from French, /eske ~ es ~ eski/ are used as introducers, /nõ ↑, ẽ ↑, pa vre ↑/ as tags. In the Indian Ocean group /eski/ tends to be confined to acrolectal usage, whereas in the Caribbean such introducers are more widespread, Haitian having developed an additional particle for negative interrogatives — compare Hai. /apa u kõtã ↑/ with Dom. /es u pa kõtã ↑/ and Sey. /u pa kõtã, nõ ↑/, all meaning 'aren't you happy?'. Tags derived from Port. /não/ or Sp. /no/ are also widely distributed, while one variety of Chabacano uses a particle /ha ↑/ in identical contexts: /ku'si bos este mana kaŋɾeho bweno bweno, ha ↑/ '(be sure) you cook these crabs really well, won't you?'. Chabacano, however, also has a specific interrogative particle /ba/, probably derived from Tagalog, which is placed after the verb in yes-no questions, or otherwise after the interrogative word.

So far, creole questions differ very little from their counterparts in European Romance. A conspicuous discrepancy occurs in phrasal interrogatives, where most creoles require QU-fronting and also pied piping of prepositions but not subject–verb inversion, as in Pap. /pa kiku bo ta kome karni/ 'why do you eat meat?' (literally 'for what you imperf. eat meat?'), Cab. /pur'ke bo pa'ga lum/ 'why did you put the fire out?', Hai. /ki mun u te wɛ/ 'who did you see?', Mau. /ki kote zot travaj aster/ 'where do they work now?', Pal. /kẽŋ bo a'ta kuʧa/ 'who are you listening to?', Sey. /lor ki u ti pe koze/ 'who were you talking about?'. Some creoles require both an interrogative word and a marker, but again without disruption of the normal declarative word order: Pri. /kwe mãda ki ti pa'ga ufogu ã ↑/ 'why did you put the fire out?' (literally 'what ordered that you put-out fire Q'). Questions without QU-fronting are occasionally found, especially in adverbial contexts, where a contributory factor may be the wish to avoid a 'dummy' copula that would otherwise be necessary; compare two renderings of 'where is your car?' in Mauritian: /u loto ki kote ↑/ literally 'your car what place?', /ki kote u loto ete/ 'what place your car is?' (see also p. 457). Crioulo stands out from the other Romance creoles in regularly forming questions without QU-fronting: witness GBi. /i kin ↑/ 'who is it?' (literally 'be who?'), /a'bo i fidʒu di kin ↑/ 'whose son are you?' (literally 'you be son of who?').

Complex Sentences
We end this section with a brief examination of more complex sentences where creoles not only differ from European Romance, but also diverge from one another, in surface organisation if not more deeply. The diversity

stems from differing requirements for overt marking of subordination. Predictably, analysts disagree as to whether unmarked structures are genuinely paratactic, in which case the dichotomy of subordination and coordination may be invalid; or whether complementisers and relativising particles present in underlying structure are deleted by low-level optional rules, in which case the categories themselves remain intact. The real difficulty can be limited to complementation and relative clauses, since indirect questions and adverbial clauses almost always require an overt marker, as in Sey. /i ti dir nu, kimajer i n arive/ 'he told us how he got there', Cab. /m baj ɲa kamiɲu, pamodi ka tiɲa nada di bebi/ 'I went away because I'd nothing to drink'. In addition, relativisation on a subject noun phrase is almost universally marked: Cha. /un tibol ki ja ki'bra kon el golpe/ 'a pot that broke on impact', STo. /migu sɛ ku bjɛj ôte/ 'the friend who came yesterday', Sey. /lakaz ki ana laport ruz/ 'the house that has a red door', Hai. /timun ki rete avɛk mãmã jo/ 'the children who lived with their mother'.

The creoles part company, however, in the way they relativise any nominal below subject in the accessibility hierarchy, and to a lesser extent also in their treatment of complementation. Indian Ocean creoles prefer a marker for relatives: Sey. /premje nuvel ki mõ tãde/ 'the first news that I heard', Mau. /mo-n gute sa dite la ki zot ti aste/ 'I've tasted the tea (that) they bought'. In these varieties, the relativisation of underlying prepositional phrases requires a marker, with pied piping of the preposition in acrolectal usage, but often its deletion in the basilect, hence: Mau. /misje-la avek ki mo ti parle/ 'the gentleman to whom I was speaking', Sey. /li ti rãtre dã lasam ki mõ pe dormi Ø/ 'he came into the room that I was sleeping (in)'. By contrast, Haitian and most other Caribbean varieties have no overt marker for simple relatives — /se te jun gasõ Ø jo rele zãpjɛ/ 'it was a boy they called Jean-Pierre'. Accordingly, they relativise underlying prepositional phrases by inserting into the surface noun phrase a complete sentence without coordination reduction — /gasõ Ø u rive ak li-a se frɛ li/ 'the boy you came with is her brother' (literally 'boy you came with him -det. is brother her'). Slightly different again are the creoles of the west African group, which lack coordination reduction but nevertheless require a relative marker, hence: GBi. /kil ke no pudi fala li/ 'what we can say (it)', /kaw ku bu e na kriadu n-el/ 'the house where you were born' (literally 'house that you were imperf. born in-it'), STo. /migu sɛ ku-N fla klu-e/ 'the friend I spoke to' (literally 'friend dem. that-1 spoke with-him').

Needless to add, the patterns for complementation cross-cut those of relatives. In Indian Ocean creoles, speakers vary in their judgements, some insisting on a complementiser while others accept its deletion in at least the following contexts: Sey. /mõ war (ki) u pa kõtã/ 'I can see (that) you're unhappy', Mau. /mo kone (ki) so frer in mor/ 'I know (that) his brother has died'. In Caribbean varieties, no marker is required for complements of assertion, though these do sometimes have a dummy head: Mar. /mwĕ kwe Ø i bõ/ 'I think he's good', Guy. /mo sere sa Ø to baj mo/ 'I put away what you gave me'. In the west African group, however, the position is more complicated. Complements of assertion may be introduced by zero or by /kuma/ 'how': GBi. /i fala Ø i ka staba el son/ 'he said he wasn't alone', /i fala kuma i na ba dʒubi si paǀpe/ 'he said that he would go and see his father'; whereas complements of wishing, ordering or suggesting are introduced by /pa/ 'for', as in: GBi. /i fala nu pa no fusi/ 'he advised us to run away' (literally 'he said (to) us for we flee'), Cab. /n kre pa seʃ fidʒ sai aɡora/ 'I want his sons to leave now'. This last pattern closely parallels an apparent innovation in Haitian which is extending the use of /pu/ as a complementiser to contexts where previously there would have been no marker: /jo te vle pu m le ãtre/ 'they wanted (for) me to come in', versus /li tan Ø nu vini/ 'he's waiting for us to come'. Innovations of this kind, whatever their motivation, have the effect of reducing the incidence of creole parataxis to the benefit of hypotactic constructions more akin, though not identical, to those of European Romance. It seems, too, that Haitian, like the west African creoles before, is marking by a grammatical device a set of semantically coherent predicates — a set very similar to that which demarcates for European Romance between indicative and subjunctive complementation or, to regress a further stage, between accusative-and-infinitive and UT-type complements in Latin (see pp. 65–70).

5   Lexis

Lexical Relationships

The high degree of lexical relationship between Romance creoles and their respective lexifiers can be illustrated by means of the standard lexicostatistical list of 100 basic concepts. On this basis, Haitian shares with French 72 per cent of strict cognates, a further 17 per cent of restructured cognates incorporating an original determiner or liaison consonant, and nine per cent of items which, while not cognate by synchronic function, represent lexical shifts that would be easily identifiable to a French speaker. Only two items would probably be unrecognisable: /ba ~ baj/ 'give', usually derived from dialectal *bailler* but probably a blend (Wolof and Hausa both have near homophones of similar meaning), and /ʃita ~ ʃinta/ 'sit down', again probably a blend, this time of Romance material (perhaps of Port. /senta/ or Sp. /sjenta/ with dialectal Fr. /sita ~ asita/).

The overall relationship between French and Seychellois is just as strong: of the 100-word list, every item can be traced etymologically to French and the great majority remain transparent. Seychellois does, however, have a much higher index of restructuring than Haitian, so that the proportions of strict cognates (53 per cent) and of restructured forms (37 per cent) differ appreciably. If Seychellois and Haitian are compared, they are found to share 63 per cent of strict cognates, a higher proportion than Seychellois shares with French, owing to a ten per cent overlap of innovations away from French, of which one is a lexical extension (the semantic range of both *connaître* and *savoir* is covered by /koné/ 'know'), and the others are shared restructurings, illustrated by /dife/ 'fire' < Fr. *du + feu*, /lalin/ 'moon' < *la + lune*, /lanwit/ 'night' < *la + nuit*, /lapli/ 'rain' < *la + pluie*, /zetwal/ 'star' < *S + étoile*.

Extending the analysis to Portuguese and Crioulo reveals an overall cognacy rate of 96 per cent including 80 per cent strict cognates. Most of the remaining items involve either a small semantic change (/fala/ 'speak, say, tell' covers the range of both Port. *dizer* and *falar*; /garganti/ 'neck, throat' covers both *colo* and *garganta*) or a preference for the less common of two near synonyms in European Portuguese (/ka'tʃur/ 'dog' < *cachorro* rather than *cão*, /kumpridu/ 'long' < *comprido* rather than *longo*). Three items are probably borrowed from neighbouring African languages, including /dʒubi/ 'see' < Mandinka /dʒubi/ 'look at'; and in two cases only, there seems to have been restructuring on a non-European model, in /ditanda/ 'to lie down' < Port. *deitar* with a causative suffix (see p. 450), and in /burmedʒu tʃau/, the nearest equivalent of 'yellow', which combines Port. *vermelho* 'red' with an intensifier meaning approximately 'bright, shiny' (see below).

A similar exercise performed on Papiamentu, however, quickly illustrates the difficulty of affiliating Papiamentu to a single lexifier. Only two items of the basic list derive from a source other than Romance: /hel ~ gel/ 'yellow' and /santu/ 'sand' are probably both Dutch, from *geel* and *zand* respectively. The largest single group, amounting to 40 per cent, corresponds to a set of lexical items which are both cognate and phonologically very similar in Portuguese and Spanish, thus providing no evidence for differential attribution. A further 26 per cent are probably cognate with Spanish, many of them positively identifiable because of their phonetic shape, as in Pap. /wesu/ 'bone' < Sp. *hueso* (Port. *osso*), /webu/ 'egg' < Sp. *huevo* (Port. *ovo*), /jen/ 'full' < Sp. *lleno* (Port. *cheio*), /rudia/ 'knee' < Sp. *rodilla* (Port. *joelho*), /huma/ 'smoke' < Sp. *humo* (Port. *fumo*). Nine per cent can, with some certainty, be identified as cognate with Portuguese, including Pap. /pretu/ 'black' < Port. *preto* (Sp. *negro*), /tera/ 'earth' < Port. *terra* (Sp. *tierra*), /foja/ 'leaf' < Port. *folha* (Sp. *hoja*), /nobo/ 'new' < Port. *novo* (Sp. *nuevo*). This leaves just over one fifth of the total, all transparently derived from Ibero-Romance but not synchronically equivalent to their European congeners. Again, most of these are difficult to attribute differentially, though the few clear instances favour Spanish: /katʃu/ 'horn' < Sp. *cacho* (designating a small horn or branch of an antler, rather than the superordinate *cuerno*), /ko'ra/ 'red' < Am. Sp. *colorado* (replacing European Spanish *rojo*),

/ʧiki/ 'small' < *chico* (formerly an adjective in Spanish but now a noun meaning 'boy'). If we now disregard synchronic equivalence and view the Romance component of Papiamentu in purely etymological terms, we find that over half of the total is not differentially attributable and that the remainder can be ascribed to Spanish and Portuguese in the approximate ratio 3:1. This would be consistent with the hypothesis that an original Portuguese pidgin, when creolised, underwent lexical expansion from Spanish. But the evidence is not so clear as to exclude several other possibilities.

A great deal of philological effort has been devoted to the detection of 'popular', archaic and dialectal antecedents in creole vocabulary. The above examples, however, demonstrate that the core vocabulary of the Romance creoles can usually be related to a more or less standard form of the European lexifier. It is therefore important to keep a sense of proportion: non-standard terms do survive in all creoles, but they are neither very numerous in the total stock nor noticeably frequent in discourse. An investigation of some 400 common terms in Haitian revealed that 92 per cent are related to French, 60 per cent having cognates in the contemporary standard language, a further 16 per cent representing creole innovations, and 16 per cent being attributable to dialectal or archaic usage. A similar investigation of a much larger corpus of Seychellois has found that items related to French amount to 86 per cent of the total, subdivided into 55 per cent cognate with standard usage, 22 per cent creole innovations and nine per cent dialectal survivals or archaisms. On a still larger corpus, but relying on rather different criteria for classification, Réunionnais has been shown to preserve a much higher proportion of non-standard French terms — some 32 per cent of its total stock.

In practice, it is often difficult to differentiate between genuine dialect words, terms which may have had a wider currency at the time of creolisation and have only subsequently become confined to remote districts, and items which may have undergone parallel but coincidental semantic changes. Established dialectalisms include: Hai. /mize/, Réu. /amize/ 'take one's time', Sey. /nik/ 'nest', Guy. /tirwet/ 'drawer', and Trinidadian /kalɔʒ/ 'kennel', /kuʃɛt/ 'baby clothes', /palavire/ 'blow, cuff', all having cognates in Norman or other western dialects; and Hai. /kabrit/, Réu. /kabri/ 'goat, kid', identifiable as a Picard or Poitevin term because of the non-palatalisation of initial /k-/. Several other creole terms share with Norman a meaning which diverges from that of the standard French equivalent: Hai. /rete/, Réu. /reste/ 'to live', Hai. /kite/ 'leave behind, let', Hai., Mau., Sey. /gete/ 'look at, watch', Hai., Réu. /visje/ 'cunning, crafty', and Guy. /sere/ 'hide, put away'; in all these cases, the slight shift in meaning follows common semantic pathways and could be coincidental. Non-standard vocabulary in the creoles lexified from Spanish or Portuguese has not been so well studied. Two incontrovertible examples from

Chabacano are /tjaŋge/ 'market' and /sakate/ 'grass', both originally from Nahuatl and still widely used in Mexican Spanish (see p. 120). They serve as a vivid reminder of the effects of the Treaty of Tordesillas of 1494, whereby Spain could only approach its outpost in the Philippines across the Pacific, via its well established colony in Mexico.

As the preceding statistics show, words of non-Romance origin make up a relatively small proportion of the core vocabulary, though their incidence may be greater in specific domains. Detailed etymologies still require investigation for many items, particularly in the Caribbean creoles, and it is therefore not always possible to distinguish between those arising directly from one of the contributor languages (which could be loosely described as the 'substrate', but see p. 425), and those due to subsequent borrowing from adstrate languages or from neighbouring creoles. The most straight-forward case is that of Chabacano, some varieties of which have always been in contact with Tagalog. Examples, mainly nouns of domestic import, include: /nana ~ naj/ 'mother', /tata ~ taj/ 'father', /anak/ 'child' (common to Cebuano and Ilongo), /dalaga/ 'virgin', /kansaŋkapan/ 'household goods', /ka'lan/ 'stove', /ulam/ 'food', /baguŋ/ 'salt fish', /kamote/ 'sweet potato', /sagiŋ/ 'banana'; and the verb /subuk/ 'watch over'. Malagasy words are widely distributed in Indian Ocean creoles, but rarely found further afield. They include: Réu., Mau., Sey. /malāŋ/ 'filthy', /taman/ 'sterile', /kelkel/ 'armpit', /sigid ~ sikid/ 'lucky charm', /kābar/ 'yam', /tatan ~ tātā/ 'castor oil', /urit ~ zurit/ 'octopus'.

In the Caribbean area, non-Romance items may derive from many more sources, among which the following west African languages have been positively identified: Wolof, Mandinka, Ewe, Edo, Twi, Yoruba, Hausa, Bambara, Diola and Kikongo. Palenquero, for instance, preserves a series of words from Kikongo: /mo'na/ 'son', /mamblojo/ 'lazybones', /kankamana/ 'witch-doctor', /ŋgombe/ 'ox, cattle', /ŋguba/ 'groundnut', and probably /ʧibumbe/ 'death'. Widely used items known to be African but still requiring etymological research, include: the terms associated with voodoo rites (see p. 430), /obja/ 'spell' (probably cognate with Twi /obia'fo/ 'witch'), /bābula/ 'drum', /gōbo /'okra', /kalaku/ 'soup made with okra', /mundoŋ/ 'cannibal' and /bonda ~ būda/ 'backside', prob-ably from Bambara /boda/. To the possible blends of Romance and non-Romance roots mentioned earlier (p. 450), we should add the St Lucian first person suppletive negatives /ma, ma:, maj/, which could be explained as morphophonemic alternants of /mwe + pa/, but may also be crossed with the Mandinka negative marker /maŋ/. A further puzzle is /piŋga ~ pīga ~ pãga ~ pãgar/, widely distributed in the Caribbean and Indian Ocean groups, and meaning variously 'be careful, take care not to, don't (as an introducer of negative imperatives)' and in Mauritian also 'lest, for fear that'. The two suggested etyma are the common Bantu verbal root /pinga/ 'prevent' and Fr. *prends garde*; both entail some semantic adjustment, with the phonological structure marginally favouring Bantu in the Caribbean and French in the Indian Ocean.

Two groups of highly characteristic words whose origin is not in doubt occur in the west African creoles: intensifiers and ideophones. Intensifiers, which are monosyllabic and non-onomatopoeic, can be very general or highly specific in their semantic range. Crioulo, for instance, has general intensifiers like /de/ and /nan/, as in /i baj dʒa nan/ roughly 'he's already left, so there!', together with specific terms collocationally limited to predicates of colour, fullness and emptiness, as in /pretu nok/ 'very black, jet black', /intʃi kun/ 'full right up', /seku kan/ 'bone dry'. Crioulo, São Tomense and Principense all possess ideophones, which are longer and more evocative than intensifiers, and can in principle modify any contentive. In São Tomense, /ˈŋwiniˈŋwini/ connotes 'smallness', /zuzuˈzu/ 'heat', /kɔkɔˈkɔ/ 'cold', /loloˈlo/ 'fullness', /fɛnɛˈnɛ/ 'brilliance', and /sasaˈsa/ 'softness'. Ideophones can only occur in clause-final position and may not be combined with any other intensifier or qualifying adverbial: STo. /e ʃka tleme ˈgidiˈgidi/ 'he's trembling all over', /kopu kɛˈbla ˈŋwiniˈŋwini/ 'the glass broke into tiny pieces (smashed to smithereens)'.

Adaptive Patterns
We have already discussed some of the modifications in phonology and morphology undergone by Romance items during creolisation (see pp. 436 and 443). Morphological restructuring is attested in differing measure in all the creoles lexified from French, but is not confined to them, witness STo. /ɔˈpɛ/ 'leg' < Port. o + pé, /ɔˈmali/ 'sea' < o + mar, /aˈfɛ/ 'faith' < a + fé, /ˈunu/ 'naked, nakedness' < o + nu, Pri. /uˈfogu/ 'fire' < o + fogo, /uˈkuru/ 'raw, rawness' < o + cru.

It has recently been suggested that the agglutination of etymological determiners, which is very unevenly distributed among the present-day creoles, should be distinguished from purely phonological restructuring involving a liaison consonant. Agglutination is particularly frequent in Mauritian and Seychellois, moderately frequent in the Gulf of Guinea and Caribbean groups, and very rare in Réunionnais, Crioulo and Caboverdiano. The suggested explanation is that the distribution coincides with that of significant numbers of Bantu speakers, whose previous linguistic experience would lead them to expect nouns to have class prefixes. They would therefore analyse de l'eau, for instance, as /de-lo/, composed of a class marker for [mass] followed by the lexical stem. Metanalysis along these lines may be a contributory factor, but it cannot be the whole story: agglutination of determiners is completely absent not only from a creole like Chabacano, which — as predicted — has no Bantu connections, but also from Palenquero and Papiamentu, which almost certainly do.

Nor is it certain that agglutination and phonological restructuring can be so cleanly separated. The critical case is the reanalysis of the liaison consonant /z-/ which, in the creoles lexified from French, necessarily correlates with the feature [+count]. In modern Haitian, at least 60 per cent of the words with initial /z-/ represent historical reanalyses, while 40 per cent or less preserve an etymological /z-/, whether or not Romance in origin. In Mauritian and Seychellois, the proportions are reversed, with only 35–40 per cent due to historical restructuring. The reason, of course, is that Indian Ocean creoles acquired many new words with initial /z-/ as a result of the unconditioned merger of the French phonemes /z/ and /ʒ/ (see p. 439), a change which must be presumed to date from the earliest phase of creolisation. Now, if Bantu-speaking slaves in Mauritius analysed /de-, di-, la-, li-/ as noun class prefixes, it would be strange if there were no trace of a parallel analysis of the large class of nouns in /z-/, almost all of which conform — albeit fortuitously — to the [+count] category. In fact, there are a few such traces: Sey. /zãɡiv/ 'type of vegetable' and /zurit/ 'octopus' both derive from Malagasy words without initial /z-/, as does /zestra/ 'overtime' < English *extra*. Similar instances of 'unmotivated' /z-/ occur in Caribbean creoles: Hai. /zanana/ 'pineapple' < Guaraní *ananá*, SLu. /zandoli/, Guy. /zãdoli/ 'lizard' < Carib *anoli*. At this remove and in the absence of documentation, we cannot say whether such forms were mediated phonologically by French speakers, or whether they were directly adapted by creole speakers to fit into a perceived morphological class. What is clear, yet again, is that speakers of Réunionnais, when faced with comparable data, arrived at a different analysis, one more in tune with metropolitan French.

Some creole reanalyses involve changes of grammatical category. We have already mentiond /kapa ~ kapav/ 'be able' and /kõtã/ 'love', deriving from French adjectives but now indistinguishable from other verbs. Mauritian has taken one further step by using /kõtã/ as a noun meaning 'boyfriend, girlfriend'. It likewise extends the use of the verbal adjunct /pãgar/ as a conjunction meaning 'lest' (see p. 465). Similar radical shifts include: Caribbean /lɛ/ < Fr. *l'heure*, now the adverb 'when', and /pito/ < *plutôt*, now the verb 'prefer' (compare Sey. /plifere/, from *préférer* perhaps crossed with *plus*); Sey., Réu. /fernwar/ 'darkness' < *faire noir*; Sey. /kokẽ/ < *coquin*, meaning both 'thief' and 'to steal'; Mau. /narjẽ/ 'nothing' < *(il) n'y a rien*; and Sey. /ferkwa/ 'why' < *faire quoi*. The original terms for 'why' and 'because' have been replaced in several creoles by periphrases; perhaps the most striking is /pamodi/, found in a basilectal variety of Caboverdiano, and cognate with Port. *pa'amor de* 'for the love of ...'!

Semantic changes and lexical shifts in creoles are occasionally spectacular but not especially numerous, even disregarding the possibility that some of them may already have taken place in a non-standard Romance input to creolisation. The most common process is semantic extension, enabling a familiar term to cover aspects of an unfamiliar environment; so Hai. /zirõdɛl/ < Fr. *S* + *hirondelle* 'swallow' refers to a large dragonfly; Guy. /kulev/ < *couleuvre* 'snake' now designates any form of reptile; and in many creoles /muʃ ~ mus/ < *mouche* 'fly' denotes also a wasp or indeed any kind of flying insect (Hai. /mjɛl/ 'bee' < *miel* 'honey' is probably an ellipsis of dialectal *mouche à miel*). One set of lexical shifts affecting several creoles seems best explained as the generalisation of nautical terminology: Hai. /mare/, Mau. /amare/, Sey. /ãmare/ 'to tie, fix, hold back' < Fr. *amarrer* 'to moor a ship' (compare STo. /maˈla/ < Port. *amarrar* now with parallel meanings); Hai. /lage/, Mau./Sey. /larɡe/ 'to let go' < Fr. *larguer* 'to untie a ship'; Hai. /ʃavire/, Mau./Sey. /savire/ 'to upset, turn over, fall over' < *chavirer* 'to capsize'. Such substitutions, whether isolated or in sets, may perhaps combine to produce a cumulative morphological effect. Consider the following examples from Mauritian: /ɡet/ 'see' < *guetter*, /rezid/ 'live' < *résider*, /plãt/ 'put' < *planter*, /ramas/ 'pick' < *ramasser*, /tap/ 'hit, knock' < *taper*, /deɡaz/ 'hurry' < *dégager*, /ɡalup/ 'run' < *galoper* (/kuri/ < *courir* now means 'flee, escape'). These may all be independent changes; but they mostly entail the elimination of an irregular verb for one that fits the preferred morphological template — a process which seems to recapitulate that whereby early Romance increased inflectional regularity by substituting derivatives in -ARE for irregular third conjugation verbs.

Lexical Creativity

All Romance creoles have inherited from their lexifiers numerous words embodying the results of European derivational processes. Does this etymological complexity remain transparent to creole speakers, and if so, are any of the processes still productive? At first sight, they are not. For instance, the economical alternation of final /-o/ and /-a/, still flourishing as a mark of gender in southern European Romance, has all but disappeared from creole. In acrolectal Crioulo, /fidʒu/ 'son' still alternates with /fidʒa/ 'daughter', and /netu/ 'nephew' with /neta/ 'niece'; likewise São Tomense still opposes /sɔɡlu/ 'father-in-law' to /sɔɡla/ 'mother-in-law'. But the more widespread pattern substitutes syntagmatic productivity for paradigmatic, witness: Pap. /jiu ˈhomber/ 'son' (literally 'child man') versus /jiu muˈhe/ 'daughter' (literally 'child woman') — structures parallelled by STo. /bwe ɔme/ 'ox' versus /bwe mwala/ 'cow', or by Cha. /pwelko maʧo/ 'boar' versus /pwelko embra/ 'sow'.

Derivational productivity, though infrequent, is not entirely lacking. We have already mentioned the non-Romance causative infix /-nD-/ of Crioulo (see p. 450). In Papiamentu, the Romance nominalising suffix /-mentu/ has been productively extended to a number of sites where its counterpart would be unacceptable in either Spanish or Portuguese, as in: /bendementu/ 'sale', /binimentu/ 'coming, arrival', /nenɡamentu/

'denial', /perdementu/ 'loss', /primintimentu/ 'promise', and even /jagmentu/ 'hunt' < Dutch *jagen* 'to hunt'. Two other affixes that have achieved some degree of productivity are: the Mauritian iterative prefix /re-/, as in /mo pe re-lav mo lame/ 'I'll wash my hands again'; and the St Lucian intensifier /de-/, illustrated by the pairs /kwaze : dekwaze/ 'crush : smash to pieces, annihilate', /pale : depale/ 'speak : rant', /viwe : deviwe/ 'return : go back and forth'.

Perhaps the best known productive mechanism of creoles is reduplication. Strictly speaking, 'reduplication' refers only to the morphological aspect of what can be a whole series of distinct though interrelated syntactic and semantic functions. It can signal: plural marking, onomatopoeia, and — depending on context — both intensification and attenuation. Plural marking by reduplication is infrequent in Romance creoles, though marginal examples occur in the west African group, as in STo. /mwala-mwala o ↑/ 'are they both women?' (literally 'woman-woman Q'). In verbs or adjectival predicates, the meaning is more commonly iterative or continuous: STo. /e pɛga-pɛga piʃi/ 'he used to catch fish regularly' (literally 'he catch-catch fish'), /e sa ŋge ka dwēʧi-dwēʧi/ 'he is an invalid' (literally 'he be person imperf. sick-sick'), Cha. /tres hora ta hil'vi-hil'vi/ it has been boiling for three hours' (literally 'three hours past boil-boil'). Intensification is a frequent effect in adjectival predicates, though this meaning may need to be signalled by repeated stress or some other phonological device, witness: Hai. /li te 'bɛl-'bɛl/ 'she was extremely beautiful', /dlo-a 'klɛ-'klɛ/ 'this water's crystal clear'; Pap. /'lebe-'lebe/ 'very slippery'; STo. /'sɛtu-'sɛtu/ 'most certainly', /'kulu-'kulu/ 'pitch black' (< Port. *escuro*); Cha. /'bwenuŋ-'bweno/ 'extremely good', /'dulsiŋ-'dulse/ 'honey sweet', /'jenuŋ-'jeno/ 'chock full' (the /-ŋ/ suffix is a regular feature of Chabacano derived from Tagalog). If, however, the reduplicated form is fully lexicalised and has only one word-stress, its force is more likely to be attenuating: Hai. /'blāʃblāʃ/ 'whitish', /'dudu/ 'sweetish'; Réu., Mau. /'ruzruz/ 'reddish'. The potential contrast is most evident in verbs, as in Mau. /li ti 'marse-'marse/ 'he trudged on and on' versus /li ti marsmar'se/ 'he went for a stroll'.

6   Conclusion

In section 2 we posed the twin questions: do the Romance creoles form a coherent typological group, and if so, is it legitimate to label them 'Romance'? We are now better placed to attempt answers.

The Romance creoles have an overwhelming preference for SVO word order (only Chabacano regularly permits the inversion of verbs and subject pronouns). They are all prepositional, and obligatorily order the thing possessed before the possessor, and the thing compared before the standard of comparison. Subject pronouns are never omitted in declarative constructions (no creole is a null-subject language; indeed, in Seychellois a 'reprise' third person pronoun is obligatory even with full subject NPs). Object pronouns follow the verb with exactly the same privilege of occurrence as full noun phrases, though in some varieties they become enclitic on the verb at normal tempo. There is usually no formal differentiation of direct from indirect objects, whether nominal or pronominal; nor does case marking commonly occur (Chabacano and Réunionnais, which both use prepositional accusatives, do so without differentiating between pronouns and full NPs). Adjectival qualifiers normally, and relative clauses always, follow their head noun; likewise, adverbial qualifiers usually follow their verb, unless they modify the whole sentence, in which case they are located initially. All creoles make frequent use of 'auxiliary' particles to express tense and aspect relations; such particles normally, and in most varieties obligatorily, precede the verb, as do any lexical expressions of modality. Yes-no questions can be formed in all creoles merely by changing the intonation contour of the corresponding statement. The majority pattern for phrasal interrogation requires QU-fronting and pied piping of any accompanying prepositions (Crioulo, however, regularly permits question formation without a movement transformation). To this extent, most Romance creoles constitute classic exemplars of typological consistency.

Their consistency is less good with respect to negative scope relations, to the ordering of determiners and possessives, and to the congruence of tense–aspect systems. Some of the discrepancies (like prenominal adjectives in certain creoles affiliated to French) can be ascribed to the lexifier; but others were either taken from a non-European contributor language or represent creole innovations. Nevertheless, the degree of syntactic consistency is impressive, especially when combined with an absence of suffixal inflection and a reduced incidence of derivational affixation. We are therefore justified in postulating a coherent 'creole type'. Moreover, since many of the features we have so far ascribed to creoles are also attested in European Romance, albeit in differing degree, it is not unreasonable to claim that the 'creole type' represents the goal towards which European Romance may be moving in terms of analytic structure and SVO organisation.

The legitimacy of the label 'Romance' for the varieties discussed here, rests primarily on their lexical affiliation. As we have seen, this can amount to 100 per cent cognacy in core vocabulary, not only in contentives but even in functors. True, cognacy is no guarantee of mutual comprehensibility, either between creoles and their lexifiers or between affiliate creoles; but synchronic intelligibility is not necessarily a good criterion for classification, and within European Romance it has generally been accorded lower priority than the regularity of lexico-phonetic correspondences. Moreover, while it is true that the creoles incorporate in their total stock features and patterns not generally present in European

Romance (serial verbs, intensifiers and ideophones are obvious examples), the differences induced by original contributor languages, or by subsequent adstrate influence, remain relatively modest. The influence of Bini and Kishikongo on São Tomense, or of Tagalog on Chabacano, is certainly noticeable, but no greater than that of Slavic and the Balkan *Sprachbund* on Rumanian. On traditional criteria, therefore, to deny the 'Romance' classification of the creoles has major implications for the unity of the European area.

A more controversial index of Romance affiliation is the degree to which present-day creoles are subject to 'decreolisation' in the direction of the acrolect or metropolitan norm. In those varieties for which adequate records survive, historical change has usually worked to decrease, rather than increase, the divergence from European Romance. For example, over the last century Mauritian has virtually eliminated the 'reprise' construction, but no longer permits the deletion of identical subject pronouns in coordinations; and Haitian has more recently introduced overt complementisers and relative markers, parallel to those of French, in contexts where previously none was required. The non-Romance element in vocabulary is particularly vulnerable to acrolectal pressure in the varieties that have traditionally maintained close contact with their lexifier, notably Caboverdiano and Réunionnais. So too are the lexical items whose register is neutral in creole, but which are instantly recognisable to European Romance speakers as low-register or even vulgar, witness Hai. /bug, neg/ 'man', /êpil/ 'many', Mau. /enpake/ 'many', /plãt/ 'place (not 'plonk')', /kujõ/ 'idiot', Sey. /dekujone/ 'to disconcert'. Better communications, improved educational provision and more frequent contact will all increase the sociolinguistic pressure on basilectal speakers to eliminate from their speech items that are perceived by acrolectal speakers as unsophisticated or worse. Of course, they may resist by focusing towards a more localised norm, and creole intellectuals and nationalists are encouraging such resistance. But the balance of available evidence suggests that, while accommodation to a European norm may be shunned in the interests of national or personal identity, factors such as urbanisation and improved education are exerting an irresistible pull on basilectal usage in the direction of a standard 'mesolect', if not of the acrolect. Such developments not only serve to underscore the increasing 'Romanceness' of the creoles; if unchecked, they will rapidly erode the validity of 'creole' as a synchronic concept.

Bibliography

d'Ans, A.M. (1968) *Le créole français d'Haïti.* Mouton, The Hague.
Baker, P. (1972) *Kreol.* Hurst, London.

—— and C. Corne (1982) *Isle de France Creole: Affinities and Origins.* Karoma, Ann Arbor.

Bebel-Gisler, D. (1976) *La langue créole, force jugulée.* L'Harmattan, Paris.

Bickerton, D. (1981) *Roots of Language.* Karoma, Ann Arbor.

—— and A. Escalante (1970) 'Palenquero: A Spanish-based Creole of Northern Colombia', *Lingua* 24: 254–67.

Bollée, A. (1977) *Le créole français des Seychelles. Esquisse d'une grammaire, textes, vocabulaire.* Niemeyer, Tübingen.

—— (1977) *Zur Entstehung der französischen Kreolendialekte im Indischen Ozean: Kreolisierung ohne Pidginisierung.* Droz, Geneva.

Boretzky, N. (1983) *Kreolsprachen, Substrate und Sprachwandel.* Harrassowitz, Wiesbaden.

Broussard, J.F. (1942) *Louisiana Creole Dialect.* Louisiana State University Press, Baton Rouge.

Carayol, M. (1977) *Le français parlé à la Réunion: phonétique et phonologie.* Presses Universitaires de Lille III.

Carreira, A. (1983) *O crioulo de Cabo Verde, surto e expansão* 2nd edn. Privately published, Lisbon.

Carrington, L.D. (ed.) (1983) *Studies in Caribbean Language.* Society for Caribbean Linguistics, St Augustine.

—— (1984) *St Lucian Creole. A Descriptive Analysis of its Phonology and Morphosyntax.* Buske, Hamburg.

del Castillo Mathieu, N. (1984) 'El léxico de San Basilio de Palenque', *Thesaurus* 39: 80–169.

Chaudenson, R. (1974) *Lexique du parler créole de la Réunion* 2 vols. Champion, Paris.

—— (1979) *Les créoles français.* Nathan, Paris.

—— (1981) *Textes créoles anciens (La Réunion et Ile Maurice): comparaison et essai d'analyse.* Buske, Hamburg.

Conwell, M.J. and A. Juilland (1963) *Louisiana French Grammar.* Mouton, The Hague.

Corne, C. (1977) *Seychelles Creole Grammar* (= Tübinger Beiträge zur Linguistik, 91). Narr, Tübingen.

Dalphinis, M. (1985) *Caribbean and African Languages.* Karia, London.

Dijkhoff, M. (1980) *Dikshonario Woordenboek Papiamentu–Ulandes Ulandes–Papiamentu.* De Walberg Pers, Amsterdam.

D'Offay, D. and G. Lionnet (1982) *Diksyonner kreol-franse. Dictionnaire créole seychellois–français.* Buske, Hamburg.

Ferraz, I.L. (1979) *The Creole of São Tomé.* Witwatersrand University Press, Johannesburg.

Gauvin, A. (1977) *Du créole opprimé au créole libéré. Défense de la langue réunionnaise.* L'Harmattan, Paris.

Germain, R. (1976) *Grammaire créole.* Editions du Levain, Villejuif.

Goodman, M. (1964) *A Comparative Study of Creole French Dialects.* Mouton, The Hague.

de Granda, G. (1978) *Estudios lingüísticos hispánicos, afrohispánicos y criollos.* Gredos, Madrid.

Hall, R.A. Jr (1953) *Haitian Creole. Grammar, Texts, Vocabulary.* American Folklore Society, Philadelphia.

—— (1966) *Pidgin and Creole Languages.* Cornell University Press, Ithaca.

Hazaël-Massieux, G. (1972) 'Phonologie et phonétique du créole de Guadeloupe', unpublished thesis, Université de Paris III.

ROMANCE CREOLES 473

Highfield, A.R. (1979) *The French Dialect of St Thomas, US Virgin Islands: A Descriptive Grammar with Texts and Glossary.* Karoma, Ann Arbor.
Jourdain, E. (1956) *Le vocabulaire du parler créole de la Martinique.* Klincksieck, Paris.
Kremnitz, G. (1983) *Français et créole: ce qu'en pensent les enseignants. Le conflit linguistique à la Martinique.* Buske, Hamburg.
Lefebvre, C., H. Magloire-Holly, and N. Piou (1982) *Syntaxe de l'haïtien.* Karoma, Ann Arbor.
Lenz, R. (1928) *El papiamentu: la lengua criolla de Curazao.* Prensa Universitaria, Santiago de Chile.
Le Page, R.B. and A. Tabouret-Keller (1985) *Acts of Identity.* Cambridge University Press, Cambridge.
Meisel, J.M. (ed.) (1977) *Langues en contact — Pidgins — Creoles — Languages in Contact.* Narr, Tübingen.
Papen, R.A. (1978) 'The French-based Creoles of the Indian Ocean: An Analysis and Comparison', unpublished thesis, California UCSD.
Peleman, L. (1978) *Diksyonnè krèyòl-fransé.* Bon Nouvel, Port-au-Prince.
Pompilus, P. (1961) *La langue française en Haïti.* IHEAL, Paris.
Reinecke, J. et al. (1975) *A Bibliography of Pidgin and Creole Languages.* Hawaii University Press, Honolulu.
Saint-Jacques-Fauquenoy, M. (1972) *Analyse structurale du créole guyanais.* Klincksieck, Paris.
Scantamburlo, L. (1981) *Gramática e dicionário da língua criol da Guiné-Bissau.* Editrice Missionaria Italiana, Bologna.
Stein, P. (1982) *Connaissance et emploi des langues à l'Ile Maurice.* Buske, Hamburg.
—— (1984) *Kreolisch und Französisch.* Niemeyer, Tübingen.
Taylor, D.R. (1977) *Languages of the West Indies.* Johns Hopkins University Press, Baltimore.
Tinelli, H. (1981) *Creole Phonology.* Mouton, The Hague.
Valdman, A. (1970) *Basic Course in Haitian Creole.* Indiana University Press, Bloomington.
—— (ed.) (1977) *Pidgin and Creole Linguistics.* Indiana University Press, Bloomington.
—— (1978) *Le créole: structure, statut et origine.* Klincksieck, Paris.
Valkhoff, M.F. (1966) *Studies in Portuguese and Creole.* Witwatersrand University Press, Johannesburg.
—— (ed.) (1975) *Miscelânea Luso-Africana.* JICU, Lisbon.
Vintilă-Rădulescu, I. (1976) *Le créole français.* Mouton, The Hague.
Vogel, C. (ed.) (1982) *La Réunion* (special issue of *Études Créoles* 4, no. 2).
Whinnom, K. (1956) *Spanish Contact Vernaculars in the Philippine Islands.* Hong Kong University Press, Hong Kong.

Maps

Map I: Language and Dialect in Spain

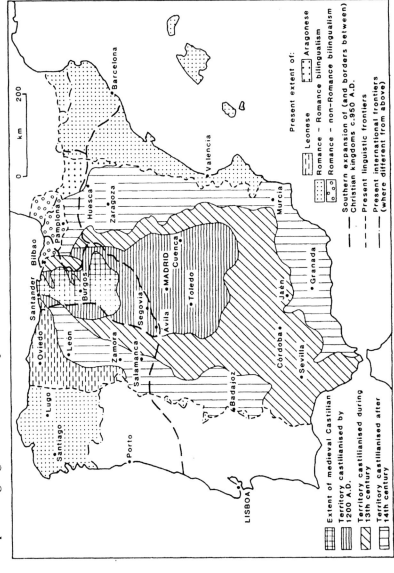

Map II: Portuguese and Galician Dialects

DIALECTS

GALICIAN

1 Western Galician

2 Eastern Galician

NORTHERN PORTUGUESE

3 Dialects of Trás-os-Montes and Alto Minho

4 Dialects of Baixo Minho, Douro and the Beiras

CENTRAL AND SOUTHERN PORTUGUESE

5 Central/coastal dialects

6 Central/inland and southern dialects

0   km   100

— — Boundary of Galician/Portuguese

— · — Portuguese/Spanish frontier (where different from above)

- - - - Dialect boundaries

——— Boundaries of Spanish regions

Map III: Portuguese in Brazil

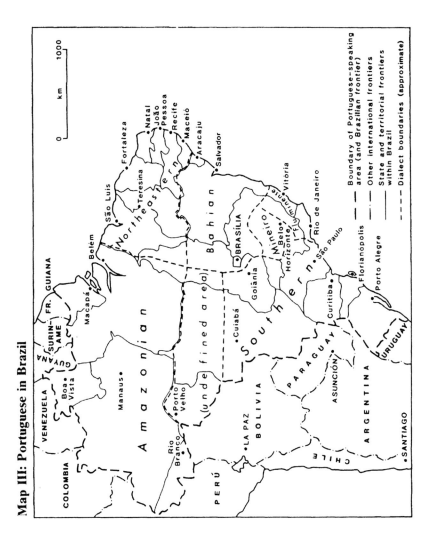

Map IV: The Distribution of Catalan

Map V: Dialect Boundaries of Medieval France

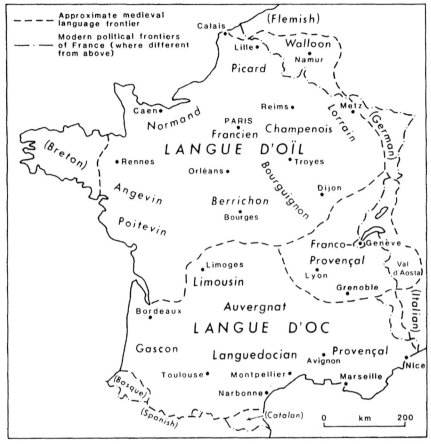

Note: For Occitan equivalents of toponyms and dialect names in the south, see Map VI.

Map VI: Occitan and Franco-Provençal

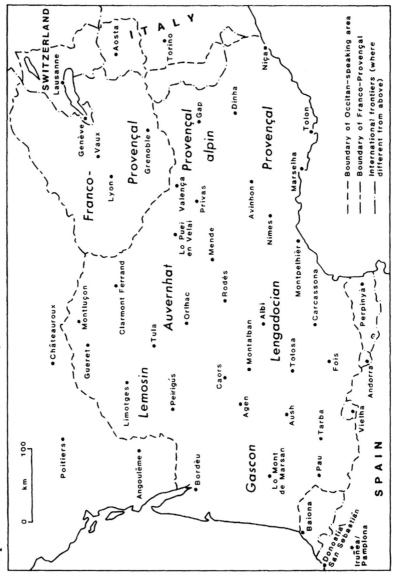

Map VII: Language and Dialect in Italy

Basel
Zürich
GERMANY
BUDAPEST
BERN
LIECHTENSTEIN
SWITZERLAND
(R-Romance)
(Franco-Provençal)
(German)
(Ladin)
AUSTRIA
Graz
HUNGARY
(Friulan)
(Slovene)
Ljubljana
Zagreb
FRANCE
(Occitan)
Lombardo
Milano
Piemontese
Torino
Veneto
Venezia
Verona
Padova
Trieste
Rijeka
Istriano
Pola
(Serbo-Croat)
YUGOSLAVIA
Ferrara
Ligure
Genova
La Spezia
Emiliano-Romagnolo
Bologna
Ravenna
Rimini
Nice
Livorno
Firenze
Toscano
N. Marchigiano
Ancona
Split
Umbro
Perugia
Abruzzese
Pescara
Dubrovnik
Corso
Ajaccio
L'Aquila
Laziale
ROMA
SC
A
A
Molisano
FP
Foggia
Bari
Campano
Pugliese
Taranto
Brindisi
(Catalan)
(Sardinian)
Napoli
N
Lucano
N
Solentino
G
A
A
Ligure
Cagliari
Colabrese
Messina
Palermo
A
N
N
Reggio
G
A
Siciliano
N
Siciliano

Istriano   Italian dialects
(Sardinian)   Neighbouring languages
A   Albanian
G   Greek
SC   Serbo-Croat
FP   Franco-Provençal
N   Northern Italian
(linguistic islands in S. Italy)

— — Boundary of Italian-speaking area
—·— International frontiers (where different from above)
– – – Boundary between Northern and Southern Italian dialect blocs
——— Boundaries of dialect groups

(Maltese)

0   km   200

Map VIII: Vowel Systems of Southern Italy (cf. pp. 32-3)

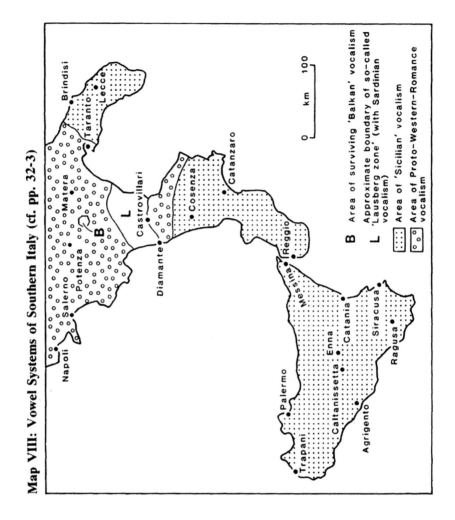

B Area of surviving 'Balkan' vocalism

L Approximate boundary of so-called
     'Lausberg zone' (with Sardinian
     vocalism)

     Area of 'Sicilian' vocalism

     Area of Proto-Western-Romance
     vocalism

Map IX: Language and Dialect in Sardinia

Towns indicated are those mentioned in the text.

Map X: The Distribution of Rhaeto-Romance

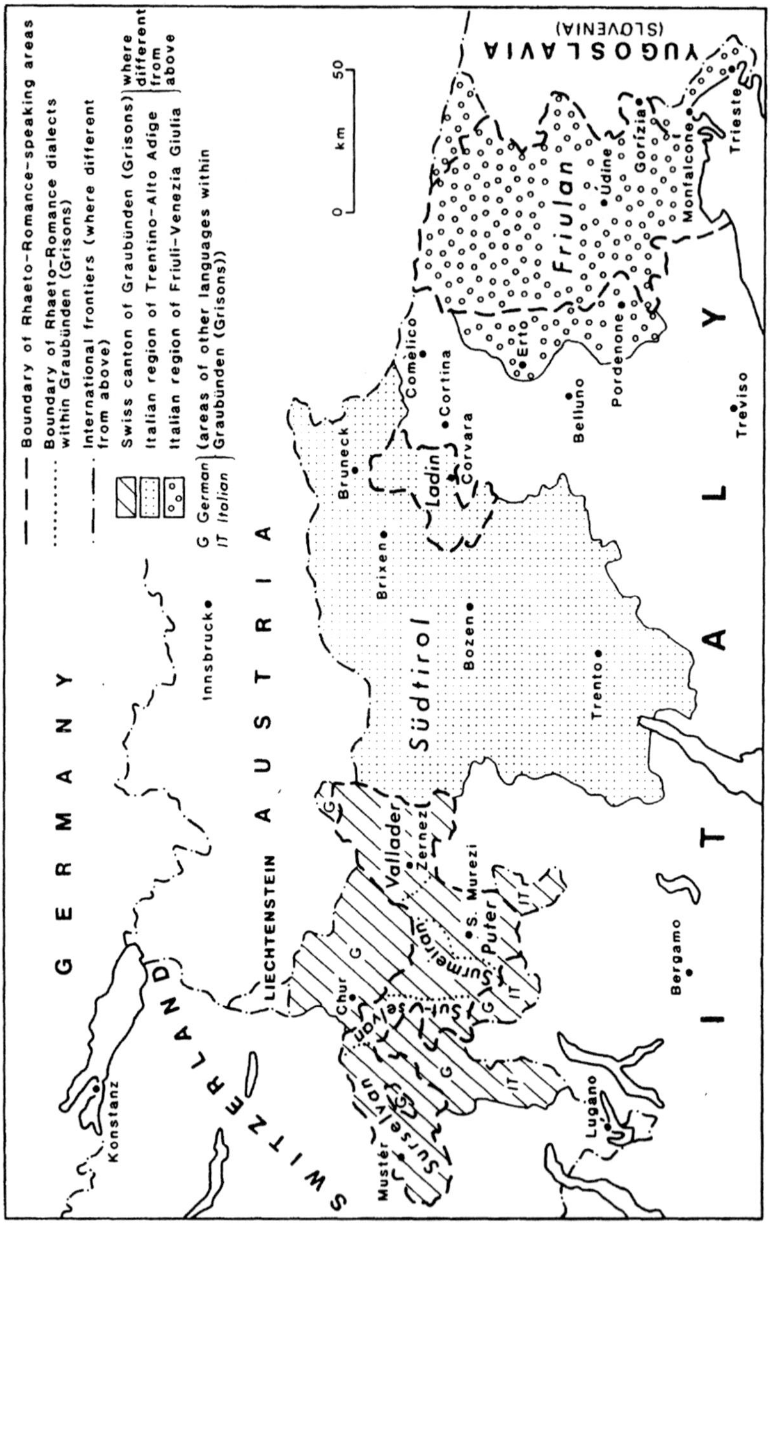

Boundary of Rhaeto-Romance-speaking areas

Boundary of Rhaeto-Romance dialects within Graubünden (Grisons)

International frontiers (where different from above)

Swiss canton of Graubünden (Grisons) } where
Italian region of Trentino-Alto Adige } different from
Italian region of Friuli-Venezia Giulia } above

G German } (areas of other languages within
IT Italian } Graubünden (Grisons))

GERMANY

Konstanz

Innsbruck

AUSTRIA

LIECHTENSTEIN

SWITZERLAND

Chur

Müster

Surselvan

Sursilvan

Sutselvan

Sut-Selvan

Surmeiran

S. Murezi

Puter

Vallader

Zernez

Südtirol

Bruneck

Brixen

Bozen

Trento

Ladin

Cortina

Corvara

Comelico

Erto

Belluno

Pordenone

Friulan

Udine

Gorizia

Montfalcone

Trieste

YUGOSLAVIA (SLOVENIA)

Treviso

Bergamo

Lugano

ITALY

0   km   50

Map XI: The Distribution of Balkan Romance

A   Arumanian

I   Istro-Rumanian

M   Megleno-Rumanian

(H)   Hungarian   } linguistic islands
(B)   Bulgarian   } within Romanian)

——————   Boundary of Balkan Romance languages and dialects

– – – –   Boundary between major dialect groups in Romanian

—·—·—   International frontiers (where different from above)

0   km   200

Index

Printed in the United States
66123LVS00001B/104

9 780415 164177